The Papers of
HENRY CLAY

The Papers of
HENRY CLAY

Melba Porter Hay
Editor

Anna B. Perry
Mackelene Smith
Kenneth H. Williams
Assistant Editors

SUPPLEMENT
1793–1852

THE UNIVERSITY PRESS OF KENTUCKY

ISBN: 08131-0061-5

Library of Congress Catalog Card Number: 59-13605

Copyright © 1992 by The University Press of Kentucky

Scholarly publisher for the Commonwealth,
serving Bellarmine College, Berea College, Centre
College of Kentucky, Eastern Kentucky University,
The Filson Club, Georgetown College, Kentucky
Historical Society, Kentucky State University,
Morehead State University, Murray State University,
Northern Kentucky University, Transylvania University,
University of Kentucky, University of Louisville,
and Western Kentucky University.

Editorial and Sales Offices: Lexington, Kentucky 40508-4008

CONTENTS

PREFACE

The Papers of Henry Clay project, which began nearly forty years ago, comes to a conclusion with this volume. This final number in the series contains documents that were discovered too late for publication in proper chronological sequence in previous volumes. In addition, it contains a calendar of unpublished documents deemed too routine to print in full or summarize, an errata for previous volumes, an essay and calendar of Clay artwork (paintings, busts, daguerreotypes, full statues, and engravings), and a comprehensive bibliography of works cited in the full series. The editors believe this edition is as comprehensive and as definitive as possible. Although additional Clay material will certainly come to light, it is doubtful that it will provide any startling new evidence about the man whose life and career is so thoroughly covered in these eleven volumes.

Dr. Robert Seager II, senior editor of the project from 1979 to 1987, has continued as consultant and has provided much sound professional advice. Assistant editors Mackelene Smith, who joined the project in 1979, Anna B. Perry, who began in 1983, and Kenneth H. Williams, who started in 1989, have continued their superb work. Without their dedication, the project would not have been completed so expeditiously.

The editorial policies that guided volumes 7 through 10 are continued in this volume except for two points: (1) when a letter referred to in the text has not been found it is so indicated by the editors; and (2) the first time a correspondent or person is mentioned in this volume, the individual is either identified, a cross-reference to the identification in a previous volume is provided, or the person is clearly indicated as "not identified." These changes were made in order to ease the burden for the researcher, since the Supplement covers a much broader time span than any of the previous volumes. As before, a majority of the letters written by Clay, as well as the most important of his incoming mail, have been printed in full. A few of the less important letters written by Clay, along with most of his speeches and much of the incoming mail, have been summarized. Marginal and peripheral Clay materials have been placed in the calendar of unpublished documents, which contains the name of the correspondent, location, and general subject of each item.

In keeping with the editorial practices established with volume 7, letter headings have been standardized and salutations, closings, and subscriptions have been omitted. Volume and page numbers are omitted in citations of encyclopedias and dictionaries that are arranged alphabetically. Abbreviations used in the notes are explained in the table below. In documents printed in full, cross-references to relevant materials in this and earlier volumes appear in notes. In summarized documents cross-references are enclosed in brackets and inserted in the text. Documents printed in full and direct quotations in summaries have been transcribed literally, as far as possible, with no silent emendations. Letters, words, and punctuation marks supplied by the editors for clarification are inserted in the text within brackets, as are identifying materials such as first names. The use of *sic* to denote errors in spelling is limited to proper names and to those rare instances in which a misspelling might cause confusion. Interlineations and raised letters have been lowered to the line and substantive decipherable cancellations have been placed in notes. Ellipsis marks at the end of a letter printed in full indicate that a brief social pleasantry that is not a part of the closing has been omitted. Readers should be aware that letters not in Clay's hand often contain errors originating in the work of an amanuensis or copyist.

One more point concerning editorial methodology must be explained. Since this volume covers virtually the entire span of Clay's adult life, most of the events discussed in these letters have previously been explained in annotations. Time and cost have not allowed for a restatement of such information; cross-references are therefore numerous.

The editors sincerely thank the Lilly Endowment, Inc., for its generous support of the early volumes. In addition, we thank the National Historical Publications and Records Commission for its many years of support for the project and the National Endowment for the Humanities for helping to fund this final volume. In addition, the assistance provided by the University of Kentucky Research Foundation and the University Press of Kentucky have been essential to making this edition possible. Special thanks are due to Dr. Wimberly C. Royster, who as vice president for Research and Graduate Studies two years ago approved this supplement and the extra year necessary to complete it. Dr. Leonard K. Peters, acting vice president for Research and Graduate Studies for the past year, has also assisted the project in many ways. We are most grateful to these institutions and individuals for their help in completing the edition.

Melba Porter Hay
March 1991

SYMBOLS & ABBREVIATIONS

The following symbols are used to describe the nature of the originals of documents copied from manuscript sources.

AD	Autograph Document
AD draft	Autograph Document, draft
ADI	Autograph Document Initialed
ADS	Autograph Document Signed
AE	Autograph Endorsement
AEI	Autograph Endorsement Initialed
AES	Autograph Endorsement Signed
AL	Autograph Letter
AL draft	Autograph Letter, draft
ALI	Autograph Letter Initialed
ALI copy	Autograph Letter Initialed, copy
ALI draft	Autograph Letter Initialed, draft
ALS	Autograph Letter Signed
ALS draft	Autograph Letter Signed, draft
AN	Autograph Note
AN draft	Autograph Note, draft
ANI draft	Autograph Note Initialed, draft
ANS	Autograph Note Signed
Copy	Copy not by writer (indicated "true" is so certified)
D	Document
DS	Document Signed
L	Letter
L draft	Letter, draft
LI draft	Letter Initialed, draft
LS	Letter Signed
N	Note
N draft	Note, draft
NS	Note Signed

The following, from the *Symbols Used in the National Union Catalog of the Library of Congress* (9th ed., rev.; Washington, 1965), indicate the location of the original documents in institutional libraries of the United States.

A-Ar	Alabama Department of Archives and History, Montgomery, Alabama
AU	University of Alabama, Tuscaloosa, Alabama
AzTeS	Arizona State University, Tempe, Arizona

CLU	University of California at Los Angeles, Los Angeles, California
COMC	Mills College, Oakland, California
CSmH	Henry E. Huntington Library and Museum, San Marino, California
CtHi	Connecticut Historical Society, Hartford, Connecticut
CtY	Yale University, New Haven, Connecticut
DeGE	Eleutherian Mills Historical Library, Greenville, Delaware
CU	University of California, Berkeley, California
DCA	Corcoran Art Gallery, Washington, D.C.
DCos	Cosmos Club Library, Washington, D.C.
DeHi	Historical Society of Delaware, Wilmington, Delaware
DeWin	Henry Francis DuPont Winterthur Museum, Winterthur, Delaware
DLC	Library of Congress, Washington, D.C.
DLC-HC	Library of Congress, Henry Clay Collection
DLC-TJC	Library of Congress, Thomas J. Clay Collection
DNA	United States National Archives Library, Washington, D.C. Following the symbol for this depository, the letters A. and R. mean Applications and Recommendations; M., Microcopy; P. and D. of L., Publication and Distribution of the Laws; R., Reel; and RG, Record Group.
DS	United States Department of State, Washington, D.C.
DSI	Smithsonian Institution Library, Washington, D.C.
DSI-NPG	National Portrait Gallery, Washington, D.C.
FU	University of Florida, Gainesville, Florida
ICHi	Chicago Historical Society, Chicago, Illinois
ICN	Newberry Library, Chicago, Illinois
ICU	University of Chicago, Chicago, Illinois
IGK	Knox College, Galesburg, Illinois
InHi	Indiana Historical Society, Indianapolis, Indiana
InU	Indiana University, Bloomington, Indiana
JSC	James S. Capley Library, La Jolla, California
KEU	Eastern Kentucky University, Richmond, Kentucky
KyBgW	Western Kentucky University, Bowling Green, Kentucky
KyHi	Kentucky Historical Society, Frankfort, Kentucky
KyLoF	The Filson Club, Louisville, Kentucky
KyLx	Lexington Public Library, Lexington, Kentucky
KyLxT	Transylvania University, Lexington, Kentucky
KyMurT	Murray State University, Murray, Kentucky
KyU	University of Kentucky, Lexington, Kentucky
L-M	Louisiana State Museum, New Orleans, Louisiana
LNHT	Louisiana Historical Society, New Orleans
MA	Amherst College, Amherst, Massachusetts
MAnP	Phillips Academy, Andover, Massachusetts
MB	Boston Public Library, Boston, Massachusetts
MBNEH	New England Historic Genealogical Society, Boston, Massachusetts

MBU	Boston University, Boston, Massachusetts
MdBP	Peabody Institute, Baltimore, Maryland
MdBWA	Walters Art Gallery, Baltimore, Maryland
MdHi	Maryland Historical Society, Baltimore, Maryland
MeHi	Maine Historical Society, Portland, Maine
MH	Harvard University, Cambridge, Massachusetts
MHi	Massachusetts Historical Society, Boston, Massachusetts
MiU	University of Michigan, Ann Arbor, Michigan
MnU	University of Minnesota, Minneapolis, Minnesota
MoHi	Missouri State Historical Society, Columbia, Missouri
MoSHi	Missouri Historical Society, St. Louis, Missouri
MoSW	Washington University, St. Louis, Missouri
MnHi	Minnesota Historical Society, St. Paul, Minnesota
NA1I	Albany Institute of History and Art, Albany, New York
NBLiHi	Long Island Historical Society, Brooklyn, New York
NcD	Duke University, Durham, North Carolina
NcRMA	North Carolina Museum of Art, Raleigh, North Carolina
NcU	University of North Carolina, Chapel Hill, North Carolina
NhD	Dartmouth College, Hanover, New Hampshire
NhHi	New Hampshire Historical Society, Concord, New Hampshire
NHi	New York Historical Society, New York, New York
NIC	Cornell University, Ithaca, New York
NjHi	New Jersey Historical Society, Newark, New Jersey
NjMoHP	Morristown Edison National Historical Park, Morristown, New Jersey
NjP	Princeton University, Princeton, New Jersey
NjR	Rutgers-The State University, New Brunswick, New Jersey
LN	New Orleans Public Library, New Orleans, Louisiana
NN	New York Public Library, New York, New York
NNC	Columbia University, New York, New York
NNMM	Metropolitan Museum of Art, New York, New York
NNMoMA	Museum of Modern Art, New York, New York
NNNGB	New York Genealogical and Biographical Society, New York, New York
NNUnionL	Union League Club, New York, New York
NRGE	George Eastman House, Rochester, New York
NRU	University of Rochester, Rochester, New York
NUtC	Utica College of Syracuse University, Utica, New York
OCHP	Historical and Philosophical Society of Ohio, Cincinnati, Ohio
OClWHi	Western Reserve Historical Society, Cleveland, Ohio
ODa	Dayton and Montgomery County Library, Dayton, Ohio
OHi	Ohio State Historical Society, Columbus, Ohio
PEL	Lafayette College, Easton, Pennsylvania
OYMHi	Mahoning Valley Historical Society, Youngstown, Ohio
PHi	Historical Society of Pennsylvania, Philadelphia, Pennsylvania
PLF	Franklin and Marshall College, Lancaster, Pennsylvania

PMCHi	Crawford County Historical Society, Meadville, Pennsylvania
PP	Free Library of Philadelphia, Philadelphia, Pennsylvania
PPAFA	Pennsylvania Academy of the Fine Arts, Philadelphia, Pennsylvania
PPiC	Carnegie Institute of Technology, Pittsburgh, Pennsylvania
PPL	Library Company of Philadelphia, Philadelphia, Pennsylvania
PPRF	Rosenbach Foundation, Philadelphia, Pennsylvania
PSC	Swarthmore College, Swarthmore, Pennsylvania
PWbH	Wyoming Historical and Geological Society, Wilkes-Barre, Pennsylvania
ScU	University of South Carolina, Columbia, South Carolina
RPB	Brown University, Providence, Rhode Island
T	Tennessee State Library, Nashville, Tennessee
TNJ	Vanderbilt University, Nashville, Tennessee
UPB	Brigham Young University, Provo, Utah
Vi	Virginia State Library, Richmond, Virginia
ViAsR	Randolph Macon College, Ashland, Virginia
ViHi	Virginia Historical Society, Richmond, Virginia
ViMtV	Mt. Vernon, Virginia
ViRMu	Virginia Museum of Fine Arts, Richmond, Virginia
ViRVal	Valentine Museum, Richmond, Virginia
ViU	University of Virginia, Charlottesville, Virginia
VtNN	Norwich University, Northfield, Vermont
VtU	University of Vermont, Burlington, Vermont
WRipC	Ripon College, Ripon, Wisconsin
WvU	West Virginia University, Morgantown, West Virginia

The Papers of
HENRY CLAY

From Peyton Short, "Greenfield," Woodford County, Ky., October 28, 1799. Reports that when "Your Brother Mr. John Clay called on me a few days ago with a verbal message from you requesting that I w[oul]d pay him the Balance of your Demand against me on a/c of the purchase of the Negro Man Dick—I was entirely destitute of the means of paying—otherwise sh[oul]d. most certainly have discharged it." Adds that he has "been daily expecting the Recpt. of a small Debt—out of which it is my fixed purpose to pay off the apprd. Balance." Now fears he will not be able to pay until his return from Cincinnati where he will go in a day or two.

Continues with a discussion of various lawsuits to which he is a party. Concludes: "Having thus with Candor, detailed to you the Ground of all those several prosecutions against me, must . . . commit my Defense to your Industry & abilities—I shall always hold my self in readiness to discharge the Debt I may incur" for legal fees. Adds that "Nothing but the Difficulty of the times could have subjected me to a prosecution for a just Debt." Copy. DLC-Short Family Papers.

For Peyton Short, see 1:2; for other documents concerning his debts, see espec. 1:25-26, 76-77, 100, 109, 111, 113, 128, 138, 423-24. For John Clay, see 1:18.

To WILLIAM TAYLOR[1]　　　　　　　　Lexington, November 1, 1799

By the direction and advice of Mr. Andrew Holmes, who informs me he is authorized by you, I have taken from Mr. [Mann] Satterwhite[2] a mortgage upon two lotts and houses in this Town to secure the debt due from him to you and also to secure a debt of about £500 due from him to Mr. Holmes; but to enable us to obtain this mortgage we were compelled to give a credit of six months for one half of the Debt and of nine months for the remaining half, the whole to carry the legal Interest of Maryland until paid. It appears to me that, if you are not in the immediate want of the money, the security for the ultimate payment of the Debt which has been thus procurred, has been very properly taken; because if the suit had progressed in the usual course of legal proceeding, as there was an error committed, for the want of the note, in the commencement of the first suit, we could not have recovered a Judgment until March; and by that time, without the mortgage, from the fluctuations to which the property of men is subject in this Country, the debt might have been insecure.[3]

It is possible that Mr. Satterwhite may effect a sale of one of the houses at least before the expiration of the time given him for the payment of the money; if he should you will receive it earlier. He has been offered Cordage for it. Would that article or any other of the produce of this Country suit you?

ALS. KyU. Addressed to Taylor in Baltimore.   1. For Taylor, see 1:19.   2. For Holmes and Satterwhite, see 1:18-19.   3. For more on this subject, see espec. 1:39-40, 54, 105-8; and below, Clay to Taylor, Dec. 2, 1800, Sept. 28, 1802, Jan. 13, 1803, and May 18, 1803.

To WILLIAM TAYLOR   Lexington, December 2, 1800

At the Federal Court for this District which is now just about to rise, I obtained Judgment for you against [John] Heugh and [Alexander] Ralston for the amount of your account against them with Interest.[1] When the suit was called, finding that they had no prospect of getting a continuance, they proposed to confess Judgment, upon my giving them a stay of execution of forty days; which I agreed to, it being the custom of the Country to give small indulgences of this kind. It is suggested by Mr. Ralston that Heugh has probably paid you in Baltimore a considerable part of the debt; should this be the fact it will readily occur to you to be proper to give me notice of it, previous to my issuing execution, as otherwise the marshall will be entitled to a commission upon the whole amount.

Adam Shepherd and Austin Hubbard[2] also came forward at the last Court and proposed to confess Judgment upon my giving them a stay of execution until the first day of May next—Knowing the difficulty of proving the account, (Mr. Hart the witness upon whom I relied in this Country for proving their acknowledgment intending to descend the Mississippi, before the suit could be tried) I consented to their proposal, and Judgment is accordingly entered up for the whole amount of your account with Interest until paid. These men say that there is compound interest charged against them upon about £20 of your account. I promised them that if it was so it should be corrected— Will you examine the statement in your possession & inform me accordingly?

With respect to the note you have against Shepherd individually, until you forward it to me I can do nothing with it. I have as I heretofore informed you security from him for the payment of the amount of that note.

The time given [Mann] Satterwhite, when he confessed Judgment, is now nearly expired, and I shall immediately order out execution against him.[3] I hope to be able to get possession of the amount of his debt shortly. By a Replevin law in this State he will have it in his power, upon giving bond & security, to put off the payment of the money three months longer; but I am inclined to think he will not avail himself of that law.

I wrote you as fully in answer to yours of the 14th. August respecting the 5725 acres of land purchased by Gittings and Smith[4] from [Jesse] Hollingsworth[5] as the information I was then possessed of enabled me. Upon farther inquiries I am confirmed in the advice which I then gave you to take back the advanced money. In addition to what I wrote respecting the quality of the land. I have since learnt that Judge Sebastion [sic, Benjamin Sebastian][6] gave no power to Mr. Hollingsworth to sell the land, and that he has since disclaimed his proceedings. Hollingsworth is dead entirely I believe insolvent.

2

ALS. KyU. Addressed to Taylor in Baltimore.   1. For Heugh and Ralston, see 1:18-19. See also 1:23, 27-28, 39-41, 54-55, 66, 70, 78-79, espec. 27-28.   2. See 1:18-19.   3. Clay to Taylor, Nov. 1, 1799. See also 1:35-40, 54-55, 105-9.   4. See 1:40-41.   5. See 1:41.   6. *Ibid.*

To WILLIAM TAYLOR   Lexington, January 29, 1802

By the last mail in a letter of the 26h. instant[1] I inclosed to you eight hundred and ten dollars, in bank notes, of which I now forward you on the other side hereof the numbers dates &c[.][2]

I most sincerely hope that no accident will occur to prevent their reaching you in perfect safety—Until I am informed of that event I shall feel the utmost anxiety—Would it not be better hereafter to cut the notes in two pieces, and transmit one half by one mail & the remainder by the succeeding mail? Or to guard more certainly against the frauds of postmasters as well as others, to remit one moiety by the Southern, and the other by the Eastern route? Such I am informed is the practice of our merchants—

It occured to me that special indorsements on the notes, in case of a fraud, might enable you if not to detect the bullion, at least to trace up the note—I therefore upon the eight largest notes indorsed "Pay the within to William Taylor Esqr of Baltimore merchant only 22d. January 1802—Henry Clay of Lexington Ky."[3]

Under the hope which I indulge that my letter will arrive safely I will add nothing to what is contained in it—

ALS. MB. Addressed to Taylor in Baltimore.   1. Not found.   2. Enclosed is a list of the note numbers, banks, date of notes, name of presidents of the banks, where payable, and amount of each note. For the difficulties involved in securing bank notes, see 1:84.   3. For Clay's account with Taylor, see 1:105-8.

Complaint, Fayette Circuit Court, *ca.* July, 1802. Clay, as "assignee of [Charles] Davidson and [John] Goddard complains of Joel Craig and Elijah Craig [1:33] in custody &c. of a plea that they . . . the defendants render to the plaintiff [Henry Clay] the sum of" 1,355 "pounds one shilling and nine pence Maryland Currency" which they owe to the plaintiff. Asserts that on June 21, 1800, Joel Craig, acting for himself and his partner Elijah Craig, "did acknowledge that he had purchased & received from the said Davidson and Goddard goods to the amount of the said sum" and had promised to pay within six months. This sum being unpaid on February 12, 1802, "the said Davidson and Goddard assigned the same to the plaintiff" who now demands the said sum of the defendants. ADS. Fayette Circuit Court, File no. 206. For this case, see 4:639.

On June 12, 1804, Clay received from Elijah Craig and son $198 "on a/c of Davidson & Goddard." ADS. Fayette Circuit Court, File no. 206.

On September 7, 1805, Clay gave a receipt to Elijah Craig for $250 "on a/c. of Davidsons & Goddards Judgt. ag[ains]t. him & Joel Craig." ADS. *Ibid.*

On July 30, 1806, Clay gave a "Separate Answer . . . to a bill of complaint against him & Mess. Davidson & Goddard exhibited in the Circuit Court of Scott County in Chancery Elijah Craig &c. Compl[aintan]ts." Clay states that "he knows nothing of the original transaction between the Complts & his Co-defendants: That the said Complts obligation, upon which the Judgt, at law was recovered, was placed in this def[endan]t's hands for collection, and from this period any information possessed by him must commence." Further states that the assignment made to him was not for his own benefit but for his "Co-defts [Davidson & Goddard]," that "the Complts made him several payments" for which he gave receipts, that "these credits are indorsed upon the execution, the first being made on the 4h Feby. 1804 & the last on the 7h. of Septr. 1805, amounting in the whole to $1048," that "subsequent to the confession of the Judgment, the Complt Elijah from time to time sought & received from this deft repeated indulgences, under express promises of payment of the debt—That at one of those periods he executed a mortgage now of record in this Office to which he refers—" ADS. *Ibid.*

Clay wrote Capt. John Hawkins [1:61; 6:1171] on August 18, 1806, reporting that "Mr. Craig & I have consented to remove his suit agt. Davidson & Goddard to Fayette Circuit Court." Asks that "the papers," including "a Copy of the Record in the suit wherein Judge. was obtained agt him," be sent. ADS. *Ibid.*

To WILLIAM TAYLOR   Lexington, August 15, 1802
By the mail on the 10h. Inst.[1] I inclosed to you bank notes agreeably to this list of numbers banks &c, which I hope you will receive before this reaches you—Since then I have received eight hundred dollars, which shall be remitted as soon as possible[.]

In my letter inclosing the above notes I stated the increased difficulty of obtaining bank notes,[2] & the probable practicability of packing the money through the wilderness at an expence less than the premium which is usually given for notes—Will you be pleased to say if I cannot procure notes, whether the expedient now proposed meets with your approbation?

ALS. KyU.   1. See 1:85.   2. See 1:84.

To WILLIAM TAYLOR   Lexington, September 28, 1802
Inclosed are bank notes amounting to five hundred dollars, for which I had to give a premium of three per Cent, and even on those terms got them with great difficulty.[1]

The gentleman by whom I intended to have sent you the doubleoons mentioned in a former letter having unfortunately broke his leg, was prevented from performing the journey which he contemplated. No other opportunity is within my knowledge—So soon as I can procure more bills I will make you a farther remittance—

In the course of the ensuing month I calculate upon receiving the balance from [Adam] Shepherd & [Austin] Hubbard—[2]

ALS. KyLoF.   1. See 1:84.   2. Clay to Taylor, Dec. 2, 1800, and Jan. 13, 1803. See also 1:18-19, 39-41, 54, 106, 109.

To WILLIAM TAYLOR   Lexington, January 13, 1802 [*sic,* 1803]
The day before yesterday I received from the Marshall, on account of the debts due you from [Adam] Shepherd & [Austin] Hubbard & Shepherd,[1] one thousand dollars & took the assumpsit of a man, on whom I can rely, for the balance due you, payable in six weeks; so that I hope shortly to be able to close my agency relative to the several debts due you in this Country.[2] At this time bank notes are not to be had—I will continue to keep a good look out, and so soon as I can command any, I will make you a remittance.[3] I have not heard whether [Peyton] Short has paid you, and consequently have not acted upon the Judg-

ment, of which by a former letter,[4] I apprized you. He is daily expected here, and if he has not discharged it I will push him with an execution.

Have you ever done any thing with [John] Armstrong since the protest of his accepted bill?[5] Be pleased to inform me, and if you have not I will thank you to send me by the mail immediately the original bill, as I expect I can get paid from the drawer in this Country. Be pleased also to forward me by the mail, the receipt of [Robert] Mickle[6] for the three hundred dollars you paid him out of [Charles Peter Stephen] Wante's Note for me.[7] As soon as I can procure Copies of the several Judgments I have obtained for you from Frankfort, I will transmit you a statement of our account.[8]

ALS. KyU. 1. See espec. 1:18-19, 109; Clay to Taylor, Dec. 2, 1800. 2. See 1:105-8. 3. See 1:84. 4. Not found. For Short's debt to Taylor, see espec. 1:76-77, 88, 109-10. 5. See 1:66. 6. See 1:101. 7. For Wante, see espec. 1:64, 100-101. 8. Writing on two blank pages of Clay's letter of Jan. 13, 1803, Taylor replies on Feb. 10, 1803, stating that "I . . . am highly pleased to find you have been successful in recovering my Dedts from Shepherd & Co—I am so much in want of money I coud wish you to forward what comes to hand as soon as it can be possible." Prefers bank notes, but warns against the danger of counterfeits. Also reports that "Mr Short paid me the 22 Octr 1802—400$" and left an order "on a Col [Thomas] Sprigg for 850$." Reports that Sprigg will not pay, and asks Clay to notify Short and get him "to settle with you the balance." Adds that he "will deliver this order on Sprigg to any person he [Short] will authorize in his concerns—The order on Armstrong was settled in Law & I got 240 Dollars cash for it—having pd 10$ Charges." Also sends "Mr Mickles acknowledgement of the Payment of 300$ about one year ago—" Wonders if Clay will "serve me in the Claim of S Wante" if he is not already "concerned on The other Side." ALS. KyU. For Sprigg, see espec. 1:70, 109-10.

To WILLIAM TAYLOR   Lexington, May 18, 1803

Your's of the 25h. April[1] has reached me—

In allowing the Credit to Adam Shepherd I was governed as stated in my letter by a receipt in your hand writing in his possession. He resides at a considerable distance from me,[2] but I will nevertheless procure the original or a Copy and forward it to you.

In making the charge of $200 as paid you by Mr. [Thomas] Hockley,[3] I was guided by one of your letters in which I think you state that you had received that sum, but was obliged previously to give bond and Security to return it, in case a certain attachment laid on Mess. Bickham and Reese[4] should not be discharged—That suit I learn is discontinued. Now I considered myself as responsible to you in case you should be ever called upon to return the money,—and upon this principle made the charge. I am pretty certain the money is in Mr. Hockley's hands, and expect that you will receive it before this reaches you: if you do not I will remit it as soon as possible after hearing from you.[5]

I have seen Mr. [Peyton] Short, who promises to pay the balance of [Haden] Edward's[6] draft in the course of a month—I have a Judgment against him, and can whenever you direct it order execution. He is a man of great & increasing wealth, and the debt is perfectly safe. I beg you therefore to submit to no sacrifice.

I am sorry that you should have the least doubt as to the propriety of two charges in my account, which you desire me to reconsider: that they are legal I have no doubt, but if they are not also conscientious I will expunge them.

The first is a charge of full Commission on [John] Heugh and [Alexander] Ralston's debt.[7] With respect to the sacrifice you made, my various letters to you will prove that I always dissuaded you against it. After the delivery bond was taken the debt was put out of all doubt, and I should have absolutely received the whole amount within a few days after the receipt of your letter informing me of the compromise. I regreted it much on your account. But you say I was not at the trouble of "receiving and paying away the money." This did not constitute one twentieth part of those Services, for the performance of which I became entitled to the 5 P[er] Cent—They comprehend corresponding with yourself & the def[endan]ts, attending to giving notices for taking depositions, superintending the Marshall, going to see the defts, who reside nearly 100 miles from me, &c &c. Besides I absolutely expended nearly $40 in employing agents for which I can now shew vouchers, but for which I made no charge against you. But if you had a right to receive a part of Heugh & Ralston's debt and thereby deprive me of my Commission, might you not also have received the whole of that debt, Shepherd & [Austin] H[ubbard] & [Mann] Satterwhites,[8] and deprived me of my Commission on them also?

With respect to the charge of Commission upon the $400 received of Short, I beg leave to remark that you lodged with me a discretionary power to remit as I deemed best, in the exercise of which I declare I always consulted exclusively your interest and advantage. When I received Edward's bill I believed it would be paid—I was disappointed. But on the return of it protested, it certainly was a new debt, and you had a right to employ any other attorney as well as myself—If you had employed any other you would have had to give 5 P Cent—You will recollect too that you receive 10 P Cent damages for the protest. I had the same routine of services (not I admit so troublesome) to perform as in the first instance—It was necessary for me to give notice of the protest, bring a Suit collect the money, repeatedly call upon the parties &c.

Fearing lest I might err with respect to these charges as I am judging in a case in which I am interested, I have consulted with several gentlemen, who have been more experienced in Collecting than myself, and they all concur with me that I am justified both by law and equity in making them.

I thank you for the polite things you are pleased to say of me. I cannot forbear remarking that I have done business for no gentleman whatever with more pleasure than for yourself. And as I desire that our accounts shall be closed in that spirit of harmony which has marked our whole correspondence, permit me to observe that I will make no further charge against you for any trouble I may be at relative to the balance of Shorts debt.

I am sorry I have been unable yet to forward you the balance due you as per my account—I assure you it is from no other cause but the difficulty of getting light money.[9] I expect Mr. H[enry] Purviance[10] will start for Baltimore in 8 or ten days; by him I will endeavour to send the Specie if I cannot procure Notes—You shall also then hear from me relative to Mr. [Charles Peter Steven] Wante's affair—[11]

ALS. KyU.   1. See 1:109-10.   2. He lived in Bardstown, Ky. See 1:19.   3. For Hockley, see 1:100.   4. For Bickham and Reese, see 1:137.   5. See 1:105, 109, 111-12.   6. See 1:70.   7. See Clay to Taylor, Dec. 2, 1800.   8. *Ibid.*; Clay to Taylor, Nov. 1, 1799.   9. See 1:84.   10. For Purviance, see 1:112.   11. Clay to Taylor, Jan. 13, 1803.

To HARRY TOULMIN[1]   Frankfort, Ky., May 10, 1804

Agreeably to your request I have endeavoured to recollect the circumstances attending the trial of Cox,[2] convicted in the District Court of Lexington for Arson. I appeared for him, as his Counsel, before the examining Court; but having no notes of the Evidence adduced, or the Authorities cited, I cannot undertake from memory to state, with any accuracy, the testimony or the Law relied upon against him. I did not appear for him on his final trial, not because I thought his case desparate or indefensible, but owing to his not being able or willing to pay my fee; and because he was not in my opinion one of that description of cases which address themselves to the feelings and humanity of the Bar.

Since the trial and conviction I have been induced to believe, from information communicated to me by several, that he was not the perpetrator of the Crime. In particular I recollect that Mr. Daniel Weible[3] now dece[ase]d, whose house was destroyed, informed me that he was satisfied Cox was not guilty—that another person was; and he wished to know how the former might be relieved, and the latter punished. I mentioned to him the course he might take, but this happened not long before his death, when from his infirmities & misfortunes he was I presume prevented from taking any decisive step. I think it just however to state that I have heard a bad character of Cox.

ALS. Henry Clay Memorial Foundation, Lexington, Ky.   1. For Toulmin, see 1:125.   2. Not found.   3. Weible was a cabinet maker in Fayette County. Charles R. Staples, *The History of Pioneer Lexington, 1779-1806* (Lexington, 1939), 66.

To EDWARD SHOEMAKER[1]   Frankfort, Ky., July 22, 1805

Your favour of the 23d. May last[2] should have been answered earlier, had I not been endeavouring to possess myself of the necessary information ever since its receipt. Among the Memoranda left in my care by Mr. [James] Brown,[3] I find he notices your claim upon [Phillips] Caldwell,[4] and states that through Mr. [William] Leavy[5] he had made you a remittance, and that for the balance of your debt he had taken an order upon Col. [Thomas] Todd & one upon Mr. [John] Jordan [Jr.].[6] The latter gentleman says he has an a/c ag[ains]t. Mr. Brown covering the demand. The order upon the former gentleman was to be paid out of a Sum due Mr. Caldwell from John Smith,[7] who says he has an account agt. Mr. Brown nearly balancing the order. In this state of the business I can do nothing until I hear from Mr Brown, to whom I shall immediately write on this subject. If the claims of those gentlemen are just the balance will be remitted to you as soon as I obtain an answer from Mr. Brown out of funds of his in this Country. If they are unjust those gentlemen I have no doubt will immediately pay up what is due from them.[8] So that in any event you may I presume calculate upon the debt being entirely safe, waiting only 'till the proper explanations take place, when you shall again hear from me. In the mean time should you have occasion to write to me be pleased to address me at Lexington, from which place my absence is only temporary.

ALS. KyU.   1. For Shoemaker, see 1:208.   2. Not found.   3. For Brown, see 1:31-32.   4. For Caldwell, see 1:2, which gives the name as Philips Caldwell; however, the name is usually spelled with two "ls." See Lewis & Richard H. Collins, *History of Kentucky*, 2 vols. (Cynthiana, Ky., 1874; reprint ed., 1966), 2:367.   5. For Leavy, see 1:9.   6. For Todd, see 1:27; for Jordan, 1:52.   7. For Smith, see 1:200.   8. See also 1:207-8, 218, 353-54, 376.

To JOHN BALLINGER[1]   Lexington, September 8, 1806

I received your favour of the 30h. August.[2] You will have no difficulty in disposing of the draft in this place to which you allude. Being in the habit of remitting money occasionally to the Eastward I will take it of you & give you the Cash at any time for it.

I heard of the unprincipled opposition which you had to encounter in your election & rejoiced most sincerely when I learnt that you had defeated it.[3] I never had any high opinion of Col. Cock,[4] but I did not suppose him capable of inventing so infamous a falsehood. His ignorance is as great as his malevolence; for if he had known any thing about the operations of the Bank, he must have been convinced that I could never have promised to supply you with money from that quarter, no individual being able to controul its measures.

I thank you for your printed defense inclosed in your letter. The people only want information to do what is right. And this production of yours was well calculated to afford it to them. I shall be glad to see Col. Knox.[5] He is an odd but I believe an honest man.

When I passed through the wilderness in 1797 I was much struck with the Spruce pine as a beautiful ever green. I am very anxious to propagate it on a little farm[6] that I am improving near this place. It would be too much to ask you to procure for me some of the small plants, but if you will get me some of the seed I shall esteem it as a favour.

I still think it is advisable to populate the wilderness, and for my own part shall have no objection to dispose of the Land upon Yellow Creek &c. on terms of mutual justice.

ALS. Courtesy of M.W. Anderson, Lexington, Ky. Addressed to Ballinger "near Barboursville [*sic*, Barbourville] Knox County Kentucky."   1. For Ballinger, who had been elected to the Kentucky legislature, see 1:601.   2. Not found.   3. The nature of the "unprincipled opposition" has not been determined.   4. Possibly Col. William Cocke, a U.S. senator from East Tennessee who explored eastern Kentucky and Tennessee with Daniel Boone. *BDAC*.   5. Probably James Knox. See 1:312.   6. "Ashland."

To JOSEPH M. STREET[1]   Wheeler [*sic*, Wheeling], Va. (W.Va.),
                                                        December 17, 1806

I forgot before I left Frankfort to request that you would forward to me at Washington your paper.[2] Whatever relates to Kentucky will be peculiarly interesting to me; and you will be so obliging as to transmit to me your paper commencing with those of the two last weeks from this time.

I have thus far advanced on my journey,[3] amidst bad weather and wretched roads, tho' I confess I have found them better than I expected. I still indulge the hope of dining on oysters at the _____ city on Xmas day.

Copy. *The Annals of Iowa*, 3rd series (April, 1901), 5:71-72.   1. For Street, see 1:246.   2. Street was a founder of the Frankfort (Ky.) *Western World*.   3. Clay was on his way to Washington to assume the Senate seat resigned by John Adair. See 1:254-55.

To Joseph H. Nicholson, "Friday morning," *ca.* January, 1807. Reports that "by the laws of Kentucky, subjecting to sale lands for taxes, a provisio is made in favour of persons labouring under the usual disabilities of two years after the removal of their respective disabilities, to comply with those laws; & he presumes that under this saving Mr. N's friend may be able to regain his land. The Sales of land for taxes, especially those made several years ago, were very irregularly conducted, and very few of them will stand the test of judicial enquiry. And, in the case alluded to by Mr. N., it is very probable that, upon investigation, it will be found that the sale is defective, independent of the minority of the proprietor. The liberty to redeem lands sold for taxes did not exist in Kentucky, until during the last Session of the Legislature, when an act was passed [1:252] giving the owner two years after the sale to redeem the land, by paying in the case of individual purchasers, 100 per Cent upon the purchase money, & in cases where the land is struck off to the State, in default of bidders, by paying 50 P[er] Cent upon the purchase money." AL. NcU.

Letter dated on the basis of the passage of the Bill for Redemption of Lands Sold for Taxes, which was passed on November 5, 1806, and the letter to Nicholson on January 25, 1807. For Nicholson, see 1:229 and *BDAC*.

To JOSEPH H. NICHOLSON   Washington, January 25, 1807
I had prepared the inclosed answer to your note,[1] intending to deliver it the next morning at the Capitol, where I expected to have the pleasure of seeing you. Upon going there I learnt that you had departed for Baltimore.

Since you left here nothing very interesting has occurred. On yesterday an application [was ma]de, at the instance of [Justus Erick] Bollman or [Samuel Swartwou]t, for a H[abeas]. Corpus, which was granted, returnable on tomorrow to the Court of this District now in Session.[2] At the earnest entreaty of Bollman an interview has been granted to him with the President [Thomas Jefferson], but the result has not transpired.[3]

ALS. NcU.   1. Enclosure is probably Clay to Nicholson, *ca.* Jan., 1807. Nicholson's note has not been found.   2. For Bollman and Swartwout and their involvement in the Aaron Burr conspiracy, see 1:272-76, 280-81.   3. President Jefferson offered Bollman immunity from prosecution if he would testify against Burr. Jefferson sent George Hay, U.S. attorney for the Virginia district, a signed pardon for Bollman, but when it was offered him in open court, Bollman refused. Thomas P. Abernethy, *The Burr Conspiracy* (New York, 1954), 196-97, 230, 233.

To JOSEPH H. NICHOLSON   Washington, D.C., February 6, 1807
Your's of the 4th. was duly received.[1] I am sorry to hear that you dislocated your shoulder but am glad that it is getting better. I reside in Lexington (K) where your letters will find me; and it will give me pleasure to be able to promote the redemption of your friends land from the hands of what I have always considered vile speculation.[2]

It is understood here that [Justus Erick] Bollman had an interview with the President [Thomas Jefferson]. What was the result is not known abroad.[3] The circumstance has afforded ground of censure upon the chief magistrate, who is supposed by some to have degraded his office in lending an ear to a man accused with Treason.

The triumvirate of Bollman, [Samuel] Swartwout & [James] Alexander have applied to the Supreme Court for a H[abeas]. Corpus. The power to *award* one is doubted by the Bench (and particularly [Samuel] Chase) and is to be discussed to day.[4] The sceptics say, that it is not within the enumerated powers vested by the Constitution, in the Supreme Court. Nothing new.

ALS. NcU.   1. Not found.   2. Clay to Nicholson, *ca.* Jan., 1807.   3. Clay to Nicholson, Jan. 25, 1807.   4. See 1:280-81. For Chase, see 1:575 and *DAB*.

To JOHN COBURN[1]   Paris, Ky., May 20, 1807

I should have earlier answered your favor of the 21. Apl—[2] but had not when I received it the contract between Mr. [Elijah] Current[3] and myself. You are entitled to a credit of $700 for the property in Lexington as paid the first of Apl. 1807, it having been agreed between us that it should be received on account of the last payment agreed to be made by Mr. Current for the land, which became due on that day. As you contemplate leaving the State,[4] it will be necessary to take a deed from you for the land recovered by Col. [Thomas] Hart,[5] and I also wish to procure a deed for the Lexington property. Will you be pleased to inform me whether you will be in this quarter before your departure, or soon after your return?

Your Law business under my care shall receive my best attention.

Wishing you much satisfaction with the Country to which you propose migrating and much happiness . . .

ALS. KyU.   1. For Coburn, see 1:72.   2. Not found.   3. Current not identified, but see 1:295.   4. Coburn became judge of the Orleans Territory in St. Louis and served there until 1809. H. Levin, *Lawyers and Lawmakers of Kentucky* (Chicago, 1897), 669.   5. For Hart, see 1:15-16. For this matter, see also 1:295.

From Peyton Short, "Greenfield," Woodford County, Ky., July 3, 1807. Encloses a copy [not found] of a letter "stating that Kincaid had forbid their delivering me any more goods on his order . . . (meaning the order for $200 as stated in his Acc[oun]t. which is the only payment of the kind he ever made me)—By this the inference seems clear that I have not recd. more goods than the amt. delivered on the 13th. of the same Month as stated in the Bill accompanying the papers submitted to the Consideration of the Referees—as also in their note to me of the same date, wherein they state that the Sum of (I believe) £40..0..5½ is the amt. delivered me on Kincaid's said Order—" Adds that "they advanced Mr. Davidson *on my Acc[oun]t* a small Sum in mdze [merchandise], as I informed both you & the Referee last Evening—" ALS. KyLoF. Kincaid and Davidson have not been identified.

From Thomas Hart, [Lexington], November 2, 1807. Assigns to Clay "value recd." on a bond from Cuthbert Banks, dated February 17, 1806, for the sum of $2,465. This bond has the "Condition . . . that if the said Cuthbert Banks shall well and truly pay to the said Thomas Hart Senr. the sum of Twelve Hundred & Thirty two Dollars, fifty cents on or before the 16h. Day of September 1808 with legal interest thereon from the 16h. Day of September 1805 then this obligation [is] to be void, otherwise to remain in full force & virtue." Copy. KyU. Endorsed by Clay: "Recd. Payment." For Banks, see 1:110.

From Harry Innes, Frankfort, Ky. January 29, 1808. Requests an investigation by the Kentucky legislature into his conduct as U.S. judge for the Kentucky district. Copy. Printed in Ky. H. of Reps., *Journal* . . . 1807-1808, pp. 105-6. For the resolutions relating to Innes, see 1:319-20.

To ADAM BEATTY[1]   Lexington, May 7, 1808
I did not receive your favor[2] until after I had addressed my letter to you, stating the event of Fitzgerald vs. Fitzgerald.[3] I am sorry that your private interests forbid your offering for the Legislature.[4] It would have afforded me real pleasure to have seen you a member of that body. I cannot advise you to become a Candidate for the Electoral office, because I doubt your acquaintance being sufficiently extensive to ensure success. In your quarter you would get votes, perhaps the bulk of them; you would no doubt also obtain some here, but still I apprehend you would not be able to command a sufficient number to elect you. Indeed I do not think that the office ought to possess any charms for you. One requiring more mental exertion would be better adapted to your talents and your youth. The office in question is generally bestowed on men of more advanced years. Nevertheless if you offer, you may count on my suffrage.

I regret that I do not practice in Clarke [*sic*, Clark County] for the sake of Miss Green,[5] of whose case I have heard, and whose claim it appears to me for justice is so well founded. I have rejected an application made in behalf of Lee.[6] And I most sincerely wish that the trial will evince the utter detestation which all virtuous men ought to display at conduct so base and unworthy.

ALS. KyLoF. 1. For Beatty, see 1:61. 2. Not found. 3. Not found. 4. Beatty was elected as a representative to the state legislature from Mason County in August, 1809. Kentucky *Gazette*, August 15, 1809. 5. Reference obscure. 6. Reference obscure.

To PRESLEY NEVILLE[1]   Lexington, August 8, 1808
I took the liberty a few days ago of inclosing to your care the first number of a set of Exchange,[2] with a request that you would obtain upon it the acceptance of Mr. Wilkins[3] and transmit it to Mr. [Luke] Tiernan of Baltimore. To guard against possible miscarriage I now send you the second number, which you will do me the favor to present & in like manner forward.[4]

I hope to be able some how or other to pay the obligation which you will place me under.

ALS. KyU. 1. For Neville, see 1:373. 2. Not found. 3. Either Charles Wilkins or his brother, John Wilkins, Jr. See 1:373. 4. For Tiernan, see 1:256. See also 1:372-73.

To [Whom It May Concern], June 3, 1809. Certifies concerning "the compilation of the Acts of the Legislature, made by Mr. [William] Littell," and published "by Mr. [William] Hunter; that I conceive the plan of the work a very good one, combining all the advantages of any digest of Legislative Acts I have seen, and some peculiar to itself, and that I have no hesitation in saying, that it merits public patronage." Copy. Printed in Ky. Sen., *Journal* . . . 1815-1816, p. 82. Enclosed with Hunter's recommendations which accompanied his letter, dated December 19, 1815, to the Kentucky house and senate. *Ibid.*, 80-84.

For Hunter, see 1:335; for Littell, see *DAB*. Littell's *The Statute Law of Kentucky* . . . was published between 1809-19 in five volumes in Frankfort, Ky., with William Hunter as the printer.

To Unknown Recipient, June 16, 1809. Introduces Maj. Jonathan Taylor [1:411], who "visits Washington in relation to the Saline belonging to the Government on the Wabash [2:165-66]." Identifies Taylor as one of the lessees of that property, and adds that the lessees "contemplate making a proposition for a renewal of the Lease, upon terms which seem to me to be advantageous to the public interest." Notes that the "heavy expences incurred by the lessees— the losses sustained by them from the extraordinary floods of last winter and spring—and the state of their preparations, whilst they give the lessees some claim to indulgence, enable them to prosecute the manufacture of the article with more effect than any others could do." ALS. MH. The seller, George D. Smith, New York City, in advertising this letter identified the recipient as "probably James Madison"; however, there is nothing written on the letter to indicate who the recipient might have been.

To ADAM BEATTY   Lexington, July 8, 1809
I received your favor of the 29 May.[1] Mr. [James] Hughes having stated to me that a probability existed of procuring the elder patent upon the land conveyed by the McConnells to [Humphrey] Marshall,[2] I was willing to wait a short time until it was ascertained whether this prior grant could be actually obtained. You were therefore right in not immediately commencing the suit contemplated. After having forborne the time proposed I will give you dire[c]tions about the institution of the suit—For the representatives of Marshall are very desirous to bring this matter to some final issue.

I was glad to learn that you were a Candidate for your County; and I sincerely hope that the people will see their true interests & elect you.[3] I feel extremely desirous that whilst you do not neglect the interests of your family you should take in the public view that prominent ground which you merit. Public sentiment is gaining strength daily in favor of adequate if not liberal salaries to our Judges of the Court of Appeals. On that bench a vacancy will I presume arise in a year or two; and I have often thought of yourself for the station. Should you have any desire for it, the object would be greatly promoted by a seat in the Legislature.[4]

ALS. Courtesy of Earl M. Ratzer, Highland Park, Ill.   1. Not found.   2. For Hughes, see 1:17; for Francis and James McConnell, 1:797, 879; for Marshall, 1:192. 3. Clay to Beatty, May 7, 1808.   4. See 1:61.

To UNKNOWN RECIPIENT   Washington, February 8, 1810
I received your favor of the 16 Jan.[1] Some time prior to my departure from Kentucky, and before I was appointed to the station which I now fill, I wrote to some of my friends here in favor of the application

of Mr. Allen of Paris for the office referred to by you.[2] This circumstance, which I thought it due to candor to state, will not however prevent me from doing justice to your pretensions. At the same time I must observe that I entertain some doubt whether any Kentuckian will receive the appointment in question, in consequence of so many distinguished offices having been already bestowed on gentlemen from that Country. The Secretary of State [Robert Smith] informed me yesterday that the nomination will shortly be made, but of whom I cannot even conjecture.[3]

We have no news from England yet as to the effect produced there by [Francis James] Jackson's dismissal.[4] I am persuaded that we shall not at present have War unless it is made upon us.

ALS. KyU.   1. Not found.   2. Possibly John Allen. See 1:38.   3. Reference obscure.   4. See 1:457. See also Clay to Daveiss, April 19, 1810.

To WILLIAM EUSTICE
[sic, EUSTIS][1]   Washington, February 20, 1810

As Chairman of the Committee[2] to whom has been recommitted; the Bill[3] authorizing a detachment from the Militia of the United States; I am requested to ask of you, a statement of the aggregate amount of the Arms belonging to the United States, actually fit for service; and the places of their deposit.

LS. DNA, RG107, Letters Rec. by Sec. of War, Jan. 1810-Oct. 1811 (M221, R35).   1. See 1:542.   2. A House Select Committee of 20 members. *Annals of Congress*, 11 Cong., 2 Sess., 1385.   3. The "Act authorizing a detachment from the militia of the United States," was recommitted on Feb. 8, 1810. The Select Committee reported the bill with amendments and the House began consideration on March 1. The bill passed the House on March 20, 1810, by a vote of 70 to 47. On April 28 the Senate postponed consideration until Dec., 1810. The act finally passed Congress and became a law on April 10, 1812. *Ibid.*, 675, 1385, 1471, 1604; 2 *U.S. Stat.*, 705-7.

To UNKNOWN RECIPIENT   Washington, March 13, 1810
I have procured for you a copy of the Map of the Rapids of the Ohio, exhibiting the scite [site?] of the proposed Canal[1] &c. It is very handsomely executed, but was attended with more expense than I expected, having cost me $20 which I have paid, and which you will be pleased to remit me.

But how shall I send you the map? It is large for the mail, & besides would be injured by folding.

ALS. OCHP.   1. See 1:162, 284-87, and Clay to Unknown Recipient, March 21, 1810.

To UNKNOWN RECIPIENT   Washington, March 21, 1810
I recd your favor with the bill remitted to pay for the Map I procured for you.[1] I have this moment delivered it to Mr. Jeffers[2] who says he will take it with him to Philadelphia.

We were yesterday engaged on the discussion of the System of internal improvements. Today a Committee has been appointed to bring in a bill to authorize the President to subscribe a certain number of shares to the Ohio Canal. I am persuaded, from the favorable indication given, that a bill will pass this body affording liberal aid for the accomplishment of the object.[3] I cannot answer for the other house.

ALS. OCHP. 1. Clay to Unknown Recipient, March 13, 1810. 2. Not identified.
3. An "Act authorizing a subscription on the part of the United States to the stock of the
Ohio Canal Company" passed the Senate on March 29, 1810. In the House it was
committed to the Committee of the Whole on March 31 from which it did not emerge.
Annals of Congress, 11 Cong., 2 Sess., 1679, 1699. For the Ohio Canal Company, see also
1:284-87.

To JOHN W. HUNT[1]   Washington, March 28, 1810
I recd. from Col. [Nathaniel] Rochester[2] a few days ago $373 which he
collected from Osborne [sic, Osborn] Sprigg[3] for advances made by Mr.
[Thomas] Hart [Jr.] for his Son in Kentucky. I now inclose a Check
drawn by the Cashier of the Branch Bank of the U.S. here on the Cashier of the B[ranch]. B[ank]. at Baltimore for that sum, which I have
made payable to yourself Mr. [Abraham S.] Barton & John Hart.[4]

We are still with[ou]t. official intelligence from Europe; and the
precise time of the adjournment of Congress cannot be fixed until we
hear from thence. But I still indulge the hope of being with you
ab[ou]t. the first of May.[5]

I have some inquiries now on foot as to the practicability of effecting the Loan which we have had in contemplation. As soon as I know
the result I will communicate it.

ALS. Henry Clay Memorial Foundation, Lexington, Ky. 1. See 1:46. 2. See 1:120.
3. Sprigg, a surveyor, had owned land in Marion and Jefferson counties. *RKHS*, 22:36;
32:174; 57:323. 4. This transaction undoubtedly was part of settling the estate of
Thomas Hart, Jr., of which Clay, Hunt, Barton, and John Hart were all executors. See
1:427. 5. Congress adjourned on May 1, 1810.

To JOSEPH HAMILTON DAVEISS[1]   Washington, April 19, 1810
I thank you for your very friendly attention to my interests. I know not
how I shall discharge the obligation which you have placed me under.[2]

The Quarter Master Department bill has passed the Senate, but I
fear it will not get through the other house.[3] Nor indeed will there be I
apprehend any military measures adopted this Session. The Fed. Gentlemen are all opposed to them, and aided by a portion of republicans
who think we ought not to engage in War for any injury whatever short
of invasion, they defeat every proposition of the kind.

Before the receipt of your favor of the 7th.[4] I had conversed with
several of the Kentucky representation, who avow a disposition to serve
you, to get you an appointment in the Quarter Master department, in
the event of the passage of the bill. They promised cooperation with
me. And if the bill should be enacted into a Law, we will endeavor to
promote your wishes on this subject.

You will have seen [Duc de] Cadore's letter to [John] Armstrong[.]
It is not known here to be official, but I entertain very little doubt of its
authenticity. Should this be the fact it certainly destroys all hope of an
arrangement with France, if we are to understand (as I do) that War
with Britain must be the price of such arrangement.[5] Nor have we
much more I apprehend to expect from England. On the 2d. of Jan.
Pinckney [sic, William Pinkney] delivered an official note to [Richard
Colley] Wellesley, and notwithstanding his pacific professions it remained unanswered as late as the 3d. March![6] Possibly we may at-

tribute this delay to the embarrassments of the ministerialists who on several great occasions in the house of Commons were left in the minority; and yet these very embarrassments it would seem to me ought to have accelerated an adjustment with us.

[James] Wilkinson is here; & the Committees raised to investigate his conduct are progressing in this duty.[7]

B[enjamin]. Howard is appointed Governor of Louisiana.[8]

I expect to be at home about the 8h. or 10h. of May monday (22d. inst.) being fixed for adjournment of Congress. You will greatly oblige me by continuing your friendly attentions to my professional business.

ALS. Courtesy of Mrs. B.F. Norflett, Harrodsburg, Ky.   1. For Daveiss, see 1:32 and *DAB*.   2. Daveiss had apparently been taking care of Clay's law practice while Clay was in Washington.   3. The Quartermaster bill was reported in the Senate on April 12 and passed that body on April 16. It reached the House on the 16th, was read twice and committed on the 17th, and was not again taken up. *Annals of Congress*, 11 Cong., 2 Sess., 598, 657, 1858, 1879.   4. Not found.   5. For the Duc de Cadore, the French foreign minister, see 1:575. For Gen. John Armstrong, U.S. minister to France, see 1:229. Reference is probably to Cadore's letter to Armstrong of Feb. 14, 1810, in which he apparently stated that in order for France to lift Napoleon's decrees, the U.S. would have to pledge "not to submit to the British edicts." For a discussion of this letter, see *State Papers and Publick Documents of the United States . . .* , 10 vols. (Boston, 1817), 7:402.   6. Pinkney's letter to Wellesley on Jan. 2 dealt with the American demand that Francis James Jackson, the British minister to the U.S., be removed. Wellesley did not reply officially until March 14, 1810. Although he implied that Jackson would be recalled, the British did not quickly replace him; instead, they left a chargé as the top-ranking diplomatic official in the U.S. for over a year. For Pinkney, Wellesley, and Jackson and this dispute, see 1:456-57. For Pinkney, see also 1:271. Pinkney's letter of Jan. 2 and Wellesley's of March 14 are printed in *State Papers and Publick Documents*, 7:414-26.   7. This second congressional investigation of Wilkinson led to a court martial and a verdict of "not guilty" rendered Dec. 25, 1811. See *DAB*; also 1:452-56, 470.   8. See 1:470.

To Caesar A. Rodney, Washington, D.C., September 15, 1810. Reports having heard that William Creighton, Jr. [1:542], U.S. attorney for the District of Ohio, contemplates resigning, and, if so, hopes that "John Monroe [1:198], at present a Judge of the Superior Court of this State," will receive the appointment. Asserts that Monroe "is a firm republican, and . . . was in favor of the election of Mr. [James] Madison." Adds that the "only obstacle to his appointment that occurs to me is, his residence in Kentucky. This he will obviate by an immediate removal to Ohio, upon receiving the Commission or an assurance of it. It is further obviated by the fact, that there is not I believe one Attorney of eminence in Ohio, who is not of the Federal tribe."

Concludes: "I mean to endeavor to procure & take in with me a pair of carriage horses; and if I should succeed in getting such as I approve they shall be tendered to you." ALS. DNA, RG59, General Records of the State Dept., A. & R., James Madison administration. Written from Lexington, Ky.

For Rodney, U.S. attorney general, see 1:311, *DAB*, and *BDAC*. Creighton remained district attorney until mid-1811. *DAB*.

To FREDERICK RIDGELY[1]   Washington, January 17, 1811
I paid to Mr. F[rancis Scott]. Key[2] the $20 which you sent by me, for which he obtained the inclosed receipt from Dr. Worthington, the security for the Costs of the suit vs Wilkinson.[3]

I am sorry to inform you that the prospect of receiving any thing from Wilkinson is extremely unpromising indeed. When he was first sued, Mr. Key informs me he spoke of giving some land in discharge of the debt; but in a late conversation which he has had with him he declared his intention to be unalterably fixed to make no distinction among his creditors but to surrender his property for the benefit of them all, and to avail himself of the insolvent law as soon as his residence here entitled him to it. He has given good bail in the action, your friend Mr. Duval,[4] who will of course take care that he is not made liable for the debt. I have conceived from the unfavorable account given me by Mr. Key, that it is scarcely necessary to apply to Wilkinson himself. Indeed it has occurred to me that he will in all probability make a merit of his insolvency. It is evident, from the tenor of the prints that have undertaken his defense, that he desires to be considered as a persecuted patriot. If he takes the insolvent oath he will avail himself of his poverty to prove 1st. that he never was a pensioner,[5] & 2dly. to shew that he has been ruined by the oppression of his enemies. I have however stated to Mr. Key that I shall be ready to co-operate with him in any way for your benefit, and that if Wilkinson makes any proposal to apprize me of it; and if it shall hereafter appear that an application to W. himself will be of any advantage I shall not fail to make it; for you know how much pleasure I would take in promoting your interest.

I hope my dear Ridgley [sic, Ridgely] you will have a parental eye upon our children. Our anxieties are continually awake about them. Mrs. [Lucretia Hart] Clay's health has been very good ever since our departure from home. My own is somewhat precarious. I have never been without cold since my arrival here, and my gums are far from being well—indeed I fear that the disorder in them is progressing. I have some thought of consulting some eminent physician here on the subject of them. What think you of it? If you deem it advisable, you will oblige me, when entirely at leisure, by giving an historical description of the disease which has affected them—such an one as will enable me to lay the case before [Benjamin] Rush or [Benjamin Smith] Barton.[6]

ALS. KyU.   1. See 1:127.   2. At this time Key was practicing law with his uncle Philip Barton Key. DAB.   3. On July 3, 1811, James Wilkinson transferred to trustees "in trust for the benefit of his creditors" all his lands in Kentucky and Ohio. He had become heavily indebted during the course of two congressional investigations. For Wilkinson's financial problems and the investigations, see 1:470; 6:997-98; Clay to Daveiss, April 19, 1810. Worthington has not been identified.   4. Possibly Gabriel Duval, who was appointed to the Supreme Court later in 1811. See 1:575.   5. Of Spain. See DAB.   6. For both Rush (1745-1813), the best known American physician of the day, and Barton (1766-1815), who worked with Rush, see DAB.

From Joshua Lewis, New Orleans, February 1, 1811. States that his "neglect of you since my residence in this Country has been so inexcusable as to leave me without apology." Adds that "I have had abundant reason to justify myself to my friends could I have persuaded myself that they would for a moment credit the malicious calumnies published against myself and the other members of the Court. These libellers are creatures of no standing and excite the indignation of every honest man in the community."

Explains that he is writing "to beg your interest in favour of your Brother John Clay, for whose welfare and happiness I . . . feel a sincere concern." Does not know what caused John's business failure, but "He certainly has saved nothing out of the wreck of his property; and his Father in law [Martin Duralde], altho' wealthy, will not . . . make him an advance during his life." Notes, however, that "his friends have the sam[e] confidence in his integrity and honour that they had prior to his misfortunes," so "can you not procure him an appointment under the Genl. Govt. should a vacancy occur or a new office be created which would give him a permanent support?" Mentions that "His Brother in law [Martin Duralde, Jr.] has lately been appointed Marshal of this District, and it is said will not accept. That office would suit your brother and he is very competent to discharge the duties of it, and I have no doubt could give security." ALS. DeHi.

For Joshua Lewis, see 1:158-59; 2:691. This letter is the one mentioned as "Not found" in 1:546, note 1. For John Clay's financial problems, see Subject Index: Volumes 1-6 in 7:707 and espec. 3:338-39. For his wife's family, see 1:574 which, however, erroneously states that Martin Duralde, Jr., became marshal of the New Orleans Territory. In fact, he did not accept the appointment due to ill health. See Dunbar Rowland (ed.), *Official Letter Books of W.C.C. Claiborne 1801-1816,* 6 vols. (Jackson, Miss., 1917), 5:143, 183-84.

The calumnies against the court to which Lewis refers are probably expressions of public indignation over the inability of the courts to deal with Gen. James Wilkinson during the Aaron Burr episode and the military occupation of the Batture in New Orleans. See 1:452-56.

From Adam Rankin, Henderson, Ky., April 12, 1811. Thanks Clay for his "attention to my requiest in my letters to you [not found], and am glad you received what was offerd and think my claim for diet will be best to be charged ag[ains]t. the officer directing me to find diet to the sick." Hopes "you will be so good as to let Mr. John Cock have which is $90 13/100." ALS. DLC-TJC (DNA, M212, R12). Endorsed by Clay: "Rankin to Clay Rect. for Money recd. at Washington City." Endorsed by John Cock: "Recd. payment, 18. Jun. 11."

For Dr. Adam Rankin, one of the first settlers of Henderson, see Edmund L. Starling, *History of Henderson County, Kentucky* . . . (Henderson, Ky., 1887), 66, 146, 259, 789-90. Not to be confused with Adam Rankin of Lexington, who appears in 1:793.

Cock is possibly John Cocke of Nelson County, Ky. G. Glen Clift, *"Second Census" of Kentucky, 1800* . . . (Frankfort, Ky., 1954).

To UNKNOWN RECIPIENT[1]   Lexington, May 27, 1811
Col. [William] Russell[2] is still in this neighbourhood, tho' he has reported himself to Genl. [Wade] Hampton.[3] His health sustained a shock when he was below before that induces his friends, and myself among others, to apprehend that he will be sacrificed if he is again exposed to so southern a clime.[4] His eyes are so weakened that I think total blindness is very far from being improbable. In the event of any active service in the South he is very desirous of participating in it; but if none such is likely would it not be practicable, without detriment to the public service, to assign him a station more congenial with his constitution & his present state of health? Such an arrangement would be very gratifying to many of us who feel an interest in his preservation.

ALS. ViU.   1. Possibly addressed to Secretary of State James Monroe or to Secretary of War Willian Eustis. This letter originally was located in the papers of Monroe's law office.   2. See 1:123.   3. For Hampton, see *HRDUSA,* 496 and *DAB.*   4. Russell had been serving on the lower Mississippi, and Clay evidently feared he would be sent back there in response to President Madison's proclamation of Oct. 27, 1810, ordering American occupation of West Florida. Russell apparently did not return to the South, however, because he took part in the Battle of Tippecanoe in the Northwest on Nov. 7, 1811. See 1:122-23, 516, 519-22 and J.M. Armstrong (pub.), *Encyclopedia of Kentucky* (Cincinnati, 1878), 138.

To Joseph H. Nicholson, Baltimore, June 14, 1811. States that he will be pleased "to render any service to yourself, or any of your friends, and particularly to the ladies who have engaged your friendly offices." Reports he has already determined that "one tract of 2000 Acres, patented in their father's name, and worth 3 or 4 thousand dollars, has been sold for taxes." In order to know whether the sale was valid, "it will be necessary to know when Peter Shepherd [1:430] died, when the two ladies who are now widows were married, and when their husbands died, and also when they respectively attained their full ages?" Has also learned "that Peter Shepherd created a trust upon his lands," and must know "where the deed was recorded, and what proceedings under it have been had."

Concludes: "I tender you my congratulations upon the affair of the President and the Little Belt, which will excite much more agreeable emotions than that of the Chesapeak[e], to which it may be plead as a sort of offset." ALS. KyU.

Clay again wrote Nicholson from Lexington on October 8, 1811, noting that he had "received the papers of the Ladies [not found]" and had turned them over to Robert Wickliffe [1:82]. Explains that Wickliffe has personal information about some of the land, "and as Congress has been convened at an earlier period than usual . . . I have thought it advisable to place their business under" his direction.

Adds that the "War spirit of our Red brethren, real or imaginary, is I believe about dissipating. Govr. [Benjamin] Howard [1:108], who has just arrived from St. Louis, stated to me that he thinks there exists no serious cause of alarm." ALS. NcU.

On December 21, 1811, Clay wrote Nicholson from Washington stating that he had transmitted "your's of the 19h. inst." to Robert Wickliffe. Adds that the "terms of the contract with your female friends are such as are very usual in Kentucky. Mr. Wickliffe is perhaps the most thrifty member at present at the Bar [of] that State; and the Ladies are exposed to no danger in placing entire confidence in his Ability and his integrity."

Is pleased "to find that the course of public measures which Congress appears to think is called for by the honor of the Nation meets your approbation. War, calamitous as it generally is, seems to me the only alternative worthy of our Country. I should blush to call myself an American were any other adopted, in the existing state of our affairs. Nor do I differ with you in the opinion that it is perhaps necessary to us, intoxicated as we have been by commercial prosperity. Even those who so much deprecate the power of the French Emperor [Napoleon], as it regards us, might I think see in the occupations of War the Nation nerving itself against his ambition, should it be directed ag[ains]t us." Adds that "On the bill from the Senate for raising 25.000 additional troops [1:602-10] there will be in the house some diversity of opinion—not so much as to the nature and object as the quantum of the force." ALS. NcU.

For the engagement between the ships *Chesapeake* and *Leopard* in 1807, see Richard Morris (ed.), *Encyclopedia of American History* (New York, 1953), 135-36. In the affair between the American frigate *President* and the British *Little Belt*, the former mistook the latter for the *Guerriere*, which had impressed a native-born American sailor. The *Little Belt* was disabled by the *President's* attack, and several of her crew were killed or wounded. *Ibid.*, 139.

18

To UNKNOWN RECIPIENT   Washington, December 7, 1811
I recd. your favor of the 4h. inst.[1] I placed your papers in the hands of
Mr. [Langdon] Cheves of South Carolina,[2] who presented them to the
house during the first week of the Session, and they were referred to
the Committee of Claims.[3] That Committee has not yet reported on
the subject, but I presume they will in due time.

The Committee of the whole house this day agreed to the Report
of the Com. of F[oreign]. relations, with the single amendment of striking out the number 10000 in the resolution proposing a Supplemental
force of regulars, and leaving the number to be inserted hereafter in
the bill.[4]

ALS. InU.   1. Not found.   2. For Cheves, see 1:616 and *BDAC*.   3. Not mentioned in *Annals of Congress*, 12 Cong., 1 Sess.   4. This actually had happened the previous day, Dec. 6. *Ibid.*, 413-20. See Clay's speech on the bill to raise an additional military
force, 1:602-10; also Clay to Wilkins, Jan. 18, 1812.

To JOSEPH GALES, JR.[1]   Washington, January 5, 1811 [*sic*, 1812]
I have sketched out two sheets of the remarks I made the other day.[2] I
should guess that the residue will occupy about another sheet. It shall
be sent to you before 1 OClock tomorrow, which I understand you as
being in time for your tuesdays paper.[3] I was much mortified at the
appearance in you paper of an ingrammaticism in the observations I
made on coming to the Chair at the commencem[en]t. of the Session.[4]

ANI. Courtesy of Dr. Thomas D. Clark, Lexington, Ky.   1. For Gales, see 1:848 and
DAB.   2. Reference is to his speech made on Dec. 31, 1811. See 1:602-10.   3. The
speech was published in Gales's paper, the Washington *National Intelligencer*, on Jan. 2
and 7, 1812. Reference here is to the portion published on Tuesday, the 7th.   4. Reference is to his speech of Nov. 4, 1811, accepting the Speakership. See 1:594.

To WILLIAM WILKINS[1]   Washington, January 18, 1812
I take great pleasure in replying to your favor of the 5h. inst.[2]

Judging as well from the acts of the body as from the known sentiments of a great number of individual members of Congress, I do not
entertain a doubt that we shall have War before the termination of the
present Session, unless England repeals her orders in Council, of which
I think there does not exist much probability.[3] As preparatory for this
event, among other measures which have been adopted, a bill has
passed to raise a Military force of 25000, in addition to what is termed
the peace establishment.[4] In commissioning the officers of this force, I
believe I am warranted in saying that all considerations of party will be
disregarded; & that merit will be promoted wherever it may be met
with. I do not hesitate to say that in any recommendation I may make,
the political character of the applicant will not at all guide me.

It will give me much pleasure to further your views, and it is due to
your immediate representative to say, that on conversing with him, in
relation to your appointment, he very promptly declared his entire
willingness to co-operate in rendering successful your application; he
also concurred with me in opinion that you were entitled to a rank at
least not less than a majority.[5]

You will be pleased to command with the utmost freedom the Services of . . .

P.S. The vacancies will be filled up gradually, and you have time enough to back your application by any recommendatory letters you may think proper to transmit here. At the same time it is advisable to do so as early as convenient.[6]

ALS. KyLoF. 1. See 1:638, *DAB*, and *BDAC*. 2. Not found. 3. War was declared on June 18, 1812, two days after Britain repealed the Orders in Council. See 1:674-75 and Reginald Horseman, *The War of 1812* (New York, 1969), 8-24. 4. An "Act to raise an additional military force" was signed into law on Jan. 11, 1812. 2 *U.S. Stat.*, 671. See also 1:602-10. 5. Wilkins's immediate representative in Congress was probably Aaron Lyle of West Middleton, Pa. *BDAC*. Wilkins apparently did not receive a commission. *DAB*; *BDAC*. 6. None have been found.

To Unknown Recipient, March 21, 1812. States that when he previously wrote "to which your's of the 19h. inst. is a reply I proposed paying you $1000 on the terms therein stated and holding myself responsible for whatever balance Mr. Watkins might owe you." Adds that "the proposition was made in consequence of an unaffected ignorance of what was the amt. he does owe you." Does "recollect . . . that he told me, some 12 or 18 months ago, that he owed about $1000, and therefore I am willing to pay that sum now; and as soon as it is ascertained by me from him and Mr. Price what further sum he does owe it shall be immediately paid." Notes that "I have no want of confidence in you, but still in such matters both creditor and debtor ought to understand each other distinctly as to the sum between them." ALS. KyU. Written from Washington, D.C.

Mr. Watkins is probably Clay's half-brother John Watkins, or possibly his step-father Henry. For John and Henry Watkins, see, respectively, 1:2 and 1:190. Price is probably Andrew F. Price. See 1:52.

On June 23, 1812, Clay again wrote reporting that "I have recd. an imperfect statement of the balance supposed to be due from Mr. Watkins to you, from which I am inclined to think there is no material variance between you." Therefore, asks him "to transmit to Mr. [John] McKim [Jr.], or Dr. [Adam] Seybert or any other gentleman here the deed with a statement of the balance you claim, and we will finally arrange the business." ALS. KyU.

For McKim, see 1:640; for Seybert, see 6:562 and *BDAC*.

To GEORGE ADAMS[1] Washington, May 7, 1812

Supposing you to be absent from Frankfort attending the Courts I have not written you for several weeks past, and presume I am to attribute to that cause my not having the pleasure to hear from you.

I received your letter[2] directing me to settle your affair with Mr. Gold.[3] It is arranged between us, subject to his brother's approbation, that you shall pay one half of the debt, that the note shall be sent to Bushnell to enforce payment of it, and that if the amt. be obtained you are to be reimbursed. If his brother ratifies the compromise I will advance the amt. for you.

The Loan has succeeded only in part. About six millions have been subscribed.[4] The Sec. of the Tre[asury].[5] is I understand highly pleased with this partial success, and expects without difficulty to raise any sum requisite for the operations of Govt.

Our Session will not I believe terminate before July.[6]

ALS. KyU. Addressed to Adams in Frankfort, Ky.   1. For Adams, see 1:211; 3:877; and the William Wirt Adams (his son's) entry in *DAB*.   2. Not found.   3. Possibly New York Congressman Thomas R. Gold. *BDAC*.   4. The "Act authorizing a loan for a sum not exceeding eleven millions of dollars" had passed the House on Feb. 25, 1812, and the Senate on March 10. On March 11 the House concurred in the Senate version. When subscriptions opened, approximately $6,118,900 were subscribed in the first two days (May 1-2). *Annals of Congress*, 12 Cong., 1 Sess., 167, 1092, 1198; 3 *U.S. Stat.*, 694.   5. Albert Gallatin.   6. It ended July 6, 1812.

To JAMES MILNOR[1]   Washington, May 21, 1812

Your return to the city of Washington affords me an opportunity of inquiring of you, if the sketch of the debate on Mr. [William] Reed's[2] motion, upon presenting the petition of the Boston merchants, which appears in the Political and Commercial Register of the 6th instant, was furnished by you? The place and manner of the appearance, for the first time, of this sketch, will apologize for the trouble I give you on this occasion.[3]

Copy. Printed in John S. Stone, *A Memoir of The Life of James Milnor, D.D. Late Rector of St. George's Church, New York* (New York, 1849), 70.   1. For Milnor—a lawyer, Pennsylvania congressmen, and later an Episcopal clergyman—see *ibid.*, 3-549 and *BDAC*.   2. For Massachusetts Congressman William Reed (Federalist), see *BDAC*.   3. On April 30, Reed had presented a petition in the House of Representatives signed by about 470 Boston merchants asking permission to withdraw their property from Great Britain and her dependencies under just and reasonable provisions. The reading of the petition was objected to on the ground that it was an insult to the House since it declared that Napoleon's Berlin and Milan decrees were still in force despite the fact that the executive had declared them repealed. Clay, the Speaker, allowed the reading to proceed. After the reading, Reed moved to refer the petition to a select committee. Milnor made a speech, in the ensuing debate, a report of which was published in the Philadelphia *Political and Commercial Register*. The author of the newspaper report was identified only as "a friend in Washington." Clay, offended by the report, which had indicated that he had "repeatedly interrupted" Milnor's speech with "intemperate warmth," wrote the above letter. Stone, *Memoir of Milnor*, 68-70. Milnor replied the same day stating that the sergeant-at-arms had delivered Clay's note "during the sitting of the House of Representatives" and that "However willing, under other circumstances, I might have been to give any information in my power on the subject to which you refer, yet, as an important principle, as it respects both my representative and personal independence, might be affected by an acknowledgment, on my part, of the right to make, and the obligation to answer, an inquiry of such a nature, I trust that my now declining it will not be attributed to any intention of personal disrespect." Copy. *Ibid.*, 71. Clay responded to this letter, also on May 21, asserting that Milnor had apparently "misconstrued the circumstances attending the place . . . and the mode of conveyance I employed" for the note and assuring him "that there existed no intention to violate your independence in any respect." Clay added: "As you have attached some degree of importance to these circumstances, altogether accidental, I have to request that, if they constitute the only bar to the information solicited, you will consider this as a renewal of my inquiry." *Ibid.* Milnor replied on May 22 that he had received Clay's second note "last evening by the Honorable Mr. [George M.] Bibb, of the Senate." He noted that "the expressions, according to my apprehension, did not impute to you an intention of violating my personal independence, nor represent the place where your note was delivered, and the mode of conveyance, as constituting the only bar to my furnishing you with the information asked for; at the same time I appreciate, as I ought, the frankness with which you have disavowed the intention alluded to." He refused, however, "your right to make, or . . . my obligation to answer, the inquiry which I understand to be renewed by your last note." *Ibid.*, 71-72. That same day Clay answered that "I am gratified to learn by your note of to-day, delivered to me by Mr. [Charles] Goldsborough, that you have placed a proper construction upon the circumstances attending the delivery of my note to you yesterday morning." Regrets that Milnor's sense of duty "will not allow you to communicate the information sought for by me. Your determination leaves to my choice a single mode of reparation for an injury of which I conceive I have cause to complain; and my friend Mr. Bibb is authorized by me to make the requisite arrangements. *Ibid.*, 72. On May 23, Milnor wrote Clay that "Being utterly unconscious of having ever offered or intended you any injury, and having received from you no information of any part of my conduct against which you consider yourself as possessing cause of complaint, the same leading principle in reference to public and private duty that has hitherto regulated my course, obliges me to deem it improper to comply with the intimation of your note of this day. For such a compliance, the most deliberate reflection that I have been able to give the subject suggests no justification, on my part, in any thing that has occurred between us, either before or since the commencement of the present correspondence." *Ibid.*, 72-73. There the matter rested. *Ibid.*, 73. For Bibb, see 1:1 and *BDAC*; for Goldsborough, see 2:188 and *BDAC*.

To JONATHAN WILLIAMS[1]   Washington, June 1, 1812

I recd. your favor of the 28h. May.[2]

The accident,[3] for which you are pleased to express your kind sympathy with me, subjected me to no other inconvenience than two days confinement, the loss of some blood &c.

I have wished repeatedly & expressed it to Mr. [Thomas] Gholson[4] to have your bill taken up. With the best intentions on the part of that gentleman, within whose peculiar province the calling it up has fallen, it has so happened that it has not been acted upon. I regret this much because the advanced state of the Session & the momentous subjects which will doubtless require our attention diminish the probability of a final disposition of it before we rise. I will urge him however to call it up, & hope there will yet be some favorable occasion of doing so.

I never was in the immediate neighbourhood of your 40000 Acres of K[entucky]. Land; but from my information and general idea of the Country in which it is particularly situated, I should not imagine the land valuable, unless indeed (which is probable) Salt water shall have been or may be found within its limits on Goose Creek. Upon that water course almost from its source to its mouth here and there Saline Water is discovered of a very excellent quality. [P.S.] 1st. June. Since writing the within a favorable opportunity offering, Mr. Gholson called up your bill, the house went into committee, it was reported & ordered to be engrossed for a third reading on tomorrow.[5]

ALS. InU. Addressed to Williams in New York City.   1. For Williams (1750-1815)—merchant, soldier, and first superintendent of West Point—see *DAB* and *BDAC*. 2. Not found.   3. Clay had fallen from a horse. Stone, *Memoir of Milnor*, 64.   4. For Virginia Congressman Thomas Gholson, see 1:614 and *BDAC*.   5. A bill for the relief of Jonathan Williams had been introduced in the House by Gholson on Jan. 24, 1812, was brought up again on June 1, and passed the House on June 8. It was introduced in the Senate on June 9, postponed on June 27, and was not brought up again. *Annals of Congress*, 12 Cong., 1 Sess., 252, 308, 933, 1479, 1483.

To GEORGE ADAMS   Washington, June 18, 1812

War is at length unconditionally declared ag[ains]t. G[reat]. Britain.[1] On the first inst the President sent a message to Congress, one of the ablest state papers I have ever seen, recommending the measure.[2] The H[ouse]. acted with great promptitude on the occasion, referring the message to the Com[mittee]. of Foreign relation, who made a long report on the 2d. in the nature of a manifesto. On the 4h. it passed the bill. It went on the fifth to the Senate where it was subjected to much delay and from which it did not emerge until the 17th. On yesterday the house concurred in some unessential amendments made to the bill by the Senate, and the president gave the measure his approbation. In the H. of R. the bill passed 79 to 49 (exclusive of my own vote & that of several other friends of the measure who were absent.) In the Senate it was carried 19 to 13. On its return to us a motion was made to defeat the bill which was negatived 85 to 44. The representation from K[entucky]. has been unanimous with one exception, Mr. [John] Pope voted against it.[3]

Mrs. [Lucretia Hart] Clay left me about 12 days ago for home. She goes under the protection of Dr. [Richard] Pindell.[4]

You will see an address of mine to the public noticing a publication of John Randolphs.[5] The matter I expect will not be carried further.

ALS. KyU. Addressed to Adams in Frankfort, Ky.   1. See 1:674-75 and Clay to Wilkins, Jan. 18, 1812.   2. For Madison's war message, see *Annals of Congress*, 12 Cong., 1 Sess., 1624-29.   3. For the various votes, see *ibid.*, 297, 1509-10, 1679-82. For Pope, see *BDAC*.   4. For Pindell, see 1:16.   5. For Clay's address, see 1:668-74; Randolph's reply is in 1:686-92.

To Richard Rush, Washington, July 1, 1812. Calls Rush's attention to the accompanying packet [not found], and notes that a bill has passed "during this Session of Congress in behalf of the Mess Sthreshlys [*sic,* Streshly or Streshley] authorizing . . . the liquidation of their a/cs." Reports that the "Senate undertook . . . to allow them the credit to which I believe them entitled, to wit between four and five thousand dollars; but the H[ouse]. (and the Senate afterwards concurred with them) thought it best to leave to the Treasury the adjustment. If it can be made with the papers herewith sent you it will save those gentlemen much trouble and expence." Inquires if other vouchers are needed, and asks, if executions are about to be issued against the men, "that you will have the goodness to direct the Atto for the K[entucky]. District to suspend proceedings on the Jud[g]ment, the debt being I believe amply secured." ALS. ViU.

Rush replied on July 2, 1812, saying that "the previous inspection of cases of this nature belongs to the Auditor," and he has therefore transferred the letter and accompanying papers to him. Adds that "care shall be taken that no intermediate execution be issued against the Messrs. Streshly's." Copy. Printed in Anthony M. Brescia (ed.), *The Letters and Papers of Richard Rush*, Series 2, microfilm edition (Wilmington, Del., 1980), Item 3, Reel 24.

An "Act for the relief of Thomas and William Streshly" had been approved on May 22, 1812. 6 *U.S. Stat.*, 109. The Streshlys (or Streshley) were formerly collectors of the excise tax in Kentucky. *Annals of Congress*, 12 Cong., 1 Sess., 94, 201, 242, 1322, 1429.

For Richard Rush, who at this time was comptroller of the treasury, see 1:878.

To WILLIAM HENRY HARRISON[1] Washington, November 7, 1812
I snatch one moment from the pressure of my official duties to thank you for your favor of the 26h. Ulto. from Franklinton.[2] I shall look with anxiety for that promised from Sandusky.[3] You will have the Presidents message.[4] It exhibits no prospect of an immediate termination of the War. Each party has rejected proposals made by the other for an Armistice.[5] I can not yet form an opinion as to the duration of the War. Looking to the interests of the parties, and the points now in difference between them, I should say it would not be long. But there is no reasoning upon the pride & folly of the enemy. I must confess too I

should not like to see the surrender at Detroit & the discomfiture at Queens town [*sic,* Queenston, Ontario] unatoned for.[6]

Much is looked for from you & your army—much, very much from my Kentucky friends and the Ohio volunteers under your command. I pray to God that expectation may not be disappointed. Tell [John] Payne, [John] Allen, [Martin D.] Hardin & [George] Madison[7] how much the credit of our State has been raised here by its recent exertions. They have a sacred trust in the duty of preserving its present reputation.

I will take an early opportunity of conversing with the President & [William] Eustis on the subject of your rank.[8] The message you see asks for more genl. Officers.

ALS. DLC-William Henry Harrison Papers. 1. See 1:424 and *DAB.* 2. Not found. 3. Not found. 4. Madison's Fourth Annual Message had been given to Congress on Nov. 4, 1812. *MPP,* 2:499-506. 5. The latest rejection of an armistice was probably that of Lord Castlereagh to Jonathan Russell on Sept. 18, 1812. *State Papers and Publick Documents,* 9:124. 6. See 1:722-23. 7. For Brig. Gen. Payne, see 1:123; for Col. Allen, 1:177; for Maj. Hardin, 1:425; for Maj. Madison, 1:314. 8. President Madison had commissioned Harrison as a brigadier general, and the commission was confirmed by the Senate on Dec. 2, 1812. On Feb. 27, 1813, after passage of a bill creating additional major generals, Madison submitted Harrison's name to the Senate for an advance to that rank. The Senate approved on March 1. Dorothy B. Goebel, *William Henry Harrison: A Political Biography* (Indiana Historical Collections, vol. 14, Indianapolis, 1926), 163-65.

Agreement, November 13, 1812. By an agreement between Thomas Tingey [4:271], "Commandant of the Navy Yard Washington," party of the first part, and [Dr.] Richard Pindell with Henry Clay as his security, parties of the second part, promise to deliver during the year 1813 fifty tons "of Kentucky best clean top'd Hempen yarns of No. 24—The yarns not to be less in *number* then [*sic,* than] *twenty four thread* yarns at thirteen Cents pr. pound." Pindell and Clay "bind themselves to . . . Tingey for account of the Navy Department in the full and penal sum of Five thousand dollars lawful money of the U S, together with return of any money or monies that may be advanced to them . . . by the Navy Department; with lawful interest thereon." Copy. DNA, RG45, Naval Records Collection, Navy Dept. Contracts, No. 2, pp. 66-67.

From Callender Irvine, Philadelphia, December 22, 1812. Has received Clay's letter of the 19th [1:747] and states: "Having made Contracts for Kentucky nitre, to a very large amount, deliverable in this City within the year 1813—and as I intend making a Contract for Gun Powder in the state of Kentucky. I do not wish to enter into any additional Contract for Nitre, prior to the passage of the Act of appropriation, by Congress, for the year 1813." Asks for the name and address "of the Gentleman . . . who is desirous to furnish nitre for Government." Copy. DNA, RG92, Quartermaster Generals Office, Commissary General of Purchases, Letterbook A, entry 35.

On March 1, 1813, Clay wrote to Irvine, attesting to the "integrity punctuality and responsibility" of Samuel and George Trotter [1:316] and Daniel Bryan [1:147], who "intend to propose a contract to you for the supply of Gunpowder for the use of the Government." Adds in a postscript: "Mr. [Martin D.] Hardin, at whose instance I wrote you on the subject of Salt Petre declines making the proposed contract. ALS. DNA, RG92, Consolidated Correspondence File, "Powder."

For Callender Irvine, son of Gen. William Irvine of the American Revolution, see 1:747 and *PMHB,* 4:422; 5:137, 234, 420, 422; 18:131, 137.

From Thomas H. Cushing, Adjutant General's Office, Washington, January 29, 1813. Reports that "on the representation of Captain [Benjamin] Price of the Regt. of the Light Artillery, an order was sent to him yesterday, to discharge John Coghlan from the Army of the United States." Copy. DNA, RG94, Records of the Adjutant General, Letters Sent.

Cushing (1755-1822), a Revolutionary War veteran, served as adjutant general from 1800-1807 and again in 1812-13. In 1812 he was commissioned a brigadier general. *NCAB,* 12:560. For Benjamin Price of Maryland, who had become a captain in 1792, see *HRDUSA.* Coghlan does not appear in the latter and has not been identified.

To UNKNOWN RECIPIENT[1] Washington, February 22, 1813
I recd. from Mr. [Robert] Wickliffe some time ago a letter[2] acknowledging the mistake which I had stated to you as having originated with him in addressing the letter to Phila. instead of Balto. He also wrote to [William] Taylor [Jr.] of that place, as I have myself done several times.[3] Under various pretexts he [William Taylor, Jr.] has shuffled off the restoration of the money. Disgusted with his conduct I have drawn upon him at sight, in favor of Scott Trotter & Tilford,[4] and threatened to expose him if he does not pay the amt. Inclosed is their letter. Mr. Wickliffe considers himself responsible as the author of the mistake, and the sum whether recd. from Taylor or not shall be paid before I set out for K[entucky].

ALS. OCIWHi.   1. Possibly William Taylor of Baltimore.   2. For Wickliffe, see 1:82. Letter not found.   3. For William Taylor, Jr., of Philadelphia, see 1:779-80.   4. For Scott, Trotter & Tilford, see 1:56.

Resolution of the House of Representatives, March 1, 1813. Request President James Madison to lay before the House "the French decree purporting to be a repeal of the Berlin & Milan decrees [1:526] referred to in his message of the 4th of November last [Clay to Harrison, November 7, 1812], together with such information . . . concerning the time and manner of promulgating the same; and also any correspondence or information touching the relations of the United States with France . . . which . . . is not incompatible with the public interest to communicate." NS, by Clay. DNA, RG59. Printed in *Annals of Congress,* 12 Cong., 2 Sess., 1151.

To UNKNOWN RECIPIENT[1] Washington, March 7, 1813
I called upon the Secy. of War [John Armstrong] upon the subject of your letters. He could make no advances until an act of appropriation passed, which did not until a few days ago.[2] I pressed him to make an advance to you, which he will do, but he will not send out specie, as he does not do that in the case of any contractor. He will accept your drafts. I think you may safely draw for eight or ten thousand dollars. He does not apprehend that there will be considerable expenditure in Kentucky in the course of the year of the contract you have made but from the nature of the subject and the uncertainty of the military operations of Government it is impossible at this time to make precise calculations. I start tomorrow or the next day for home, with the prospect of bad roads, and with an afflicted heart for the misfortunes of our town.[3]

ALS. NN.   1. Probably Dr. Frederick Ridgely. See 1:784.   2. "An Act making appropriations for the support of the military establishment and of the volunteer militia in the actual service of the United States" for 1813 had become law on March 3, 1813. 2 *U.S. Stat.*, 822-23.   3. Reference is to the Battle of the River Raisin in Jan., 1813, in which many Kentuckians had been killed. See 1:814 and Horseman, *The War of 1812*, 84-85.

Bond to the Commonwealth of Kentucky, April 12, 1813. Clay, John Hart, and E.W. Craig bind themselves to pay the sum of $60,000 to to Commonwealth, the bond to become void when John Hart fulfills his legal obligations as executor of the Last Will and Testament of Nathaniel G.S. Hart [1:64]. DS. KyHi.

For John Hart, Clay's brother-in-law, see 1:374, *passim;* for Craig, see 2:163.

To UNKNOWN RECIPIENT   Lexington, April 12, 1813

I have returned to my original intention of placing my sons[1] under your care. Presuming that the places you were kind enough to retain for them in your family were filled, I sent a message the other day to Mr Young[2] requesting him to take them, and my servant now calls upon him for an answer. Should he not find it convenient, I must go down myself and look about for a suitable situation for them. The eldest who, when I saw you in Lex., was just recovering from a fever will be too weak for ten or twelve days yet, to commence his school exercises, and I wish them to start together. In the mean time you will have the goodness to consider them both as entered with you on this day.

ALS. KyLoF.   1. The two eldest sons: Theodore Wythe Clay (b. 1802) and Thomas Hart Clay (b. 1803). See 1:871.   2. Possibly John D. Young, clerk of Fayette County Court and a member of the board of trustees of Transylvania University. See 1:829, 841.

To William T. Barry, May 1, 1813. Receipt for $140 paid by Barry, "of which forty are for the hire of George and the balance to be credited to a lot sold by me to [John P.] Wagnon." ADS, Fayette Circuit Court, File 823.

For Barry, see 1:261; for Wagnon, see 1:152. George is probably the slave mentioned in 1:786, 833, 1006, not the one mentioned in 1:950. For the lot sold to Wagnon, see 1:383.

From ISAAC SHELBY[1]   Frankfort, May 16, 1813

Before this reaches your hands, you will no doubt be informed of the mournfull disaster that befell Colo. [William] Dudleys Ridgment [*sic*, regiment] on the 5th. inst. opposite Fort Meigs[2]—A more careless in considerate waste of Human blood cannot be found upon the Annals of North America—I have seen a Copy of General [William Henry] Harrisons official dispatch to the Secretary of War [John Armstrong] on the day this Misfortune happened—To my mind it is a mere plaister to cover his own mistake. It cannot be supposed by any rational mind that Colonel Dudley would have rushed his handful of men into the midst of several thousand British and Indians, had he been aware of their force, or had he have received orders to retreat upon Spiking the Enemys Cannon—He received his orders from Genl. [Green] Clay,[3] who had them verbally from an other Man to whom Harrison had communicated his designs—Genl Harrison states in his letter of the 5th. to the Secy. of War. That ["]when our Men had spiked the Enemys

Cannon their work was done, but that confidence which always attends Militia when Successfull proved their Ruin, that although there was time Sufficient to return to the boats before a reinforcement arrived to the Enemy, our men remained upon the Ground in Spite of repreatted calls made across the river to bring them back." can any rational mind believe that in the confusion and tumult, that must have existed on that occasion, that any calls across the river at least half a mile distant could be heard by Colo. Dudley or any of his Men—or that he had the smallest apprehension of the danger he was exposed to by delay—on the other hand Harrison must have been aware that his Verbal orders might readily have been misunderstood, passing as they did through different hands—he knew too the great Superiority of the Enemy, and it was his duty the moment Colo. Dudley, appeared on the heigths on the opposite shore to have sent a boat a cross the river, apprising him of the danger of delays, and ordering him possitively to cross the river so soon as he had spiked the Enemys Guns—but here the Ginerals presence of mind seems to have forsaken him and to remove public impressions attributes all the misfortune to the impetuosity of the Militia whose lives in fact have been sacraficed for the want of that information which might Easily have been conveyed in time to them—[4]

A certain—Webster[5] who lived near Lexington & who surrendered with those that Survived made his Escape the night after the Action, arrived at the St. Marys on the 11th. inst. says that the Slaughter was very great, that upwards of three hundred were killed, that Colo. Dudley & his Major, My son,[6] was among the Slain & that the Indians tomahocked all the wounded, that the Enemy was five thousand Strong—This Mournfull Event has I assure you deadened the feelings of many of our best patriots, and abated their Confidence in the Commanding General it will have an unhappy effect upon future calls on Kentucky for Men[.]

[7]When I consented last year to Serve as the chief Magistrate of this State, it was under a beleif I should be able to render Services to my Country in the event of a war with the Savages, having had a long and an intimate knowledge of Indian affairs, and under that impression, have taken the liberty both last year an[d] this, to make Various lengthy Communications to the War Department. In very few instances have I been answered except by a bare Acknowledgment of the receipt of my letter—If the Smallest discretion had been confided to me, the Post at Camp Meigs could have been reinforced before the Pennsylvania and Virginia Brigades were discharged, which in all probability would have prevented the Siege of it. & that inconsiderate waste of Human blood that has resulted from it, & which Kentucky must long deplore[.]

It is said here, and the report comes from high Authority, that the Secretary of War has declared "the Militia of Kentucky will not be paid[.]"[8] I lament deeply that their services have been premature, & although I shall at all times hold it my duty as Governor of Kentucky to do what may legally be required of me by the President of the United States. I am free to declare to you that as an individual, my Confidence in the Administration expecially as it relates to War Measures in the western Country *has greatly abated*, and I shall feel but little inclination in future to see a greater proportion of the best blood of Kentucky put to hazard in the General cause than what would be our equal share in the War[.]

I have thus my dear Sir, written you a longer letter than I intended, & from the perturbed State of my feelings excited by the Awfull Calamity that has befallen my friends & Country Men, many of the Ideas may seem to you new and incorrect—but some of them have existed before the present moment.

I pray God that my forebodings as to future events in the Western Country may not be reallised[.]

[P.S.] I have no objection to any part of this letter being communicated to the Secy of War[.]

ALS. KyU. 1. For Isaac Shelby, see 1:317 and Lowell Harrison (ed.), *Kentucky's Governors 1792-1985* (Lexington, Ky., 1985), 1-6. 2. See 1:783. 3. See 1:3, 23, 782-83, 799. 4. Immediately on their arrival at Fort Meigs, Harrison had ordered Gen. Green Clay and Col. William Dudley to launch a sortie against the British. They were to spike the guns and retreat. The initial attack of the Kentuckians, led by Dudley, was successful in spiking the guns, but they delayed their retreat too long and were overwhelmed by a sudden counterattack by the British and the Indians. About 500 Kentuckians were taken prisoner in addition to approximately 150 who were killed. Horseman, *The War of 1812*, 100; Harry L. Coles, *The War of 1812* (Chicago, 1965), 119. 5. Probably Dudley Webster of Fayette County. William H. Perrin (ed.), *History of Fayette County, Kentucky* (Chicago, 1882), 432. 6. Maj. James Shelby had been captured, not killed, at Fort Meigs and was later parolled. Anna M. Moon, *Sketches of the Shelby, McDowell, Deaderick, Anderson Families* (Chattanooga, 1933), 29-30. 7. At this point a pointing hand symbol appears. 8. See 1:808-9, 815-16.

To JOHN ARMSTRONG   Washington, May 25, 1813

I shall be very glad if the wishes of Mr. [John M.] McCalla, as expressed in the inclosed letter, in relation both to the muskets and pieces of light artillery, can be complied with. May I expect the favor of an answer.[1]

Applications have been repeatedly made to me by officers of various ranks in the army to have them transferred from the Corps to which they are attached to other corps, on account of misunderstandings between themselves and other officers. Is that ever indulged and under what circumstances?

Copy. Printed in *Document Transcriptions of the War of 1812 in the Northwest, Letters to the Secretary of War . . .* (Columbus, Ohio, 1961), 7:853. 1. This is the letter indicated as "Not found" in note 1 on 1:801. For McCalla, see *ibid.*

To WILLIAM WIDGERY[1]   Washington, July 1, 1813

I had expected that you would have given me a sketch of the condition and views of the political parties in your quarter. Are you seized with apathy, and do you mean to acquiesce in the retention of power by those who have gained it in your State, without struggle? I hope our friends do not despair, but will be able at your next elections to displace those who are so wantonly abusing their authority.[2] The remonstrance of your legislature was laid before us the day before yesterday.[3] It excited some warmth, but was finally laid upon the table. I was glad to see it accompanied or rather followed by that of the minority, breathing the most patriotic and animated spirit.

We are on the taxes at this moment—the most agreeable subject, you well know, in the whole compass of legislation! I hope and believe they will be laid, but I fear some of our Eastern friends will desert us.[4]

The President [James Madison] has been extremely ill, but is on the recovery, and judging from present appearances, out of all danger.[5] His death would at this moment be a great national calamity.

ALS. KyU.   1. For Massachusetts Congressman Widgery, see *BDAC*.   2. In the fall congressional elections in Massachusetts, 17 Federalists and 1 Republican were elected. *Niles' Register* (Dec. 31, 1814), 7:285.   3. The Memorial or Remonstrance of the Legislature of Massachusetts against the War of 1812 was introduced in the House on June 29, 1813, and ordered to be printed. *Annals of Congress*, 13 Cong., 1 Sess., 334-41.   4. An "Act for the assessment of direct taxes and internal duties" was passed by the House 97-70 on July 8. On July 22 it passed the Senate by a vote of 20-11. *Ibid.*, 46, 65, 411; 3 *U.S. Stat.*, 22-34.   5. Madison had been critically ill from a bilious fever. Irving Brant, *The Fourth President, A Life of James Madison* (New York, 1970), 543.

From Robert Brent, Army Pay Office, Washington, September 16, 1813. Encloses [not found] "an unsealed dispatch for Lieut. Ashton Garrett [2:877]," appointing him paymaster for the 7th Regiment of Infantry as recommended by Clay. Sends it to Clay "lest A. Garrett should have left Lexington within a short time, in which case it might remain in the Post Office." Copy. DNA, RG99, Records of the Office of the Paymaster General, vol. 5.

To [WILLIAM SIMMONS][1]   Washington, December 14, 1813
Availing myself of your polite offer of yesterday, I transmit to you the papers 1st. which entitle Col [John] Allen's widow[2] to a pension under the act of the last Session of Congress,[3] and 2dly. a power of Atto. from the Exor of Capt. [Nathaniel G.S.] Hart authorizing me to draw whatever arrearages of pay are due to his Estate.[4] His death was on the 23d. of Jan. the day subsequent to the defeat of [James] Winchester,[5] in which action he was wounded. His Death is abundantly proven in the volume of testimony collected at the last Session by the Committee of the H[ouse]. of R[epresentatives]. C[ol.] Hart was, at the time of his death, Inspector Gen[eral] of the N.W. army, and as such I presume there are arrearages of pay due to him, as well as in virtue of his rank of Capt. I thought I had a power of Atto. from Mrs Hart,[6] his widow, to draw her pension, but do not find it. I shall however have one in a few weeks. The act provides that the "widow or children shall be entitled to receive half the monthly pay to which the deceased was entitled at the time of his death." Consequently Capt. Hart's widow will be entitled to half of the aggregate pay to which he was entitled both as Capt—and Inspector Genl.[7]

I beg your early attention to this subject—and to be informed if the papers to which you have access sufficiently shew the right of Mrs. Hart to her pension, without the aid of any others.

ALS. KyLoF.   1. Simmons, from the accountant's office of the War Department, has been determined to be the recipient of this letter. See Simmons's reply below.   2. For Allen and the pension claim, see 1:177, 841, 843-44, 863.   3. For the act to provide for the widows and orphans of slain militiamen, see 1:817.   4. For Hart, who had been killed at the River Raisin, see 1:64, 699.   5. For Brig. Gen. Winchester, see 1:696.   6. Ann (or Anna) Gist Hart. See 2:100.   7. On Dec. 17, 1813, William Simmons wrote Clay from the first auditor's office in the War Department reporting that he had "adjusted the Account of the late Capt. Hart for the bal[an]ce of his pay &

Subsist[en]ce as Captn. & Deputy Inspector General." The amount of $189.16 for Mrs. Hart "will be paid to you at this Office," as will the first instalment of Mrs. Allen's pension. Copy. DNA, RG217, 1st Auditor, Accountant's Office, War Dept., Letter Sent, Letterbook 2, p. 391. On Jan. 4, 1814, Clay sent Simmons "a power of Atto. from Mrs Hart empowering me to draw her pension." ANS. DNA, RG217, 1st Auditor, Accountant's Office, War Dept., Letters Rec'd. Simmons replied on Jan. 6, stating that "I have settled the Accot. of Mrs. Hart for her half pay from 23d. Jany. to 23d of July 1813 being the 1st 6 Months half pay . . . to which she is entitled as the Widow of the late N.G.S. Hart Captn & Depy. Inspr. Genl." Copy. DNA, RG217, 1st Auditor, Accountant's Office, War Dept., Letters Sent, Letterbook 2, p. 436.

To MANUEL EYRE[1]   Washington, January 16, 1814

When we were in Philada[2] your good lady mentioned to Mrs. [Lucretia Hart] Clay that she knew of a person well adapted for the situation of Governess, to take, in a private family, the management and education of girls. Will you be good enough to drop me a line giving me some more precise information about the person in question? I should like to know her qualifications, expectations, and disposition to a residence in Kentucky.[3]

ALS. Courtesy of Dr. Thomas D. Clark, Lexington, Ky.   1. For Eyre, see 9:500. 2. Probably in Oct. or Nov., 1813. See 1:834, 836, 839-40.   3. This evidently did not work out, because in May, 1814, Amos Kendall became the tutor for the five older children—Theodore, Thomas, Anne, Susan, and Lucretia. William Stickney (ed.), *Autobiography of Amos Kendall* (New York, 1949), 115-16.

To MANUEL EYRE   Washington, January 23, 1814

I recd. your obliging favor of the 19h. inst.[1] Mrs. [Lucretia Hart] Clay will not accompany me on my intended voyage to Gottenburg,[2] but will return to Lexington in Kentucky.

I shall sail from N. York in the John Adams, and expect to pass through your City in the course of the next week, perhaps early in it.[3] I will endeavor to have the pleasure of seeing you.

ALS. KyLoF.   1. Not found.   2. For Clay's appointment as a peace commissioner and his trip to Europe, see espec. 1:852-53, 863, 866, 875.   3. Clay did not sail until Feb. 25. See 1:875.

To DAVID PARISH[1]   Washington, January 23, 1814

I recd. your agreeable favor of the 20h. inst.[2] I know not how adequately to express my grateful sense of the repeated instances of your kindness to me. I did not find myself at liberty to decline the duty which the Government has been pleased to assign me in the mission to Gottenburg, altho' it is full of responsibility and presented very few attractions to me.[3] Having determined to accede to the wishes of the President [James Madison] I signified to him that, waving all private considerations, I should hold myself ready to march at a moments warning. It is his desire that there should be as little delay as possible, in the departure of Mr. [Jonathan] Russell and myself from America; and I have accordingly fixed upon next friday for leaving this City, provided the Secy. of the Navy [William Jones] shall be informed by that time (as is probable) that the John Adams will be ready to sail on my arrival at N. York; if not I shall leave here as soon after that day as he receives this information.[4] I think therefore that I shall be in Philada. in the course of the next week, and probably early in it.

Upon determining to go, I turned my attention towards you as being most competent to give me the best advice on the subject of the pecuniary and other arrangements it will be incumbent on me to make. The letters you have promised will therefore be extremely acceptable to me, and should you have left Philada. before my arrival there I must ask the favor of you to place them in the hands of some one that will take the trouble of giving them to me.

On reaching N. York, where I expect to join Mr. Russell it will be my wish to sail at the earliest possible moment.

The recent intelligence from Europe exhibits a total revolution in the state of public affairs there. The power of [Napoleon] Bonaparte, if not annihilated, will at least be subjected to such restraints that it will cease to be the source of universal apprehension.[5] I sh[oul]d. join with yourself and with the people of Europe in rejoicing at the event, if I were quite sure that its consequences would not be pernicious (and I am far from asserting that they will be) to my own Country. For I am free to confess (it may be a narrow and selfish sentiment) that my first and greatest solicitude is for the welfare of America. If the Emperor Alexander[6] and the other Continental powers, who have so successfully opposed the daring ambition which sought to reduce every thing upon land to its sway, will equally prescribe limits to that no less inordinate ambition which aims to make every thing subservient to it upon the Water, then indeed will the late events challenge the gratitude and admiration of the world.

ALS. DeHi. 1. See 1:857. 2. Not found, but see 1:856-57. 3. See 1:852-53. 4. See 1:863, 866, 875. For Russell, see 1:774. 5. By this time Napoleon had been defeated by Russia, and France was being attacked on all its frontiers. In April, 1814, Napoleon abdicated, and he was exiled to Elba in May. William L. Langer (ed.), *An Encyclopedia of World History*, 4th ed. (Boston, 1968), 645-50. 6. Tsar of Russia. See espec. *ibid.*, 645.

To ROBERT FULTON[1]   Washington, January 27, 1814

I have to acknowledge the receipt of two of your favors.[2] That inclosing the testimony in behalf of your Steam Battery[3] I put, with its inclosure, into the hands of Mr. [William] Lowndes,[4] the intelligent Chairman of the Naval Comm[itt]ee. I am happy to inform you that before and since the arrival of Commodore Lewis,[5] the subject has attracted much attention. The sentiment is general not merely of passive acquiescence, but of positive conviction in its utility. I have not seen one (and I have conversed with many) who is not fully persuaded of its immense importance. And I have not a doubt of Congress making provision for testing, by fair experiment, its value, when the subject is brought before them. This I understand will be speedily done, if the Executive determine their powers incompetent to adopt the Engine.[6]

I thank you for your kind congratulations about my mission.[7] In accepting it, I was sensible of the difficulty and responsibility which I assumed, but at the same time made up my mind for a firm and resolute discharge of my duty. If the flattering anticipations which are made as to the result shall be realized I will be happy.

I hope to have the pleasure of seeing you and Mrs. [Harriet Livingston] F[ulton]. in N. York in about ten days. Mrs. [Lucretia Hart] Clay is deterred from accompanying me by the season.

ALS. NHi. 1. For Fulton (1765-1815), pioneer in steam transportation, see *DAB*. 2. Not found. 3. Clay was a strong supporter of Fulton's proposed steam frigate or steam battery. On May 9, 1814, Congress passed a bill authorizing $1,500,000 for the construction of one or more floating batteries built according to Fulton's plan and under his supervision. Cynthia O. Philip, *Robert Fulton, A Biography* (New York, 1985), 324-29. 4. For Lowndes, South Carolina congressman, see *BDAC*. 5. Probably Jacob A. Lewis, who became a captain in the U.S. Navy in 1814. Edward W. Callahan (ed.), *List of Officers of the Navy of the United States and of the Marine Corps From 1775-1900 . . .* (reprint ed., New York, 1969), 331. 6. See note 3 above. 7. See 1:852-53.

Memorandum "which may be useful in the event of my death," n.d., *ca.* January-February, 1814. Explains: "My private and other most valuable papers are contained in the Case in the small sitting room. They are arranged in bundles with labels indicating the contents of each." Notes due, deeds, and bills of sale were also contained in separate bundles. Discusses his financial affairs: "The principal debt I owe is for the purchase from [George] Nicholas's Estate [1:146] of the farm formerly belonging to it. For that my bond, with Mr. [George M.] Bibb as my surety, is held by Genl. Sam. Smith [1:196]." Has directed "James Adams of Pittsburg[h] [1:563] to send to Smith and Buchanan of Balto . . . a quantity of about 25 or 30 ton of yarns. . . . The amt. of Sales I have directed to be applied to the credit of my bond [2:95-96]."

Continues: "The next most considerable transaction I have to settle is my agency for [Henry] Purviance's trustee. The amt. with which I am chargeable will appear from two reports made to the Fed Court in the suit of [Samuel] Moale ag[ains]t. Purviance [1:493-94]." Although he retains "papers relative to Col. [Thomas] Hart's Estate . . . with that subject John Hart is more familiar than myself." Concludes by listing a series of specific debts due to him. ADS. DLC-TJC (DNA, M212, R11). Editors have determined that Clay probably drew up this document while making preparations for his departure for Europe.

To UNKNOWN RECIPIENT[1]   Washington, February 1, 1814
I find, with much regret, that Dr. [Adam] Seybert[2] declines accepting the place of Secy. to the Legation—May I ask the favor of a line, addressed to me at Phila. informing me who is designated?[3] And also if the President [James Madison] will permit H[enry]. Toland Jr. to be attached to the mission?[4]

ALS. InU. 1. Probably addressed to Secretary of State James Monroe. 2. For Seybert, see Charles F. Adams (ed.), *Memoirs of John Quincy Adams*, 12 vols. (Philadelphia, 1876), 6:562 and *BDAC*. 3. Christopher Hughes became secretary to the mission. See 1:867 and Chester G. Dunham, "The Diplomatic Career of Christopher Hughes," Ph.D. dissertation, Ohio State University, 1968. 4. For Toland, see 2:295. He did not become a part of the mission.

From James Monroe, Washington, February 12, 1814. Transmits "to our ministers to whom the negotiation with G[reat] Britain is intrusted" a message "just handed to me by Mr. [Rufus] King of the Senate." Trusts it will receive the consideration it deserves, although "Not having even read it I can give no aid in forming a correct estimate on that point." Copy, by J. Russell. RPB. For King, see 1:774 and *BDAC*.

To E.I. DUPONT[1]   New York, February 16, 1814

I recd. your favor of the 14h.[2] with the packet which it covers, and which I shall take great pleasure in delivering to its destination. I thank you for your polite offer about the Shepherd's dogs, of which if you can preserve me a pair by my return from Europe you will oblige me much.

The specimen of Cloth which you sent me to Philada, though good, not being such as would attract admiration abroad I sent to your agents in that City. But I have had the good fortune here to find an excellent piece from your establishment, some patterns from which I will take with me. Be pleased to make to Mr. [Peter] Bauduy[3] the respects of . . .

ALS. DeWin.   1. For Eleuthere Irenee Dupont, see *DAB*.   2. Not found.   3. For Bauduy, see 1:175.

To JAMES BROWN   New York, February 20, 1814

Just as I was leaving Washington a bill was presented to me for acceptance drawn at 60 days by Tho. Pindell for upwards of $8000.[1] The ground upon which he was induced to draw was a claim upon the Navy Dept. for a like sum, the receipts evidencing which he transmitted to me. I could not think, situated as I was, of accepting and leaving unsettled a bill for so considerable a sum, and I suffered the bill to be noted. This gave me less concern, because I took pains to prevent Tom's credit from suffering, by explaining to the Cashier of the Office of pay and deposit of the B[ank]. of Columbia the transaction, and *placing in his hands the above receipts*, with a request to liquidate the demand with Mr. [William] Jones[2] and discharge the bill. I wrote to Tom informing him of what I had done and not done, and thus afforded to him the opportunity before the 60 days expire of making any other or further provision in the affair.

I recd. for Mrs. [John] Allen $180 which I remitted to Mr. [Martin D.] Hardin in a post note drawn by the B[ank]. of Washington before I left that City.[3] I have written to Mr. McKee,[4] upon whom the bill you refer to has I understand been drawn.

Mr. [Jonathan] Russell has at length joined me. He arrived last evening and we sail on tuesday or wednesday.[5]

ALS. KyU.   1. For Pindell, see 1:589.   2. For Jones, see 1:811.   3. See 1:841-44, 863.   4. Possibly Samuel McKee. See 1:252 and *BDAC*.   5. See 1:875.

From [John Speyer], Stockholm, April 11, 1814. Has heard through letters from Reuben G. Beasley "of the President's [James Madison] acceptance of the proposal of the english government, to treat for the accommodation of differences between the United States and Great Britain . . . and of Your appointment [1:852-53], to act in concert with Messrs. [James A.] Bayard and [John Quincy] Adams, as Commissioners." Reports that he has received no instruction from the State Department on this, although "It would have been my wish as early as possible to pay to the Swedish government the attention usual on Such occasions by official notice of the object of the intended meeting in Gotenburg [*sic*, Gottenburg]." Notes that the British government "has already done this." L. DNA, RG84, Foreign Service Posts, Sweden. Addressed to Clay and Jonathan Russell.

For Speyer, U.S. Consul at Stockholm, see 1:887; for Beasley, see Clay to Crawford, August 18, 1814.

From Samuel Angus, Gand (Ghent), August 2, 1814. Thanks Clay and Jonathan Russell for "presenting me with a Silver urn" which he "will always preserve . . . as a token of your approbation." ALS. RPB. Angus was captain of the U.S. corvette *John Adams.* See 1:870.

From William H. Crawford, Paris, France, August 4, 1814. Reports that "Your friendly letter of the 25th ulto. [1:950] was handed me by by [*sic*] Mr. Benson [*sic,* Adrian Benjamin Bentzon]."

States that Count de Caraman, "secretary of the French Legation in the U.S. on the 2d. Instant delivered me dispatches from the Secretary of State [James Monroe] for this Legation and for the American envoys at Gottenburg.—The dispatches for you are Stated to be of great importance." Promises to send one set by Myers, who "is to set out for that place tomorrow morning," and another by Morton and Jonathan Russell who "will set out the next day."

Mentions that Count de Caraman "sailed from N York on the 6th. of July" and "[Isaac] Chauncey expected to sail with his new vessels on the 10th of that month." Adds that "Mr. [James] Monroe refers me to the news papers for the Naval and Military operations which had taken place. Of these we have received tolerably correct accounts thro' English News papers." Believes that "the Maritime States with the Emperor of Russia [Alexander I] at their head, will effectually interpose their good offices between the United States and G. Britain.—Even France it is supposed will be able to have some weight upon this question."

Notes that Caraman "informs me that no fortified camp has been formed on Long Island, and that no other force has been collected in that place, than the ordinary garrison.—I strongly fear that a land force debarkened on Long Island will hazard the safety of New York."

Says he has asked to return to the U.S., and "my request is granted, but time to select a successor is demanded."

Reports that "It is impossible to foresee the time that will be consumed in obtaining a definitive answer from this Govt upon the claim of the American Merchants for the unjust Spoliation committed upon them.—I am informed that the Prince of Benevento [Count Charles Maurice de Talleyrand-Perigord] is to attend the Congress at Vienna." Emphasizing his desire to return to the U.S. before winter, states: "As you are in Europe I think you would confer an obligation upon the Government, if you would consent to suceed me in this appointment.—The Mission in which you are engaged, has dissolved the connexion which existed between you and the H[ouse] of R[epresentative]'s and I thought might be an inducement with you to desire to remain a few years in Europe, before your return.—If the appointment would be acceptable to you, I would with great pleasure suggest the propriety of your appointment to Mr Monroe in my first dispatches, which I intend to send by the John Adams.— This communication is confidential."

Mentions that he gave Henry Carroll the sum of $500 as he was leaving Paris, and suggests that "As you engaged to pay his expences, It will be proper that he should make out a list of his expences & submit them to your approbation. . . . You will also determine whether your engagement covers the expences of his residence in Paris, or only his expences in Coming to & returning from this place." Copy. DNA, RG84, Foreign Service Posts, France (R15).

For Crawford, see 1:867; *DAB; BDAC.* For Bentzon, see 1:950. "Myers" is probably Christopher Meyer. See 1:961. For Georges-Joseph-Victor de Riquet,

Count de Caraman, see 6:107. For Commodore Chauncey, see 1:990 and *DAB*. For Talleyrand, see 1:997. For Henry Carroll, see 1:887. For Clay's response to Crawford's proposal to recommend Clay as his successor, see 1:972, 990, 993-94. Albert Gallatin succeeded Crawford as minister to France, serving from 1815-23. Richardson Dougall & Mary Patricia Chapman, *United States Chiefs of Missions, 1778-1973* (Washington, 1973), 55.

To WILLIAM H. CRAWFORD   Ghent, August 8, 1814

Mr. [Anthony St. John] Baker, Secretary of the British Commission,[1] called on us yesterday at 11:00 o'clock to announce their arrival the preceding evening and to say that they would be glad to see us and exchange of our powers at their lodgings today at 10:00 o'clock. The message of Mr. Baker was delivered to Mr. [James A.] Bayard, who informed him that an answer would be sent in the evening. We accordingly communicated to them that we should be very happy to meet with them confer with them and to exchange copies of our powers, but that some other place would be more agreeable to us than their own lodgings, and Mr. [Christopher] Hughes[2] was instructed to suggest Le Pays Bas, the Hotel which we lately left.

Mr. Baker called last evening to say that our proposition was acceded to, and accordingly we shall have an interview with the gentlemen today at the Hotel Le Pays Bas at one.

By letter from Paris Last evening[3] I find that Mr. [George-Joseph-Victor de Riquet, Count de] Caraman has arrived and brought your new commission. We are also expecting to receive instructions through the same channel, and I hope he has some private letters for me. I have indeed heard indirectly from home, but it would be infinitely more agreeable to receive letters.

I am notified that [Isaac] Chauncey had done nothing in the month of June.[4] Otherwise the general complexion of the American news is quite enlivening.

Copy. DLC-William H. Crawford Papers.   1. For Baker, see 1:949.   2. See 1:867. 3. Not found.   4. See 1:990.

To WILLIAM H. CRAWFORD   Ghent, August 18, 1814

I had written a long letter[1] in reply to your obliging favor by Mr. [Henry] Carroll,[2] but no private opportunity being likely to occur shortly, and not choosing to trust it to the mail, I have concluded not to send it at present, if I should trouble you with the persual of it at all. I am rejoiced to find that whatever difference of opinion exists between us regards the mode rather than the substance of things, and that even this difference will probably be done away by the dilatory movements of the other party. Mr. [Reuben G.] Beasley, upon enquiry as to the time when the Commissioners would leave London, with the view of sending by them a pacquet to this place, was informed by Mr. [William R.] Hamilton,[3] the Under-Secretary, that his pacquet would be in time if delivered in all last week. We might therefore look for them this week if they had not already disappointed expectations equally well founded which they themselves had authorized. The treatment we have experienced is perhaps without example in the annals of diplomacy or even in that code by which gentlemen regulate their intercourse with each other. We however take things here very patiently, and you will learn with satisfaction that there exists amongst us the most entire harmony. We have taken a house for our joint occupation, into which we shall enter about the first of next week.

I congratulate you upon the news from America, in what in the aggregate is encouraging, although no single item exhibits any thing very brilliant. The [word illeg.] I think is safe, and the Wasp has again stung the enemy. We derive some compensation for [Isaac] Chauncey's delay in getting out, in the alleged capture of 300 men, including two or four port captains, near Sachetts harbour, and in the bravery with which Oswego was defended.[4] The successful [result] of the N. York elections (of which I understand you have accounts at Paris) will have a good effect at home and abroad.[5]

I owe you an apology for my apparent neglect of your kind and friendly invitation to make your Hotel my home when I make my intended visit to Paris. Your obliging letter of _____ May was never received by me until Mr. [Albert] Gallatin's arrival here. I shall embrace with much pleasure your obliging offer.[6]

I regret extremely that I have it not in my power to supply the charm which exists in your file of the intellect.

[P.S.] I thank you for your communication about the [words illeg.]. I presume he speaks the French language which I am determined my sons shall never feel the want of that I do. If to his professional qualifications, he adds a good moral character, his [word illeg.] ignorance of the English language would form no objection. When I have the pleasure of seeing you I will determine if I engage him. In the meantime you will lay me under an obligation to you to obtain what information you can conveniently, as to *essential* points in his character.[7]

Copy. DLC-William H. Crawford Papers.   1. Not found.   2. Probably Crawford to Clay, August 4, 1814.   3. For Beasley, U.S. agent for prisoners in London, see 1:868; for Hamilton, British undersecretary of state for foreign affairs, see 1:909 and *DNB*.   4. The *Wasp* was a 22-gun sloop. See 1:949, 975; 2:7; also Horseman, *The War of 1812*, 150-51. Chauncey's new ships had been blockaded at Oswego Falls after the British attack on Oswego in May, 1814. Kate Caffrey, *The Twilight's Last Gleaming, Britain vs. America 1812-1815* (New York, 1977), 217-18; Horseman, *The War of 1812*, 173-74.   5. In the April elections in New York the war party [Republican] won every seat except one in the state senate and gained control of the assembly. This enabled the Republicans, for the first time during the war, to enact a large volume of wartime legislation. Ray W. Irwin, *Daniel D. Tompkins: Governor of New York and Vice President of the United States* (New York, 1968), 178.   6. Reference is to Crawford's letter of May 15. See 1:910-12. Clay did not leave for Paris until Jan. 7 where he remained until March 19, 1815. See 2:4, 11.   7. Reference obscure, but probably a reference to a possible teacher for Clay's children. See 1:942 and Crawford to Clay, Sept. 19, 1814.

To CHARLES TAIT[1]   Ghent, August 19, 1814

My visit to Europe having been as yet confined to Sweden and my journey from Gottenburg through Denmark, Germany and Holland to this place, I can offer very little for your amusement or information, as to the Country. The climate, judging solely by my experience, is execrable. No summer, no sun, eternal clouds, and damp weather. Holland and this Country are as productive as it is possible for a highly cultivated & rich soil to be. In the former, their Canals, their rich meadows extending as far as the eye can reach, without fences, and separated only by ditches fitted with water, and covered with innumberable herds of the finest cows I had ever beheld, exceeded my expectations, much as they had been raised. This Country is only inferior to Holland. Both sustain perhaps as large a population as possible in their social condition.

The B[ritish]. Comm[issioner]s never joined us until about ten days ago.[2] We have had several conferences with them, the amount of which is communicated to our Government by the John Adams. I cannot commit to the casualties of a letter their nature—One thing only I will say that we shall make peace or fail to make it on grounds which will unite all parties at home.

Our friend [William H.] Crawford stands extremely well with our Countrymen at Paris. He has been particularly kind to me, and I hope to have the pleasure of seeing him.[3]

I cannot say exactly at what time we shall take our departure for America. I am more than ever attached to my native home, and to my friends there, amongst the first of whom I shall, I hope with your permission, continue to regard you.

ALS. A-Ar.   1. See 2:580.   2. See 1:952-59.   3. Clay saw Crawford during his stay in Paris in Jan.-March, 1815. See 2:4, 11.

From William H. Crawford, Paris, August 22, 1814. Reports having received Clay's letter of August 11 [1:960-61], which was delayed because, as postmarks indicate, it "has come from the other side of the Channel." Contends that "If the *British government is seriously* disposed *to conclude the war,*" they will not insist upon the sine qua non *"with which their ministers have opened the negotiation."* Adds that "your letter does not define the *limits of the territory to be set apart*" for the Indians, "nor the nature, or extent of the *alteration which they desire in the boundary between their provinces and the United States.* It is inferred that this *barrier* is to be formed at *the sole expense of the United States* and that the *alterations in the boundary* are to be advantageous, *to the enemy and* [the] course injurious *to us.*" Has believed "Since the *month of April . . . that peace could not be made* during *this year.*" Thus, his "greatest solicitude" has been that the negotiations be broken *"off upon demands that will have a* decided *tendency to produce unanimity in the further perpetuation of the war.*" Thinks their demand for an Indian barrier "cannot fail to produce the happiest effects." If they insist upon this sine qua non, asks why the U.S. commissioners should prolong the negotiation "for the purpose of asking *a decision which you already know.*"

Believes "Your opinions of the views of the British Commissioners upon one of the controverted points is confirmed" and that "this point will present the greatest obstacle to the success of your labors.—The other propositions cannot be seriously pressed if there is any disposition or desire to make peace. . . . these may be put in advance and pressed with warmth for a season, and—the merit of relinquishment, will be urged as an additional reason for your yielding in the other point." Expects that Lord Castlereagh "has passed into Ghent before this.—I wish you had to negociate with him" instead of those "with whom you have to do." Notes that Castlereagh "has been bred up in the Cabinet, and deeply skilled in the intrigues which are carried on in the political Cabinets of Europe."

Had hoped "to have had your views upon the question presented for your consideration in my last [Crawford to Clay, August 4, 1814], before I closed my dispatches for the Government.—An early communication of your decisions might have enabled me, to accomplish the object of my wishes before the winter should set in.—As it is I presume that it must be deferred until the spring."

Encloses "one of Gardner's [sic, Barent Gardenier] papers, which contains his and [William] Coleman's views on the work in which you are engaged.— From what is stated by the editor, I presume that 'observer' is by the pen of G.M. the orator.—What profanation of divine things, for a man whose whole life has been one continued libel upon virtue, and Christian Morality, to take upon himself the Ministry of these holy things? Nothing is more disgusting than an affectation of religion, but when this affectation is assumed for political purposes, depravity has reached its summit.—The man whose whole life presents a continued succession of benevolent & just actions, has a claim-to attention, if he should chuse to censure the immoral or mistaken conduct of his rulers, but the demagogue whose every action has inflicted a wound upon morality takes upon himself the task of Censor morum, no other sensations is excited but that of the deepest execration." Copy, partially in cipher. DNA, RG84, Misc. Letters Sent, France. Direct quotations translated from the cipher appear in italics. This is one of six known letters between Clay and Crawford from this time period written partially in cipher. It, along with the letter from Crawford to the American Commissioners of May 28, 1814 [1:926-27] and Clay to Crawford of August 11, 1814 [1:960-61], are all in the cipher known as WEO25, while Crawford to the American Commissioners of April 8, 1814 [1:872-75, translated in the errata of this volume], Crawford to Clay of September 14, 1814 [see below] and Crawford to the American Commissioners of October 14, 1814 [1:986-88] are in the cipher WEO28. The charts used to decipher the coded parts of these letters are in Ralph E. Weber, *United States Diplomatic Codes and Ciphers 1775-1938* (Chicago, 1979).

For Lord Castlereagh, Robert Stewart, see 1:774; for Gardenier, former Federalist congressman from New York, see *BDAC;* for Coleman, editor of the New York *Evening Post,* see *DAB.* For the British insistence on a boundary to protect the Indians from U.S. encroachment as a *sine qua non,* see espec. 1:952-57, 963-65.

From William H. Crawford, Paris, August 28, 1814. Has received Clay's letters of August 9 [not found] and August 22 [see above]. States that "I am happy to learn that the decision which you have made, corresponds with the opinion which I Should have given, if your letter of the 11th [1:960-61] had reached me in due time. . . . If they intend to make peace, this sine qua non is put in advance, with a view to be given up, if necessary, and the impressment, upon which they have affected so much indifference, will be substituted in its place. My impression is however decidedly that they have never intended to make peace.—I presume they conceived that we were prepared to admit their claim to impress and therefore chose what they thought was the best sine qua non, which we would reject."

Believes the "publication of the official papers must produce a great effect, both in the United States and in Great Britain." Predicts that when the English learn "that the property tax, and all the other war taxes are to be continued for the purpose of protecting their Indian Allies, and for the purpose of depriving us of the possession of the Lakes, and changing the line, whilst *their maritime rights* have been thrown in the background, this thinking people will believe, that the gratification of their resentments will cost them rather too dear." Adds that the mercantile class, especially the shipping interest, "will feel that the present state of England, is precisely that which is most injurious to them," as most shipping will be transferred "to neutral bottoms."

38

Discusses the dilemma derived from the "seizure of the vessels at Liverpool, with cotton from Amelia Island," noting that "The principle then is, that property found in a neutral Port, and purchased there for a Neutral account, can be affected by a Blockade of the Ports from whence it was originally exported.—If the original exportation took place in violation of this blockade, there may be some plausibility in the Seizure.—But if the original exportation was in the vessels of the Belligerent, how does the case of blockade apply to it." Points out that it would be virtually impossible for an admirality court to "ascertain whether the original exportation was by a Belligerent or a Neutral vessel." Adds that he has "presented a note to all the Ministers of the maritime states (except those where we have Ministers) enclosing a copy of the Presidents proclamation relative to the blockade of our coasts, and to neutral trade." Copy. DNA, RG84, Misc. Letters Sent, France.

For the British sine qua non regarding the Indians, see espec. 1:952-57, 963-65. For President Madison's proclamation of June 29, 1814, declaring the British blockade of the U.S. coast to be illegal and instructing all public and private armed vessels of the U.S. to render all possible aid to neutral vessels proceeding to U.S. ports, see James D. Richardson (comp.), *A Compilation of the Messages and Papers of the Presidents 1789-1902*, 10 vols. plus supplements (Washington, D.C., 1904), 2:528-29.

This letter is the one indicated as "not found" in note 2, 1:979.

From William H. Crawford, Paris, September 14, 1814. States that James Monroe has "directed me to give Mr. [John] Vanderlyn a passage in the Argus, if he should go direct from France to the United States." This is "his only chance of returning in a public vessel. . . . No person can obtain a Passport for the Neptune, but thro' the American Envoys." Adds that "You are the best judges whether Mr. Vanderlyn can embark on board that vessel without incommoding yourselves and suite."

Reports that "The person [Justus Erick Bollman] referred to [in] my letter of yesterday [1:975-77] states *that the President* [James Madison] *is drunk* every day of his life [and] *that Mr.* [James] *Monroe and General* [John] *Armstrong insult each other every day in the street* and that they must fight, or subject themselves to insults from others."

Reports also that "various insinuations" have been made "against the conduct of our Ministers at Ghent" which were probably collected "in London & which were fabricated there by our renegade Americans or by the retainers of the present Ministry." Adds that "*He states that Mr.* [George B.] *Milligan went to England* [to] *speculate in American produce* and that *our ministers* were engaged in these transactions *instead of* pursuing *the true interest of the nation.*"

Is convinced that the person making these statements cannot be relied on, and "I am somewhat at a loss to determine upon the inducement which has led him to make these statements."

Concludes: "Gen[er]al. LaFayette has been here all the week in the expectation of seeing you and your Colleagues, but I presume he will set out in a few days for his country seat." ALS, partially in cipher. DNA, RG84, Misc. Letters Sent, France. Direct quotations translated from the cipher appear in italics. The code used for this letter is WE028. See Crawford to Clay, August 22, 1814, for a discussion of the codes.

For Vanderlyn, an artist, see 1:978, 980. For Bollman and Clay's comment in reply to this letter, see 1:272, 281, 975-79; see also Bollman entry in *DAB*. For Milligan, see 1:883.

To Lloyd Jones, U.S.S. *Neptune*, September 16, 1814. Report they have "given you a credit with Messr Baring Brothers & Co. of London for a sum not exceeding one Thousand pounds Sterling." Add that this is to be used only "for the support of the crue & for the safty of the Ship under your command." Copy, signed by Clay, James A. Bayard, John Quincy Adams, and Jonathan Russell. PHi. Written from Ghent.

On October 1, 1814, Jones, writing Clay in Ghent from the *Neptune* near Antwerp, states that he has received Clay's letter of "the 28th ult [not found]," and "I went in search of the Baggage which arrived last evening & recd one case & two Bales for You which is safe on Board." Adds that he received yesterday four packages for Jonathan Russell and has "just learnt that a Case or trunk from England for my ship which I hope is Mr [Christopher] Hughes's" has arrived. Copy. *Ibid.* For Jones, see 1:886.

From William H. Crawford, Paris, September 19, 1814. Has received a letter from Mr. McClure "who is now on a tour to Switzerland, in which he says he can obtain for you a Pistalozzian [*sic,* Pestalozzian] teacher of the best—Character & reputation, but that if you intend to take him out with you, some time must be given him to prepare for the voyage." Believes $250 a year may "be sufficient to engage this man." Adds that "Mr. [Henry] Jackson who is with Mr. McClure is much pleased with Pistalozzi's School."

Mentions that " _____ [Justus Erick Bollman] has called upon me" but "did not mention his interview in London [Crawford to Clay, September 14, 1814].—Upon the dissentions in the cabinet, which I mentioned in that letter he was explicit.—he visited the seat of Government a few days before he set out and received his information from the inhabitants of the place." States that he could determine the truthfulness of the statements neither from Bollman's manner nor countenance. Still believes his stated motive is false. Reports that "He asked me if I thoug[h]t there was any reasonable prospect of Peace. I replied that the questions of peace or, continuance of the war depended entirely upon the result of the Congress at Vienna; He seemed to acquiesce in this opinion." Believes the present negotiations "justify this opinion.—You will not leave Ghent until Lord—Castelreagh [*sic,* Castlereagh] shall believe that he distinctly sees the result of the Congress at Vienna." Thus, does not "expect to see you at Paris before the 1st. of December, & probably a month later [Clay to Crawford, August 18, 1814].—From the policy already developped, you will find no difficulty to determine upon the ultimate measures which will be adopted to detain you at Ghent."

Concludes: "I am extremely glad to hear that Lord [Rowland] Hill's expedition is postponed until the next year.—The nation will know the result of your efforts before this formidable expedition will be debarked upon its coasts." Copy. DNA, RG84, Misc. Letters Sent, France.

For Henry Jackson, secretary of the U.S. legation in France, see 2:12. Johann Heinrich Pestalozzi (1746-1827), a Swiss educational reformer, ran a boarding school in Yverdon. See Kate Silber, *Pestalozzi: the Man and His Work* (New York, 1973). For Clay's desire to hire a teacher for his children, see 1:942. For the Congress of Vienna, see Sir Charles K. Webster, *The Congress of Vienna 1814-1815* (New York, 1963).

In the early summer of 1814, the British government had considered sending a large force under the command of Lord Hill to undertake an invasion of Louisiana. The project was postponed because of difficulties in establishing peace in Europe and tension with the Russians. A modified plan of invasion was later adopted. Horseman, *The War of 1812,* 226.

To LLOYD JONES   Ghent, October 22, 1814
I learnt with some surprise by Mr. [Albert] Gallatin that you had fixed upon monday for sailing.[1] When you left here I had no idea that you

thought of going so early, and indeed understood you to say that you would be time enough if you took your departure the last of next week. My porcelain has not yet arrived, though it ought to have been here this day. I look for it every day, and unless you have very strong reasons for an immediate departure, I must request that you will remain until wednesday or thursday next, by which time I will have it on board, or the Neptune may sail without it. My colleagues I am sure will have no sort of objection to this detention—Indeed I understand that the time of your sailing is altogether an affair of your own[.]

The Bail that arrived the other day I expect is for me, and contains I suppose a plateau; but the China[2] itself is yet behind.

ALS. NNC. 1. Jones did not sail at that time. See, for example, Clay to Jones, Dec. 24, 1814. 2. See 2:62.

To CHARLES TAIT   Ghent, October 25, 1814
I had the pleasure of writing you a line by the John Adams, since when we have been kept here by an unexpected protraction of the negotiation with which we are charged.[1] You will be put in possession of the whole subject through the Secy. of State [James Monroe].

The events in your quarter engage most my attention and solicitude. The loss of our Capital filled me with grief, less for the loss of property than the loss of honor.[2] This, I thank God, is in some measure recovered by the encouraging victories on Champlain, and the repulse before Baltimore.[3]

The wanton destruction of the Capitol and President's house has excited in Europe, as far as I have learnt, but one sentiment of reprobation. I heard the event, when, in the interval of business, I had taken a short excursion to Brussells,[4] and could not help reflecting on the contrast which the two Cities presented. At Brussells, though it has been the continual seat of War, and been occupied at various times by all the great powers, the public edifices have escaped for ages the Barbarian torch. It is the same throughout all this Country.

Although the affairs of Europe are by no means settled, and France in particular begins to open her eyes upon her fallen and degraded condition, I think the American statesman ought to act, in relation to the enemy, upon a supposition that no diversion or co-operation was to be expected in this quarter. Talleyrand is said to have demanded at Vienna that other powers, in imitation of France, shall return to the condition of 1792.[5] And it has been said with not less truth than humor that Lord Wellington has his head quarters in Paris and his army in Flanders. Yet much as France undoubtedly decries this Country, and feels her recent disgrace, I doubt her going to War. The warlike chief [Napoleon] who lately directed her power is no longer on the throne, and Louis [XVIII] dreads still more a state of War than the possible commotions which may attend that of peace.[6]

If my wishes could be accomplished I should be now with you; but I know not when I shall have that pleasure. I expect to return in the Neptune, which is ordered to Brest to receive us.

Make my respects to our worthy and inestimable friends [George M.] Bibb and [John] Mason . . . [7]

ALS. A-Ar. 1. Negotiations continued to drag on with demands on both sides being constantly modified in response to the war in America and conditions in Europe. Horseman, *The War of 1812*, 250-69. 2. See *ibid.*, 194-204 and 1:982. 3. See Horseman, *The War of 1812*, 204-8. 4. See 1:982. 5. Reference is to the conditions existing in Europe before the beginning of the War of the First Coalition in 1792. Langer, *Encyclopedia of World History*, 630. For the outcome of the Congress of Vienna, see Webster, *The Congress of Vienna*, 155-64, *passim*. See also 1:997. 6. For Napoleon's brief return to the throne in 1815, see 2:11-12. 7. For Mason, see 1:99.

From William H. Crawford, Paris, November 11, 1814. Reports that the "letter of Mr [Jonathan] Russel[l] enclosing the last note of the B[ritish]. L[egation] was handed to me by Doctor Boswell.—I think Mr Russel complains of the ambiguity & uncertainty in which that note leaves the negotiation, rather too strongly." Sees the points to be discussed as reduced to three: "The fisheries, the territory east of the Penobscot, and the boundary line of the U.S. west of the lake of the Woods." Adds that the "Indian barrier is manifestly merged, and arranged in the article which you have accepted.—From the understanding which I have of the previous notes of the British plenipotent[iary]. the military possession of the Lakes formed a part of their Sine Qua non. If so, it is already disposed of.—If I could confide in the sincerity of the British Ministry, I would now say that peace is not only practicable but very probable.—If they are not sincere, they are extremely foolish." Believes the "English nation without an exception would have supported them upon the Question of Impressment," but "I strongly suspect that the American government would have found it extremely difficult to rally the nation upon this point."

Contends that "If peace is not made the war will be prosecuted in a manner to secure an honorable one at the end of two campaigns at farthest." Thinks that if this happens, the U.S. will have officers and soldiers "who will not suffer by a comparison with the best troops in Europe." Notes that "The left division of our Army under [Gen. Jacob J.] Brown, has established an imperishable reputation," while "The right division under McCombs [*sic,* Brig. Gen. Alexander Macomb] has given evidence of its gallantry, and will no doubt equal the left, when it has the same opportunities of establishing its reputation.—The center under Gen[er]al Izzard [*sic,* George Izard], I confidently hope; has established its claim to the confidence, & to the respect of the nation.—The capture of [Sir Gordon] Drummond will place the reputation of our Army upon the proud eminence to which our navy has already raised itself." Believes the U.S. can "then make peace with the national confidence that we shall not again be forced to recur to arms from the conviction of our weakness, and incapacity to repel aggressions."

Has heard rumors that the negotiation at Vienna "is likely to fail. . . . I do not believe this. If it fails you will succeed." Is convinced that at the French court "English influence carries every thing" and that "this government would not be able to preserve its Neutrality upon any point upon which the British Minister should choose to be importunate." Adds that the "augmentation of British Troops in Belgium gives this government pleasure rather than pain.— To these Troops . . . it looks for protection against the malcontents, who increase every day in number and influence." Copy. DNA, RG84, Misc. Letters Sent, France.

The "last note" of the British Legation to which Crawford refers was probably that of October 21 [see 1:991] rather than the one of October 31 [see 1:998]. For the article regarding the Indian barrier which had been accepted by the American commissioners, see 1:985. For the initial British demands, see 1:953. For Gen. Brown, see 1:990, 994; for Brig. Gen. Macomb, 1:992-94; for Gen. Izard, 1:990; for Drummond, 1:990 and *DNB*. See Horseman, *The War of*

1812, 180-93 for the battles during this period; also Caffrey, *The Twilight's Last Gleaming*, 251-68, *passim*.

From William H. Crawford, Paris, December 12, 1814. States: "I believe you will be able to terminate the war, and I congratulate you upon the probable success of your labors.—After so far abandoning the principle of Uti possidetis, as they have already done, I see no difficulty on that point.—It is not probable that the navigation of the Mississip[p]i will present insurmountable obstacles to the return of Peace." Believes the negotiation "ought not to be Broken off on our part, by slight obstacles."

Has heard through private letters that the people in the South "march greatly in advance of the Government, upon the important subject of taxes.—They demand of their representatives, the imposition of taxes to the utmost wants of the Government." Adds that the "resolution of the Legislature of New York, and the other measures of that body, tending to increase the military force of the nation, is highly honorable to the State and to the federal party there, and cannot fail to have an influence upon the decisions of the enemy.—The measures of Massachusetts, and the exertions of the Boston Editors, who no doubt, promulgate the views of the Essex Junto, are calculated to counteract the salutary measures of New York.—If the other new England States yield to the impulse of the Boston faction, I shall rejoice to see a Peace signed before the history of the contemplated convention shall be known in Europe."

Believes that Massachusetts is "incurable" and "I shall regret any measure which hereafter shall be intended to conciliate them.—I should rejoice at a reconciliation between the two parties South of New England. I think the thing practicable.—The long opposition which has been made by this party [Republican] to many of the principles which formed a part of their [Federalist] Creed, when in power, and the experience which we have had of the impropriety of some of our attacks when we were in the minority removes many of the difficulties to this reconciliation.—For myself, I am willing to abandon my opposition to the Navy, and to consent to a System which shall provide for a regular and uniform increase of that species of force.—All men, who now act as good Americans ought to act, should be considered as members of the Majority, and entitled to an honorable confidence. The rest should be considered as Englishmen in principle and practice.—The adoption of this course, would place the unprincipled faction of Boston, in the point of view, which they so really merit.—They deserve the contempt of every honest American, and I hope they will meet with their just reward." Asserts that "The Majority will never be convinced of their error, by the treasonable practices of the Essex Junto.—The Boston federalists will never convince the people of the other states, of their attachment to the constitution, and to the union, by the adoption of unconstitutional measures, with a view to overthrow the federal constitution.—These measures are manifestly not calculated to restore Massachusetts to her former weight in the union.—Whilst she pursues these measures, if she has any weight in the councils of the Nation, She manifestly has more than She ought to possess."

Mentions that his private letters have not revealed who may likely be James Monroe's successor. Hopes it will be a Federalist, because "many of them have given sufficient evidence of their American feelings." Fears "Mr [Alexander J.] Dallas's plan of a National bank is too gigantic" and would be "extremely difficult—to put . . . in operation at this moment." Copy. DNA, RG84, Misc. Letters Sent, France.

New York Gov. Daniel Tompkins had called a special session of the legislature in September, 1814, and it had passed several laws increasing the number and pay of the militia and the funding for fortifications. Irwin, *Daniel D. Tompkins,* 178-79.

For the Essex Junto, see 1:773; for Massachusetts's opposition to the war which led to the Hartford Convention, see Coles, *The War of 1812,* 243-46.

Monroe at this time was serving as both secretary of state and as interim secretary of war. Monroe retained the office of secretary of state for the remainder of Madison's term, but Alexander J. Dallas, the secretary of the treasury, followed him as intermin secretary of war on March 14, 1815, a position he held until August 8, 1815, when William H. Crawford assumed the office. Joseph N. Kane, *Facts About the Presidents* (New York, 1974), 35. For Dallas and the national bank bill, see 2:7 and *DAB.*

To LLOYD JONES   Ghent, December 24, 1814

I have sent down this evening my baggage from Paris, and expect it will reach Antwerp tomorrow morning.[1] I have also sent my servant Frederick [Cana][2] to attend to its being placed on board, and beg you to give him any assistance in your power. I hope the delay in its arrival has subjected you to no inconvenience.

ALS. PHi.   1. Clay to Jones, Oct. 22, 1814.   2. See 1:915.

To WILLIAM H. CRAWFORD   Ghent, December 25, 1814

In this moment of hurry I seize one [minute] to say to you that we signed a Treaty of Pea[ce today.][1] Its terms are different from what was expected [when] the War was made, but not perhaps dishono[rable] under existing circumstances. The Passama[quoddy] Islands remain [w]ith the possessor at th[e time] of the exchange of ratifications of t[he treaty], subject to future decision. We gain the unencumbered Navigation of the Mississippi, or lose the right of fishing in British waters—

I expect to have the pleasure next week of embracing you, when I will explain all—[2]

ALS, manuscript torn. DLC-HC.   1. See 1:1006 and Clive Parry (ed.), *The Consolidated Treaty Series,* 231 vols. (Dobbs Ferry, N.Y., 1969), 63:421-30.   2. For Clay's departure for Paris, see Clay to Crawford. August 18, 1814.

From Thomas Sumter, Jr., Rio de Janeiro, January 8, 1815. Had written to Clay on June 30, 1814 [not found], in order "to make you acquainted with what information I possessed here, and . . . to use that as the only mode then within my reach of communicating with our government." Writes once more "to put at your disposition whatever information I can obtain here, which may possibly be turned by you to any advantageous purpose for us."

Reports that the "antient and new connections between England & Portugal, the force and arrogance of the one, and the . . . apparent feebleness and humility of the other" may "establish the belief which England wishes to inspire, that this government [Brazil/Portugal] is satisfied with these pretensions, and means to be contented in the condition to which they are calculated to reduce it." Believes "this is by no means the fact." Thinks the Prince [Dom John] hopes "to fortify himself gradually and silently against" British influence, "by family & commercial alliances; and thereby, to escape immediate concussions with her, and . . . to postpone for a while, if not forever, his return to Europe." Adds "that it would be a great blessing to him and his nation if the councils of continental Europe should take it upon them to do more for his independence than he thinks he is capable of doing . . . for himself."

States that "I have not received any letters from the government of the United States, since the change of affairs in Europe must have suggested to the President the propriety of giving instructions relative to his policy and my conduct in the case of the Princes removal from Brazil to Portugal." Notes that "My commission was for Brazil," and a difficulty exists now "in consequence of the arrival here of Admiral [John P.] Beresford . . . to carry or escort the Prince to Lisbon." Considers "This expedition" to be "a diplomatic manoeuvre intended to have some effect at Vienna and in Portugal; but, chiefly, to mollify the fanaticism of the English nation and the opposition on the . . . Slave trade." Notes that before the "end of the war," the British "preferred his stay here," but following the war "it was the natural policy . . . to desire the restoration of that [colonial] system as extensively as possible." England also wants "to prevent the rise of a maritime power here." Explains: "By the treaties of 1810, the colonial system cannot be restored here without the consent of England, and she presses the Princes return; it is plain, therefore, that he must settle a regency here if he returns, or she must give her consent to the re-establishment of the colonial system—I believe she has consented to re-establish the colonial system, with her guarantee of the colony." Contends that "whether the Prince returns to Lisbon, or stays here, it is his policy to make his subjects in Portugal believe that he is going; that the colonial system will be restored, on which their prosperity is supposed to depend, and equally to make the Brazilians believe, that he will never go; that the colonial system will not be restored; and that the slave trade will not be abandoned." Has, therefore, made "a direct enquiry into the Princes intention," and has urged "many arguments against the change of residence either near or remote."

Refers to the people of Brazil, saying that "their hostility to Englishmen depends upon their religious prejudices . . . which is at least as dear to them as any religious sentiment." Contends that "if the Prince were to leave the country in the hands of his own subjects, none or few of the English would dare to stay in it." Adds that "Besides the spark of spirit struck out of the government by the affair at Fayal, the depredations of the English upon the African Ships have lately excited . . . animosities against them in all parts of Brazil."

Discusses the attack on an American cruiser at Fayal and reports that "About the same day that government received the despatches from Fayal, a Portuguese Vessel entered this port, bringing . . . a British Lieutenant & prize crew put on board a Slave Ship (lately recaptured by her own crew.) by two British Frigates the Niger & Laurel under the American flag. The Prince liberated the prisoners, but ordered a price to be inserted in his Gazette . . . stating the fact to be proved, of the capture being made under false colours."

Deplores "the hypocrisy of England" in respect to the slave trade when "her own colonies . . . are now overstocked with Slaves." Believes "All these circumstances must tend surely to encrease the Princes disposition and that of his Cabinet to remain where they are for the present," but fears they might still be "pressed by their friends the English to go." Maintains: "I should not doubt the propriety of my government maintaining a minister in Portugal, if the colonial system should be restored in these dominions." Ponders what he should do in the absence of instructions of his government if the Prince leaves. Concludes that "My present impression is, that it would be most correct for me to refuse to go, without orders to do so from home." Asks: "But as the intercourse with Washington is very precarious, I beg the favor of you, Gentlemen, to consider the circumstances I have exposed to you, and to this government; to combine them with such views as they are supposed to be connected with in Europe; and, exercising your better judgement, to tell me freely your opinion of the conduct I have so far pursued in this matter; and to give me your advice on that which I ought to pursue in the case that the Prince should go in a British squadron, or in one of his own, leaving this a colony either in the hands of his own troops or in those of England." Thinks he can receive their answer before the Prince "can be ready to go . . . by reason of the unprepared state of his marine . . . and the number of his attendants and the bulk of such an apparatus as he would chuse to accompany him to Lisbon." Believes England's actions "in sending a Ship here to carry or escort him to Europe, and appointing an embassy to meet him there, have had the effect to make other sovereigns believe that he was already determined to return thither—They have sent their ministers to Lisbon instead of Rio."

Concludes: "The question therefore, whether I ought or not to follow this Court under any of the circumstances herein presented, resolves itself into a question of individual policy, as it regards the United States." Hopes their "presence in Europe, and your knowledge of the current politics of its courts, may enable you to judge well of what may be the interest of the United States in this matter; and knowing, as you must, the train of their affairs, as well as the tenor of their Policy adapted to the new circumstances of all nations. I shall depend upon your anticipations of the sentiments of the government much more then I can upon my own uninformed judgment." ALS. DNA, RG59, General Records of the State Dept., Misc. Duplicate Despatches, Box 2, folder 7. Addressed to the commissioners at Ghent with a duplicate to William H. Crawford at Paris.

For Thomas Sumter, see 2:428. Portugal's Prince Regent Dom John and his family had escaped capture by Napoleon's forces in 1807 by fleeing to Brazil. A Treaty of Alliance between Portugal and Great Britain was concluded on February 19, 1810; however, a January 22, 1815, treaty between the two countries annulled the alliance, restricted the Portuguese slave trade, and abrogated the Loan Convention of 1809. A convention on January 21, 1815, provided for indemnifying Portuguese subjects for slave vessels which had been detained by the British. On January 16, 1815, Brazil was raised to the rank of a separate Kingdom, equal to the mother country, and the following year Prince Dom John succeeded to the throne as John VI of the United Kingdom of Portugal, Brazil, and Algarves. He did not return to Portugal until 1821 when a liberal revolution there forced him to do so. See C.R. Boxer, *The Portuguese Seaborne Empire, 1415-1825* (New York, 1969), 200; Charles E. Nowell, *A History of Portugal* (New York, 1952), 181; Parry, *Treaty Series*, 61:41-101; 63:453-72.

For British admiral Sir John P. Beresford, see *DNB*.

To Captain Lloyd Jones, U.S.S. *Neptune*, January 31, 1815. Repeat previous instructions "that if in your Opinion the value of the ship on her return home will be so much encreased as to exceed the expense of coppering, you will cause it to be done." Mention that "As the expence will be much less than in England it would seem advisable to provision and fit the Ship completely for her voyage before you leave Brest." Add that if "the work can be accomplished so as to enable you to be at Plymouth by the first of April, it will be within the time that we propose embarking from that Port for America." Instruct him to let them know the amount needed to pay these expenses before they leave Paris "about the 20th of the ensuing month." ALS, by James A. Bayard, signed also by Clay. PHi. Written from Paris.

Bayard and Clay again wrote Jones on February 25, informing him that they had received his letter of February 20 [not found] indicating that the ship "would be ready to proceed to Plymouth by the 1[s]t of April." State that "That part of our baggage not necessary for immediate personal use we have sent to the ship and . . . it ought to arrive at Brest by the 15th of March. After its arrival you will be at liberty to chuse your own time to make the passage to Plymouth so as to be there the 1[s]t. week in April."

Order Jones "to lay in ten dozens of claret & three of brandy on account of Messrs. [George B.] Milligan [John Payne] Todd & ourselves." Add that "Mr. [Albert] Gallatin has not yet returned from Geneva—upon his arrival, arrangement shall be made on the subject of the additional funds you require." In a postscript, note that they have placed "in the hands of Hottinguer & Co. of Paris one thousand franks for . . . the purchase of Wines &c" and that "Any deficiency shall be made good to you in England." *Ibid.*

For Todd, see 1:942. See also 2:3-4, 9, 43-44. Jones reached Plymouth at least by the end of May, 1815. He sailed from Plymouth on June 18 and reached Wilmington on July 31. See 2:39, 62. Clay and Gallatin sailed from Liverpool in July on the *Lorenzo* rather than the *Neptune*. Gallatin had made a trip to Geneva, Switzerland, on January 12, 1815, to visit the city of his birth. Raymond Walters, Jr., *Albert Gallatin, Jeffersonian Financier and Diplomat* (New York, 1957), 289-90.

To LLOYD JONES   Paris, March 3, 1815

On the 15th. of Feb, I sent to the Waggon office ten packages marked H.C. from number 5 to number 14 inclusive, which were stipulated to be delivered at Brest in 25 or 26 days, and which I wish to be put on board the Neptune. At the same time my servant Frederick [Cana] sent a trunk marked HC No. 1. likewise to be put on board; and by the same conveyance some other packages were sent for Mr [James A.] Bayard, Mr. [Christopher] Hughes and Mr [George B.] Milligan, of which I presume you will be duly advised. In one of my packages, or in Fredericks there are some shirts which you ordered at Gand. [Ghent, Belgium] and which we received from Mr. Hughes for you.

Inclosed is a receipt for the delivery of my packages and some others. I paid here two thirds of the price of transportation, and there remains to be paid at Brest the other third, that is to say 64 franks and 21 Centimes. I must ask the favor of you to advance that for me, and I will return it as soon as I have the pleasure of seeing you. By the terms of the contract indeed they are not entitled to receive it, if the articles are not delivered in the time specified; and I did not pay it here to quicken their diligence. But if they do not deliver the articles in time I wish you to exercise your own discretion as to paying them. At all events I do not wish the packages to be placed under any difficulties, as to their getting out of their possession into yours—

I know you will do whatever is in your power to preserve those packages free from injury. And if I thought it necessary to venture a request on the subject it would be, that particular care might be taken of package No. 6, and that package No. 5 which contains glass might be set up edgeways.

I doubt whether they will arrive before about the 20h. instant.

Mr. Bayard and I will leave here on monday next for London, and I hope to have the pleasure of seeing you early in the month of April at Plymouth.[1] Mr. [Albert] Gallatin has not yet arrived from Geneva.[2]

P.S. I promised Ms. Fenwick to mention to you that amongst Mr. [William] Shaler's[3] baggage on board the Ship, is a package covered with sacking cloth, which contains things of a very delicate nature, and which may be easily spoiled by the damp; and to request that you would have them placed in a dry situation.

ALS. PHi. 1. Clay remained in London until July 4. See 2:59. 2. Clay & Bayard to Jones, Jan. 31, 1815. 3. For Shaler, see 1:865-66.

To LLOYD JONES
Paris, March 7, 1815

I wrote you a few days ago[1] that I had sent on to the Neptune ten packages of my own numbered from 5 to 14 inclusive, and one of Fredericks [Cana], my servant, which I expected would arrive at Brest on or before the 20th. instant. I requested your kind attention to these articles, and also desired you to pay 64 franks and 20 Centimes, which would be due for the Waggonage provided the delivery of the articles was in the time contracted for. If the delivery was not made in time I submitted it to your discretion to pay or not that sum as you might deem reasonable and just.

I have now to inform you that I have deposited with the house of Hottinguer to your credit 65 franks to pay the balance of the waggonage; and request that at the same time you draw for the 1000 franks which Mess. [James A.] Bayard [George B.] Milligan [John Payne] Todd and myself have placed at your disposal for provisions, you will draw for the 65 franks.[2] Or if you shall have drawn for the 1000 franks before the receipt of this letter, that you will nevertheless find means to get the 65 franks, as I shall leave Paris under that expectation.

Mr. Bayard is unwell, and Mr. [Albert] Gallatin not yet arrived.

ALS. PHi. 1. Clay to Jones, March 3, 1815. 2. Clay & Bayard to Jones, Jan. 31, 1815.

To LLOYD JONES
Paris, March 14, 1815

I have sent the bearer Francois Jaucrot, [sic, Arnail-Francois, Marquis de Jaucourt][1] one of my servants, to go on board the Neptune and await my arrival there. You will be good enough to receive him. I have directed him to ask your permission to have my cases sent from this place to be put on board in some dry and safe place.

Mr. [Albert] Gallatin has at length arrived.[2] Mr. [James A.] Bayard has been and is still extremely ill.[3]

I shall go in a day or two to England, and hope to have the pleasure of seeing you by the time heretofore mentioned.[4]

I offer you my congratulations upon our complete success at New Orleans, where the assailants have experienced the greatest loss ever sustained by one party in any battle fought in America.[5]

ALS. PHi. 1. See 2:16 2. From Geneva. See Clay to Jones, Jan. 31, 1815. 3. Bayard suffered from an ulcerated throat and fever. Elizabeth Donnan, *The Papers of James A. Bayard* in *Annual Report of the American Historical Association for the Year 1913*, 2 vols. (Washington, 1915), 2:378. 4. Clay to Jones, Jan. 31, 1815. 5. See 2:11.

NOTES ON CONVERSATIONS IN BRITAIN
May 11, 1815[1]

7th June. We again recd. from Mr. [Frederick John] Robinson, Mr. [Henry] Goulburn and Dr. [William] Adams[2] an invitation to call at the same place this day at 2 OClock. Mr. Adams being included in it, we all three accordingly attended. They notified us that they had received a Commission from their Govt. to enter upon the negotiation to which our previous interviews related. Mr. [Albert] Gallatin and I observed to them that considering the delay which had unexpectedly intervened, but which we had no doubt was altogether unavoidable on their part, we had, before we received their note requesting this interview, asked and obtained an interview with Lord Castlerea[g]h for the purpose of stating to him that we felt ourselves obliged to exercise the right which we had reserved to ourselves of withdrawing from the negotiation, and leaving it in the hands of Mr. [John Quincy] Adams, the Commission under which we had proposed to act, being several as well as joint. The British Commrs expressed a wish that whilst we remained in London we would attend the meetings and participate in the discussion. This we consented to, and proceeded to an exchange of our respective powers which we did by each party examining the original power of the other, and interchanging Copies thereof.

The B. Commissioners then remarked that on the subject of the India trade they had before stated the expectation on the part of their Government of an equivalent for the privilege of the circuity of the outward voyage from America, which equivalent they had intimated might be obtained in some accommodation to be granted by us in the Fur trade. That they were now instructed to say that without an equivalent their Government could not consent to the circuity of our outward voyages. But they yet hoped that we might find it practicable to grant the equivalent; and they thought that, without interference with the political considerations which had induced our Government to decline renewing the intercourse with the Indians inhabiting our territories, the equivalent might be granted in the Fur trade. We stated that we did not know what accommodation in that respect they desired; and although we pressed them on this point we could not arrive at any distinct development of their views or wishes. It was stated by one of us that we had not understood them as demanding specifically an equivalent for the privilege of circuitous trade with India at the former interview—They said that that was certainly the way they had intended to be understood, and they thought they so expressed themselves.

We then proceeded to remark that we had prepared a projet of a Commercial Convention, which we would then hand them, if they pleased, and that afterwards a projet upon the other subject which had been spoken of in our former interviews would be delivered to them. That as the Commercial topic was subject to least difficulty, and as certain principles had seemed to be already agreed upon between us, we supposed it would not take up much more time in arranging it; and that it was possible it might be completed before our departure.

They assented to this course, received our projet, and promised to return us an answer on friday next, when it was agreed that we should again meet at the same hour.

9h June—The same parties again met at the same place. The B. Commissioners informed us that they had not been yet able to arrange an answer to our projet, but that they would certainly be prepared with one in what we should ourselves deem a reasonable time. Mr. Gallatin and I stated that we had thought of leaving London on the succeeding monday, and if they could inform us by that day when they would be prepared with an answer, it would enable us to govern our movements, which they promised to do.

[See the correspondence which passed between the American and British Plenipotentiaries for the sequel and for further explanations][3]

AD. DLC. 1. Clay used the notes from May 11 to write his and Gallatin's letter to James Monroe of May 18, 1815 [2:30-37], which bears a striking similarity to the notes up to this point and are not herein repeated. However, the remainder of the notes has not been found in any other letter or report and is printed here in full. 2. For Robinson, see 2:20; for Goulburn and Adams, see 1:915. 3. Insert in brackets has been added in Clay's hand.

To David Shriver, Cumberland, Md., December 20, 1815. States that he has "a note of Michael C. Sprigg Esq. given to the late Capt. [Nathaniel G.S.] Hart," and asks: "Will you oblige me by applying to him for the amount, and if it cannot be obtained but by suit telling me what Lawyer I had better send it to?" ALS. KyU. The attached note is for $104.00, dated November 10, 1808. For Shriver, see 4:305; for Sprigg and Clay's receipt of the note, see 2:100.

To ALBERT GALLATIN[1]   Washington, December 31, 1815
It has been contended, I understand, in the Senate, that the second clause of the second article[2] of the Convention[3] places British vessels, although coming from ports into which ours are not admitted, on the same footing with American vessels; and that it is not restricted to the case of British vessels coming from the British European possessions. This construction is supposed to be fortified by the omission of the clause proposed in the second article of our projet in the following words: "Such only excepted as may be bound from or to British possessions to which vessels of the United States are not permanently admitted."

I do not think the above construction warranted by the instrument, especially when we consider the last paragraph of the same second article which was inserted expressly to guard ag[ains]t. it.

My impression of the cause of the omission of the clause proposed by us in the second article of our projet is, that it was thought to be rendered unnecessary by the insertion of the exception of the West Indies & the British possessions on this Continent—Will you tell me if your recollection accords with mine?

ALS. MHi. 1. Name of recipient supplied by editors, based of Gallatin's reply of Jan. 4, 1816 [2:124-27]. This letter is the one indicated as "Not found" in 2:127, note 1, of Gallatin's letter. 2. For article 2, see 2:57-58. 3. See 2:57-59.

From Caesar Augustus Rodney, Dover, Delaware, January 7, 1816. States that he has sent "Col. [Allan] McLane [2:129] a letter of introduction to you, requesting your aid & influence in his favor, on the subject of a claim he had on [the] government." Also asks "your assistance & exertion, in support of the only Democratic county, New Castle, in this state." Explains that "This state consists of three counties New Castle, Kent & Sussex," and "By the last census . . . Sussex contains more people than Kent or New Castle." Complains that the last session of the legislature imposed "nearly two thirds of the state tax on New Castle," and that the pretext for this "was an assessment made of the property taxed by the U. States." Points out that the new assessment for New Castle was greater than the amount had been previously for all three counties combined, and asks Clay's influence in attempting to remedy the problem. AL, incomplete. DeHi. For Clay's reply, see 2:129. This letter is probably one of those indicated as "Not found" in 2:129, note 1.

To JAMES MONROE[1] Washington, February 7, 1816

In reply to your letter of the 5h. inst.[2] I would observe, that Russellville is about 160 miles from Lexington and Frankfort, in the South Western extremity of the State of K[entucky]. and Frankfort is about 22 miles West from Lexington. I am not acquainted with the comparative extent of circulation of the paper of Mr. [William] Hunter,[3] and that published at Russellville, but from the location of the latter I should think it ought to be retained.[4] The K[entucky]. Gazette (lately published at Lexington by Tho[mas]. Smith)[5] is the *oldest* print in the State, and I imagine circulates more extensively than that referred to by you as being published by Mr. Hunter, who I believe is no longer the Editor. This latter paper has, on the other hand, the advantage of being edited at the seat of the State Govern[men]t; though it is not the official gazette.

The [Lexington] Reporter is decidedly the best paper in the State, and has the extent of circulation before noticed. If I were to determine which of the papers it should be substituted for, I should say that of Mr. Hunter.

ALS. MHi.   1. Name of recipient has been supplied by editors, based on internal evidence.   2. Not found, but see Clay's letter to Monroe on Feb. 2, 1816, in 2:160-61 and in *FCHQ*, 25:206. The latter adds the endorsement: "H. Clay Feby 5 Requested him to designate the paper in place of which he wished the Reporter Substituted." 3. William Hunter had been one of the founders of the Washington (Ky.) *Mirror* and later of the Frankfort *Palladium;* however, in 1809 he sold the latter. At various times he also was a publisher and binder of books, owner of a bookstore, editor of the Louisville *Gazette*, and clerk for the U.S. Treasury Department. William H. Perrin, *The Pioneer Press of Kentucky . . .*, Filson Club Publications No. 3 (Louisville, 1888), 24-26.   4. Charles Rhea was the publisher of the Russellville *Weekly Messenger*. Edward Coffman, *The Story of Logan County* (Nashville, Tenn., 1962), 127, 147, 216.   5. The first issue of the Lexington *Kentucky Gazette* was issued in August, 1787. Perrin, *Pioneer Press of Kentucky*, 10. Thomas Smith succeeded John Bradford as editor of the *Kentucky Gazette* in 1809. In 1814, he and his partner John Beckley sold out to Fielding Bradford, Jr., and in Feb., 1816, Smith joined his brother-in-law, William W. Worsley, as publisher of the Lexington *Reporter*, which the following year was renamed the *Kentucky Reporter*. Clarence S. Brigham, *History and Bibliography of American Newspapers, 1690-1820*, 2 vols. (Worcester, Mass., 1947), 1:163, 166. For Worsley see also 2:160-61. The statement in the note [2:161] that "Apparently Worsley declined the favor," is erroneous. The *Reporter* published the laws throughout the summer of 1816, so apparently it was not until 1817 that Worsley declined, as stated in Richard M. Johnson to John Quincy Adams, Dec. 9, 1817. *FCHQ*, 25:206-7.

To JAMES MADISON Washington, February 8, 1816

I fear that I cannot add to the stock of information of which you must be already possessed respecting Genl LaFayette's lands.[1]

When in Paris, I was informed by him that he had sold all his lands to Sir John Coghill,[2] except one location near or adjoining the City of N Orleans containing I think less than 500 acres, of which he retained perhaps a moiety. He was desirous then to know whether the land could be held in virtue of his location. This question depends upon the true construction of the acts of Congress granting and directing the mode of locating his lands.[3] By the act which first authorized him to go into the State of Louisiana to locate his lands, it was provided that no location should contain less than 1000 Acres. By a subsequent act this limitation was brought down to 500 Acres. His location near the City contains less than 500; but the question is whether he may not hold on upon what it does include, and abandon the residue of the location? In determ[in]ing upon the true interpretation of th[e] Acts of Congress, it may be important to know the pre[cise] state at present of the location, when it was made [&c—] information which I presume the Comm[issio]n[er]. of the Lan[d] office can supply.

I should think that an attention to the Marq[uis's] interest would require that his claim, under the above location, should be immediately asserted or abandoned; if asserted, that measures should be adopted to produce a decision with as little delay as possible, if abandoned that the location sh[oul]d. be transfered to some other tract of valuable land.

I understand that Mr. [Armand Allard] DuPlantier,[4] the Marquis's agent, is yet alive.

ALS. NN.   1. See 2:115-16, 330-33.   2. See 2:114-16   3. See 2 *U.S. Stat.*, 236-37.   4. See 2:115.

To TENCH COXE[1]   Washington, February 25, 1816

The controversy between the two houses of Congress on the proper interpretation of the Treaty making power,[2] relative to which you favored me with the perusal of a sensible essay,[3] is likely to terminate by a drawn battle, or a victory on the part of the popular—branch. A conference between the two branches has resulted in a modification of the bill passed by the Senate, satisfactory to the house, and which will probably be approved by the other body.[4]

The whole difficulty of the question, as in a thousand other cases, perhaps consists in too much inattention to the proper definition of terms. In the *formation* or *ratification* of Treaties Congress has nothing to do. Not so with regard to their *fulfillment*.

I have to thank you for the Compilation & Views on our Manufactures, which I duly recd.[5]

ALS. PHi.   1. For Tench Coxe (1755-1824), Philadelphia merchant and member of the Continental Congress, see *DAB* and *BDAC*.   2. The issue of a conflict between a treaty and a law of Congress had been raised during debate on a bill to put into effect the provisions of the Commercial Convention with Great Britain of July 3, 1815. See Clay's speech on the subject in 2:123-24. The note on 2:124 states the House bill was rejected by the Senate but fails to add that a Senate bill eventually passed which achieved the same objective by declaring of no effect all discriminating duties in conflict with the treaty. See 3 *U.S. Stat.*, 255, and Robert L. Meriwether (ed.), *The Papers of John C. Calhoun, 1801-1817*, (Columbia, S.C., 1959), 1:313-14.   3. Not found.   4. See note 2, above.   5. Not found.

To WALTER KIRKPATRICK[1]   Washington, March 28, 1816

I am much pleased to learn, by your favor of the 17th. inst.,[2] that your private views do not urge your immediate return to New Jersey; and that you can remain at Ashland until we get there. I still think Congress will adjourn on if not before the first of May, and I hope to be able to reach Kentucky in that month.[3]

Will you have the goodness to request John Watkins or John Hart (who will probably get to Lexington before this letter) to pay you any sum of money you may want not exceeding one hundred and fifty dollars?

ALS. NjHi.   1. Not identified.   2. Not found.   3. Congress adjourned on April 30, 1816.

To THOMAS MORRIS[1]   Lexington, June 16, 1816

I have determined to send my sons to Mr. [Lewis] Bancel's Academy,[2] and must tax your kindness with making for me the necessary arrangement. One of my sons is 13 and the other 12[3] which I believe I before communicated to you, and if I mistake not you said that the circumstance of age was not absolutely indispensible. I intend them to take their departure in the month of August so as to reach New York about the first of September. They have made some progress in their education, about as much as boys of their age generally do. They have been through Virgil, know a little of Greek, of Geography, Arithmetic &c &c. I will thank you to put Mr. Bancel in possession of the circumstances above mentioned and ascertain from him definitively if they will be received if sent—It would be highly inconvenient for them to proceed under any uncertainty.

I will thank you to present my respects to Mrs. Morris[.] P.S. Be pleased to direct your letter via Washington & Marietta to me at this place.

ALS. NhHi.   1. For Morris, See 2:138 and *BDAC*.   2. See 2:253-54.   3. Theodore Wythe and Thomas Hart Clay, respectively.

To RICHARD BLAND LEE[1]   Lexington, June 30, 1816

I recd your letter[2] requesting to be furnished with the names of fit persons to be appointed Commissioners under the late act of Congress.[3] As I presume you have written to all the members to the same effect I will confine myself to my own District, and at present to Fayette County, which includes Lexington. I recommend John Bradford, Charles Humphreys, Oliver Keene, Richard Higgins and Matthew Elder.[4]

With regard to the other two Counties, composing my district, not having yet full information, I will send you hereafter the names of suitable persons.[5]

The Commissioners will want to be informed on the subject of compensation. Not having the law before me will you state for their information what may be expected on that subject?

ALS. KyLoF.   1. For Lee and his reply, see 2:214. This letter is the one indicated as "Not found" in note 1 of the reply.   2. Not found.   3. For the act, see 2:214, note 2.   4. For Bradford, see 1:136; for Humphreys, 1:431; for Keene, 2:90; for Higgins, 1:299; 2:98, 866, 904; and for Elder, 1:304.   5. No further recommendations have been found.

From Robert Brent, Washington, July 23, 1816. Reports that he has sent to Major Voorhies "the Copy of the law in favour of Colo. William Dudleys detachment, and directed him either to pay them in person or place the funds necessary for their payment in the hands of Charles Carr Esqr." Has "also suggested . . . how very improper it is to pay the Militia of Kentucky with any other money than the notes of the Kentucky Banks as the D[ra]fts. sent by me to him were drawn on the banks of New Y[ork]." Copy. DNA, RG99, Records of the Paymaster General, vol. 9, p. 320.

For Brent, see 2:237. He had also been mayor of Washington, D.C., 1802-12. Constance McLaughlin Green, *Washington Village and Capital, 1800-1878* (Princeton, N.J., 1962), 31, 36, 39, 43, 51.

Voorhies is probably Peter G. Voorhies, who had been Kentucky district paymaster when he received his discharge from the army in 1815. See 2:899 and Francis B. Heitman, *Historical Register and Dictionary of the United States Army . . .* (Washington, 1903), 990.

For Charles Carr, an early sheriff and farmer in Fayette County, see 1:84 and Perrin, *History of Fayette County,* 591.

For the law in favor of Dudley's detachment, see 2:167.

To ROBERT BRENT   Lexington, August 2, 1816

In the settlement of the accounts of Col. [William] Dudley's[1] regiment a question has arisen whether the militia men are entitled to the usual allowance per month for clothing? Or whether the provision made for their benefit at the last Session[2] is limited simply to pay to the exclusion of every thing else? On this question my opinion has been asked by Messr. [Peter G.] Voorhies and Mr. [Charles] Carr. It involves so much responsibility to one or both of those gentlemen, and I am at the same time so destitute of the requisite information to form a correct judgment, that I have advised a reference of the question to you. If, according to usage in similar cases, or according to any liberal interpretation of the law, the Regiment be entitled to receive a compensation for clothing, their services and their sufferings justly entitle them to it, and I hope they will be permitted to receive it.

An early answer[3] addressed to Charles Carr Esqr or to me at this place will facilitate the final adjustment of this business, already too much delayed, and will at the same time oblige . . .

ALS. KyU.   1. Brent to Clay, July 23, 1816.   2. See 2:167   3. Not found.

To PORTER CLAY[1]   Lexington, August 2, 1816

Your letter[2] by Mr. Bartlett[3] I recd. & should have answered by him, but for his earlier return than I expected, and my counting upon seeing you at [John] Higbee's.[4]

Mr [John] Pope voted in opposition to the resolutions of 1799 ag[ains]t. the Alien & Sedition laws.[5] Sufficient publicity was given to this fact yesterday in the course of the discussions. I do not think that so late as the present time that the publication of his bank speech would have any particular effect. A publication of his speech made at Campbell's Spring on the War would have had an excellent effect, but I fear it is too late at present.[6]

I have not the smallest doubt of the result of the Election. The confidence of my friends, always great, was strengthened by the events of yesterday.

ALS. MA. 1. For Porter Clay, see 1:96. 2. Not found. 3. Possibly Thomas Jefferson Bartlett of Versailles. See 5:555. 4. See 2:182, 221. 5. For the Kentucky and Virginia Resolutions against the Alien & Sedition Laws, see 3:170; 9:249, 716. For Pope's stand on this, see Orval W. Baylor, *John Pope, Kentuckian* (Cynthiana, Ky., 1943), 114-16. 6. Pope was Clay's opponent in the 1816 congressional race. Although Pope's biographer places the last debate between Clay and Pope at the Lexington cattle show on July 25, George D. Prentice's biography of Clay and this letter indicate that the final one occurred on August 1. In addition to using Pope's vote against the Kentucky Resolution of 1799, Clay also called attention in the campaign to his opponent's speech in 1811 in favor of rechartering the Bank of the United States and supporting strong action against the British and his later vote against war with Britain. Pope attempted in his speech at Campbell's Well to explain his vote against war. George D. Prentice, *Biography of Henry Clay* (New York, 1831), 123-27; Baylor, *John Pope*, 114-22; and 2:181-82, 216-21, 231, 233.

To PETER IRVING[1]   Lexington, August 30, 1816

I learnt with great pleasure, my dear Sir, by your letter of the 8h. of May,[2] which not finding me at Washington followed me to this place, that your health, so bad when I parted with you at Liverpool, was nearly re-established. I hope your contemplated visit to the continent has completely restored it; and that you may also have derived much pleasure from renewing your acquaintances at Ghent. I am very anxious to hear from you, and shall continue to expect the letter which you have been so good as to promise me until it arrives.

I have written to [the] Government in behalf of [Reuben G.] Beasley as you desired. I understand that there are many applicants for the vacant Consulship at Bordeaux, and being uninformed as to their respective merits & pretensions I can not venture to anticipate the fate of your friend's application.[3]

I have nothing to offer you of news from this distant region. You will however I am sure take an interest in learning that upon my return from Europe, after an absence of nearly two years from my family, I found them all in health, my children much grown, and a progress made in their education greatly exceeding my expectations. I spent last winter with Mrs. [Lucretia Hart] Clay, as we expect to be the approaching one at Washington. I have sent my two eldest boys[4] to [Lewis] Bancel's Academy in N. York.[5]

I now, my dear Sir, wish to avail myself of your kindness in the execution of a commission, which I hope you may execute without much trouble.

Our Country is admirably adapted to the rearing of Cattle, and the improvement of the breeds has become an object of general attention. I have had repeated applications, since my return, to import some cattle, and am desirous, as well for my neighbours as myself, to import two males & two females. Can you procure them for me & have them shipped? I believe the beef and the milch races are distinct; and in that case I should like a male and female of each breed. But the object being to get the best breeds your information and judgment would be entirely satisfactory. As to age, I should think about two year olds would be the best, and if the females were recently impregnated it would be very desirable. Besides the chance which such a circumstance would give of multiplication, I believe animals are more tenacious of life in the pregnant state than any other. The port to which I should prefer their being shipt is Baltimore or Alexandria, most convenient to this Country. I have thought the present a favorable period to get out these cattle on account of the low freights, and the low price of Agricultural produce in England.[6]

I am so utterly ignorant of the expence attending this business, in all its branches, and am besides so remote at present from the Cities, where alone a remittance could be made, that I have not effected one; and shall have to depend upon your making the advances in the first instance of such sums as cannot be made payable in America, and I will reimburse you in such manner as you may please to direct.

If the Cattle should be purchased & sent to Balto., they may be directed to the care of [Alexander] McDonald & [Nicholas G.] Ridgley [sic, Ridgely][7] of that place; if to Philada. to the care of [Alexander] Scott, [George] Trotter & [John] Tilford there.

Wishing you that greatest of all blessings, health, & all other blessing's . . .

ALS. NjMoHP.   1. For Irving and his reply, see 2:252-53. This letter is the one indicated as "Not found" in 2:253, note 1.   2. Not found.   3. Beasley received the appointment of U.S. consul at Le Havre, France, in Dec., 1816. U.S. Sen., *Executive Journal*, 3:61-62.   4. Theodore Wythe Clay and Thomas Hart Clay.   5. See 2:253-54; and Clay to Morris, June 16, 1816.   6. Clay was one of the earliest importers of Hereford cattle. See 2:314-15, 329-30, 345-46; Perrin, *History of Fayette County*, 182.   7. See 2:315.

From John Bradford, Lexington, October 3, 1816. Certifies as justice of the peace that Henry Clay appeared before him and swore under oath "that in April 1813 William Saterwhite [sic, Satterwhite; 1:590-91] . . . being indebted to him for rent, offered in payment thereof a negro slave named George . . . but not having any particular use for the s[ai]d slave, he the sd Clay first declined purchasing him, but upon the sd Slave applying to him and expressing a wish . . . that he would purchase him he determined to buy him, and accordingly did buy him of sd Satterwhite and received from him a Bill of sale [1:786]. . . . That not having any employment for the said slave in his own service, he hired him out, for a few months, to [David] Megowan [1:486] and Bulls [sic, John Bull; 1:789] who again hired him to Allen Davis [1:114], who advertised him in . . . the [Lexington] Reporter." Adds that Clay subsequently traced George through Ohio "where he was apprehended as a fugitive, and confined in the jail at Chilliothe [sic, Chillicothe], from which he made his escape and thro the State of Pensylvania [sic] to Philadelphia" where he was seen by Thomas Satterwhite [3:814] "and measures were adopted to arrest him, but before they were executed, he again disappeared." Clay was then informed "last summer" that the slave was in New Haven in Connecticut, "passing as a freeman . . . under the name of William Carr." Describes George at the time Clay purchased him as "a waiter in the tavern of the said Satterwhite in Lexington"; he was "in the prime of life, about five feet nine or ten inches high (by supposition) dark complexion, knock kneed, and he thinks a plausible fellow."

Thomas P. Satterwhite, who had lived with William Satterwhite when Clay purchased George, swears to Bradford that "he accords in the description" given of George by Clay "in the preceeding affidavit; to which he adds that besides being knock kneed the sd slave bent back considerably about the knees and legs when in a standing position: That in Novr. 1814 he saw the sd slave in Philadelphia and he appeared to recognise and avoid him, that he gave information thereof, but before the requisite papers could be obtained from Kentucky George disappeared. That George while living in the sd Satterwhites tavern learnt something of the business of a barber and could shave persons. . . . That some weeks ago Joseph W. Edmiston described to this deponant a black fellow, whom he saw some time during the last summer in New Haven and from the description given of him by the sd Edmiston, he the sd Satterwhite believes him the afores[ai]d slave George." ADS. CtY. See also 1:1006.

Memorandum on Legal Profession in Kentucky, *ca.* 1817. States that the "Judicial establishment of Kentucky consists of a Court in each of the several Counties . . . which has criminal, equity and law jurisdiction; and a Court of dernier resort, to which appeals in civil cases from all those subordinate tribunals are carried." Reports that "subjects of usual controversy are the titles to land and such contracts as may be supposed to arise out of the transactions of a society having some commerce and manufactures but chiefly addicted to agriculture." Notes that the most successful lawyers make $4-5,000 per year, while "Admission to the Bar is easy and requires no previous residence." Adds that "The present is a favorable moment for a lawyer of talents and industry to make an establishment there, several of the most considerable lawyers having from various causes quit the Bar."

In respect to the climate, states that it is "uncommonly fine from the first of May to the middle of November," but "winters are rather too humid." Productions in the area are horses, cattle, sheep, hogs, hemp, maize, wheat, rye, etc. Concludes: "Lexington is the chief town, and living there is very cheap." ADI. InU.

To JONATHAN RUSSELL[1] Washington, January 8, 1817
Will you do me the favor to dine with me on tuesday next at ½ after four?

You must excuse the air of ceremony in the distance of the day. The truth is (to be candid) that we sent from home some table furniture which has not yet arrived, though it ought to have been here long since, and as I wish to have some of the fashionables with you, I have mentioned that day to take the chance of its arrival. In the mean time I should be glad to see you as often as possible. I would call at your lodgings but for the uncertainty of finding you there. As for myself I shall be at home every evening this week except friday.

You will have the goodness to send me an early answer—Should you be engaged on tuesday, be pleased to name some day when you will not be.

ALS. KyU. 1. Identification of recipient made by Paul C. Richards, who sold the letter to the University of Kentucky.

From Commissioner of Public Buildings [Samuel Lane], Washington, January 20, 1817. Reports that "for carrying into effect the act of Congress entitled 'an act making an appropriation for enclosing and improving the Public Square [2:193] near the Capitol' the first consideration . . . was to digest a plan which should combine with the requisite degrees of convenience & elegance that durability which it is believed ought to be consulted in public works of this description." Notes that "After determining the plan," it was offered "to the competition of the public," and "a contract entered into . . . under which great part of the work has been executed." Continues: "It was however soon ascertained that the sum appropriated would fall considerably short of completing the whole, and this appears to have been occasioned in part by the original estimate not having been made to embrace the whole of the square. The paper marked A, contains an estimate of the sum which would be required for this purpose amounting to $52,242,45 and leaving a deficiency of $22,242,45, to be supplied by future appropriation if the wisdom of Congress should so direct." Copy. DNA, RG42, Records of the Office of Public Buildings and Grounds, 1791-1867, Letters Sent. Addressed originally to the "President of the United States" with a notation in the margin that it was withdrawn and sent to Henry Clay.

"An act making further provision for repairing the public buildings, and improving the public square" was approved on March 3, 1817. It appropriated $100,000 for repairing public buildings and $38,658 for completing the enclosure of the public square. 3 *U.S. Stat.*, 389-90.

For Samuel Lane, who had been nominated and confirmed as commissioner of public buildings on April 29, 1816, see 2:665 and U.S. Sen., *Executive Journal*, 3:53.

To THOMAS MORRIS   Washington, February 5, 1817

I have the pleasure to inform you that my sons [Theodore & Thomas] arrived yesterday, without having met on their journey with any accident.[1] The young gentlemen look very well and are certainly much improved.

I hasten to acquit myself of the pecuniary obligation under which I stand to you, by transmitting the inclosed order for $184:16. I know not how I shall ever have it in my power to extinguish another and greater debt which I owe for the kind attentions of yourself and lady to my boys. Of the magnitude of that debt I had formed no adequate conception until I saw the young gentlemen, who speak in the highest terms of the kindness of yourself, your excellent Lady & indeed the Whole family. I pray you for yourself & for them to accept my sincere thanks. We have a strong motive to visit your City in the spring or summer, as you have obligingly wished, if for no other purpose than to make our personal acknowledgements. Whether we shall be able to gratify this desire depends upon circumstances.

ALS. MBU.   1. Clay to Morris, June 16, 1816, and 2:253-54.

To GEORGE C. THOMPSON[1]   Washington, February 22, 1817

I recd. your favor[2] by Capt. Moore,[3] to whom I should have cheerfully rendered any services in my power, in the dispatch of his business, if it had been necessary. He told me to day that he had nearly completed it.

The public events in K[entucky]. to which you refer have indeed excited much surprize, not with me so much as with others.[4] I cannot bring myself, however, yet to believe that the cause in which your father has so long struggled & in which I have had the pleasure of co-operating with you, is lost. Kentucky may be under an eclipse, for a moment, but her light cannot I trust be extinguished.

There is much speculation here as to the new Cabinet, and this topic engrosses now exclusive attention.[5] It is certain that J. Q. Adams will be Secy of State. Mr. [William H.] Crawford will remain in the Treasury, if he pleases (and it is not known whether he pleases or not to remain) [Benjamin W.] *Crowninshield will not give up the Ship;* and it is rumored that the place of Secy. of War will be offered to our friend Col [Isaac] Shelby.

Make my best respects to your father [George Thompson][6] & believe me . . .

ALS. KyLoF. 1. See 1:159. 2. Not found. 3. Possibly Thomas R. Moore of Clark County, Ky. See 4:414. 4. Reference is probably to the political disturbance in state government which resulted from Gov. George Madison's death in office in Oct., 1816, and the subsequent actions taken by his successor, Gabriel Slaughter. When Slaughter removed Charles S. Todd as secretary of state and replaced him with John Pope, the Kentucky legislature attempted unsuccessfully to pass a law providing for a special governor's election. See *BDGUS*, 2:512 and John F. Dorman, "Gabriel Slaughter 1767-1830, Governor of Kentucky, 1816-1820," *FCHQ* (Oct., 1966), 40:343-48. 5. For Monroe's Cabinet, see Clay to Russell, March 20, 1817. 6. See 1:458.

To PETER IRVING   Washington, March 18, 1817

I have been intending for months past to write to you, but the pressure of official business during the Session of Congress has obliged me to defer this gratification until the present moment.

I recd. the letter which you did me the favor to write me from Liverpool on the 1st. Novr.;[1] and thank you for the kind manner in which you have assumed the execution of my commission respecting the Cattle.[2] As the spring has now commenced I shall begin to look for their arrival by some of the vessels which it will doubtless bring in. My anxiety to possess those cattle is increased, and I hope you will be able to procure & transport them without much difficulty.

The distress of Europe has been felt, though in a very mitigated degree, in this Country.[3] Our apprehensions, resulting from the scantiness of the last Crop, will pass off, however, without any thing like general suffering. In the Commercial, Manufacturing & Navigating interests of our Country there has been & continues some depression. The elasticity of our Country is happily such that it will soon rise above this momentary depression. And you must have seen, with particular satisfaction, that as far as respects the concerns of our Government, no people ever had more cause to be proud of their condition. Our revenue especially flourishes even beyond example in our own astonishing history.

I have had the pleasure of seeing your brother a good deal during the Session.[4] He has enjoyed, I think, better health & spirits than usual. But you have no doubt heard often from him.

The termination of our own War[5] and the calm of Europe have deprived the political parties in our Country of the instruments with which they annoyed each other. And party names are in a considerable degree losing their force. New combinations will probably arise. One good effect however has clearly attended the Republican administration (besides many others) that our free institutions are placed on a solid basis not likely to be disturbed for centuries to come.

I shall be extremely happy to hear from you often; & pray you to offer my sincere regard to your brother[6] & your amiable brother in law & sister.[7]

ALS. KyU. 1. See 2:252-53; also 2:314-15, 329-30, 334-37. 2. Clay to Irving, August 30, 1816. 3. For the economic recession in Europe, see M. E. Barlen, *The Foundations of Modern Europe* (London, 1968), 173. 4. William Irving was in Congress from 1814-18. *BDAC* and *CAB*. 5. Of 1812. See 1:1006. 6. Probably his brother Ebenezer, who was a partner with Peter in the firm P. & E. Irving and Co. See 2:253. However, it could refer to Washington Irving, who was also in Europe in 1817. See Washington Irving's entry in *DAB*.   7. Henry and Sarah (Irving) Van Wart. See 2:315.

To JONATHAN RUSSELL   Washington, March 20, 1817

I recd. your favor from N. York, inclosing my public account.[1]

You will have seen the Cabinet arrangements, of which you were pretty well informed prior to your departure from the City. [Isaac] Shelby's determination upon the offer to him of the department of War has not yet been received. And [Benjamin W.] Crowninshield talks of postponing his decision, in regard to remaining in that of the Navy, until he goes home.[2] The mission to St. James's will not be filled until Mr. [John Quincy] Adams's return; and the person who will succeed him, if determined upon, is not known.[3]

I recd. a letter from [Christopher] Hughes, under date the 24h. Decr.,[4] in which he desires me to say to you that he is very sensible of your kindness, in writing some letters from England to Stockholm, to give him a welcome reception, and that he intends to write to you.

Mr. [James] Madison is yet here. I dine with him today at the Presidents. In a few days I shall set out for Kentucky, whence I expect to return in all June—I am looking out to see a particular event announced, with respect to which I sincerely wish you all possible happiness.[5]

ALS. KyLoF.   1. Not found.   2. Monroe's first Cabinet was comprised of: State—John Quincy Adams (entered upon duties Sept. 22, 1817); Treasury—William H. Crawford; War—Isaac Shelby declined, John C. Calhoun appointed Oct. 8, 1817; Attorney General—Richard Rush until Oct. 30, 1817, followed by William Wirt, appointed Nov. 13, 1817; Postmaster General—Return Jonathan Meigs, Jr.; Navy—Benjamin W. Crowninshield until Oct. 1, 1818. Kane, *Facts About the Presidents*, 41. See also 2:316-17.   3. Richard Rush succeeded Adams as minister to the Court of St. James's. See 2:373.   4. Hughes had been appointed secretary of legation to Sweden and expected to be the highest-ranking American diplomat there; however, Jonathan Russell, who had been minister to Sweden, came home briefly and then returned to Sweden. Russell remained minister until Oct. 22, 1818, and Hughes became chargé d'affaires, the ranking U.S. diplomat in Sweden, on Jan. 21, 1819. Dougall & Chapman, *U.S. Chiefs of Mission*, 144. See also 2:231, 233, 259, 390-91, 426-27.   5. Reference is to Russell's marriage on April 2, 1817, to Lydia Smith. See 2:373.

From Robert Brent, Office of Paymaster General, Washington, April 1, 1817. Sends "a packet which is addressed to the agent for paying pensions under the acts of Congress on that subject relative to the representatives of Officers or privates who are killed or die in the Service." Mentions that the packet "Contains a blank bond to be executed by the agent; If the funds are placed in the hands of a private individual," instructions for such an agent, and "a list of the pensioners and a further letter of instructions accompanying this list together with blank receipts." Believes "if the Branch Bank of the United States be in operation on your arrival at Lexington, it will comport more with the views of the Government, that this institution be made the organ of payment." Concludes: "I must solicit you to pardon me for the trouble I give you in this business, but believing, as I do, that you feel equally anxious that the representatives of meritorious individuals of your state, should as promptly and with as good faith as possible, receive what the bounty of the Government had extended to them, I can think of no better mode of carrying my wish into effect . . . than by giving you this trouble, assuring you at the same time that I shall feel both honor and pleasure in an opportunity of testifying the obligation I shall feel." Copy. DNA, RG99, Records of the Office of the Paymaster General, vol. 10, pp. 102-3.

Brent again wrote Clay on May 10, 1817, saying he had received Clay's letter of April 29 [not found] "with the receipt of the Cashier of the office of Discount and Deposit at Lexington for 11.412 35/100 Dollars ... for the pay of the half pay pensioners of ... Kentucky." *Ibid.*, p. 173.

For the most recent acts dealing with pensions to widows and orphans of those killed in military service, see 2 *U.S. Stat.*, 704-5; 3 *U.S. Stat.*, 73-74, 103-4, 285-87, 373-74, 394-95.

From Thomas Todd, Frankfort, Ky., June 1, 1817. Thanks Clay for taking care of his business "& shall readily avail myself of your kind offer to attend to my concerns in the City." Reports that he has "requested Mr John Henry our agent in Jefferson, to transmit to you such sums of Money as he has received for the rents of land & hire of negroes for the last year . . . I beg the favour of you to receive such sum as he may transmit & procure a similar warrant to the one last transmitted, it answered my purpose better than the mode I had suggested & was greatly preferable on the score of safety."

Notes that "I have for five weeks been closely confined in Court & on to-morrow shall set out for Nashville & shall not return for eight weeks[.] I most cordially wish that the next Congress will be more liberal than the last & make some provision to relieve us from this arduous duty of attending the Circuit Courts, but that unfortunate measure the Compensation bill has almost blasted every hope."

Mentions that "It was a source of much gratification to us, at seeing . . . the expression of public sentiments of gratitude, & the affectionate & cordial farewell, of the Citizens of the Metropolis at the departure of . . . Mr & Mrs. [James] Madison—they were the effusions of the heart sincerely regretting the departure of those whose worth they knew, whose benevolence they had experienced, whose virtues were acknowledged & whose absence would be seriously felt by all classes of Citizens." ALS. KyU.

For the Compensation bill and its repeal, see, 2:172, 287. U.S. Supreme Court justices continued to ride circuit until 1891. See 26 *U.S. Stat.*, 827.

Two days after his term ended, Madison was presented with farewell resolutions at a mass meeting in Washington. Many balls and dinners were given in honor of the Madisons in the month before their departure from Washington on April 6, 1817. Irving Brant, *James Madison*, 6 vols. (Indianapolis, 1940-61), 6:418; Brant, *The Fourth President, A Life of James Madison*, 607.

John Henry is possibly the John R. Henry who married Mrs. Barbara F. Todd in Louisville in October, 1830. G. Glenn Clift, *Kentucky Marriages, 1797-1865* (Baltimore, 1966), 61.

To RICHARD C. ANDERSON, JR.[1]　　　　　Lexington, July 1, 1817
I find by your favor of the Ulto. that you estimate too highly the tender I made, through your father,[2] of my services in Selecting a situation, during the ensuing winter, in Washington. It was made from a knowledge of the few comforts which that place affords. And really six months, the probable duration of a long Session of Congress, constitute so large a share of ones time that it is quite desirable to be well lodged, well situated and in an agreeable mess. I have, however, no doubt that if Mr. [John J.] Crittenden[3] & you should come on early in the Session, and before the first places are occupied, you will be able to make a Satisfactory arrangement in these particulars.

Should I have it in my power, in any other respect, to render you service, I beg you to consider me as fully disposed to do so.

ALS. CSmH.   1. Richard Clough Anderson, Jr., of Kentucky had been elected to his first term in the U.S. House. See *BDAC*.   2. For Richard C. Anderson, Sr., see 1:72.   3. See 2:419.

To PETER IRVING   Washington, August 13, 1817

I should have earlier acknowledged the receipt of your several favors, and those of your House, respecting the cattle which you had the goodness to procure for me,[1] but having received them in Kentucky, I defered answering them until my return to this City, which happened a few days ago.

The Cattle all arrived safe at Baltimore. The oldest heifer calved there, and remains in the neighbourhood. The other three were started on their journey to Kentucky, and on the road the young bull unfortunately died by eating clover. After the other two had travelled about 180 miles their feet became so tender (for the operation of shoeing Cattle is but little understood in the Southern parts of the U. States) that it was necessary to stop them. On my way to this place I came by where they were and found that they had so far recovered as to justify venturing them again on the road; and I expect they are accordingly now on the road to Kentucky.

The bull is a very fine animal. His color, figure, size & limbs are very good. I should have liked him better if a part of the flesh about his neck & shoulders could have been transfered to his hind quarters. The heifer I did not think extraordinary; though I understand the one near Baltimore, and for which I shall send in a few days is uncommonly fine. I shall not, upon the whole, regret my attempt to introduce these Cattle into our Country, if I can get what remains safely to Kentucky. Whatever may be my fortune, in that respect, I pray you, my dear Sir, to accept my sincere thanks for the trouble you have taken upon yourself in making the best selection, and for your kindness in the whole business.

I have this day remitted to Mess. P. & E. Irving & Co. of N. York[2] a sum which I hope will be sufficient to make the indemnity of your house complete at Liverpool.

Our Country continues to enjoy the greatest prosperity. The crops already cut, and those which remain to be gathered, are unusually fine, as I had recently an opportunity personally to witness, during a long journey from the West here, and as all accounts concur in stating. Some of the interests of the Country, the Navigating, Manufacturing & Commercial, continue to complain indeed of some of that distress which is felt in Europe by these branches of industry. It is acknowledged however that we feel it in a much less degree, and even what we do experience is daily diminishing.

The President [James Monroe] is now absent from this City, on an extensive tour which he has undertaken around the frontiers of our Country.[3] You will have seen from the papers, with which your friends no doubt supply you, that he has been every where received, even in places where it might have been least expected, with demonstrations of the greatest respect, if not attachment. He will not return until the last of September to the seat of Government.

Party animosity has very sensibly abated. Confidence in the Government every where exists. A national character is formed. And there is a buoyancy in the spirits of the public every where exhibited.

Mr. [John Quincy] Adams has reached America. It is believed here that he will be replaced at the Court of St. James's by Mr. [Richard] Rush, the Attorney General.[4]

You have not informed me whether you ever executed your intention of visiting Ghent, and if you did, how you found *all* our friends there.

A brother in law of mine James Brown Esq. late a Senator of the U.S. from Louisiana, and his Lady [Ann "Nancy" Hart Brown],[5] a sister of Mrs. [Lucretia Hart] Clay, are travelling in Europe for amusement. They are at present in France, but intend to visit England prior to their return. Should you meet with them I beg you to make their acquaintance.

I shall be glad often to hear from you . . .

ALS. NNC.   1. Clay to Irving, August 30, 1816; and March 18, 1817; and 2:252-53, 314-15, 329-30, 334-37.   2. Not found, but see 2:334-37.   3. President Monroe made a sweeping tour to inspect the defenses of the country, visiting the Atlantic seaboard cities from Baltimore to Portland, Maine, then traveling to Detroit and back to Washington via Zanesville, Ohio, Pittsburgh, and Fredericktown, Maryland. Arthur Styran, *The Last of the Cocked Hats, James Monroe & the Virginia Dynasty* (Oklahoma City, 1945), 348.   4. Clay to Russell, March 20, 1817.   5. See 1:32.

From George Bomford, Ordnance Department, Washington, August 26, 1817. States that "Instructions have been forwarded . . . to Majr. [Abram R.] Woolley (of the Ordnance) near Pittsburgh—to prepare for the State of Kentucky the following arms": "500 Sabres—500 pairs of pistols and 60 Harpers ferry Rifles." Adds that the sabres and pistols are enroute to Pittsburgh and the rifles are undergoing repairs. Copy. DNA, RG156, Records of the Office of the Chief of Ordnance, Misc. Letters Sent.

For Bomford, see 4:736. Maj. Woolley was transferred from ordnance to infantry in 1821. *HRDUSA*, 1060.

To JOHN C. CALHOUN[1]   Washington, December 3, 1817
I have just heard of your safe arrival,[2] & congratulate both that event & your recent appointment;[3] with regard to the latter however not without some feeling of regret at our loss of you in the H. of Representatives.

You will have to appoint a first Clerk in your department forthwith. It is an appointment in which your personal convenience as well as the public interest, must be much concerned. Maj [Christopher] Van De Venter[4] (to whom I by leave introduce you) is, unless I am greatly deceived, precisely the person you want. Educated at West Point well acquainted with tactics, familiar with the actual condition of the Army, & conversant with all its details, he will be of vast relief to you. Such is the character I have of him by letters, & from Gen. [Joseph G.] Swift.[5] & other officers: & such is the character which I think he deserves from what I know of him. I therefore, write with his friend in expressing to you a wish for his appointment to the situation in question.

Copy. MiU.   1. For Calhoun, see 1:910 and *DAB*.   2. He had arrived in Washington on Dec. 2. Charles M. Wiltse, *John C. Calhoun: Nationalist, 1782-1828* (Indianapolis, 1944), 142.   3. As secretary of war. See Clay to Russell, March 20, 1817.   4. For Van De Venter, see *HRDUSA*, 982.   5. For Swift, see 4:232.

To WILLIAM D. LEWIS[1]   Washington, January 25, 1818

I recd. your favor of the 13h. Sept. last[2] from St. Petersburg. I had previously received several of your obliging letters which afforded me much gratification. You must not attribute my failure to acknowledge them to any diminution of my esteem and regard for you, which I assure you, most truly, remains unabated. You will recollect that I told you that you would find me a lazy and unprofitable correspondent. The truth is that, when I am absent from this metropolis, I have nothing interesting to communicate; and when I am here I have a pressure of occupations and engagements that does not leave me one hour of freedom.

Your last letter required, however, that I should break silence lest you should think me indifferent to what concerns you. I went to see the Secy. of State [John Quincy Adams] shortly after the receipt of it and found that he had been already fully apprized of your affair with Mr. [John Leavitt] Harris.[3] And I am happy to inform you that no impression has been made on the Executive, in consequence of that affair, unfavorable to you. The tenor I was told of Mr. [William] Pinkney's communications in relation to it was such as to do you justice.[4] Of course I did not ask to see them. I enquired if the Consulate at St. Petersburg were vacant or was likely to become so? And I was informed by Mr. Adams that it was not vacant, nor did he know that it would become so.[5] I stated to him that if any appointment were to be made I wished to recommend my friend Lewis. As the Government was apprized of the occurrence between Mr. Harris and you (and as I knew nothing else of him) I did not feel myself authorized to urge his dismission; and therefore made no interposition with that object.

Our Country continues to enjoy a high degree of prosperity, great in itself, and greater still by a contrast with the condition of the powers of Europe. The Federal party, as a party, is almost extinct, and seeks to sink all traces of itself into a general oblivion which it encourages of all party distinctions. The subject of the Independence of Spanish America, in which I take a very lively interest, may possibly lead to the formation of new political Sects.[6] You are so far removed from the scene that you can survey it almost without emotion. And yet, if I am not mistaken greatly in your character, you are not indifferent to the liberty & happiness of so considerable a portion of our Species, inhabiting too your native continent. Our Government, I believe, sincerely wishes success to the cause; but it indulges apprehensions, with regard to the powers of Europe, which I think groundless, and which I fear may restrain it from doing even the little which I think we ought to do, and which in my opinion would not compromit our peace or neutrality.

All my family is with me. We shall however return to K[entucky]. in May or June. I have sons as big, if not so old, as you. They are pursuing their education & I hope will some day make your acquaintance.

[Christopher] Hughes, poor fellow, from whom I lately received a letter dated at Stockholm, is terribly non-plus'd by the unexpected & to him unwelcome return of Mr. [Jonathan] Russell.[7] I presume however that you hear directly from him. [Henry] Carroll is here, but has a scheme for going to the Missouri in the Spring to fix himself there for life. [William] Shaler is still in Algiers, and most discontented with the Turk.

Make my respects to your brother,[8] and be assured that, whether I shall prove to be a good or bad correspondent, it will always give me pleasure to hear from you . . .

ALS. KyLoF.   1. For Lewis, see 1:880; 9:144 and *DAB*.   2. Not found.   3. In July, 1817 Lewis had been imprisoned in Russia at the instance of Harris, who was U.S. consul at St. Petersburg. The two men continued their personal quarrel, and, back in the U.S. in 1819, they fought a duel in which Lewis wounded Harris. For this conflict, see Lewis's entry in *DAB*.   4. William Pinkney of Maryland was minister to Russia. *BDAC*.   5. The office did become vacant with the resignation of Pinkney on Feb. 14, 1818. On April 16, George Washington Campbell of Tennessee was appointed to the post. Dougall & Chapman, *U.S. Chiefs of Missions*, 136.   6. For Clay's involvement in the issue of Spanish American independence, see Subject Index: Volumes 1-6 in 7:764-65.   7. Hughes's letter not found. For Russell's return to Sweden, temporarily displacing Hughes as ranking U.S. diplomat there, see Clay to Russell, March 20, 1817.   8. For his brother, John D. Lewis, see 5:570.

From Robert Brent, Office of the Paymaster General, Washington, January 27, 1818. Reports that "Your note of the 23d. instant, addressed to Mr. [George] Boyd of the War Department [2:432], covering the cases of the widows Truman [*sic*, Sarah Trueman] and [Elizabeth] Radford, has been referred to this office." States that the "half pay pension claims, of these widows . . . can be established, and, if you think proper, reported to the agent for the state, at Lexington . . . to be paid by him . . . or, accounts can be forwarded to the attorney /Mr. [Samuel C.] Smith/ . . . and a remittance, afterwards, made to him." Copy. DNA, RG99, Records of the Office of the Paymaster General, vol. 11, pp. 110-11. See also 2:432, 438. For George Boyd, see 1:981; for Smith, see 2:438; for Trueman and Radford, see 2:432.

On February 11, 1818, Brent again wrote Clay concerning the pension claims of Mrs. Prudence Elliott and the widows Trueman and Radford. In respect to Mrs. Elliott, reports that "there is no power authorizing you to receive the arrearage of her pension, which is all that is deficient, in the case." For Trueman and Radford, sends "duplicate accounts for the signature of Dr. Smith, their Attorney." Encloses a draft for $350, "being the amount of the arrearages of pensions due Mrs. Trueman and Radford." Copy. DNA, RG99, Records of the Office of the Paymaster General, vol. 11, p. 149. For Mrs. Elliott, see 2:237, 438.

Brent wrote again on February 13, 1818, enclosing "for Mrs. Elliott, a certificate of pension, which you will be pleased to forward to her." Copy. DNA, RG99, Records of the Office of the Paymaster General, vol. 11, p. 150.

To John C. Calhoun, Washington, January 30, 1818. Recommends John W. Carlisle for appointment to West Point, "If . . . he is not too far advanced in years to be admitted." Adds: "Should that even be the case, it is worthy of consideration whether an exception . . . might not be made in his behalf, uniting in himself, as he does, the strong claims of an unprotected orphan, and the child of a distinguished Revolutionary officer." ALS. DNA, RG94, Application Papers of Cadets, 1818, no. 66. Endorsed on verso: "Appd. Jany 31-/18."

On January 31, 1818, Clay wrote William S. Dallam that he had "recd. your letter respecting young Carlile [*sic*]" and had written the secretary of war "to get him admitted into the Military Academy." Promises: "If that application fail, I will endeavor to procure for him a Midshipman's warrant." ALS. KyU. For Dallam, see 1:176.

Carlisle is listed with the class of 1818 under the category "failed to report for examination" or "rejected as unqualified for admission." *House Docs.*, 21 Cong., 1 sess., no. 79, p. 197. He is not listed in Callahan's *List of Officers of the Navy.*

To MAGDALEN ASTOR BENTZON[1]

Washington,
February 10, 1818

A parent myself I know, when one is bereft of the object of his hopes and affections, in the unexpected but doubtless wise dispensations of providence, how difficult it is for another to offer any thing which can mitigate the grief that tears his afflicted bosom. And yet I can not refuse to myself to say to you how sincerely Mrs [Lucretia Hart] Clay and I sympathize with you in the late melancholy event. Indeed the whole City has been filled with distress in consequence of it, as was manifested on Sunday last by the immense concourse of people, including many of the highest officers of Government, as well as the foreign ministers and members of Congress, who attended to pay the last respect & perform the last duty to the remains of your son [John Jacob Bentzon].[2]

When you write to Mr. [Adrian B.] Bentzon I pray to you to convey to him my sentiments of regret, on account of the late mournful calamity, and to accept for him & yourself assurances of the respect . . .

ALS. CSmH; courtesy of San Diego County Committee, The National Society of Colonial Dames of America.   1. Mrs. Bentzon was the eldest daughter of John Jacob Astor. John Upton Terrell, *Furs by Astor* (New York, 1963), 285.   2. Her 8-year-old son had recently drowned in the Tiber River. *Ibid.*

From Joseph Crockett, Jessamine County, Ky., March 1, 1818. Reports that he has "seen an act of Congress, making provisions for the poor and indigent officers and soldiers of the late Revolutionary War" which "is evincive of great liberality of the members comprising the present Congress." Believes that, although he is poor, he doesn't "come within the provisions of the law." Notes, however, that most of his "brother officers . . . received commutation for five years' pay," and feels he is entitled to "the same liberality." Explains that he was in "a distant portion of Kentucky" where he "didn't receive timely notice of their liberality."

Details his years of military service from 1774 to 1782, adding that he moved to Kentucky in 1784 and has lived there ever since. Asks: "Be kind enough to inform me whether I come within the act of Congress passed for the benefit" of Revolutionary soldiers. Copy. Printed in Samuel W. Price, "Biographical Sketch of Colonel Joseph Crockett: A Paper read before the Filson Club at its meeting April 6, 1908," *Filson Club Publications No. 24* (Louisville, 1909), part II, pp. 8-10.

For Crockett, see 2:351; for the law recently passed by Congress, see 2:681.

Clay presented Crockett's matter to Congress and by special act, Crockett was placed on the pension roll. He was also aided by an act of May 15, 1828, which placed the general officers and commanders of regiments who had served in the Revolutionary War and the War of 1812 on the retired list with captain's pay. Crockett, however, lived only a few months after the act went into effect. Price, "Biographical Sketch of Colonel Joseph Crockett," 11. See also 4 *U.S. Stat.*, 269-70.

To ROBERT WICKLIFFE   Washington, March 12, 1818

I receved your letter of the   and I have drawn on you for $1200 receved by you from General [Samuel] Hopkins[1] for me, in favour of Col. [Richard M.] Johnson,[2] who has occasion to use the money in K[entucky] and gave me the amount here.

I will write and obtain either the chancellor of Maryland's[3] assent to my holding the land in the grant which I purchased (and in that event you shall be concerned) or an authority to sell &c the supream Court has decided that a devise of land to trustees, who are citizens, to sell and pay the proceeds to aliens is good and valid, this secures me with [William] Lytle.[4] Mr Holly [*sic*, Horace Holley],[5] the president of the [Transylvania] University, is detained in Philada. by sickness. He will come on here a[s] soon as he recov[er]s[.] I shall bring on the Patriot question next week—[6]

Copy. KyU.   1. A blank space appears instead of the date of Wickliffe's letter, which has not been found. For Hopkins, see 1:123 and *DAB*.   2. Probably Richard M. Johnson [1:721], but possibly his brother James.   3. For William Kilty, chancellor of Maryland in 1818, see *DAB*.   4. Clay to Lytle, July 2, 1818. See also 1:348-49; 2:383, 416, 877.   5. For Holley, see 1:583.   6. Reference is to one of his speeches in support of the "Patriot" cause of South American independence. See 2:492-562.

To UNKNOWN RECIPIENT   Washington, March 15, 1818

A disposition appears to be felt in Russellville and in that neighborhood in Kentucky that some of the directors of the Nashville branch [of the Bank of the U.S.] shall be taken from that quarter.[1] Should the Bank of the U.S. be willing to gratify that disposition, I would recommend as suitable persons Col. Anthony Butler,[2] Amos Edwards,[3] William W. Whitaker[4] and Robert Latham,[5] if four should be appointed, and if less, to be taken in the order here named.

The Committee of Ways and Means has reported in favor of the Bank on the question of pledges of stock &c. raised by Mr. Forsythe [*sic*, John Forsyth].[6]

ALS. KyLoF.   1. In fact, the Nashville branch was not created until 1827. Ralph C. H. Catterall, *The Second Bank of the United States* (Chicago, 1903), 384.   2. For Butler, see 2:166.   3. For Edwards, see 5:1009.   4. For Whitaker, see 3:128.   5. Possibly Dr. Robert Latham of Hopkinsville, Ky. Clift, *Kentucky Marriages, 1797-1865*, 90.   6. For Forsyth, see *BDAC*.

To ELIJAH HUNT MILLS[1]   Washington, March 22, 1818

I recd. your favor of the 18h March,[2] and asked leave of absence for you, according to your request, for the remainder of the Session, which was granted by the House.[3] I participated in the regret, which was generally felt, at losing you so soon, after you had taken your Seat, especially as the Session was becoming more interesting. This regret is increased by the communication contained in your letter, that your absence will prevent us from having the pleasure of hearing your vindication of the great doings &c. in Boston during the late Tour—[4]

ALS. KyLoF. 1. For Mills, see *DAB* and *BDAC*. 2. Not found. 3. For the leave of absence, see U.S. H. of Reps., *Journal*, 15 Cong., 1 Sess., 359. 4. Probably a reference to President Monroe's tour of the nation's defenses. See Clay to Irving, August 13, 1817.

From ISAAC SHELBY

N.p., March 22, 1818

I was on a Journey for a fortnight from home, when your favour of the 8th. Ulto.[1] was handed to me by the Post Master of Danville which will account for my not answering it sooner.

The Treaty of [Richard] Henderson & Co. with the Cherokees was at Wattauga [*sic*, Watauga], in March 1775.[2] and I am informed the Deed then made to Henderson & Co. by the Cherokees has for some purpose since been recorded in the Clerks office of Hawkins County in East Tennessee. That purchase by Henderson &c. extended no farther South then the waters of the Cumberland river—It began at the mouth of the Kentucky river and up the same to the head of the Most Northwardly branch thereof then So. East to the top of powals [*sic*, Powell's] mountain & Westwardly along the same to a point from whence a Northwest course would strike the most Southwardly branch of the Cumberland river—thence down said river including all its waters to the Ohio river & up the Ohio to the Begg.—but there has been other Treattys by which the said Indian title to all the land South of the Ohio river in this State has been extinguished—Vizt. At a Grand Treatty held at Lancaster in Pennsylvania in the year 1744.[3] in presence of the Governor of that province [George Thomas]. the Commissioners from other provinces and many other Gentlemen who attended. The Six United Nations of Indians ceded to the Crown of Great Britain all the Lands on the South side of the Ohio. and conveyed the same by Deed to Thomas Lee & William Beverly [*sic*, Beverely] Commissioners for Virginia in behalf of the crown. This conveyance was further confirmed by an other Deed for the same land and track of country. made by the several Nations, on the Ohio, Tributaries & Dependents of the Six Nations at a Solemn treatty held at Logs Town in the year 1752[4] for a valuable consideration paid by the Commissioners from Virginia being Joshua Fry, Lunsford Lomax, and James Patton on behalf of the Crown of Great Britain—which Deeds were still further confirmed at the Treatty of Fort Stanwix in 1768.[5] When the six nations in presence of Sir William Johnston; the Governor of New Jersey, the commissioners from Virginia, & Pennsylvania, ceded to the crown of Great Britain the Lands of the South side of the Ohio as low as the mouth of the Cherokee river, (now Tennessee river) and up the same to the head on the Northside thereof. The Commissioners for Virginia at the last mentioned Treatty were (as well as I now recollect) Thomas Walker & Andrew Lewis.

I had occasion near forty years ago to enquire into the extent of the different Treattys in relation to the Western lands & the above is the substance of the notes which I have on that occasion—And I well recollect when the Land Law of Virginia was on its passage before the Assembly of that State in 1779. That the claim of Henderson & Co. to their having extinguished the Indian title to this Country was Defeatted by the introduction of those Treatties[.]

Thus Sir have I stated all that I recollect in relation to your enquiries. it will be of little service except to point to documents which may establish the point you desire—I have no doubt but the Deeds of Cession of those several treaties may yet be found among the Archives of Virginia[.]

Mrs. [Susanna H.] Shelby Joins me in our cordial respects to your Lady [Lucretia Hart Clay]. P.S. At the date of the above treatties all the lands bordering on the Ohio. was deemed as the property of the Six Nations. it was never doubted until the purchase of Henderson & Co. in 1775. and the Cherokees then with very great reluctance signed the deed to him for the Kentucky Country. They made many protests to avoid it. and wanted to confine him to the waters of the Cumberland river but finding they could not get his merchandize otherwise they said it was what he would to go to that dark bloody land, & signed his Deed evidently against their wills.

ALS. DNA, RG107, Sec. of War, Letters Received, S-215 (12). 1. See 2:436-37. 2. For Henderson's Treaty of Sycamore Shoals, see 2:437. 3. For the Lancaster Treaty, see Joseph S. Walton, *Conrad Weiser and the Indian Policy of Colonial Pennsylvania* (Philadelphia, 1900), 93-121. 4. Logstown was located on the Ohio River below the present site of Pittsburgh. For the Logstown Treaty, see *ibid.*, 193-94. For Lee and Beverely, see *ibid.*, 97. 5. For the Treaty at Fort Stanwix [Rome, N.Y.], see Kenneth P. Bailey, *The Ohio Company Papers, 1753-1817* (Arcata, Calif., 1947), 12-14. For Fry, see *ibid.*, 242; for Lomax, *ibid.*, 2; for Patton *ibid.*, 233.

To RICHARD C. ANDERSON, JR. Washington, April 29, 1818

You will like to know something of the movemen[t] of your brother.[1] When you left the City he came to m[y] house and remained with my sons until the day befo[re] yesterday, when Theodore [Wythe Clay] & he sat out in the stage to join Mr. [Nathaniel] Silsbee at Baltimore.[2] I gave to Mr. Silsbee $300, one hundred & fifty for each of the boys, and particular instructions in writing relating to them both. They left here in good spirits and I hope their affection for each other will continue. Mr. Silsbee and the boys have all promised to inform me of the manner in which they may locate themselves at Cambridge.

I shall commence my journey tomorrow or next day & hope to reach home about the 25h. My best respects to your father—P.S. Mr. Silsbee's illness was the cause of the boys not getting off sooner[.]

ALS. CSmH. 1. For his brother, Larz Anderson, see 2:620. See also Clay to Anderson, Sept. 15, 1818. 2. For Silsbee, see 2:620 and *DAB*. See also *ibid.* and 2:725-26.

To JOSEPH GALES, JR. Lexington, May 30, 1818

I reached home a few days ago, after a journey of much fatigue, particularly during the first part of it.[1]

Inclosed are your notes, with some few corrections, of my concluding remarks on the question of Internal Improvements, which I am particularly desirous should appear in the [Washington *National*]

Intell[*igence*]r. after the misrepresentation of what I said, on that occasion, which first appeared in a Connecticut paper. I presume the delay in transmitting them will be without inconvenience, as I have not yet received the Speech, to which they are a kind of supplement, and which you promised to forward to me.[2]

I have been received in Kentucky with a kinder & more cordial welcome than I ever experienced on any former occasion—All sorts of testimonies of esteem & confidence have been given me—

I will thank you to make my respects to Mr. [William W.] Seaton—[3]

P.S. You will see in the [Lexington *Kentucky*] Reporter an extract from an interesting letter from Buenos Ayres. It was received by me from Breckenridge [*sic*, Henry M. Brackenridge],[4] though I do not wish his name mentioned.

ALS. MHi.   1. His journey home from Washington. See Clay to Anderson, April 29, 1818.   2. Reference is to Clay's speech of March 13, 1818 [2:467-91], which was not published in the *Intelligencer* until Sept. 19 and Oct. 6.   3. For Seaton, see 1:848. 4. Brackenridge's letter to Clay of March 3, 1818 [2:443-46], was printed in the *Reporter* on May 27, 1818. For Brackenridge, see 2:387.

To WILLIAM LYTLE   Lexington, July 2, 1818

I understand that in your suit with [John] Mays heirs in the Federal Court the fact is controverted whether any such man as Charles de Warnsdorf[f] ever existed. Inclosed is the Copy of a receipt from Warnsdorf to [John] Campbell and [John] Connolly from the records of the General Court in Virginia attested by several witnesses, which proves his existence. I send it to you, lest you should not have known of such a document.[1]

Are you likely to be, during the present Summer, in this place, and if so at what time? I should be glad to see you that we might have a final arrangement of our business. The suit for a part of the Hotel is still prosecuting.[2]

A decision took place at the last term of the Supreme Court by which it would seem that your Compromise with Byewaters [*sic*, Robert Bywaters] &c. was altogether unnecessary & that they had no pretense of claim.[3]

ALS. OCHP.   1. For Lytle, see 1:44.   2. For Warnsdorff, Campbell, and Connolly, as well as their involvement in this case, see 1:306-7, 348-49, 495-96, 829; 2:127, 416. The receipt mentioned has not been found, but by a deed, special warranty, dated Nov. 1, 1810, and recorded May 20, 1818, Deed Book G, p. 415 in the Office of the Court of Appeals in Frankfort, Ky., Charles de Warnsdorff, for the sum of five shillings, conveyed to Henry Clay and Fortunatus Cosby 2,000 acres, comprising the Warnsdorff patent. D. KyLoF. An identical deed of the same date from John Connelly to Fortunatus Cosby and Henry Clay is recorded in Deed Book G, p. 413. *Ibid.* Both of these deeds were made in obedience to a decree of the General Court of the State of Kentucky, at their May term, 1810, in suit in Chancery, *Cosby and Clay* v. *Connelly and DeWarnsdorff.*   2. See 1:348-49, 561, 578; 2:383, 416.   3. For Bywaters, see 1:418. Reference to the Supreme Court case decided in 1817 is to either *Johnson* v. *Pannel's Heirs* or *Shipp* v. *Miller's Heirs*, both Kentucky cases involving land disputes. G. Edward White, *The Marshall Court and Cultural Change, 1815-35* (New York, 1988), 766-74, 777.

To THOMAS A. SMITH[1]   Lexington, July 7, 1818

Col. James Johnson[2] has it in contemplation to send a considerable distance up the Missouri, a steamboat which he has built for the purpose.

The experiment is worthy the enterprize which distinguishes Col Johnson, and if successful must impress the Indians in that quarter favorably in regard to the power and force of the U. States. It will however be attended with hazard and with much expence. To diminish the latter as much as possible is desirable, and I presume you have it in your power to assert in effecting this object by giving him the transportation of men, baggage and means. I understand that the President [James Monroe] has refered him to you; and I have great pleasure in recommending him to you as worthy of your confidence in all respects & is entitled to your best services[.][3]

ALS. MoHi.   1. For Smith, see 6:200.   2. For Johnson, soldier, congressman, and brother of Richard M. Johnson, see *DAB*.   3. Johnson did receive a contract in 1819 to supply federal troops on the Missouri and Mississippi rivers. *Ibid.*

To RICHARD C. ANDERSON, JR.

Lexington,
September 15, 1818

Inclosed I transmit to you some letters relating to Lars [*sic*, Larz Anderson] and Theodore [Wythe Clay] which will afford you, in the perusal of them, similar pleasure to that which I have experienced.[1] I remitted to Mr. [Nathaniel] Silsbee some weeks ago $150 and requested him to use it as well for your brother, if wanted, as for Theodore.[2] I have some thought of visiting Cambridge next month,[3] and in that case I shall set out from this place about the 5h. Can you not go? I should like very much to have the satisfaction of your Company. I offer you, most sincerely, my congratulations on the occasion of your recent honorable re-election. Do me the favor to present my respects to your father . . .

ALS. CSmH.   1. Letters not found, but see Clay to Anderson, April 29, 1818. 2. See also 2:275-76, 619-20.   3. See 2:614.

To George Boyd, War Department Pension Office, Washington, September 26, 1818. States that "William Pamer, a pensioner on the Virginia Roll, wishes to avail himself of the late act of Congress [2:681] and to have his present pension substituted by the greater one allowed by that act." Explains that he "wishes the arrearages of his old pension & the new one as it accrues to be paid at . . . Lexington." ALS. NhHi. For this claim and the confusion respecting the surname, see 2:594, 680-81.

On April 15, 1819, Clay wrote Secretary of War John C. Calhoun stating that "Mr. William Parmer has been making an effort for a year past to have himself Transfered, as a pensioner of the U. States, from the Virginia roll to that of Kentucky, payable at Lexington." Asks that this transfer be made. ALS. KyLoF. Endorsed: "Let the transfer be made." ALS. *Ibid.*

From William H. Crawford, Secretary of the Treasury, Washington, December 15, 1818. Submits a statement in reply to a resolution of the House of Representatives of December 3, asking for the amount of public and private sales of public lands in the Alabama Territory. Notes that the statement comes from the office of the commissioner of the General Land Office and does not include sales made in July, August, and September at Huntsville, "as no returns have been received from that district for those months." Adds that "Extensive sales were made in that district and in the Alabama District in the month of

Novr last, the returns of which have not been received." Explains that when the banks resumed specie payment in 1817, "the receivers of public money and the collectors of taxes and the Customs, were instructed generally to receive no Bank notes which could not be converted into specie upon demand." Also, a bank in Huntsville created by the territorial legislature "has been made the immediate depository of the public money received at the land office at that place," and the "money received and deposited there has been credited to the Treasurer of the U. States as specie." Clarence E. Carter (ed.), *Territorial Papers of the United States*, 26 vols. (Washington, 1934-), 18:492-93.

To GREENBERRY RIDGELY[1] Washington, December 31, 1818

I recd. your letter of the 26h.[2] The motion respecting the Establishment of a Territorial Government in Arkansas, to which you refer, was merely the initiative step. It will probably be some weeks before that motion ripens into a law.[3] It has not even passed one of the houses, and will not for some time to come. I should think that your presence here in February will be sufficiently early to pursue your object. However you will probably observe in the news papers the progress of the measure, and if you will merely remind me where a letter will find you I will say to you when you had better repair hither.

Applications for such appointments are generally made through the Secretary of State, or directly to the President. You must not be too sanguine. There is such a crowd of candidates for every vacant that it is the merest lottery, and perfectly uncertain who draws the prize.

ALS. KyLoF. 1. For Ridgely, see 2:418. 2. Not found. 3. "An Act establishing a separate territorial government in the southern part of the territory of Missouri" was approved on March 2, 1819, and Arkansas officially became a territory on July 4, 1819. 3 *U.S. Stat.*, 493-96. Ridgely wanted to be appointed secretary for the Arkansas Territory. See 2:676-77, 679.

From William H. Crawford, Secretary of Treasury, Washington, February 6, 1819.

Sends documents requested by the House of Representatives in a resolution "of the 16th inst" asking for "a statement of the tracts of land rese[r]ved for the establishment of towns in the Alabama territory, specifying the price at which said lands have been sold, and such other information as may be in . . . possession" of the secretary of the treasury. Adds that "The reservation made at the mouth of the Cahaba, has been selected by the Governor of the Alabama territory for the permanent seat of Government. . . . The reservation made at the foot of the Muscle Shoals on the southern bank of the Tennessee has not yet been laid off into town lots. No return has been made by the Register of the land office of the sale of the lots in the town of Marathon at the head of Muscle Shoals; the price at which they sold cannot therefore at this time be ascertained." Copy. Carter, *Territorial Papers of the United States, Alabama Territory*, 18:559.

For William W. Bibb, Territorial governor of Alabama, see *BDGUS*, 1:5. St. Stephens had become the territorial capital of Alabama in 1817. The capital was changed to Cahaba in 1820, to Tuscaloosa in 1826, and to Montgomery in 1846. Emanuel Friedman (ed.), *Collier's Encyclopedia*, 24 vols. (New York, 1985), 1:429.

To JOHN COBURN Washington, February 20, 1819

I have recd. your two favors.[1] There is no prospect at present of a continuation of the U States road Westwardly from Wheeling.[2] It will take place some time or other altho' one may not be able exactly to say when. My best efforts, whilst I continue in Congress, shall be directed to the accomplishment of that favorite object.

I understand that there is no intention at present to establish any office of distribution at Maysville.

I am very happy to find that my opinions on two subjects which I have greatly at heart, that of Internal Improvements & that of the Patriots,[3] are approved by one in whose judgement I have so much confidence as I have in yours. I hope you will also have seen in my unavailing efforts on the Seminole question[4] a proof of my attachment to Liberty & the Constitution.

ALS. KyLoF.   1. Not found.   2. See 2:187-89, 479-80, 563, 667; and American System: internal improvements, in Subject Index: Volumes 1-6 in 7:694.   3. Reference is to those attempting to liberate South America from Colonial rule.   4. See 2:636-62.

From Thomas Scott, Jessamine County, Ky., October 22, 1819. Sends a petition [not found] asking for a military pension. States that "I truly am Reducd, to Low Sircumstances by a Late suit which went against me for about $1250" and which "oblidgd, me to Sell part of my Land to Raise the money, which ocations both myself & family to Live, frequently without the Comfortable acomodations of Life." Believes he should receive compensation for his military services in the militia, adding that "tho I am poor Yet I Claim Rank among the highest patriots of our Nation." Explains that he has nine sons, "all Stanch Republicans, three of them Servd, in the Late War, one is Now a Colonel in the Militia & two more Captains, & Nothing Could give them greater Encouragement then to see patriotism Rewarded." ALS. DLC-TJC (DNA, M212, R14). For Scott, see 1:68.

From Samuel Hodges, Jr., Port Praya, St. Iago, Africa, November 13, 1819. Reports seeing in an American paper "an extract of the report of the Committee employed to select a suitable place for colonizing the Free Blacks of the United States in Africa; and was not a little astonished at the report, particularly as it relates to the place they consider most suitable, and their opinion that it is impracticable to undertake the Colonization." Believes that "the Island of Bulam [sic, Bulama; now Bolama] . . . is the most suitable place on the western shores of Africa for colonizing the Free Blacks of America, because the soil is fertile . . . and the air Salubrious." Contends that such a colony "will draw all the trade of the natives from the main in Hides, wax and Ivory, and from the Portuguese settlement on the river—Considerable will be drawn from the natives at the head of the Gambia." Acknowledges that the English and Portuguese will throw obstacles in the way, because it will "draw all the Trade from their settlements above; and be a powerful means of intimidating them in pursuing that horrid and inhuman traffic the slave trade, of which many are at present engaged." Notes that Bulama is uninhabited and "now belongs to the King of Kanaback, and can be purchased of him for a trifling compensation."

Believes the expense of colonizing has been exaggerated. Offers to transport the freed slaves at the cost of $50 per person, instead of the $100 estimated by the committee. Solicits Clay's support in "drawing the attention of the Society from the unhealthy climate of Sherbra, and fixing on Bulam as the most suitable place for founding a colony in Africa." Has addressed Clay because he is convinced "that you are an enemy to that abominable traffic the slave trade, and are anxious of checking insulted humanity." ALS. DLC-HC (DNA, M212, R4).

For Hodges, see 4:364. After its formation in 1816, the American Colonization Society first sent the freedmen to the island of Sherbra, which proved to be unhealthy. T. A. Osae, *A Short History of West Africa* (New York, 1968), 229. Bolama Island on the west coast of Africa came to be a part of Portuguese Guinea, which in 1974 became Guinea-Bissau. *The Encyclopedia Americana International Edition*, 30 vols. (Danbury, Ct., 1986), 13:586-88.

To Thomas M. Randolph, Governor of Virginia, December 13, 1819. Informs him "that James Pleasants Esqr. did this day resign his seat in the House of Representatives . . . as a member from Virginia." ALS. Vi. Written from the House of Representatives. For Randolph, see 1:271; 2:158. For Pleasants, who had just been elected to the U.S. Senate, see 3:626 and *BDAC*.

To SIDNEY P. CLAY[1]   Washington, January 4, 1820

I have expected to see you here for some weeks. Your father[2] informed me that he had consented to your passing the Xmas holydays here, and presuming you would avail yourself of his permission, I omitted, upon my arrival at this place, to inform you that he had put into my hands some money for you. I have one hundred and fifty nine dollars which he desired me to pay to you, from time to time, as you might want it. Should you desire it to be sent to you inform me.[3]

ALS. NjP.   1. See 2:817.   2. Green Clay.   3. Clay to Sidney P. Clay, Jan. 9 1820.

To SIDNEY P. CLAY   Washington, January 9, 1820

In reply to your letter of the 7h.[1] I have to say that the discussion of the Missouri question[2] will probably begin tomorrow or next day; and, unless some unexpected turn should arise in the affair, the debate on it will probably last ten days or a fortnight.[3] If your object in coming here should be to attend the two houses of Congress there is every reason to believe that you will have opportunities enough to attend the debates.

I transmit your inclosed a check on the Bank of the U. States at Philadelphia for $100.[4]

ALS. KEU.   1. Not found, but see Clay to Sidney P. Clay, Jan. 4, 1820.   2. For the Missouri question, see Missouri Compromise in Subject Index: Volumes 1-6 in 7:747 and Glover Moore, *The Missouri Controversy, 1819-21* (Lexington, Ky., 1953).   3. For a discussion of the House debates on the Missouri compromise in Feb. and March, 1820, see Moore, *The Missouri Controversy*, 99-107.   4. Not found, but on Jan. 29, 1820, Clay sent Sidney P. Clay a check for $59 on the Bank of the United States. ADS. KEU.

To JAMES L. EDWARDS[1]   Washington, January 16, 1820

My note to you[2] to which yours of yesterday[3] is in reply was founded upon a letter of Thomas Church, the guardian of the heirs of John Gardner,[4] in which he stated that the officers of the B[ranch]. Bank at Lexn. had informed him that they were not upon the Pension roll of K[entucky].; and the inquiry whether the arrearages of the pension would be paid there was made upon the supposition that they were not upon that roll but would now be transfered to it. Perhaps the letter which you suggest that you will write to the Agent at Lexn. will be the most effective way of setting the matter right; and I will thank you to address such a letter accordingly.

74

ALS. Courtesy of Everett N. Rush, Jr., M.D., Louisville, Ky.   1. For Edwards, see 2:594.   2. Not found.   3. See 2:754-55.   4. For Church, see 1:998; for Gardner, 2:755.

From William Wirt, Office of the Attorney General, Washington, February 3, 1820. Reports he has received from Major Joseph Wheaton the order of the House of Representatives of January 28, 1820, as well as accompanying documents, requesting an opinion of the attorney general on Wheaton's claim. Expounds at length on the duties of the attorney general as set forth in the law and concludes that the order of the House does not fall under his official duties. Points out that in answer to another case "referred to me, officially, by the House of Representatives in the session of 1818-19: in the hope that if it was thought advisable to connect the Attorney General with the House of Representatives, in that character, of Legal Counsellor, which he holds, by the existing law, towards the President & heads of departments, a provision would be made, by law, for that purpose. No such provision having been made, & believing as I do, that in a Government purely of Laws, it would be incalculably dangerous to permit an officer to act, under colour of his office, beyond the pale of the Law, I trust that I shall be excused from making any official report on the order with which the House has honored me." Copy. DNA, Letters Sent by Attorney General's Office (M-T411, R1), pp. 81-83. For Wirt, see 2:398.

Wheaton, a former deputy quarter-master general in the army, was petitioning for payment for whiskey which he had supplied to the navy in 1812. His petition was tabled on February 7, 1820. U.S. H. of Reps., *Journal,* 15 Cong., 1 Sess., 55; *ibid.,* 16 Cong., 1 Sess., 38; *Annals of Congress,* 16 Cong., 1 Sess., 991, 1137. For Wheaton, see *HRDUSA,* 1022-23.

On the same day, Wirt again wrote Clay reporting that "I have heard nothing yet of the plea in the case of John Anderson v. your Sergeant at Arms [Thomas Dunn]. If it comported entirely with the convenience of the counsel who conducts the defence, in the Court below, I should be glad to see the precise ground on which the controversy is to rest, before the meeting of the Supreme Court, on Monday; because after that time my engagements in Court will render it much less convenient to me to make the investigation which I suppose will be nec[e]ssary in the case." Wants to know if Clay has had time to determine "whether it is my *official* duty to appear in this case? the question is a very short one—the act makes it my duty 'to prosecute and conduct all suits in the supreme Court in which *the U.S.* shall be concerned.' Is the sergeant at arms the representative of the U.S. in this instance?—Is the House of Representatives the U.S.?" Continues: "I confess that in a question which is made one of unconstitutional oppression between an individual & the House of Representatives, singly, I confess, I confess [*sic*] that I can not discern very distinctly how the U.S. at large can be said to be more concerned on the one side than on the other." Adds that "I shall be perfectly willing to take up this case, officially, if such be your construction of the act of Congress." Copy. DNA, Letters Sent by Attorney General's Office (M-T411, R1).

For John Anderson and the origins of this case, which resulted in a reprimand from the House of Representatives, see 2:424-25, 428-30. The case of *Anderson* v. *Dunn* was heard at the February, 1821, term of the U.S. Supreme Court. See 6 Wheaton, 204-35.

To PETER B. PORTER[1]   Washington, March 7, 1820
I was in hopes to have sent you by this day's mail a letter from Mrs. [Letitia Breckinridge] Porter,[2] but although the Western mail duly arrived there was none for you. I transmit one from her addressed to

poor Walker,[3] which may probably afford you some information concerning her. The letter to her friend I forwarded to its address.

What is the news in New York? I suppose all there is bustle and commotion, the respective friends of the two great rival candidates each claims success for their favorite.[4]

Nothing new here.

Copy. OHi.   1. For Porter, see 2:162.   2. For Mrs. Porter, see 1:168.   3. Probably David Walker, recently deceased Kentucky congressman. See 2:566, 786.   4. In the 1820 gubernatorial race in New York, DeWitt Clinton defeated Daniel D. Tompkins by a vote of 47,447 to 45,990. *BDGUS*, 3:1073. For Clinton, see 2:370.

From Nathaniel B. Rochester, Rochester, N.Y., April 8, 1820. Has heard from Albert H. Tracy, congressman for this district, that "the Committee of Commerce and Manufacturers have reported a bill for prohibiting the exportation of produce to the British possessions on the continent of America." Asserts that such a policy would cause ruin "to nearly half the people of this state, particularly" in Genesee County, "which embraces not less than 300,000 inhabitants, mostly agriculturalists, and occupying the most fertile and best improved part of the State, and whose dependence for a market for their surplus produce is at Montreal." States that most farmers are in debt for their land "which they purchased with full reliance on a market at Montreal for their surplus produce, but which they never can pay for if they shall be deprived of that market and utter ruin must be the result." Adds that "The merchants and traders at this place are about to forward a memorial to Congress on the subject." Copy. NRU.

For Tracy, see *BDAC*. For the bill referred to, see 3:729.

To SPENCER ROANE[1]   Washington, May 13, 1820
Being about to retire from the House of R[epresentatives].[2] I had intended, previously to that event, to put into your hands, as in those of one whose friendly notice of me, in early life, I still recollect with gratitude, the refutation of an opinion which, I understand, has been entertained by some in Virginia, that the instances in which I have ventured to differ from the present administration of the General Government are attributable to disappointment and chagrin.[3] I had even prepared a letter to that effect which I intended to address to you. But I have concluded to let that, with other calumnies of which I have sometimes been the object, during my public career, die a natural death, undisturbed by me. I have thought, too, that I am best vindicated by the success which my exertions have been finally attended with, in the adoption of the resolution proposing a recognition of the Patriot Governments of South America,[4] the subject on which the most signal instance of that difference of opinion has occurred. The friendship which, I flatter myself, you feel for me will induce you to share with me in the gratification I have derived from this testimony of the favorable sentiments of the H. of Representatives towards the great cause of Spanish America, even if your judgment (which I hope it does not) disapprove the particular proposition. P.S. If you have a fugitive Copy of Mr. [James] Madison's resolutions, printed by the order of the Virginia Assembly, at its last Session, may I ask the favor of it from you?[5]

ALS. KyU.   1. See 2:490.   2. For Clay's temporary retirement, see 2:794-95, 821-22.   3. See 2:491, note 27.   4. See 2:817-18 for the resolutions which had been adopted on April 4, 1820. For Clay's support of South American independence, see Subject Index: Volumes 1-6 in 7:764-65. For Monroe's recommendation for U.S. recognition of the independence of the South American governments, see 3:186.   5. Probably a reference to Madison's *Exposition of the Federal Constitution. Contained in the Report of the Committee of the Virginia House of Delegates . . . in answer to the resolutions of the General Assembly . . . commonly called Madison's report . . .* (Richmond, Va., 1819).

From Spencer Roane, Richmond, Va., June 3, 1820. Reports receiving Clay's letter [Clay to Roane, May 13, 1820] "on my arrival at this place from the country, three days ago." Thanks him "for the favourable Sentiments towards me which are expressed" in it, adding that "I have seen with pleasure the distinguished progress you have made, in life." Notes that he has "sometimes had occasion to differ from you, respecting our public affairs" and has "expressed that difference of opinion, freely." Asserts that "As for the *calumnies* which you have understood have been circulated in Virg[ini]a. against you, I am ignorant of them." Promises that "If you have been injured, and I could be the humble means of affording you any relief, it would give me pleasure to do it.—As for your differing in opinion from the president [James Monroe], I owe it to the same Cause that you have made explanations to me on the subject. Connected as I am to him by the ties of private friendship, I, nevertheless, do not believe him to be infallible. I can readily excuse in others a privilege in relation to him, which I have, often, exercised myself."

States that he would have sent Clay a copy of James Madison's "reflections" if he had received the request while Clay was in Washington [Clay to Roane, May 13, 1820], but "the expence of the postage to Kentucky, deters me." Hopes it is the wish of Clay and "the western Country . . . to unite with Virga. on the great subject of preserving the *federal* character of our Government." If so, "you and they may receive much light from a work which I hope will be shortly published, at this place. It is from the pen of the celebrated John Taylor of Caroline. . . . He is a farmer, is 67 years of age, & has no Earthly view but the public Good." Contends that "Nothing but such a work as that, can awake our Countrymen from the sleep of Death with which they are threatened, in relation to 'the rights of the states and of the people.'"

In reference to South American affairs, states that "I am not acquainted with them: but I . . . wish well to the Cause of liberty, throughout the Globe. My first maxim, however, is, that 'Charity begins at Home.'" Copy. DLC-Sylvanus Cadwallader Papers.

John Taylor's (1753-1824) work, which was published in 1820 in Richmond, Va., was *Construction Construed and Constitutions Vindicated.* For Taylor, see 2:264-65 and *DAB.*

To THOMAS M. RANDOLPH   Lexington, June 5, 1820
Towards the close of the last Session of Congress a letter was received by me,[1] as Speaker of the H[ouse]. of Representatives, from Col. [George F.] Strother,[2] a member of that house from Virginia, communicating his resignation of his seat. Amidst the hurry of business, always incident to the termination of the Session, I am apprehensive that I omitted to acquaint your Excellency with the fact, 'though I should suppose that the publication of the Journal, in which it was announced, would be deemed sufficient evidence of it. Lest, however, that it should not, I have now the honor to give the necessary information that your Excellency may adopt such measures thereon as may appear to you to be proper.

ALS. Vi.   1. Not found.   2. Strother had resigned from the House on Feb. 10, 1820. He subsequently served as receiver of public moneys in St. Louis, where he died in 1840. *BDAC.*

From Return Jonathan Meigs, Marietta, Ohio, July 11, 1820. States that he is sending a copy of a letter [not found] which "will explain to you the disagreeable relation in which I stand /officially/ to your worthy Freind Capn. [John] Fowler." Notes that "I am not ignorant of the estimable Character of Capn. Fowler and the high regard which his fellow Citizens entertain for him. . . . But I cannot justify myself in adopting a more moderate Course than the one proposed in my Letter to him of the 10th instant." If Fowler fails "to comply with my proposal I ask of you the favor to select some suitable Gentleman for his Successor." ALS. KyLxT.

Meigs was postmaster general [2:574], while Fowler was the Lexington, Ky., postmaster. Fowler was removed from office in 1822 because of a defalcation of $9,000. Ila Earle Fowler, *Captain John Fowler of Virginia and Kentucky . . .* (Cynthiana, Ky., 1942), 103. See also 3:34.

From JOHN J. AUDUBON[1]   Cincinnati, August 12, 1820

After having Spent the great part of Fifteen Years in Procuring and Drawing the Birds of the United States with a view of Publishing them; I find Myself possessed of a Large Number of such Specimen as usually resort to the Mid[d]le States Only, having a desire to complete the Collection before I present it to My Country in perfect Order, I intend to Explore the Territories Southwest of the Mississip[p]i.[2]

I Shall leave this place about the mid[d]le of Sepr for the purpose of Visiting the Red River, Arkansas and the Countries adjacent, and Well aware of the good Reception that a few lines from one on Whom our Country looks up with respectful Admiration, would procure me; I have taken the liberty of requesting such Introductory Aid, as you, May deem Necessary to a Naturalist, While at the Frontier forts and Agencies of the United States[.]

Copy. Printed in Howard Corning (ed.), *Journal of John James Audubon Made during His Trip to New Orleans in 1820-1821 . . .* (Boston, 1929), 226-27.   1. See 3:104.   2. For this trip, see Alice Ford, *John James Audubon* (Norman, Okla., 1964), 113-18, and *DAB.*

To JOHN J. AUDUBON   Lexington, August 25, 1820[1]

I received your letter of the 12th inst[2] and now do myself the pleasure to transmit to you inclosed such a letter[3] as I presume you want—I suppose a general letter would answer all the purposes of special introduction, which I should have been at a loss to give as I do not know the particular points which you may Visit—and even if I did, I might not have there any personal acquaintances—

Will it not be well for you before you commit yourself to any great Expense in the preperation and publication of your Contemplated Work to ascertain the success which attended a similar undertaking of Mr [Alexander] Wilson?[4]

Copy. Printed in Corning, *Journal of John James Audubon*, 65.   1. This letter is not dated but probably was written at the same time as the letter of introduction enclosed with it. See, below, note 3.   2. Audubon to Clay, August 12, 1820.   3. Clay's letter of introduction, written at Lexington on August 25, 1820, stated that "I have had the satisfaction of a personal acquaintance with Mr. John J. Audubon; and I have learn[e]d from others who have known him longer and better, that his Character and Conduct have been uniformly good." Added that Audubon would be making a journey "with a laudable object connected with its Natural History" and recommended him as "a Gentleman . . . well qualified . . . to excute the object which he has undertaken." Copy. Printed in Corning, *Journal of John James Audubon*, 65-66.   4. For Wilson and his work, see 3:104.

To Thomas Scott, Columbus, Ohio, September 11, 1820. Regrets he cannot recommend Scott for the "Office of Atto. for the U. States in this District," because of "the rule which I have prescribed to myself of not interfering in the appointment to offices out of the State of which I am a Citizen." Proclaims his "high estimate" of Scott's "professional skill, learning, and capacity." ALS. DNA, RG59, A. and R. (Series 331, Box 53). Written from Columbus. For Scott, see 2:874.

To WILLIAM KEY BOND[1]   Lexington, September 28, 1820
In reply to your letter of the 25h. inst.[2] I have to say that I think it will be best to transmit to the Clerk such a letter as the inclosed,[3] which if Mr. [Thomas] Scott & you approve it, you can sign and forward. If notwithstanding, the Attachm[en]t. should issue, we will not be responsible for the measure nor I think affected by it. Perhaps you might add (as you are better acquainted with him than I am) a word of advice to the Clerk not to issue it, at least without consu[lting] Judge [Thomas] Todd. The order of the Court commands him to issue the Atta[chment] returnable to the first day of the next term. *When* I rather think is a matter within his sound discretion. I cannot account for Mr. [John C.] Wright's[4] conduct. It would be a mockery of justice to allow the Atto[rney]. for the U.S. to oppose in its incipient stage a proceeding, even admitting it to be of a criminal nature, and after he is overruled, to let him take the sole control of the affair.[5]

ALS. KyU.   1. See 3:539-40.   2. Not found.   3. Not found.   4. For Wright, see 2:874.   5. See also 2:874, 900-901; and Clay to Scott & Bond, Nov. 6, 1820.

To THOMAS SCOTT   Frankfort, Ky., November 6, 1820
& WILLIAM KEY BOND
My absence from Lexington has prevented my earlier answering the letters[1] of Mess. [William] Creighton [Jr.] and Scott, in regard to the actions of False Imprisonment, brought by Mess [John L.] Harper & [Thomas] Orr of the Bank of the U. States &c.[2]
    The strong wish of the Bank is to withdraw the cases from the jurisdiction of the State Tribunals, the demurrer which has been filed, and certain decisions of the Supreme Court stand in the way of accomplishing this wish. Still I think it will be well to attempt 1st. yet to withdraw them and that failing 2dly. So to shape the causes as to confer jurisdiction upon the Supreme Court, through the instrumentality of bills of exceptions, by way of appeal from the State tribunal of dernier resort.
    1st. If the officer could be prevailed upon, by intimations of his having made a False return on the summons, or by other means, to amend his return, I suppose you would then have a right either to plead denovo[3] or to move to quash the return[.] Whether he amends his return or not, I would present a petition from the Bank, in the

mode provided by the act of Congress to remove the causes to the Circuit Court of the U.S. and if it be refused except to the decision. It is a case in which the parties were not necessarily joined in the action, and it would seem to be hard that a def[endan]t sh[oul]d. be deprived of his right to the jurisdiction of the Federal tribunal by the arbitrary act of the pl[ain]t[if]f in connecting his name with that of others. Should the Court overrule (as it probably will) the application for the removal of the causes, I would then move to quash the return on the summons because the Sheriff has not shewn *how* he executed it. Taken litterally it means that he has summoned The President Directors & Company of the Bank of the U. States, which is impossible, as they are an ideal being. If he means that he has summoned their legal representative he ought to have stated who that is that the Court not he might judge of the sufficiency of the return. Should the Sheriff obtain leave to amend his return, your difficulty will be less, as in that case the right, now probably lost, would be restored of questioning the sufficiency of the execution of the process. If you fail in all these preliminary efforts, we must then attempt

2 To make every point by which the causes may be so moulded as to give jurisdiction to the Supreme Court.

As the demurrer is put in, perhaps you had better argue that if it will not preclude you from pleading the general issue after the opinion of the Court upon it shall be intimated. In Kentucky and in England, you may plead to the merits, by waiving the demurrer after the opinion of the Court is suggested. If your practice is different you had better withdraw the demurrer, and plead the general issue. and also a plea of justification, alleging that the assault & battery and imprisonment supposed were in consequence of the service of the Capias which issued from the Ct. Court of the U. States. To this latter plea, they will reply that the deputy was not sworn, to which you will demur, and in that or in some other way spread upon the record for the Supreme Court the point, whether an oath was necessary. Supposing the Court to decide, as the Circuit Court did that an oath was indispensible, I would then move the Court to instruct the Jury that the defendants are not liable, in these actions, for the default of the Marshall, in not taking the oath required by law, and except if the decision be against you[.]

I concur with you entirely in thinking that the Corpora[tion] is not liable for a tort and could not be legally joined in the actions with the other defendants. Besides the reason usua[lly] met with in the Books in support of this opinion, its justice is further illustrated by the consideration, that the Corporation being a trust, the cestuy que trust,[4] who has had no agency in the tort, ought not to be liable for it, but the persons alone who have committed it ought to be held responsible. If the State Courts would certainly agree with us in this opinion there would be no difficulty; but as they may entertain a different opinion it is desirable, for the interest of the Bank, that every legal defence, of which it can avail itself, should be made[.]

I shall be glad to be informed of the progress of the causes[.] When will they be tried in the interior, and when in the Supreme Court?[5] If I can possibly attend at their trial in the latter I will do so, if I can be allowed to appear in them.

ALS. KyU.   1. Not found.   2. For Harper and Orr, and their arrest, see 2:723, 874, 900-901; 3:646-47.   3. That is, to plead anew.   4. That is, he who has a right to a beneficial interest in and out of an estate, the legal title to which is vested in another; the person who possesses the equitable right to property and receives the rents, issues, and profits thereof, the legal estate of which is vested in a trustee.   5. See 3:647.

To THOMAS T. CRITTENDEN & GORHAM A. WORTH[1]

Frankfort, Ky.,
November 15, 1820

I recd. your letter of the 4th. inst[2] addressed to me at Lexington, which was forwarded to me at this place, inclosing Copies of two notes, one made and the other indorsed by Jacob Fowler,[3] belonging to the Bank of the U.S. with a request to bring suits if Judgment can be obtained earlier than by bringing them some weeks hence, otherwise to postpone the commencement of them.

The Federal Court of this District has two terms, one commencing the first monday in May and the other the first monday in November. The fall term had of course begun before your letter reached me. By a rule of Court writs served *thirty days* before the commencement of a term, in money cases, entitle the pl[ain]t[iff]s to have their causes put upon the issue docket and tried at the first term, unless the def[endan]t will swear and his counsel will certify that he has a substantial defence. We cannot therefore by bringing these suits now obtain judgments before May, and we probably may get Judgments at that term by commencing them some weeks hence. As your object will be to charge the indorsers, I think the cases will stand upon somewhat better ground, as it respects them, if the writs were issued and made returnable to the present term. Should that be done there will not exist so much facility in getting continuances at the next. As there will however be time enough to bring the suits & make the writs returnable to the present term after I again hear from you (provided you write immediately on the receipt hereof) I shall defer bringing the suits until I obtain your further orders.

Mr. [Ezekiel] Salomon is appointed Cash[ie]r. to the N. Orleans branch & passed through this place yesterday to his post in that City.[4]

ALS. KyU.   1. For Crittenden & Worth, see, respectively, 2:579, 902.   2. Not found.   3. For Fowler (1765-1850), a surveyor and frontiersman who came to Kentucky early in life, see Elliott Coues (ed.), *The Journal of Jacob Fowler*, 2nd ed. (Lincoln, Neb., 1970), 5-6, *passim*. See also Clay to Worth, Nov. 27, 1820. For two of the cases in which the B.U.S. sued Fowler, one involving a $312 debt and the other $283.40, see U.S. Circuit Court (7th Circuit), Reel 1541, Complete Record, Book U, Nov. term, 1822, Box 21. (Kentucky Federal Court Records for the Eastern District of Kentucky have been microfilmed by the Church of Jesus Christ of Latter Day Saints, and copies are held by the Special Collections Department, Margaret I. King Library, University of Kentucky, Lexington).   4. See 2:907.

From Gorham A. Worth, Office of the Bank of the United States, Cincinnati, November 20, 1820. Reports receiving Clay's letter of the 6th [2:901-2] "covering one from the President of the Bank of the U. States [Langdon Cheves] informing the Agents of your having been engaged generally as Counsel for the Bank, both in Kentucky & Ohio." Mentions that "Our solicitor Mr. [William M.] Worthington [3:287] will give you the necessary information relative to the Bill in Chancery against the Bank of Cincinnati [2:621]." Adds that "When Mr [Thomas] Wilson [2:165] left this office on his return to Philadelphia, no particular order was given by him on the subject of bringing Suits," and no instructions have been received from Philadelphia. Thus, "the Agents are at a loss what Course to pursue." Relates that "I have . . . determined to act, & to distinguish between those whose notes fell under protest in consequence of the discontinuance of the Office, & those whose paper had been due and protested previously—& who have manifested but little or no disposition to secure or to pay." States that of nearly "a million of dollars" due, he has "selected about 200,000 Doll[ar]s & placed the papers in the hands of the Solicitor with instructions to institute suits immediately." Yet, feels that "even this step may be considered as of doubtful propriety," since "it is difficult to determine what measures—would be the wisest, *Lenity* or coersion." Asserts that while allowing more time might enable "The most desperate" to "be strengthened, the interest at stated periods collected, and the whole rendered ultimately safe—On the other hand, to wave the present *term* would be giving to the parties *nine Months* longer to shuffle and negotiate . . . and enabling them by an ill-times lenity to set the Bank at Defiance." Copy. DLC-U.S. Banks: 1774-1856.

This is the letter indicated as "not found" in note 1, 2:908. For Clay's reply, see 2:907-8.

To GORHAM A. WORTH   Frankfort, Ky., November 27, 1820
Considering that the recourse against the indorsers on the two notes given by C[hasteen]. Scott and Jacob Fowler,[1] copies of which you sent me, might be hazarded, if the present term of the Federal Court were allowed to be passed without commencing suits on them, I have ordered writs to be issued & the Marshall goes down this week to serve them. I have thought it proper to communicate the fact to you that you may be apprized of it in any arrangement the parties may make. What is the situation of Hugh Glenn?[2] Is it worth retaining the recourse ag[ains]t. him? It will facilitate a recovery agt. the indorser Jacob Fowler to erase the name of Glenn.

ALS. KyLoF.   1. Clay to Crittenden & Worth, Nov. 15, 1820; Clay to Crittenden, Worth, & Jones, May 1, 1821. Chasteen Scott served in the Kentucky Senate from 1836-38. Collins, *History of Kentucky*, 2:771.   2. For Hugh Glenn, see 5:849-50 and *DAB*.

To LUCAS BRODHEAD[1]   Washington, January 17, 1821
Just as I was mounting my horse to depart from Columbus, your letter of the 23d. Ulto.[2] with the opinion of the Court in Mr. [Lucas] Elmendorfs[3] case was handed to me, I defered therefore answering it until I should reach this place, I have since examined the opinion, and although it is not one of those cases in which it can be said with confidence what will be the final decision of the Court, I am disposed to think favourably of it. If as you suppose, the objects for which the *Surveys* call are proven to be notorious there cannot be a doubt of Mr. Elmendorf['s] Success, I apprehend however that you are mistaken on that point—this I shall ascertain by an examination of the Record, Judge [Thomas] Todd with whom I had some conversation about the case, speaking merely from memory, said that he thought there was difficulty in some of the other calls of the Entry, if the point about the

lenght of time of the making of the Surveys were gotten over—I do not see any such difficulty noticed in the written opinion—

on the subject of a fee; the usual fee in the Supreme Court is five hundred Dollars, and less than $300. is I am told never taken, I am willing to appear in behalf of Mr. Elmendorf for $250. Certain and $800. to depend upon the contingency of establishing the Entry by the decision of the Supreme Court. There is plenty of time before the cause will be reached on the Docket of the Supreme Court for me to hear from you, In the interim I will procure the transcript of the Record, and study the case, The precedents from the Court of Appeals are here—[4]

Copy, by Robert Scott. KyU.   1. See 4:714.   2. Not found.   3. See 3:195.   4. For the case, see 4:714.

To LANGDON CHEVES   Washington, January 18, 1821

Col. Rich[ar]d. M. Johnson informs me that he has made an application to the Bank of the U States, in behalf of himself & his connexions, to be allowed to discharge the debt which they owe that Institution in Kentucky, in real estate at valuation:[1] and he has added that the real estate which they propose to give consists principally of first rate land in the Elkhorn region and Ohio bottoms. As a general rule, it must certainly be adverse to the Interest of the Bank to vest any portion of its funds in such inactive & unmanageable property as real Estate is; but there must be exceptions to it, arising out of the circumstances and condition of debtors, and I am persuaded that the case of Col: Johnson presents one. From the calamitous change in the times, he candidly owns, what I think Mr. [Thomas] Wilson must have become satisfied of, that they are unable to pay the debt alluded to, if payment be demanded in specie. Persistance in such a demand would make their situation hopeless, and even deter their numerous friends from lending them that pecuniary assistance which they would otherwise be disposed to afford. I am induced to believe that they have friends who would largely and liberally contribute towards extricating them from this load of debt, if real estate were received; and I think it probable that, if they convey such estate as I have suggested, and it should be correctly valued, the Bank will be ultimately remunerated or nearly so. I do not believe that instances of such enormous & fraudulent valuations as some of those which shocked Mr. Wilson & myself at Cincinnati,[2] are likely to occur in Kentucky; at least I should hope not. If the Board at Lexington were charged with the execution of the arrangement with Col: Johnson, I feel confident that it would be able so to regulate the subject of valuations as to do justice to both parties.

There are considerations belonging to the case of Col. Johnson, arising out of his public services, his distinguished enterprize, and the esteem in which he is every where held, that I am quite sure the Bank will give all the weight to which they ought to receive, in deliberating upon his proposition.

Copy. DNA, RG107, Letters Received, Unentered, J-1821.   1. For the Johnsons' financial problems, see espec. 3:89, 99, 102, 121-25, 485, 557-60, 759, 811-13.   2. Much of the debt owed to the B.U.S. by Ohio banks, as well as individuals, was secured by mortgages on greatly over-valued real estate. The over-valuation was due more to the drop in western land prices than to actual fraud, so that, eventually, when land prices rose, the B.U.S. profited from the lands it had obtained through foreclosures and, in fact, acquired much of the property comprising the city of Cincinnati. See Ernest L. Bogard, "Taxation of the Second Bank of the United States by Ohio," *American Historical Review* (Oct., 1911-July, 1912), 17:312-31, espec. 321; C.C. Huntington, "A History of Banking and Currency in Ohio before the Civil War," *Ohio Archaeological and Historical Publications* (1915), 24:235-539, espec. 291. See also 3:13.

To GEORGE A. OTIS[1]   Washington, January 21, 1821

Since my arrival at this place within a few days past I have received your letter of the 2d. Ulto.[2] with its inclosure. I congratulate you on the progress which you h[ave] made in the translation & publication of your work,[3] which I am eager to see entire.

I return you the Subscription paper forwarded to me, with some signatures.[4] Several of my colleagues either declined subscribing or had previously subscribed.

Wishing you great success in the sale of your book[.]

ALS. KyU.   1. For Otis, see 2:860.   2. Not found.   3. See 2:860.   4. Evidently, a subscription list for advance orders of the book.

From James Smiley, Bardstown, Ky., February 13, 1821. States that "from what I have seen in the papers, a reduction of the Officers and Soldiers of the U.S. Army will take place, Capt. [Samuel] Spotts with whom I am particularly acquainted is altogether worthy . . . was in three engagements at Orleans, in which he distinguished himself as a brave Officer, if you can be of any service to him for any appointment you will confer an obligation on your sincere friend." ALS. DNA, RG94, Adjutant Generals Office, Letters Received, Sam Spotts, 1821.

For Smiley, see 2:233 and *HRDUSA*, 893. For Spotts, see *HRDUSA*, 912. For the bill reducing the military establishment, see 3:15.

To MRS. M. BECKLEY[1]   Washington, February 16, 1821

I received the letter[2] which you wrote to me respecting Capt. [John] Fowler. My friendship for him, and my desire that he should retain the post office, he knows well. They are unabated. He will not lose the office, on account of the alleged losses of money. But he is greatly in arrear to Government, even beyond what I had supposed, and unless he makes some satisfactory arrangement very soon as to that arrearage he will be deprived of it. The Post Master General [Return Jonathan Meigs] will not finally act until the close of the Session.[3]

ALS. Courtesy of Turner McDowell, Glen Falls, N.Y.; copy in ViU.   1. Probably Maria Prince Beckley, who lived with the John Fowlers in Lexington. Edmund & Dorothy Berkeley, *John Beckley* . . . (Philadelphia, 1973), 52-55, 286, 288.   2. Not found.   3. See 3:33-34; 6:916; and Meigs to Clay, July 11, 1820.

From William S. Cardell, New York, February 28, 1821. Explains that he has been delegated by "The society whose general principles and objects are explained in the enclosed circular [not found] . . . to communicate to you their choice of you as one of their counsellors." Reports that the "officers of the institution are Hon J[ohn]. Q Adams, President, Judge [Brockholst] Livingston Judge [Joseph] Story Mr. [William] Lowndes-V[ice] Pres[iden]ts. Doct A[lexander] McLeod Recording Sec. Doct [John] Stearns (Pres. N. York State Med. Soc.) Treasurer. " Mentions several other counsellors who have already accepted. These include Daniel Webster, Chancellor James Kent, and Washington Irving. States that they have also received cordial communications from the seven chosen as honorary members: John Adams, Thomas Jefferson, James Madison, James Monroe, John Jay, Charles C. Pinckney, and John Trumbull.

Believes $10-$20,000 will be raised for the organization in New York City "by private subscription," and adds: "We ought not to suppose other parts of our Country wanting in the necessary patriotism or pride to support a national institution of this kind." ALS. KyLoF.

See Clay to Cardell, March 9, 1821, in which Clay accepts the appointment as a counsellor for the American Academy of Language and Belles Lettres. The purpose of this organization was to "collect, interchange, and diffuse literary intelligence; to promote the purity and uniformity of the English language; to invite a correspondence with distinguished scholars in other countries speaking the English language." Lexington *Kentucky Gazette*, May 3, 1821.

For Cardell, see 3:181; for Brockholst Livingston, 1:643; for Joseph Story, 2:405; for William Lowndes, Clay to Fulton, January 27, 1814; for Alexander McLeod, New York City clergyman and author, *DAB*; for John Sterns, 9:494; for James Kent, 3:473 and *DAB*; for Charles C. Pinckney, 2:102; and for John Trumbull, 6:95.

To S. WILSON[1]   Washington, March 3, 1821

I received your letter of the 27 Jan.[2] and I assure you, most sincerely, that it would be very gratifying to me, if I could be instrumental in procuring for you such an appointment as would be agreeable to you and as you ought to accept. At present, more than ever I have known, are the pressure and solicitation for office great. The hardness of the times is the immediate cause.[3] The Land offices are sought after with great avidity & vacancies are not unfrequently filled upon anticipation. At this time there is no prospect of getting one of them for you. And in regard to the office of Consul, be assured, Sir, by one who is well acquainted with the subject that you ought not to get one, if you could. Except, I believe, that at London and Paris, there is no salary attached to a Consulate. It devises all its importance from its supposed Commercial advantages, and these depend again upon capital, or credit, and commercial knowledge. Almost every one who obtains the office is disappointed as the present editor of the Kentucky gazette can tell you from experience.[4] If, however, on my return home, you persist in your wish to obtain such an appointment, it will, I repeat it, give me much satisfaction to aid you.

I learn, from home, that my son Thomas [Hart Clay] is again put under your direction.[5] I approve entirely of it; and if you can reclaim him from his habits of indolence (I believe he has none worse) you will do me an essential favor.

ALS. KyLoF.   1. Possibly Samuel Wilson, who was head of the Forest Hill Academy in Jessamine County, Ky. See 1:667.   2. Not found.   3. For the Panic of 1819 and the subsequent depression, see Catterall, *Second Bank of the United States*, 22-92; Bray Hammond, *Banks and Politics in America* (Princeton, N.J., 1957), 251-85; Murray N. Rothbard, *The Panic of 1819; Reactions and Policies* (New York, 1962).   4. Joshua Norvell of the *Kentucky Gazette* had been nominated as consul to St. Bartholomew on Jan. 22, 1821, and confirmed on Feb. 5. U.S. Sen., *Executive Journal*, 3:236, 240.   5. Apparently at Forest

Hill Academy; however, Thomas entered the U.S. Military Academy at West Point in July, 1821. See Clay to Morris, Feb. 25, 1822.

To WILLIAM S. CARDELL   Washington, March 9, 1821

I owe you an apology for not having earlier answered the communication, which you have done me the honor to make,[1] of my having been appointed one of the Counsellors of the American Academy of Language and Belles Lettres. I was not at all insensible to the distinguished proof which the Society has been pleased to give of its favorable opinion of me. But the truth was, that I doubted whether I ought to accept or not a situation, in which I apprehended that I could make no actual contribution towards promoting the object of the institution, from my remote residence and from other causes which I need not enumerate. And I yet am inclined to think that it would be better to substitute some other more useful name to mine. Nevertheless, entertaining an anxious wish for the success of the Academy, and of every similar effort, I will, with great pleasure, accept the place designated for me, if such casual and contingent aid as I may have it in my power to render, shall be deemed satisfactory. At all events, I pray you to present to your associates my respectful thanks for the honor confered on me, and accept assurances of the high respect which is felt for you and them . . .

ALS. MH.   1. Cardell to Clay, Feb. 28, 1821.

To James Monroe, Washington, March 9, 1821. Recommends Edmund Law to be "Secretary to the Board of Commissioners under the Florida treaty." Has had "an intimate acquaintance with him for several years past" and is "persuaded that he would execute the duties of that office with the greatest propriety," because he has great "personal merit, and a modesty which is very rare." Concludes: "I need not advert to the circumstances of the benevolent, intelligent and disinterested character of Mr. Law's father [Thomas Law], so well known to you, to fortify his application." ALS. DNA, RG59, Applications and Recommendations.
    For the Adams-Onis (Florida) Treaty, see 2:678. For Edmund Law, see 6:322; for Thomas Law, 6:190.

From William H. Crawford, Washington, March 23, 1821. Reports that he has sent this day two drafts to the Bank of the United States at Philadelphia—"1 for $300. & the other for $220. with directions that the amount shall be entered to your Credit."
    States that "Nothing has been done towards the organization of the Floridas, since the appointment of the Governor [Andrew Jackson]. It has been determined not to select the commissioners from the principal commercial cities. Mr [George] Hay will not be appointed. You will perceive that decisions which have been made are principally negative."
    Mentions that he is "uncertain whether the U S B[ank]. will offer proposals for the loan." Believes Langdon Cheves "will probably have great influence with the board." Believes "he will be wrong if he does not urge the bank to take the whole loan. The four millions that I propose now to raise will not be more than enough to adjust the demands now pressing upon the Treasury, more than $2.000.000 of which, draw interest at the rate of six per cent. The remain-

86

der of the sum authorized to be borrowed, will not be raised until the end of the year if it is practicable to satisfy the demands upon the Treasury without it." Notes that "the whole balance of $1.391.000 will be inadequate to" pay the Revolutionary War pensioners, while "The military appropriation act appropriates . . . only $1.200.000." ALS. KyLoF.

George Hay was the son-in-law of James Monroe. Adams, *Memoirs of John Quincy Adams*, 5:322.

On March 3, 1821, Congress had passed an act [3 *U.S. Stat.*, 635] authorizing the government to borrow a sum not exceeding $5,000,000 at a rate not exceeding 5% to meet the federal deficit. The Bank of the United States was allowed to lend all or part of the sum, and it did, in fact, lend the entire amount. Rafael A. Bayley, *The National Loans of the United States from July 4, 1776 to June 30, 1880* (Washington, 1881), 62-63. For further information on loans made during Crawford's tenure as secretary of the treasury, see *ibid.*, 61-66, and William F. DeKnight, *History of the Currency of the Country and the Loans of the United States from the Earliest Period to June 30, 1896* (Washington, D.C., 1897), 57-62. See also 2:850-51.

To THOMAS T. CRITTENDEN,   Frankfort, Ky., April 27, 1821
GORHAM A. WORTH,
& GEORGE W. JONES[1]

Will you transmit to me the original notes, copies of which you sent me last Fall, against [Jacob] Fowler &c. at or near New port [*sic* Newport, Ky.]?[2] The Federal Court will commence its Session here in May, and I shall then want them.

I shall have occasion to address you shortly on the affairs of the Bank under your care—

ALS. OCHP.   1. For Jones, see 3:234.   2. Copies not found, but see Clay to Crittenden & Worth, Nov. 15, 1820; Clay to Worth, Nov. 27, 1820; Jones to Clay, Nov. 8, 1822.

CIRCULAR[1]   Lexington, May 1, 1821

Having been engaged by the Bank of the United States as its counsel to exercise a general superintendence over its Law business in the two States of Ohio and Kentucky, as some what connected with that object, I have been requested to suggest some system by which collections, from Marshals and other public functionaries, of monies belonging to the Bank, upon executions and other law process, ought to be regulated I now proceed to comply with that request.

Of the importance of some regulations upon that subject there can be no doubt, when the amount is considered, which it has been and may be, unfortunately necessary to put in a course of litigation from any one of the Western offices. In devising these regulations, the material purposes to be accomplished are 1st. To provide for the exertion of a vigilant attention, in the offices respectively, to the progress and final termination of causes, from the time of their commencement to the ultimate recovery or absolute loss of the debts which they were intended to secure. And 2dly. To secure the payment to the several offices of the money which may be recovered by course of Law, with as little delay, risk and expense as possible. Each office ought, at all times, to be able promptly to exhibit the exact state of its business, as well that in litigation as that which is not. But this it would not be able to do, if, after delivering over to its Solicitor evidences of debt for suits, it did not continue to keep a watchful eye upon their progress and final issue.

To effectuate the first object I would recommend that some particular clerk in your office be specially charged, under the general superintendence of your Board, and the particular directions of the Cashier, with keeping the accounts against persons whose debts are put in suit, and with your Law business generally: that he also keep, for prompt occasional reference, a docket or manual, exhibiting the causes of the Bank which have originated in your office, and having various columns in which shall be shown 1st. the parties names. 2dly. On what the suit is founded. 3dly. The indorsers names. 4thly. Against whom, for what amount, and in what Court Judgment has been rendered. And lastly a large column for an account of the proceedings after judgment and general remarks presenting the actual condition of each case. The object of this docket is to exhibit, in one collective view, the precise state of your law business, and consequently additions should be made to it, from time to time, and immediately after the respective terms of courts in which that business is distributed, as far as may be practicable, so as to fulfill that object. And that it likewise be made the duty of the same Clerk to see to the timely registry of all deeds, mortgages, and other instruments required by the law to be recorded, and carefully filing away, in your office, the originals after they have been duly registered; and generally that he attend to such out-of-door business connected with the Law interests of your office as the Solicitor or Counsel of the Bank cannot. 2ndly. Whenever money is collected by the Marshal or Sheriffs it ought to be paid into the Bank with as little delay, hazard and expense as possible. This object, it seems to me, will be best attained by requiring of those public officers to make all payments directly at your office. Whatever confidence may justly belong to the gentlemen in the employment of the Bank, at its several offices, it may be assumed as a general rule, inculcated by all experience, that the risk, delay and expense of money getting to its ultimate destination are, for any given period, in proportion to the number of hands through which it passes. The Marshals and Sheriffs should be instructed therefore to make payment, in all instances, of money received by them for your office, directly into the office. If, as may happen, these officers will not come to the Bank to make payment the before mentioned Clerk should be required to call on them, receive the amount in any particular case, and immediately pay it over to the office. The same Clerk should also be charged with the duty of attending, from time to time Marshals and other public sales, on executions of the Bank, when there may be reason to apprehend that there will be any collusion, or to force the sale, if necessary In the performance of the various duties which I have intimated, your office will of course be assisted by the advice and counsel of the professional characters retained by the Bank. I need not add that I shall take particular satisfaction, whenever called upon, to communicate any which it may be in the power to give . . .

DS. OCHP.   1. Sent to the Western offices of the Bank of the United States in Ohio and Kentucky. Enclosed in Clay to Worth *et al.*, May 1, 1821.

To WILLIAM CREIGHTON, JR.   Lexington, May 1, 1821

Inclosed I transmit a bill[1] which I have prepared for an injunction against the collection of the tax imposed on the Bank of the U. States by the act of Ohio passed at the last Session of the Legislature.[2] The pending injunction perhaps might be considered as constituting a sufficient restraint upon the Auditor against proceeding under the last act; but as there is some question on that subject, we had better I think leave nothing to hazard and procure another injunction. As I presume you will concur in the opinion, will you have the bill sworn to by yourself or Mr Claypole [sic],[3] give the requisite notice, and obtain an injunction from Judge [Charles W.] Byrd?[4] There being plenty of time I hope nothing nothing [sic] will be omitted which is necessary to give effect to the injunction.

I also send you inclosed a Calendar which I have prepared on the subject of cases put in suit by the different Western offices, and the mode of making collections from Marshalls &c. It is not unlikely that several or all of its suggestions may be unnecessary at your office as being already acted upon.

I shall on some future occasion & in due time address you on the subject of the act of the last Session of the Legislature intended to operate as a species of outlawry—[5]

Is the present mind of the Grand Jury at Columbus a fair indication of public opinion generally in Ohio, in regard to the proceedings of the Legislature towards the Bank, or ought it to be considered as expressing one peculiar to that place?

ALS. KyU.   1. Not found.   2. For the Ohio tax law, see 2:723; 3:111-16.   3. For Abram G. Claypool, see 4:62, where his first name is erroneously given as Abraham.   4. For Byrd, see 3:173. For more on the proceedings, see William T. Utter, *The Frontier State, 1803-1825*, vol. 2, in Carl Wittke (ed.), *The History of The State of Ohio* (Columbus, Ohio 1942), 301-9.   5. See above, note 2.

To GORHAM A. WORTH, THOMAS T. CRITTENDEN, & GEORGE W. JONES   Lexington, May 1, 1821

Inclosed I transmit to you a Circular[1] which I have prepared for the several Western offices of the Bank of the U. States, in Ohio and Kentucky, on the subject of debts which have been put in suit, and the mode of making collections from Marshalls and other public officers. I recommend to you the observance of the rules which it suggests as far as they are applicable to the constitution of your agency.

I hope there will be particular attention paid by you and Mr [William M.] Worthington to the timely execution of the Subpoenas against the Bank of Cincinnati, and all other legal process which were not served in season returnable to the last term of the Federal Court.[2]

I shall address you again before long in regard to the act of Ohio,[3] passed at the last Session, which had for its object the denunciation of a sort of outlawry against the Bank of the U States.

ALS. OCHP.   1. Circular, May 1, 1821.   2. See 2:621; Clay to Cheves, Jan. 18, 1821.   3. See 3:63.

To GEORGE W. JONES, GORHAM A. WORTH, & THOMAS T. CRITTENDEN

Lexington, May 20, 1821

I have duly received your favor of the 15h. inst.[1] and will have the cases of [Jacob] Fowler and [Chasteen] Scott disposed of according to the arrangement which you have made.[2] You are, I presume, aware that if the mortgage is upon real Estate, lying in this State, the laws of Kentucky and not those of Ohio must regulate its registry &c. and that according to a late act it must be recorded within sixty days from its date.[3]

With respect to the affair of the Bank of Cincinnati, subsequent reflection has strengthened my conviction of the correctness of the principles, on which the suit in Chancery is founded.[4] It is a suit, however, in which I fear there will be considerable delay, owing to the number of the parties &c. If therefore you could get good real Estate, with indisputable titles, at a fair valuation, I think it is advisable to accept it. Would it not be best for the Bank to specify the property which it wishes to offer, and for you to treat directly with it as to the price, without the intervention of Commissioners to value it?

It will give me great pleasure to aid you in your arduous duties; and I think that there had better be as few references to the parent bank as possible, because our local knowledge must enable us in the general to have a better view than can be taken in Philada.

P.S. Be pleased to say in your next, if I must issue *Executions*, for the Costs against Fowler and Scott.

ALS. OCHP. 1. Not found. 2. Clay to Crittenden & Worth, Nov. 15, 1820; Clay to Worth, Nov. 27, 1820; Clay to Crittenden, Worth, & Jones, April 27, 1821. 3. See Ky. Gen. Assy., *Acts* . . . 1820, p. 114, sec. 4. 4. See espec. 2:621 and Clay to Cheves, Jan. 18, 1821.

To CAESAR A. RODNEY

Frankfort, Ky., June 6, 1821

I received your letter of the [1]May relative to the case of Capt. [James] Barron.[2] Having also recd. that of the Judge Advocate (Mr [Henry] Wheaton)[3] with the Interrogatories prepared for me, I have made my deposition, and transmit it by the mail which carries this, addressed to Mr Wheaton at New York. I shall be happy to learn that the Captain is found not to be obnoxious to the charges made ag[ains]t. him[.][4]

The Italians have made such a miserable out of it, that I am mortified & chide myself for having ever allowed my feelings to become interested for them.[5] In South America, events are occurring which communicate very different sensations. There they are marching steadily on to Independence & to Freedom.[6]

ALS. DeHi. 1. A blank space appears at this point; letter not found. 2. For Barron, see 1:481-82; 3:107. 3. For Wheaton, see 2:915. 4. See 3:107. 5. For the failed revolutions in Naples and Piedmont (Sardinia) in 1820-21, see 2:863; 3:80-82. 6. For Clay's support of South American independence, see Subject Index: Volumes 1-6 in 7:764-65.

To JOHN C. CALHOUN

Lexington, June 23, 1821

I ought earlier to have made my respectful acknowledgments to you for your obliging and prompt attention to my request respecting the appointment of my son Thomas [Hart Clay], as a Cadet at the Military

Academy at West point.[1] Thomas resolved to accept the appointment forthwith, is now on his way to West point, and will I presume arrive at that place during this month.[2]

ALS. DNA, RG94, Adjutant General's Office, Cadet Applications, 1821/11.   1. See 3:82-83 and Clay to Morris, Feb. 25, 1822.   2. Thomas's letter of acceptance, addressed to Calhoun and dated June 4, 1821, is in DNA, RG94, Adjutant General's Office, Cadet Applications, 1821/11.

To WILLIAM MURPHY[1]   Lexington, June 23, 1821

The two Judgments recovered at the late Circuit Court of Mason against Mess. [Richard L.] Waters, [Joseph K.] Sumrall, [Thomas M.] Duke & yourself in the name of Mr. [Matthew T.] Scott, but for the benefit of the Farmers and Mechanics Bank, have been assigned to me.[2] I understand the Judgments to have been got, and the executions to have issued, at the request or with the concurrence of the sureties. The endorsement, to take paper of the Commonwealth Bank or the State Bank, has been omitted, because I can, in paying my own debts, make no use whatever of the former, and a very limited one of the latter, and because of the constantly depreciating state of the paper.

If time, further than even is allowed by the law, is wanted, I am disposed to give it, provided the ultimate security of the debt is rendered perfectly safe. Or, if it would be an accommodation to take the notes of the Bank of Kentucky, I would take them for half the debt, provided they are paid me within thirty days.

Receiving the debt for the purpose of paying my own, I trust that you and the other gentlemen will be satisfied that every easement which I can consent to, consistently with that object, will be ch[eer]fuly accorded.[3]

P.S. Be pleased to communicate the contents of this to the other gentlemen concerned with you.

ALS. KyU.   1. For Murphy, see 3:88   2. For these men and the judgments, see 3:88.   3. See also 3:95, 97-98, 100, 423-44, 439-42, 455-56, 497-98. This letter is indicated as "Not found" in 3:97-98, note 1.

To GORHAM A. WORTH &   Lexington, July 6, 1821
THOMAS T. CRITTENDEN

I have received a letter[1] from the President of the Bank of the U.S. [Langdon Cheves] in relation to the securities transfered or pledged by the Miami Exporting Company for payment of the debt which it owes to that Bank;[2] and I have been requested by him to communicate with you on the subject of it.

With respect to the right of the debtors, the evidences of whose debts have been transfered or pledged to the B.U.S. to pay their debts in the notes of the Miami Exporting Co., I think that they can have no such right after they have notice of such transfer or pledge. The act of Ohio of the 18 Feb. 1820,[3] which allows debtors of a Bank to discharge their debts in the notes of such Bank, even in the hands of assignees must, I think, be construed to mean assignments which have been made in trust for the Bank. To suppose that the Legislature meant to vest in the debtor the right to discharge the debt, after it became the property of another, and after his knowledge of that fact; would be to attribute the greatest injustice to the act, if not to make it unconstitutional. Nor do the words of the act seem to me to require such interpretation. If, before notice of the assignment to the Bank of the U S, any of those debtors had *acquired* and *retains* the notes of the Miami Exporting Company, he will have a right to offset the amount of such notes against his debt.

I must therefore repeat the advice which I have already given to you to notify all persons, whose debts have been as aforesaid, put into the hands of the agents of the B.U.S. by the M. E. Co. in security of its debt, that you hold their debts & that payment of them to you will be expected. As to the form of this notice, and whether it is verbal or written, that is not material, provided it is substantially given & is susceptible of proof here after, if necessary. To guard however against accidents, you had better have it in writing. I would also advise that you accompany this notice with a demand if the debtors have any and what offsetts against their respective debts? And if in any case they can make out that, prior to their knowledge of the transfer, they became possessed of the notes which they still retain of the M. E. Co., you had better offer to receive all such notes & to credit the debt with the amount. A refusal to surrender them will probably prevent their being used as a credit hereafter.

I continue also to think that you ought, without delay, to have a distinct understanding with the M E. Co. (if it has not already been had) about your suing those debtors. In cases where the debt has been *legally* transfered, if you give time to the debtors, or forbear to bring suit, the responsibility of the M. E. Co. as assignees will be destroyed. In cases where the debt has not been legally transfered, but a mere deposit has been made with you of the evidences of it, it will be advisable for you to demand of that Co. such legal transfer. And I shall be glad to give you, from time to time, any professional advice in my power about all or any of those cases.[4]

ALS. OCHP.   1. Not found.   2. See 2:621; 3:99-100.   3. See 3:100.   4. This letter is indicated as "Not found" in 3:99-100, note 2.

From George Gibson, Washington, July 14, 1821. Reports that Secretary of War John C. Calhoun has instructed him "to contract for the delivery of subsistence Stores at Council Bluffs. This arrangement will enable Genls. on the Missouri & particularly those moving high up that River, to make proposals with great probability of Success." Copy. DNA, RG192, Office of Commissary General of Subsistence, vol. 2, p. 345. For Gibson, see 2:714.

To WILLIAM MURPHY   Lexington, August 4, 1821
When your letter of the 24h. Ulto.[1] arrived here, I was gone to Louisville, from which I have just returned to day. To that cause is owing the delay in my' reply to your's.

I should not like to say that I would receive the sum you mention in paper of the State Bank, without a positive assurance of paying it by a precise and a short time. The truth is, that I have a use, in the payment of my debts, of a certain amount of that paper; and beyond that I could not apply it. Now I have several sources to depend on to get that limited supply of it. If I could count, with entire certainty, on any one of these sources, I could make arrangements as to the others. If I were to say to you that I would receive it, without such an engagement as I have mentioned above, I should be at a loss to know whether it would afterwards suit your convenience to pay it. If the money were now offered me, I would take it.

I think however that there is a mistake about your not having a right to pursue your mortgage against the mills, without first paying off the debt. The actual condition of Mr. [Richard L.] Waters, and your having entered into a replevy bond indicate such a just ground to apprehend that you will ultimately suffer as I think entitles you to go into equity, to have the adverse pretensions to the Mills put out of the way, so as to subject them to the satisfaction of the debt for which you are responsible.[2]

ALS. KyLoF.   1. Not found.   2. Clay to Murphy, June 23, 1821.

To GEORGE W. JONES, GORHAM A. WORTH, & THOMAS T. CRITTENDEN

Lexington,
August 6, 1821

The period assigned for the commencement of the operation of the act passed by the Ohio Legislature, at its last Session, "to withdraw from the Bank of the U States the protection and aid of the laws of this State in certain cases,"[1] being near at hand, I take the liberty of addressing to you some observations on that subject. It has been impossible for the Bank to accede to the conditions, on its performance of which, the Legislature declares that the act shall be in-operative; and although we might reasonably expect from the character of the act, that it would remain a dead letter, and not be attempted to be enforced, it is better to be prepared for the opposite contingency.

The act prohibits, from the first day of September next, any Judge, Justice of the peace or other judicial officer, from receiving the acknowledgment or proof of the acknowledgment of any deed of conveyance of any kind in which the Bank may be interested; and also any recorder from receiving into his office or recording any such deed of conveyance.

With respect to this part of the act I would advise that, in all cases where you may take deeds to the Bank, you proceed exactly as if the act in question had not passed. I would recommend you to apply to a judge of the Court of Common pleas to receive the acknowledgment of the deed; if he refuses to receive it, get him to indorse and sign such refusal on the back of the deed. If he refuses to make such indorsement, get the indorsement made and attested by other persons. Should the Judge comply with the act of Ohio, I would advise you then to apply to the most convenient justice of the peace, and follow, in respect to him, the same course as is suggested in relation to the Judge of the Common pleas. If there are several judges of the Court of Common pleas residing in the County where the land conveyed lies, I would apply to each of them. Should the acknowledgment of the deed be received by either the Judge or Justice, you will then apply to the Recorder of the proper County to receive and record the deed. If he refuses to receive and record it, get him also to indorse that fact upon the back of it; and if he refuses to make and sign the indorsement, get it certified by some other persons.

The act next prohibits, from and after the same first day of September, any Notary public appointed by the State from making a protest or giving notice of a protest of any bill of exchange or promissory note &c.

In respect to this part of the act, I would advise you to ascertain from the Notaries of your place if they mean to conform to it. If all of them do, then let any bill of exchange or promissory note, which it may be necessary for you to have protested, be protested by some respectable and substantial person, in the presence of at least two witnesses, and treat this protest and give notice in all respects as if a Notary had acted. But if any one Notary will act; as if the Legislature had not interposed, I would advise you to employ him as heretofore.

Congress having made provision for the denial by the Legislature of Ohio, of the use of the Jails of that State,[2] it is not necessary for me to make any further remarks on the act in question. The object, you will perceive, of the advice which I now give is to be able to exhibit hereafter proof that the Bank was ready and willing to comply with those general laws of Ohio which regard the acknowledgment and registry of deeds, and the protest & notes of protest of bills of exchange and promissory notes, notwithstanding the act of the last Session; and to entitle the Bank to insist, that its interests shall not be affected or impaired, if the functionaries of Ohio have determined to lend themselves to the enforcement of that act.

ALS. OCHP. 1. See 3:63. 2. A resolution, passed by both houses on Feb. 2, 1821, and approved on March 3, stated that if a state withdrew the use of its jails, the U.S. marshal could hire a convenient place to serve as a temporary jail. 3 *U.S. Stat.*, 646-47. See also 3:114-15.

To GEORGE W. JONES, GORHAM A.   Columbus, Ohio,
WORTH, & THOMAS T. CRITTENDEN   September 8, 1821

Mr. Maddox Fisher,[1] who will present you this letter, being indebted to your Agency, is desirous of making some arrangement of his debt. He renewed, I understand, his note at Chillicothe, and had the amount passed to your Credit. If you accepted the Certificate which he obtained from that office, I suppose it will operate as a discharge of so much of his debt at Cincinnati, and he would now be liable upon his note at Chillicothe. But it is to be wished to close the transaction. When I knew him he was, and I believe yet is, a man of perfect integrity & I presume his debt to be ultimately good. I have told him that I was quite sure of your disposition to give him every accommodation consistent with those general rules which it is necessary for you to observe. And I shall be glad if you will co-operate with him in securing the debt giving him such indulgence as you can[.][2]

ALS. OCHP. 1. For Maddox, see 1:170, 567, 870; 4:506. 2. On May 9, 1825, Clay, writing from Washington to George W. Jones, reported that "I cannot refuse to comply with the request of Mr. Maddox Fisher that I would interpose in his behalf to obtain some further indulgence from the Bank; for the payment of the debt which he owes it." Mentions that he has known Fisher for "upwards of 25 years as an honest man and good

Citizen," and that Fisher says "he pays the interest regularly and has paid the Costs, and that the debt is well secured." Hopes that "you will extend to him all possible indulgence."
ALS. OCHP.

To WILLIAM MURPHY   Lexington, September 18, 1821

I regret to have to say to you that I find, since my return home, that I cannot receive the sum which Col. [John] Pickett wishes to pay in notes of the Bank of Kentucky.[1] If I were to receive them I should be unable to apply them to the payment of my debts, without incurring the ruinous loss which would be sustained by converting them into that medium which will alone be received from me.

I lost the night that I reached Washington (last friday night) between Maysville and that place my surtout which was tyed to the saddle behind. It was a brown coat with a velvet Cape & almost new. Mr. Arbis [?] sent a servant the next morning to look for it, but I have not heard with what success. I certainly lost it between those places, as I saw it attached to the saddle as I crossed the river. If you can assist me in the recovery of it I shall be obliged to you.

ALS. KyLoF.   1. For Pickett and the debt, see 3:423-24.

To BENJAMIN C. HOWARD[1]   Lexington, September 22, 1821

I have duly received your letter of the 5h. inst.[2] On the subject to which it relates I have to say, that my agency, as a trustee of the Mess. Purviances,[3] was limited to this State and did not extend to any of the adjoining States; that the offer made by me for the land appertaining to the trust, refered to in your letter as being contained in one of mine to Mr. Jeffray,[4] was not accepted; and the land to which I presume that offer applies, that is to say about 20.000 Acres of land in [Richard] Hendersons Grant near the mouth of Green river in this State, remains to be sold. The present is a very inauspicious period to effect a sale, owing to the depression of real estate every where, and the condition of our local currency. I have unsuccessfully offered it for a dollar an acre. Sales might be accomplished of small parcels (a hundred or two acres at a time) but they would be very troublesome and expensive; and I have prefered waiting for the reflux of better times, if they should ever come.

There are some balances[.] One on former sales which I am endeavoring to get liquidated, and which I hope to collect (though most probably in our depretiated money) 'ere long.

ALS. MdHi.   1. For Howard, see 6:143 and *BDAC*.   2. Not found.   3. Henry, Robert, and Samuel Purviance. See 1:112, 494, 548.   4. Letter not found; Jeffray not identified.

To THOMAS T. CRITTENDEN   Lexington, November 3, 1821
& GORHAM A. WORTH

In reply to your favor of the 29h. Ulto.,[1] requesting to be informed what notes were handed to me at Columbus, by Mr. [William M.] Worthington, I have to say that I received & retained only two, one given by James Taylor[2] to Hubbard Berry[3] for $18500, dated 26 Sept. 1820 and payable sixty days after date;[4] and the other given by James B.

Taliaferro & Charles Thornton[5] to James Taylor for $700 dated the same day and also payable sixty days after date. For both of these notes Genl. Taylor informed me that he held himself liable, and he engaged to renew them at the office here, in the course of this month, otherwise I shall sue him.[6]

ALS. OCHP.   1. Not found.   2. For Gen. Taylor of Newport, Ky., see 1:31 and Armstrong, *Biographical Encyclopedia of Kentucky*, 309.   3. For Berry, also from Newport and the nephew of James Taylor, see *VMHB*, 25:81, and Horace E. Hayden, *Virginia Genealogies* (reprint ed., Washington, 1931), 682.   4. See also Clay to Jones *et al.*, Dec. 7 and Dec. 17, 1821.   5. For Taliaferro (b. 1796), the son of Robert T. Taliaferro and Ann Taylor, see *WMQ*, 2nd series, 9:312. For Charles Thornton of Orange County, Va., who moved to Oldham County, Ky., about 1812, see *WMQ*, 1st series, 6:109-10. The Taylor, Taliferro, and Thornton families intermarried, and it seems likely that James B. Taliaferro and Charles Thornton, along with Berry, were also nephews of Gen. James Taylor. Hayden, *Virginia Genealogies*, 682.   6. See 3:69-70.

To GEORGE W. JONES, THOMAS T. CRITTENDEN, & GORHAM A. WORTH

Frankfort, Ky., December 7, 1821

On the third inst. I took from James Taylor of New Port [*sic*, Newport, Ky.] his note for $20.836 payable & negotiable at the Lexn. off[ice]. to the Bank of the U.S. on the 26h. May next, being for $20.074:50 his own note with int[erest]. up to that day and cost of protest, and for $761:50 the note of [Charles] Thornton &c with like interest & cost which two latter notes were sent to me by you from the Cincinnati office.[1]

As a security for the payment of the above note I have taken a mortgage to the Bank from the maker of it upon 1200 Acres of land, part of [Hugh N.] Mercers[2] Military survey lying on the Ohio above New Port, which has been estimated to me by good men at 30$ per acre. This mortgage which I shall send to you certified by the Clerk of the Ct. of Appeals, must be recorded in the Campbell County Ct. office within sixty days from its date.[3]

ALS. OCHP.   1. See Clay to Crittenden & Worth, Nov. 3, 1821.   2. For Mercer, see 3:396.   3. See also 3:393, 395-96, 406-8.

To WILLIAM CREIGHTON, JR.

Frankfort, Ky., November [*sic*, December] 10, 1821[1]

With infinite regret, I have to tell you that I find it impossible for me to reach Chillicothe in time for your Supreme Court there. The Courts here are yet in Session and it is not even known when they will adjourn, but they certainly will not in time to enable me to present myself, as I wished, in your town by the 20h. instant.

Inclosed I transmit you a Copy of the opinion of this Court[2] on the question of the validity of the acts of the Marshall of this State, who has not qualified according to the act of Congress, of which I have supposed you may make a favorable use on the trial of the actions of [Thomas] Orr & [John L.] Harper against the Bank.[3] You will recollect that the object of the Bank is to have the cause so prepared as that it may be taken to the Supreme Court, if the pl[ain]t[iff]s should succeed.

ALS. KyU.   1. Not only was this letter postmarked on Dec. 13, but Clay wrote on Dec. 3 that the Federal District Court in Frankfort, which he was attending, would continue for two more weeks [3:144]; thus, he must have dated this letter Nov. 10 when it should have been Dec. 10.   2. See 3:143-45.   3. See 2:723, 874, 900-901; 3:14, 50-52, 112, 114, 646-47; Clay to Scott & Bond, Nov. 6, 1820.

To GEORGE W. JONES, THOMAS T. CRITTENDEN, & GORHAM A. WORTH

Lexington,
December 17, 1821

I transmit you herewith the mortgage which I took from Genl. James Taylor to secure the ultimate payment of his note, refered to in my last from Frankfort.[1] By our laws this mortgage must be recorded in the office of Campbell County Court within sixty days from its date, and it is sent to you for the purpose of having that ceremony performed, after which you had better send the original to the office here to be retained to act upon if finally necessary. In taking Genl. Taylor's note, he contended that he was entitled to two credits 1st. for a certificate of deposit for $1500 with which he was charged, without being credited with the amount in his bank book and 2dly. for 1000$ with which he thought he was erroneously debeted. Without admitting either of those credits, I gave him a receipt specifying that his execution of the note which I took from him should not prejudice his claim to them or any other credit, if it were well founded. You had better have the matter investigated and explained to the satisfaction of both parties.

I am very anxious that the witnesses, whose attendance was prevented at the last September term of the Federal Court at Columbus, should be gotten to attend punctually at the approaching term in January.[2] I hope that your Solicitor will take the necessary means to secure their attendance. If the distance from Cincinnati to Columbus were 100 miles, their depositions might be taken under the act of Congress providing for the case of taking depositions de bene esse; but if I am not mistaken it wants a few miles of being 100. You are no doubt apprized of the Solicitude of the Bank to bring the suits upon the docket to as early a termination as is practicable.

P.S. If either of the witnesses should be again in custody, an affidavit of that fact should be at Columbus on the first day of the term, that a writ of habeas corpus may be obtained from the Court to have him carried to Columbus to testify &c &c.

ALS. OCHP.   1. Clay to Jones *et al.*, Dec. 7, 1821. See also Clay to Crittenden & Worth, Nov. 3, 1821.   2. See 3:155-56.

To RICHARD C. ANDERSON, JR.

Lexington,
December 19, 1821

I am truly sorry that you should have had so much difficulty in the affair of the Pension.[1] The affidavit is an indispensible requisite, without which the item, in the settlement of the account of the Bank at the Treasury, would be disallowed. I return you the power and the receipts. The Cashier informs me that, if you will get the duplicate receipts signed by the Pensioner himself and transmitted to the office, the money will be forthwith paid to you or your order.

I mentioned to you that I could, without inconvenience, advance you the money, until you were enabled to obtain the amt. of the Pension. I send you a check for $283 72/100 (the exact amt. of the pension) on the office at Louisville. This sum you must *certainly* have replaced there or in the office here by the first of April, and I shall not want it before that time. It is a part of the amt. of a bill which I drew on St. Louis when I was at Louisville last summer. I will thank you to say to Mr. [Edward] Shippin[2] that Col. [Thomas Hart] Benton, on whom the bill was drawn, informed me that he had paid it in Specie.[3]

I pray you to believe that, far from considering myself troubled, I have much satisfaction in endeavoring to serve you in this matter, as I should have in any other—

Wishing you a pleasant journey home . . .

ALS. CSmH.   1. Reference obscure.   2. For Shippin, cashier of the Louisville branch of the Bank of the United States, see 3:340.   3. For other business dealings with Benton, see, for example, 2:892; 3:346.

To GEORGE W. JONES   Lexington, December 22, 1821
THOMAS T. CRITTENDEN

Inclosed I transmit to you an agreement[1] which I have entered into with Mess. [Thomas D.] Carneal[2] and [Charles S.] Todd,[3] subject to your ratification, or rejection. Mr. Carneal, I believe, is the only party to the bill who can be considered responsible; the condition of all the others being such as to render, in my judgment, a recovery of the amount of it from them perfectly hopeless. As to him there was a difficulty about the notice, which was sent to Cincinnati, instead of the post office nearest to him. Such, at least, I was informed by the office here was the state of the fact. Under these circumstances I concluded that it was best to take the property described in the agreement rather than risk the loss of the debt, on the point of notice, by urging the suit. If you concur with me in this arrangement, be pleased to notify the other party in writing of your ratification of it, and I will thank you also to take measures to have the valuation effected. On being informed of which I will have the agreement carried into full effect by receiving a conveyance &c.

P.S. I wish you to exercise your own judgments, with the most entire freedom, without being at all affected by what I have done.

ALS. OCHP.   1. Probably a reference to the agreement of Dec. 21, 1821, mentioned in 3:415, note 9. In that agreement, Todd and Carneal gave to the Bank of the U.S. "towards satisfaction of the said debts with their interest and costs, the undivided half of a House and Lot in the Town of Louisville, situated on Main Street nearly opposite the Post Office . . . the legal title to which is in said Carneal." If the property was appraised at a lower sum than the debt, "the deficiency shall be paid by the said Todd and Carneal and if it exceeds the said amount, the excess shall be credited to the said Todd on some debt due by him, to the said Bank to be mutually designated by the said Clay and Todd." This agreement had to be ratified by the agents of the bank within six months. George W. Jones approved the agreement on behalf of the Bank on June 14, 1822. DS. OCHP. 2. For Thomas D. Carneal, son of Thomas Carneal, see 1:125, 654. Thomas D. Carneal was one of the founders of Covington, Ky. See also James F. Shaffer *et al.*, *Piatt's Landing Eastbend* (Cincinnati, 1978), 9-10. For one of Carneal's debts, amounting to $150, see U.S. Circuit Court (7th Circuit), Reel #1541, Complete Records, Book U, Nov. term, 1822, Box 21.   3. For Todd, see 2:713. For his debt to the Bank of the U.S., see 3:415.

To THOMAS DOUGHERTY[1]   Maysville, Ky. December 29, 1821

I am thus far on my way to Columbus [Ohio], Richmond [Va.] and Washington. I shall be detained at the first ment[ione]d. place until about the 14h. Jan. and shall then proceed, with all practicable dispatch, to the Metropolis of the antient dominion via Washington.

I have great solicitude to know whether my son [Thomas H. Clay] has had any, and what, share in the unpleasant incidents which have occurred at West point,[2] during the last month or two. To obtain that information I have taken the liberty to inclose this letter to him,[3] in which I have requested that he will transmit an answer under cover to you; supposing that, upon its receipt, you will be able to give it the direction which will ensure its quickest arrival at the place where I may happen to be.

I saw Mr. & Mrs. Tilford[4] on the evening of the 26th. at a large party in Lexington; and of course they were both well. He spoke of setting out in about ten days for the Eastward. . . .

ALS. KyU.   1. For Dougherty, clerk of the U.S. House, see 2:589.   2. Sylvanus Thayer, superintendent of the U.S. Military Academy 1817-33, instituted several educational and disciplinary reforms which led to a number of rebellious actions by cadets throughout the early years of his tenure. Stephen E. Ambrose, *Duty, Honor, Country: A History of West Point* (Baltimore, 1966); Thomas J. Fleming, *West Point: The Men and Times of the United States Military Academy* (New York, 1969); Joseph Ellis & Robert Moore, *School for Soldiers: West Point and the Profession of Arms* (New York, 1974).   3. Not found. 4. Robert & Mary Ann Dougherty Tilford. See 3:289.

To Unknown Recipient, *ca.* late December, 1821. States that "You will have heard that P[hilip]. Barbour [2:280] is elected Speaker [3:150]—Altho' I am much gratified with the event, I think it w[oul]d. have been better to have taken [Caesar A.] Rodney as tending more to allay the excitement produced by the Missouri question." ALS. CSmH. Dated only "Lexn. Monday." For the Missouri Compromise, see Subject Index: Volumes 1-6 in 7:747.

To GEORGE W. JONES   Columbus, Ohio, January 7, 1822
I received your favor of the 3d. instant relating to the case of Mr Ennis.[1] By the mortgage which he made to the Bank [of the United States] the legal title to the property conveyed by it became vested in the Bank, and there remained in Mr. Ennis what is called an equity of redemption. Under the arrangement which you have made with him I understood it has been agreed to receive this property in absolute payment of the debt for which it was pledged. It appears to me therefore that the most correct mode of completing this and all similar transactions is to obtain a deed releasing the equity of redemption, after reciting the mortgage and the agreement to receive the property in payment. The deed should be acknowledged or proven and registered in the usual way. Such a deed may be prepared by your Solicitor, as for want of the mortgage and an adequate description of the property I cannot prepare it here. When the business is thus consummated, there will be no danger from other judgments or liens subsequent to your mortgage. It is I think of no consequences whether satisfaction is formally entered of Record or not of the Judg[men]ts; but at all events such an entry had better not be made until such a release as I have intimated is executed.

ALS. OCHP.   1. Not found. Ennis not identified.

To THOMAS MORRIS   Washington, February 25, 1822

My son Thomas [Hart Clay], whom I put last summer at West point, left that establishment about a month ago, and I have not since heard from him. Indeed I did not know, until several weeks had elapsed after his departure, that he had left it; and the fact was communicated to me at Richmond.[1] I will not conceal from you that I entertain strong fears that he has not gone home, as he avowed it his intention to do, when he left the point; and that I am apprehensive that he remains in the City of New York—He was supplied with money at the point to pay off his debts there, and to take him home. I wish, my dear Sir, to trouble you with endeavoring to ascertain for me whether he is in New York; or what has become of him? If there, what he is doing? And if you find out that he is there, or where he is, to give or send the inclosed letter to him. I do not wish any advances made to him of money without my previous approbation. Your own parental feelings will excuse the liberty I take, and enable you to judge what are mine.[2]

P.S. I shall remain here about two weeks.

ALS. NhHi.   1. Note 2 on 3:83 states that Thomas entered the U.S. Military Academy in July, 1821, "but failed to qualify at the examinations the following September." In fact, records in the archives at the Academy indicate that he was admitted on August 31, 1821, at the age of 17 years, 7 months, and that at the mid-year examinations held in Jan., 1822, he was found deficient in mathematics and was recommended for discharge. The discharge became effective on Feb. 28, 1822. Information supplied by Dorothy Rapp, USMA Archives.   2. See also Clay to Morris, March 8 and 21, 1822.

To UNKNOWN RECIPIENT[1]   Washington, February 26, 1822

I have just received your favor of the 8h. inst.[2] transmitting the check which I gave you on the office at Louisville. I am mortified & surprized that it was not paid. It ought to have been, because they know that my draft has been paid, and they had no authority to receive payment in any thing but specie. Moreover, Col [Thomas Hart] Benton informed me that it was paid in that medium, before I left Lexington.

I had determined to write you from Richmond, but defered it until my arrival here. In regard to our *public object*,[3] we have not been able to get Virginia to accede to either of the two propositions which we submitted; although we were given to understand that she would refer *all* matters arising under the Compact. To such a comprehensive reference our powers did not extend; and we thought it useless to open a negotiation upon it. The two States can at any time take up the whole subject, if they please, and refer it to the Tribunal of the compact. I think Kentucky has nothing to apprehend from such a general reference. Virginia has however made *no complaint*, and the House of Delegates abstained from expressing any opinion for or against our laws. In that course the Senate will probably concur—I do not think that the transactions at Richmond can do us any possible injury, and may benefit us, here. We expect to try the cause in a day or two.[4]

Our reception at Richmond was distinguished by every possible mark of cordiality, hospitality and kindness. My old friends were particularly attentive to me; and if there existed any alienation on their part from me (which I am now disposed to doubt) it has been entirely effaced.

100

There has been a strange state of things here. A divided Cabinet and distracted counsels. *All* the prominent members of the Cabinet looking to the succession, and the friends of each rallying around him, presents a state of things extremely to be deprecated as it regards the public business.[5] It is one, at the same time, that I believe has done essential injury to the parties concerned. At this moment matters are more quiet, but it is the quietude of smothered jealousy and resentment. My name has not been thrust upon the public, and my friends here have generally deported themselves with great prudence. Their confidence & my own is strong. And I think the sequel will prove that all our anticipations will be realized. On this subject I cannot enter into details, which I will as soon as I have the pleasure of seeing you.

I ought to add that in our effort at Richmond we encountered every species of difficulty which the activity of private correspondence & communications could throw in the way. Herring[6] preceded us, and visited every mess of the members, and incessantly occupied himself with our affair. He professed however to be favorable to a general reference—

ALS. CSmH.   1. Although the extant letter does not contain the recipient's name, the Huntington Library lists the recipient as Richard C. Anderson, Jr.   2. Not found.   3. Reference is to the appointment of Clay and George M. Bibb as commissioners from Kentucky to Virginia to conduct negotiations under the Occupying Claimant law. See 3:91, 151, 158, 160-71.   4. Reference is to *Green v. Biddle*. See 3:91, 208-9, 392-93, and Subject Index: Volumes 1-6 in 7:773.   5. John Quincy Adams (State), John C. Calhoun (War), and William H. Crawford (Treas.) were all potential 1824 presidential candidates. For a discussion, see Wiltse, *John C. Calhoun: Nationalist*, 240-62. 6. Probably John S. Herring. See 3:385.

From James Chambers, Maysville, Ky., February 27, 1822. Addressing Clay and George M. Bibb, sends "Two Certificates for Revolutionary Services as you will Discover, William Warrington, is an old man he has been wo[u]nded in the Service of his Country he has a large Family. & a Cripple from the wounds." States that Warrington "no Doubt Could Receive a pension but his old pride will not allow him to apply for it, but earnes[t]ly, Requests the Interposition of his Friends to procure for him a Warrant for What ever land may be justly due him." Notes that "the other Certificate of James Warington [*sic*] will Shew for its Selfe," but adds that he is "Very much Respected but Wretchedly poore."

Writes with reluctance because "Humanity & Justice Requires it," and asks them to use their influence in Richmond, Va., with the representatives of Accomack County "to procure, Warrants for those Worthy Citizens who procured the liberty we now enjoy." ALS. KyLxT.

For Chambers, see 3:248. James Warrington served in the Virginia State Navy during the American Revolution. William Warrington has not been found. Stratton Nottingham, *Revolutionary Soldiers and Sailors from Accomack County, Virginia* (Onancock, Va., 1927), 53.

To William Creighton, Jr., Chillicothe, Ohio, March 1, 1822. States that because he was detained in Richmond, Va., the case of *Bouldin & wife* v. *Massie's Heirs et al.* came up in his absence, "but it was taken care of by the other Counsel" and today "the Court . . . delivered an opinion in favor of the town of Chillicothe."

Reports that "My reception at Richmond was cordial and hearty in the extreme. I saw a great many of my old friends, and rubbed the rust off of the chain of our friendship, and made many new ones. Altho' we did not succeed in the particular object of our mission, what was done will not have a bad effect, but I am inclined to think a good one, on the cause here [Clay to Unknown Recipient, February 26, 1822]." ALS. KyU. Written from Washington, D.C.

The Supreme Court ruled that the patent issued on a military land warrant under the law of Virginia, is *prima facie* evidence that every prerequisite of the law was complied with. For this case, see 7 Wheaton, 122-57 (1822).

To JOHN C. CALHOUN   Washington, March 2, 1822

I am requested to communicate the inclosed proposition[1] for the sale of powder to your department. It is made by respectable Citizens of Lexington in K[entucky]. upon whose faithful compliance with it entire reliance may be placed. Will you favor me with the means of communicating to them an answer to it? Or refer it to that branch of the Department which can decide upon it, with instructions to put me in possession of the answer?[2]

ALS. DNA, RG156, Office of the Chief of Ordnance, vol. C. Endorsed on verso: "Encloses Mr. Boswells proposal for manufacturing powder for the U.S. Ansd. 4 March, 1822."   1. Not found.   2. On March 4, 1822, George Bomford from the Office of the Chief of Ordnance writes Clay that Secretary of War Calhoun has turned over to him the "proposition from Mr. Joseph G. Boswell for the sale to the United States of a certain quantity of Gunpowder." Reports that "from the large quantity of powder now on hand . . . it is not contemplated, nor deemed expedient, to enter into new engagements for the supply of that article at present; nor are there at this time any appropriations for that object." Promises, however, that the proposal "will be preserved on file." Copy. DNA, RG156, Records of the Office of the Chief of Ordnance, Misc. Letters Sent. For Boswell, see 1:850.

To THOMAS MORRIS   Washington, March 8, 1822

After having written to you today on the subject of Thomas [Hart Clay], I received your letter of the 5h. inst.[1] I thank you most sincerely for the kind interest which you have taken in him. The truth is, and I say it with infinite pain, that I have lost all confidence in his stability. I would yet indulge the hope that he has some sense of honor and propriety left. And yet $100 was advanced to him at West point upon the pledge, as I am informed, of his honor, to proceed directly home. I neither have the ability nor inclination to supply him with money to waste in dissipation and idleness in the Cities. He has cost me $500 since he left home in June last, and one half of it after he had made me a solemn promise to limit his expences to his allowance as a Cadet. Nothing can be more ridiculous than an idea of entering the Patriot service,[2] which may be considered as substantially terminated, which never offered any but illusory inducements to Foreigners, and for which he has no adequate qualifications. The Marine Corps is full; and if it were not, I could not think of asking the public to take into its service, a son of mine, in whose firmness and consistency of conduct, I have so little confidence. In short, he fills me, my dear Sir, with inexpressible distress.

If he will nevertheless join me here to return home, I will thank you to advance him a sum not exceeding Sixty dollars to defray his expences and pay what he states he owes. I must rely on your judgment and discretion, in determining whether you think he will, upon receiving the money, come or not[.] I do not think I shall remain here longer than the 20h. instant.[3]

I quit this painful & mortifying subject, with the repetition of my thanks for your obliging attention to it, and assurances of my cordial esteem and regard.

P.S. I stay at Brown's Hotel.

ALS. NhHi. 1. Not found, but see Clay to Morris, Feb. 25, 1822. 2. That is, the South American independence forces. 3. Clay to Morris, March 21, 1822.

To THOMAS MORRIS   Washington, March 21, 1822

I have delayed transmitting the inclosed check to you for the amount which you had the goodness to advance to my son [Thomas Hart Clay], in the hope that when I sent it I could inform you of his having joined me.[1] In that I have been as yet disappointed. He has not arrived here, but I learn that he is in Philadelphia, where it is probable he is waiting for me, having heard of my intention to go there. I shall leave this place on sunday for that City, where business will detain me two or three days. I will be obliged to you to address me a line at that place informing me if you receive the check. For your kind attentions to Thomas I pray you to accept my sincere thanks. I could not wish for an opportunity of returning similar services, but it would give me pleasure to have any other mode of testifying a sense of the obligation under which you have placed [me] . . .

ALS. NhHi. 1. Clay to Morris, Feb. 25 and March 8, 1822.

To JOHN D. GODMAN   Washington, March 22, 1822
& JOHN P. FOOTE[1]

I have received the letter which you did me the favor to address to me on the 6h. instant,[2] with the first number of the Western Quarterly Reporter,[3] which accompanied it; and I pray you to accept of my thanks for this gratifying mark of your attention. You have my best wishes for the highest degree of success. An American must see, with lively satisfaction, literary advancement in any quarter of our common country; and this feeling must be greatly increased, in contemplating it in the West, a boundless field so little as yet trodden, on which there have, nevertheless, been many unsuccessful efforts heretofore. These efforts resemble those which are made by a stout hearty child, when he first attempts to walk. Far from being discouraged by repeated failures, he perseveres fearlessly until he stands firm and erect. That the Reporter may assume and maintain this position is the ardent wish . . .

ALS. NjMoHP. 1. For Godman (1794-1830), see 3:447-48; for Foote, see 3:868 and Henry A. Ford, *History of Cincinnati, Ohio* (Cleveland, 1881), 267. 2. Not found. 3. *The Western Quarterly Reporter of Medical, Surgical, and Natural Science* was first published in March, 1822. See Godman's entry in *DAB*.

From THOMAS HART BENTON   Washington, April 9, 1822

Mr. [Jonathan] Russell will give me the remainder of the Ghent business. He only waits for the letter which he sent containing his reasons, and which the President has not yet been able to deliver, or to say positively that it was mis laid. If he does not get it soon, he will use the copy that he retained and his own memory, and will shew the views taken by you and himself.[1]

The Nashville Clarion has republished all the Nos. of the Western Citizen[2] (at my instance) and will keep an eye to the progress of that and other writers. The same have been republished in Missouri.

The Ohio members are warm and true. I think the friends of the "army candidate"[3] are beginning to shew signs of despair at this place.

You must have heard, or seen in the public prints, that the President [James Monroe], after seeing two of his army nominations rejected, had withdrawn all the rest from the Senate. It was done with the known intent of nominating the rejected ones over again.—[4] Thus far the thing has not worked well for the administration. It is becoming a question of honor & of rights with them, and the symptoms get worse for the President and his War Minister [John C. Calhoun].

I received yours from Phil.[5] Mr. Russell had a letter from his son, who, altho a boy, could tell what he heard men say. It was all agreable to you. If Pennsylvania and Ohio go for you, *the game is up.*[6] The two would carry enough in the east and west to settle the question almost without struggling. I look upon these two states as the *hinges.*

[P.S.] I am getting along very well in the Senate with all my local bills.

ALS. KyU.   1. For the duplicate letter controversy, see 3:204.   2. Not found in available issues of the *Clarion.*   3. Probably a reference to Sec. of War John C. Calhoun.   4. See 3:202.   5. Not found.   6. In the 1824 presidential election, Andrew Jackson won 152,901 popular votes and 99 electoral votes, John Quincy Adams won 114,023 popular and 84 electoral votes, William H. Crawford won 46,979 popular and 41 electoral votes, and Clay won 47,217 popular and 37 electoral votes. In Pennsylvania, Jackson received 36,100 popular votes to 5,441 for Adams, 4,206 for Crawford, and 1,690 for Clay. Jackson received all 28 of Pennsylvania's electoral votes. In Ohio, Clay received 19,255 popular votes to 18,457 for Jackson and 12,280 for Adams. Clay received all 16 of Ohio's electoral votes. Since no candidate received a majority, the election was determined by the House on Feb. 9, 1825, from the top three candidates. Adams was elected president by the 13 votes of Maryland, Kentucky, Ohio, Missouri, Maine, New Hampshire, Vermont, Massachusetts, Connecticut, Rhode Island, New York, and Illinois. Jackson received the 7 votes of Pennsylvania, South Carolina, Alabama, Mississippi, Tennessee, Indiana, and New Jersey, while Crawford received the 4 votes of North Carolina, Virginia, Delaware, and Georgia. Arthur M. Schlesinger, Jr. *et al.* (eds.), *History of American Presidential Elections 1789-1968*, 4 vols. (New York, 1971), 1:380, 409.

To LANGDON CHEVES   Wheeling, Va. (W. Va.), April 11, 1822

I present to you Col. C[harles]. S. Todd, who will deliver you this letter, and whom I beg you to receive as a gentleman of honor and intelligence. His affairs connected with the Kentucky Offices have been before the Board at Philada., and he now wishes to obtain the discharge of his Bail[1] or an assurance that, during his contemplated absence from the U.S.,[2] proceedings will not be had against his Bail. There appears to me to be every motive to accede to his wishes (for the considerations which he will communicate to you.) and none to oppose them.

ALS. KyU.   1. See 3:415 and Clay to Jones & Crittenden, Dec. 22, 1821.   2. He was returning to Colombia as a diplomatic agent for the U.S. See 3:247.

To WILLIAM CREIGHTON, JR.
Wheeling, Va. (W. Va.),
April 12, 1822

I am this far on my way home. During a short sojourn which I made in Philadelphia, I saw a great deal of Mr. [Langdon] Cheves on the business of the Bank. The Board has a strong wish to obtain Judgments in all cases of suit brought or to be brought. I stated to him the allowance which I had thought reasonable for the Solicitors of your office; and altho' there exists a determination to practice the most rigid economy, which is absolutely necessary to the prosperity of the institution, I believe there was no dissatisfaction with that allowance. I will thank you to favor me with an early communication of the exact state of your Law at present in regard to the lien which is acquired by judgment or execution upon the Estate of the debtor. Does it still commence with the Judgment? what is its duration? what circumstances, short of satisfaction of the judgment, affect or destroy it? Must real estate command a certain & what proportion of its value? Does a Judgment in one County bind property in another? If the Estate will not sell for the required proportion of its value, is the lien affected & how? Is the law of valuation temporary or permanent? Does it extend to mortgages & trusts? On all these points I desire the earliest information. You had a bill pending on this general subject before the last Legislature, of the fate of which I have not heard.[1]

ALS. KyU. No. 1 of date.   1. See 3:232, 234.

To WILLIAM CREIGHTON, JR.
Wheeling, Va. (W. Va.,),
April 12, 1822

Having written you on business,[1] I am now about to address you on politics. I think I have now a pretty good view of the whole ground, as it stands at present, in regard to the next Presidency. My confidence, from the prospect, is greatly strengthened & Confirmed in ultimate success. Mr. [John Quincy] Adams may be considered as hors du combat. His partizans are early deserting him, and I assure you that the question is surrendered as to him. In Virginia no body is generally thought of, but Mr. [William H.] Crawford or me, and I have every reason to suppose that if she were now to decide it would be in my favor.[2] But she means to hold back and throw her weight in the scale where it will effect most; and upon that very principle, which all her politicians profess, she must give me her support. New York will, from all the information I have received, decide in the same way.[3] In Pennsa. the Secretary of War [John C. Calhoun] is making a movement, but it is artificial and will prove abortive; and there is not a doubt, he being out of the way, that she will decide for me.[4] Against the Secretary of the Treasury [Crawford] there are inconquerable prejudices in that State, arising among other causes, from the supposed obloquy which he threw some years ago upon foreigners.[5] They tell me that in West Pennsa. all parties are united in my favor. In short, my dear Sir, assuming the point of a zealous & firm union of the West there is not a doubt with me, if Ohio takes the lead, that the wishes of my friends twill be accomplished.[6] These are two points to be well weighed; one is not to obtrude my name prematurely upon the public notice; and the other is

105

not to lie back too long. Hitherto our course has been in conformity to the first; and I think it will be time to begin, during the next summer, to act on the latter. I say Ohio should take the lead, the moral effect of which will be great both in the West and East. It will demonstrate that there are not even any dregs left of the Missouri question;[7] and will undeceive those to the East who have wickedly bottomed their ambitious hopes on that question. It will powerfully influence Indiana and Illinois.[8] Ohio is entitled by her weight to take the lead, And if she does so in behalf of a Citizen in another State, and that a Slave State, the influence of her disinterested example will be incalculably important[.]

My own judgment tells me that the time for her to act will be next winter; the way, by a public expression of her wishes through a Legislative recommendation.[9] If therefore the supposition is well founded that she is for me, the disposition must exist to obtain her choice in the effectual manner. At Washington, I was informed by one of your delegation that the whole of your representation, without exception, was for me; and I communicated the views here expressed to Mr. [John] Sloan[e],[10] than whom I have no heartier supporter. Should you concur with me, it will be expedient by conversations & otherwise to prepare for a decisive movement at Columbus next winter. After Ohio has thus broken the ground, Kentucky and other States will follow in all probability.[11] When all the neutral States (a term which I apply to those not having Candidates of their own,) observe that the West presents an unbroken & firmly compacted front, they will, upon those National considerations which they will admit should influence their decision, be disposed to take sides with the West.

Shall I go into the next Congress? I wish your judgment on that question. There are many pros and cons. I understand that there is a disposition at home to force me into it, at all events.[12] Let me hear from you soon.

P.S. I have a great body of the most encouraging information, the details of which would be too long for a letter, but which I will communicate when I shall have the pleasure to seeing you.[13]

ALS. KyU. No. 2 of date. Letter marked "(Confidential)." 1. Clay to Creighton, April 12, 1822, no. 1 of date. 2. In the 1824 presidential election in Virginia, Crawford won 8,489 popular votes to 3,189 for Adams, 2,861 for Jackson, and 416 for Clay. Crawford won all 24 of Virginia's electoral votes. Schlesinger, *History of American Presidential Elections*, 1:409. See also Benton to Clay, April 9, 1822. 3. In the 1824 presidential election in New York, electors were chosen by the state legislature; Adams received 26 electoral votes, Crawford 5, Clay 4, and Jackson 1. *Ibid.* See also Benton to Clay, April 9, 1822. 4. For Pennsylvania's vote in the 1824 presidential election, see Benton to Clay, April 9, 1822. 5. Crawford's remarks on immigrants had been made in his 1816 report on Indian affairs. Chase C. Mooney, *Willaim H. Crawford, 1772-1834* (Lexington, Ky., 1974), 222-23. 6. Ohio did not endorse any candidate at its 1822 legislative caucus. See 3:341. For Ohio's vote in 1824, see Benton to Clay, April 9, 1822. 7. See Subject Index: Volumes 1-6 in 7:747 for the Missouri Compromise. 8. In the 1824 presidential election in Indiana, Jackson received 7,343 popular votes to 5,315 for Clay and 3,095 for Adams; Jackson received all 5 electoral votes. In Illinois, Jackson received 1,901 popular votes to 1,542 for Adams, 1,047 for Clay, and 219 for Crawford; Jackson received 2 electoral votes and Adams 1. Schlesinger, *History of American Presidential Elections*, 1:409. 9. See note 6, above. 10. For Sloane, see 3:130. 11. See 3:301. 12. See 3:274. 13. This letter is the one indicated as "Not found" in 3:206, note 1. Creighton's reply is in 3:204-6.

To THOMAS DOUGHERTY   Maysville, Ky., April 15, 1822

I received the letter[1] which you did me the favor to address to me at Wheeling, in regard to the Carriage of the late Mr. [William] Pinkney. I regret that the office which I requested you to perform for me about it, should have been the occasion of any dissatisfaction of Commodore [John] Ro[d]gers.[2] I certainly never did suppose him capable of lending himself to any imposition; nor ought he to have imagined any such imputation implied by the enquiries I requested you to make. You will remember that the first information I got respecting the Carriage was at breakfast at your house; immediately after which we went to see it. I certainly bought it under the impression (how made I cannot say, perhaps from a view of the carriage itself) that it was a *new* carriage a little used, but not essentially injured. It turns out that I was mistaken in that particular, not I admit by the fault of the Commodore. It appears that it is an old carriage fitted up recently not for sale but for the use of Mr. P.s family. It is thought however that it is not essentially impaired. I am perfectly content to take it, and there is an end of the matter.

I have had a boisterous passage down the river which is compensated by its rapidity. My best respects to Mrs. [Nancy Scott] Dougherty.[3]

ALS. KyU.   1. Not found.   2. See 3:183, 263.   3. For Mrs. Dougherty, see *RKHS*, 54:359.

To ADAM BEATTY[1]   Blue Licks, Ky., April 16, 1822

I was anxious to have seen and conversed with you, as I passed through Washington [Ky.], but my extreme anxiety to see my family, after near four months absence, prompted me to proceed on my journey. And yet I might as well have stopt, for I am likely to be detained here this day by the badness of the weather.

I do not know whether you approve or not of that effort which my friends are about to make to place me in the Chair of the President, as the successor of Mr. [James] Monroe.[2] Whatever may be your opinion of it, I am sure that I may safely rely on your friendship in confiding the subject of this letter to you. The prospect, I assure you, is most encouraging and such as to afford the best grounds for calculating upon ultimate success. I have been always sanguine of such a result, *assuming the zealous and hearty co-operation of all the Western States;* and of such a co-operation I cannot doubt, from the information which I have received. What other competitor can stand upon ground so broad, firm and commanding? In the South there is likely to be great division; and the candidate, and probably only candidate, of the North[3] has so far lost all prospects of prevailing, that wherever I have recently been he is considered as hors du combat.

The Middle states, from New York to North Carolina inclusive, presenting no candidate themselves, will have a most powerful influence on the question; and from the circumstance of their neutrality it may be supposed that they will give great weight to those impartial and national considerations which should be well weighed in determining their judgment. All those considerations, unless I greatly deceive myself, concur to favor the wishes of our quarter. And accordingly the intelligence which I have received from several parts of that portion of the Union is highly flattering. In Virginia no one is generally thought of but Mr. [William H.] Crawford and myself, and I have strong reasons to believe that her great weight will be given to my support.[4]

From New York I have less information, but that which I have is good.[5] It appears to me that there are peculiar besides general views of the subject which that State must take that will attach her to the West. Every thing considered, New York and the West are doubtless those quarters which have the strongest claims. N. York wishes, of course, to obtain the Presidency; but it has so happened that all her more distinguished Citizens are thrown in the back ground. She can bring forward no candidate at the next election. She desires nevertheless to obtain the honor of that high office as soon as she can. If she give her weight to the North or to the South, she will leave her great Western rival in the possession of all her present pretensions, with those strong additional ones that will arise out of the lapse of time, and the rapid growth of the West, between the end of Mr. Monroes terms, and that of his successor. By supporting the West now, she will satisfy claims in this quarter, and may then step in as a matter of course. She will do more; she will not only get rid of a rival, but she will make a powerful friend. If she lend herself to the support of the New England Candidate, her own claims will in no inconsiderable degree be merged in those of New England. Moreover; between the West and New York there are many strong points of affinity. A large part of that State is Western. Many of her sons have migrated to the West, particularly to Ohio. By means of the great canal she is brought into direct contact with Ohio; and when the further link shall be completed from the Lakes to the Ohio River, she will be brought into contact with the very heart of the Western States. There are numerous points of coincidence, in the opinions of the Western people and those of New York, on subjects of National policy.

Should you unite with my other friends in desiring to secure my election, it has appeared to me that you might communicate with good effect some of the preceding views, and others corresponding with them, that will suggest themselves to you, to Mr. W[illiam]. Rochester and his father [Nathaniel Rochester].[6] Both of them have deservedly much influence, particularly the old Colonel; and their position in the Western part of the State is well adapted to form a rallying point. I have other friends in that qua[r]ter (Genl. P[eter]. B. Porter &c) who will promptly co-operate with them. I do not certainly know the opinion of either of them. At Washington, I did learn that William was favorably disposed, but I did not receive the information from himself and do not know how far it can be relied on. It is important to make a strong impression to the East of the fact of the cordial union in the West; and respecting this, I repeat, there can be no doubt. If you should think proper to address either or both of them the sooner it is done the better.

It has been three weeks since I left Washn. At that time the period of adjournment of Congress was uncertain. It was not however expected to be earlier than the first of next month.[7]

Ought I to go into the next Congress? It is an important question on which I should like to have the benefit of your judgment. I have been disinclined to go; but many of my friends are very urgent in their persuasions to me to offer—[8]

ALS. Courtesy of Earl M. Ratzer, Highland Park, Ill. Letter marked "(Confidential)." 1. The reply to this letter is in 3:192-95. This letter is the one indicated as "Not found" in 3:194, note 1. 2. See Election of 1824 in Subject Index: Volumes 1-6 in 7:714-19. 3. John Quincy Adams. 4. For Virginia, see Clay to Creighton, April 12, 1822, no. 2 of date; also Benton to Clay, April 9, 1822. 5. For New York, see *ibid.* 6. Beatty's letter to Rochester is in 3:194-95. 7. Congress adjourned on May 8, 1922. 8. See 3:274.

From Henry St. George Tucker, Winchester, Va., April 28, 1822. Reports that "Should the Southern States, find the probability of electing the Southern Candidate remote, they would—at least Virginia would—vote against John Quincy [Adams]. Should the Northern people be compelled to give up Adams, I presume their vote would be very much divided between the Western and Southern Candidates, in which event, the Western uninimity would be decisive." Believes Virginia "will probably pursue the course you intimate of saying nothing until she goes to the polls." Thinks public opinion in Virginia indicates "a decided dislike to Adams, and some apprehension that Mr. [John C.] Calhoun who is much and deservedly admired is too young, too ardent and too high toned for her politicians. . . . I think Mr. [William H.] Crawford is upon the whole looked on most favourably in Virginia, tho there seems to be no very active feeling in his behalf." Believes Virginia "ought to hold back with a view of throwing her weight into either scale as she may find most for the interest of the Union." Hopes also that "we will take care to prevent the degradation of having 'a chip of the old block'—of electing to the first office in the country a man who deserted his fathers sinking cause, as rats will leave a sinking ship— while in the other hand, we must not deliver over the reins of government to the hands of a consolidatist." ALS. DLC-HC (DNA, M212, R4); typed copy in InHi. For Tucker, see *DAB* and *BDAC.*

For the popular and electoral votes in 1824, see Benton to Clay, April 9, 1822; for Virginia's vote, see Clay to Creighton, April 12, 1822, no. 2 of date. The "chip of the old block" is a reference to John Quincy Adams and his switch from his father's Federalist party to the Republican. Marie B. Hecht, *John Quincy Adams* (New York, 1972), 178-81.

To ADAM BEATTY   Lexington, April 30, 1822
I derived particular satisfaction in learning from your letter of the 17h. inst.,[1] which I duly received with its inclosure, that you approved of the attempt which my friends contemplate making to elect me as Chief Magistrate of the U.S.; and I am greatly obliged by the letters[2] which you have addressed, in promotion of that object to Col. [Nathaniel] Rochester and his son [William B. Rochester]. When you shall hear from them, on the subject, you will add to my obligation to you, by communicating to me their views. Mr. Elmendorf is a Client of mine, for whom I argued a Cause in the Supreme Court at the last term; but I really do not know his residence.[3] His christian name is Lucas. I understood that the member from his district, his friend, favored my wishes.

Whatever doubt I ever had as to the *time* of my name being brought forward, that is whether it should be at the next or the succeeding election, is removed by the fact that my juniors, in age and in public service, are held up to the public notice. If in them it be not premature, much less is it so in me. There will be Caucus's in the several states or at Washington or both. In any event, the expression of public opinion through the Legislative Assemblies in the several States will be highly useful. It should not be made too soon, nor too late. I think in the West, for many obvious and strong reasons, Ohio should take the lead;[4] and I think the next winter Session will be the time for her to commence. My opinion is, that she will have a more deciding influence, on the approaching election, if she take up a person from a Slave-holding State, than any other single State in the Union. The effect of her example will be powerful on both sides of the Alleghany. Although I do not entertain a doubt of her favorable disposition, it may perhaps be necessary to stimulate her to take so conclusive a stand as that would be of making a recommendation, at the next Session of her Legislature. The impartiality of her position, as it regards me; her superior numbers to what any other Western State contains & other considerations would seem to justify her in coming out at that period. I submit to yourself and other friends in your vicinity the propriety of pressing this matter on those Citizens of Ohio with whom you may have intercourse. *After* Ohio shall have manifested her wishes Tennessee, Kentucky[5] and other Western States might usefully imitate her example.

As to Pennsylvania[6] I have strong reasons to believe that her decision will be ultimately favorable to me. It was generally admitted, when I was there, that she would lend her support to either the Secretary of War [John C. Calhoun] or me; and I feel strongly persuaded that the effort, which is making to attach that State to his interests, will be found unavailing. It would be very erroneous to draw any conclusion from what you see in the Papers of that state, the articles which they contain, on that subject, being the productions of a few, often the same person, manufactured for the special purpose of looming. The attempt for him, I believe, is founded on no adequate basis, and will ultimately explode.

I am still considering whether I shall be a Candidate for the next Congress. I have many friends abroad and at home who think I ought to do so.[7]

ALS. Courtesy of Earl M. Ratzer, Highland Park, Ill.   1. See 3:192-95; also Clay to Beatty, April 16, 1822.   2. See 3:194-95.   3. See 3:193, 195; also Clay to Brodhead, Jan. 17, 1821.   4. See 3:341.   5. The Tennessee legislature recommended Jackson. See 3:274. For Kentucky's nomination of Clay, see 3:301.   6. Benton to Clay, April 9, 1822.   7. See 3:274.

From Langdon Cheves, Cincinnati, May 30, 1822. States that "You are generally acquainted with the circumstances of the large debt due to the Bank U States, contracted at the late office at Cincinnati, by the late John H Piatt of that place." Notes that "the debt is secured by mortgage of property supposed to be equal in value to the amount of the debt." Sends a copy of the mortgage and a copy of the proposition of Piatt's administrator to the bank and requests Clay's opinion [Clay to Jones, June 19, 1822].

Details "some of the doubts and objections which occur to us on the subject." Asks if administrators in Ohio have "any authority over the real Estate or can they acquire any *as* administrators"; also, who are Piatt's heirs since he left a widow but no children; "will not the creditors always have a claim on the Equity of Redemption until the foreclosure . . . & if the Bank were to sell the property without such foreclosure could it make a good title & be Safe in giving the usual covenants for good Title & warranty?" Understands that the wife "has renounced her Dower," and wonders "has she then any claim to one third of the income of the property for five years as proposed?" Feels the "Bank is suposed to be indulgent but it has no authority to be generous with the property of the Stockholder." Further, "What are the rights of the Bank as to the rents & income of mortgaged property?" Wants to know "what time will it take . . . and what will be the ordinary expenses thereof." Notes that Piatt's estate now owes the bank $40,000 and by May 1, 1823, "there will be due about $100,000 on account of principal and Interest."

Turns next to "other concerns of the Agency, at Cincinnati." Asks that in regard to pending lawsuits Clay "will give any instructions to Mr. [George W.] Jones . . . which you may deem useful & calculated to obtain judgments in as many cases as possible in September next." Has asked Jones to send Clay copies of laws passed at the last session of the Ohio legislature which concern "the operation and effect of Judgments and Executions." Wants Clay "to communicate to him as soon as may be necessary duly to protect the Interests of the Bank." Adds that "our liens generally may require your superintending care and advice what ought the Agent to do in relation to mortgages, Judgments & executions, respectively?" ALS. OCHP. This letter is indicated as "Not found" in 3:233, note 1.

For Piatt's estate, as well as Clay's answer to this letter, see 3:228-34; see also Clay to Jones, June 19, 1822.

On June 19, 1822, George W. Jones wrote Clay from Cincinnati saying that he had received a copy of Cheves's letter to Clay of May 30. Sends "By the present Mail . . . in pamphlet form [not found] the Laws of this State made by the Legislature at its last sitting [Clay to Creighton, April, 12, 1822, no. 1 of date]." Wants "your Advice and Instructions on the effect of any of those Laws touching the interest of the Bank."

Mentions "some debts in Indiana" and asks for the name of an attorney he can engage to collect them. Asks what to do in cases "where the Drawer of a Note is out of the State and the Endorser is in this or any other State."

Refers to "the agreement you entered into with Messrs. [Charles S.] Todd and [Thomas D.] Carneal," and reports that "To avoid the unpleasantness of a Suit in this case I receded from the determination of not adopting a reference to others for *the value of the property* to be taken in discharge . . . of debt." States that he had "formerly clearly understood" that Carneal "held the title to the property under his Controul to save himself from the danger of loss on account of that debt and at the same time remarked that he could divert it to other claims . . . which I felt disposed to doubt [Clay to Jones & Crittenden, December 22, 1821]."

Concludes with a reference to "Several debts . . . in Kentucky," and says he is thinking of turning over "those in the neighborhood of this place" to Thomas T. Crittenden "unless the whole can be more conveniently taken [under] your direction." ALS. OCHP.

To GEORGE W. JONES
Lexington, June 19, 1822

Inclosed I transmit to you a Copy of a letter which I have written to Mr. [Langdon] Cheves[1] in reply to one which I received from him,[2] and of which you have been also furnished with a Copy. The written notice, advised in that letter to be given to the tenants in possession of the property mortgaged to the Bank by the late Mr [John H.] Piatt,[3] I would recommend you immediately to give, forbidding them to pay rents accrued or accruing on that property, to his representatives. If after they receive such notice, they should nevertheless make payment of the rents to those representatives, the payment will be in their own wrong, and they will be compellable again to make it to the Bank. If there be a compromise this notice will do no harm; and if the compromise be defeated, we shall then experience the advantage of the notice. Inclosed I transmit a form of notice to be used, and it should be delivered by some person who will be able hereafter to prove it if necessary. From the nature of your arrangement with the Bank, you will be objected to as an incompetent witness, and in all cases, therefore, where it may become necessary to resort to witnesses, you had better engage some person to whom that objection will not apply.

I have not received one line from you respecting the provisional agreement which I entered into with Col. Charles Todd and Mr. [Thomas D.] Carneal,[4] although information might have been very material, if the Cause had been reached at the late term of the Federal Court. Col Todd may be considered as insolvent, at least nothing at present can be co-erced out of him. If the agreement should not be ratified (about which I repeat I have not the slightest personal sensibility) it is important that I should know what proof can be furnished at Cincinnati to charge Mr. Carneal as indorser.

You are apprized of the solicitude which the Bank feels to have their Causes in the Federal Court at Columbus tried at the approaching term. I unite my entreaties to theirs that you and your Solicitor will omit no step whatever to ensure a full preparation for the trials.

ALS. OCHP. 1. See 3:228-34. 2. Cheves to Clay, May 30, 1822. 3. John H. Piatt—Cincinnati lawyer, banker, and businessman—had died in 1822 in prison for debts he had acquired while providing supplies to the Army during the War of 1812. Although Congress passed an act in 1820 for the relief of Piatt from the debt of $46,112.56 and another in 1824 to pay his estate $63,620.48, the U.S. Supreme Court ruled in the case of *Piatt's Administrator (Grandin)* v. *United States* in 1874 that the government owed the estate an additional $131,508.90, but they did not add the interest due from 1820-74. 89 *U.S. Reports*, Wallace, 22:496-513. Shaffer, *Piatt's Landing Eastbend*, 17-21; Charles G. Miller, *Donn Piatt: His Work and His Ways* (Cincinnati, 1893), 16-18. See also 3:228-34. 4. Clay to Jones & Crittenden, Dec. 22, 1821; Cheves to Clay, May 30, 1822.

To GEORGE W. JONES   Lexington, July 5, 1822

Your letter of the 19h. Ulto.[1] having arrived here during my absence from home, the delay in answering it is owing to that circumstance. Previously to the receipt of it, I had transmitted to you a copy of my answer[2] to the letter of the 30h. of May from the President of the Bank of the U.S.[3] which I presume you duly received. In that answer I spoke of the effect of the act of the last Session (winter) of the Ohio Legislature upon the recovery of debts in that State.[4] I do not know that I can add any thing further at present to what I have there said. But I shall, at all times, take particular satisfaction in giving you any aid or advice in my power to promote the interests of the B. of the U.S. and I pray you to apply to me, with the most perfect freedom, from time to time, as you may have occasion to consult me.

In regard to the debts due to the institution in Indiana, for the collection of which you request me to recommend some attorney, I would propose David Hart Esq.[5] of Vincennes, who has transacted some business very satisfactorily for me, and of whom I have heard otherwise a good report. I should think that you had better advise him to commence the suits which it may be necessary to bring in the Federal Court, to which tribunal I know the Bank wishes in all cases at once to appeal, rather than to the State Courts. In cases of notes executed in Ohio where the drawer is out of the State, and the indorser in it, or vice versa, I think two actions may be carried on at the same time against both of them, and that you are not bound to bring successive suits, first exhausting the property of the drawer. In the event of the recovery of two judgments you would not be entitled to double satisfaction; but upon obtaining the amount in either you would have to abstain from enforcing the other. The provision of the Law of Ohio, which required the Clerk to certify which of the defendants is principal debtor and which are the suretior or bail, and directs him to first issue execution against the principal, applies I think only to *joint* judgments; and not to cases where, from the different residences of the parties, you are bound to proceed against them separately.

I observe what you state with respect to the provisional agreement which I entered into with Mess [Charles S.] Todd & [Thomas D.] Carneal.[6] I made that agreement because, upon the state of the fact as it appeared to me, a recovery against Mr. Carneal was extremely doubtful, and I was inclined to think the law strictly was against us, that is supposing the notice to him to have been sent to the P. office at Cincinnati, without his instructions, special or general. If he had given directions that notices to him should be sent to that post office, I should have thought otherwise. In making the agreement, as you were aware, I did not intend to compromit you; but on the contrary it was my intention to leave you perfectly free to ratify or reject the agreement, and particularly if the state of fact were different from what I understood it to be, and was such as to entitle us to recover. I was aware that Mr. Carneal held the title to the property at Louisville as an indemnity, but if he were not otherwise responsible, I did not think that that fact could make him so further than for the value of the property. I was perfectly persuaded, as I am yet, that nothing can be coerced out of Col. Todd. Under this view of the subject it was that I made that provisional arrangement, which I should be sorry was the occasion of any loss to the Bank. Whatever honorable obligations Mr. Carneal may have been under, I distinctly understood that he intended to question before the Court his responsibility upon the ground of want of legal notice of the protest. I think the rule which you have adopted of submitting property to the valuation of others as seldom as possible a very good one.

It is probable that the debts in your immediate neighbourhood due from persons residing within this State can be best taken care of by Mr. [Thomas T.] Crittenden. I should be glad that you would avail yourself of his professional services whenever you can, as I think he has some claims upon the institution. If there be any cases however which are likely to be much litigated, I think they had better be brought in the Federal Court.

I have not received the pamphlet which you had the goodness to send me; but it is not material as I expect to be in Ohio in a short time. I propose passing by Cincinnati to see you, if in my power.

ALS. OCHP.   1. Cheves to Clay, May 30, 1822.   2. See 3:228-34; Clay to Jones, June 19, 1822.   3. Cheves to Clay, May 30, 1822.   4. See 3:232, 234; Clay to Creighton, April 12, 1822, no. 1 of date.   5. See 3:135.   6. Clay to Jones & Crittenden, Dec. 22, 1821.

To GEORGE W. JONES   Lexington, July 6, 1822

I duly received your letter of the 29h. June.[1] The notice given to the tenants of the property mortgaged by the late Mr [John H.] Piatt,[2] I advised lest the compromise should fail, about which the parties are treating. If, upon the termination of any lease, or upon a tenant quitting the demised premises, a tenant should be willing to take possession under and a loan from the Bank, I have no doubt this may be lawfully done, provided there is no resort to force. I think however, you had better take no step of this kind 'till you hear from the Bank, after my letter is received. Should the compromise be broken off, it was my intention that we should commence proceedings to the next term of the Fed. Court both for the purpose of foreclosing the mortgage, and of recovering from the tenants in possession the rents and profits &c. Should there be any change of tenants, you had better give the same notice to the new ones. I suppose they will generally refuse payment of the rents to both parties until the question is settled between them. If any of them should be disposed to make payment to the Bank, upon being indemnified for so doing, such indemnity might be given.

If Mr. [Nicholas] Longworth[3] is right in supposing that we cannot foreclose until the last instalment is due, and that in the mean time the representatives of Mr. Piatt are entitled to the possession and the accruing rents,[4] then indeed we ought to pause before we decline accepting the terms offered, or even others more unfavorable. But I think he is laboring under error. The law of Ohio which authorizes a foreclosure by Scire facias,[5] may not permit that to be done until the last instalment of a debt is due. But that law furnishes a cumulative remedy, without repealing the old one. And if it did repeal the old one, the repealing law would not probably operate in the Federal Courts. By the old remedy, there can be no doubt of our right to foreclose, upon the non-payment of any part of the debt; and that the Court of Equity will direct, from time to time, sales of the mortgaged Estate, as the instalments successively fall due.

With respect to any other Estate of Mr Piatts not mortgaged if the Admon apply it, in a course of administration, contrary to law, they will be liable under these office bonds. They are not bound as you seem to suppose, to make a saleable distribution of his effects, but, among creditors of equal dignity, may prefer one or more to the others.

I will thank you to have made out for me a full transcript of the record and judgment in the case of Genl. [William] Lytle.[6] You ought

114

to take particular care that the lien, created by that judgment, is not impaired and for this purpose to prosecute executions in due time. The prosecution of these is necessary also to enable you to go into other Counties where he may have property. Without losing the benefit of the lien already existing in our favor, I have thought of bringing an action in the Federal Court to obtain a judgment there which would probably bind his property throughout the State[.]

My idea of the compensation proposed to Mr. [William M.] Worthington was that it covered all services rendered by him as Solicitor, and that he was freely to render these. I think he ought to be satisfied with what was proposed, but if he is not, and will not attend to the business, we must get some body else. I have not yet seen him, nor do I know in what part of the State he is. The objection you state to his brother will be conclusive.

ALS. OCHP. 1. Not found. 2. Clay to Jones, June 19, 1822. 3. For Longworth —lawyer, horticulturist, and one of Cincinnati's wealthiest men—see *DAB*. 4. On Sept. 2, 1822, Clay, as counsel for the bank, served notice on Nicholas Longworth, Benjamin M. Piatt, and Philip Grandin, administrators of John H. Piatt, and on Piatt's heirs "that on the Sixth day of the present September Term" of the U.S. Circuit Court for the District of Ohio "we shall move the said Court . . . for an injunction to restrain you from proceeding to Collect any Rents . . . upon the property Mortgaged by the said John H. Piatt . . . and also for the appointment of a Receiver of all such Rents." D. OCHP. The "bill and exhibit" for this suit, in Clay's hand and dated Sept. 4, 1822, is in *ibid*. 5. A writ of statutory origin used both as an original writ to obtain a judgment where none has before existed and as a writ of execution or continuation of a judgment previously entered. The term applies not only to a certain writ, but also to the action or proceeding instituted under the writ. 6. Clay to Wickliffe, March 12, 1818; Clay to Lytle, July 2, 1818.

From THOMAS HART BENTON
Nashville, July 12, [1822][1]

I came here on the 7th. Mrs. [Elizabeth McDougal] Benton came with me to Abingdon [Va.], from which point she returned.

In Virginia,[2] and in this State,[3] the Presidential election was the constant theme. In the former yourself and Mr. [William H.] Crawford have the chief favor; in this state it seems clear that your interest is decidedly the best.

A new aspirant is expected to be disclosed here in the person of Gnl. [Andrew] Jackson. It is generally believed that he will be *caucussed* for at the general assembly which sits on the 22d. ins[tant].[4] It seems that [Felix] Grundy[5] is to manage that affair. This will surprise you, but I have it from a man of honor in this town, that Grundy himself told him so; and some of our friends, to whom I have mentioned it, say it is just what they would expect. His deportment seems to be suspicious, for he has abstained from making any declarations to me, altho I have given him many opportunities. He is in fact vehemently suspected by all our friends here, notwithstanding the voluntary pledges which they know that he has made.—How the *caucus* will go is matter of speculation; but the better opinion is, that, if the thing is pushed, a majority will recommend him.

I find your interest stronger in the state than I had expected. Many that I had not counted upon, have made warm professions to me. Gov. [William] Carroll[6] will be active and efficient. He and I have been enemies, growing out of my affair with Jackson;[7] but, "the times have changed, and we change with them." Mutual friends have proposed and effected peaceful terms for the future, without reference to what is past.

Col. [John] Williams will have opposition, got up, it is supposed by the influence of Genl. Jackson. Mr. W[illia]m. Blount is to oppose him; lately in the H[ouse]. of R[epresentatives]. a man of no force, and who will say *yea* and *nay* according to the impulsion of those who make him.[8]

Great efforts will be made to arrange a district that will not elect [Newton] Cannon to the next congress. If that object is accomplished it is probable that a young man, Genl. [Sam] Houston, formerly a Lieut. in my regt. will be elected.[9] He is now and always has been greatly attached to me. Mr. [George W.] Campbell[10] is not doing any thing, and it i[s] thought that his influence will be nothing at all in any question with the people.

ALS. KyU.   1. Although the year is not given, internal evidence indicates this letter was written in 1822, just before the Tennessee legislature endorsed Jackson for president. See 3:265.   2. For Virginia's vote in the 1824 presidential election, see Clay to Creighton, April 12, 1822, no. 2 of date.   3. For Tennessee's vote in 1824, see Clay to Meigs, August 21, 1822.   4. Actually, the Tennessee house endorsed Jackson on July 20 and the senate followed suit on August 3. See 3:265.   5. For Grundy, see 1:172 and *DAB*.   6. For Carroll, see 3:157.   7. See 1:820.   8. For Blount, governor of Tennessee from 1809-15 and subsequently a congressman, see *BDAC*.   9. Clay to Meigs, August 21, 1822.   10. For Campbell, see 1:878 and *BDAC*.

From THOMAS HART BENTON   St. Louis, August 1, 1822

Yours of the 15 ult.[1] arrived by the last mail. Major [Richard] Graham[2] had set out one or two days before to Fort Osage, 300 miles up the Missouri, to wind up the Factory establishment at that place, and is not expected to return under a month or more. I will apply to him as soon as he gets back, and if he declines payment, I think it may be enforced as the undertaking appears to be personal and absolute.

I had anticipated your suggestion with respect to *my* correspondence with Mr. [Jonathan] R[ussell]. Seeing that the whole was coming out before I left Washington, I have since taken no step, and shall not. The people here are for R. and [John Quincy] Adams' letter only enrages them.[3]

I wrote you from Nashville, on my way through Ten[nessee]. about the 12th. ult.[4] giving you the result of my observations in that state, and which I think may be relied upon to the whole extent stated.

In this State my most sanguine expectations are exceeded by the accounts which I daily receive. The leading men, and the body of the people, are both for you, the latter so decidedly that it is believed any prominent man would only hurt himself by going against you. Gov. [Alexander] McNair[5] authorizes me to assure you of his zealous support. I apprehended opposition from a party heretofore opposed to *me,* but several of the best of them have assured me of their support let who will come against you.—It is a rule with me, when I have succeded against any opposition, to break its force by conciliating the best.—In Illinois you have doubtless have [*sic*] friends, both among the body of

116

the people and the leaders, and from their position they must come into the western system. [Joseph] Phillips and Brown [*sic*, Thomas C. Browne] are the leading candidates for Gov.[6] both western men; McLane [*sic*, John McLean] is pressing [David P.] Cook closely,[7] and [John] Reynolds opposes [Jesse B.] Thomas for the Senate.[8] These are also western men. Mr. [John] Scott is opposed here by Judges [Alexander] Stuart and [Jean B.C.] Lucas.[9] The former declares publicly for you; the latter is governed exclusively by his own inherent wickedness and no calculations can be made about him. The re-election of Mr. S. is h[ow]ever considered certain.

My affectionate remembrance to Mrs. [Lucretia Hart] Clay and family, and believe me truly yours.

ALS. KyU. 1. Not found. 2. For Graham, see 5:427. 3. See 3:204. 4. Benton to Clay, July 12, 1822. 5. For McNair (1775-1826), the first governor of Missouri, see *BDGUS*, 2:837. 6. In the 1822 gubernatorial race in Illinois, Edward Coles was elected with 3,854 votes over Joseph Phillips, who won 2,687 votes, and Thomas C. Browne, who won 2,443. *BDGUS*, 1:366. 7. Cook, incumbent Illinois congressman, won reelection to the House over John McLean (not to be confused with John McLean of Ohio). For McLean and Cook, see *BDAC*. 8. Jesse B. Thomas, incumbent senator from Illinois, defeated John Reynolds. *BDAC*. For Thomas, see 2:775-76. 9. John Scott [2:579], incumbent congressman from Missouri, won reelection over Alexander Stuart and Jean Baptiste Charles Lucas [6:1127; *DAB*]. For Stuart, who became a circuit court judge in St. Louis in 1823, see Howard L. Conrad, *Encyclopedia of the History of Missouri*, 6 vols. (New York, 1901), 6:117.

To RETURN JONATHAN MEIGS[1]   Lexington, August 21, 1822
You will have heard of the recommendation of Genl. [Andrew] Jackson for the Presidency.[2] That measure has been produced by the following causes, and possibly others. 1st It has been prompted by persons to the Eastward, friendly to other Candidates, to produce divisions in the West. 2dly. It has been adopted to affect the local elections within the State of Ohio, and particularly those of Senator [John] Williams, Genl. Cock [*sic*, John Cocke], and Col. [Newton] Cannon,[3] who are unfriendly to Jackson. And 3dly. It has been concurred in by many members of the Legislature, as a compliment due from his own State to the Genl., which it was expected he would decline. What course he will adopt is unknown and is uncertain. Whatever combination of motives may have produced the recommendation, its first effect will be unfavorable to the success of the West, as indicating a division, where unity and cordial co-operation were anticipated. How is this injurious effect to be counteracted? Will it not be best to do it, by similar manifestations of public sentiment made through other Legislative Assemblies in my favor? And ought not this to be done during the next fall and winter Sessions? If (as all my information leads me to believe) the other Western States will unite in supporting me, no ill effect can result from the movements of Tennessee. For it will then be seen to the Eastward that there is no other division in the West than that of Tennessee on the one side, and *all* the West, on the other. And when this is demonstrated there is reason to believe that Tennessee herself (if even serious in recommending the General) would not longer persist in a vain and hopeless object. But this development of Western sentiment ought to be early made, so as to prevent compromitments to the Eastward, whilst

117

an *apparent* and, as it may be supposed there, an extensive division exists among us here. If, in this view of the subject, I am right would it not be most expedient that Ohio, the great State of the West, should *early* in the next Session of her Legislature, declare her sentiments?[4] Will you, my dear Sir, turn this matter over in your mind, and let me have your full sentiments addressed to me at Columbus, for which place I start the day after tomorrow.

My information, from all parts of your State, testifies that there is a decided majority among you in favor of me; and some of my friends tell me that the measure of a Legislative recommendation of me has been already thought & talked of. This must have been before they knew or even suspected what has occurred in Tennessee. That event appears to me to increase very greatly the force of the considerations which unite in favor of a Legislative Nomination of me—

My information from Louisiana; from Mississippi; from Missouri; from Indiana & Illinois; and even from Tennessee itself, continues to be in a very high degree encouraging.[5] I do not speak of the East because you are probably as well informed, as it respects that quarter, as I am.[6]

ALS. InU. Letter marked "(Confidential)." 1. For Meigs, see 1:724 and *BDAC*. This letter is indicated as "Not found" in 3:282, note 1. 2. By Tennessee. See 3:264-65. 3. In 1823, Tennessee Senator John Williams was defeated for reelection by Andrew Jackson. Congressman John Cocke of Tennessee was reelected, while Congressman Newton Cannon was defeated by Sam Houston. *BDAC*. See also 3:265, 460, 492. 4. See 3:341. 5. In Louisiana, presidential electors were chosen by the legislature in 1824, and Jackson won 3 electoral votes there to 2 for Adams. In Mississippi, Jackson won 3,234 popular votes to 1,694 for Adams and 119 for Crawford, with Jackson receiving all 3 of the state's electoral votes. In Missouri, Clay won 1,401 popular votes to 987 for Jackson and 311 for Adams, with Clay receiving all 3 electoral votes. Jackson won 20,197 popular votes in Tennessee to 312 for Crawford and 216 for Adams, with Jackson receiving all 11 electoral votes. Schlesinger, *History of American Presidential Elections*, 1:409. For the vote of Illinois and Indiana in 1824, see Clay to Creighton, April 12, 1822, no. 2 of date. For the 1825 presidential election in the U.S. House, see Benton to Clay, April 9, 1822. 6. This letter is answered in 3:282.

To GEORGE W. JONES   Lexington, October 7, 1822

There has been delay in answering your letter of the 21st. Ulto.,[1] which I duly received; with its inclosures, in consequence of a severe attack of fever, from which I am just recovering.

I still think that a Circular, or general notice in the news papers, addressed to the debtors of the Bank against whom Judgments were recently recovered at Columbus, requesting them to come forward and make satisfactory arrangements with you, might do good, and could not possibly be harmful. The Bank is not strictly bound to give any such notice; but it would afford further evidence of that spirit of forbearance and moderation, which has constantly characterized its conduct, and of which it is well enough to continue to entitle itself to the credit. Whether the notice be given or omitted, if the debtors do not come forward to make & actually make with you satisfactory arrangements, I think there can exist no motive for longer delay in ordering executions against all the negligent, and I advise you to direct the Clerk to issue executions and put them into the hands of the Marshall accordingly.

In respect to the case of Mr. [Hugh] Glenn I concur with you in thinking that he had better be taken in execution at the suit of the Bank.[2] You will therefore direct the Clerk to issue CaSas'[3] against him and deliver them to the Marshall, apprizing him that the defendant is now in custody. I would send the order to the Clerk from this place, but it will reach him as soon to issue from you; and circumstances may have arisen, since the date of your letter, to affect the question. It will be the duty of the Marshall to apply to the District Judge in regard to a place of confinement, if the use of the State Jails is denied to him.[4]

If the Mess Breckinridges of Indiana[5] have property liable to the Foreign attachment in Ohio, undoubtedly it will be better to resort to that process there rather than sue them in Indiana.

Will you be pleased to forward to the Bank at Philadelphia a Copy of the agreement which you entered into, under my advice, with the Adm[inistrat]or[s] of John H. Piatt?[6]

Be pleased to apprize me of the appointment of a Solicitor, when it takes place. In the mean time, and at all times, I shall be happy to offer you any advice that you may require, and which is in my power to give.

ALS. OCHP. 1. Not found. 2. Clay to Worth, Nov. 27, 1820. 3. Ca. Sa. is an abbreviation for capias ad satisfaceiendum, a writ for the arrest and imprisonment of a judgment debtor until the claim against him shall be satisfied or otherwise discharged according to law. 4. For the Ohio law denying the use of its jails to the B.U.S., see 3:61, 63. 5. Not identified. 6. Clay to Jones, June 19, 1822.

To WILLIAM MEREDITH[1]   Lexington, October 8, 1822

Your letter under date the 12h. Aug.[2] reached this place whilst I was attending the Fed. Court at Columbus in Ohio, and followed me thither. On my return home, I had an opportunity of seeing Majr. [John] Brown (who resides at Maysville) the surviving partner of Brown and [David] Bell.[3] He says that the account of Hawthorn and Kerr[4] against Brown and Bell (which I presume is the one you allude to) was paid by him many years ago part to Mr. James Brown, and part to a Mr. Drake, I think upon the order of Mr. Brown[.]

I believe Majr. Brown to be mistaken in this statement, as I am quite sure that Mr. James Brown cannot have recd. the money since he left this Country in 1804 for Louisiana. And if he had received it prior to that time, he would not have put the papers in my hands. You may have an opportunity of ascertaining from himself, during the approaching Session of Congress, if Majr. Brown's statem[en]t. be correct, and in that event I am persuaded he will instantly pay over any money in his hands.

There has been great delay in this business, which I regret extremely. It has been chiefly owing to the fact that Majr. Brown has not resided within the jurisdiction of any Court in which I practiced. I thought the a/c had been sent to some local Atto[rny]. in his neighbourhood, but I believe I was mistaken.

From the interest which has accrued upon the a/c, in consequence of the great lapse of time, the Fed. Court would not have jurisdiction of the case. And in that Court I will bring suit, if it be deemed necessary, after you hear from Mr. Brown. In that case, it will be necessary to prove the a/c. Can that be done? It is sworn to, I observe, by Mr. Hawthorn, but his affidavit would not be evidence in this State.

ALS. NN.   1. For Meredith, see 3:275.   2. See 3:274-75.   3. For John Brown and David Bell, see 3:275.   4. Not identified.

From George Gibson, Office of Commissary General of Subsistence, Washington, October 22, 1822. Writes that John Viley of Scott County, Ky., "has bid for the important contract at Council Bluffs, and has made reference to you." Wants to know "your opinion of his ability to fulfil this contract," because "It is of the utmost importance that the contract for Council Bluffs should be given to a responsible, capable and active man, as its fulfilment will require the exercise of much enterprise, industry, talent & Capital." Copy. DNA, RG192, Office of Commissary General of Subsistence, vol. 3, p. 148. See also Gibson to Clay, July 14, 1821.

Viley was probably the father of John M. Viley (b. 1823) of Georgetown, Ky. William H. Perrin, *History of Bourbon, Scott, Harrison and Nicholas Counties* (Chicago, 1882), 619.

Fort Atkinson had been built at Council Bluff on the Nebraska side of the Missouri River in 1819. It served as a staging and outfitting area for a number of western explorations. William J. Peterson, *The Story of Iowa*, 4 vols. (New York, 1952), 1:255.

To JOHN SLOANE   Lexington, October 28, 1822

I have duly received your obliging favor of the 16h. inst.[1] from which I regret extremely to learn that it was the indisposition of your family which prevented you from visiting Columbus, where I hoped to have had the pleasure of seeing you, during the late term of the Federal Court. Upon my return from Ohio I was seized with a violent fever, which gave my friends some alarm, and from which I have just recovered. We have had a year of great calamity, whether we regard the number or the standing of the individuals, of whom death has deprived us.

I thank you for the information which you have kindly communicated, respecting the state of public sentiment, in regard to the Presidential election, in the part of Ohio east of the Scioto. (I think I possess accurate knowledge of it in all other parts of the State; and if I do the zeal and unanimity which prevail in my behalf are not surpassed by what exists in this State. Several of my friends assured me, during my attendance on the Federal Court, that there was much reason to believe that the Legislature would, at the ensuing session, announce the wishes of the State, by some public act.[2] The value and importance of such an act I continue to think would be incalculably great. Of that I am assured from all parts. Indeed my opinion is that it would be more decisive of the question than any other one circumstance. It would have great influence in Pennsylvania, in New York, in Virginia, in short throughout the Union.) An intelligent and well informed friend writes me, from New York,[3] that the best effect will be produced in that State[4] from a public declaration of the Legislature of Ohio. That same friend tells me that the National Advocate in that State has been put in motion by [Martin] Van Buren,[5] and that the part it is taking for Mr. [William H.] Crawford has given great and general dissatisfaction among the Republicans.

120

Our Legislature has commenced its Session in this State. I understand that there is a strong and general disposition, among the members, to make some public nomination of me, and that it will certainly be done in the course of the Session.[6] With some of my friends there is a wish to wait to see if Ohio will not take the first step; and if they do not wait it will be because there will not be time, to hear from your Legislature, before our's adjourns.

In your State, the only ground on which some of my friends apprehended that the Legislature might not do any thing, was that they were not aware of any prominent and experienced men who would be returned as members; that young members would be diffident; and that [Thomas] Worthington, the most experienced, was extremely uncertain in his movements. How far those apprehensions are well founded you are the most competent judge. But I should suppose that there could not be wanting influential & experienced members enough to give direction to such an affair. In the Senate, indeed, I know there are Mr. Kelly (sic, Alfred Kelley], if he be friendly inclined, as I understand he is, and Genl. [Allen] Trimble,[7] or either of them, to say nothing of others can have no difficulty in taking the lead on such an occasion.

You enquire about the movement in Tennessee.[8] That resulted from one of all of three causes 1st. As a compliment to Genl. [Andrew] Jackson from his own state—2dly. to affect local elections, those of Senator [John] Williams, Genl. Cock [sic, John Cocke] and Genl [Newton] Cannon particularly,[9] and lastly it was stimulated by some Eastern politicians to produce the appearance of division in the West. From what I have heard I have very little doubt that it will, in the sequel, be abandoned or not pressed by Tennessee. In that event, I do not entertain the smallest doubt that Tennessee will unite her support of me to that of Ohio and the other Western States. Govr. [William] Carroll of Tennessee, after his return to Nashville, from a recent Session of the Legislature of that State, writes[10] me: "Since I last wrote you, I have seen many of our most influential Citizens, from all of whom I learn that you will be unanimously supported in this State, in preference to any other gentleman, Genl. Jackson only excepted. That is the sentiment of our Legislature, and if the name of Genl. Jackson should be withdrawn previous to their next Session, you will be recommended unanimously by that body."

Gov. Robinson [sic, Thomas B. Robertson][11] communicates his belief that Louisiana will support me. And I hear from Mississippi, Alabama, Missouri, Illinois and Indiana the most favorable and encouraging accounts. Indeed, should Ohio take the step which is anticipated, I have not the smallest doubt of a cordial co-operation between all the States from Ohio to the gulph of Mexico.[12]

I think the contest will be between Mr. Crawford and me. Mr. [John Quincy] Adams has obtained a decided advantage over Mr. [Jonathan] Russell, without advancing, in the smallest degree, his interests in the pending election; and any support which he receives will be limited to New England, and even there they will be divided.[13] The support which some of the Southern States will give to Mr. Crawford, principally because they are opposed to internal improvements and to manufactures, and that which he will derive from the Treasury influence in the large Cities, will place him a-head of any of the Cabinet Competitors, and confine in my opinion, the contest to us. I am told that, since Mr. [John C.] Calhoun's prospects are evidently on the decline, there is much movement in Pennsylvania in my behalf; and my friends there are very confident of that State supporting me.[14]

Col. [Richard M.] Johnson has a good prospect of being reelected to the Senate next week.[15] The principal difficulty which he has had to encounter has been that some suspicions were entertained of his zeal on the Presidential election. He has made very explicit declarations, to obviate it, both on paper and by parol.

I shall be glad to hear from you, both from Ohio and Washington City, where I shall have the pleasure I trust of seeing you during the Session of the Supreme Court.

I fear our friend [Levi] Barber[16] has lost his election in your State.

ALS. MH. Letter marked "(Confidential)." 1. See 3:294-95. This letter is the one indicated as "Answer not found" in 3:295. 2. See 3:341. For Ohio's vote in the 1824 presidential election, see Benton to Clay, April 9, 1822. 3. Peter B. Porter. See 3:290-91. 4. For New York's vote in the 1824 presidential election, see Clay to Creighton, April 12, 1822, no. 2 of date. 5. The *National Advocate* was a pro-Bucktail newspaper in New York City, edited by Mordecai M. Noah. For Noah, see 3:291; for Van Buren, see 3:188. 6. See 3:301. 7. For Worthington, see 1:322; for Kelley, see 5:439; for Trimble, see 3:309 and *DAB.* 8. See 3:264-65. 9. Clay to Meigs, August 21, 1822. 10. Letter not found. 11. For Robertson, governor of Louisiana 1820-22, see *BDAC.* 12. For the votes of Louisiana, Mississippi, and Missouri in the 1824 presidential election, see Clay to Meigs, August 21, 1822; for Illinois and Indiana, see Clay to Creighton, April 12, 1822, no 2. of date; for Ohio, see Benton to Clay, April 9, 1822. In Alabama in 1824, 9,443 popular votes were cast for Jackson, 2,416 for Adams, 1,680 for Crawford, and 67 for Clay, with Jackson winning all 5 electoral votes. Schlesinger, *History of American Presidential Elections,* 1:409. 13. For the total popular and electoral votes cast in 1824, see Benton to Clay, April 9, 1822. 14. For Pennsylvania's vote in the 1824 presidential election, see *ibid.* 15. He was reelected. See *BDAC.* 16. See 3:282 and *BDAC.*

To NICHOLAS LONGWORTH　　　　Lexington, November 4, 1822
I recd. your obliging letter of the 27h. Ulto.[1] and thank you for the interest which you kindly took in my recovery from my late indisposition[.]

I shall be greatly indebted to you for the very acceptable present of the fruit trees; and the addition to them of the Citron and Cape Jessamine places both Mrs. [Lucretia Hart] Clay and me under further obligations to you—

I expect to be in Washington late in January, and shall be very glad to meet you there, if your business does not bring you away before that time.

Wishing you great success in the objects which take you to the Eastward[.]

ALS. OCHP. 1. Not found.

From George W. Jones, Office of the Bank of the United States, Cincinnati, November 8, 1822. Reports that since writing on November 2 [not found], "I discovered that the information of the Deputy Marshall having been here was unfounded—I have had a visit from Col. [William] Doherty the Marshall," and "to the business of the Bank his attention is promised." States also that "Mr.

[Harvey D.] Evans has finished a very complete Docket embracing the whole business . . . for which his charge is $50."

Mentions that he has received a note from Hugh Glenn, "dated at Newport [Ky.] requesting to know the amount of his Debt and Endorsements—of which I furnished a Statement of upward 117.000 [Clay to Worth, November 27, 1820]." Notes that Glenn is called to Frankfort on business and that he says "he is still anxious to make an arrangement." Suggests that "should he not reach Frankfort before you proceed against him, it may perhaps be proper for the Marshall to visit Newport."

Reports that the "case of Genl. [William] Lytle . . . is on the Docket [Clay to Wickliffe, March 12, 1818]—Is the case of [Evans] Dozier & [Charles] Thornton in your hands [Clay to Crittenden & Worth, November 3, 1821]?" Refers to a debt of some $7,000 owed to the bank by Jacob Fowler [Clay to Worth & Crittenden, November 15, 1820]. Explains that "A mortgage was given by Jacob Fowler on lands in Boone County," and he has since heard that there is "some difficulty as to title," to the land, which is described in the mortgage as the farm on which Chasteen Scott resides. Adds that "the attention of Counsel may therefore be necessary to protect the interest of the Bank."

Asks Clay to inquire from Thomas D. Carneal about the difficulty involving "the tract received by Mr. [Thomas] Wilson from Mr. Carneal [Clay to Jones, November 21, 1822]." ALS. OCHP.

For Doherty, see 3:156; for Dozier, see Myrtice C. Kraft, *Campbell County Kentucky Marriages, 1795-1840* (n.p., 1961), 14. For the Dozier and Thornton case, involving $200 in debt and $500 damages, see U.S. Circuit Court (7th Circuit), Complete record, Book S, May term, continued 1822, Reel 1540, Box 19. For Evans, see 3:504.

To GEORGE W. JONES   Frankfort, November 19, 1822

Your two letters, under the dates of the 2d.[1] and 8h.[2] instant, addressed to me at Lexington, have followed me to this place, where I am attending the Federal Court, and I have just received both of them, with the transcript of the record inclosed in the latter. I will in a few days write you at large upon their contents. At present I address you merely to remind you that, according to the arrangement which we entered into with [John H.] Piatts adm[inistrat]ors,[3] at Columbus, they were to answer our bill in Chancery and also the heirs, *provided we furnished them with a copy of it a certain number of days (I think thirty) before the next Court;* and to request your particular attention to a compliance with that condition.

I am like yourself without any letters of business from the Bank of the U.S. (except one short letter) since I parted with you at Columbus.

ALS. OCHP.   1. Not found.   2. Jones to Clay, Nov. 8, 1822.   3. Clay to Jones, June 19, 1822; see also 3:233-34, 415.

To NICHOLAS LONGWORTH   Lexington, November 20, 1822

I received your obliging letter of the 4h. instant[1] and tender you many thanks for the fruit trees &c. which you have sent me, and of which a bit is contained in your letter. The continued rains which have prevailed so much this fall have affected very much our roads, & I have not received the trees yet from Louisville, but I do not doubt that they will come safely.

I have examined the deed executed by Mr. [John H.] Piatt, and the acknowledgment of Mrs. [Martha A.] Piatt, since I received your letter.[2] It appears to me that the acknowledgment is sufficient under the act of Ohio of February 1820.[3] It is true that it is rather in the form which is observed when it is intended to convey the Estate of the wife in fee. But it is nevertheless substantially agreeably to that act. And if it were not a deed possessing all the requisites of a conveyance of a greater Estate it would be good to pass a life Estate. This is my opinion; but if gentlemen of the Bar in this differ from me, this diversity of opinion furnishes an additional motive for compromise.

I would write to the Bank again on the subject of receiving Real Estate; but I have so often communicated to them my sentiments that I doubt whether any letter from me at this time would have any good effect.

Wishing you an agreeable & successful trip . . .

ALS. Courtesy of Henry C. Thacher, Lexington, Ky.   1. Not found, but see Clay to Longworth, Nov. 4, 1822.   2. See 3:228-34; Cheves to Clay, May 30, 1822; Clay to Jones, June 19 and July 6, 1822.   3. Clay to Worth & Crittenden, July 6, 1821.

To WILLIAM CREIGHTON, JR.   Lexington, November 21, 1822

I recd your obliging favor of the 8h inst.[1] and am greatly indebted to you for its interesting contents.

The General Assembly of this State took the occasion of an informal meeting of the members of both houses, on the 18h. inst. to confer about Comm[issione]rs to be appointed under the recent Convention with Va.,[2] to recommend a suitable person as President. One hundred & five members (out of 138 composing the whole body) attended, and they did me the honor unanimously to recommend me. Of the absentees some were sick, some out of town, a few opposed to caucusing &c. &c. I understand a general solicitude was felt that Ohio should have first acted;[3] but if any expression of public opinion were to be made here it was found altogether impracticable to wait for your Legislature, as they talk of adjourning here in a week or two. And it was generally agreed that some public declaration of their wishes should be made in the course of this Session. I am told that their proceedings are judicious and unassuming. I hope my friends with you will see all this, in a proper light, and without any disapprobation.

Among the many reasons which give to Legislative caucus's a decided preference over one at Washington, since the Secretaries are considered of course Candidates[4] ought not a private Citizen, who is not surrounded by official parade, patronage &c. to be brought out, if his name be offered at all, by such respectable portions of the Community as State Legislatures?

Jacob Burnett [sic, Burnet] of your State, and Hugh L. White of Tennessee were appointed Commissioners.[5] No other gentlemen were proposed. Mr [John] Rowan is associated with me as Agents to attend the Board &c.[6]

I am very much pleased to find that your business will carry you to Columbus during the first of the Session; and I shall look with much anxiety for a letter from you from that place.

124

My health continues good. Hoping that of yourself and family is perfectly re-established.

ALS. KyU. Letter marked "(Confidential)." 1. Not found. 2. See 3:215-18, 326. 3. A committee from the Kentucky legislature, composed of William T. Barry, John Rowan, J. Cabell Breckinridge, B. W. Patton, Richard C. Anderson, Jr., John J. Crittenden, and George Robertson, wrote to the Ohio legislature in Nov., 1822, to explain why they had proceeded in their recommendation of Clay for president and to ask Ohio "to act in unison with Kentucky." DS. OCLWHi. 4. Reference is to the desires of Cabinet members John Quincy Adams (State), William H. Crawford (Treas.), and John C. Calhoun (War) to be elected president in 1824. 5. They had been appointed to a claims commission set up under the Adams-Onis Treaty. For Burnet, see 3:289 and *DAB;* for White, see 3:326 and *DAB.* 6. For Rowan and his involvement in this matter, see 1:178; 3:326.

To GEORGE W. JONES   Lexington, November 21, 1822

I proceed now to reply to your two letters of the 2d. and 8h. inst.[1] more fully than I could do from Frankfort.

I have ordered a Writ against [Hugh] Glenn with instructions to the Marshall to use his best exertions to serve it, and hold him to bail.[2] I cannot learn that he has been to Frankfort or intends coming there. He has a suit with the Government which may possibly bring him. I do not understand from your letter how he obtained his release from his confinement in Cincinnati, whether it was for want of the CaSa, or after the service of the CaSa.

In cases where Judgments are obtained and mortgages are held, as the mortgaged property cannot be sold, in virtue of the judg[men]t. (at least it being very doubtful it is not prudent to do so) it will be best to urge the proceedings as fast as may be practicable on the mortgage, and in cases where the rents may be an object to notify the tenants not to pay them to the mortgagor as was done in [John H.] Piatts case.[3] There must be a number of mortgages on which it is necessary for you to proceed, and as the Court is near at hand what will you do, if no Solicitor is appointed? If I had them here I could prepare the bills in Chancery on them; for I prefer the bill in Chancery to the Scire facias, which indeed we cannot use, in cases where there are any instalments not yet accrued. If you do not hear of the appointment of a Solicitor by the Bank had you not better engage Mr. [Thomas T.] Crittenden contingently or absolutely?

I concur substantially with you about the expediency of the Bank taking from their debtors, in many instances, real Estate; in other words taking from them that alone which they have to give. If the Bank had an option; if the reception of real estate were only an accommodation to the debtor, the question would assume a different aspect. It is in vain to attempt to extract from a debtor what he has not got, or more than he has got. I have presented these views to the Board through Mr. [Langdon] Cheves frequently. I would do it again, if I thought it would have any effect. It is possible that I shall visit Philada in the Spring, and in that case more can be accomplished by personal explanations than by letter. I think I should receive the house, offered you at $5500 or $5000 and which you say can be rented at $450 per annum for five years, in payment; unless you can consult the Bank before it is necessary to complete the arrangement.

I think you are laboring under some mistake in regard to mortgages. The law of Ohio requiring property to command two thirds of its value does not apply to the foreclosure of mortgage by bill in Ch[ancer]y. It was so decided in Ohio at the last Sept. term in a cause in which I was concerned; and it has been so decided, on an analogous law in this State, in the Federal Court at Frankfort. When a mortgage is foreclosed and the Estate is sold, there [no] longer exists any right of redemption, and the debtor becomes entitled to a credit against his debt for the nett amount for which the property sold, and the purchaser acquires a right in absolute fee to the Estate. To recur again to the subject of mortgages; I yet think, as I told you when I had the pleasure of seeing you, that where the mortgaged property constitutes all that the Bank can rely upon or is likely ultimately to obtain, there does not appear to me to be any adequate motive for forbearing to proceed to foreclose the mortgages; and that in such cases it will be better for you to proceed accordingly on the falling due of the first instalment forthwith. Where the debt is undoubtedly safe, or where it is probably safe, and the debtor appears to manifest, by his exertions, a disposition to pay it, indulgence may be given.

I think Mr. [Harvey D.] Evans's charge for the docket reasonable.[4] It is less by half than was paid here for one not so large. I would advise the advance to him of a proportion of his fees. The practice in Ohio is not to pay the fees until the Judgment; but as a large number of Judgments were obtained at the last term, and others may be procured at the next, it is well to keep the officers in a good disposition, since they have much in their power, to accommodate you or not. I shall have occasion to write you from Frankfort respecting the actions brought agt. [Thomas D.] Carneal & Piatt, and I will then inform you of the condition of the debt agt. [Evans] Dozier & [Charles] Thornton, which I believe I had the direction of.[5]

I have made some enquiries concerning the title of Jacob Fowler[6] to the Land which he mortgaged to the Bank and although they have not been entirely full as yet, there is much reason to apprehend difficulty about it. I will endeavor to prosecute them still further. That debt I am afraid is in great hazard. Can you not proceed to enforce the mortgage? that is, is no part of the debt due? If it be, I am persuaded you had better act upon it.

I have seen and conversed with Carneal about Pennell's bottom. He states that there is a tax claim of about 300 Acres (one half only of which affects his moiety) which he mentioned to Mr. [Thomas] Wilson, prior to his conveying the Land to the Bank;[7] that the sale for taxes was not valid; that he has a suit pending against the purchaser, or his tenant, in the local Court; and that the contract with Mr. Wilson has a provision for the contingency of the establishment of the Tax claim. If the Bank has a deed from Carneal for the whole tract sold by him to it, including his Proportion of the tax claim, I rather think that it would be better to bring an Ejectment against the persons asserting it in the Federal Court at Frankfort—

126

Mr. Carneal says that there is no impediment to effecting a division of the land with Genl. [James] Taylor—I shall See him probably in a short time, and will sound him on the subject.

I think the instruction given by you to the Marshall to levy the executions on Whites Farms conveyed to his Son in law was perfectly proper. I would advise, that they be sold, and purchased by the Bank. We will then bring Ejectments to obtain the possession. If a suit in Chancery should be necessary it will be time enough to bring it after I see you, which I hope to do on my way to Columbus.

The delay in hearing from Philadelphia is much to be regretted. I presume it results from the intention of Mr. Cheves to retire, and his being engrossed with more important objects.

ALS. OCHP. 1. Jones to Clay, Nov. 8, 1822; that of Nov. 2 has not been found. 2. Clay to Worth, Nov. 27, 1820; Clay to Jones, Oct. 7, 1822. 3. Clay to Jones, June 19, 1822. 4. Jones to Clay, Nov. 8, 1822. 5. Clay to Jones & Crittenden, Dec. 22, 1821; Clay to Jones, June 19, 1822; Jones to Clay, Nov. 8, 1822. 6. Clay to Worth & Crittenden, Nov. 15, 1820. 7. Jones to Clay, Nov. 8, 1822.

To GEORGE W. JONES   Frankfort, December 11, 1822

I brought a suit for the Bank in the Federal Court of this State against [Evans] Dozier and [Charles] Thornton upon a small note of $200.[1] It abated as to Dozier by his death. Judgment was recovered at the last May term against Thornton, and upon the execution which issued against him the Marshall has returned No Estate. I fear the debt is lost. Has Dozier any administrator or Exor, and is it worth pursuing them?

Inclose[d] I transmit dedimus's to take depositions in the suits brought against [Thomas D.] Carneal & [John H.] Piatt upon the notes which you gave me.[2] It is necessary to prove notice &c. If it were put into the Post office for Carneal, it will be necessary to shew by proof to what office it was directed; and then it may be needful to take the deposition of the Post Master, whose name I do not know, and therefore the dedimus's only authorize the taking of [Griffen] Yeatman's[3] deposition. On this subject I will converse with you when I shall have the pleasure of seeing you.

ALS. OCHP. 1. Jones to Clay, Nov. 8, 1822. 2. Clay to Jones & Crittenden, Dec. 22, 1821; Clay to Jones, June 19, 1822. 3. For Griffen Yeatman, owner of Yeatman's Tavern and a notary public who served as city recorder for Cincinnati, see Charles T. Greve, *Centennial History of Cincinnati and Representative Citizens*, 2 vols. (Chicago, 1904), 1:529-30, 534; Lewis A. Leonard (ed.), *Greater Cincinnati and Its People, A History*, 4 vols. (New York, 1927), 2:390.

To RICHARD C. ANDERSON, JR.   Lexington,
December 16, 1822

I transmit you the inclosed letter from [Philemon] Beecher,[1] the contents of which will be, I have no doubt, particularly satisfactory to you. I send it because, should you be able (as I trust you may be) to take the trip of which we spoke, it may be there useful. I accompany it by a letter from Mr. Hanson[2] giving me some information about Vermont, which I think may be relied on. Capt. [Samuel] Breck,[3] the gentleman ment[ione]d. by Mr. Hanson, is a person of great respectability from N.

England. It accords with what I had reason to believe were the dispositions of Mr. Mallory [*sic,* Rollin C. Mallary],[4] the most popular representative from that State.

ALS. CSmH.   1. For Beecher, see 3:872 and *BDAC.*   2. Letter not found. Possibly Samuel Hanson. See 3:132, 346.   3. For Breck, see 3:549.   4. For Mallary, see 3:53 and *BDAC.*

To Edward Coles, Edwardsville, Ill., December 20, 1822. Introduces "my friend" B. Reed McIlvaine of Lexington, "one of our most respectable and intelligent Citizens" who is visiting Illinois on business.

States: "I avail myself of this opportunity to offer you my hearty congratulations upon the occasion of your recent election." ALS. NjP.

Coles, a Democratic-Republican, had been elected governor of Illinois on August 5, 1822, by a vote of 3,854 to 2,687 for Joseph Phillips and 2,443 for Thomas C. Browne, both of whom also were Democratic-Republicans. His inauguration was held on December 5, 1822. *BDGUS,* 1:366. For McIlvaine, see 2:787.

To RICHARD C. ANDERSON, JR.   Lexington,
December 25, 1822

I owe to the confidence I have in your friendship and discretion the transmission to you of the inclosed letters.[1] You will perceive, from their perusal, that the result which they announce is not in accordance with our hopes, nor with the opinion of Genl. [Philemon] Beecher contained in his letter to me, which I heretofore forwarded to you.[2] But for that, and other similar communications, it does not however surprize me. On the contrary, they inform me of what I had previously feared and anticipated. Taking the whole of the information together it is, I think, far from being discouraging. It rather demonstrates my strength. For it shews that with a combination against me of the whole force of *all* my competition, aided by the times, by those prejudiced against caucusing, and by intrigue, I failed in getting a nomination only by two or three voices; and that there is yet a strong probability of such a nomination being made during the present Session of the Legislature of Ohio.[3]

The effect which I most deprecate is that which is likely to be produced by this event on the Indiana and Illinois Legislatures.[4] If notwithstanding what has occurred those Legislatures (and most particularly Indiana) shall concur in a nomination, I shall have the more reason to place a high estimate upon it, and upon the exertions of my friends who contribute to produce it.

I leave here on saturday. Let me hear from *you* at Washn. And in all events & in every contingency consider me most . . . P. S. Give my best respects, if you go to Indiana, to Govr. [William] Hendricks,[5] in whom I have the highest confidence[.]

ALS. CSmH.   1. Enclosures not found.   2. Beecher letter not found, but see Anderson to Clay, Dec. 16, 1822.   3. See 3:341 and Clay to Creighton, April 12, 1822, no. 2 of date.   4. Neither Indiana nor Illinois endorsed Clay. See 3:551-53 and Schlesinger, *History of American Presidential Elections,* 1:363.   5. For Hendricks, Indiana governor 1822-25, see 3:518 and *DAB.*

To JOHN SLOANE   Lexington, December 27, 1822

I recd. only by the last mail your obliging favor of the 4h. instant.[1] The events at Columbus will have reached you ere this. Considering the combination of circumstances to prevent a nomination, the result has not surprized me.[2] Nor is it discouraging. It proves incontestibly what you and other friends have constantly told me that Ohio will be favorably disposed towards me. From what I learn I think it not improbable that a nomination will yet be made during the Session of the Legislature.[3] If the information which shall be received from Washn. should satisfy some gentlemen from the reserve that their favorite in New York will not be run I think such a nomination will certainly take place—[4] Be the event what it may I am very thankful to yourself and other friends for your kind exertions.

I leave here tomorrow for Washn via Columbus, where I do not apprehend I shall be long detained. Expecting therefore shortly the pleasure of seeing you, and offering you the compliments of the season . . .

ALS. MH.   1. Not found.   2. See 3:341.   3. It did not.   4. DeWitt Clinton was their favorite candidate. The information from Washington was in letters intended to convince the Ohio legislature that Clinton was not going to be a candidate. See 3:331, 340-41; also Clay to Este, Jan. 22, 1824.

To Nicholas Longworth *et al.,* Cincinnati, Ohio, January 1, 1823. As counsel for the Bank of the United States, notifies the administrators and heirs of John H. Piatt [Clay to Jones, June 19, 1822] "that on the fourth day of the approaching January term (1823) of the Circuit Court of the U. States for the District of Ohio we shall move the said Court by our Counsel for an injunction to restrain you from proceeding to collect any rents now due or which shall hereafter accrue upon the property mortgaged by the said John H. Piatt to us on the 13h. day of October 1820 and also for the appointment of a Receiver of all such rents." ADS. OCHP.

To RICHARD C. ANDERSON, JR.   Columbus, Ohio,
                                                    January 5, 1823

I arrived here this day. The day before yesterday another meeting of the members of the Ohio Legislature to the number of 90 took place (the total number of the whole body is 103).[1] It was determined to proceed to a nomination; thirty three declined voting. Of the 57 who did vote 50 were for *me,* 5 for [DeWitt] Clinton, 1 for [John C.] Calhoun and 1 for [John Quincy] Adams. The thirty three composed those who from timidity or from prejudices against caucusing, were opposed to any nomination. In fact, I am *well assured* that a majority of that thirty three, almost amounting to entire unanimity were in my favor. I hasten to give you the above intelligence. It happened extremely well that the event took place prior to my arrival.

P.S. The communication from the Kentucky Com[mitt]ee of correspondence was well recd. here.[2]

ALS. CSmH.   1. See 3:351.   2. Clay to Creighton, Nov. 21, 1822.

From Nicholas Biddle, February 4, 1823. Reports receiving "Your letter of the 28th ulto [3:354-55]," and discussing "the cause between the Bank & the State of Ohio" with the bank's board of directors. States that the directors have instructed him "to inform you that such is the respect with which your opinions are habitually regarded, that they would not hesitate to incur any additional expence which you might recommend . . . even tho' the early misfortunes of the Bank impose on them the duty of practising the utmost" economy; yet since his suggestion that they might want to hire a second attorney was "rather for the Bank than for yourself," they assure him they believe he can make a "most ample vindication of its rights . . . against the counsel over whom you have already triumphed, or against any combination which may be brought against you." Concludes: "The Board therefore consider that they have confided the interests of the institution to one abundantly able to defend them," and "will remain entirely satisfied that nothing will be lost from any failure of zeal or ability in their distinguished counsel." ALS. NjR.

For Biddle, the new B.U.S. president, see 3:348-49 and *DAB*.

To BENJAMIN WATKINS LEIGH[1]

Washington,
February 4, 1823

I duly received your obliging favor of the 2d. instant.[2] I had no doubt that the omission to answer my two letters,[3] addressed to you subsequent to that in which I inclosed you my report to the Kentucky Legislature,[4] did not proceed from the want of those friendly feelings of regard which I felt must be cherished for me on your side, as I know they were retained on mine. Indeed they did not require nor did I expect any particular notice of them from you. I should, immediately after my arrival here, have written you, but that, whilst the Kentucky question was pending at Richmond[5] I felt an unwillingness to hold any communication with friends there from causes which every honorable man must justly appreciate. These causes I presume have now ceased, by the most unexpected expression of the pleasure of the Senate of Virginia: For although a strange enquiry was made of me the other day, through Mr. [James] Barbour[6] of the Senate, at the instance of Genl [Henry St. George] Tucker, I apprehend that there is not any serious intention to preserve in the amicable effort to produce, by means of a friendly tribunal organized by the two parties, an accommodation between the two States. That enquiry was whether Mr. [John] Rowan and I would be willing to proceed with the Board here without the clause of guarranty.[7] I gave to it, without seeing Mr. Rowan, the only answer which it could receive that is, that I could not recognize in Genl Tucker any other than a distinguished member of a deliberative Assembly composed of upwards of 220 gentlemen; that whenever *that* Assembly would make a proposition it would be received and treated with all possible respect; and that there was no equality in the condition of Genl Tucker and ourselves. I need not say to you that Mr. Rowan, on being informed of the enquiry made of me and of my answer promptly approved of it.

The issue of our joint labors in your Senate is most extraordinary; and such as must be condemned by all of the impartial world who choose to look into the matter. Opinions to that effect have been expressed here to me by gentlemen from other States, in language so strong that I will not even repeat it. You declined the propositions which Mr. [George M.] Bibb and I made you.[8] It was not very friendly to reject at least that which proposed a reference. You know my sentiments on that head; and I have almost the dying words of Judge [Spencer] Roane, an illustrious but at the some time a haughty and high-minded Virginian, in coincidence with them. We did not ask you, after rejecting our overtures, to institute any fresh ones of your own. You voluntarily chose to open a negotiation. How we received you, my dear Sir, I will not say; but I will say that our reception of you was all that veneration for Virginia, and a high opinion of her representative could make it. I was appointed to treat with you; and whilst I firmly believe that neither sought to obtain over the other any advantage, I do think that, if there were any inequality, it was to our prejudice. In regard to the clause of guarranty what is it but a stipulation by the agent that his constituent shall abide by his acts? That the tribunal to be organized shall not be a solemn mockery? It was a necessary accessory to your powers, and fairly comprehended in their spirit, if not expressed in their language. If Virginia committed any error, it was not in what her Commissioners did, but in what she authorized; not in what occurred at Lexington, but in that which originated at Richmond. And when good faith between States shall be at an end; & when there is no longer identity in the individual existence of a Commonwealth, but a succeeding Legislature shall hold itself free to absolve itself from the engagements which its immediate predecessor has fairly controuled or authorized with another people, and not 'till then, will a justification be found for the recent vote of the Senate of Virginia.[9] Such are my sentiments and the whole world may know them.

But I confess to you I was not prepared for the addition of the insult which has been offered with the injury which has been done to Kentucky. I was not prepared to hear the base and false insinuation against her good faith and fair dealing, which I am shocked to learn has been made, in the selection of Commissioners. No State; nor private gentleman ever acted with more scrupulous delicacy in the choice of an umpire to settle any question than was observed by Kentucky. She would have scorned to choose any one who she knew had formed an opinion in her favor; and I know that gentlemen, in the course of the consideration of the subject, were put aside, although no opinions were known to have been formed by them, upon the mere possibility that, from their residence amongst us, they might have contracted a bias in our favor.

I am unapprized and indifferent as to the course which is meant now to be pursued by those councils which have produced the rejection of the guarranty.[10] They may be disposed, without the aid of their new ally, the Supreme Court, to seize upon the Lands below the Tennessee. If such be their pleasure, let them come and take them. The Land at least will make no resistance. And if the people upon it or near it should happen to exhibit, upon the occasion, some little spirit, in the maintenance of what they believe to be their rights, it will be a misfortune resulting from the blood descended to them from their ancestors.

For you, my dear Sir, in all the turns of affairs; for your manly, frank and honorable deportment whilst amongst us; for the zeal & fidelity with which you urged the just pretentions of your own State; and for the kindness with which I understand you have always spoken of ours, I pray you to believe that we shall all long cherish the most lively and friendly recollections. In the failure of the experiment which was made to preserve unimpaired the antient friendship which existed between our two States, you have nothing to reproach yourself. And it belongs to those who have occasioned that failure, as statesmen, now to bring forward their measures to vindicate the rights of Virginia, as Virginia understands those rights. And I venture to say that at this moment they feel the inextricable embarrassments of the position which they have taken.

P.S. If it will not give you any trouble, I should esteem it a particular favor if you would desire Mr. [William] Mumford,[11] the Clerk of the H. Of Delegates to send me a Certificate of the day on which the May Session 1779 of your Legislature, and every other Session to that of the fall 1785 inclusive, terminated. Did you try our cause in the Federal Court for Ephraim [*sic*]?[12]

ALS. CU.   1. For Leigh, see 2:727 and *DAB*.   2. Not found.   3. Probably those of Nov. 18 and 21, 1822. See 3:326-27. This letter is the one indicated as "Not found" in 3:378, note 1.   4. See 3:304-5.   5. For the conflict between Kentucky and Virginia concerning the Virginia act of 1789, which allowed Kentucky to become a state, see 3:215-18, 301-4, 377-78, 390, and Clay to Unknown Recipient, Feb. 26, 1822. 6. For James Barbour, see 2:320 and *DAB*.   7. Clay to Creighton, Nov. 21, 1822. 8. See espec. 3:207-8.   9. See 3:378.   10. See *ibid.* and 3:390.   11. See 3:159.   12. The estate "Euphraim" left by Clay's father. See 2:726-27; 3:320, 378, 551, 801, 897, 900.

To George Bomford, Chief of Ordnance, Washington, February 27, 1823. Sends samples of gunpowder made by "Some neighbours of mine," and reports that "They are desirous to contract for the delivery of a quantity of the article" to the government. Asks whether or not any is "wanted or likely to be shortly for the public service?" ALS. DNA, RG156, Records of the Office of Chief of Ordnance, Letters Received.

On March 5, 1823, Lieut. Col. George Bomford replied from the Ordnance Office that there "is now in the public magazines, a full supply of gun powder" and that "no appropriations, for an additional supply have been made or requested for some years past." Notes that one of the samples sent "was partly lost, by the breaking of the bottle which contained it—the two remaining samples, have been proved." Copy. DNA, RG156, Ordnance Office, Misc. Letters Sent, vol. 8, 1820-23.

For Bomford, see 4:736 and *DAB*.

To DAVID JENNINGS[1]   Washington, February 27, 1823

The interest which you kindly take, in my behalf, in regard to the next Presidency, induced you to express a wish at Columbus that I would write to you. I now comply with the promise which I made you on that occasion. Standing as I do in a relation to the public, which subjects me perhaps to much erroneous information, I have to make many allowances in what I receive. Making however very liberal ones, I think I may say that my prospects are highly encouraging, and not surpassed, if they are equalled, by those of either of the other gentlemen.[2] I am indebted for this favorable state of things, in a great degree, to the recent Western demonstrations and particularly that made at

Columbus.[3] I have the most undoubted assurances of receiving the undivided support of Louisiana; and I think there is no doubt of the co-operation of the nine Western and South Western States.[4] From New York,[5] Pennsylvania[6] & Virginia[7] our intelligence authorizes the belief that there is a rapid increase in the strength of our cause. It is however not probable that either of those States will indicate by any unambiguous act, its preference before next winter. Upon the whole, there is every ground to entertain high hopes, and no occasion for the least despair. The members & other gentlemen from your quarter will I am persuaded confirm to you this view of things.

ALS. KyU.   1. For Jennings, see 3:872 and *BDAC.*   2. William H. Crawford and John Quincy Adams.   3. See 3:351.   4. For the election of 1824, see Benton to Clay, April 9, 1822.   5. For New York's vote in 1824, see Clay to Creighton, April 12, 1822, no. 2 of date.   6. For Pennsylvania's vote in 1824, see Benton to Clay, April 9, 1822.   7. For Virginia's vote in 1824, see Clay to Creighton, April 12, 1822, no. 2 of date.

To BENJAMIN WATKINS LEIGH   Washington, March 6, 1823
I duly received your obliging favor of the first instant[1] covering a copy of the Resolution of Virginia, to be communicated to Kentucky, in respect to the convention which we concluded between the two States. I thank you for the opportunity which you have thus given me of perusing the final act of your Legislature on that subject, and which I presume has been transmitted by your Governor to the Executive of Kentucky.[2]

You will have seen the fate of our Occupying claimant laws before the Supreme Court.[3] The manner of the decision has been as unhappy as the decision itself will be unsatisfactory. It was communicated as the opinion of three judges to one. Those three were [Bushrod] Washington, Duval [*sic*, Gabriel Duvall] & [Joseph] Story, Judge [William] Johnson being the dissentient.[4] Thus a minority of the Court, Judge Washington acting as its organ, (and after all that has recently occurred will not many of the people of Kentucky be disposed to regard him, however erroneously, as a sort of party to the controversy?) pronounces a judgment, which has the most tremendous effects of any ever delivered by a judicial tribunal. Judge [Brockholst] Livingston[5] gave no opinion, being indisposed. Although there has been doubtless great delay in the cause, as there was no reason for accelerating the decision of the particular case, it being in fact compromised, I was in hopes that the Court would have seized the circumstance of Judge Livingstons illness as affording a reason for postponing the decision.

We shall make, I fear, an unavailing effort to get it reheard or suspended. Had the Court defered it until the next term, it might not have been impracticable perhaps to have prevailed upon Kentucky to waive insisting upon the guarranty! Though I strongly suspect, my dear Sir, from a conversation which I have recently had with Mr. [Edwin S.] Duncan[6] of your Senate, that the guarranty was only a pretext, with the majority of that body, for rejecting the Conventions. If the maintenance of our quieting laws be hopeless I need not tell you that the General Assembly of Kentucky would not be prevailed upon to submit to a Board of Commissioners the question merely of your warrants.

I shall take my departure from this City in a few days, and beg you to believe that I shall carry back with me the sentiments of the highest esteem & regard for you which have been inspired by your conduct throughout the whole course of the unfortunate business between our two states.

ALS. ViRVal.   1. See 3:390.   2. For Gov. James Pleasants of Virginia, see *BDGUS*, 4:1633-34. For Gov. John Adair of Kentucky, see *BDGUS*, 2:512-13. See also 3:215-18, 378.   3. In the case of *Green v. Biddle*. See 3:91, 208-9, 392-93.   4. For Washington, see 1:278 and *DAB;* for Duvall, 1:575; for Johnson, 1:280-81 and *DAB*.   5. For Livingston, see 1:643.   6. For Duncan, see 3:641-42.

To LUCAS ELMENDORF   Washington, March 8, 1823

I have this moment received your own letter of the 2d. Inst. and one from Mr. [Lucas] Brodhead of the 19h. Ulto.[1]

Your cause argued at the last term is not yet decided. It has been mentioned to the Judges informally (the only way that it could be decorously done) both by Mr. [Isham] Talbot[2] and me. The Chief Justice [John Marshall] told me that he was anxious to have Judge [Thomas] Todd present, and also to see if the Court of Appeals in Kentucky would not settle the question, between their conflicting decisions, about an entry dependent upon a previous survey. I stated to him that you were very anxious for a decision, and that I thought there was enough in the record to support your entry, without determining that contested point. He said that he was about to look into the record to see if that could be done; and I will again remind him of your wishes.

There is not the remotest prospect of getting the adjourned question from Kentucky, which has recently come up, decided at this term, which will probably close this day week. I shall inform Mr. Brodhead accordingly.

Virginia did not ratify the Convention with K[entucky]. and the Supreme Court persists in its opinion against the validity of our Occupying claimant laws.[3]

ALS. KyU.   1. Neither letter has been found, but see Clay to Brodhead, Jan. 17, 1821.   2. For Talbot, see 1:121.   3. Clay to Leigh, Feb. 4 and March 6, 1823.

To Whom It May Concern, March 17, 1823. Attests that "I have known for some years the bearer hereof Mr. [John James] Audubon, a naturalized citizen of the United States, as an ingenuous, worthy and highly respectable gentleman" who "resided several years in . . . Kentucky and has been engaged for some time past in exercising his fine talent for painting on objects connected with the natural history of the U. States." Notes that Audubon is going to Europe "to avail himself of the artists and opportunities of that quarter, in executing some of his sketches and designs, so as to give them a wider diffusion," and recommends him "to the good offices and kind reception of the American ministers, consuls and public agents abroad, and to the hospitality and good treatment of all other persons." Copy. Printed in Alice Ford (ed.), *The 1826 Journal of John James Audubon* (Norman, Okla., 1967), 377.

To MIGUEL SANTA MARIA[1]   Washington, March 20, 1823

I received the letter which you did me the favor to address to me from Mexico in September last,[2] through Mr. [William] Taylor[3] the American Consul at La Vera Cruz; as I have since received the correspondence[4] which you did me the honor to transmit to me in regard to the circumstances which led to your retirement from Mexico.

You do me only justice in supposing that I continue to take the liveliest interest in all that concerns the welfare, reputation and glory of the new Governments lately established on this Continent. My first and greatest wish was for their Independence on [sic, of] Spain. My next is that their institutions shall be so formed as to secure the greatest quantum of practical liberty, believing such free institutions to be best adapted to the promotion of the intelligence the dignity and the happiness of the greatest number of our species. Nevertheless, the respective forms of your Constitutions present interesting considerations solely for the several communities for which they are proposed, with which Foreigners have nothing to do but to rejoice when they resolve wisely, and to grieve when they behold any of them led astray by the glare and ridiculous pageantry of Monarchies in all their modifications. The late events in Mexico have given me infinite regret. [Agustin de] Iturbide has sacrificed immortality for a giddy hour.[5] He might have entitled himself to be enrolled with the great deliverers of their country in the old world; with the [George] Washingtons and the [Simon] Bolivars of the new. As it is if he preserves his head and his throne from the perils which menace both, he will be classed, by the impartial historian, among the vulgar herd of licentious military chieftains and unprincipled usurpers, and be considered as one who has surrendered the laudable ambition of perpetuating the happiness of millions of his fellow beings for the vicious indulgence of his criminal passions; who has prostrated a whole people that he might elevate a contemptible thing, called an Emperor.

As far as I have been able to judge of your own affair at Mexico, I think you have been ill treated. But you must have left without reluctance a scene which you could not have witnessed without disgust.

Mr. [Richard C.] Anderson [Jr.] who will deliver you this letter, lately appointed Minister from the U. States to Colombia is among the most highly esteemed of our fellow Citizens, has been the steady friend of South America,[6] and a particular friend of . . .

ALS. CSmH.   1. For Santa Maria, the Colombian minister to the U.S., see 4:444. 2. Not found.   3. For Taylor, see 4:188.   4. Not found.   5. For Iturbide, see 3:207. On May 19, 1822, Iturbide had induced a section of the Mexican Congress to elect him emperor. Langer, *Encyclopedia of World History*, 843.   6. See 3:335.

To CHARLES S. TODD   Washington, March 20, 1823
I received your favor under date the 2d. of Decr. last[1] at the City of Merida; and heard with great pleasure through that and other channels of your progress prosperity and cordial reception. We have now just learnt that you have safely arrived at Bogota.[2]

Mr. [Richard C.] Anderson [Jr.], appointed Minister to Colombia, will convey to you all the news relating to public affairs and to what concerns myself in particular. We had hoped that in the arrangement of the South American missions something better would have been done for you than has been; but you know how those matters are disposed of here. What will you do? I suppose return.[3]

Your father's [Thomas Todd] health was not good when I left K[entucky]. about Xmas. He could not attend the Supreme Court. But I hope you will hear from him through Mr Anderson more favorable accounts, as well as good information from your own family.

Col. [Isaac] Shelby is busily engaged in making preparations to repel the attack of [William C.] Preston, in regard to the conduct of Col. [William] Campbell at the battle of Kings mountain; and I am gratified to tell you that he will I think completely vindicate himself & make good all that he has said.[4]

Our friend Col. [James] Morrison[5] is now with me at this place, I fear upon his last legs. His long and perilous indisposition has been the cause of my detention here.

I shall return in a few days.

With my best wishes for your success and happiness & safe return to N America[.]

ALS. IGK. 1. Not found. 2. See 3:247. 3. See 3:413-15. 4. At the Revolutionary War Battle of King's Mountain, fought on Oct. 7, 1780, William Campbell, Issac Shelby, and John Sevier had all been colonels of equal rank, but Campbell had received most of the credit for the victory because he had been the designated officer-of-the-day. Also, Shelby and Sevier had fought on the front lines of the battle but believed Campbell had stayed in the rear to avoid the fighting. On July 1, 1822, Seiver's son published in the Nashville *Gazette* four letters between his father and Shelby, written from 1810-12, in which they discussed Campbell's actions. William C. Preston, Campbell's grandson and later a U.S. senator from South Carolina, responded in late 1822 with a defense of his grandfather which was published in several papers. Shelby replied in a pamphlet, "Battle of King's Mountain," published in April, 1823. For this controversy, see Lyman C. Draper, *King's Mountain and It's Heroes* (New York, 1881; reprint ed., 1971), 558-91. For William C. Preston and Col. William Campbell, see *DAB*. For Sevier, later governor of Tennessee, see 1:123. 5. For Morrison, see 1:87; for his death, see 3:409-10.

To BENJAMIN WARFIELD[1]   Frankfort, Ky., May 15, 1823

I recd. your letter of the 9h. instant[2] with the transcript in the case of Samuel vs Monson.[3] I think damages and costs ought to have been awarded and I have therefore filed the record.

I cannot interfere to indulge Mr. Samuel[4] further for the reason assigned by you that I am an assignee. I will take Commonwealth's paper at its value in the market. The debt does not belong to me. No indorsement must be made. If a seizure of property is made & a sale advertized I will thank you to take care of my interests or to apprize me of the day of sale the property to be sold & the valuation of it & probability of sale.

I thank you for your kind wishes and enquiries respecting the Presidential election. All that I need say in this letter and until I see you is that, judging from such information as I possess, I believe my prospects superior to those of any of the other gentlemen.[5]

Give my respects to Col. Brown.

ALS. KyU. 1. For Warfield, see 1:304-5. For his reply, see 3:425-26. This letter is one of the two indicated as not found in 3:426, note 2. 2. Not found. 3. This case has not been found. Monson was possibly either Samuel or Thomas Monson of Nicholas County, Ky. Ronald V. Jackson *et. al.* (eds.), *Kentucky 1820 Census Index* (Bountiful, Utah, 1976). 4. Not identified, but see 3:426. 5. For the 1824 presidential election, see Benton to Clay, April 9, 1822.

To GEORGE W. JONES   Lexington, May 16, 1823

I have received from Mr. [Nicholas] Biddle, President of the Bank of the U. States, a letter under date the 3d. instant,[1] accompanied by two letters to you of the same date, embracing various instructions relative to the interests of the Bank confided to your care. He requests me to make to you any suggestions, in regard to the subject matter of those instructions, which may appear likely to be useful, and then to transmit the letters to you, with those suggestions. It is, therefore, in compliance with his request that I now address you.

The instructions furnish a further proof of the liberality of the Board. They relate to points on which we have so fully and frequently conversed, and are in themselves so explicit that I do not know that it is necessary for me to communicate to you any particular observations upon them. But there are one or two circumstances on which I will take the liberty of making a few remarks.

We were both much shocked with the nature and sensible of the possible extent of the evil which first began to exhibit itself, I believe, last fall, by which a change of the property of debtors of the Bank was attempting, through the means of sales for taxes due the State or the Corporation. This fraud may be attempted as well in cases where the Bank holds a lien upon the property as in those in which it has no lien, specific or general. It is more important, if possible, to arrest in the threshhold the evil, because of the very great difficulty there would be in establishing to the satisfaction of the Courts of justice, the fraudulent intent of the sale, in cases where all the requisites of the law had been observed in making it. With respect to property in and about Cincinnati I should suppose that, by a proper understanding with the officers charged with the Collection of the State and City revenue, there could be no difficulty in your ascertaining, time enough to prevent any prejudice to the Bank, the property of most of its debtors that was likely to be sold. As to sales for taxes,

1st. In cases where the Bank holds a mortgage or any other specific lien. I can have no doubt that it has a right, in all such cases, to purchase in the property when sold for taxes; and I think it is better to buy rather than to prevent the sale by the voluntary payment of the tax. By purchasing, if it be of the whole mortgaged property, the title of the Bank is at once consummated, without foreclosure of the mortgage. Even if the sale for taxes should be hereafter deemed invalid, for either irregularity or want of power on the part of the Bank to buy, I think it would nevertheless have the same lien upon the property, for the reimbursement of the tax, as originally the State or City respectively had, at whose instance it was sold. By purchasing at the sale the Bank will add to its old lien the new title which it acquires, and the one may serve, in various ways, to fortify and strengthen the other.

2. With respect to sales of the property of debtors of the Bank, where it has no specific lien, created by deed, or actual levy of an execution, I think the Bank would have no right to purchase, under the charter. Still you will at once perceive the utility of keeping a vigilant eye upon all such cases. And you might yourself or where your attendance was impracticable, you could get some one to attend

the sale, and, by bidding for the property, prevent its fraudulent sacrifice.

Other fraudulent conveyances, on the part of some of the debtors of the Bank, have been, and no doubt will continue to be practised. In regard to these, where the fraud is manifest or susceptible of easy proof, it would be well, if we have a judgment, to proceed to sell the property by execution, totally disregarding the fraudulent conveyance of it. If the proof of the fraud is difficult, or if the case is doubtful or complicated, or if there is no judgment on the part of the Bank, we had better proceed by bill in equity. It follows, that each case must depend upon its own peculiar circumstances. I have already informed you in person and need not repeat that I shall, at all times, be ready promptly to advise you, upon being informed of any particular case.

I have perused the form of a contract for building which accompanies one of Mr. Biddles letters. It appears to me to be well adapted to its purpose. The point, I apprehend, of most difficulty in cases of those building contracts, will be that of the fidelity with which the work is executed. To secure yourself as much as possible against slighted or slovenly work, you should retain much power in your own hands. That object is perhaps sufficiently accomplished by the third article in the project of an agreement. It would be also advisable expressly to guard against a failure, in the fulfillment of the contract, by a stipulation, that unless the building should be completed in the manner and by the time mentioned and agreed upon, the debtor is not to be credited any thing for what may be done.

The Mechanics, who erect a building, have no lien, by the *laws* of Ohio, for their labor upon it, but if they had the draft of a contract which has been prepared at Philadelphia would guard effectually against the assertion of such a lien.

I have not received the depositions which you were to have taken in the cases of [John H.] Piatt and [Thomas D.] Carneal[2] &c. I fear, for the want of them, or of some other proof of notice in regard to the notes of Canby[3] and Gray,[4] I shall be unable to obtain Judgments at the present term of the Circuit Court of the U States for the Kentucky District.

As I shall have occasion soon to address you again I will now only add that I remain . . .

ALS. OCHP. 1. Not found. 2. Clay to Jones, June 19, 1822; Clay to Jones & Crittenden, Dec. 22, 1821. 3. Probably Dr. Israel T. Canby of Boone County, Ky., and later of Indiana. In 1817 Canby had married the daughter of Robert Piatt, and in 1820 they sold 810 acres of land to Thomas D. Carneal. Shaffer, *Piatt's Landing Eastbend*, 22-28. 4. Possibly John T. Gray of Jefferson County, Ky., whose debt to the B.U.S. amounted to $1,244. U.S. Circuit Court (7th Circuit), Reel #1539-40, Complete record, Book R, May term, 1822, Box 18.

To NICHOLAS BIDDLE Lexington, May 18, 1823

I duly received your favor of the 3d. instant[1] with two letters of instruction &c. for Mr. [George W.] Jones, the agent of the Bank at Cincinnati, which I have deliberately perused. I have forwarded them on to Mr. Jones, accompanied by a letter from myself,[2] of which a copy is inclosed herein.

Supposing it to be impracticable that a Commission could be organized at Philada., to consist of directors of the Board, or others possessing its entire confidence, to repair to Cincinnati, and there by personal observation and enquiry to enable themselves to determine in each case of a debtor to the Bank desirous to compound &c., I think the next best scheme has been devised in the letters which you have forwarded for my examination. In respect to the subject of improvements, they convey a large power to Mr. Jones. If there were (I believe there is not any) disposition on his part towards abuse, what security have you against his admitting debtors who are perfectly solid paying off their debts by ameliorations? Or against allowing for improvements what greatly exceeds their value? I should think that you ought to require from him frequent reports of cases which he has permitted to be brought within the range of these powers. That there are many instances in regard to your Western debtors, and particularly at Cincinnati, of whom you had better take payment in almost any thing you can get, is but too true. And I cannot but think very favorably of property at Cincinnati.

I do not know that it is necessary to add to what I have written to Mr. Jones any thing in respect to sales for taxes of real property. The general principle of the Laws of all the States, as far as I have been able to obtain information of them, is that the lien of the Commonwealth for the taxes accrued & accruing is paramount to every other lien created upon the land. Supposing therefore a sale to be effected for taxes, in conformity to the provisions of any of those laws, it must vest in the purchaser a perfect title, according to the sale, that is if it be for the whole tract, of the whole tract; if for a part, of that part. The sale operates so as to extinguish any previous incumbrance. If the purchase, at the sale, be made by a previous incumbrancer, it operates then cumulatively, that is it adds to the pre existing title of the incumbrancer. In any case the actual purchaser at a tax Sale has only to pay the amount of the tax due & costs of Sale.

The Copy of the arrangement with Mr. [John H.] Piatt, that is with Mr. [Nicholas] Longworth as his representative, which you state to be inclosed in your letter was not there.[3] I presume it was left out by mistake in folding up the letter to me—I shall afford, with great pleasure, any co-operation in my power to the execution of that arrangement, as I shall with like pleasure render any other services in my power to the Bank and which you may command.

ALS. MH.   1. Not found.   2. Clay to Jones, May 16, 1823.   3. Clay to Jones, June 19, 1822.

From Nicholas Longworth, Lexington, M[ay] 20, [1823]. Reports that the day he left Cincinnati, he called twice on George Jones "to learn if he wish[e]d to write," and that he promised "to bring one . . . before I started" but did not do so. In respect to the law of descents which "I understood you had written to him" about, states that "the Ordinance of Congress regulating descents was in force at the time of D[aniel] Conners death." Mentions that he has obtained a certificate of Judge Jacob Burnet, who "did not understand Mr. Conner had heard from any of his friends or relations in Ireland from the time he left it."

Informs Clay that "My present debt & liabilities to the Bank [of the United States], are such as to excite serious alarm—My debt is 52,000 $, three fourths of which was endorsements taken in my own name on the failure of the principals." Adds that he is also bound for $60-70,000, some of which he will be compelled to pay, and has other debts which must exceed $35,000. Has tried to work out with Jones and the B.U.S. board in Philadelphia an agreement for dealing with the debts. Asserts that if Clay does not think the contract is fair and believes it should not be executed, then "I do not wish it, altho my desire to have it" completed "has given me more anxiety than all the other circumstances of my life." ALS. OCHP. Dated only as "Tuesday 20M _____ ." The basis for supplying May 20, 1823, as the date is that the contract Longworth made with the B.U.S. was drawn up in 1823, and May was the only month in that year where the 20th day fell on a Tuesday.

See also Clay to Jones, July 15, September 24, September 30, 1823; Jones to Clay, September 24, 1823.

To GEORGE W. JONES   Frankfort, Ky., May 28, 1823

I am here attending the Federal Court whose Session commenced on the first monday of this month, and is likely to continue for a week or two longer. The cases against [Thomas D.] Carneal[1] and [John H.] Piatt[2] were continued for the want of proof of notice; the depositions which you were to have had taken not having arrived. I regret this the more because the effect of the continuance *may* be to continue the causes until next May, in consequence of a rule of practice here. In taking the depositions, you will bear in mind that notice is to be given to the defendants. Mr. Carneal shewed me an agreement, by which you have undertaken not to press him until efforts to recover the money from [Israel T.] Canby and Piatt shall prove unavailing.[3] Is there not some disadvantage in such an arrangement, as no suit is brought against Canby? I obtained Judgment against Johnson.[4] The case against [Hugh] Glenn[5] will be in a state to authorize Judgt. at the next Court. Glenn was here and stated to me that he had important business to transact at St. Louis, but was restrained from going there by the apprehension that you might cause his arrest in Indiana, Illinois or Missouri; upon other Judgments recovered against him at Columbus. I promised him to express to you the opinion and advice that as we have him bound by the suit here, so that he would return to relieve his bail, it would be unnecessary to cause his arrest whilst in transitu to transmit important business. I comply with that promise in now mentioning the subject to you. I added to him, that I did not believe you contemplated any such arrest as he feared.

The circumstances of the case of Genl. [William] Lytle[6] have surprized me very much. It appears to me that there is not even colorable ground for the motion which was made to set aside the Judgment. But as that motion was lost by the division of the Court (a result just as clear and as certain, as if the Court had been unanimous against it) it is strange that the Court did not rescind the order restraining the emanation of the execution. That order was itself an extraordinary exercise of power. If there should be persistance in the refusal to issue it, I should think it would be better to apply to the Superior Court at its next Session for a Writ of Procedendo to the Inferior Court.

I hope you will not forget, and will also impress upon the Solicitor of your office, the importance of making full preparation for the trial of all the causes upon the docket of the Federal Court at Columbus in September next. This is the more necessary because you know that the January term, being in the depth of winter, most always fails. I shall not have it in my power also to attend at the next January term.

Mr. Carneal informed me that you had agreed with him to receive the Louisville property, without valuation, in full discharge of the debt for which he is bound, as the indorser of Col. [Charles S.] Todd.[7] Is that correct? And is the suit to be struck off the docket?

ALS. OCHP.   1. Clay to Jones & Crittenden, Dec. 22, 1821.   2. Clay to Jones, June 19, 1822.   3. Clay to Jones, May 16, 1823.   4. Probably in the case of the *B.U.S.* v. *Henry Johnson* or the *B.U.S.* v. *John T. Johnson.* See 3:431. For John T. Johnson, see 2:605.   5. Clay to Worth, Nov. 27, 1820.   6. Clay to Lytle, July 2, 1818.   7. Clay to Jones & Crittenden, Dec. 22, 1821.

To ALLEN TRIMBLE   Frankfort, Ky., May 28, 1823

My attendance on the Federal Court at this place has delayed my acknowledgment of the receipt of your agreeable favor of the 7h. instant,[1] which I received in due course of the Mail. I thank you for the valuable information and views which it contains.

I do not doubt that the intrigue on the part of W———n to which you refer or any other intrigue which would advance his pretensions would be attempted by him.[2] I have, in the whole course of my life, scarcely known a man, of his moderate capacity, more restless, more devoid of public principle, and more disposed, by all sorts of means, to elevate himself. I was told last Spring at Wheeling that he thought he ought to be made President. We ought to be vastly indebted to the moderation which now limits his aspiration to the second office in the Union. I cannot believe, however, that he has the least prospect of obtaining it. You have a hundred men in Ohio of more public worth, and of higher and better claims to the office than he possesses. I think I know enough of the people of Ohio to be assured that, if it were possible for them to be caught in a Vice President trap, it must be baited with some thing very different from Tho. Worth———n. You and the rest of my friends will doubtless keep an eye upon his movements, and as you know him thoroughly you will have no difficulty in detecting this plot, and at the proper time and in the proper way exposing it. The people of Ohio have too much solidity of judgment to allow their choice of a President to be controlled or affected by such a mere nominal office as that of Vice President.

You will have seen the proceedings at Louisville, and will have no difficulty in comprehending them.[3] In that town there happens to be concentrated many of the connexions of Mr. Pope, who have been for years assailing me. They have a paper[4] dedicated to their object which has been incessant in its attacks and abuse. After exertions equal to what are employed in a contested county election, as I have been well assured, you have seen what an abortion they have made of it. My friends disagreed about the mode of treating it, some thinking that it was best to pay no attention to it, others believing that as the call was

141

for *Genl.* [Andrew] *Jackson's* friends exclusively it might be improper for any others to attend, and all believing it of no importance. If my friends had thought it merited an exertion, they could have, by an overwhelming majority, have controlled the proceedings of the meeting: For you may rest assured that there is not a village, or County in Kentucky in which there is a majority against me. A similar meeting has been since attempted at Bowling green [Bowling Green, Ky.], where there happens to be a few malcontents. My friends turned out, and the utmost number I am informed that could be got for Genl. Jackson amounted to ten persons!

The information which I continue to receive from all quarters, on this subject, remains as encouraging as ever. And my friends may rest assured that, however the question may ultimately be decided, my prospects, at present, are greatly superior, in my opinion, to those of any of the other gentlemen. The claim which is set up for Mr. [William H.] Crawford of New York is without foundation. That State cannot be affirmed truly, at this time, to have a decided preponderance for any one; and unless I am greatly deceived my interest there is better than that of either of the others. I possess this advantage over either Mr. [John Quincy] Adams or Mr. Crawford, that a decision by N. York for me secures unquestionably my election, whilst the same cannot be asserted as to either of them. Further, a decision by N. York against either of them puts him incontestibly hors du combat which cannot be said of my case.[5]

I shall be in Ohio in September to attend the Federal Court. Should circumstances bring you to Kentucky I pray you to call & make my house your head quarters. Give my respects to Collins . . . [6]

ALS. NjP.   1. Not found.   2. Thomas Worthington.   3. A meeting had been held on April 24, 1823, in Louisville for the purpose of considering the expediency of recommending Andrew Jackson for president. A motion was made at the meeting *not* to consider making any nomination. This motion was defeated by a vote of 170-164. The Jackson forces in charge of the meeting, recognizing that a nomination of Jackson would not pass, immediately adjourned the meeting. Nevertheless, a victory was claimed for Jackson in the account of the meeting given in the Louisville *Public Advertiser* on April 26, 1823, which stated: "The vote was considered as conclusive as to the nomination of Gen. Jackson." Frankfort *Argus of Western America*, April 30, 1823.   4. Louisville *Public Advertiser*.   5. For New York's vote in the 1824 presidential election, see Clay to Creighton, April 12, 1822, no. 2 of date.   6. Probably Capt. Joel Collins. See 3:351.

To GEORGE W. JONES   Lexington, June 1, 1823

I received in due course of the Mail your letter of the 27th.[1] Ulto. mentioning that friday the sixth inst. is assigned for the argument of a motion of [William] Lytle against the Bank of the U.S.[2] before the Supreme Court, for a mandamus to be directed to the Court of Common Pleas to shew cause why the Judgt. obtained against him by the Bank in the latter Court should not be set aside, and expressing a wish that I should attend to assist in the opposition to the motion, what it is expected will be supported by eminent Counsel.

I regret extremely that it is not in my power to attend from two causes, one is, that the Federal Court is yet in Session and will continue beyond the day appointed for the argument of the motion, and probably until the 14h. instant, and the Bank, besides other Clients, has im-

142

portant Causes before that Court which require my attention. The other is, that I have a daughter, in the last stage, I fear, of a deep consumption, whose death we have daily but too much reason to apprehend, and from whom I cannot think of separating myself by so distant a journey.[3] I am glad to learn from you that you do not entertain serious apprehensions of the motion. It is totally unsupported, as far as I comprehend it, by any principle, precedent, or reason applicable to the case; and I should like extremely, under other circumstances, to give expression to the opinions which I entertain upon it and to the sentiments of surprize which have been excited in hearing of the importance and consideration which have been attached to such a proceeding. If the motion should happen to be continued, or if it should not be (as I understand from your description of it that it will not be) final and conclusive of the question, I shall take particular satisfaction in opposing it on some future occasion when I can attend at Cincinnati.

I regret that you did not send on the depositions taken in the cases of [John H.] Piatt[4] and [Thomas D.] Carneal[5] for reasons mentioned in a former letter.

Will you not visit us this summer? We shall be very much gratified to see you and Mrs. Jones here.

ALS. OCHP.   1. Not found.   2. Clay to Lytle, July 2, 1818.   3. Clay's daughter, Lucretia Hart Clay, died June 18, 1823. See 3:431.   4. Clay to Jones, June 19, 1822.   5. Clay to Jones & Crittenden, Dec. 22, 1821.

To GEORGE W. JONES   Lexington, July 2, 1823
I received by the last mail both your letters, under date the 23d. and 28th. with the inclosure in the latter.[1]

In the case put by you in your first letter, in regard to the Estate of Genl. [William] Lytle, there can be no doubt that his wife will not be entitled to dower.[2] A lien which exists previous to a marriage cannot be encumbered by dower. Mrs. Lytle would not therefore be entitled to it either as respects the mortgage or the Judgment of the Bank. At the last term of the Federal Court in this State, after full argument in a case of a mortgage held by the Bank, the Court decided that, whenever the mortgaged estate was insufficient to discharge the debt, and the mortgagor was insolvent, the mortgaged property might be taken possession of, under an order of Court, and a Receiver of the rents and profits be appointed. This decision is in conformity to the opinion I gave the Bank in the case of [John H.] Piatts mortgage.[3] I do not think that the claim set up for repairs, for a proportion of the taxes for 1822, or for a proportion of the Salary of the Collector of the rents, is well founded. All these demands must be considered as merged in the compromise. If that compromise is now to be set aside in whole or in part, the Bank might have a demand for interest, for the rents which accrued between the time of the notification of the tenants and the 17h. Sept. &c. &c.

I am sorry that the efforts to make an arrangement with Mr. [Hugh] Glenn have been so unsuccessful.[4] Immediately upon the receipt of the transcript of the record, I sent a memorandum to the Clerk to issue a Capias,[5] which I presume is by this time out, and I requested the Marshall to be very particular in regard to Bail. The demand he made upon you through Col. Carr[6] of a proces verbal[7] of what passed between you I imagine is a mere russe de guerre and should create no concern.

The September [term] is approaching, and I hope you will bear in mind the necessity of thorough preparation for the trial of the causes depending in it.

ALS. OCHP.   1. Not found.   2. Clay to Lytle, July 2, 1818.   3. Clay to Jones, June 19, 1822.   4. Clay to Worth, Nov. 27, 1820.   5. That is, a writ to be executed by seizing, in some instances, the property, in other instances, the person of the defendant.   6. Possibly Francis Carr, one of Cincinnati's first city aldermen. Greve, *History of Cincinnati*, 1:508.   7. That is, an official report or a formally attested account of proceedings held before a public officer and the result thereof.

To CHARLES MINER[1]   Lexington, July 4, 1823

I received your very obliging favor of the 19h. Ulto.[2] and owe you many thanks for the communications which it contains, and the kind feelings which dictated them.

There is some foundation for most of the previous confessions made by the leaky supporter[3] of Mr. [John C.] Calhoun to your friend.[4] With respect to the great effort to be made to elect that gentleman, the past tense as well as the future might have been employed. I am disposed to doubt for the sake of the President [James Monroe] himself, his intermeddling in that object, otherwise than by promotions of the friends of the Secy of War [Calhoun]. Mr. [Return Jonathan] Meigs was my friend, and that circumstance may have contributed to his ejection. I have no doubt that he will be succeeded by some friend of Mr. Calhoun, whose influence in the affair of appointments evidently is predominant; and I think it probable that Mr. McClean [*sic,* John McLean] of Ohio will be appointed.[5] But the election of Mr. Calhoun, after all, is almost next to impossible. The very means employed to produce it, will as heretofore, operate to his prejudice. Where is the interest to elect him? Give him So. Carolina & yield him also Pennsylvania (contrary to all probability) and it is impossible to take him into another State. He may every where have some warm admirers, and a few zealous supporters, but, except in those two States, he has no practical interest to be counted upon in any other. I do not think it is in the compass of all the accidents in the Chapter, aided even by intrigue, to secure his election.

I think the contest at present may be fairly considered as confined to three. If New York[6] and Penna.[7] should fail to indicate their respective preferences so long before the election as to operate upon the American public generally, the probability is that the election will devolve on the H[ouse]. of R[epresentatives].[8] On the contrary, if New York should declare her choice within the next eight months, by some unambiguous act, the result would be as follows:

If that choice should fall on Mr. [William H.] Crawford, there is an end to Mr. [John Quincy] Adam's pretensions, and the contest would then be between Mr. Crawford and me.

If on Mr. Adams, there would be an end to Mr. Crawford's pretensions, and the contest would be between Mr. Adams and me.

If for me, my election would take place by not less than two thirds of the Union[.]

In the first and second suppositions, the contest would be somewhat doubtful. New England would hold the balance between Mr. Crawford and me. I should, I think, enter it with a plurality of votes.

In the second supposition much would depend upon Penna. but I think I should get against Mr. Adams nearly all South and West of New York.

Mr. Adams is undoubtedly stronger in the West than Mr. Crawford. He has every where some interest, 'though not an available interest in a contest with me. Mr. Crawford has no where, except in East Tennessee, any interest in the Western States. In a contest between them, I believe Mr. Adams would get the Western vote with the exception *possibly* of Kentucky and Missouri.[9]

I write you in confidence & subscribe myself . . .

ALS. PWbH. Letter marked "(Confidential)." 1. For Miner, a Pennsylvania newspaperman and congressman, see 3:326 and *DAB*. 2. See 3:435-38. 3. Richard Haughton. See 3:435-37 4. William H. Dillingham. See *ibid*. 5. See 4:837. 6. For New York's vote in 1824, see Clay to Creighton, April 12, 1822, no. 2 of date. 7. For Pennsylvania's vote in 1824, see Benton to Clay, April 9, 1822. 8. *Ibid*. 9. For Missouri's vote in 1824, see Clay to Miegs, August 21, 1822.

To ADAM BEATTY   Lexington, July 6, 1823
I recd. your obliging favor of the 30h. Ulto.[1] and thank you for the friendly communications which it contains. I regret extremely W[illiam]. [B.] Rochester's retirement from Congress, as he would have been in that body enabled to have rendered me the most essential service.[2] Wherever he may be I have no doubt that he will omit no fair occasion to promote my interests.

My information from Albany, during the late Session of the New York Legislature, assured me that my friends were more numerous than those of any other Candidate.[3] Genl. [Peter B.] Porter who was there, during almost the whole Session, and who frequently wrote to me, stated that he had scarcely a doubt that I would obtain a majority of the *whole* Lesiglature, if any nomination were made during that Session; but he expressed at the same time the belief that no nomination would be made, and added that my friends did not intend to press one. Col. Rochester is mistaken in the supposition that Mr. [William H.] Crawford would have been nominated, if any one had been. After the Session of Congress was over, Mr. [Martin] Van Buren went to Albany and made every effort to procure a nomination of the Secretary of the Treasury without success. The weak measure was finally resorted to of recommending a Congressional Caucus, from which no body dissented. My recent information from that State continues to be encouraging. Genl. Porter is very sanguine. My information from Penna. is also highly encouraging,[4] and if it is to be credited, there is no doubt that my strength is greater in that State than that of any other Candidate. In Virginia[5] Mr. Crawford is probably the strongest and I next.

The contest may be considered at present as confined to three. If New York, within the course of the next seven or eight months, declares her preference by some unequivocal act, the result would be as follows:

If that preference should be for Mr. Crawford, there will be an end of Mr. [John Quincy] Adams's pretensions, and the contest would then be between Mr. Crawford and me.

If for Mr. Adams, the contest would then be between him and me, and there would be an end of Mr. Crawfords pretensions.

If for me, I have no doubt that my election would be secured by two thirds of the Union.

Should the State of New York make no such indication of her choice,[6] and the vote of Pennsa. should also be a matter of uncertainty, then I think there will be no election by the people, and the H. of R. must decide;

Unless there should be a Congressional Caucus, and its recommendation should be acquiesced in; on both of which points I entertain strong doubts. The tranquillity of the present period; the extinction of party; the difficulty of settling the elements of a Caucus; the extensive discussions among the great body of the people of the Presidential question, all tend to render the formation of a Caucus doubtful, and to bring its decision into controversy. Would any State which has fixed its judgment give up its favorite and support one, to whom it might be opposed, because he happens to be recommended by some 70 or 80 gentlemen at Washn.? It is a settled principle of a Caucus that the minority must support the choice of the majority. Can the members of Congress from committed States undertake to pledge their States to support any other person than him as to whom a preference has been manifested?

My friends may rest assured that my prospects are good—better I sincerely believe than those of any other Candidate. At present I look upon Mr. Adams as my most formidable competitor. The circumstance that operates most to my disadvantage is Genl. [Andrew] Jackson being still held up by Tennessee, 'though I verily believe he cannot get out of that State into any other. But there is a moral influence from there being two Candidates from the same section, which is injurious to both.

ALS. Courtesy of Earl M. Ratzer, Highland Park, Ill.   1. See 3:446-47.   2. See 3:377, 445, 447.   3. For New York's vote in 1824, see Clay to Crieghton, April 12, 1822, no. 2 of date.   4. For Pennsylvania's vote in 1824, see Benton to Clay, April 9, 1822.   5. For Virginia's vote in 1824, see Clay to Creighton, April 12, 1822, no. 2 of date.   6. See 3:572.

To GEORGE W. JONES   Lexington, July 15, 1823
I transmit you herewith the opinion which I have formed on Mr. [Nicholas] Longworth's title.[1] I have also sent a Copy of it to the Bank at Philadelphia for the examination of the Parent Board.

I have received your favor of the 2d. instant;[2] and have thought of the several suggestions which it contains. It does not appear to me that the Judgments obtained against Mr. Longworth, as an indorser, in the name of the Bank itself, prior to the agreement, and which were of course known to it, constitute one of these liens or encumbrances on his title which he is bound to remove in order to comply with his agreement. Those Judgments cannot of course affect the property so far as the title is in Mrs. [Susan] L[ongworth].[3] And so far as it is held in the name & right of Mr. Longworth, I think the Bank w[oul]d have inserted a stipulation in the contract requiring the paymt. of those judgments, as being necessary to enable him to make a clear title if such had been its intention or expectation.

If the conveyance to [George P.] Torrence & Ormsby,[4] under the order of sale, be set aside or treated as null, then the title to the whole 300 lots according to the opinion which I have formed would be in Mrs. L.

ALS. OCHP. 1. Jones to Clay, Sept. 24, 1823; see also 3:498. 2. Not found. 3. Susan Howell, daughter of Silas Howell, had first been married to Daniel Connor (or Conner). She married Nicholas Longworth in 1807. Her sister was the wife of Thomas D. Carneal. Shaffer, *Piatt's Landing Eastbend*, 9; see also Nicholas Longworth's entries in *DAB* and *CAB*. 4. For George P. Torrence, a Cincinnati judge, see Harry R. Stevens, *The Early Jackson Party in Ohio* (Durham, N.C., 1957), 14, 22. Ormsby is possibly Peter B. Ormsby. See 1:407; 3:431. Ormsby, and probably Torrence, were administrators of Daniel Connor's estate. See Jones to Clay, Sept. 24, 1823.

To GEORGE W. JONES   Lexington, July 30, 1823

My absence from home at the Olympian Springs prevented my earlier acknowledging the receipt of your letter of the 11h. instant.[1] to which I will now proceed to reply in the order of the several subjects which it embraces.

I adhere to the advice which I heretofore gave you in relation to the proceedings against Genl. [William] Lytle.[2]

I have received a letter from Mr. B[enjamin]. M. Piatt in relation to the claim for taxes and for the Agents compensation, which has been set up, in behalf of the Admon of J[ohn]. H. Piatt.[3] I have replied to him, or rather shall answer him, in substance as I wrote to you, that is that the claim is not, in my opinion, well founded. I refer you to my letter to him. As it is my intention to pass through Cincinnati, on my way to Columbus, the final completion of the arrangement with them had better perhaps be deferred until that time.

The transcript of the Judgment & proceedings against Jesse Hunt[4] was sent to me last winter by the Bank to have him arrested in the City of Washington, but it arrived too late to effect the object, and I either returned the transcript to the Bank, when I was in Philadelphia, or left in Washington, I am not certain which, but I believe the former. If it be not too late, I think it will be well for you to direct Mr. [Harvey D.] Evans to send a Copy of the Judgment (shewing the amt. of debt & Costs) to the Cashr. of the office of d[iscoun]t. & deposit at Washn. City, with a direction to have a suit brought, if Mr. Hunt be there. I think it will be advisable for you to obtain a Copy of the Conveyance which Mr. Hunt has made to his son, and at the next term of the Fed. Court a bill in Chancery had better perhaps be filed to set aside the conveyance as fraudulent. At least this is a course about which we can consult, if nothing better can be done.

ALS. OCHP. 1. Not found. 2. Clay to Lytle, July 2, 1818. 3. Benjamin M. Piatt (b. 1779), a Cincinnati lawyer and judge, was the elder brother of John H. Piatt and an administrator of John's estate. Miller, *Donn Piatt*, 16-21. For John H. Piatt's estate, see Clay to Jones, June 19, 1822, and 3:333-34. 4. For Hunt, see 3:389.

To GEORGE W. JONES   Lexington, August 2, 1823

I received your letter of the 29th. Ulto.[1] transmitting some observations of B[enjamin]. M. Piatt Esqr. respecting a claim to dower which it is apprehended may be asserted in some of the lots which have been conveyed by the representatives of John H. Piatt deceased to the Bank of the U. States.[2]

I do not think that the claim is well founded in lots No. 6 and No. 7 because, if I understand correctly the statement of Mr. Piatt, the *legal* title was never conveyed by [Charles] Vattier to Washburn.[3] Washburn had only an equitable interest, in which a wife cannot be endowed. Such however is the common law, and must be the law of Ohio, unless it has been changed by some statute, of which I have no knowledge.

The claim to dower in lot No. 31 has more foundation. To that lot or the part of it in which the dower is claimed, Washburn it seems had a legal title; and if the dower has not been forfeited, the wife of course may lawfully assert it. But I think her claim would be restricted to the value of the property at the time & in the state it was transfered by the husband; and that she could only claim that value from the time she makes a lawful demand.

Considering these as the only obstacles to the completion of the arrangement made with the Bank; and that if the dower shall be established there are persons bound to indemnity, who you think are responsible & competent to effect it, I would advise the transfer to the widow of one half of the amount which the Bank agreed to pay her in debts. With respect to the other half, it may remain until I visit Cincinnati, which I hope to do towards the last of this month on my way to Columbus, at which time I will examine more fully into the business.

ALS. OCHP.   1. Not found.   2. Clay to Jones, June 19, 1822, and July 30, 1823; see also 3:233-34.   3. Vattier at one time owned an important tract of land in the area which became downtown Cincinnati. See 3:233-34. Washburn has not been identified.

To JOHN SLOANE   Lexington, August 12, 1823

I received your favor of the 29th. Ulto.[1] requesting a Copy of the Journals of the Convention of our State, containing the votes of its members on the subject of slavery.[2] They will not shew what I presume you desire to establish from them, or I would obtain a Copy & transmit it to you. I infer from your letter that you desire to exhibit evidence of my opinions on that question. I was not a member of the Convention. The propriety of a gradual emancipation of slaves (such as had been adopted in Pennsylvania) was a question much agitated in this State in 1798 and 1799, and was one, among the considerations, which led to a call of a Convention to revise our Constitution. The late Col. George Nicholas and Jno. Breckinridge[3] (at that time the most distinguished citizens in this State) opposed the measure. The honble James Brown, now Senator from Louisiana, then a resident of this town, and I supported it. I espoused the cause of gradual emancipation in the circles, public assemblies and public prints.[4] We were beaten at the polls, but we brought to them a highly respectable minority. If the Slave interest had not been quite so strong we should have succeeded. I observe, in a late Chillicothe paper, a pretty correct account is given of the part which I acted, on that memorable occasion, & of some of the personal consequences of it to myself. My opinions are unchanged. I would still in Kentucky support a gradual emancipation. So I would in Missouri. The question I think in any State is a good deal affected by the proportion of the African to the European race. In this State I do not think that so great as to endanger the purity and safety of society. But I nevertheless believe that this question of emancipation of slaves, as our Federal Constitution now stands, is one exclusively belonging to the States respectively and not to Congress. No man is more sensible of the evils of slavery than I am, nor regrets them more. Were I the Citizen of a State in which it was not tolerated, I should certainly oppose its introduction with all the force and energy in my power; and if I found myself unhappily overruled, I would then strive to incorporate in the law, by which their admission was authorized, the principle of a gradual emancipation.

In thus disclosing to you, My dear Sir, most truly & frankly my past & present sentiments, I pray you to understand the communication for yourself alone. It does not appear to me to be proper or delicate that I should be received, in any way, to testify on the subject of my own opinions. You are capable of justly appreciating this feeling.

My information on the other subject of your letter continues to be from all quarters highly encouraging.[5] I reserve the details of it for the occasion when I shall have the pleasure of seeing you.

ALS. MH.   1. Not found.   2. See 1:8.   3. For Nicholas, see 1:146 and *DAB;* for Breckinridge, 1:22-23 and *DAB.*   4. See 1:3-8, 10-14.   5. Reference is to the 1824 presidential election. For results, see Benton to Clay, April 9, 1822.

To WILLIAM CREIGHTON, JR.   Lexington, August 21, 1823
& WILLIAM K. BOND

I regret extremely that the state of my health and the means which I am adopting for its restoration will not allow me to attend at the approaching term of the Fed[eral]. Court in Ohio. I had hoped until within these few days that I should be able to go; but I find that I am too weak to undertake the journey, which my physicians also positively forbid. I must ask the favor of you, therefore, to represent me in all cases of the Bank [of the United States], whether from your office at Chillicothe, or the agency at Cincinnati, that may be brought on for trial. If you should in any case desire assistance Mr. [Charles] Hammond, Mr. [David K.] Este, or Mr. [Philip] Dodderidge, or Col [Henry] Brush,[1] I am sure, will cheerfully afford it in my behalf.

In other causes also in which I am concerned, altho' the Bank may not be a party, I must rely on your friendly attentions. Will you have the goodness to examine if a sale has been made in Cunningham agst. Vause &c (in Ch[ancer]y.) and if the report of Commis[sione]rs[2] has been made to direct the Clerk to send me a copy of it? It need not be confirmed by a final decree until further direction.

ALS. KyU.   1. For Hammond, see 2:874 and *DAB;* for Este, see 3:287; for Dodderidge, see 3:8 and *DAB;* for Brush, see *BDAC.*   2. Case not found.

To WILLIAM CREIGHTON, JR.   Lexington, August 23, 1823

I wrote you and Mr. [William K.] Bond yesterday [*sic*] informing you of my inability to attend the approaching Federal Court at Columbus.[1] I have regretted extremely that I could not go on many accounts, public professional and private. But if I had have gone I might have prevented altogether the success of an experiment to re-establish my health which I am now making and about which my physicians are very sanguine. Indeed, as the medicinal course which has been presented to me comprehends the use of mercury, there was considerable hazard in the journey. By great attention, I hope to acquire sufficient strength and health for the arduous vocations of the ensuing winter.

I was very desirous to have gone to Ohio to have ascertained by personal observation the state of things there in relation to the Presidential election. The disposition of that state is still contested within and without it.[2] I am assured that the supposed uncertainty of its vote materially influences Virginia.[3] I believe myself two facts in regard to it, and if they really exist, it is very important to impress Virginia with their truth. The first is that the State will *certainly* support me; and the other that it will certainly not support Mr. [William H.] Crawford, if from any cause I should be out of the way. From the information I have obtained (and upon no one do I rely more than on you) I presume in the Scioto Country there is a large & decided majority in my favor; and that the same may be said of the Country through which the great road passes from Chillicothe to Wheeling, including New Lancaster & Zanesville & St Clairsville. How stands it elsewhere? Mr. [Charles] Hammond thinks that Mr. [John Qunicy] Adams has many supporters, and that Mr. Crawford is very obnoxious in the Miami Country. Do you concur with him? How is the [Western] Reserve? Your opportunities of obtaining information, during the Court, will be good; and I will thank you to let me know the result of your enquiries. How did the members who voted for me in Caucus last winter[4] succeed, or are likely to succeed at the elections? Is it likely that the Legislature will make any further declaration upon the subject?[5] Upon the supposition of a general attendance of the members and a large majority concurring there is no doubt of the utility of such declaration.

My information from New York is highly encouraging, and if the West remain united on the object my confidence in ultimate success is rather increased than diminished since I saw you.

On the question of a Congressional Caucus, my opinion is that there will be none, or if there be one that it will do nothing, or if they make a recommendation that it will have but little effect.[6]

1st. On the first point; the difficulties of constituting a Caucus will be found, I apprehend, insuperable. Who are to be admitted? Who excluded? Then, never heretofore has there been such a popular agitation of the subject as during the present period. Never before was there such a state of parties; and it must be confessed that the best defense of a Caucus is to be found in the condition of opposing parties.

2. If there be a caucus, the same divisions that exist in the nation will be found there. Who will give way? It is a vital principle of a Caucus (and will be probably the first resolution proposed.) that the minor-

ity shall yield their favorites, and support that person designated by the majority. On that resolution it will split. How can the members from the committed States undertake to support any other than him in whose behalf they have given decided indications? Would those from Tennessee, for example, undertake to support any other than Genl. [Andrew] Jackson?

3. But if after great contention and much management, there should be a designation made, it would probably be by a bare majority, and instead of tranquillizing the Country it would apply a torch to it. All the prejudices would be lighted up. Intrigue, Corruption &c &c would be charged. The people would be told that an infamous contrivance had been adopted to wrest from them the elective franchise—that a sort of Pretorian cohort at the metropolis was disposing of the Chief Magistracy &c. &c. So that I am inclined to think the Caucus recommendation would not only be ineffectual, but it is not clear that it would not injure him who might obtain it.

And yet it must be admitted that if there be no Caucus it is pretty certain there will be no popular election. Is that at last an evil so great as engrafting practically upon the Constitution the principle of a Caucus? If we have one now, we must ever have one. The Constitution has provided for the contingency of a non election. It is true that the States vote in their Corporate capacity; but then they are limited to one of three persons in whose favor large portions of the Community shall have previously indicated their preference & their confidence. What limitation is there upon a Caucus?

If Virginia & New York call out for a Caucus, it is because either they cannot respectively agree upon a Candidate, or because they hope to accomplish, by the instrumentality of a Caucus, the election of one whom they could not elect without it. Upon the latter supposition, interest is the motive. Ought those who have not the same interest to concur in the object?

I must depend upon your friendly exertions to prevent injury by my absence at this time from Columbus, and to acquire & communicate such information as you may think useful—

Give my respects to the gentlemen of the Bar generally and to Genl. [Allen] Trimble.

ALS. KyU.   1. Clay to Creighton & Bond, August 21, 1823.   2. For Ohio's vote in 1824, see Benton to Clay, April 9, 1822.   3. For Virginia's vote in 1824, see Clay to Creighton, April 12, 1822, no. 2 of date.   4. See 3:351.   5. They did not.   6. See 3:634-35, 640-41.

To GEORGE W. JONES   Lexington, August 23, 1823

I have very great regret in communicating to you that the state of my health is such as to oblige me to decline going to Columbus, at the approaching term of the Federal Court. I had cherished, even to the last moment, the hope that I should be able to attend; but I am admonished by both my debility and my physicians that I must not undertake the journey. They say that the good effects which are anticipated from a course of medicine, and of regimen, on which they have put me, would be greatly hazarded if not entirely lost by the journey, besides other perils to which I should be exposed. Under these circumstances I am compelled, most reluctantly, to decline the journey.

I hope and believe that the interests of the Bank [of the United States], in Court, will sustain no prejudice by my absence. Whenever it may desire continuances of any of its causes, the fact of my absence from indisposition will furnish an incontestible ground. In cases that may be ready for trial, and which it may be desirable should be brought on, notwithstanding my absence, I have written to Mess. [William] Creighton [Jr.] and [William K.] Bond requesting them to appear in my behalf,[1] as Mr. [Charles] Hammond will also do, where he is not engaged in opposition to the Bank. It will be well enough, I think, to take judgment against [William] Lytle in the action I brought at the last term against him on the judgment of Hamilton.[2] He will oppose this upon the ground of the local proceedings which he has instituted to get rid of that judgment; but there is nothing in them, and I think the Court will so decide.

It is my intention as soon as my strength and health will allow of it to go to Cincinnati, especially if you should desire to see me there in regard to any of the business of the Bank. I have supposed it might be necessary in order to close the [John H.] Piatt affair &c.[3] Can that be conveniently done without my going there?

I transmit along with this letter, letters for Mess. Creighton and Bond and Hammond, which you will oblige me by taking with you if you go to Columbus, or if you do not forwarding them by Mr. [David K.] Este or some other safe hand.

ALS. OCHP. 1. Clay to Creighton & Bond, August 21, 1823. 2. Clay to Lytle, July 2, 1818. Hamilton has not been identified. 3. Clay to Jones, June 19, 1822.

To GEORGE W. JONES   Lexington, September 17, 1823

I recd. your letter of the 6th. instant[1] by Mr. [Thomas] Wilson transmitting sundry notes to bring suits upon, for which I have handed to him my receipt. I could not ascertain from your memorandum whether [John] Leathers as well as [Jamison] Hawkins lived in this State and whether each of them was to be sued upon his endorsement of the other's note as well as maker of his own.[2] The indorsers and makers of notes cannot, by the laws of this State, as by those of Ohio, be comprehended in the same suit, but must be sued separately. This creates additional costs, which in small cases, such as those of Hawkins and Leathers, becomes a matter worthy of consideration. We must get Mr. [Griffen] Yeatman to attend at Frankfort as a witness. Cincinnati, being within 100 miles of Frankfort, we have not a strict right, under the act of Congress, to take his deposition; and the directions which I heretofore gave to have his deposition taken in the case of the indorsers upon the note of [Israel T.] Canby were to guard against the possible accident of his death. I still wish, from the same motive, those directions complied with. I sent you dedimuss for that purpose, and notices should be given to [Thomas D.] Carneal and [Benjamin M.] Piatt.[3] But if Yeatman does not attend as a witness, they will get, or rather we shall have to get, the causes continued until the May term. We shall want no witness in any of the notes now sent by you, as the makers of the notes alone will be sued, unless we should sue Hawkins and Leathers as indorsers, for which I shall wait your directions.

I have also received your letter of the 10h. instant, and thank you for the information which you have communicated respecting the letter which Mr. [Nicholas] Longworth is to make;[4] and which I shall not fail to take into consideration, when I shall examine into his title. And I shall be obliged to you by any further suggestions, on that subject, that you may happen to think of making. I have not yet been furnished with a copy of his agreement with the Bank.

With respect to the attachment of James Glenn's[5] alleged interest in the Steam Boat Vulcan, now perhaps lying at Louisville, to make the attachment efficacious; the Boat should be taken possession of by the public officers, unless security should be given (which the defendants might decline) to have her forthcoming upon the Judgment being rendered by the Court. If the Boat should be detained, and be prevented from making her accustomed voyages, in consequence of our attachment; and it should upon a judicial investigation turn out that James Glenn had no interest in her, her real owners would be entitled to damages for her detention. This renders it necessary that we should be reasonably certain of making it appear to the Court that James Glenn is in fact interested. We should not go haphazard to work. You have not stated to me the proof which can be adduced. You only mention "there is reason to believe." I think it will be better to ascertain before hand what testimony you may be able to produce and communicate information of it to me; upon which I should be able to form some opinion as to the probable event of the controversy. Or as we shall I expect obtain a Judgment at the next Court against Hugh Glenn,[6] perhaps a better course will be to levy the execution against him on the Boat and try the right of property in that way. If it becomes expedient to resort to the remedy of attachment the transcripts of the Judgments against Hugh & James Glenn will furnish sufficient basis to proceed upon. In the case of Daniel Holloway,[7] and all similar cases where the debtor is out of the State, and there are persons within it having effects of his in their hands or being indebted to him, I think it would be advisable to resort to an attachment, and summon the residents as garnishees. In cases of this description there is no rush to encounter, except the costs of the proceeding. If the residents should have effects or be indebted to the absentee, these means can be applied to the payment of your debt.

I brought a suit formerly against John McKinney [Jr.] as the indorser in the case of E[vans] Dozier and C[harles]. Thornton, but I cannot at this moment ascertain whether Judgment was rendered against him.[8] If not, and the writ has not been served upon him, he must be proceeded against in Indiana, as we cannot make him a party to the Judgment against the principals. In that case you will take steps to have him sued there.

ALS. OCHP. 1. Not found. 2. John Leathers lived in Campbell County, Ky., and Jamison Hawkins in Boone County, Ky. Jackson, *Kentucky 1820 Census Index.* Each was sued for a debt of $207.50. U.S. Circuit Court (7th Circuit), Reel #1541, Complete record, Book U, Nov. term, 1822, Box 21, pp. 409-13. 3. Clay to Jones & Crittenden, Dec. 22, 1821, and Clay to Jones, June 19, 1822. 4. Clay to Jones, July 15, 1823. 5. Probably a brother of Hugh Glenn. 6. Clay to Worth, Nov. 27,

1820.   7. Case not found.   8. For McKinney, see 3:418. See also Clay to Crittenden
& Worth, Nov. 3, 1821.

To GEORGE W. JONES   Lexington, September 18, 1823

I have this day ordered suits in all cases without exception on the notes
you transmitted to me by Mr. [Thomas] Wilson. I find that Mr. [Grif-
fen] Yeatman will be wanted as a witness at Frankfort against [Thomas
D.] Carneal as the indorser of the Johnsons note and against Lindsey as
the indorser of that of John & Noble.[1] Without his attendance we shall
be unable to recover Judgments in those cases or in the former ones
against [John H.] Piatt & Carneal.[2] When the Clerk makes out the
Docket for the next term I will forward Subpoena's for him. I do not
understand, from your memo. whether [John] Leathers is a resident of
this State, or whether you wish him sued as the indorser of the notes of
[Jamison] Hawkins or Hawkins as the indorser of Leather's notes.[3] Are
these men good for any thing? If insolvent, is it worth while putting
the Bank to the expense of suits against them. Has not [Jacob] Fowler
given a mortgage to secure his debt?[4] If so, had we not better proceed
upon the mortgage also? You are aware that we are entitled to sue although all the installments have not fallen due, to secure payment of
which the mortgage was executed. By operating on mortgages we have
the important advantage of getting rid of the valuation laws, both in
Ohio and Kentucky.

I cannot prepare a bill in Ch[ancer]y against the Farmers and Mechanics Bank[5] on the memo. which has been sent me. Your solicitor
had better perhaps prepare one, in doing which that which I formerly
drew against the Bank (I think) of Cincinnati, and which I presume is
on file in your office would assist him. If it be wished that I should
draw it, I will thank you to get him to make out a Brief of the case,
which should comprehend 1st. An account of the manner in which that
Bank stands indebted to your's. 2dly. the names of all the officers of
that Bank as the period of its ceasing to transact business. 3dly. the
names of the Stockholders as far as may be practicable. 4dly the same
as to the debtors of that Bank and 5ly. the name of the person or persons who are supposed now to have the custody of its books and papers. The bill should be shaped for a discovery also of the debts &
effects of that Bank &c.

ALS. OCHP.   1. No further references to these cases have been found.   2. Clay to
Jones, June 19, 1822; Clay to Jones & Crittenden, Dec. 22, 1821.   3. Clay to Jones,
Sept. 17, 1823.   4. Clay to Crittenden & Worth, Nov. 15, 1820.   5. See 2:621.

From George W. Jones, Cincinnati, Ohio, September 24, 1823. Writes "to communicate some information . . . in relation to Daniel Conner the former husband of Mrs. [Susan] Longworth [Clay to Jones, July 15, 1823]." Reports that
Connor "has a brother in Ireland of whom he was known to speak with affection, and to express an intention of sending for him." Adds that Nicholas Longworth's denial of this is "such as to impeach his veracity and cause greater
suspicion on other points not clearly established."

Also mentions that he has "received your letter of the 18th. inst [see
above]" and that "some doubt was expressed by Robert Piatt in relation to the
authority of Embree & Howell to use his name" because Robert Piatt [Clay to

Jones, September 30, 1823] doesn't remember granting a power of attorney. Adds, however, that he has since found the power of attorney which was signed before a justice of the peace in Kentucky. Asks about the process for proving the signatures and wonders if it will be required to exhibit the power in court. Reports that "The principle, of Suit upon a Mortgage for part of the Consideration has not been practiced here if a levy can be made upon *the whole* of the Mortgaged property for *a part* of the debt, we shall the sooner be enabled to look to other sources for any deficiency after the Mortgaged property shall have been expanded." States that "Mr. [David K.] Este will prepare the Bill in Chan[cer]y. against the Farmers & Mecha[nic]'s Bank and will communicate with you upon the subject."

Asks Clay's advice on charges made by Thomas Heckewelder after "I consented to have him served at Columbus for not more than five or six cases." Mentions also the debts owed by James and Hugh Glenn [Clay to Jones, September 17, 1823] and the steps which may be taken to collect from them.

Adds on September 25 that "I have seen both Genl. [James] Findlay & Judge [Jacob] Burnet since I wrote the foregoing" and that "the latter is very positive of having frequently . . . heard Mr. Conner speak of his younger brother." Notes that Burnet had been engaged to write Connor's will, but Connor "was taken ill and was not well enough on the return of Mr. Burnet to proceed with it"; also, a brother or uncle living on the island of Jamaica was mentioned. Believes that Longworth may "be disappointed in his expectation of convincing you that the title is good—and pursue a course to compel the acceptance, he will lead to inquiries in Ireland and Jamaica that will probably deprive him of all the rights which the Statute of limitations may in a short time fully secure." ALS. OCHP.

Embree is probably either Jesse Embree, who was a member of the Cincinnati Society, or Davis Embree, who was an officer of the Cincinnati Royal Arch Chapter. Thomas Heckewelder was sheriff in Cincinnati. Greve, *History of Cincinnati*, 1:528-29, 571. For Robert Piatt, cousin of John H. Piatt, see Shaffer, *Piatt's Landing Eastbend*, 10-18, 21. For James Findlay, see 3:7. Howell has not been identified.

On September 25, 1823, Clay wrote in a memorandum that on April 24, 1823, Longworth had contracted with the B.U.S. "to convey to it certain real property in discharge of debt due from him to that institution, at its Cincinnati office" and that he "has shewn to me certain title papers to enable me to form an opinion of his ability to execute such a conveyance as he has covenanted to make." Finds that he must have additional papers and information in order to make "a conclusive judgment as to the validity of Mr. Ls. titles." This must include: (1) "The chain of title from John Cleves Symmes to Daniel Conner, former husband of Mrs. Longworth"; (2) a verification of the circumstances by which Mrs. Longworth "claimed the property as heiress of her former husband"; (3) a "transcript of the record of all the proceedings in and out of court by which the estate was sold, at the instance of Mr. [Peter B.] Ormsby the administrator of Mr. Conner"; (4) the "mutual conveyances or quit deeds which passed between Mr. & Mrs. Longworth . . . and Mr. Ormsby"; (5) for that property belonging to Longworth in his own right, "I wish to see all the titles from the original grantee of the U. States down to Mr. Longworth," and prefers that "Mr. [George] Jones or the Solicitor" of the B.U.S. at Cincinnati compare the description of the estate contained in the deed to "the property itself to ascertain if it be correct and adequate." ADS. OCHP.

For John Cleves Symmes—New Jersey congressman, judge, founder of Cincinnati, and father-in-law of William Henry Harrison, see *BDAC* and Leonard, *Greater Cincinnati and Its People*, 2:609, 611.

To GEORGE W. JONES   Lexington, September 24, 1823
I recd. your two letters under date the 18h. and 20th. instant[1] with the inclosure in the latter, by Mr. [Nicholas] Longworth, who has submitted to me the papers respecting his title to the Estate to be conveyed to the Bank.[2] The papers are not complete, and I am not therefore able at present to furnish a conclusive opinion on the validity of Mr. Longworth's title. I have given to him a list of such additional papers, and the particulars of such further information as I shall want to form an opinion. When I have completed the examination I will transmit to you a written opinion. The correctness of the description of the property, as contained in the deed which he has prepared, can be better tested on the ground than here, and I would therefore be glad if your Solicitor would examine it to see if it be accurate. I will thank you also to request him to send me a Copy of the act of descents of Ohio, in force at the period of the death of Mr. [Daniel] Conner, the former husband of Mrs. [Susan] Longworth.[3] I have the present act, but I wish to compare the two together.

If this letter should find Mr. [Thomas] Wilson yet at Cincinnati be pleased to say to him that I have not written to him under the supposition that he will have left your City and that I shall address him on the above subject at Philadelphia. P.S. I inclose a Copy of the Memo. given to Mr. Longworth.[4]

ALS. OCHP.   1. Not found.   2. Clay to Jones, July 15, 1823.   3. *Ibid.;* Jones to Clay, Sept. 23, 1823; Clay to Jones, Sept. 30, 1823.   4. Not found.

To GEORGE W. JONES   Lexington, September 25, 1823
By the contract between Mr. [Nicholas] Longworth and the Bank [of the United States] he was to convey the property which it agreed to receive from him, upon his return to Cincinnati;[1] and he was to have confessed judgment for the undischarged portion of his debt at the last term of the Federal Court at Columbus. He informs me that shortly after his return he stated to you that he was ready to make the deeds and offered to make them; and that he also stated to you that he was ready to confess judgment, according to the contract, but that you mentioned to him that it was not material & might be postponed until the other part of the contract was fulfilled. I wish to be informed by you of the correctness of these statements that I may give to them such weight as they may deserve on a consideration of the whole subject. Perhaps you had better have a conversation with him previously to communicating with me.

ALS. OCHP.   1. Clay to Jones, July 15 and Sept. 24, 1823; Jones to Clay, Sept. 24, 1823.

To GEORGE W. JONES   Lexington, September 30, 1823
I have duly received your letter of the 24h. instant[1] to which I will reply in the order in which the several topics of which it treats are placed by you.

The information which you have communicated respecting Daniel Conner having a brother shall be duly weighed when I again take up

156

the subject of Mr. [Nicholas] Longworth's title. If I understand the ground upon which he rests his title it is that Daniel Conner died without heirs capable of inheriting; that his brother being an alien could not inherit; and that in such cases, by the law of Ohio, existing at his death, his wife became his heir. On all these points I am yet to be satisfied.[2]

I am glad you have found Robert Piatts power of Atto. Whether it will be necessary or not to exhibit it in Court depends upon circumstances.[3] By the rules of the Court, if he denies the authority by which his name was indorsed he must deny it upon oath. If he does not so deny it we are not bound to exhibit and prove it. But it will be safest to be prepared for the worst. And I therefore advise that the power be sent, and if there be a subscribing witness to it living within this state or, if out of this State, within 100 miles of Frankfort he must be summoned. If there be no witness then the Justice of the peace before whom he acknowledged the power must be Summoned. It will also be necessary to prove the signatures of the attorneys, which must be done by a subscribing witness, if there were one, and if none by any other person acquainted with their signatures.

I have ordered suits against both [John] Leathers and [Jamison] Hawkins upon their respective notes; but have not sued each as the indorser of the other.[4]

I have not I perceive succeeded in impressing you with the advantages of suing upon a mortgage, made to secure several installments, before all of them become due. The Law of Ohio and the Law of Kentucky are exactly alike. By suing on the mortgage you get a sale of the mortgaged property, *without the valuation laws* being applied to the case. If the party be in doubtful circumstances and the mortgaged property is thought insufficient to secure the debt, you can at the first Court get an order to take the property out of the possession of the defendant and have a Receiver of the rents appointed. As the successive installments fall due you obtain orders in the same suit, from time to time, for the sale of the mortgaged property. If the mortgaged property be indivisible, I conceive the Chancellor would decree its sale upon terms to meet the several installments as they become due. By proceeding to get a Judgment at law, you cannot, according to the opinion of Judge [Thomas] Todd, sell with your execution the mortgaged property; and if you could you would be exposed to the valuation laws of the State. My practice is to sue both upon the notes at law, and upon the mortgage in Chancery, unless the def[endan]t is notoriously insolvent, and then to save costs I sue upon the mortgage alone. By prosecuting both remedies, if the deft has any other than the mortgaged property it is levied upon with the execution upon the Judgment at law and the suit in Ch[ancer]y covers all that is pledged.

I see in the mortgage of [Jacob] Fowler which is inclosed a most unusual stipulation, guarding against the above course, that there shall be no foreclosure until the last installment becomes due.[5] This will prevent my filing a bill to foreclose; but it does not prevent an ejectment being brought to obtain possession of the mortgaged property. But the utility of that step depends upon two enquires which I will thank you to

157

answer 1st. whether the mortgaged estate is productive and 2dly. whether it amply secures the debt. If it does it would hardly be worth while to trouble ourselves with the possession and renting out the property.

There has been no decision either in Ohio or Kentucky that the Bank shall pay, or shall not recover, costs, in cases under $500. My own opinion is that it is entitled to recover them in such cases; but the Court has intimated an opinion that it is not entitled to recover them. The Clerks in both Courts have not therefore taxed the costs to us, 'though in neither have they been taxed against us. The question is not of such amount as entitles us to carry it to the Supreme Court, or I would take it there; and if I can prevail upon the Judges to divide pro forma I will yet take it up by adjournment. The law is the same in both States on this question of jurisdiction. I found my opinion on the provision in the Charter to which you refer.

The amount of costs or rather fees which has been paid to the Clerk here is much greater than Mr [Harvey] Evans's bill. Perhaps you had better advance him the amount subject to have his account corrected hereafter if upon scrutinizing it I shall find any errors in it. There will be no risk in this course as he will have other fee bills against you.

With respect to Mr. [Thomas] Heckewelders charge I think it better be not paid until the instruction of the Court is obtained as to the propriety of it.[6] Where a witness is summoned to attend a Court at the same time in several cases, in strictness I think he is entitled to claim for his attendance and for his Mileage in but one of them, and he may elect which he pleases. I understood at the Septr. term of last year that the witnesses could not be gotten to attend on those terms, and that there was an acquiescence in their charging in all the cases in which they were summoned to testify. To the Bank it is of no consequence where it is sure of reimbursement out of the defts. But where they are insolvent, or the allowance is not taxable, it becomes material. I think therefore you had better pay to him the amount in one of the cases, selecting if you can one in which the Bank will be reimbursed, and reserve the others for the order of the Court.

If the Steamboats in which you suppose the [James & Hugh] Glenns and Levi James to be interested should come to Cincinnati, you had better have them levied upon there, as the right of property can be better tried there than at Louisville, where the witnesses do not reside.[7]

James Glenn cannot be released as an insolvent debtor without conforming to the act of Congress in such cases, which requires him to swear that he is not worth twenty dollars. He may possibly indeed convey away all his property and then take the oath.

I will send you the note to which [John] McKinney [Jr.] is a party as soon as I can obtain an order of the Court for it, as it is now on file in the Clerks office.[8]

ALS. OCHP.   1. Jones to Clay, Sept. 24, 1823.   2. Clay to Jones, July 15, 1823. 3. Jones to Clay, Sept. 24, 1823.   4. Clay to Jones, Sept. 17, 1823.   5. Clay to Crittenden & Worth, Nov. 15, 1820.   6. Jones to Clay, Sept. 24, 1823.   7. Clay to Jones, Sept. 17, 1823. Levi James was a resident of Bourbon County, Ky. Jackson, *Kentucky 1820 Census Index.*   8. Clay to Jones, Sept. 17, 1823.

To GEORGE W. JONES   Lexington, October 25, 1823

Inclosed I transmit Subpienas for Mr. [Griffen] Yeatman and other witnesses in the cases of the Bank of the U.S. ag[ains]t. [John H.] Piatt[1] and [Thomas D.] Carneal[2] for the 29h. day of the term, which if I have made no mistake in calculation will be the 5h. Decr. You had better get them to acknowledge service of the Subpoenas and return them inclosed to the Clerk of the Court, paying the postage to Frankfort—As I shall have left the Court at that time, Mr. [James W.] Denny[3] the Solicitor of the Louisville office will represent me, aided by Mr. [Robert] Wickliffe; so that the witnesses should be urged to attend, if possible. Benjamin Stephens,[4] the Justice who attested Piatts power of Atto. must also be summoned. Should we unfortunately fail agt. Piatt, on a/c of the power being transcended, is there not danger of its affecting our recovery against Carneal under the arrangement you made with him? It will not affect it, unless that arrangement should.

In considering [Nicholas] Longworth's case my opinion was predicated on the right of [Daniel] Conner's relations, if he has any, to inherit notwithstanding their alienage.[5]

Will you have the goodness to desire Mr [David K.] Este to write me an expose of the condition of the causes for your Jany term.

ALS. OCHP.   1. Clay to Jones, June 19, 1822.   2. Clay to Jones & Crittenden, Dec. 22, 1821.   3. For Denny, see 3:4.   4. For Stephens, who had immigrated to Kenton County, Ky., about 1807, see Collins, *History of Kentucky*, 2:759.   5. Clay to Jones, July 15, 1823.

To WILLIAM MURPHY   Lexington, October 26, 1823

I duly recd. your letter.[1] I have prevailed upon the Bank [of the United States] to consent to receive your note upon discount in lieu of an equivalent amount of my own debt, and to promise you at least four renewals, provided the discount is regularly paid, which will give you until Septr. next. I have no doubt that they will give you longer if it should be necessary and in the mean time a punctual attention is paid to it.[2] But the Bank never consents to diminish a security which it has; and as Mr. Ward's[3] name is to the bond it requires that his name or that of some other equivalent person shall be put to the note. I shall probably then have to add my own guarantee—Inclosed is a statement with the interest computed up to the 4h Novr. and the form of a note—[4] You must also send the discount say $33:60—

The note should be here by sunday next, or sooner if practicable— As I am on the eve of my departure it should be here before I go, otherwise you may not get the business done—

P.S. Address your letter to Jas. Harper[5] Cashier of the off. of Dr. & Dr.

ALS. KyLoF.   1. Not found.   2. For Murphy's debt, see 3:88.   3. Probably David L. Ward, the owner of the steamboat *Exchange* and the estate near Louisville known as "Hayfield." J. Stoddard Johnston (ed.), *Memorial History of Louisville From its First Settlement to the Year 1896*, 2 vols. (New York, 1896), 1:85, 233; Collins, *History of Kentucky*, 2:362. For Ward's debts, see 1:737; 2:81-82, 466, 575, 888; 3:118-19, 346.   4. The enclosure indicated a debt of $3,204.30.   5. For Harper, see 2:179.

Legal Document on November 1, 1823. Clay, "sole acting executor of James Morrison," nominates "Martin Duralde [Jr.] and James Erwin jointly and severally for me and in my name as executor aforesaid to demand sue for recover and receive the amount due to the Estate of the said deceased upon a mortgage executed by John K. Smith" to Morrison "on a Sugar plantation and Negroes in Louisiana on the Mississippi river to secure the payment of fifteen thousand dollars with interest." Further, "I do . . . empower my said Attorneys . . . to Sell assign and transfer the said mortgage. And to grant receipts, acquittances or releases as the case may require." ADS. LN.

This document applied to the case of *Henry Clay* v. *Nathaniel Cox et al.,* File No. 6480, First Judicial District Court of Louisiana. The case file is in the City Archives Collection at the New Orleans Public Library.

For Martin Duralde, Jr., see 1:575; 3:198. For James Erwin, see 3:495-96, 502. For John K. Smith and his debt to James Morrison, see 3:43-44, 594. See also 5:399, 1019-20; 6:960-61.

To GEORGE W. JONES   Lexington, November 8, 1823

I have duly received your favor of the 3d. instant.[1] I think you are perfectly right in waiting for the determination at Philadelphia on the case of Mr. [Nicholas] Longworth.[2] I have sent there a copy of my opinion.[3] I formed it upon the supposition of the capacity of the alien relations of Mrs. [Susan] Longworth's former husband to inherit, if he has any. The only point I think is that of the dower—

I informed you from Frankfort of the continuance of the cause against [John H.] Piatt;[4] and consequently that it is unnecessary for the witnesses to attend at the present term. Upon examining the agreement with [Thomas D.] Carneal[5] (of which you have sent me a Copy)[6] I am inclined to think that it will not obstruct our recovery against him, if we shall be defeated against Piatt. Still if you can make a satisfactory arrangement with the parties, as advised by my letter from Frankfort, I think it had better be done.

ALS. OCHP.   1. Not found.   2. Clay to Jones, July 15, 1823.   3. Not found.
4. Clay to Jones, June 19, 1822.   5. Clay to Jones & Crittenden, Dec. 22, 1821.
6. Not found.

To GEORGE W. JONES   Washington, December 12, 1823

I have duly received your letter of the 17h. Ulto.[1] in relation to the business of Mr. [Israel T.] Canby and his indorsers.[2] It appears to me that, from what you state with regard to his responsibilities when the contested note was indorsed by [John H.] Piatts[3] attorneys, the amount of them was such as to authorize that indorsement. As I have not the power with me here and speak from my recollection of its terms, it is possible that I may be mistaken in them 'tho' I think I am not. Still if you can make a compromise, of which time shall be the basis, and ultimate security of the debt the object, I would advise it to be done. If no such compromise can be effected it will then be necessary to shew in detail all the responsibilities of Mr Canby at the time the note was indorsed on the trial of the Cause, and testimony must be furnished accordingly at Frankfort.

If Piatt should be released upon the ground of a violation of the authority given to his Attorneys, I really have some fears whether [Thomas D.] Carneal[4] may not be released also upon the agreement you made with him. I think he will not and ought not be, because I understand the agreement to mean only that an effort shall be *first* made to get the money from the other parties; but I have not absolute confidence in this opinion. I think you had better order a suit in Indiana against Canby, unless he can be taken in Ohio. The original note can be sent from Frankfort in time to bring that suit. I have also to acknowledge the receipt of your letter of the 10h. Ulto. with the one inclosed from Mr. [David K.] Este,[5] to whom I shall write in a few days.[6] I regret extremely the misunderstanding with Mr. [Harvey] Evans; and hope that Mr. Este will be able in January at Columbus to restore those amicable relations which, on every account, are desirable. If he chooses to purchase at the Marshall's sales I know of no law to prevent him. If amenable to any tribunal, it can only be a moral one, and there his conduct would be judged & determined upon as it happened to be fair or otherwise. With respect to his fees, the law prescribes his rights and our obligations, and with that we must comply. The question of Costs, in cases under $500, is embarrassing. The truth is that Judge [Thomas] Todd has intimated in Kentucky pretty distinctly an opinion that we are not entitled to Costs. I have wished to get him to revise that opinion, and if he will not change it, to bring the question in some way before the Supreme Court. There is great difficulty in doing that, and other solid reasons have also existed for not making prematurely questions of jurisdiction, in the Bank cases, before the Supreme Court. The Board at Philadelphia, I think, was long since apprised that the recovery of Costs was doubtful, if not against us, in those small cases; and still, there were so many reasons for preferring the Federal tribunals, that they were nevertheless disposed to use them, even in that class of cases, rather than the State Courts.

I shall be glad to hear from you whenever you may suppose that I am able to render to the Bank any service from this place.

ALS. OCHP.   1. Not found.   2. Clay to Jones, May 16, 1823.   3. Clay to Jones, June 19, 1822.   4. Clay to Jones & Crittenden, Dec. 22, 1821.   5. Neither letter has been found.   6. See 3:539-40.

To WILLIAM CREIGHTON, JR. & WILLIAM K. BOND

Washington,
December 15, 1823

Mr. [David K.] Este, the Solicitor at Cincinnati of the Bank is engaged against it in the actions of the Bank [of the United States] against Stone, Mack, Bates & ad.[1] May I ask the favor of you to represent me at Columbus in those cases, and in any others, if there be any others, in which he cannot from any cause appear? And you will greatly oblige me by continuing your kind attentions to my business generally in the Fed. Court. I hope to be able to attend in September next, and to dispose of the greater part of it at that time. My health continues to be very good.

ALS. KyU.   1. For Ethan Stone, see 3:539-40; for Andrew Mack, 4:531. Bates has not been identified.

To WILLIAM CREIGHTON, JR.

Washington,
December 22, 1823

I recd. your obliging favor of the 10h. instant.[1] On the point of Mr. [DeWitt] Clinton being a Candidate it is asserted and denied, believed an[d] disbelieved, both here and in New York. It is difficult to form an opinion as to the truth. I am inclined to think that his being brought out depends upon contingencies.[2] If, as is most probable, there shall be no popular election; and if also he thought that he could obtain votes enough to make him one of the three, from among whom the selection must be made by the H[ouse]. of R[epresentatives]. he would be held up. But where can he get votes enough to accomplish that object?

There has been a considerable effort making, it is understood, to get up a Caucus here, but it not being as much encouraged as its partisans could have wished, it is postponed for the present, and will probably *not* be renewed until the 15h. or 20h. of January. My friends believe that in a general caucus I should be one of the two highest, if not the highest. No one, in such a Caucus, would get a majority at first; and they further believe that a majority could only be concentrated on me, because there is a stronger disposition among the friends of all the Candidates to support me than there is to support either of the others. But a general caucus cannot be got. The Tennessee delegation which, with one exception, is unanimous for me next to Genl. [Andrew] Jackson, will not attend a Caucus. And now the Maryland delegation, in which I have as many, if not more friends, than any other, will not it is supposed attend, in consequence of instructions from their Legislature.[3]

It is on all hands conceded that, if the election goes into the H. of R. and I should be one of the three highest, my election is much more probable than that of any other. Supposing the three highest to be [John Quincy] Adams, [William H.] Crawford and me, the probability is that I should receive the vote of 12 states on the first ballot. This shews the importance of my friends adhering to me, and guarding against any risk of my not being one of the three highest.[4]

In Maryland there is not much likelihood of there being a general ticket, owing to the influence which would be given to Baltimore, in such a ticket.[5] If they elect by districts I am certain of two and probably five or six.

Will the Legislature at Columbus recommend the persons who are to compose your electoral college?[6]

I have not communicated to Mr. Brent the name of the Post Master General [John McLean] as the author of the letter you received.[7]

ALS. KyU.   1. Not found.   2. Clay to Sloane, Dec. 27, 1822; Clay to Este, Jan. 22, 1824.   3. See 3:634-35, 640-41.   4. Benton to Clay, April 9, 1822.   5. In the 1824 presidential election in Maryland, 14,632 popular votes were cast for Adams, 14,523 for Jackson, 3,364 for Crawford, and 695 for Clay. Jackson received 7 of Maryland's electoral votes, Adams 3, and Crawford 1. Schlesinger, *History of American Presidential Elections*, 1:409.   6. The choice of presidential electors in Ohio was made on the basis of a state-wide popular vote rather than by districts or by the legislature. Stevens, *Early Jackson Party in Ohio*, 137.   7. Reference obscure.

To WILLIAM CREIGHTON, JR.   Washington,
December 28, 1823

You will expect from me my views of the present state of the Presidential question. & I will now give them. 1st As to the point of a Caucus.[1] I think there will be none. A considerable effort is making to get up one by the 15th or 20 of next month. The friends of Mr [William H.] Crawford are those who are principally making it, and they are actuated as much by considerations connected with themselves as from motives of friendship to him. The major part of the friends of all the other Candidates is opposed to a Caucus, and they constitute together nearly three fourths of Congress. I think the cause of a Caucus is rather losing than gaining ground. The Penna. delegation is almost unanimously opposed to it[.] Nearly a moiety of that from N. York is also adverse to it[.] If a Caucus of all the members of Congress was to be assembled, comprehending Federalists, or all the Republican members excluding Federalists, one of two results would happen, I think that it would come to no agreement, or if it united in a recommendation of any one it would be me. And the reason for this opinion is that the friends of all the Candidates would more readily unite on me than either of the others. In a Caucus constituted in either of the two modes suggested, on the first ballotings, no one would have any thing like a majority. Mr Crawford and I would stand, I think, the highest and be nearly equal, Mr [John Quincy] Adams next, Mr [John C.] Calhoun next and Genl [Andrew] Jackson the lowest. If, therefore, any practical result should be obtained, it could only be by the friends of some of the Candidates yielding their favourites and uniting with the friends of some of the others. Genl. Jackson's & Mr Calhoun's would first make the sacrifice. And it is well known that, with very few, if any, exceptions, they would concentrate on me. I should now be the highest and perhaps have a majority; but if not on the final voting, whether Mr Adams or Mr Crawford should be surrendered I should, I think, unquestionably receive a majority. If therefore considerations of expediency were alone consulted my friends would probably go into Caucus, but for one circumstance, and that is, that the delegations from Tennessee & Maryland en masse, as well as many of the friends of Mr Adams & Mr Calhoun, from other States, will not attend a Caucus. And I cannot afford to lose the weight which would be thus abstracted. A caucus composed of members, to the exclusions of the delegations, and *parts* of delegations which would thus absent themselves, might and probably would come to a conclusion very different from that which would flow out of a general Caucus either of all Congress or of all the Republicans members.

2dly Upon the supposition of there being no Caucus. In that event there will certainly be a devolution of the election upon the H of R which you know is restricted to the three highest on the list. Those three would, judging from the present state of public sentiment be Mr Adams, Mr Crawford & me[.] In that event, I believe, on the first ballot in the H of R, I should receive the votes of 12 States, that is the nine Western & South Western States and S. Carolina, Maryland, and Penna.[2] Public Sentiment may be mistaken or may change, and those may not happen to be the three highest. I offer no speculations on that contingency.

The ultimate course of N. York continues to be a matter of great uncertainty. The people of that State have most unequivocally manifested a wish to have the election of Electors transferred to themselves from the Legislature. The Governor will probably recommend such a change[.] And the house of delegates will almost unanimously, it is believed pass a Bill to that effect.[3] I think it may be positively affirmed that in the event of such a change, Mr Crawford will not receive the suffrage of that State, but that it will be given to Mr Adams or to me and I think most probably to me.[4] But it is said that the Senate of N York will [nega]tive the contemplated change, & that this is already ascertained[.] It is also asserted that a majority of the Senate is favorably disposed towards Mr Crawford. I regard this as a mere electmanouevre intended to promote the Caucus cause here by creating confidence and hope with the partisans of the Secretary of the Treasury. I do not believe the Senate of New York will be able to resist the united voice of the people, their immediate representatives & the Governor, in favor of the change but if they were I should still doubt whether they would not lose their object in a joint Ballot of the two houses[.]

What increases the embarrassment of foreseeing the final course of N. York is, that if a Law passes to change the mode of appointing the Electors, Mr [DeWitt] Clinton may, and in that event would probably, be brought out.[5] I do not think he will otherwise be a candidate. The knowing ones here say that in no event can he obtain the vote of that State. There certainly must be a most extraordinary change of public sentiment in that State if he should receive its vote[.]

I think it may be positively affirmed that Penna. will not vote for either Mr Crawford or Mr Adams.[6] Certainly it will not with out [a] Caucus recommendation of one or the other of them by an overwhelming majority—An event which cannot happen[.]

You are at liberty to make any use of this communication among my friends that you may think proper, except that of publishing it as coming from [me] . . .

LS. KyU.   1. See 3:634-35, 640-41; Clay to Creighton, Dec. 22, 1823.   2. Benton to Clay, April 9, 1822.   3. Featherstonhaugh to Clay, April 24, 1824.   4. For New York's vote in the 1824 presidential election, see Clay to Creighton, April 12, 1822, no. 2 of date.   5. Clay to Sloane, Dec. 27, 1822; Clay to Este, Jan. 22, 1824.   6. For Pennsylvania's vote in 1824, see Benton to Clay, April 9, 1822.

To JAMES ERWIN   Washington, December 29, 1823

I have not had the pleasure of receiving one line from you. I have not before written to you from two causes, one is the multitude of my engagements, and the other the uncertainty of where a letter would find you. I have had the satisfaction of making the acquaintance of your father[1] and often seeing him. My health is much better.

My prospects brighten on the subject of the Presidency. If they had a Caucus they would be able to agree upon no one but me. But they will not have one, 'though great efforts are made for it.[2] The Election will probably go to the House, and if I am one of the three highest, I think there is a moral certainty of my election.[3] The sole point of danger is that [Andrew] Jackson may so interfere with me as to exclude my being one of the three highest. In this view of the subject, Alabama[4] is extremely important. If I were sure of that State there would be no hazard from Jackson's interference. But I apprehend he will take it. I am certain of two or three, if not of all the votes of Maryland;[5] and yielding to Jackson Alabama, I should be still one of the three highest, unless he takes from me both Louisiana[6] and Mississippi.[7] The whole Tennessee[8] delegation is for me, except [John] Cocke, after Jackson. New York[9] is still undecided, but strongly inclining to me. If the three highest should be [William H.] Crawford, [John Quincy] Adams and me, leaving out Jackson and [John C.] Calhoun, I should on the first ballot receive in the H[ouse]. of R[epresentatives]. the vote of 12 states, that is the 9 Western & S. Western States, and Pennsa.[10] Maryland and South Carolina.[11] Crawford is very ill[12] and has been so since Septr. Some of his friends fear that he will lose his life or his sight. He had a violent inflammatory rheumatism, and the disease has fixed itself on his eyes, the use of both of which he is now interdicted.

I hope you and Anne [Brown Clay Erwin] will not be in a hurry to leave Ashland. I pray you both to consider that you oblige me by remaining there. Give my love to her, and accept assurances of the affection of . . .

ALS. T.   1. Andrew Erwin. See 3:496.   2. See 3:635, 641.   3. Benton to Clay, April 9, 1822.   4. Clay to Sloane, Oct. 28, 1822.   5. Clay to Creighton, Dec. 22, 1823.   6. Clay to Meigs, August 21, 1822.   7. *Ibid.*   8. *Ibid.*   9. Clay to Creighton, April 12, 1822, no. 2 of date.   10. Benton to Clay, April 9, 1822.   11. Clay to Erwin, Jan. 7, 1824.   12. Clay to Creighton, Jan. 1, 1824.

To WILLIAM CREIGHTON, JR.   Washington, January 1, 1824

I enclosed the Enquirer to you today principally for the purpose of shewing you the course which has been taken in the No[rth] Car-[o]l[in]a Legislature, by the friends of Mr. [William H.] Crawford, to nominate an electoral ticket there.[1] My friends at Columbus understand better than I do what may be most adapted to the habits & sentiments of the people of Ohio. But it would appear to me advisable that a bold and decisive course should be taken; that my friends of the Legislature (the more numerous the attendance the better) should meet and nominate persons to be electors, who should be well selected both for their local positions and their public characters.[2] A decided demonstration for me made in this way would have two effects 1st. It would secure ultimate success and 2dly. It would prevent [DeWitt] Clinton from coming out. He is now hesitating.[3] What inclines him to be a Candidate is a belief that he can get Ohio. What would decide him not to be is a conviction that he cannot obtain the vote of that State. He has been deceived by the movements at Steubenville and Cincinnati.[4]

Some of my friends at Columbus are afraid of a Caucus to nominate electors. Call it by any other name. It is concert; and it will prevail without *concert* in opposition. And if they also hold a Caucus or public meeting, why then they can say nothing against yours. Decision by Ohio is all important and at this time. Every where my prospects are brightening in this quarter—*Some of the friends of several of the other Candidates already begin to talk of taking shelter with my friends.* A caucus will not be got up here, unless a minority of the republicans holds it.[5]

which I think they will not venture to do. *I should not be at all surprized if the friends of Mr. Crawfords en masse* in N. York determined in the course of two months to quit him and to unite with mine. In all their movements, I remain of course passive & still. My friends tell them that while they have made up their mind to come over, they will be received, but they must surrende[r] at discretion; that they cannot support their Candida[te] &c. and that no terms can be granted, because we treat with nobody.

By the bye, and entre nous, the Secretary of the Treasury is dangerously ill. He has never recovered from his attack of last Septr. which was a violent [manuscript torn; words illeg.] his life or his sight.[6]

ALS. KyU. Letter marked "(Confidential)." 1. On Dec. 24, 1823, a caucus of about 100 Republican legislators met in the North Carolina senate chamber and formed a ticket of 15 Crawford electors. Thomas E. Jeffrey, *State Parties and National Politics: North Carolina, 1815-1861* (Athens, Ga., 1989), 26. 2. See 3:744. 3. Clay to Sloane, Dec. 27, 1822; Clay to Este, Jan. 22, 1824. 4. See 3:546. 5. See 3:634-35, 640-41. 6. For Crawford's illness and its effect on his presidential campaign, see Mooney, *William H. Crawford*, 240-41, 263-68.

To MATHEW CAREY   Washington, January 2, 1824

I recd. to day your favor[1] with Lewis' work[2] for which I am greatly obliged to you, altho' as I wrote you yesterday[3] I had been able to obtain a Copy here—

The Com[mitt]ee. on Manufactures will report, as the Chairman informed me, on Monday next.[4] I have great hopes of success. Believing as I most sincerely do that the prosperity of our Country mainly depends upon the naturalization of the arts among us, my best and most zealous exertions will be faithfully employed to that great end. I think we have nothing to fear in the house; and if Genl. [Andrew] Jackson adhere to us, nothing in the Senate; for his vote there may be of material consequence.[5] With the compliments of the season . . .

ALS. PPRF. 1. Letter not found. For Carey, see 3:729, note 22. 2. Probably Enoch Lewis (1776-1856), whose *The Arithmetical Expositor . . .* was published in Philadelphia in 1824. See *DAB* and *NUC*, 330:441. 3. Not found. 4. On the Tariff of 1824. See espec. 3:561, 727, 756. 5. Jackson voted for the tariff. *Annals of Congress*, 18 Cong., 1 Sess., 743.

To JAMES ERWIN   Washington, January 7, 1824

I duly received your favor of the 12th Ulto. from N. Orleans[1] and hope this letter will find you arrived at Ashland. I wrote you a few days ago.[2] Nothing new has since occurred. I am satisfied that the entire recovery and preservation of my health is in my power, if I can take the necessary exercise, and particularly on horseback—This I endeavor to do, whenever the weather admits of it.

My election to the Presidency I think is certain, if I can be made one of the three highest, from among whom the H[ouse]. of R[epresentatives]. will undoubtedly, from present appearances, have to make the selection[.] Mine would in that event be certain, whilst I think it equally certain that Genl [Andrew] Jackson could not be elected, if he should even be one of the three highest.[3] He may possibly prevent either of us being among the three highest. He will probably obtain the vote of Alabama, and I think of Mississippi also. I some times fear that he will take Louisiana from me. If I get Ohio,[4] Kentucky,[5] Louisiana,[6] Indiana,[7] Illinois[8] and Missouri,[9] I think with my prospects on this side of the Mountains I shall be made one of the three highest. I do not believe that the chance of my getting New York is surpassed by that of any other Candidate. I may say that I shall *certainly* receive two votes, probably more, in Maryland.[10] I have good prospects in Pennsa.[11] in New Jersey[12] and in So. Carolina.[13] If [William H.] Crawford, [John Quincy] Adams and I should be the three highest, it continues to be generally thought that my election in the H. of R. is secure[.]

Mr. Crawford's health is now better.[14] That of your father [Andrew Erwin] is good.

Give my love to Anne [Brown Clay Erwin] and believe me . . .

ALS. PP.   1. Not found.   2. Clay to Erwin, Dec. 29, 1823.   3. Benton to Clay, April 9, 1822.   4. For Ohio's vote in 1824, see *ibid.*   5. In the 1824 presidential election in Kentucky, Clay won 17,331 popular votes to 6,455 for Jackson. Clay received all 14 electoral votes. Schlesinger, *History of American Presidential Elections*, 1:409.   6. For Louisiana's vote in 1824, see Clay to Meigs, August 21, 1822.   7. For Indiana's vote in 1824, see Clay to Creighton, April 12, 1822, no. 2 of date.   8. For Illinois's vote in 1824, see *ibid*.   9. For Missouri's vote in 1824, see Clay to Meigs, August 21, 1822.   10. For Maryland's vote in 1824, see Clay to Creighton, Dec. 22, 1823.   11. For Pennsylvania's vote in 1824, see Benton to Clay, April 9, 1822.   12. In the 1824 presidential election in New Jersey, Jackson won 10,985 popular votes, Adams 9,110, and Crawford 1,196. Jackson received all 8 electoral votes. Schlesinger, *History of American Presidential Elections*, 1:409.   13. In the 1824 presidential election in South Carolina, electors were appointed by the state legislature, and all 11 electoral votes were cast for Jackson. *Ibid.*   14. Clay to Creighton, Jan. 1, 1824.

To JOSEPHUS B. STUART[1]   Washington, January 9, 1824.
I ought before to have acknowledged my obligation for the information obligingly communicated in your letter of the 26h. Ulto.[2]

On the question of a Caucus here, I have to say, that I still think there will be none, unless (which is not probable) the desperate expedient of holding one of a minority is resorted to, which I do not believe.[3] My friends have no fear of the result of any Caucus, composed either of all the Republicans, to the exclusion of the Federalists, or of all Congress, comprehending the Federalists. In a Caucus, composed in either of those two modes, they believe that the result would be favorable to me, *because on no one else could a majority be concentrated.* But they have no idea of attending a Caucus, which shall exhibit the aspect of a faction—a caucus in which *all* the friends of one of the Candidates shall be present, and a *few* only of those of the others. They have no idea, in short, of playing the part of mere figuranti. The recent event at Richmond[4] will not have the slightest effect in promoting here the cause of a Caucus. I give you the impressions which prevail here among the Sober and discreet. All eyes are now turned on Albany; and events there are consequently expected with great solicitude.[5]

If the friends of Mr. [DeWitt] Clinton still believe that Ohio will support him let them consult the delegation from that State here. I believe almost every member will say that he has no prospect of obtaining its suffrage in a contest with me—[6]

I write in confidence and remain . . .

ALS. KyLoF.   1. For Stuart, see 3:399.   2. Not found.   3. See 3:634-35, 640-41.   4. See 3:561-62.   5. See 3:572.   6. For Clinton's candidacy, see Clay to Sloane, Dec. 27, 1822; Clay to Este, Jan. 22, 1824. For Ohio's vote in the 1824 presidential election, see Benton to Clay, April 9, 1822.

To ALLEN TRIMBLE   Washington, January 13, 1824

Inclosed I transmit to you two letters which I have just recd. from Albany, one from Genl. Geo. McClure,[1] a distinguished member of the N. York Legislature, the other from a Dr. [Josephus B.] Stuart who was at Columbus last January.[2] I send them to put you in possession of correct information as to the condition of things there at the opening of their Legislature. There are many concurring letters from members of the N. York Legislature to the members from that State in Congress. You may rely upon it that there is greater probability at this time of my getting the vote of N. York than that any other person will obtain it.[3] And that effect will be powerfully promoted by decision at Columbus among my friends there.[4] We hear very little at present about Mr. [DeWitt] Clinton. The report of the intention of his friends to bring him out seems to have almost entirely died away.[5]

ALS. NjP.   1. Letter not found. For McClure, see 3:463.   2. Not found, but see Clay to Stuart, Jan. 9, 1824.   3. For New York's vote in 1824, see Clay to Creighton, April 12, 1822, no. 2 of date.   4. See 3:744.   5. Clay to Sloane, Dec. 27, 1822; Clay to Este, Jan. 22, 1824.

From Baptis Irvine, January 19, 1824. Writes that "A *band*, who had plotted to take away the lives & fame of strangers, who had no relations of any kind with *them*, surely ought to forfeit their own." Wants an investigation, though "the hope of it would perhaps be quixotic, without the support of my own government. In order to convince you, and *the President* of the subtle & guileful co-operation of [Cortland L.] Parker,—not to say *instigation*," gives as an example the following: "The super cargo, *Isaac Reid*, (nephew of Mr. [Robert] Patterson, of the Mint, and an acquaintance of mine at Washington, (Penn.) from our boyish days) had requested Capt. [Robert T.] *Spence*, to demand the property seized here; telling him, that he was an American citizen &c. *Spence*, as I hear, resolving to proceed cautiously enquired of Parker, about him. For, who would suspect *an American agent* of conspiring against American citizens or cargoes &c. None of us dreamed of such possibility at *that* time. Parker, wrote him in reply, that Reid had been deeply concerned with [H. LaFayette Villaume] Du-Coudray [-Holstein], and *was to have been* made Intendant of Porto-Rico! A more malignant false-hood was never coined." Asserts that "Reid never for an instant had any but a commercial object, viz. to receive the stipulated paymt. for cargo—or, in case of non-fulfilment of contract, to convey the merchandize *to the best market*." Adds that Reid reproached Parker for this "infamous falsity" and demanded his contract with Ducoudray, which Parker refused to give him. Asks: "Now, if P. took steps so false, so base and daring, to prevent American property from being even demanded, can you longer doubt *that he* had it seized—for the most dishonest designs?—To him and to Cantzlaar conjointly, *I* am debtor for all the good offices done me here! Yet the [Dutch] governor [Cantzlaar] is the responsible man." Adds, however, "But, C. is no less *fearful* than tyrannical: therefore a *word* from an American agent could have quashed all roguary & persecution." ALS. DNA, RG59, Misc. Letters. This letter is an addendum to that of January 18, 1824 [3:594-96]. See also 3:600, 618-19, 775.

For Irvine, see 3:596, 775. For Parker and Ducoudray-Holstein, see 3:596. Robert Patterson of Pennsylvania had been appointed director of the mint by

President Thomas Jefferson on December 20, 1805, and approved by the Senate on December 23. U.S. Sen., *Executive Journal*, 2:7, 10. For Captain Spence, see 5:114. Reid has not been further identified.

To DAVID K. ESTE

Washington, January 22, 1824

I duly received your two letters under date the 8h. inst.[1] for which be pleased to accept my thanks. I regret extremely the failure again of the Court at Columbus. It was what I feared. We have heard nothing from [Thomas] Todd; but I presume his indisposition prevented his attendance. I hope some adequate provision will be made, during the present Session of Congress, to prevent the recurrence of the evil.[2]

The proceedings of the meeting at Columbus, gotten up by Mr. [DeWitt] Clintons friends, have reached us through various channels, which concur with the account you have given of them. The scene of disorder and tumult was truly discreditable; but the result upon the whole was encouraging to my friends.[3] If the election come to the H[ouse]. of R[epresentatives]. as is now probable, there is very little diversity of opinion here as to my success, if the election be to be made from [John Quincy] Adams, [William H.] Crawford and myself, which is also most probable.[4]

I regret that our friend the General will not obtain the appointment to Mexico.[5] I am not in the secrets of the Cabinet, but I understand that he will certainly not be appointed. Be pleased to give him my best respects.

ALS. ViHi.   1. Not found.   2. For the failure of the judges to attend the court at Columbus and the unsuccessful attempt in 1824 to reform and expand the Federal circuit court system, see 3:551, 596-97.   3. On Jan. 8, 1824, the friends of Clinton had met in the Presbyterian Church in Columbus to attempt to nominate Clinton for president; however, Clay supporters blocked the nomination and the meeting became disorderly and adjourned inconclusively. Stevens, *Early Jackson Party in Ohio*, 78.   4. Benton to Clay, April 9, 1822.   5. Probably William Henry Harrison, whom Clay later suggested for the post. Dorothy Burne Goebel, *William Henry Harrison: A Political Biography* (Indiana Historical Collections, vol. 14, Indianapolis, 1926), 238-39.

To ADAM BEATTY

Washington, February 15, 1824

I duly recd. your letter of the 29h. Ulto.[1] and thank you for the views which you present in respect to the Tariff. Of all subjects it is the most disagreeable affair of legislation. The numerous conflicting and irreconcilable interests render it impossible to do all that I could desire. We must do the best we can. Woolens are one of the most difficult articles of the whole Tariff, in consequence of the Southern opposition. We are now engaged in the discussion of the bill; and I entertain strong hopes of success.[2]

There was a caucus of Mr. [William H.] Crawfords friends last night. Sixty four members of Congress only united in his recommendation.[3] I think it will completely prostrate him, if he ever had any prospect, which I never believed.

The upper district of Maryland[4] will *certainly* support me; and probably two or three others. I stand well in New Jersey;[5] though it is impossible to say at present whether that State will be for [John Quincy] Adams or me. All our information from Albany is highly favorable.[6] It is known that there is a majority of the legislature for me; so at least friends & foes have written from that place. All the family of my old friend Col. [Nathaniel] Rochester are exerting themselves to the utmost for me. From Richmond also we have cheering intelligence.[7]

You will excuse this short letter & believe me . . .

ALS. Courtesy of Earl M. Ratzer, Highland Park, Ill.   1. Not found.   2. See espec. 3:561, 727, 756.   3. See 3:634-35, 640-41.   4. For Maryland's vote in 1824, see Clay to Creighton, Dec. 22, 1823.   5. For New Jersey's vote in 1824, see Clay to Erwin, Jan. 7, 1824.   6. For New York's vote in 1824, see Clay to Creighton, April 12, 1822, no. 2 of date.   7. For Virginia's vote in 1824, see *ibid.*

To JOSEPHUS B. STUART   Washington, February 15, 1824

I duly recd. your obliging letter of the 9h. inst.[1] and several other previous communications, of the value of which I pray you to believe me highly sensible, although, from the multitude of my engagements, I have not been able to make regular acknowledgments of them.

I understand that those who were opposed to a Caucus here deemed it best to absent themselves from that which took place last evening, so that the actual and naked state of Mr. [William H.] Crawford's strength should be distinctly exhibited.[2] The result has corresponded with that expectation. After the greatest exertions but 66 could be got to attend, of whom he had 62 besides two proxies. Of that 62 some 18 or 20 are known to act contrary to the wishes of their respective States. If they be deducted, he will only have recd. some forty odd including those who come from your State, and whether they have conformed to public sentiment or not there you best know. The movement is considered here as a complete failure, rather tending to prostrate than to second the views of his friends. The public prints will inform you correctly of the whole proceeding. We shall wait with anxiety to learn the effect that it may produce at Albany.

ALS. KyLoF.   1. Not found.   2. See 3:634-35, 640-41.

To HORTON HOWARD[1]   Washington, February 19, 1824

I duly recd. your letter of the 7h. inst.[2] and will give to the memorial[3] to which it refers the attentive consideration which is due to the highly respectable source whence it has emanated. A friend, from well considered principles, to the freest toleration of Religion, I shall be happy to be able to give to the memorial a conscientious support. Your sect is a most interesting portion of the general community. Averse to War, lovers of order and of law, industrious, economical it deserves serious enquiry whether your labors may not be left to a peacable direction by which the sum of production may be augmented, whilst others, having no such scruples as you possess, may be employed in the military service of the Nation. If a time should indeed ever arrive when it would become necessary to exert the entire physical force of the Country, in defence of its liberties its institutions and its religion, there might be more doubt, whether your sect could be excused from the common struggle. Such a time I hope will never come.

ALS. ODa.   1. For Howard, see 5:439.   2. Not found.   3. Probably a reference to the memorial of the Society of Friends asking Congress to meliorate the condition of slaves within the District of Columbia. The memorial had been introduced on Dec. 10, 1823, and was laid on the table on Feb. 20, 1824. U.S. H. of Reps., *Journal*, 18 Cong., 1 Sess., 44, 245.

To FRANCIS P. BLAIR[1]   Washington, February 29, 1824
I sent by the last mail the last Waverley Novel[2] addressed to you, which I intended for Mrs. [Eliza Gist] Blair, with whose permission you may read it. I have not had time to read it myself. It is not very well spoken of. My health continues to be in such a state as to enable me to get through, some how or other, my multifarious vocations. These have prevented my writing as often and as much as I wished to my Frankfort friends. In regard to the affair of the Presidency (about which, you know, one of my calm and philosophical cast can feel no solicitude) all that I have to say is that I think Mr. [William H.] Crawford will not be even one of the three who will go into the H. of R; that [Andrew] Jackson, [John Quincy] Adams and myself will go there; and that I shall be elected. If I do not go into the House, I think Adams will be elected.[3]

[Ichabod] Bartlett made a written apology to me for his unprovoked affront.[4] I forgave him. The apology was so explicit and full that I have not desired it to be the subject of any particular conversation.

My best respects to Mrs. Blair.

ALS. CtY.   1. For Blair, see 3:10-11.   2. Possibly *St. Ronan's Well*, published in Dec., 1823. For the impact of Sir Walter Scott's Waverley novels in the United States, see Moray McLaren, *Sir Walter Scott* (London, 1970), 142-43, *passim*.   3. Benton to Clay, April 9, 1822.   4. For Bartlett and his attack on Clay, see 3:612-14. For his apology, see 3:616-17.

To WILLIAM EUSTIS   Washington, March 20, 1824
I have the honor to inform your Excellency that the seat of John Bailey,[1] who had been returned a member of this House, from the Norfolk district in the State of Massachusetts has been declared, by a vote of the House of Representatives, to be vacant.

ALS. MHi.   1. Bailey's election had been contested on the ground that he was not a resident of the district which had elected him. On March 18, 1824, the house refused to seat him. He returned to Canton, Mass., was reelected to the seat and served from Dec. 13, 1824, to March 3, 1831. *BDAC*.

To JAMES PLEASANTS   Washington, March 20, 1824
I have the honor to inform your Excellency, by order of the House of R[epresentatives]. that the Hon[ora]ble William Lee Ball,[1] a member of that House returned from Virginia, hath departed this life; and of consequence his seat is vacated.

ALS. Vi.   1. Congressman Ball of Virginia had died on Feb. 28, 1824. *BDAC*.

To MATHEW CAREY   Washington, April 21, 1824
I am sorry to hear of your retirement. But you have done your duty, and have rendered the most essential service to a good cause. The fate of the cause in the Senate, I am sorry to say, is very doubtful.[1]

Copy. Printed in *Mathew Carey Autobiography*, Research Classics, no. 1 (Brooklyn, N.Y., 1942), 130.   1. For Carey's publications in support of a protective tariff, see 3:729, 745-46.

From JOHN McKIM   Baltimore, April 22, 1824

I thank you for your attention—Indavouring to lay a duty on sheathing Copper I am convinced that If the House had been in Possession of the facts, that it was of Importance to the Country that it should have been a unanimous vote in its favour, there is not an article belonging to a ship, that is Imported, that does not pay a duty, Except sheathing Copper—

Our Exports to the whole of South America are now very greate, we must take the productions of that country in Payment, for our produce and Manufactures, and copper is now Recd. from the Whole of South America, but Particularly—from Chilli [*sic*, Chile]; And If our Manufactories are destroy[ed] by the large Importation of Sheathing Copper, our Merchants will be disapointed in their Remittances, for I do Assure you, the Pig Copper that we have been in the Habit of giving from 16 to 20 cents pr lb. for, will not bring 12½ cents And there is several mines Opened in the United States, the Ore will not bring one cent pr lb. Besides Incouraging this Infant Manufacturer the Government would raise a Good deal of money out of the Sheathing Copper, that now pays *no duty,* And the British are sending it in, in large Quantities and selling it 2 to 3 cents pr lb. under What it costs, the Obj[ect] of which is very plain, to Destroy the 3 only factorys in the United States;

Now all We Want on this Article, is 2 to 3 Cents pr lb, or place it at the same duty the Brasian [*sic*, Brazilian] Copper pays, say 15 pr lb. advalorem—

I Request that you Will speake to Mr. [Josiah S.] Johnston,[1] and any other of the Senators that you think proper, and have it placed on the Tariff in the Senate.[2]

ALS. NjHi.   1. For Johnston, see 3:339.   2. For Clay's motion to amend the tariff bill to provide a duty on manufactured copper, see 3:733-34. For the tariff, see 3:756.

From GEORGE FEATHERSTONHAUGH[1]   Duanesburgh, N.Y.,
                                                       April 24, 1824

Having watched with great interest the progress of the Tariff Bill in the House of R[epresentatives]: the news of its final passage has given me the most lively Satisfaction.[2] Believing it to be a measure, which if it should become a Law, will gradually introduce more substantial Comfort amongst us, than any other which could be devised; and which will help to take down a little the pampered sufficiency of the Commercial men of our Community, now almost insupportable, I most sincerely rejoice at what has been done, and feel grateful to the steady supporters of the Bill, especially to yourself. We are all satisfied that without your great Exertions it could not have been Carried. Such a Law will seal the natural union betwixt the Agricultural and manufacturing branches of industries. I am particularly pleased with the liberal protection our Raw Material Wool has assigned to it. I remember fifteen months ago in Washington Expressing my Opinion to you on that Subject.

The people in the interior of this State, are just beginning to acquire a few clear ideas on the Subject of national industry, and how it will be affected by such a Tariff. I have passed the Winter at the Seat of our State Legislature, for the purpose of becoming acquainted with the members, and of awakening them to this important matter. Whether the Tariff passes into Law or not, I intend this Summer to publish a pamphlet,[3] with a view to diffuse in the most Extensive manner proper ideas about it, and to prepare the minds of the Members against their meeting in Albany in November next to choose Electors.[4]

As important Consequences may flow from that meeting, I shall avail myself of this occasion to give you my opinion of the materials of which it must be constituted, assured that you will attribute no motives to me, but such as I should wish to make acceptable to yourself.

Mr. [William H.] Crawford's Friends are certainly not numerous in our Legislature. Out of 160, I would not at present warrant him more than 56. The Republican Party is very strong in this State, but not united on this subject. Offence has been taken not to the Character of Mr. C-d, but to the manner in which he has been brought forward. Of the remaining 104, General [Andrew] Jackson may have 20, but since his nomination for president by the Clintonian men of this State, his chance has become very bad. The party here unites but in one thing, having the utmost horror of Clintonianism. Some of his Friends in the Legislature, voted him out of the Canal Commission the other day, lest they should be suspected of it. The Friends of Mr. [John Q.] Adams, and the Friends of National Industries, will dispose of the remaining 84. Mr. Adams has Friends but they are Extremely [word illeg.] Their interests are the same with those of the Friends of national industries, who are warmly attached to Mr. Clay. If a judicious Effo[r]t then is made this summer, to unite the Agricultural and Manufacturing interests, I think such a [word illeg.] can be made next November, as will make Mr. Clay the leading contender of our State. And it is personally known to me, that the leading friends of Mr. Crawford, would unite in it, if his case were desperate.[5]

Such are the Views I entertain, with favourable opportunities for Observation. Another Circumstance that the party stands committed to support Mr. [Samuel] Young for Governor, and he is entirely with the [word illeg.] of national industry.

ALS. NAlI; copy in MnHi.   1. For Featherstonhaugh, see 4:34.   2. For the Tariff of 1824, see 3:561, 726, 756.   3. Not found.   4. For the attempt in New York to change the mode of selecting presidential electors, see 3:477, 768-71, 787-88, 820-21, 869-70, 889.   5. For New York's vote in the 1824 presidential election, see Clay to Creighton, April 12, 1822, no. 2 of date.   6. For Young, see 3:376, 511.

To JAMES HARPER   Washington, April 24, 1824

The very great protraction of the present Session of Congress will prevent my reaching K[entucky]. until towards the last of the ensuing term of the Fed. Court which I regret extremely. I have written to Mr. Crittenden[1] and to Mr. [James W.] Denny to represent me in the Bank causes and particularly to take Judgments for me in plain causes, allowing the controverted ones to remain open until I get out. Congress I think will adjourn on the 17h. May[2] and I shall lose no time afterwards in getting home. Have you brought any new suits? Has the Marshall collected and paid over the am[oun]t. of [David L.] Ward's note which I assigned to the Bank?[3] Be pleased to write me by the return mail, as there will be time for me to hear from you before I leave this place.

I am extremely sorry to inform you that the Supreme Court did not give its opinion on the Kentucky relief laws.[4]

ALS. KyLxT. 1. Probably John J. Crittenden. 2. It adjourned on May 27. BDAC. 3. See 2:888; 3:118-19, 346. 4. Three cases—*Wayman* v. *Southard, B.U.S.* v. *Halstead,* and *B.U.S.* v. *January*—which were designed to test the validity of Kentucky's stay and replevin laws were argued before the Supreme Court in March, 1824, but the decision was not rendered until Feb., 1825. Charles Warren, *The Supreme Court in United States History,* 2 vols. (Boston, 1937), 1:647-51. For the continuing controversy over Kentucky's relief laws, see Kentucky: New Court (Relief) party and Kentucky: Old Court (Anti-Relief) party in Subject Index: Volumes 1-6 in 7:739-40.

From John G. Jackson, Clarksburg, Va. (W.Va.), May 6, 1824. Has read in the Washington *Daily National Intelligencer* "Your truly great Speech upon the Tariff [3:683-730]." Believes it proves "your unquestionable claims to the reputation of a great debater (&, which is of more value) of a great Statesman." ALS. InU.

For Jackson, a judge and formerly a congressman, see *BDAC.* Clay's speech was published in the *Intelligencer* on April 19-20, 1824.

From George Feathersonhaugh, May 12, 1824. Reports that "Genl. [Stephen] V[an]. Rensselaer had . . . sent me your speech [3:683–730]" on the tariff. Notes that "I certainly admire my friend Mr. [Daniel] Webster, as all men must who have had opportunities of judging of the vigour of his capacious mind, but his speech is a plea for his Boston Constituents, he is against it because of them, but he is for those parts which favour their present interests." Adds that "Mr. [Joel R.] Poinsett too in a Letter the other day, predicts the most lugubrious results." Asserts that while it is "distressing to differ from such estimable" men, "if I had been in Congress . . . I would have voted with you to the last tenpenny." Predicts that "You have sown your seed in places where it will come to a ripe harvest. I look to the day when all these gentlemen will make their acknowledgments."

Turns to the "Question of next President," noting that "I at the very first moment told Mr. [Martin] Van Buren that my preferences were for you and would not change. We have been going on thus ever since but Mr. [William H.] Crawford and yourself have been considered on all sides as the only candidates of the Republican Party, the effort on the part of Mr. Crawford's friends during our last Legislature has been to persuade the members that you were entirely out of the question, first you was sick, then you had received the last unction; your appearance in the speakers chair however wonderfully revived you, and new stories were brought forward." Points out that "last winter in Albany . . . we succeeded in the great object of preventing the Crawfordites from drawing the Legislature into approving of the caucus nomination, this was much wished, but could not be accomplished, and they gave it up, being afraid of shewing their own weakness. If Mr. Crawford is withdrawn there is no doubt, but we shall get an electoral Ticket in your interest." Promises that "your friends in this state will not be idle this summer," and states that "I propose to take some very particular pains with the members which my situation and connection with the landed men give me opportunities of doing." Asks for suggestions as to how to contribute to Clay's "advancement and ultimate success," indicating that "personal trouble [is] no consideration." ALS. NA11; copy in MnHi.

For Stephen Van Rensselaer, see 3:214. For Joel R. Poinsett, see 2:238. For Webster's speech against the Tariff of 1824, see *Annals of Congress,* 18 Cong., 1 Sess., 2026-68. For the Tariff of 1824, see 3:561, 727, 756. For Poinsett's opposition to the tariff, see James F. Rippy, *Joel R. Poinsett, Versatile American* (Durham, N.C., 1935), 82-85.

Van Buren supported William H. Crawford for president while maintaining a friendly attitude toward Clay. This led to confusion as to his motives and intentions. John Niven, *Martin Van Buren, The Romantic Age of American Politics* (New York, 1983), 126, 131-35, 146-55.

For New York's vote in the 1824 presidential election, see Clay to Crieghton, April 12, 1822, no. 2 of date.

To JOHN G. JACKSON   Washington, May 15, 1824

I received you obliging letter of the 6h. inst.[1] in which you are pleased kindly to express your favorable opinions of the Speech which I delivered in the H[ouse]. of R[epresentatives]. on the Tariff.[2] I have received and read them with particular satisfaction, as giving strength and confidence in my own. I am happy to be able to inform you that the bill having passed the Senate, 'though with material alterations in some particulars, is likely to be finally consummated.[3]

I avail myself of the occasion to assure you of my friendly recollection of our former acquaintance and cordial intercourse, and to tender you the best wishes for your prosperity . . .

ALS. InU.   1. Jackson to Clay, May 6, 1824.   2. See 3:683-730.   3. See 3:561, 727, 756; Clay to Carey, Jan. 4, 1824.

To JAMES MADISON   Washington, May 25, 1824

I was particularly gratified to be favored from yourself with your sentiments on that interesting subject which has engaged so much of the attention of Congress during its present Session; and it gave me a good deal of satisfaction to find, on perusing your letter of the 24h. Ulto.,[1] that my opinions were not widely different from your's. I think there can be no doubt of the impropriety of the interference of Government, in the direction of labor and capital, between the different members of society, so far as it respects our own Country; but I have supposed that it ought to interfere, in behalf of our own people, against the policy and the measures of Foreign Governments. If the U.S. were disconnected with the rest of the world, I should be opposed to the principle of the Tariff. In the actual relations in which we stand to other powers, I can not but think that the circular of the Emperor of Russia [Alexander I][2] describes accurately the situation of a people whose Government does not protect their industry. A community of nations, some of which do whilst others do not protect their respective industry, would resemble a condition of society filled with Corporations and Monopolies. The monopolists and the Corporators would carry every thing before them.

The exceptions which you state to the general principle which you lay down are so many as to comprehend almost all the objects which would appear to me to require the aid of Government.

The bill, you will have seen, has finally passed.[3] The measure of protection which it affords is short of what many of its friends wished; but considering the sensibilities which have been awakened, and the real or imaginary diversity of interests which exist in our Country it is perhaps better that we should advance slowly. I have no doubt with you

175

that friends & foes will be alike disappointed. I cannot however but hope and believe that, altho' we shall not be able immediately to recognize distinctly any particular effect of the Tariff we shall see, after a few years, that it will have accomplished much.

I pray you to communicate to Mrs. [Dolley] Madison my respectful Compliments and to accept for yourself as well as her my best wishes for the continued health and prosperity of both of you.

ALS. NN.　1. See 3:740-43.　2. See 3:716-17, 729.　3. See 3:561, 727, 756, and Clay to Carey, Jan. 4, 1824.

To GEORGE W. FEATHERSTONHAUGH
Washington, May 26, 1824

I cannot leave this City without acknowledging my obligations for your obliging letter of the 12h. inst.[1] I congratulate you on the final passage of the Tariff.[2] The measure of protection which it extends to Domestic industry is short of what it should have been. But we have succeeded in establishing the principle, and hereafter I apprehend less difficulty will be encountered in giving to it a more comprehensive & vigorous application.

In respect to the Presidency, on which you are so good as to express your favorable opinions of me, I can add but little to the stock of information which is derivable from the public prints. Events in your State are most likely to influence its decision,[3] and of these you are more competent to judge than I can be. You may place absolute reliance on these points 1st. that my friends will persevere in their endeavor, under any circumstances, to secure my election. 2dly. that the states of Ohio, Indiana, Kentucky, Illinois, Missouri and Louisiana are firm and immovable in my support.[4] 3dly. that I shall divide Maryland[5] with the other candidates and 4thly. that, if I am not excluded from the H[ouse]. of R[epresentatives]. I shall be elected. Some manifestations in my behalf have been recently given in New Jersey,[6] of the value of which you can make a better estimate than I can. My friends have been thinking of running Chancellor [Nathan] Sanford[7] for the Vice Presidency, and should they ultimately determine to do so, I apprehend that there will not be much difficulty in his obtaining the support of those States which I have above mentioned. On this matter they will not finally decide until they have some reason to believe that he will be acceptable to New York.

Entre nous, it is believed here that [William H.] Crawford cannot possibly outlive the summer.[8] Within a few days past he has become much worse, and paralytic symptoms have exhibited themselves. A veil has been kindly thrown over his actual situation, which is certainly creditable to humanity; but it will not be practicable or proper to conceal it much longer from the public.

I shall take the liberty of giving a letter of introduction to you my friend J[osiah] S. Johns[t]on, Senator from Louisiana, who intends passing the ensuing summer principally in your State, and who you will find to be an intelligent & discreet gentleman.

I am glad to tell you that Mr. [Lewis] Eaton[9] is very well thought of here, as a sensible, judicious & honest politician.

ALS. KyU.   1. Featherstonhaugh to Clay, May 12, 1824.   2. See 3:561, 727, 756;
Clay to Carey, Jan. 4, 1824.   3. For New York's vote in the 1824 presidential election,
see Clay to Creighton, April 12, 1822, no. 2 of date.   4. For Ohio, see Benton to Clay,
April 9, 1822; for Illinois and Indiana, see Clay to Creighton, April 12, 1822, no. 2 of
date; for Kentucky, see Clay to Erwin, Jan. 7, 1824; for Missouri and Louisiana, see Clay
to Meigs, August 21, 1822.   5. For Maryland, see Clay to Creighton, Dec. 22,
1823.   6. Several meetings in behalf of Clay's candidacy were held in Paterson, N.J.,
but he had little support in New Jersey outside of Essex County. Herbert Ershkowitz, *The
Origin of the Whig and Democratic Parties: New Jersey Politics, 1820-1837* (Washington, 1982),
39. For New Jersey's presidential vote, see Clay to Erwin, Jan. 7, 1824.   7. For Sanford, see 3:577, 799, 833, 841, 864.   8. Clay to Creighton, Jan. 1, 1824.   9. For New
York Congressman Lewis Eaton, see *BDAC*.

To HORTON HOWARD   Lexington, June 12, 1824

I ought earlier to have acknowledged the receipt of your letter of the
16 January last,[1] with the accompanying Map of the Delaware district,[2]
executed with so much neatness by your son. Be pleased to accept of
my thanks for this proof of your obliging attention to me. Although I
do not know that I shall have occasion myself for any of the valuable
information which the Map presents, it is not unlikely that some of my
friends may, in which case I shall be able to promote the laudable object which you had in view, in the publication and distribution of it.

ALS. ODa.   1. Not found.   2. A map maker, Howard published a number of maps
of Ohio, including, presumably, one of Delaware, Ohio. *NUC*, 256:604; R. Carlyle Buley,
The Old Northwest Pioneer Period, 1815-1840, 2 vols. (Bloomington, Ind., 1950), 1:235, 286;
2:525.

To JOHN G. JACKSON   Lexington, June 19, 1824

I thank you for the excellent Speech addressed by you to the people of
Harrison County,[1] relative to the proposed Convention in your State,[2]
of which you did me the favor to transmit me a Copy.[3] The effort now
making to reform the Constitution of your State (if indeed you now
have one) will excite much interest every where. I shall view with deep
concern its progress and its result. Although it does not belong to me
to judge of what may be fitting for your State, I cannot nevertheless
forbear from expressing my entire concurrence with you in the views
which you have taken on most of the great points of Government, and
especially that which relates to the Elective franchise. Here we experience, I think, no inconvenience whatever from the most extended exercise of it.

It is very remarkable how uniform the arguments against reform
always are, wherever employed. Reverence for the work of our Ancestors, wildness of the spirit of innovation, the safety and prudence of
adhering to those institutions which have stood by us so long, are the
themes dwelt upon at Constantinople, Madrid, Paris, London, and in
Virginia. I congratulate you upon the prospect, which is presented in
the State of our common nativity, of their being deprived of their
magic influence.

ALS. InU.   1. Jackson had delivered a speech on the need for a constitutional convention in Virginia in April before the militia and had repeated it the following week on
election day. For this and the movement for a constitutional convention, see Dorothy
Davis, *John George Jackson* (Parsons, W. Va., 1976), 259, 279, 312-13.   2. Such a convention was finally held in 1829. See 7:576.   3. Not found.

To HENRY H. GURLEY[1]   Lexington, June 21, 1824

I hope this letter will find you safely returned home, and that you found your family and friends all well. The object on which I wish to trouble you at present is one in which I am sure your humanity will second my request. The late Capt. Nath[anie]l G.S. Hart (the brother of Mrs. [Lucretia Hart] Clay and Mrs. [Ann Hart "Nancy"] Brown) who was killed at the disatrous battle of Raisin,[2] took with him a servant, of whose fate we never received a satisfactory account but who we feared had fallen in the general massacre. Recent intelligence induces us to believe that he is yet alive and in the possession of a gentleman opposite to Baton Rouge. Mr. John Trimble,[3] a respectable citizen of Ohio, saw and conversed with him this Spring. He informed Mr. Trimble that he was sold some few years ago at or near St. Louis by the Indians who had taken and held him in captivity. He is in the possession of a Mr. Ayriatt or Arytt (so the name of the gentleman was pronounced to Mr. T. 'though it may be incorrectly spelt) a lawyer residing opposite to Baton Rouge.[4]

Isham (for that is the name of the boy) is a black man of low statue, about forty or forty five years of age, at this time, of agreeable countenance, and rather soft voice. He knew all the members of Col. [Thomas] Hart's family, and is acquainted with the names and many particulars of most of the inhabitants of Lexington at the time he left it in the summer of 1812. He belonged to Col. Hart (the father of Mrs. Clay) but is now and has been for several years past entitled to his freedom. He was in the service (having some years then to serve) of the widow [Susannah Gray Hart] of Col. Hart, who permitted him to accompany her son, being a faithful good natured and excellent servant. I am the sole surviving Exor of Col. Hart, and as such would have a clear right to take possession of and hold him, if he were a slave; but it is my wish that he should enjoy the freedom to which he is entitled and be permitted to return here, if he desires it.

Now what I should be glad that you would do is to satisfy yourself of the identity of the man, and if you believe him to be the person in question, to take the necessary measures to effect his liberation or his return to me. If any authority be necessary to invest you with for that purpose from me as Exor of Col. Hart I do hereby convey it in the most ample extent.

Mr. [Thomas] Smith, who is connected with my family, has written to my son and Mr. [Martin] Duralde [Jr.] on this subject, which I mention because some steps may have been taken by them to accomplish the object of this letter. I am not sure that my son was not too young, when Isham left, to recollect him.

I need not say to you, my dear Sir, that this is a matter deeply interesting to our feelings. Indeed we have forborne as yet to make any communication concerning it to Mrs. Hart, who yet lives. The return of Isham among us might afford a melancholy satisfaction. I pray your kind & prompt attention to the affair.

P.S. Mr. Smith also wrote on the above subject to Mr. [Hugh] Alexander P.M. at Baton Rouge.[5] The requisite proof to identify the man shall be supplied from this Country if necessary.[6]

ALS. LNHT. 1. For Congressman Gurley of Louisiana, see 3:249 and *BDAC*. 2. For Hart's death see Clay to Simmons, Dec. 14, 1813; 1:699; 2:622-23. For Ann Hart "Nancy" Brown, see 1:150. 3. For Trimble, brother of Ohio governor Allen Trimble, see Mary McA. T. Tuttle & Henry B. Thompson (eds.), *Autobiography and Correspondence of Allen Trimble Governor of Ohio* (reprint ed., Columbus, Ohio, 1909), 80, 128, 238. 4. Not identified. 5. Name supplied by Judy Bolton, Hill Memorial Library, Louisiana State University. 6. Clay again wrote Gurley on June 22, 1824, reporting that he had been informed that "Mr. Fielding Bradford of St. Francisville can identify the person of the negro man Isham . . . and I have no doubt that he will promptly lend any aid in his power towards the ascertainment of the fact." ALS. LNHT.

To Phineas Savoury [*sic*, Savery] *et al.*, Providence, R.I. August 16, 1824. Thanks them for offering to make him an honorary member of the Franklin Society of Brown University. Accepts with pleasure, but regrets that there is "little probability . . . of my ever being able to participate with its members in their highly useful discussions and deliberations." ALS. RPB.

Savery received the A.B. degree from Brown University in 1824 and the M.D. from Harvard in 1827. *Historical Catalogue of Brown University . . . 1764-1906* (Providence, R.I., 1905). The Franklin Society was one of three literary societies at Brown in the 1820s. Walter C. Bronson, *The History of Brown University, 1764-1914* (Providence, R.I., 1914), 233, 239.

From George W. Featherstonhaugh, Duanesburgh, N.Y., September 20, 1824. Reports on observations he has made on New York politics during a journey of three weeks. Continues: "At the close of the Extra Session of our Legislature in August we counted 32 persons, personally known to me, and whom we thought were to be depended upon for you, in preference to all other Candidates with the exception of perhaps two for Gen. [Andrew] Jackson." Notes that "Col. [William R.] King of Alabama of the Senate, talks with much apparent Candour of the certain success of Gen. Jackson in Louisiana [Clay to Meigs, August 21, 1822]." Points out that there are 160 votes in the New York legislature, and, in order to "make an uniform Electoral Ticket for Mr. [William H.] Crawford there must be 81 votes, deducting the 32 from the 79 thus left for all others, there would only be 47 for [John Quincy] Adams." States that Martin Van Buren "affects in the coolest manner to consider the thing as settled, and ventured to say quite in a serious way the other day . . . that the success of Mr. Crawford's Ticket was already a matter of history." Asserts, however, "There has in truth never been a moment in which Mr. Adams has not been considered as strong a man as Mr. Crawford in our present Legislature—therefore the giving [of] 81 votes to the latter and only 47 to the former is to say the least of it an impudent Absurdity. Mr. V.B. however is playing a deep and active Game. He and his Emissaries are unwearied in their Endeavours to shew that under any Circumstances you cannot get into the H[ouse]. of R[epresentatives]. & that the Cause of Mr. Crawford is the Cause of the Republican party. That the demonstrations made in your favour are merely to secure you some Eminence at the close of the Game. By such arts they hope to cajole your supporters here into their Ranks." Predicts that "your Friends in the N.Y, Legis[latur]e. will Effectually hold the balance betwixt Crawford and Adams, preventing either of them from getting the Ticket . . . should any thing happen to Mr. Crawford you will certainly get the Electoral Ticket of this State; but not, I am pretty sure with the full consent of Mr. V. Buren. Why I cannot tell [Featherstonhaugh to Clay, May 12, 1824]."

Explains also that the "leading Friends of Mr. Adams have freely told me, that the great point with them is to Exclude Mr. Crawford, and that to effect this they are willing at any time to divide the Electoral Ticket with us . . . My answer has uniformly been, that our great Object was to get you into the H. of R. that I believed your Friends would not do you so great an injury as to talk of making Bargains."

Reports that "in about 3 weeks I publish a pamphlet addressed to the farming interest here, but intended for the members. It will be a plain Story for plain people. I shall explain the Tariff [of 1824] and your part in it [3:561, 727, 756], and shew the necessity of discarding all the old rips of Politicians, and of beginning de novo."

Sends "a Bath newspaper with your nomination [3:840-41] and that of Mr. Sandford [*sic*, Nathan Sanford]," and asks: "What do you think of Mr. S's nomination?" ALS. NA11.

For New York's vote in the 1824 presidential election, see Clay to Creighton, April 12, 1822, no. 2 of date; for the election of 1824, see Benton to Clay, April 9, 1822. For Sanford's nomination for vice president, see 3:577, 798-99, 822-23, 833, 841, 864. For William R. King, see 2:255 and *BDAC*.

From Thomas Hart Benton, St. Louis, September 22, 1824. Reports that he has traveled through half of Missouri's counties and will soon visit the remainder. States: "The only place in which I have found serious opposition to you is in a part of the . . . Cape Girardeau district." Hopes he helped "to remove the only objection, *that you had no chance.* On the contrary I represented that your chance was better than ever; that a resort to the H[ouse]. of R[epresentatives]. was now certain [Benton to Clay, April 9, 1822]; and that you were foremost." Asserts that "[Andrew] Jackson is the only man that interferes with you," but "he can do nothing at all in the state," even though he is strongest in St. Louis. Adds that "We are at a loss about a V[ice]. P[resident]. to go with you. We have seen what was done in Ohio and Kentucky on the subject of Mr. Sandford [*sic*, Nathan Sanford]; but we have not learnt whether the people of those states will take him up [3:577, 798-99, 822-23, 833, 841, 864]." ALS. KyU.

For Missouri's vote in the 1824 presidential election, see Clay to Meigs, August 21, 1822. For the outcome of the 1824 presidential election, see Benton to Clay, April 9, 1822.

To GEORGE W.   Lexington, October 10, 1824
FEATHERSTONHAUGH

I have just received your obliging favor under date the 20h. Ulto.[1] and thank you most heartily for the sketch which you have drawn of the state of politics in New York. It agrees substantially with the opinions of other friends which have been communicated to me.

You enquire what strength out of N. York I possess? I have entire confidence in my obtaining the votes of Ohio, Indiana, Illinois, Missouri, Louisiana and Kentucky. The aggregate of these is 46. It is *possible* that I may lose one in Illinois. With regard to Louisiana, Col. [William R.] King is entirely mistaken.[2] Genl [Andrew] Jackson is the third Candidate only in that State. The result of the election in the City of N Orleans[3] made a momentary impression that he might receive the vote of that State; but it was more than counterbalanced by contrary results in other parts of the State. All the information from that quarter which has reached here is perfectly concurrent that the vote of the State will be confered on me. The Govr. elect,[4] who passed through here some weeks ago, so stated. And no later than yesterday a letter was received from Mr. [Dominique] Bouligny,[5] a distinguished

180

French gentleman, late a member of the Senate of Louisiana, and now a Candidate for the Senate of the U.S. affirming most confidently that the vote of the State w[oul]d. be given to me, and that Genl Jackson was the third Candidate in point of strength.

Passing the mountains with 46 votes or 45 at the least, it is not necessary for me to open the chapter of chances and probabilities on the other side of them. You will be best able to judge of events there. If the vote of N. York alone were added to that which I have mentioned, there would be very little uncertainty in the final issue.[6] But if Mr. [William H.] Crawford should lose N. York, or if from any cause he should be withdrawn, I entertain very little doubt but that the vote of Virginia would be cast on me.[7] Not that Virginia loves me more, but because she hates me less, than the other Candidates. All the events which have occurred from the 4h. of July last inclusive have tended to alienate that State from Mr. [John Quincy] Adams. And Genl. Jackson is the last of the Candidates that she would take.

In reference to the prospects of Mr [Nathan] Sanford, I think there is no hazard in saying that he will receive the votes of Ohio and Kentucky, and most probably of all the States favorable to me.[8] If he does not obtain the whole, it will be in consequence of the want of demonstrations of a disposition to support him to the Eastward. In that view of the subject, the recent nomination at Bath will have the best effect.[9] I feel considerable solicitude in regard to the Vice Presidency, on account of the American policy. If Mr. [John C.] Calhoun is elected we shall have, in a body already nearly equally divided as to that policy, the presiding officer against us.[10] I *know* that his opinion is that the Tariff of 1816 went far enough, and that he was opposed to that of the last Session. But if he were favorably inclined towards that policy, he would be controled by his Southern position. If, during the next Administration, we should have both the President and Vice President against us, what should we be able to effect in advancing the internal prosperity of the Union? There would be reason to apprehend that we should lose the ground, little as it is, which we have gained. I have been surprized at the supineness of that portion of the American public, favorable to domestic industry, in relation to the Vice Presidency.

President [Horace] Holl[e]y saw Mr Secretary Crawford about four weeks ago at Frederick town, on his return from the Virginia Springs. Mr. Holley says that his articulation, his gait and his general appearance bore conclusive evidence of his paralytic attack.[11] Should he be withdrawn, I think the votes of Delaware, Virginia, N Carolina and Georgia in the H[ouse]. of R[epresentatives]. will be given to me.[12] And this is not the effect of any understanding between us or between our friends. All insinuations of any such understanding are utterly destitute of foundation. I have come to none, I shall have none, with any one.

I know not what to say in regard to the future in your State; and therefore I shall say nothing.

I am unable to account for the opposition to me which you impute to Mr. [Martin] Van Buren.[13] It is inconsistent with all his professions to my friends and to me. To them he has, again and again, said that he hesitated between Mr Crawford and me; that he should be alike satisfied with the election of either of us; and that his decision to support Mr Crawford proceeded from a belief that he was more likely to be sustained elsewhere than I was.

I shall be eager to see your pamphlet.[14] If I could make any contributions to it (which is not probable) it is too late for them to reach you in time for its publication[.]

ALS. KyLoF. Letter marked "(Confidential)." 1. Featherstonhaugh to Clay, Sept. 20, 1824. 2. For the votes of New York, Indiana, and Illinois in the 1824 presidential election, see Clay to Creighton, April 12, 1822, no. 2 of date; for Ohio, see Benton to Clay, April 9, 1822; for Louisiana and Missouri, see Clay to Meigs, August 21, 1822; for Kentucky, see Clay to Erwin, Jan. 7, 1824. 3. See 3:823. 4. Henry S. Johnson was Louisiana's govenor-elect. See *BDGUS*, 2:558. 5. For Bouligny, see 3:900. 6. For the outcome of the 1824 presidential election, see Benton to Clay, April 9, 1822. 7. For Virginia's vote, see Clay to Creighton, April 12, 1822, no. 2 of date. 8. See 3:577, 798-99, 822-23, 833, 841, 864. 9. See 3:840-41. 10. See 3:669, 814, 833, 846. 11. Clay to Creighton, Jan. 1, 1824. 12. Benton to Clay, April 9, 1822. 13. Featherstonhaugh to Clay, May 12, 1824. 14. Not found, but see Featherstonhaugh to Clay, Sept. 20, 1824.

To GEORGE W. JONES Frankfort, Ky., November 6, 1824
Inclosed, I transmit you a Certificate of the payment of Mr. [John] Rowan's two notes which you placed in my hands.[1] Be pleased to inform me if it be satisfactory, if it comprehends the Costs, and if the notes may be delivered to him. I have not made the computation, but I think he informed me that he had made some other payment.

The Cincinnati Causes will not be tried this Court; and therefore you need not attend. They will probably not be reached, and the burning of the Capitol[2] and the illness of Judge [Thomas] Todd[3] will abridge the term, which has already extended to four weeks.

ALS. OCHP. 1. Not found. 2. The Kentucky Capitol at Frankfort burned on Nov. 4, 1824. Collins, *History of Kentucky*, 1:31. 3. Clay to Todd, March 20, 1823.

To GEORGE W. Washington, December 9, 1824
FEATHERSTONHAUGH
Your favor of the 4h and 10h of November addressed to me at Lexington,[1] and that of the 17h.[2] directed to this place have all been received here. I thank you for them. It would be useless and unprofitable now to make any observations upon the singular issue of the election at Albany.[3] Whatever differences of opinion may exist among my friends, as to the true course of policy which they ought to have pursued, I am perfectly satisfied that they were guided by their best judgments, in the difficult circumstances under which they were placed; that there was uncertainty and hazard in either of the alternatives which I find were presented to their choice; and that, if a more favorable result has not been obtained, it is not owing to the want of firmness fidelity and zeal on their part.

Had our expectations to the West been realized, the actual state of the vote at Albany would have been less material. But there unfortunately we have been also disappointed, owing to the propagation of tales of my being withdrawn so late as to accomplish their object before they could have been contradicted—to the possession of the press in the Atlantic cities exclusively by the other Candidates, and to the belief industriously inculcated by the partizans of all of them that I could not enter the H[ouse]. of R[epresentatives]. We have not yet heard from Louisiana,[4] but I am prepared, from the operation of the same causes, to receive unfavorable intelligence from it. I owe you many thanks for your disinterested exertions in my behalf, as also for your kind offer to repair to this City, where however it cannot be necessary for you to come for the friendly purpose indicated by you.

Altho' the particular public interests which chiefly led you to espouse my cause cannot receive from me, in the high office in question, the support which you and other friends anticipated, we may, nevertheless, I think, hope that, under any administration, they will be taken care of. That of domestic manufactures has struck such a deep root (if I am to credit what I have heard since my arrival) that it cannot fail to flourish. In this view of the subject we ought to repress any regret or mortification at the final result of the election, be that what it may.[5]

ALS. KyLoF.   1. Not found.   2. Not found.   3. Clay to Creighton, April 12, 1822, no. 2 of date.   4. Clay to Meigs, August 21, 1822.   5. Benton to Clay, April 9, 1822.

To John Hare Powel, December 24, 1824. Thanks him for his note of December 14 [not found] which accompanied a copy of "the 'Memoirs of the Pennsylvania Agricultural Society.' " Adds: "Sharing, with you, a high degree of interest in the subjects of which this volume treats, I shall seize the earliest leisure moments to enjoy the satisfaction of perusing it." ALS. PHi. Written from Washington, D.C.

For Powel, see 8:122 and *DAB*. Powel had been one of the founders of the Pennsylvania Agricultural Society and wrote numerous articles for agricultural journals.

To Horatio Gates Spafford, Troy, N.Y., December 25, 1824. Thanks him for the "Copy of your highly useful Pocket guide along the line of your noble Canals." Anticipates "the day when, aided by the valuable information which it contains, I shall be able to view those truly great works." ALS. NjMoHP. Written from Washington, D.C. For Spafford, see 4:232.

From George W. Featherstonhaugh, Duanesburgh, N.Y., January 31, 1825. Reports receiving Clay's letter of January 21 [4:34]. Mentions that "Bologna Hemp seed has been brought to New York" from Italy, but he does not know whether or not any can be procured. Asks if Clay wants him to try to obtain some. Explains that he "resided sometime in the Bolognese territory" and is acquainted with their excellent hemp, which "when dressed is as glossy and beautiful as yellow floss silk." Believes it is "the want of attention, and spoils in the various processes betwixt the seed and the Dressing, that makes the difference" between it and American-grown hemp. Deplores "the stifling of so much national wealth & private comforts" by such carelessness, noting that "Last Autumn I found in N York no less than 500,000 lbs. of inferior Saxony merino Wool, in store in the very teeth of the Tariff and selling for fifty per centum more than the native Wool of an equal quality simply because this last was not clean and well put up."

In regard to the presidential election, reports that Andrew Jackson's party "in this state has less respectability about it than any other—Such a man as he is should have something more in his favour than a veni, vidi, vici, and being called Old Hickory, to be called to the direction of this promising and rising nation." Adds that while the election of John Quincy Adams "will not make some of us prodigiously happy here," it will put to rest for some time the question of a Northern president. ALS. NAll. Copy in MnHi.

For the presidential election of 1824, see Benton to Clay, April 9, 1822. For New York's vote in 1824, see Clay to Creighton, April 12, 1822, no. 2 of date.

From John C. Calhoun, Department of War, Washington, February 5, 1825. Sends, in compliance with a resolution of the House of Representatives, copies of papers relating to the work of the commission appointed by the president "to treat with the Creek Indians for the extinguishment of their claim to lands lying within the state of Georgia." Copy. DNA, RG75, Bureau of Indian Affairs, Letters Sent, vol. 1.

James Meriwether and Duncan G. Campbell had been appointed on July 16, 1824, to negotiate with the Creek Indians for an exchange of territory. See *House Docs.,* 18 Cong., 2 Sess., no. 72, pp. 1-41. The resolution was introduced in the House on January 31, 1825, and agreed to on February 1. The House received Calhoun's reply on February 8. U.S. H. of Reps., *Journal,* 18 Cong., 2 Sess., 190, 192, 215. For the treaty, which was concluded on February 12, 1825, see Parry, *Treaty Series,* 75:89-93. See also 4:501-2.

To WILLIAM CREIGHTON, JR.[1]   Washington,
February 7, 1825

I recd. your obliging letter of the 25h. Ulto.[2] I must beg you to excuse my not having before written to you during this Session. Attribute it to any other cause than that of a want of the highest regard for you. The day after tomorrow we are to decide the Presidential question. I think Mr. [John Quincy] Adams will be elected, 'though it is not yet ascertained whether it will be on the first ballot, or whether we may not have a protracted balloting.[3] I wish the first result.

You will have seen what a conspicuous figure I have recently made in the public prints. This attack proceeds from those who wish now to be President, that is to say from some of the friends of [William H.] Crawford and [Andrew] Jackson, and those who wish to be President four or eight years hence, that is to say some of the friends of [John C.] Calhoun and [DeWitt] Clinton. The former wish to drive me from my purpose, the latter from the field of competition.[4]

Shall I, under all the circumstances of abuse which surround me, go into the Department of State, if it should be offered to me? Whether it will be or not I really do not know.

Col. [William K.] Bond is here.

ALS. KyU. Letter marked "(Confidential)." 1. This letter is indicated as "Not found" in 4:76, note 2. 2. Not found. 3. Benton to Clay, April 9, 1822; see also 4:62. 4. See 4:45-48. Also in the Subject Index: Volumes 1-6, see Election of 1824: House election phase [7:716-17]; Election of 1828: Corrupt Bargain issue & related campaign literature [7:719].

To GENERAL [SAMUEL SMITH][1]   Washington, March 25, 1825
I recd. your letter of yesterday with its inclosure which is returned.[2] Mr. [Christopher] Hughes's instructions[3] will be received this day by

Mr. ⸱ ⁴ to be forwarded to him. A duplicate of them will be sent to New York to go by the packet of the first of the next month. He is not directed as to the duration of his abode at Copenhagen, which will be regulated by his own discretion exerted on facts which may appear to him but of which we have not the possession.

I am not at liberty to speak at present of the dispositions which the President has made about the English Mission.⁵ The public considerations which have guided him I think you would approve of. If they had admitted of your appointment, I could not doubt that you would have fulfilled the duties of the position with zeal & your accustomed ability.

When I asked why should there be an opposition? I was not ignorant of the wishes of some to organize one—But they have no lament, nor will we supply them with any aliment.

ALS. MdHi.　　1. Although this letter is addressed only to "Dear General," the editors have determined that the recipient was Christopher Hughes's father-in-law, General Samuel Smith, with whom Clay had much correspondence concerning Hughes's appointment. See for example, 4:85-86, 119. For Smith, see 1:196 and *BDAC*.　　2. Not found.　　3. See 4:138-40.　　4. The name has been erased.　　5. Rufus King received the appointment. See 4:193-94.

To PETER FORCE¹　　　　　Washington, *ca*. March 28, 1825²

On a hasty perusal of my address³ I remark only two errors. One is in the 4h. column and 18h. line from the top, the word "this" is used instead of "his." And the other is in the 48h. line (counting from the bottom) of the fifth column the word "protests" is used instead of "protocols." In the impressions not yet made be pleased to have those errors corrected.

I will thank you to send by the bearer half a dozen of the pamphlets, if any of them are prepared.

ALS. DLC-HC (DNA, M212, R6).　　1. For Force, see 3:809.　　2. Dated only "Monday"; however, the address referred to in the letter was published in the Washington *Daily National Journal* on March 28, 1825.　　3. See 4:143-65.

To SAMUEL L. SOUTHARD¹　　　　Washington, *ca*. April, 1825

Strong and frequent representations have been mad[e] to me of the general wish in Balto. that you should have two of the Sloop[s] of War, lately authorized,² built there, will you allow me to suggest the prospriety [*sic*, propriety] of gratifying it, if consistent with the public interest.

ALS. NjP. Letter marked "(Private)."　　1. For Southard, see 3:437 and *DAB*.　　2. By an act of March 3, 1825, the building of up to ten sloops of war was authorized and an appropriation of $500,000 made. 4 *U.S. Stat.*, 131. No sloop was built in Baltimore during the J.Q. Adams administration. See K. Jack Bauer, *Ships of the Navy, 1775-1969* (Troy, N.Y., 1969), 25-26.

To JAMES TALLMADGE [JR.]¹　　　　Washington, April 7, 1825

I received today your friendly and obliging letter of the 4h. instant² for which I owe you many thanks. I concur with you entirely in thinking that the publication of my address³ would have been unnecessary if I had been as well known to all my countrymen as I have the honor to be to you. My retirement from the service of my district seemed to me to furnish a legitimate occasion for the address; and then there was one or two points (especially that of my relations to Mr. [John Quincy]

Adams) on which I wished to make some explanations to the public. The effect of my valedictory has greatly exceeded all my expectations. Letters from the most eminent men of our Country are daily, in great numbers, pouring in on me, from all quarters, which the address had reached time enough to admit of their transmission. These letters speak in a tone of approbation the most decisive and encouraging. Among others I had, yesterday, the honor of receiving two such letters from the Chief Justice of the U.S.[4] and the C. Justice of Virginia.[5]

In regard to Genl. [Andrew] Jackson's N. York correspondent,[6] I sought to repress rather than enlarge. I knew that the public prints would make him sufficiently known.

I believe, my dear Sir, I know every thing that occurred during the election at Albany of electors.[7] I regard it now however entirely as past history. I was greatly surprized, considering Mr. [DeWitt] Clinton's high character and great attainments as a Statesman, that *he* should have preferred Genl. Jackson.

I am gratified to learn that there is a cordial union in your State between Mr. Adams friends and mine. The Administration will be proud of the support of N. York, and it will do every thing to deserve it, by striving to do every thing to merit that of the whole American public. With a friendly recollection of our service together in the H[ouse]. of R[epresentatives].

ALS. T.   1. For Tallmadge, see 2:410; 9:897; *BDAC.*   2. Not found.   3. See 4:143-66.   4. John Marshall. See 4:211-12.   5. Francis T. Brooke. See 4:213-14.   6. Samuel Swartwout. See 4:46, 161, 166.   7. See 3:866; Clay to Creighton, April 12, 1822, no. 2 of date.

To BENJAMIN WATKINS LEIGH   Washington, April 14, 1825

I return you inclosed the answer transmitted in your favor of the 11h. inst.,[1] sworn to and properly certified; and I also return the other papers forwarded, supposing you may have occasion for them.

I certainly have no reason to complain of the importuance of the officers as to the payment of their fees. I send a check for $112:44/100,[2] the sum mentioned in your letter, and, if it will not give you too much trouble, I will thank you to divide the amount justly between them and send me their fee bills.

ALS. ViHi.   1. Not found.   2. See 4:251.

To Edward Everett, May 2, 1825. Expresses his pleasure at being made an honorary member of the Bunker Hill Association, "formed to commemorate one of the most important military events in our History." Asks Everett "to convey to the Society the sensibility with which I accept the highly distinguished honor which it has been pleased to confer on me." ALS. MHi. Written from Washington, D.C. For Everett, see 2:598.

To FRANCIS McALEAR   Washington, May 3, 1825
[*sic*, McLEAR][1]

I am truly mortified and concerned about your petition to Congress to obtain relief from the Judgment of the Fed. Court in Kentucky.[2] Finding it impracticable to get the business through that body, at its late Session, I directed the Clerk[3] to get out the papers which he did and placed them on the Speaker's table. I read them and was satisfied that your case entitled you to redress. I intended to send them to the Treasury department, but in the hurry of business towards the close of the Session omitted doing it, under the hope that after the Session I should have more leisure to attend to the matter. I accordingly sent to the Clerk for them and regret to have to tell you, as you will see from the inclosed note,[4] that they are mislaid.

Under these circumstances all that I can advise is that you should proceed to replace them by getting another petition prepared supported by documents and affidavits as the last was. Upon receiving these, you may rely on my prompt attention to the affair and, if the Executive has the power, you may I think confidently expect redress.[5]

In the mean time, I should think as the enforcement of the Judgment has been so long delayed, a further forbearance might be extended, until your application is decided on.

ALS. KyLoF. Addressed to McLear in Lexington, Ky.   1. McLear, born in Ireland, had served in the American forces during the War of 1812 and in 1814 had moved from Philadelphia to Lexington. He was a grocer and liquor dealer and, for a time, a justice of the peace. *RKHS*, 51:46.   2. Two judgments, each for $150.01, had been issued against McLear in the United States District Court for Kentucky on May 13, 1817. Order Book H, 11-12. On Feb. 2, 1818, he had initiated a petition to Congress for "Remission of fine for violation of the license laws." On Jan. 26, 1825, the House of Representatives had "Ordered, That leave be given to withdraw the petition and papers." U.S. H. of Reps., *Journal*, 18 Cong., 2 Sess., 167; *Digested Summary and Alphabetical List of Private Claims Which Have Been Presented to the House of Representatives from the First to the Thirty-First Congresses...*, 3 vols. (Washington, 1853), 2:408.   3. Matthew St. Clair Clarke. See 3:499.   4. Not found.   5. No further action has been found.

To EDWARD EVERETT   Washington, May 17, 1825

Upon receiving your letter of the 11th instant,[1] requesting by the direction of the Committee of Foreign Affairs, a communication of the instructions that have been given to the Minister of the U. States in France, touching the claim of Baron [Pierre Augustin Caron] de Beaumarchais, I did suppose that an instruction had been given to Mr. [Albert] Gallatin, our late Minister, or to our present Minister in France [James Brown] respecting that particular claim; but upon a careful research, which I have directed, no such instruction has been discovered.[2]

By a reference to Mr. Gallatin's correspondence with this Department, it appears that to an inquiry made of him by the French Minister of Foreign Affairs in the year 1822, whether he was prepared to embrace the claim of the Baron de Beaumarchais in a negotiation upon the subject of claims, he replied in the affirmative. In this, however, he probably allu[d]ed to no other than the instruction of the 7th May, 1816, by which he was authorized in general terms to negotiate a convention which should provide, among other things, for "claims of French subject[s] against the United States."

Copy. InHi.   1. Not found.   2. For the Beaumarchais claim, see 3:313.

To JOHN H. JAMES[1]   Maysville, Ky., May 24, 1825

My detention at this place to day enables me to acknowledge the receipt of your kind letter of the 22d. instant.[2] I am infinitely obliged by the friendly intention to give me the compliment of a public dinner at Cincinnati. And I own to you that my inclination is to accept it; for, after the gross and malignant attack lately made on me, I have thought that I ought not to decline or repress any testimonies which the public might be spontaneously disposed to render me. Still, if I could be persuaded that a public dinner, given to me at Cincinnati, would be considered as offensive to a majority, or even a large portion, of the Citizens of that place, or might lead to a disturbance of the peace of society, I should feel it to be my duty to decline the honor. On that point I should be glad to know more than I do at present.

I will answer the public invitation, which I have received, from Lexington, upon reaching home.[3] If I determine to accept the invitation, I will give at least a weeks notice of the time of my arrival in your City. I apprehend it will not be in my power to visit you before the last of June or the first of July.[4]

ALS. KyLoF. Addressed to James in Cincinnati.   1. For James, see 8:499.   2. Not found.   3. Not found.   4. See 4:528-32.

To FINIS EWING[1]   Lexington, June 16, 1825

Your letter of the 28h. April,[2] addressed to me at Washington, arrived there after I left that City, and followed me to Kentucky. I believe I received the preceding one, to which you refer, but I am not sure that I did.[3] If I did, you must attribute my failure to answer it to the pressure of public business and correspondence, and not to the want of sin[cere] regard for you. My new office [manuscript torn; words missing] roses, and I cannot often enjoy the luxury of [personal] correspondence.

I thank you for the account you give me of public sentiment in Missouri, in respect to the late Presidential election.[4] It coincides with information which I have received through other channels, and agrees with the progress of public opinion in other parts of the Union. You will have seen my address to my Constituents,[5] who are now giving me the most conclusive and gratifying testimonies of their entire satisfaction. I have never been heretofore, at any time, received with half the enthusiasm which has marked my late return to Kentucky.

I can with truth affirm that the President [John Quincy Adams] and the members who compose his administration are animated with the best intentions and the warmest zeal to promote the public good. And, if they fail, in any instance, to perceive and advance it, the error must be ascribed to the head, or to adverse causes. In respect to appointments to public office, there is great solicitude always to select those who are honest faithful & capable. Previous pledges or committments for them, always embarrassing, will be avoided; and when vacancies occur the pretensions of the different applicants will be justly weighed, without favor or partiality. With respect to Mr. [Benjamin H.] Reeves,[6] I entertain a high opinion of him; from character, and in the event of the office's, to what you allude, becoming vacant, it will be advisable that recommendations of him should be forwarded to Washington, [word missing] the fullest consideration will be given to them, and [words missing] it would be a deviation from the rule [words missing] indicated (and of which I think you will approve) to make any prior promise further than what I have now stated.

I shall return with my family to Washington in a couple of weeks. With my best wishes for your health & prosperity . . .

ALS, manuscript torn. UPB. 1. For Ewing, see 4:569. This is the letter indicated as "Not found" in 4:569, note 1. 2. Not found. 3. Not found. 4. For Missouri's vote in 1824, see Clay to Meigs, August 21, 1822. For the results of the presidential election, see Benton to Clay, April 9, 1822. 5. See 4:143-65. 6. For Reeves, see 4:569.

To GEORGE THOMPSON   Lexington, June 24, 1825

Your servant having arrived here in the night & departed very early in the morning I could not conveniently by him acknowledge the receipt of your very friendly letter of yesterday.[1] I thank you for it. Having had the honor to enjoy your friendship, from our earliest acquaintance, (which has not been short) it gives me great satisfaction to learn from you that I still retain it. The approbation of such friends as you compensates for all the undeserved censure of which I have been recently the object.

I heard of your touching interviews with [Marquis de] La Fayette.[2] I regretted that I could not witness them. The meeting must have been mutually gratifying, and the recollections which it recalled were no doubt highly pleasing. I expect to see him in Washington, prior to his return to Europe, and will not fail to deliver your message.

I have seen, with mortification and disgust, the late scurrilous attack upon you. It carries however its own antidote, and it ought to inflict no pain. You should drop it and despise it.[3]

I have lamented that I could not see you before I take my departure.[4] Wherever I go or may be rest assured, my dear Col., that I shall cherish a lively recollection of your esteem and regard . . .

ALS. KyLoF. 1. Not found. 2. Thompson and LaFayette had met at Transylvania University on May 16, 1825. Lexington *Kentucky Reporter*, May 30, 1825. See also 4:19. 3. This paragraph has been stricken through. Reference obscure. 4. See 4:489, 585.

From Henry St. George Tucker, near Richmond, Va., June 30, 1825. Reports that he is resigning because "My various infirmities, and particularly my—almost total loss of hearing, added to a degree of Debility . . . renders me incapable of discharging the Duties of my present office of Judge of the United States for the Eastern District of Virginia." Asks "that this Letter may be accepted as my Act of Resignation, and that you will . . . communicate the same to the president [John Quincy Adams]." ALS. DNA, RG59, Entry 339, Box 10.

To NORBORNE B. BEALL[1]   Lexington, July 3, 1825

As intimated in my former letter, I shall leave home on Wednesday morning and sleep at Frankfort. On Thursday I shall dine at Shelbyville, and passing the night, perhaps, with Col. C[harles]. S. Todd, I shall reach Middletown by 12 OClock next day (friday)[.] If convenient I shall be glad to find you at Genl Dabney's.[2] I will remain with you on friday night, and go to Louisville the next Morning. I wish to set out for Cincinnati on sunday,[3] if a boat shall leave Louisville on that day.

ALS. KyLoF. 1. For Beall, see 1:493. 2. Possibly Isaac W. Dabney, who is listed in the 1830 Kentucky census as a resident of Jefferson County. Jackson, *Kentucky 1830 Census Index.* 3. For Clay's speech in Cincinnati, see 4:528-32.

To WILLIAM LYTLE
Lebannon [*sic*, Lebanon], Ohio,
July 18, 1825

I wished to have seen Mr. [John] Rowan and yourself on the subject of the Stable & lot attached to the Kentucky Hotel, which I acquired from you.[1] I sold the lot, shortly after I obtained it, for $1800: A great part of the purchase money remains unpaid. Mr. Rowan is bound to me for the balance (principal and interest) which amount now to near $2000. You bought the title of Mr. [Robert] Wickliffe, but not having paid for it, he will refuse to convey it, and if there should be much further delay on your part a Court of Equity would probably not compel him to convey, if it would now do so. Mr. Wickliffe holds my bond given for a title, and is desirous to rescind the contract with me and to compel me to refund what I recd. with interest, which would amt. to perhaps as much if not more than he is to get from you. Such however is his view and that of Mr. John T. Mason[2] who is associated with him in interest.

I am extremely desirous that this business should be settled and would be glad if you would obtain and make to me the title of the lot.[3]

ALS. OCHP. 1. See 4:507-9. 2. For Mason, see 4:52. 3. See also 4:564-65.

To WILLIAM LYTLE
Lebannon [*sic*, Lebanon], Ohio,
August 4, 1825

I recd. your letter of the third instant.[1] It was my wish when at Cincinnati to have seen you on the subject of the business between you and Col. [James] Morrisons estate, as, in a personal interview, explanations could have been given and received better than on paper.[2] But circumstances did not allow me to have such an interview.

Altho' I have all proper confidence in your statements, the caution which it is necessary for me to observe in the transaction of business as Col. Morrisons executor, makes it desirable that I should have some precise information,

1st. as to your authority for selling his interest in the 100 and 125 acres. Extracts from his letters would do. Mr [Robert] Scott seems to be satisfied on that head, but I should prefer myself to judge of the authority. and

2dly. Some statement shewing for what Col. Morrisons interest in those two tracts was sold by you. No paper that I have here furnishes that information.

The deed and assignment and the receipt which you have prepared all bear date in the last year, and the two former are prepared for execution in Kentucky. An alteration will be necessary in these particulars.

As to the land located in the names of O'Harra [*sic*, James O'Hara] and [Nicholas] Bausman I believe we have not titles.[3] Being in want of information on that matter, all that I can now say is that whatever is right & proper shall be done.

I hope to be able to leave here in two or three days.

190

P.S. The receipt is [manuscript torn] you desired—It can be again forwarded to me, with the date altered, if the business can now be completed.

ALS. OCHP.   1. See 4:564-65.   2. See also 3:878; 4:394.   3. See 3:878.

To DANIEL WEBSTER   Washington, October 3, 1825
I have received your favors of the 28h. Ulto.[1] and feel greatly obliged by your kind suggestions on the British Colonial trade. I find that opinions are not united on the policy of a mutual discontinuance of the discriminating duties. The amount of the effect of their abolition, I think, is that we should gain by the direct trade with the British Colonies and lose by that of which those Colonies would by the medium or entrepot. It is not easy to say whether the loss and gain would neutralize each other. I apprehend that it would be very difficult to prevail on the British Government to consent to the same unrestricted importation and exportation from their Colonies as their own vessels enjoy.

Political affairs stand well in the West. In my own State the great body of both the State parties (the Reliefs and Anti-reliefs)[2] were friendly to me; but some of the Leaders of the first were otherwise affected. The late auspicious change is good for the State and for me. Mr. [DeWitt] Clinton is preparing for a Campaign,[3] but whether he will take the field or not, three years hence, depends upon intermediate demonstrations. There is no danger from him; and, upon the whole, I think his late trip to the West did not advance his interests. Wherever he came in contact with the people the fact fell far below the imagination of his greatness. It was often said, in the Miami Country, that they would not exchange their Governor (the unaffected and worthy [Jeremiah] Morrow,[4] whom you know) for the Governor of New York.

We are moving on harmoniously and I think well in the Administration[.] The Creeks and Governor [George] Troup[5] were happily disposed of, for the present. Then Genl [Edmund P.] Gaines, who ought not to have written at all but upon his official business, wrote some indiscreet and silly letters.[6] The demand to arrest him could not be complied with; but disapprobation has been conveyed to him of his use of the pen. I am deceived if all do not agree that what has been done here has been properly done, when it comes to be known.

I thank you for your kind advice about my health. It is not bad, nor yet very good. I continue to take daily exercise on horseback, and I cherish the hope that, by the system which I have prescribed to myself, I shall restore it. I wish I could act more on the Austrian Minister's[7] maxim of confiding to others what they might do; but really, in my office, I have very little assistance.

P.S. Mr [Rufus] Kings[8] health was bad on his arrival in England. Cheltenham's[9] waters improved it, but he has not more than reached London now.

ALS. KyU.   1. See 4:695-99.   2. Clay to Harper, April 24, 1824.   3. Public meetings in Virginia, Ohio, and Buffalo, N.Y., nominated Clinton for president, but he died in Feb., 1828. Dorothie Bobbé, *DeWitt Clinton* (New York, 1933), 277-92.   4. See 3:130.   5. Calhoun to Clay, Feb. 5, 1825.   6. See 4:677. For Gaines, see *DAB*.   7. Lewis Charles Lederer. See 4:903.   8. See 4:193-94; Clay to Smith, March 25,

1825.   9. Cheltenham Springs, an English watering place with saline springs, lies eight miles east northeast of Gloucester on the Chelt River. *Lippincott's Gazetteer of the World* (Philadelphia, 1922).

From Edmond Charles Genêt, New York City, October 6, 1825. Although not a personal acquaintance, writes that "I have always viewed you, Sir, not only as an eloquent Orator, But as a friend of mankind, an able Republican statesman, and a zealous supporter of the useful arts." Reports: "In my youth, I have also been placed on the political scene, But, unfortunately, compelled, by the most exalted orders, to promote, on this continent, in one year, what the slow operative hand of time has required many more to accomplish. My efforts unsupported by an unsettled Republic, who has not known how to support herself, have only served to accelerate my fall, under the pressure of the enemies of Democracy, to despoyl me of all the fruits of an unspotted carrier of 14 years faithful Services, in the diplomatic department of france, and to leave me entirely destitute, with no other reward, but the interior satisfaction of having in all my public acts and measures, implicitly obeyed, what my Duty was to consider as the orders and instructions of the government of my country.—At the last breath of her existence as a Republic, under the Directory, the french Nation, has however, it is true, attested my innocence and honour by the most consolatory and reinstating Decrees transmitted to me with a flood of fulsome adulation by their versatile Minister of foreign relations Talleyrand; But, it was too late, that acknowledgment of their error and ingratitude was immediately succeded by the *double usurpation* of the Ambitious and insatiable Buonaparte [Napoleon Bonaparte], to which I peremptorily refused to assent, and being disgusted, for ever, of European politics, I have definitely adopted the United States, where I have enjoyed, as a simple citizen, all the Blessings of Domestic rural and philosophical retirement, without ever being moved to quit that happy situation, by the pressing invitations of my french family, in the highest favour with the new Dynasty." Notes that whereas his time was "formerly lavished to watch and report the little intrigues of courts, the mean secrets of cabinets, or the afflicting divisions of parties," it is now devoted to "my duties as a husband, a father and a citizen, to promote litterature, agriculture, manufactures, public improvements, in a State become the World for me."

Asserts that "in those moments of true worship, consecrated to the study and admiration, of the . . . Splendid temple of Nature, that I have turned my attention to the causes of Motion, and ascertained the existence of the upward force of a principle of levity and action . . . which had always been overlooked by Mechanists." Adds that "on the strength of that new force, in Mechanics" he has "laid the foundation of a new system of Mechanical arrangements" and has petitioned "you, Sir, . . . to grant me a patent." Proclaims that he has "not trusted my own opinion and calculations alone; On the contrary I have solicited the severest scrutiny of my new system, from Mathemathicians, philosophers Mechanists, and civil Engineers of known experience and talent, and their flattering reports, which I possess, have encouraged me, as I am poor, to claim a Patent, in order to secure, for myself and heirs, the benefit of my labours. You will accordingly, Sir, oblige me, infinitely, if by your recommendation, you can accelerate the expedition of that favour, having reason to believe that my means to facilitate the internal water communications and the drawing of vessels or boats over rail ways and inclined planes, as well as to procure vertical lifts, will meet with immediate experiment in this State and other States, where undulating and mountainous countries, have hitherto opposed insurmountable difficulties to the extension of the canaling system." Also hopes that someday men "will navigate the air in my Aerouants, with as much confidence as they now navigate the water."

Encloses a copy of an address he made to the legislature of New York "relative to the construction of a ship *canal* around the obstructions of the Hudson." ALS. DNA, RG59, Entry 212.

Genêt, the French diplomat who was known as Citizen Genêt when he outraged the Washington administration with his actions soon after his arrival in the U.S. in 1793, settled in the U.S. after Washington refused to extradite him, became an American citizen, and married a daughter of Gov. George Clinton of New York. See Morris, *Encyclopedia of American History*, 125-26. Genêt's *Address on the Several Subjects of Science, Useful Knowledge, Public Improvements. . . . Delivered on the Fifth of February, 1824, in the Assembly Room of the Capitol* was published in Albany, N.Y., in 1825. On October 31, 1825, he was granted a patent on his "Hydrostatic, aerostatic machinery." Edmund Burke (comp.), *List of Patents for Inventions and Designs, Issued by the United States from 1790 to 1847* (Washington, 1847), 223.

To THOMAS I. WHARTON[1]   Washington, November 21, 1825

I received, in due course of the mail, your obliging letter of the 16h. instant,[2] and thank you for the friendly sentiments of personal regard which it expresses. It will afford me gratification to be able, in personal intercourse with you, when you visit this place, as you propose doing next winter, to reciprocate them. As to the affair of the claims of our Citizens on France & Holland, and I may add, indeed, several other European Governments, I confess I have no very sanguine hopes without some strong movement in Congress towards those Governments. We have been so shamefully robbed, by all the powers of Europe, that each feels secure, in his denial to us of justice, from the impunity of his particeps. It is worthy of serious consideration whether it w[oul]d. not be politic (I am sure it would not be unjust) to select the stoutest of them and make an example of him by strong measures. If we were to take the Bull by the horns (I do not mean John Bull) the rest of the flock wd. follow. However perhaps it will be best for the claimants to wait & see if the President [John Quincy Adams] sh[oul]d. take any and if any what notice of the subject in his message, and then to act accordingly.

The selection of Cadets for the W[est]. P[oint]. Academy usually takes places in March. As I presume I shall have the pleasure of seeing you before that time I will reserve, for that occasion, what I would recommend in regard to your kinsman. . . . [3]

ALS. KyU.   1. For Wharton, see 3:468.   2. See 4:831-32.   3. The grandson of William Rawle, Sr. See 4:831-32.

To FRANCIS P. BLAIR   Washington, December 16, 1825

I received your letter of the 28th November.[1] I began to conclude that you had cut me, from the long interval since I had written you, without a reply. Although I think you have recently erred in your adherence to party contrary to your own principles, I beg you to be assured of my continued esteem.[2] I have seen too much of political strife, and know too well the repugnance which men of honor have to even an apparent abandonment of their party, to allow myself to think unkindly of you, for what I must nevertheless characterize as an amiable deference, on your part, to the less correct judgment of others. . . .

[The paper states: "After entering into a long discussion of State politics, the letter concludes thus:"]

If the extent of my friendships were measured by the length of my letters to you, there are few who would share it with you in the same degree. I rarely pass from the first page of my sheet, not from the want of inclination, but from the want of leisure from the incessant duties of a most laborious office, now more than ever burthened by the presence of Congress.

Copy, extract. Printed in Washington *Globe*, March 16, 1841.   1. See 4:859-62. 2. Reference is to Old Court/New Court. See Clay to Harper, April 24, 1824.

To WILLIAM CREIGHTON, JR.   Washington,
December 26, 1825

Your letter of the 22d. Novr.[1] inclosing a note of Frances Purves for $650, given to Hugh Fullerton,[2] with a request that I would forward it to England to try and have it collected, has been received, and I have transmitted the note to Mr. John A. King,[3] secretary &c. in London. I thought that the best disposition I could make of it, and I presume he will attend to it[.]

I have recd. your favor of the 10h. instant.[4] I thought I had a Copy of the will of Col. Morrison with me, but upon searching for it I find I was mistaken; and it is now too late to direct one to be sent from Kentucky in time for the approaching term of the Federal Court. Could you not get an order of the Court to make the deed to the legal representatives of James Morrison?

I have heard nothing of any attempt to remove Col. [William] Doherty. He need entertain no fears whatever of losing his office, if, as I presume to be the case, there are no established charges against him of misconduct in it.[5]

I should have been highly pleased, under the circumstances, with the mission to Panama,[6] and would sooner go on it than on any foreign mission whatever; but situated as I am I cannot leave this Country. We shall however be well represented there. I think the resolutions at Columbus ought not to be attempted without a strong probability of there being carried by a large majority.[7]

ALS. KyU.   1. Not found.   2. Not found; Purves and Fullerton not identified. 3. For King, see 4:328; for the note, see 4:945.   4. See 4:892-93.   5. See 4:893. 6. For the Panama Congress, see Subject Index: Volumes 1-6 in 7:769.   7. See 4:794-95.

To EBENEZER B. WILLISTON[1]   Washington, January 18, 1826
I recd. your letter,[2] communicating a request that I would forward to you Copies of my Speeches on the Tariff[3] and on the recognition of S[outh]. America,[4] which you kindly wish to insert in some collection of American speeches which you are preparing.[5] I send you a printed Copy of the Tariff speech, which is the only one of which I have preserved any printed Copy. I have a manuscript copy of the other, and also of my Seminole speech[6] (which, if any thing I have said is worth preserving, well deserves it.) If you cannot do without my manuscript, you shall have it—it is a copy made from the [Washington *Daily National*] Intell[*igence*]r. by a young man in this place.

Should any circumstances prevent your intended publication, be pleased to return what I send, and let me know if you must have the above manuscript.

ALS. VtNN.   1. For Williston (1801-37)—a professor at a military academy in Norwich, Vt., and later president of Jefferson College in Missouri—see *CAB*.   2. Not found.   3. It is uncertain to which of his many tariff speeches he refers, but see, for example, 3:683-730.   4. See Spanish America in Subject Index: Volumes 1-6 in 7:764.   5. Williston's *Eloquence of the United States* was published in Middletown, Conn., in 1827.   6. See 2:636-62.

To EBENEZER B. WILLISTON   Washington, February 13, 1826

Indisposition has delayed my answer to your favor of the 25h. Ulto.[1]

By this mail I transmit you manuscript copies of my speeches

1st In the opening and reply on the first occasion of bringing forward the South American subject.[2]

2 On the Seminole War and[3]

3dly. On the New Army bill[4] during the late War. The Copies are taken from the files of the [Washington *Daily National*] Intell[*igence*]r, and have recd. scarcely any corrections from me; but I believe they are correctly copied. These, together with the Tariff speech,[5] I should like to be published; and yet I am afraid that they will occupy too much space in your work,[6] where, perhaps, I ought to have none. If you omit either, that, in reply, on the S[outh]. American subject, I should prefer to be left out. But I pray you to consult your own interests and inclination exclusively, and if you omit all I shall not be discontented. All that I w[oul]d. ask, in the latter contingency, is that you wd. have the goodness to return the papers.

ALS. VtNN.   1. Not found, but see Clay to Williston, Jan. 18, 1826.   2. See 2:508-41.   3. See 2:636-62.   4. See 1:754-74.   5. Clay to Williston, Jan. 18, 1826.   6. *Ibid.*

To Baron Durand de Mareuil, Washington, March 9, 1826. In reply to "your note of the 28h. Ulto. [5:137–38] which has been submitted to the President," which explained his desire to have assisted at the funeral of John Gaillard, Clay states that he does "not know by whose authority the arrangement" of the funeral procession was made, although it was probably by a committee of the Senate. Notes that "The attendance or not of any of the persons comprehended in the arrangement was altogether optional & voluntary," and it was not expected that such an occasion "would, by any one, be deemed fit to raise questions of mere precedence, in the line of procession which should follow him to the grave." Adds that no official invitations were given. States that President John Quincy Adams has directed him to explain "the principles which regulate the conduct of this Government in respect to the Foreign Ministers" whom it accredits: "The Government of the U.S. recognizes, in the most liberal extent, all the rights, privileges and immunities which appertain to the diplomatic character, according to the public law." Asserts that prompt attention is always paid to any complaint of the violation of the rights of foreign ministers, but that "The Government does not undertake to regulate the ceremonies to be observed in our social or festive circles, nor in solemn processions." Mentions that while de Mareuil has on several occasions expressed dissatisfaction with ceremonies, this is the first time he has put it in writing. Thus, although the president would have preferred to avoid replying in writing, he has deemed it "proper to give this answer the opportunity of an equally permanent preservation." ALS, draft. CSmH.

For Baron De Mareuil, see 4:331. For John Gaillard, see 3:318.

To CHARLOTTE MENTELLE[1]
Washington, March 11, 1826

I thank you for your letter of the 26 Ulto.[2] It is always agreeable to us to receive such details, and no one more kindly communicates them than yourself.

We have sent James [Brown Clay], under the auspicies of Bishop [Philander] Chase, to Ohio.[3] The Bishop passed two or three weeks here at my house, and James became attached to him, as I had long been. We could not have confid[ed] him to better hands, but parting with him cost us some sacrifices—and has reduced our once large family to poor little John [Morrison Clay], his mother [Lucretia Hart Clay] and I.

Our health continues not very good. Mrs Clay, from sympathy, or from want of the exercises of Ashland, is beginning to share the dispeptia with me.

ALS. Courtesy of William W. Layton, Millwood, Va.   1. For Mentelle, see 1:121.
2. Not found.   3. For Chase and his school, see 3:470; 5:188.

To Elijah Warner, Lexington, August 11, 1826.
For the sum of $1,000 sells "a negro woman named Priscilla [3:310] or Scilla together with her five children, John, Joe, Caroline, Dick, and Maria." ADS. Courtesy of Robert H. Poindexter, Cynthiana, Ky. For Warner, see 4:462.

On December 26, 1827, Thomas P. Hart [1:475] for Eleanor Grosch Hart [1:96, 394] signed a promissory note, providing that "On the 25th day of December 1828 I promise to pay Henry Clay or order, Thirty dollars . . . for the hire of his negro woman Phillis [1:385] for the year 1828." Also promises to clothe her and pay the taxes on her for the year. Document is endorsed by Robert Scott [1:404]: "Mrs. Hart hired Phillis for for [sic] E. Hart the year 1829—and I believe her son Capt Thos. P. Hart gave his note for the hire, but if he did I have lost or mislaid it—" ADS. DLC-TJC (DNA, M212, R16).

To HENRY SHAW[1]
Washington, September 23, 1826

During my absence from this City your two favors of the 27h. August[2] and 10h. Septr.[3] arrived. I thank you most cordially for them. I see in them new and strong proofs of a friendship on which I have placed great value. I think you are deceived as to the coldness of Mr. [John Quincy] Adams. He has, I assure you, on many occasions manifested a warm interest in all that concerns me. And I do not think that he has any undue partiality in the quarter that you suppose. [Elijah H.] Mills[4] was very steady and efficient in the support of the Administration. I should be sorry to see him displaced by an inferior man. [Henry W.] Dwight[5] has always appeared to me to be a good fellow, and he has in several instances evinced a warm regard for me.

On the subject of your last letter, I regret that the absence of the President prevents my laying your views before him. In regard to Mr. [John] Savage[6] I have a strong attachment to him, and high respect for his abilities and worth. You know we served together in the H[ouse]. of

R[epresentatives]. The President is expected about the 15h. or 20h. of next month, and when he comes I will not fail to make known to him the suggestions with which you have favored me.

My health has improved on the journey[7] which I have just terminated, and I hope to be able to sustain all the fatigues of the approaching campaign. The cause of the administration is constantly acquiring additional strength; and I concur with you, in thinking that we have nothing to dread, if it should conduct itself hereafter, as I am persuaded it will, with prudence.

ALS. NNC.   1. For Shaw, see 3:186.   2. See 5:649-52.   3. See 5:675-77.   4. For Mills, see *BDAC*.   5. For Dwight, see 3:376.   6. For Savage, see 3:187.   7. See 5:695.

To JOHN GREEN[1]

Washington, September 29, 1826

Immediately on the receipt of your letter of the 20h. Ulto.[2] which reached the City before I did, I had a conversation with Mr. [Richard] Rush on the subject of it, who put into my hands the inclosed Copy[3] of a letter which must have reached K[entucky]. shortly after the date of yours'. He has the most friendly dispositions towards the Asylum which have no other control than that which arises from a sense of official duty. He persuades himself that that letter will prove satisfactory; but if it should not I will undertake to say from him that mutual explanations will lead to the most liberal exercise of the discretion with which he is invested, subject only to the limitation which has been indicated. My own office affords me full employment; and even if any error were committed in another, not under my direction, it would not be very just to ascribe it to me, or to hold me responsible for it.

I should have been very glad to have seen you on my late visit to K. I was relieved from an anxiety about your election,[4] prior to my departure. I offer you my cordial congratulation on your success, and on that of the cause in Kentucky which you have expoused. You have something more, in both branches of the General Assembly, than a majority of one, which Mr. [Nathaniel] Macon[5] considers the best majority in the world. I hope the power thus obtained will be judiciously exercised, & so as to advance the character and prosperity of the State.

ALS. Danville-Boyle County Historical Society, Danville, Ky.   1. For John Green (the Younger), see 5:6.   2. See 5:632-34. This letter is the one indicated as "Not found" in 5:634.   3. Not found.   4. For Green's election to the Kentucky senate, see 5:634.   5. For Macon, see 1:819.

From William Thornton, Washington, October 5, 1826. Complains that "Soon after you commenced the duties of your present appointment you informed me that you would never recommend me to any mission to South America but would do anything to serve me in my present office." Explains that he had sought such a mission, "because it was a country scarcely investigated, and I had made various branches of natural history and drawing particular studies, which I thought would enable me to render more services to my country" than those who have so far filled such stations. Recalls informing Clay that three members of the House and three from the Senate had "waited on the late president [James Monroe] to recommend me to the mission to Colombia previous to the appointment of Mr. [Richard C.] Anderson [Jr.]," and Clay's reply "that the president asked the gentlemen if they would give the appointment to me were they in his situation and received an answer in the negative." Asserts that "I have asked several of the gentlemen if such a question was ever proposed: but not one of them recollected it." Admits that "We were then in negotiation for the Floridas, but as three complaints had been made against me to our government by the Duke of Infantado, when regent of Spain . . . for the pieces intended to rouse the patriots to independence, and the constitutions etc. that I wrote, a question might have arisen . . . whether it would be politic to send me, while such a negotiation was pending, especially as we had, during the whole struggle, professed compleat neutrality." Also recalls that Clay asked "if I was not too old?" Points out other older persons who have obtained appointments, and concedes that "It is true that I have grown old in the service of the United States, and though my duties have increased four fold my salary is less now than the day I was appointed by the great [George] Washington."

Explains that the "late secretary of State [John Quincy Adams] promised to mention me to the late president as an envoy to Guatimala [sic, Guatemala]," but the president decided to leave the appointment to his successor. Says he felt sure of receiving the appointment, but William Miller was appointed, and when he died, John Williams was then appointed. Adds that "The late secretary of state once observed to me that he considered me as identified with the South Americans because I had written and published so much in their favor." Points out that both Colombia and Bolivia lack an envoy and that he would like to be appointed to the former. Asks Clay to "condescend to do me the favor to reconsider" his opposition to such an appointment, "and if you should still not deign to be my friend you at least shew no inclination to be my enemy: for you have never had any cause to consider me but as a sincere friend." Copy. Courtesy of William Thornton Papers.

For Thornton, see 1:324. Thornton had written *Outlines of a Constitution for a United North & South Colombia* . . . (Washington, D.C., 1815).

William Miller was confirmed as chargé d'affaires to Guatemala on March 5, 1825. After Miller's death, John Williams of Tennessee was appointed on December 26, 1825, and confirmed on December 29. U.S. Sen. *Executive Journal*, 3:436-37, 461, 469.

To HORACE HOLLEY   Washington, October 17, 1826

I received your letter of the 5h. inst.[1] transmitting inclosed one from Mrs. [Mary Austin] Holley to Mrs. Allen,[2] which shall be forwarded with the first despatches.

I sent by the last mail a Copy of tables arranged by Dr. Lovell[3] of observations made on the thermometer, for several successive years, at different points in the West and the East, for the use of the [Transylvania] University. It is to be regretted that similar observations were not made in the valley of the Mississippi, and especially in that of the Ohio.

The papers will give you all the news I possess. Political prospects are bright in this quarter. The elections in New Jersey[4] and Maryland[5] have terminated in favor of the Administration. This result is more important because both of those States (one giving a majority and the other an undivided vote) were for Genl. [Andrew] Jackson in the Electoral Colleges, at the last election.[6] In New Jersey the issue was fairly made up, and contested with great warmth and animation. We are not without strong hopes even of Pennsa.[7]

Mrs. [Lucretia Hart] Clay joins me in respectful compliments to Mrs. Holley.

ALS. KyLoF. 1. Not found. 2. Possibly Elizabeth Hart Allen, wife of Heman Allen, the U.S. minister to Chile. For Heman Allen, see 3:377 and *CAB*. 3. Not identified. 4. See 5:756. 5. See 5:742-43, 756. 6. For Maryland's vote in 1824, see Clay to Creighton, Dec. 22, 1823; for New Jersey's, see Clay to Erwin, Jan. 7, 1824. 7. See 5:87, 353-54, 731, 755-56, 796-98, 1000-1001.

From Nathaniel Rochester, Rochester, N.Y., November 22, 1826. Has been informed that the administration intends to remove Abelard Reynolds as postmaster at Rochester, an office he has held since the post office was first established there. Believes the Federalists want to do this because Reynolds is "a uniform republican"; however, his absence from Rochester to attend the legislature to which he was recently elected is the stated reason. Asserts that Reynolds is willing to resign from the legislature in order to keep the job if Postmaster General John McLean so desires. ALS. NRU.

For Reynolds, see the entry on his son Mortimer F. Reynolds in *NCAB*, 8:80.

To THOMAS I. WHARTON   Philadelphia, November 28, 1826[1]
I return, with many thanks, the Cloak which you lent me, under the hope that you have not wanted it as much as it has benefited me.

I beg you to make my respects to Mrs. [Arabella Griffith] Wharton, and to say to her that, among the many regrets which I feel this morning in leaving this City that is not the least that I have not had the pleasure of seeing her during my short sojourn.

ALS. KyU. 1. Although only the date Nov. 28 is given, editors have determined that this letter was written in 1826 when Clay was in Philadelphia. See 5:947, 949.

To JAMES LLOYD[1]   Washington, December 2, 1826
I recd. your favor of the 18h and 21st. Ulto. and thank you for the extracts inclosed.[2]

I have not the smallest objection, nor am I aware of any impropriety whatever as to any reference you may think proper to make to the letter which you did me the favor to write in June 1825,[3] nor to my letter to which it was an answer.[4] I think however that you had better defer any publication until you shall have had full opportunity to peruse and consider the papers which will be submitted to Congress. I am greatly deceived if one Government was ever put more clearly in the wrong by another than those papers will shew G. Britain to have been placed by this Government.

I will send Mr. [William] Huskissons speeches in a day or two.[5] The President [John Quincy Adams] now has them.

ALS. KyLoF. 1. For Lloyd, see 1:465. 2. Letters not found, but see 5:921. 3. See 4:477-86. See also Clay's reply in 4:601-603. 4. Not found, but see 4:337-38 for a similar letter to Samuel Smith. 5. See 5:855-56; see also 5:1007-8. For Huskisson, see 4:89.

From Anne Royall, New Haven, Conn., December 2, 1826. Sends a copy of her book for "deposit in your office to secure the copyright as the book was snatched from the press before I could get it secured in the usual way." Has been "told that my merely leaving a copy in the State Department it would secure the right, but if any particular form is requisite you will of course apprize me."

Expresses sorrow "that your kindness to me subjected you to the lash of the [Washington *United States*] *Telegraph* but such things are an advantage to you as the man who crys treason when there is no treason is intitled to. no credit—I am a friend to [Andrew] Jackson coming from the same country but my friendship for him does not blind me to the merit of Mr. [John Quincy] Adams." ALS. MeHi.

For Royall (1769-1854), who from 1826-31 published ten travel volumes and later edited newspapers, see *DAB*. Royall had been in Washington raising subscriptions to publish her novels. The *Telegraph* published a list of her patrons, which included Clay and John Quincy Adams, and it charged that Clay had paid the subscription out of the contingent fund of the State Department. Washington *United States Telegraph*, November 7, 1826.

To THOMAS I. WHARTON   Washington, December 22, 1826

Mr. T[homas]. Smith of Lexington (K.) informs me that he has written to you for the purpose of getting to you to contract for the printing of some Speeches &c. of mine, on which too much value is placed.[1] Mr. Smith may be entirely relied on for the execution of any engagement into which he may enter.

My son,[2] just arrived from K[entucky]., brought with him the MS. copies of some of the Speeches, taken from the public prints of the dates of their publications. These and others which were here Mr. Smith wishes to be forwarded to you, if you have made the contemplated contract. And the object of this letter is to ascertain if you have contracted for their publication? And if they now are or when they will be wanted for that purpose.

Allow me also (on my own account) to enquire if your leisure and convenience will admit of your superintending the publication, that is the arrangement of the speeches in the order of time of their delivery; and the correction of typographical & other incidental errors.

ALS. KyLoF.   1. See 6:415.   2. Probably Theodore Wythe Clay.

To JOSIAH STODDARD JOHNSTON   *ca.* 1827[1]

Mr. Rufus King arrived at Liverpool 26 June 1825. He was presented and delivered his letter of Credence on 11h. Novr. 1825. The lateness of the time was owing to the dispers[i]on of the British Cabinet. Before presentation he could not regularly transact official business— Certainly not enter on any negotiations.[2]

The B[ritish]. acts of P[arliament]. of 1825[3] were recd. at the Dept of State on the 22d. Septr. 1825, *after my return from Kentucky.* I was detained on my return by the illness of my daughter:[4]

In 1825 I left Washn. for Kentucky 14h. May and returned 21st. August[5] leaving my family on the road to follow me, with my sick child who died.

In 1826 I left Washn. about the 27 June & returned 19 Septr.[6] (See [Washington *Daily National*] Intell[*igence*]r & [Washington *Daily National*] Journal)[.]

ALS. PHi.   1. Dated only "Friday morning." This was probably written to provide information for Johnston's speech of Feb. 23, 1827, on the subject of colonial trade. See 6:239-40.   2. See 4:194, 821.   3. See 4:180.   4. Eliza Clay. See 4:546-47, 586. 5. See 4:335, 589.   6. See 5:492, 695.

To THOMAS I. WHARTON   Washington, March 11, 1827
I received your letter,[1] and communicated to the Judges of the Supreme Court your wish, about the office of Reporter. There will be no appointment made until the next term, should Mr. [Henry] Wheaton accept the Foreign place lately confered on him which, 'though probable, is not absolutely decided.[2] This delay will afford you time to bring forward and support your claims. If the appointment were made now, I think it not unlikely from what I have heard that Mr [Richard] P[eters]. [Jr.] would get it, from previous commitments of some of the Judges.[3] In a conversation I had last evening with Judge [Robert] Trimble,[4] I learnt that all the Judges are very favorably impressed in regard to you. Perhaps at the next term you may, therefore, prevail.

I have transmitted a packet for Mr [Thomas] Smith to your care by the mail. If he should be absent be pleased to open it. It contains a sketch[5] which has been prepared by a friend, and which I wish may be subjected to your severe criticism and amendment if you think it necessary.

ALS. KyLoF.   1. Not found.   2. For Wheaton's appointment to the mission in Denmark, see 6:389, 616-17, 626.   3. Richard Peters, Jr., received the appointment, and the first *Reports of the U.S. Supreme Court* published by him were those in 1828. See *CAB.*   4. For Justice Trimble, see 1:222.   5. Possibly a reference to the memoir mentioned in Clay to Wharton, March 24, 1827. See also 6:415.

MEMO ON PROCEEDINGS   Washington, *ca.* Mid-March, 1827[1]
OF CONGRESS
The proceedings of the last Session of the Congress which closed its term on Monday last, and especially those of the Senate will receive the serious consideration of the people of the U States. It is our purpose hereafter to notice them more particularly. It need not be disguised that towards the close of the past Session, we presume by some of those "combinations" of what Dr. [John] Floyd, in his late address at Richmond,[2] made a previous confession, the Opposition obtained a small majority in the Senate. We will select only a few prominent instances to shew how this majority was disposed to use the ephemeral power so obtained.

1. The Wool bill (that measure so important to the great farming interests of our Country) was, in effect, rejected by the casting vote of Mr. [John C.] Calhoun, the Vice President.[3]

2 A committee appointed by the majority of the Senate made a report, on the subject of the Georgia controversy,[4] of what 3000 Copies were ordered to be printed for distribution among the people of the U States, countenancing and encouraging the Governor of Georgia.

3. The bill for converting a portion of the six per Cent debt into a debt, bearing an interest of five per Cent, which passed the H[ouse]. of R[epresentatives]. was lost in the Senate. By the failure to pass a bill last year, in consequence of the now acknowledged errors of Mr. Louis McLane,[5] the Country lost about $90.000. By the failure of the Senate to pass this bill it loses a like sum.

4 The Colonial bill was lost by the refusal of the Senate to agree to an amendment of the H. of R. without which the measure would have

humiliated this Country.[6] And now G. Britain is left in possession of the monopoly of the navigation concerned in the intercourse, unless the President feels himself authorized to close our ports under the act of March 1823.[7]

Whatever regret will be felt at the course pursued by the Senate in the above instances, the people will derive much satisfaction from knowing that that of their immediate Representatives, was directly the reverse of it. We must add, as one of the remarkable incidents occuring at the last Session of the Senate, that Duff Green, the editor of a paper notorious for the scurrility of its columns, and its utter disregard of all decency and truth, received the votes of twenty three SENATORS of the U States to be the printer of the Senate.[8]

AD, in Clay's hand. DLC-HC (DNA, M212, R4).   1. This document is undated, but internal evidence suggests it was written following the conclusion of the 19th Congress, 2nd Session; however, Clay states in the document that Congress ended on "Monday last," when the 19th Congress, 2nd Session ended on Saturday, March 3, 1827.   2. At a dinner in Feb., 1827, Floyd had criticized the Adams administration and had asserted that a combination was forming which would wrest power "from those hands so unworthy to hold it." Richmond *Enquirer*, Feb. 22, 1827. For Floyd, see 6:200 and *BDAC*.   3. On Feb. 28, 1827. See 6:200.   4. For the Georgia controversy, see 4:501-2. On Feb. 5, 1827, the Senate had appointed a Select Committee to investigate the situation between Georgia and the Creeks. The committee reported on March 1 and the Senate adopted a resolution on March 2 to request the president to continue efforts to obtain from the Creeks a relinquishment of any claims to land in Georgia. U.S. Sen., *Journal*, 19 Cong., 2 Sess., 147-50, 166, 260, 267, 274.   5. For McLane's statement that the treasury deficit resulted from errors made in previous years, see *Register of Debates*, 19 Cong., 2 Sess., 643-45, 1267, 1306, 1345-46, 1352. For McLane—congressman and senator from Delaware and later minister to Great Britain, secretary of treasury, and secretary of state—see *BDAC*.   6. See 6:239-40.   7. See 3:729.   8. For Green, see 4:379; for his election as printer, see 6:373.

To JAMES TALLMADGE   Washington, March 24, 1827

I duly recd. your favor of the 21st. inst.[1] The Foreign correspondence authorized to be published by the resolution of 1818 has not yet been selected and published.[2] I am now about to have that done. A copy of the Journal is now sent you and I hope you will receive it safely by mail.[3]

I wish, my dear Sir, that I could enjoy the respite from labor which you suppose the adjournment of Congress admits. The office in which I am allows of but very little recreation—too little I fear for my almost exhausted constitution[.][4]

ALS. MBNEH.   1. Not found.   2. See 6:154, 297-300.   3. See 4:816; 6:414-15.   4. Tallmadge's reply is in 6:378-79. This letter is the one indicated as "Not found" in note 1, although Tallmadge says he is replying to Clay's of "the 22th [*sic*]."

To THOMAS I. WHARTON   Washington, March 24, 1827

I received your favor of the 23d. instant.[1] With respect to the papers printed by order of the British Government on the subject of a new Criminal code, I will write to Mr. [Albert] Gallatin and request him to procure a Copy for the use of your Commission, which will be better than if you were to write yourselves.[2]

The renewal of our Commercial treaty with England[3] is among the subjects on which Mr Gallatin is instructed and is now negotiating. The result will be soon known.

I thank you for your kind attention to the Memoir,[4] and to the Miniature. Be pleased when Mr. [James B.] Longacre[5] is done with the latter to have it put in a gold frame and safely returned to me.

ALS. KyU.   1. Not found.   2. For Clay's letter to Gallatin, see 6:351; see also 6:519-20, 758-59. In 1826 Wharton, Charles Shaler, and Edward King had been appointed by the Pennsylvania legislature as a commission to revise the state's penal code. For a discussion of their report, see Negley K. Teeter & John D. Shearer, *The Prison at Philadelphia: Cherry Hill* (New York, 1957), 20-23.   3. For the commercial treaty of 1815, see 2:57-59, 611; for negotiations leading to and renewal of the treaty, see 6:520, 534-36, 551-52, 577, 582, 608-9, 679-80, 704, 716, 722-23, 750, 806, 827-28, 855, 1026.   4. See 6:415.   5. For Longacre and the miniature, see 6:433.

To DAVID TRIMBLE[1]   Washington, April 7, 1827

I received your letters under date the 25th ultimo,[2] and I will endeavor to procure for you the letter of resignation of Mr [John Quincy] Adams, of his seat in the Senate of the United States.[3] I will also send you in the course of a few days a volume of my speeches, lately published in Philadelphia, which contains the address and particular speech you desire.[4] I am very much gratified to find that you entertain no fears as to the result of your election.[5] [Francis] Johnson and [Richard A.] Buckner, I learn from the former are both safe,[6] and I hope you will be so, but to make your election sure, a duty enjoined as well by Holy Writ as by patriotism, you must spare no exertions. You have an active, indefatigable, and boisterous competitor, and you should be particularly guarded against a ruse de guerre. I shall write to Owens,[7] as you desire, though I feel some difficulty, as to what I ought to say to him. After you have made the grand tour of your District, do write me, and let me know how "the land lies."[8]

ALS. OC1WHi.   1. For Trimble, see 1:580 and *BDAC*.   2. Not found.   3. On June 8, 1808. Adams supplied the letter which Trimble wanted to use in his stump speeches. Adams, *Memoirs of John Quincy Adams*, 7:255.   4. See 6:415.   5. Henry Daniel defeated Trimble in the 1827 Kentucky congressional election by a vote of 4,163 to 3,811. *Guide to U.S. Elections*, 550.   6. Also, in the 1827 Kentucky congressional election, Richard A. Buckner defeated William Owens by a vote of 3,527, to 3,247, while Joel Yancey defeated Francis Johnson 3,268 to 3,169. In all, 10 Jackson Democrats and 2 Adams administration supporters were elected to Congress from Kentucky. *Ibid.* For Buckner, see 4:79; for Owens, see 6:1010; for Yancey, see 3:335; for Johnson, see 3:42 and *BDAC*.   7. Probably William Owens. No such letter has been found.   8. On the 1827 Kentucky elections, see also 6:926-29, 959-60, 966, 970-71.

To SAMUEL BELL[1]   Washington, April 18, 1827

I am happy to be able to inform you that we have very cheering intelligence from the West and from Pennsa. in respect to the prospects of the Administration and Mr. [John Quincy] Adams's reelection.[2] I am perfectly satisfied, from comparing the accounts which I receive, that we shall not only maintain our ground but acquire additional strength in the West. Mr. Adams will obtain the votes of all the States beyond the mountains which gave him their suffrages in the H[ouse]. of R[epresentatives]. and Indiana superadded.[3] The development of the means, the ultimate aims, and the effect of the success of the opposition are producing in that quarter the best influence. A letter which I recd. this day from Mr. [John] Test[4] (who you know voted formerly for Genl. [Andrew] Jackson) contains the strongest assurance of the ultimate vote of Indiana being given to Mr. Adams. He details changes of individuals and other circumstances which amount to the most perfect evidence that we shall not be disappointed in that result.

In Pennsa. every thing is working well. The vice of timidity and apathy is giving way to confidence and exertion. Meetings of the people have been, and others will be, held favorable to the Administration. And if no adverse cause shall arrest the progress of converſion in that State, I think there is every reason to hope that it will be true to its real interests, which the intelligent portion of the Pennsa. public now sees are sustained by the present Administration, and would be jeopardized by the success of the Opposition.

In the mean time, we should not relax in exertions any where, not even in New England, and especially not in N Hampshire. I do not know what may be the disposition of your people, nor would it be proper for me to dictate any course to them; but if I might take the liberty of making a suggestion I would observe that I think the best effect out of your State would be produced by resolutions of your Legislature, at the approaching Session, in approbation of the Administration and in condemnation of the Opposition. These resolutions would inspire confidence, and put at rest the question which is made out of your State, as to its final vote. They would also serve to neutralize the effect of Mr. [Levi] Woodburys course, and add strength to your own. One of the arts of the Opposition is to make a *shew* of force, and there is certainly much concert and co-operation on their side. This should be met by concert and co-operation on ours, and by real demonstrations of popular sentiment.[5]

The results of the Elections in Virginia are less unfavorable than were to have been anticipated. I regret the loss of Mr. [Alfred H.] Powell,[6] but it is to be attributed mainly to local causes. His district is composed of only two Counties, each of which appears to have adhered with remarkable unanimity to its own Candidate, and unfortunately his antagonist resided in the most populous County.

I shall be glad to hear from you at your leisure . . .

ALS. NhHi. Letter marked "(Private and Confidential)." 1. For Bell, see 6:447. This is the letter indicated as "(Clay letter not found)" in 6:447, note 7. 2. See, for example, 6:445-47. 3. See 6:362 and Benton to Clay, April 9, 1822. 4. Letter not found. For Test, see 4:709 and *BDAC*. 5. For developments in New Hampshire, see 4:447. 6. Powell had been defeated by Robert Allen. *Guide to U.S. Elections*, 550. For Powell, see 5:381; for Allen, see *BDAC*.

To NATHANIAL SILSBEE   Washington, May 28, 1827

I have to acknowledge the receipt of and to thank you for your obliging letter of the 23d. inst.[1] which contains a clear if not entirely satisfactory account of the condition of public affairs with you. It will be cause of much regret if Govr. [Levi] Lincoln should adhere to his determination to decline running for the Senate. I agree with you that, in that event, it would be desirable that Mr. [Daniel] W[ebster]. should be returned, if such should be the pleasure of your General Court.[2]

I am glad to find that there is reason to hope we shall not lose you.

(Confidential) It will be satisfactory to you to know that the affair at Rio [de Janeiro] looks worse in the papers than the facts attending it justify. Mr. [Condy] Raguet acted altogether, in his demand of passports, upon his own responsibility, and it may be at least doubted whether there was justifiable ground for a measure so serious.[3]

ALS. MHi.   1. See 6:584-86.   2. Webster was elected on June 7, 1827, after Lincoln had earlier declined. Charles M. Wiltse & Harold D. Moser (eds.), *The Papers of Daniel Webster: Correspondence*, 7 vols. (Hanover, N.H., 1974-86), 2:214-17. For Lincoln, see 4:851-52.   3. See 6:295, 317-18, 603-4.

To HENRY H. GURLEY   Washington, June 1, 1827
Dr T[obias]. Watkins[1] of this place, has addressed a letter to yourself and to the other members of the Western delegation, requesting from each a statement in relation to the charge brought forward, under the sanction of General [Andrew] Jackson's name, against my friends and myself, in regard to the late Presidential election.[2] The object is to obtain a mass of evidence, to be published hereafter, if circumstances should render it necessary.[3] May I hope that you will answer the Doctor's letter?

LS. LNHT.   1. For Watkins, see 3:371.   2. See 6:557-58, 572-73, 681-83, 1071. 3. See 6:1394-96.

To SAMUEL BELL   Washington, June 3, 1827
I received this day your obliging favor of the 24h. Ulto.[1] and thank you for the very satisfactory account which it contains of public affairs in N. Hampshire. I am glad to find that the friends of the Administration have become sensible of the utility of concert and open exertion, and of the propr[i]ety of tearing off the mask from those who profess neutrality or friendship, whilst they are secretly and actively engaged in promoting inimical designs, I never myself doubted that any part of New England would finally be opposed to Mr. [John Quincy] Adams's re-election;[2] but I confess I entertained apprehensions that by the forbearance or supiness of his supporters in N.H. mischief would be done there or elsewhere. Your kind letter dissipates these apprehensions. From other quarters, the information generally is very encouraging. In Kentucky, where we shall have, early in August next, the first warm contest, I must be greatly deceived, if the Administration does not maintain, not only its present numbers from that State in the H[ouse]. of R[epresentatives]. but acquire some addition.[3] Ten out of the eleven votes in Maryland may be fairly anticipated; and things wear a very promising aspect in Pennsylvania.[4]

I shall leave here on the 10h. for Kentucky via Pittsburg[h] to be back by the 1st August.

You will hear with satisfaction that the late affair at Rio de Janeiro has been arranged at this place.[5]

ALS. NhHi.   1. Not found.   2. See 6:362.   3. Clay to Trimble, April 7, 1827. 4. For Maryland, see 7:482; for Pennsylvania, see 6:363.   5. See 6:295, 317-18, 603-4, 612, 614-15, 629-30, 634-35, 641, 1180-81; 7:393, 416-17, 420, 479.

To PHILIP R. FENDALL   Steubenville, Ohio, June 23, 1827
I must refer you to the News papers for an account of the reception which they have given me in the Western Country, and which has greatly exceeded in its cordiality my expectations.[1]

I hastily prepared a sketch of my Speech at Pittsburg[h] and in the last paragraph according to my recollection of it there is a want of precision, which I should be glad to be corrected in its publication in the [Washington *Daily National*] Intell[*igence*]r. and [Washington *Daily National*] Journal. The clause (I write from memory) now stands: "I have yet another cherished resource, of which He only can deprive me who gave it. *It is the consciousness of the rectitude with which I have ever faithfully served my Country.*" The last sentence should be, "It is the *power* of consciousness, which assures me that I have ever faithfully" &c[.]²

I will thank you to get Mess [Peter] Force & [Joseph] G[ales]. & [William W.] Seaton to make this modification, if they feel authorized upon my request to make it, without *formally* noticing the alteration in their papers.

I hope to get a passage tomorrow in a Steam boat at Wheeling. In that case, I think I shall get to Lex[ingto]n. before the end of the month.³

ALS. KyU. 1. See, for example, 6:687, 700-703, 705-6, 712-13, 763-79, 783, 796. 2. See 6:700-703 for Clay's speech in Pittsburgh. In the version printed in both the Washington *Daily National Journal* and the Washington *Daily National Intelligencer* on June 28, 1827, the sentence read: "It is the consciousness of the rectitude with which I *know* I have faithfully served my country." 3. Clay was in Maysville, Ky., on June 26 and in Lexington by June 29. See 6:719, 728.

To NORBORNE B. BEALL   Lexington, July 9, 1827

I received, with unaffected pleasure, several days ago your obliging favor of the 2d. instant.¹ Far from considering it, as you intimate, any bore, I am thankful for your kind recollection of me, and for the valuable information it communicates. I hope the flattering anticipations you make will be realized, as they ought to be, if truth and justice prevail.

I have also recd. this day your favor of the 6h. inst.² You have most justly appreciated the importance of Genl. [Andrew] Jackson's letter.³ I consider that letter as insuring his condemnation, and my triumph. He must be condemned whether he received the statement or not which he describes. In the first case, because he concealed it; in the second because it is impossible that it can be established, since it is not true. If he gets a man (and I have no more idea than the man in the moon, from any thing I know, who he can get) to verify the statement, he has already invalidated the testimony of that man by the advice which he represents him to have given. And his testimony must be further discredited by that of every friend I had in Congress—So that in any event I must stand acquitted and Genl. Jackson convicted.

I should be glad if you could procure and transmit to me at Washington a statement from the Jackson man ment[ione]d. in the postscript to your last letter,⁴ that it was Mr. [James] Buchanan, by whom Genl. Jackson expects to prove the charge. I should like to have it, because there are different statements of the person refered to, made by General Jackson's intimate friends or connexions. I have as little objection to Mr. B. as almost to any other man, having it in my power to prove in regard to him what amounts to something very variant in its nature from any proposal originating with me or my friends.⁵

206

I thank you for Mr. [Charles A.] Wickliffes address, which I shall read at my leisure. I have no desire or intention to interfere in that gentleman's election.[6] He has some connexions my regard for whom concurs with other considerations to restrain me from any interposition against him. But *he* has no right to drag my name before the public in aid of his cause, without confining himself strictly to truth. If I have been rightly informed he has not always done that. I understand that he has said that I had expressed to him, in private conversation, an approbation of Mr. [George] McDuffie's proposition, at the Session before the last, to amend the Constitution, or of the same principle.[7] This is not true. When I was a member of Congress different proposals were made to amend the Constitution, by districting the U. States, for some of which I voted; but Mr. McDuffie's proposition was widely variant from any of them, and I never did express to Mr. Wickliffe any opinion upon that. It does not follow that because one may happen to be a friend to a given proposal to district the U.S. that he is therefore friendly to every proposal with the same object. Nor that, if he be a friend to an amendment of the Constitution at a period of perfect calmness, he is to support any amendment, looking to the same object, brought forward, in a season of great excitement, for a special & a personal purpose.

I have also been told that Mr. Wickliffe alleges that I endeavored to prevail upon *him* to vote for Mr. [John Quincy] Adams. Such an allegation is entirely untrue. I never sought in my life to influence Mr Wickliffes vote on that, or any other question.

I authorize you to correct his statements, if they have been made as represented to me, in the above particulars.

I have regretted very much that I could not visit my friends at Louisville. I could not do it without such a neglect of business, public and private, as they would disapprove. I shall leave here for Washington on the 16h. instant.

I am happy to assure you that prospects are bright on public affairs in every quarter and in every way. Intelligence from various points has reached me since my arrival in K[entucky]. of the most gratifying kind. It confirms your views of N. York.[8] And in Pennsa.[9] a current, deep, strong and rapid, is now running in favor of the Admon which must carry the vote of that State to Mr. Adams, unless something occurs to check it.

I shall always hear from you, My dear Sir, with peculiar pleasure; for I assure you, with entire sincerity, that the steadiness of your friendship is a source of great gratification . . .

ALS. KyLoF.   1. Not found.   2. Not found.   3. Reference is to Jackson's letter asserting his belief in the corrupt bargain charge. See 6:718-19, 728-30, 840-41. 4. Reference obscure, since the letter has not been found.   5. For Buchanan's role in the corrupt bargain charge, see 6:682-83, 819-20, 839-41, 886-89, 891-92, 899, 922, 949, 966, 1030-31, 1035-36, 1162, and entries under Buchanan, James in the indices of volumes 7-10 and in Subject Index: Volumes 1-6, in 7:701.   6. Wickliffe defeated Lee White in the race for Kentucky's 9th congressional district by a vote of 3,856 to 1,982. *Guide to U.S. Elections*, 550. For Wickliffe, see 3:728; for his claim that Clay had tried to talk him into voting for John Quincy Adams, see 6:1014-15.   7. See 5:278-79. For McDuffie, see 3:567 and *BDAC*.   8. Jackson carried New York State over Adams in 1828 by a popular vote of 140,763 to 135,413. Jackson received 20 electoral votes to 16 for Adams. Thomas H. McKee, *The National Conventions and Platforms of all Political Parties . . . Popular and Electoral Vote* (New York, 1906; reprint ed., 1971), 25-26.   9. Jackson carried Pennsylvania over Adams in 1828 by a popular vote of 101,652 to 50,848. Jackson received all 28 of the state's electoral votes. *Ibid.*

From WILLIAM HENRY HARRISON   North Bend, Ind., September 23, 1827

I received your letter of the 6th. Inst[1] on Tuesday last. It was delayed in reaching me several days by being directed to Cincinnati instead of Cleve[land] which is the Post Office nearest to me.

I inclose herewith the statement you request.[2] As you did not say in what shape you wished it to be written I have authorised our friend Josiah J.S. Johnston Esqr. to give it that which will best meet your wishes supposing that you would not like to do it yourself. The copy of Govr. [John] Branch's speech was not inclosed with your letter But I saw it since the receipt of your letter in a Cincinnati Paper.[3] I regret that you had forgotten that I informed you that Mr Branch had spoken against your appointment which I certainly did, altho I cannot conceive that it has any bearing on the main Point, for I cannot now see any thing in the speech which would have induced me to have determined otherwise than I did.

ALS. CU-B.   1. See 6:1003-5.   2. For Harrison's statement, see 6:1005.   3. See 6:1004-5. For Branch, see 6:573-74.

To JOSIAH S. JOHNSTON   Bath, Va. (W.Va.), October 6, 1827

I transmit inclosed the promised statement.[1]

We arrived here on the third, since which I have been unwell with a slight bilious attack. It is unattended by fever, and will not I hope prevent my reaching the City by the 11h. or 12h. instant.

I have nothing new, being out of the way of all that could be news to you. Be pleased to present me affectionately to Mrs. [Eliza] Johnston, and believe me always . . .

P.S. The statement is sent in the rough state in which it has been first written.

ALS. KyLoF.   1. See 6:1114-17.

To BENJAMIN WINER[1]   Washington, December 26, 1827

I have received your friendly letter of the 14h. instant[2] communicating the substance of a conversation between yourself and Mr. [John] Test in which he stated my avowal to him, a short time after my arrival at Washington in the Fall 1824, of a preference for Mr. [John Quincy] Adams over Genl. [Andrew] Jackson. I do not doubt that the conversation between us took place, and that I expressed to him such a preference, although it had escaped my recollection.

A mass of testimony has been collected to establish the fact of my fixed resolution to vote against Genl. Jackson, if I were called upon to vote. It may probably be shortly published;[3] and I should have been glad to have added to it that of Mr. Test, especially as he voted for Genl. Jackson. If he thought proper to state the fact to some Editor, and allow him to publish it, either under Mr. Test's name or upon his authority it would perhaps have even better effect than if he were to transmit a statement directly to me.[4]

I cannot close this letter without making my warm acknowledgments for the kind interest manifested in your letter towards me.

ALS. UPB. Addressed to Winer at Cincinnati, Ohio.   1. Not identified.   2. Not found.   3. See 6:1394-96.   4. No such statement has been found.

From Robert Walsh, Jr., *ca.* 1828. Sends Clay "a Prospectus of the Biographical work which I mentioned to you." Promises that "It will be executed with much care and directed from authentic materials." Asks Clay to suggest "the names of any worthies, of the West, who might be introduced into it." Hopes Clay will find "a moment of leisure in which to pen the memoranda concerning your own career, that you have kindly promised." ALS. DLC-TJC (DNA, M212, R14).

For Walsh, see 7:309 and *DAB*. This letter has been dated April 4, 1845, in a strange hand; however, it appears that Walsh was referring to the biographical sketches he was planning to write for the *Encyclopaedia Americana,* edited by Francis Lieber and published between 1829-33. See Walsh's entry in *DAB*.

To JOSEPH E. SPRAGUE[1]   Washington, February 18, 1828

I have to thank you for your obliging letter of the 14h. inst.[2] communicating the course proposed by your General Court, in reference to the Administration.[3] I am very grateful for the kind intentions which are intimated towards me. The resolutions of approbation of the Administration will do good. Although *you* of Massachusetts know well the state of public sentiment there, it is not known, and is misrepresented in the Valley, for example, of the Ohio. My friend [Henry] Shaw has proven himself the faithful and sincere friend that I always believed him.

You will have heard of the important event at Albany.[4] It cannot fail to have much effect (and I hope good) on general politics.

We shall have a tremendous scuffle in K[entucky]. I hope and think we shall succeed.[5] I adhere to the opinion that Mr. [John Quincy] Adams will get a greater Western vote, than both he and I together received at the last election.[6]

ALS. CLU. Addressed to Sprague in Salem, Mass.   1. For Sprague (1782-1852)— an attorney and postmaster in Salem, Mass., who also served as a member of the Massachusetts General Court—see Wiltse, *Papers of Daniel Webster: Correspondence,* 2:195. 2. Not found.   3. In June, 1828, a meeting was held in Concord, Mass., to organize a statewide drive in support of the Adams administration. *Ibid.,* 2:355-56; James S. Chase, *Emergence of the Presidential Nominating Convention, 1789-1832* (Chicago, 1973), 85. 4. Probably a reference to the death of DeWitt Clinton on Feb. 11, 1828, but also possibly a reference to the recent caucus nomination of Andrew Jackson made by the New York legislature. Clay managed to view both of those events in an optimistic fashion. See, for example on the former, 7:93, 103, 113; on the latter, 7:94.   5. See 6:362; 7:429. 6. See 6:362.

To NORBORNE B. BEALL   Washington, March 21, 1828

I received your favor of the 5th instant,[1] and thank you for the very satisfactory and interesting information, which it contains. Your letters breath such a friendly and cheering spirit that I always derive pleasure from the receipt of them. Accounts from other parts of Kentucky corroborate the encouraging intelligence which you communicate.

Whatever contrary impressions may be attempted, I give it to you as my firm and honest conviction, that if our friends succeed by a handsome majority in the Kentucky elections in August next,[2] the reelection of Mr. [John Quincy] Adams is not merely probable, but certain.[3] The adverse effect of the unfavorable issue of our elections last year,[4] more than any thing else, occasioned the depressing events of last Autumn.[5] Its favorable termination this year, will, I am quite sure, work directly the other way. We have just heard the result of the New Hampshire election, on which our opponents had counted with the greatest confidence. They have sustained a Waterloo defeat. The election of the Governor, and large majorities in both branches of the Legislature has been triumphantly carried, with a degree of unanimity which, it is said, has not been experienced in that State for thirty years.[6] The reaction in New York commenced soon after the elections of last Fall, and after the tricks were developed by which their unexpected results were brought about. The death of Mr. [DeWitt] Clinton[7] has added great strength to it, and intelligence from all parts of the State assures us that all our expectations and hopes in respect to that State will be yet realized.[8] From 24 to 30 votes are anticipated by our friends, for Mr. Adams. Without entering into further details I have the satisfaction to assure you, that at no time, for many months, have prospects been more bright and auspicious.

I recommended young Floyd, as I informed you I would, to the Department of War.[9] Whether any appointment has been since made, such as he wants, I really do not know; but I will take an early opportunity of inquiring.

Congress is likely to have a very protracted session, I think.[10] The house is now engaged in the discussion of the Tariff bill, reported by the Committee of Manufacturers, which nobody believes has the least prospect of passing in that shape.[11]

LS. KyLoF. 1. Not found. 2. See 7:429. 3. See 6:362. 4. Clay to Trimble, April 7, 1827. 5. Probably a reference to the fact that anti-administration forces had won control of both houses of Congress and had triumphed in the 1827 Kentucky congressional elections. See 6:362, 1363-64; 7:429. 6. In the March, 1828, New Hampshire gubernatorial race, John Bell defeated Benjamin Pierce by 21,149 votes to 18,672, and the National Republicans/Federalists captured two-thirds of the seats in the state legislature. The legislature then elected Samuel Bell, the new governor's brother, to the U.S. Senate. In Nov., Adams carried New Hampshire. Donald B. Cole, *Jacksonian Democracy in New Hampshire, 1800-1851* (Cambridge, Mass., 1970), 72-73, 75, 78-79. 7. Clay to Sprague, Feb. 18, 1828; 7:93. 8. Clay to Beall, July 9, 1827. 9. Not found. 10. The 20th Congress, 1st Session lasted from Dec. 3, 1827, to May 26, 1828. *BDAC.* 11. For the Tariff of 1828, see Congress of the United States: "Tariff of Abominations" in index on 7:660.

To CHARLOTTE MENTELLE Washington, March 24, 1828

I received your favor of the 10h Feb[1] in due course of the mail, and was thankful for it as a public proof of friendship. I must hope that you will not draw any conclusions unfavorable to my high estimate of that friendship from my having so long omitted to acknowledge. You can appreciate, and make due allowances for a correspondence so exceedingly extensive that, altho' often the source of satisfaction, is nevertheless very oppressive.

210

Mrs. [Lucretia Hart] Clay, I believe, will not visit K[entucky]. this year. Nor have I positively decided whether or when I shall. My business and inclination would carry me there, but I tremble (on account of my health, always delicate) to encounter that great excitement which I should find. And yet my health would be benefited by travelling, if I could quietly travel, without the stimulus of perpetual crowds.[2]

W[illia]m [C.C.] Claiborne[3] is yet with us, as is our grandson,[4] who now goes to school.

I pray you to make my respects to Mr. [August Waldemarde] M[entelle].[5] and Mrs. Clay unites with me in offering you assurances of our continued friendship.

ALS. Courtesy of Dr. Thomas D. Clark, Lexington, Ky.   1. Not found.   2. Clay did go to White Suphpur Springs and on to Kentucky. See 7:375, 397, 399.   3. For Claiborne, see 3:780.   4. See 6:703-4.   5. For Mentelle, see 1:121.

To HEZEKIAH NILES[1]   Washington, March 29, 1828

The regretted death of Dr. [William] Thornton[2] leaves vacant the Situation of Superintendent of the Patent office. Being desirous to avail the public of your services in it, I offer you the appointment, and hope it may suit your views to accept it. The salary is fifteen hundred dollars per annum. An augmentation of the Salary has been repeatedly recommended, and more than once by me. I think it ought to be made, but whether that will be done or not you will judge for yourself. It is, I think, just in itself, and the receipts of the office would fully warrant the increase.

I shall be glad to hear from you as soon as you can conveniently make a decision . . . [3]

ALS. COMC.   1. For Niles, see 3:247.   2. Thornton had died on March 28, 1828.   3. For Niles's reply, see 7:210-11.

From WILLIAM W. WORSLEY   Philadelphia, March 30, 1828

Your friendly favour of the 24th instant is received[.][1] I regret exceedingly that it is out of my power to accept your kind invitation to take the City of Washington in my route to Kentucky. I need not say that it would give me great pleasure to see you; and I should be gratified by communing with our friends from Kentucky on the subject of the approaching campaign in our State. I shall proceed from this place in a few days to New York; from thence, by way of Hartford, to Boston, and return to Kentucky by way of Albany, Buffaloe [sic, Buffalo], &c; so that I shall at no time be nearer the City of Washington that I am at present,

There is a subject on which I have for some time intended to address you. There is in Louisville a Mr. John Bull,[2] formerly of the firm of Megowan & Bull, carpenters, in Lexington. This individual has, with much industry, circulated a report to your prejudice. Had he the same standing in Louisville which Mr. [David] Megowan[3] has in Lexington, I should not deem it necessary to give the matter a moment's consideration. As I have never heard Mr. Bull tell his story myself, I do not know exactly what it is; but it is something to this effect:—That Megowan & Bull did a considerable job of Carpenter's work for you; that you disputed their account[4] and docked them very much; that you exacted time from them, and then bought your own paper at an usurious discount. To all whom I have heard mention this story, I have vouched that it is a gross fabrication—at least so far as dishonorable conduct of any kind is imputed to you. If you have a recollection of the circumstances of the transaction, I would thank you to communicate them to me, that I may have it in my power to rebut any charge to your prejudice by giving a true history of the Case. Among mechanics particularly, a story of this kind uncontradicted, is calculated to do much injury. They constitute as it were a distinct class in society, and an injury, or supposed injury, done a single member, is resented by the whole fraternity. I have the satisfaction, however, of informing you, that a very large majority of the most respectable and intelligent mechanics of Louisville are your friends. Indeed, it seems to me, (with some few exceptions) that in our State at least, you are opposed only by unprincipled and designing knaves or stultified fools.

I have been informed both in Pittsburgh and this place, that there have been a great many changes in Pennsylvania in favour of the administration; but I am fearful that they will not be sufficiently numerous to give the vote of the State to Mr [John Quincy] Adams.[5] Such appears to be the opinion of many of our friends here, whilst others speak with much confidence of success. I should not be astonished if the approaching election were to be decided by the vote of Kentucky;[6] and how distressing, how humiliating will it be, to the highminded Citizens of that state, if her vote should be given to her bitter reviler and base caluminator.[7] The heart sickens at the contemplation of the bare possibility of such a result. I will not believe it—and yet when I recollect the result of the late congressional elections, I am filled with the most gloomy apprehensions.[8] The ignorant and degraded class of our population are nearly all against us—and the numbers of that discription of people who push forward to the polls are really formidable. Scarcely one of them remains at home during an election. Many of our elections are lost by the inertness of our friends in remaining on their farms, whilst their more active opponents are swimming rivers and risking their lives to get to the polls. . . . [P.S.] A letter within a week or ten days from this time, will find [me] in New York. Address to the care of Messrs. Collins & Hannay.[9]

ALS. DLC-HC (DNA, M212, R3). Letter marked "Private." 1. Not found. 2. For Bull, see 1:789. 3. For Megowan, see 1:486. 4. Account not found, but see 1:789; 2:683, 708. 5. Clay to Beall, July 9, 1827; 7:460. 6. See 6:362-63. 7. Reference is to Jackson's "slander" of Kentucky troops at the Battle of New Orleans. See 2:11-12. 8. Clay to Trimble, April 7, 1827. 9. Not identified.

Agreement between Robert Scott, Ozborne Henley, and Henry Clay, April 25, 1828. Agreement puts in writing the terms agreed on the previous October in forming a business for the manufacture of cotton bagging in Lexington, Ky. Under the terms: (1) the firm shall be named Scott, Henley & Co. and shall be continued for five years; (2 & 3) Scott and Clay are "to advance to the Firm as its interest may require it," the sum of $6,000, including what they have already advanced; (4) Henley "is to attend specially and exclusively to the management of the Factory" and is to receive $160 annually "besides his equal share of prof-

212

its when a dividend may be made"; (5) Scott "is to keep the accounts," do the correspondence, and take the waggoners' receipts, for which he will be paid $150 annually besides his share of the profits; (6) Clay is not expected to perform any of the labors of the business, but he is "to have an equal voice in all its deliberations"; (7) should any partner advance the firm "a sum over and above that stipulated to be put into the concern, he shall receive an interest of six per cent per annum"; (8) should any partner "fail to advance in equal proportion to the sum herein stipulated, as the wants of the firm may require it, then he shall after the 30th day of June next," pay 6% interest "per annum on half the difference between him and the party who may have made the greatest advances to the concern, so as to equilize the advances of each to be paid semi annually until his advances shall be equal to that of the others"; (9) no party shall receive money or property from the firm without the consent of the other two, "except such sums as are herein stipulated, and such sum or sums as he may have advanced over and above the amount of stock herein stipulated"; (10) neither party shall dispose of his interest without the consent of the other two; (11) neither party "shall endorse for the firm, the paper of any individual, or company, without the concurrence of all its members"; (12) if any party should die, it shall be optional with the two survivors whether the firm shall be continued for the five years of the agreement, but if they continue, they shall make reasonable provision for payment of the sum due the estate of the deceased; (13) on dissolution of the partnership, there will be a prompt payment of all debts and an equal division of assets. ADS. DLC-TJC (DNA, M212, R16).

For Henley, see 2:256; 7:29-30.

To Whom It May Concern, June 5, 1828. Introduces the "bearer hereof, Prince [Abduhl Rahahman]," who "is a Moor, reduced to captivity near half a century ago." Notes that "The Executive of the United States has obtained him from his master [Thomas Foster], with a view of restoring him to his friends and country." States that Prince and his wife Isabella intend visiting some of the Northern cities of the U.S. and recommends him to all. Copy. Printed in Portsmouth (N.H.) *Journal and Rockingham Gazette,* August 30, 1828.

For Rahahman, see 6:158, 351-52, 933-35; 7:30-31; 8:28, 34. Rahahman died on July 6, 1829, soon after his return to Africa. Washington *Daily National Journal,* November 9, 1829.

To DANIEL WEBSTER   Lexington, July 24, 1828
Your letter of the 7h. inst. with its inclosure found me here.[1] The inclosed[2] will explain to you the disposition of the latter, which will be transmitted to Washington, and thence to Boston, where it may arrive in a few days after the receipt hereof.

Our friends are animated zealous and confident. My belief is that we shall succeed, in the pending election, after a hard contest. Two weeks more will decide the question, and the fact will be better than any conjecture, which is all that I could now offer.[3]

My health has improved; 'though gradually; and only in such degree as to leave me rather to hope for what is to come, than to be entirely satisfied with what I have.

[James] Clark[4] is with me today, and partakes of the general confidence. A favorable rumor from Louisiana, which has just come, will benefit us, if confirmed, as it must be, or refuted, in a few days.[5]

ALS. Henry Clay Memorial Foundation, Lexington, Ky.   1. See 7:376-77.   2. Not found.   3. For the August, 1828, Kentucky state election, see 7:429; for Kentucky's vote in the 1828 presidential election, see 6:362-63.   4. For Clark, see 1:119.   5. Probably a reference to the recent Louisiana state elections. See 7:403.

To NORBORNE B. BEALL   Washington, November 18, 1828
I duly received your letter[1] respecting the most extraordinary letter of
Genl [Edmund P.] Gaines to the Editor of the "Advertizer."[2] I concur
with you entirely in your remarks upon that reprehensible production.
But for existing circumstances I should advise some strong measure to
be taken in regard to the General. As they are it is most likely that
nothing will be done but to leave him to the just rebuke of public opinion, and to the animadversion of Mr. [John Quincy] Adams' successor
[Andrew Jackson]. I have also received your friendly letter of the 5th
instant,[3] which I perused with much interest. I lament extremely that
its just reflexions upon the existing state of things are but too strongly
justified by all past history, and I fear have too much foundation in the
condition of human nature improved as we had flattered ourselves it
was. I agree with you that the President elect has a path before him
strewed with thorns. If he can carry the nation through all its present
difficulties and his own, prosperously and safely, preserving the Union,
the Constitution and our liberties, I will acknowledge, at the close of
his career, that I have done injustice to his temper and capacity. Meanwhile I shall be a "looker on in Venice," anxious and struggling, in
whatever station I may be, to preserve those great principles of freedom and policy to which I have hitherto dedicated my public life. My
confidence in their success, it is true, is shaken. But they, have been so
interwoven with my very soul, that I will not abandon the hope of their
final success and triumph whilst reason and life endure.
     With respect to the existing Administration all the members of it
will proceed with diligence and fortitude to perform their duties to the
last. And they will turn over to their successors the public trusts which
have been committed to their hands, with the sincere desire that they
may there find a safe repository, and that the Republic may be benefited by the new stewardship.
     I expect to return to Kentucky in the Spring, where I hope to enjoy
in tranquillity the society of those tried friends whose fidelity has been
tested in the severe ordeals through which I have passed. Among that
number there is not one, my dear Beall, whom I more highly appreciate than yourself.

LS. KyLoF.   1. Not found.   2. Gaines had written a letter on Oct. 4, 1828, refuting various allegations of Jackson's misconduct. Louisville *Public Advertizer*, Nov. 1, 1828.   3. Not found.

From HENRY SHAW   Lanesborough, Mass., November 24, 1828
The agony is over.[1] It would be vain to reason upon the result—we
must abide it—your friends will glory that in retiring from office for
the present, you will bear back with you, the same frank & open and
sustained Character with which you entered Public life—An Administration is put down, by a Cossack Hourra [Andrew Jackson]—what are
we to think of that Intelligence and Virtue, of which the Coast [*sic*,
cost] has been so large—and what are we too think of the permanency

of Institutions, where at both ends of the Confederacy the leading Men lye under the imputations of Treason—The number of desperate Men are too rapidly increasing, to afford much confidence in the hope, of Immortality to the Republik—The feeling of the South is not stronger on this subject, nay it is infinitely less fixed, than in the North—common Men look at, and calmly talk about, a separation! I have been astonished at what I have heard—But we must go on, while we can, allaying all excitements, repressing every treasonible suggestion—The Publick sentiment towards yourself will immediately soften, and the friends of the Rivals will soon open the way for the return to power of the really great & good Men. could I influence the conduct of my friend [Clay], from now 'till March, it should be calm, compliant and dignifyed—reproaching no one, but yielding with respectfull deference to the voice of the People. sur[e]ly he who has risen with so much grandeur can for once fall with grace—above all things I would maintain towards the Head of the Govt. an equiable and cordial feeling—the race will perish with him. It has been unfortunate both in its principles and its associations—your friends, your real ones, will now show their devotion, and when the occasion arrives will put forth with vigor all the exertions requisite!—Mr. [Charles] King[2] of the [New York] American has already got up 3 Candidates, & poor Mordecai the Jew, is calling for the real Republican Party,[3] while Duff Green & Col [Russell] Jarvis, have Amicably separated[4]—Let us look on and enjoy the game—how unlucky poor Jonathan [Russell] is—but it is not all him—you know his bitter past—If he had been content with [Seth] Hunts conviction, he might have passed into a comfortible oblivion—at it stands, for heaven sake let him go—he has done you a favor by accident, that perhaps no other Man could, and altho he makes himself your foe, he has really proved a friend—I marvel at Jonathans folly!—[5]

upon the whole It is best that Hickory [Jackson] should come in—you could not have carried on the Govt. for 4 years more, if Mr. A[dams]. had succeeded—a majority of Congress against you, and an opposition consolidated by defeat, and animated by the hope of ultimate success, would have worn you out—you can now gather up your Laurels & repose upon them—let the People take time to reflect, the result will be Auspicious—I hope to give you a call during the winter—long before this I should [have] written you, but I had no good thing to tell—The time of need is at hand, tell me what I can do—I rejoice To hear that your health is nearly re established—take care of it, for your own and your Countrys sake—be governed by circumstances, and make few Publick declarations of what you will, or will not do—Take this arrogant counsel, as it is intended. . . .

ALS. DLC-HC (DNA, M212, R3). 1. See 6:362-63; 7:45, 482, 533, 535. 2. For King, see 2:21 and NCAB, 5:419. See also 7:537-38. 3. Mordecai M. Noah, pro-Jackson editor of the New York Enquirer, called for a return to earlier party and platform distinctions, "the old divisions of party, democratic and federal." The Jackson party would embrace the "republicans of '98," and sustain "those principles which were achieved in the civil revolution of 1800. New York Enquirer, Nov. 8, 19, 1828. 4. For Jarvis, see CAB. His split with Green is discussed in his pamphlet, To the Public. Statement of Russell Jarvis Regarding the Difficulties Between Himself and Duff Green Arising Out of the Dissolution of Their Partnership in the United States Telegraph, Washington, D.C. (Washington, 1829). 5. For Seth Hunt and his conviction on the charge of libelling Jonathan Russell, see

3:271-72; 6:551, 963-64. For the Russell/Adams controversy and Clay's involvement, see 3:204, 224-26, 252-57, 269-74; 7:337-38, 533, 540.

To ANNA MARIA THORNTON[1]
Washington,
December 15, 1828

Mr. Clay's respects to Mrs. Thornton, with the papers herewith returned[2] which accompanied her note of the 11h. inst.[3] all of which, according to her request, have been first perused by him, and afterwards by the President [John Quincy Adams] and Mr. [Richard] Rush.

Mr. C. who has the most friendly feelings and sympathies for Mrs. Thornton would gladly afford her any advice,[4] if any presented itself to him, which was likely to be available. But none such has suggested itself.

It has never been the practice of the Executive Government to interfere with public offices so as to coerce acts of justice between Debtor and Creditor. Such an interference would lead to endless embarrassment and difficulty. The President would have to assume the office of the tribunals in deciding questions which properly belong to them. If a creditor cannot through the agency of the Laws, regularly administered, obtain satisfaction of his debt, it would be a very doubtful policy, if not questionable in a constitutional or legal point of view, for any Executive interposition.

ALS. DLC-Thornton Papers. Letter marked "(Private & Inofficial)." 1. For Mrs. Thornton, widow of William Thornton, see 7:525. 2. Not found. 3. Not found. 4. Mrs. Thornton evidently was seeking help in collecting debts owed to her late husband.

From Charles R. Vaughan, Washington, December 30, 1828. Acknowledges the receipt of a note from Clay, "dated this day [7:583] . . . communicating, in conformity with the 3rd Article of the Convention, signed at London on the 29th day of September of the last year, the evidence which the Government of the United States intends to submit to the Sovereign, to whom are to be referred, the points of difference which have arisen in the Settlement of the Boundary, as described in the 5th Article of the Treaty of Ghent." Also notes receipt of a trunk, "containing written and printed evidence" which he promises to "transmit to His Majesty's Government, by a special Messenger." LS. DNA, RG59, Notes from British Legation, vol. 15 (M50, R15).

For Vaughan, see 3:179-80. For the convention, see Great Britain: Convention of 1827 to Arbitrate Northeastern boundary in Subject Index: Volumes 1-6, 7:730.

MEMO
ca. Late 1828-Early 1829[1]

Plural commissions, constituted for diplomatic service, are most frequently liable to divisions and dissensions among the members. This is the testimony of all experience. The cause is to be found in the want of congeniality in tempers, dispositions and attainments, and in jealousies to which most men are too often prone. But in that, which was entrusted by the Government of the U.S. with the important duty of treating at Ghent for peace with G. Britain, although composed of a larger number than customary, an extraordinary degree of harmony prevailed. From their remoteness from their Country, and the consequent difficulty of free and frequent intercourse with the Government, they labored under a great disadvantage, to which the British Commission was not exposed. They were often thrown upon their own responsibility, and this was especially the case when they took upon themselves to reject the sine qua non of the British government without even referring it to their own,[2] which might have led to a rupture of the negotiations and a protraction of the war. But they did not hesitate to assume that responsibility, and to conduct the correspondence without the benefit of consulting their Government.

The British Commissioners, on the other hand, transmitted every important note they received from the American to the British ministry and obtained in substance if not in express terms the answer which they were to return. Thus the American Commissioners were in fact treating with the whole British ministry. How honorably they acquitted themselves has been decided by the united voice of Europe & America.

On one point alone did any serious division arise among the American Commissioners, and that related to the Navigation of the Mississippi and the Fisheries. By the third article of the definitive treaty of peace of 1783 between G B and the U.S.[3] it had been stipulated by the contracting parties "that the people of the U. States shall continue to enjoy unmolested the right to take fish of every kind, on the Grand Bank and on all the other banks of New Foundland; also in the Gulf of St. Lawrence, and at all other places in the Sea, where the inhabitants of both Countries used at any time heretofore to fish; and also that the inhabitants of the U States shall have liberty to take fish of every kind on such part of the coast of New Foundland as British fishermen shall use (but not to dry or cure the same on that island), and also on the coasts bays and creeks of all other of his Britannic Majesty's dominions in America; and that the American fishermen shall have liberty to dry and cure fish in any of the unsettled bays harbors and creeks of Nova Scotia, Magdalen islands and Labrador, so long as the same shall be unsettled; but so soon as the same or either of them shall be settled, it shall not be lawful for the said fishermen to dry or cure fish at such settlement without a previous agreement for that purpose, with the inhabitants, proprietors or possessors of the ground."

By the eighth article of the same treaty the parties further contracted that the navigation of the river Mississippi, from its source to the ocean, shall ever remain free and open "to the subjects of Great Britain and the Citizens of the U. States."

In the treaty of 1794, negotiated by Mr. [John] Jay,[4] it was further stipulated that the river Mississippi shall according to the previous treaty of peace be entirely open to both parties; and that all the ports and places on its Eastern side, to whichsoever of the parties belonging may be freely resorted to and used by both parties, in as ample a manner as any of the Atlantic ports or places of the U States, or any of the ports or places of His Majesty in Great Britain."

At the dates of both of these treaties Spain possessed the sovereignty of the whole Western Side of the Mississippi from its mouth to its source; and of both sides from its mouth to the thirty first degree of latitude north of the Equator. From that point to the source of the river, the residue of the Western side belonged to the U States, except that it was supposed that the British territory would bind on a small portion of the upper part of it, when the line come to be marked from the Lake of the Woods as provided in the definitive treaty of peace.

The U. States and G. Britain, therefore, being the sovereigns of only a part of one bank of the river, and Spain being the exclusive sovereign of its mouth, a stipulation for its free navigation from its source to its mouth, between the two first named parties, could not affect the rights of Spain and could operate only so far as the contracting parties themselves had a right to give it effect, that is to the extent of their respective territories binding on the river. If they had a right to navigate it within the jurisdiction of Spain, that right could not be founded upon their compact, but upon the laws of nature, which give to nations who inhabit the banks of the upper part of a river the right of free access to and from the ocean, altho a different nation may be the Sovereign of the mouth of the river. It will be seen, in the sequel, that G. Britain could have had no such natural right, because she was not in the condition which it requires, that is she was not in fact the Sovereign of any part of either bank of the river.

The situation of G. Britain and the U. States, at the epoch of the treaty of Ghent,[5] was totally different from what it was, in fact, or supposed to be at the dates of the treaties of 1783 and 1794. Subsequently to this latter period, in the year 1803, the U. States acquired by treaty the province of Louisiana,[6] and consequently obtained all the rights of Spain, in regard to the Mississippi as they existed in the years 1783 and 1794. Further; prior to the treaty of Ghent it had been ascertained that the line designated in the treaty of 1783 to run from the Lake of the Woods to the Mississippi, would not strike that river at all but would pass above its source. Thus the U. States were at the period of that treaty the sole and exclusive proprietor of the river Mississippi from its Mouth to its Source. It being within their jurisdiction alone, G. Britain now had no more right to demand its free navigation, than she had to demand that of the Hudson, or any other river of the U. States.

The American government had been informed, prior to the preparation of instructions for the Commissioners at Ghent, that G. Britain intended to attempt our exclusion from the Fisheries; and they were instructed not to allow our rights to be brought into discussion. They were further instructed not to renew the stipulation in Jays treaty by which each party was allowed to trade with the Indians inhabiting the territory of the other, nor to agree to the subjects of G Britain having any right to the navigation of a river exclusively within our jurisdiction.

At any [sic, a very] early period of the negotiations at Ghent the British notified the American Commissioners that they would not agree, without an equivalent, to the renewal of our liberty to catch and cure and dry fish within the British exclusive jurisdiction; but they did not contest our right to fish on the high seas of the Grand Bank and other banks of New Foundland.

When the American Commissioners were engaged in preparing the projet of a treaty to be offered to the other party, a question arose among them, in consequence of the above notification, what should be proposed in regard to the Fisheries? They appear to have been divided on the point, whether the stipulation in relation to them contained in the treaty of 1783 did not expire with the breaking out of the recent War, or whether from the peculiar character of that treaty, being one by which an empire was served, and a new power acknowledged, the stipulation did not survive the war. Mr. Clay and perhaps all the other Commissioners except Mr. [John Quincy] Adams believed that the general rule of the public law applied to the case, and that the stipulation ceased with the declaration of War. Mr. Adams entertained the contrary opinion. All were of course desirous that we should not lose any right or liberty which we had enjoyed prior to the War. It is clear that if the stipulation survived the War, and was from its nature imperishable, no new stipulation was necessary to give it validity.

In consequence probably of the doubt on that subject, Mr [Albert] Gallatin proposed to insert in the projet of a treaty an article providing for the renewal, on the one hand, of the rights and liberties to us in the fisheries, and on the other of the right to the navigation of the Mississippi to G. Britain, as they had been provided for in the treaty of 1783. To the introduction of such an article Mr. Clay objected, and a long animated and anxious discussion ensued, conducted principally by Mr Gallatin, on the one side & Mr Clay on the other. It is described by him, in a letter addressed in 1822, to Jonathan Russell,[7] one of the Comm[ission]ers, and since published by him in violation of the confidence in which it was addressed to him, as having been [Here copy from the letter, or state the account of it without adverting to the source][8]

Finally after putting the proposed article to the vote, Mess Adams, Gallatin and [James A.] Bayard were in favor and Mess Clay and Russell against it. Upon perceiving the state of the vote, Mr. Clay informed his colleagues that he felt in candor bound to say to them that he would affix his signature to no treaty which contained such an article. After this declaration Mr Bayard left the majority, and uniting with Messrs. Clay and Russell made a majority against the insertion of the article and it was therefore not proposed.

The arguments which were urged pro and con on that interesting occasion are no where, that we are apprised of stated at full length. They can only be gleaned from documents or supposed from the nature of the subject.

In behalf of the article it was probably contended that we ought not to come out of the War with the loss or jeopardy of any right or liberty that appertained to the nation prior to its commencement; that it was at least not clear that such would not be the fact if the treaty were silent in regard to the Fisheries; that in such case it would give a subject to a powerful opposition to the admon at home to handle ag[ains]t. the Administration; that the right of navigation of the Mississippi, the contemplated equivalent to the British for the grant to us of the liberty in the Fisheries, within their exclusive jurisdiction, was one which could not be, and had not been, used by them to our prejudice; that the instructions from our government related generally to the whole affair of the Fisheries, without discriminating between those which existed on the high seas and those within the British exclusive jurisdiction, and that if the discrimination had been made in the instructions, or if the American Gov. had received the notification which had been given to the American Commissioners, respecting the exercise of the fishing liberty within the British jurisdiction, authority w[oul]d. probably have been given for the article proposed.

It is presumable that Mr Clay insisted on the other side that the article could not be proposed without a positive violation of the instructions of Government; that if the supposition were to be indulged that the discrimination had not been looked to which existed between fishing on the high seas and on British limits, and, if the Government were acquainted with the notification which had been given, it was by no means certain, but highly improbable, that the authority would have been given to renew the one privilege in consideration of the other; that there was no connection between the two subjects, none in the treaty of 1783, none in their nature, and the local position of the Mississippi and the fishing grounds were as remote from each other, as their natures were distinct. That if G.B. had not, prior to that period, availed herself of the stipulation in the treaties of 1783 and 1794, it might have been because of the obstacles which Spain presented, who had denied us the exercise of the right of navigation until the year 1795 and, shortly after, again interrupted it. That from the period of 1803, when, by the treaty of Louisiana, we acquired the incontestable right to the navigation, our relations with G.B. had been, during a great part of the time such as not to admit of her enjoying it. That the right to navigate the Mississippi would give her free access to the Indians of the N.W., and we knew how she might exert an influence over them to annoy us and disturb our frontiers by past experience. That it was wrong to select from all the rivers of the U.S. the noblest and to subject it, tho altogether within our limits, to conditions from which all others are free. That the U. States now, by our acquisition of Louisiana, stood in a totally different predicament from what they did in 1794 and 1783. That Great Britain had no territory, it was now known, touching the river. She could have no ground to ask its navigation which would not apply to the Potomac or any other American river, and she could not ask it but for some unfriendly or improper purpose. That the people of the West had been always justly sensitive to whatever related to the navigation of the Mississippi; and that they would regard the proposed article as an unnecessary sacrifice of a paramount interest of theirs for an object with which it had no sort of connection. That the liberty of fishing within the G. British jurisdiction in question was restricted and contingent our fishermen not being at liberty to cure and dry their fish on the island of New Foundland, nor on the unsettled bays harbors and creeks of Nova Scotia, Magdalen Islands and Labrador except so long as they remained unsettled, without the permission of the inhabitants. And that it was best to conform to instructions and to leave the subject where they had directed it to be left, and depend on future negotiations.

It had been already stated that a majority by the accession of Mr Bayard, decided not to offer the proposed article. In lieu of it they adopted the following clause in their note to the British Commissioners, prepared & proposed by Mr Clay [Here copy it][9]

Subsequently the British Commissioners returned their Contre Projet of a treaty, among the articles of which was one proposing to renew to the British nation the right to navigate the Mississippi, without any equivalent. Upon consideration of this article by the American Commissioners, the question arose what answer should be given to it. Mr Clay proposed that it should be stricken out and not made a part of the treaty; but the same majority which had been originally in favor of coupling the Fisheries and the navigation of the Mississippi together were now in favor of accepting the British article with the condition that there should be a renewal of all our rights & liberties in the Fisheries as they existed by the treaty of 1783; and in this way it was proposed to accept the British article. Mr. Clay having announced to his colleagues his settled purpose to subscribe no treaty which should comprehend such an article did not repeat the annunciation of his unalterable determination, lest it should be understood as a menace. Upon the proposition of the article, with this modification, the British Commissioners declined accepting it, and it was concluded to abstain from inserting any article in the treaty in respect to the Fisheries or the navigation of the Mississippi.

Thus was the father of rivers forever, it is to be hoped, released from any foreign encumbrance in respect to navigation; whilst on the other hand by a treaty with Great Britain concluded in 1818 the American right in the Fisheries has been satisfactorily secured. And thus has the wisdom of the course insisted on by Mr Clay been fully demonstrated.

AD, in Clay's hand. DLC-HC (DNA, M212, R6). Printed in Lexington *Herald*, Dec. 27, 1914, with minor differences in punctuation, abbreviations, and capitalization.   1. Although this document is undated, the editors have concluded that it may have been prepared after the publication in Oct., 1828, of Clay's 1822 letter to Jonathan Russell [3:252-57].   2. Crawford to Clay, August 28, 1814.   3. See Great Britain: Treaty of Paris (1783) in Subject Index: Volumes 1-6 in 7:724.   4. See Great Britain: Jay's Treaty (1794) in *ibid*.   5. See Great Britain: Treaty of Ghent (1814); issues discussed at Ghent; other dimensions of the discussions in *ibid*., 7:727-28.   6. See Louisiana Purchase Treaty and Louisiana (Orleans) Territory in *ibid*., 7:742.   7. See 3:252-57. 8. Brackets and statement inserted in Clay's hand.   9. Brackets and statement again inserted in Clay's hand.

To Anna Maria [Mrs. William] Thornton, February 16, 1829. States that he has received Mrs. Thornton's note "acknowledging the receipt of his Check for $500, the price of the D[utchess]. of Marlborough, and enclosing a check in his favor for $13 on account of the expences of sending for Rattler, with which he is entirely satisfied." ALS. DLC-Thornton Papers. See 7:525.

To THOMAS MORRIS   Washington, March 12, 1829
I am afraid that you have thought unfavorably of me for not answering your letter[1] and transmitting to you the sum you advanced for my unfortunate and heedless son.[2] But I beg you to be persuaded that I have not been insensible to the kindness to me which prompted you to afford him that relief. He has inflicted on me indescribable pain, and I

have perhaps allowed it to operate too much on my mind. I ought certainly not to have permitted it to delay so long an acknowledgment of your generous interference in his behalf.

I now send you a check for $103 the amount you advanced, with many thanks.

ALS. MBU.   1. Not found.   2. Thomas Hart Clay. See 8:2-3 and Clay to Wharton, March 24, 1829.

To THOMAS I. WHARTON
Near Cumberland, Md., March 24, 1829

Your favor of the 6h inst.[1] was duly received prior to my departure from Washington. I scarcely need say how greatly obliged I am by your friendly attention to Thomas [Hart Clay]. I regret that his enlargement cannot sooner take place. If he could be liberated by the 27h or 28h of this month he might overtake us at Wheeling, with which we would be exceedingly delighted. Be pleased to say to him that I expect a sufficient portion of the $150 check will be applied in aid of what remains in your hands to the payment of his board. There will be doubtless some persons from K[entucky]. in Philadelphia, about the time of his discharge, perhaps from Lexington, with whom he might be induced to return home. Mr. [William W.] Worsley who is now with you I am sure would afford his friendly offices.

I have had a sort of triumphant march through Maryland. Crowds flock around me every where, exhibiting a degree of enthusiastic attachment surpassing all expectation. I have had literally a free, as well as a triumphant passage; for the taverns and the turnpike gates are thrown open to me, without charge. Dinners, suppers, addresses &c. follow in rapid succession, and my feeble frame is hardly strong enough to sustain the affectionate demonstrations of what I am the object.[2] many of the Jackson men unite in offering them, whilst others of that party are still shy.

ALS. KyU.   1. See 8:2-3.   2. For Clay's trip home, see 7:633.

To PHILIP R. FENDALL
Lexington, May 18, 1829

I have been inexpressibly mortified about the case of Dr. [Tobias] Watkins, both on his and public account.[1] Your letter of the 7h. inst.[2] just received conveyed the first particulars which I have received, and that does not undertake to be very accurate. I shall, I presume in a few days know the whole. I sincerely hope that it may appear, in the sequel, that he has been guilty of no impropriety; but if he has been, painful as it will be to abandon him to his fate, he must be left to abide by the consequences of his own misconduct. Violations of public duty should be neither justified or countenanced in friends or foes. On the other hand, if he has not acted improperly[,] I trust it will so appear, and, in that event, he ought to be zealously sustained.

I perceive that the spirit of proscription has reached you and other friends.[3] Well; you must bear it like men. I think the public will ultimately condemn it. I made this a copious topic of discussion in a Speech which I addressed last Saturday to about 3000 gentlemen at a rural entertainment.[4] You will probably shortly see it in the prints.

My friends who voted for [Andrew] Jackson are rapidly returning to me; or rather, as they say, they have never abandoned me. If I were to offer for Congress, I have reason to believe not only that I should be elected with perfect ease but without opposition from any quarter[.] But I have finally resolved to offer neither for Congress nor for the Legislature.

The [Washington *Daily National*] Journal has been conducted with great spirit and ability of late, and is gaining fast upon the public favor in this quarter. I have very little doubt that the number of its subscribers might be considerably augmented, in this State, on application by an authorized agent. I shall be glad to learn that you may find it your interest to be associated in editing it.[5] But if you should ever revert to the idea of establishing yourself here or else where in the West to pursue the practice of the law, be assured of the continuation of my disposition to serve you all in my power. I have not yet resolved to return to the practice. I have much repugnance to it, but I may possibly engage in a qualified manner in it.

I shall be glad often to hear from you. I feel indeed in much want of a correspondent in the City to keep me advised of what is not always contained in the News papers. I felt greatly at a loss to comprehend the affair of Dr. Watkins; and your letter, altho' more satisfactory than any thing which has reached me, does not supply the requisite information. With unalterable regard . . .

ALS. KyLoF. Addressed to Fendall in Baltimore, Md.   1. For Watkins's conviction for defrauding the government, see 8:60.   2. Not found.   3. Fendall, who had been a clerk in the State Department under Clay, had been dismissed by Martin Van Buren, the new secretary of state, in April, 1829. Adams, *Memoirs of John Quincy Adams*, 8:147. 4. See 8:41-54.   5. Fendall served as editor of the *Journal* in 1829-30. William E. Ames, *A History of the National Intelligencer* (Chapel Hill, N.C., 1972), 247.

To NORBORNE B. BEALL   Lexington, July 14, 1829

I have received your favor of the 11h. inst.[1] In respect to the proposition of Mr. Sudduth,[2] I can do nothing with propriety, until the arbitration of the case of [George] Nicholas heirs &c. ag[ains]t. me which is to take place next month. It is not the [Samuel] Smith debt but another upon [Thomas D.] Owings in which the heirs expect to derive some benefit; and I think there is a mortgage on the Furnace to secure this other debt.[3]

It appears to me that some arrangement might be advantageously made, such as Mr. S. suggests, but until the decision of the above arbitration, I can not cooperate.

You think the Administration has arrested the course of proscription; but have they not nearly exhausted the subjects of it?[4] Except some Clerkships &c in Washington and a few post offices not worth having, what more cases remain on which it could act?

If my Speech[5] produced the effect you attribute to it (and which others have also attributed to it) I should rejoice exceedingly, because it will have saved some few families from starvation. As to the effect on the Nation at large depend upon it the Administration, by going as far as it has gone, has done itself all the mischief which could flow from that subject. The public had heard of so many removals that the novelty ceased to strike; and all that remain in office might have been expelled without producing the sensation that some half a dozen cases did in the first instance.

But is it true that the Adm[inistrati]on has stopt? I see new cases daily. You seem to suppose that Jackson will take advice from me, or, which is in effect the same thing, that he will be affected by my opinions publickly expressed. On the contrary, I believe that such are his feelings and passions towards me that I am persuaded he would, to gratify them, take the side opposite to me on any question whatever; and that on the particular subject he would continue, merely because I disapproved of proscription.

Pray make my best regards to Majr. Massie,[6] to whom I hope you communicated the apology I left in your charge.

When shall I see you? I shall be in Bardstown on the 28h. 29h. & 30h. inst. Can't you conveniently meet me there? I presume you have laid by your Crop, or by that time that you will have done so. I intend also to go to Mud Lick[7] the week after the Election.[8] I should be happy to meet you at one of the above places.

ALS. KyLoF.   1. Not found.   2. Probably James Sudduth, county clerk of Bath County, Ky., 1812-51, as well as state representative (1834) and senator (1855-59). John A. Richards, *A History of Bath County* (Yuma, Az., 1961), 357; Collins, *History of Kentucky,* 2:771. The "proposition" mentioned probably relates to the statement in a letter to James Sudduth, April 2, 1830, in which Clay states that he is not ready to sell mortgage interest in 249 acres. This document appears in 8:880 in Calendar of Unpublished Letters and Other Documents.   3. For Thomas D. Owings, see 1:133. For the origin of these cases, see espec. 1:135, 474-75, 597; 2:118-19.   4. On proscription, see espec. 8:42-48.   5. See 8:41-54.   6. Possibly Henry Massie of Jefferson County, Ky. Jackson, *Kentucky 1820 Census Index.*   7. Boone County, Ky.   8. See 8:22, 35, 83.

To ROBERT R. RICHARDSON[1]   Lexington, July 15, 1829

I have been so occupied with the trial of young [Charles] Wickliffe (of whose honorable acquittal you will have heard)[2] and with other engagements that I have not before been able to find time to acknowledge the receipt of your obliging letter of the 12h. Ulto.[3] I shall be much indebted to you by the communication, from time to time, of such events passing with you as may be interesting, according to your friendly offer. I never think of Balto. without a thousand agreeable associations. And whatever concerns it, or its patriotic and high spirited population, it will always be gratifying to me to learn.

We are going on here pretty much as you left us. The place adjoining me (owned by [George] Trotter [Sr.])[4] containing about 100 Acres, which we wished you to purchase, has been sold for $7500, principally cash. The same party that assembled with you and Mrs. R. at Mrs. Hart's[5] often meet there and frequently talk of you.

On public affairs, I have the pleasure to inform you that daily developements are made, which place beyond doubt that Kentucky will not support the present administration in its tyrannical course of proscription.[6] The Jackson party begin to feel that some body else is acting as President than the person for whom they voted. The testimonies of personal attachment & confidence which I constantly receive are of the strongest and most affectionate character.

Mrs. [Lucretia Hart] Clay joins me in respectful Compliments to Mrs. Richardson. I pray your acceptance of those of Yr's with constant regard . . .

ALS. KyLoF. Addressed to Richardson in Baltimore, Md.   1. Not identified.   2. See 8:9-10.   3. See 8:68.   4. See 3:785.   5. Probably Susannah Gray Hart (Mrs. Thomas, Sr.), but also possibly Eleanor Grosch Hart (Mrs. Thomas, Jr.).   6. On proscription, see espec. 8:42-48.

To THOMAS I. WHARTON   Lexington, July 15, 1829

I have duly received your favor of the first instant[1] with the receipts of the Cabinet maker and Waggoner for the Sofas' which you were good enough to order for me and for which you have advanced one hundred and twenty eight dollars.[2] Mr. [James] Erwin, my son in law, will call on you in a few days after the receipt of this letter and reimburse you that sum. In the mean time, be pleased to accept many thanks for your kind attention to this affair. You perceive by the article which I have procured that I mean to go to sleep. You think the people will not allow me to remain quietly in private life. That they have already much reason to be dissatisfied with the present [Andrew Jackson] Administration is most true; and that they will have more is to be feared. But it does not follow that I shall be called upon to assist in remedying the disorders of the State. Other and more skilful physicians may be necessary.

Pray have you heard any thing about a proposal which it is said that the Cabinet at Washington means to make the British Government to admit mutually the productions of the respective Countries at a fixed rate of duty, say 25 or 30 per Cent? I have been told, but I cannot credit, that such a proposal is contemplated. Ask my friend Mr. [Mathew] Carey what he would think of it. It would have as pernicious influence upon the prosperity of this Country as the famous treaty between Portugal and G. Britain produced in Portugal.[3]

ALS. KyLoF. Addressed to Wharton in Philadelphia.   1. Not found.   2. See 3:30-31, 36.   3. For the Methuen Treaty, see 10:640.

To CHARLES R. VAUGHAN   Lexington, July 18, 1821 [sic, 1829][1]

I have duly recd. your favor of the 1st. instant.[2] The rifle shall be delivered to you by or before the meeting of Congress. I will make some arrangement, through [Robert] Letcher[3] or Clarke [sic, James Clark], for the transmission to me of the Lithographic portrait of the dog which Mr. [Christopher] Hughes has forwarded to your care for me. Poor Hughes! he will be sensibly affected by his recall, unless some equal or better situation should be provided for him, of which I have not heard.[4] I wish his successor may do as well as I am persuaded he would have done.

Always desirous that a good understanding may continue between our two Governments, I take pleasure in your communication of your satisfaction with the present American administration.

You will lose an agreeable associate in Mr. Ousley [sic, Sir William Gore Ouseley].[5] He always appeared to me to be amiable, intelligent and well disposed. I presume that Mr. [Charles] Bankhead[6] continues with you. In that case I pray you to communicate our best regards both to him and Madam. Do me the favor also to assure Mr. Doyle[7] of my friendly recollections.

What is the cause of the distress of Manufacturers in G.B. and in France? Is it to be attributed to the excess of the producing power of machinery?

Johnny [John Morrison Clay][8] goes to school and is grateful for your friendly remembrance of him.

The summer's heat this week is very great here. I hope you suffer less from it at Washington than we do.

ALS. All Soul's College, Oxford University.   1. Although the letter is clearly dated 1821, this letter must have been written in 1829, since it is a reply to one dated July 1, 1829, and all other letters pertaining to the subject of the rifle are likewise dated 1829.   2. See 8:71.   3. For Letcher, see 2:764-65 and *DAB*.   4. See 7:566-67; 8:71, 105-6, 161-62 and *DAB*.   5. For Ouseley (1797-1866), attache at the British embassy in Washington, see *DNB*.   6. For Bankhead, British envoy to Washington, see the entry on his grandfather John Bankhead, noted Irish Presbyterian minister, in *ibid.*   7. Not identified.   8. Clay's youngest son. See 3:496.

To NORBORNE B. BEALL   Lexington, August 13, 1829

In answer to your favor of the 10h[1] I have the pleasure to inform you that Judge [Francis T.] Brooke[2] ha[d] a brother by the name of John,[3] who was probably in Williamsburg about the time mentioned by you, and who is now dead. He died near Fredericksburg, to which place you had better direct your enquiries. The Judge lives near it.

Our State Elections have terminated very well,[4] better than I had anticipated. Their successful issue compensates the unfavorable results of those for Congress. The prostration of the [Thomas P.] Moore faction is very encouraging[.][5]

I go today to the Olympian Springs where I should be happy if business or inclination would carry you.

ALS. KyLoF.   1. Not found.   2. For Brooke, see 1:16 and *DAB*.   3. See 1:525.   4. See 8:22, 35, 83.   5. For Moore, see 3:764; *DAB* and *BDAC*.

Speech at Mt. Sterling, Ky. August 21, 1829. To an assembly estimated at 800-1,000, states that "More than twenty years had passed since he was in habits of personal intimacy with the inhabitants of this town, and what scenes had been witnessed in the world—in our own country, since that period. The war [of 1812], a glorious war, had been waged for the assertion of our rights and principles on land and sea." Notes that he had played a part in these events. Then, alludes to the independence of South America, the Missouri question, and the tariff, pointing out his position on these issues and asserting that the people of Mt. Sterling "were almost unanimous in approving and eulogising his conduct on all those questions."

Refers to the corrupt bargain charge levied against him following the election of 1824 when he had been, "without any agency of his own, . . . mentioned as a candidate of the Presidency." Avers that "the calumnies and atrocious slanders with which he had since been pursued was . . . unparalleled." Asks what he has ever done to deserve such censure. Looks to the "impartial justice" of another world but is consoled "by the approval of his own conscience, that he had discharged his duty to the best of his abilities."

Explains that William H. Crawford's health left him no choice except Andrew Jackson or John Quincy Adams and that "he made [the] choice of Mr.

226

Adams, believing it to be in accordance with" the will of his district. Asks, "If he had voted for Jackson, after expressing such opinions as he did of him, during the question on the Seminole war [2:636-62], what would have been said of him?" Believes only the people in his district have a right to complain about his choice, and they have proved again and again that they agree with him. Challenges "any man to come forward and show how he violated his duty." Even if his choice were wrong, thinks he should not be assaulted as he has been.

Referring to the corrupt bargain charge, scorns the opportunity to try to prove his innocence, but "if there is any one now within the sound of my voice, who thinks he can prove it upon me, I challenge him . . . to bring it to fair trial in a court of justice, and I'll put down the ungenerous assumptions." Then, explains his reasons for accepting the office of secretary of state: "It was not . . . through a desire for office," because he had refused offers made him by presidents James Madison [2:88-89, 226, 233] and James Monroe [2:391, 488]. Adds: "I would have considered the lowest place in the cabinet of Mr. Madison more honorable than the highest under Messrs. Adams and Monroe, or even under the present Chief Magistrate, and yet I did not deign to accept." Thus, "it was not love of office, but love of country which induced me to fill the post I held under the last administration. . . . I had not viewed Mr. Adams in a favorable light. I had fears and doubts about the soundness of his principles; and I knew that by accepting an office in which I would have an opportunity to meet him in council, I would be enabled to keep him in the straight path of duty, even if he was inclined to deviate from it." Explains that Adams's conduct soon dissipated his fears "and proved to me that they were unfounded." Admires Adams's support for the tariff, opposition to the conduct of Georgia, protection of the Indians from "utter annihilation," and conciliatory policy towards the South American republics.

Concludes by saying that "however we differ as to the respective merits of two men, of John and of Andrew. . . . We should all be united in preserving the constitution and laws . . . we should support the American system, without which we can never be free, independent and happy." Notes there are some who say we should give up the tariff out of respect to southern opinion, but asserts that "Of all the maxims of republican government there is none that should be regarded with more respect, than that which imposes upon the minority the necessity of acquiescing in the will of the majority." Copy. Printed in Frankfort *Argus of Western America*, September 16, 1829, taken from the Mt. Sterling *Whig* of August 22, 1829. For Clay's comments on the accuracy of this version of his speech, see Clay to Thomas, October 5, 1829.

For the election of 1824 and the corrupt bargain charge, see Election of 1824 and Election of 1828 in Subject Index: Volumes 1-6 in 7:714-19.

To FRANK THOMAS[1] Lexington, October 5, 1829

Since my return from the Green river County,[2] Mr. [Thomas] Smith has shewn me a sketch, by whom made I know not, of my speech at Mount Sterling,[3] which appears to have been addressed to you. It is in the general remarkably accurate, and is certainly a much fuller as well as more correct representation of what I said on that occasion than was published in the Mt Sterling paper. Still I do not wish its publication, for t[w]o reasons, the first of which is that I do not think it of sufficient importance; and the second that I do not mean at any time to be forced to publish any speech by the garbled accounts of it from an inimical source. One of the conditions on which I consented to address the [m]eeting was that my speech should not be published. To that I adh[ere.] My indisposition to the publication does not proceed from any objection which I have to my expressions [o]r even my thoughts being known to the whole world; but because I do not wish to present myself too frequently before the public. I have in the course of th[e] last three weeks made some half a dozen Speeches, two of which occupied more than three hours in the delivery[.] None of them have been or will be published.[4] And yet I never made one in my life that appeared to give so much satisfaction as the two did at Russellville and Hopkinsville[5] to the whole audiences. I caused a paragraph to be inserted in the [Lexington *Kentucky*] Reporter denying the correctness of the Sketch published at Mount Sterling. With that I am content.[6] There were several gross inaccuracies in that Sketch which I could point out if I had it, and it was necessary. One was in relation to the *time* the offer was made me of the Dept. of State, and my motives for accepting it. Another was in attributing to me the sentiment that I would give up the Union sooner than the American System. I said that if a minority could at any time rise up, on any subject and in any part of the Union, and by threats of its dissolution control the majority that Union would not be worth preserving. Much as I prize the American System, I love the Union still more.

There was nevertheless enough of truth in some parts of the Sketch to deceive a careless reader who had heard the speech.

I am sorry to trouble you so much on a little affair [real]ly not worth it. As to any thing the Editor of the pap[e]r at Mount Sterling (I forget the name)[7] can say write or do, it is absolutely beneath my contempt.

I will thank you to make my respects to the gentleman who furnished you with the Sketch, and to inform him that it is my wish it should not be published.

Be pleased also to communicate my regards to Mrs Thomas and Mr. and Mrs. Howard . . .

ALS. Mt. Sterling Public Library, Mt. Sterling, Ky. Also printed in an unnamed and undated newspaper taken from the Detroit *Free Press*. 1. Not identified. 2. See 8:101, 104. 3. Speech in Mt. Sterling, August 21, 1829. 4. See 8:101, 104. 5. *Ibid.* 6. For the Mt. Sterling version, see Speech in Mt. Sterling, August 21, 1829. 7. The Detroit *Free Press* identified the editor as a Mr. Dowling.

Speech to Shakers, October 15, 1829. While on his way to a barbecue in Harrodsburg, Ky., stops at Shakertown and is provided with dinner and presented a piece of cloth "as a testimony of their high respect for his public services and character."

Clay responds that "It would be uncandid to say, that I concur with you in your religious practices. But this is your affair, not mine. It is in its social aspect that I contemplate and have ever admired your society. The example which it exhibits of industry, economy, regularity and fidelity to engagements cannot fail to communicate a salutary influence around you. These valuable qualities more than redeem any error, if there be error, in your religious creed, which only HE has a right to decide who governs the universe and judges us all. Entertaining these views of your institution I should regret the existence of any dissentions among you which might threaten a dissolution of your interesting community; and I sincerely hope that none such may arise. With my best wishes for its prosperity, and for the individual happiness of all its members, I pray you to express to them my grateful acknowledgment, for the proofs of their respect and friendship, with which I have been this day honored." Copy. Printed in Frankfort *Argus of Western America,* November 4, 1829.

Speech on Lexington & Frankfort Turnpike, Lexington, October 30, 1829. At a meeting at the courthouse Clay makes a report on subscriptions on the "middle route" of the Lexington & Frankfort Turnpike [8:132], noting that only $12,000 had been subscribed in Frankfort and expressing regret that only $33,000 had been raised in Lexington. Also presents a draft of an act of incorporation and offers the following resolutions: (1) that it is expedient to organize a company to build a turnpike between Lexington and Frankfort by "the McAdam's method"; (2) that an application should be made to the Kentucky General Assembly now in session to renew the act of incorporation for that object; (3) that a committee of three be appointed to make that application; and (4) that the meeting will forbear expressing a preference on the route at this time. Then, speaks "on the advantages of Turnpike roads to the citizens of both town and country." The resolutions were all adopted. Copy, summary. Printed in Lexington *Kentucky Reporter,* December 16, 1829.

From the Selectmen of Rodney, Mississippi, *ca.* March 15, 1830. State: "We have seen with a sense of deep regret, the unjust and malevolent imputations with which party spirit recently assailed you with an unremitting and relentless assiduity; but we derive much satisfaction from the belief that it has resulted in an increased and still increasing confidence in the integrity of your political character; while it has also proved that you possess a fortitude that can resist persecution, and an interpidity of spirit that can withstand the frowns of party and of power." Copy, excerpt. Printed in *Niles' Register* (April 24, 1830), 38:156.

Clay replied to the Selectmen of Rodney that "I have, indeed, been the subject of most unmeritted and unjust imputations. Amidst them all I have felt myself sustained by the conviction that I did not deserve them, by the support of a large portion of the virtue and intelligence of the country, and by the persuasion that, if I did not survive them, other tribunals, to which all human conduct must be finally submitted, would pronounce a right judgment upon mine." *Ibid.*

These excerpts have been dated by the editors based on the fact that Clay was in Natchez on March 13 and 14, 1830, and probably reached Rodney the following day. See 8:179-81.

To ROBERT P. LETCHER   Lexington, April 1, 1830
I received yesterday your very acceptable favor of the 10h. and 11h. Ulto.[1] through Mr. [Richard] Chiles.[2] Its contents are highly curious and interesting. When at N[ew]. O[rleans]. I understood that a confidential friend of Mr. [John C.] Calhoun then there had received a letter from him stating expressly that [Andrew] Jackson would not be a Candidate for re-election. It was some time ago stated in a Northern paper that Mr [Martin] V[an]. B[uren]. had addressed a confidential circular to his friends in different parts of the Union announcing the same fact. Assuming the truth of these statements it would follow that the late announcement of Jackson as a Candidate for re-election was a mere russe de guerre.[3] Still, in the distracted condition of the party at Head quarters, it may be found expedient again to bring him forward and we ought to stand prepared for any event.

I have no doubt, with you, that he would no longer be formidable; if the knowledge which you possess at Washington of his incompetency, and of the state of his cabinet[4] could be brought home to the great body of the people. There lies the difficulty. Whatever would lend to that desirable end should be encouraged and promoted by all means by our friends at Washington. In that view of the matter, and in that only, I think with you that the rejection of [Isaac] Hill, [Amos] Kendall &c would be highly beneficial.[5] It would demonstrate to the public that he is not invulnerable, and it would destroy the magic of his name.

[Thomas] Chilton's defection will do much good.[6] He is known to the public at large only as a member of Congress, as a warm Jacksonian, and as the mover of the resolution of Retrenchment.[7] His public confession of utter disappointment in all his anticipations must have great effect. Would it be possible to get some of those whom you represent to be on the anxious seats to make jointly or separately a similar address to the public?

I am sometimes written to for the purpose of knowing whether I am to be a Candidate for the next Presidency; whether the time has not arrived for a formal annunciation of my name; what I shall do if Jackson is again a Candidate &c. To all which I reply that I certainly do not mean to present myself as a Candidate; that whether I am to be or not, under any and every contingency must depend upon the people or portions of the people; and that having entire confidence in the zeal fidelity and attachment of my friends at Washington, they are the most competent to decide whether, when and how I shall be announced as a Candidate.

On that point it seems to me that some consultation and distinct understanding should take place among our friends prior to the adjournment of the present Session of Congress. Whilst it is expedient to do nothing prematurely, but to leave to the full developement the dissentions among the other party, we must not forget that we also want some cement to bind our friends, not in Congress but elsewhere, together. Several friends in Maryland have written to me that the election last fall was lost for the want of a banner; and that to prevent the same result in the more important election, in that State, next fall, they deem it essential that my name should be publicly put forth.[8] I do not intend to intimate that they are certainly right; but I make the communication for the consideration of yourself and other friends.

In Louisiana such is the strength of our cause that I should not fear the result with any competition.[9] And I do believe that Mississippi[10] may be counted upon in considerable confidence, if Jackson is not a Candidate, or if the public can be made sensible of the true state of things at Washington.

I will not trouble you with details about my visit to the lower Country. It was attended with the highest gratification, without a single incident to mar the satisfaction which I derived from it. When I attended the Legislature of Louisiana, which was altogether unexpected, the members, without previous concert, and without distinction of party, rose in a body to receive me.[11] At Natchez I found myself at a large public dinner surrounded equally by the two parties, with a Jackson man on my right and an [John Quincy] Adams man on my left.[12] Wherever I went the crowd pressed around me with intense curiosity and with the most hearty welcome.

What has become of Majr. Jonathan Taylor? and what are the prospects of the bill for our relief?[13]

You will have heard of the depression in the price of hemp. It is equally great in the article of Cotton bagging, which sold whilst I was at N.O. and Natchez at 16 Cents per [word illeg.] Surely this is not a time when either the interests of the Cotton planter or of the Manufacturer require the adoption of Mr. [James K.] Polk's insidious proposition.[14]

[Daniel] Webster's speech has been universally read and greatly admired.[15] Tell him that I congratulate him on his complete triumph. Our friends generally in that singular debate in the Senate have sustained themselves well.

Will you get an appropriation for the Maysville road?[16] And what prospect exists for our poor University?[17]

ALS. KyLoF.   1. Not found.   2. Chiles operated Chiles Tavern on Strode's Road in Fayette County. Lillie T. Edsall, *Chiles Tavern in Fayette County, Kentucky* (Lexington, 1944).   3. See 8:191-92.   4. See 8:169-70, 181-82.   5. Hill was rejected, Kendall confirmed. See 8:171. For Kendall, see 2:54; for Hill, 4:855.   6. For Chilton, see 5:920; for his defection from the Jackson party, see 8:189.   7. See 7:71   8. See 8:24, 237.   9. In the 1832 presidential election in Louisiana, Jackson won 4,049 votes to 2,528 for Clay. McKee, *National . . . Popular and Electoral Vote*, 32-33.   10. See 8:368.   11. See 8:185.   12. See 8:179-81.   13. Clay, as executor of the Morrison estate, had been sued by Taylor in two cases. Taylor's name omitted by editors in Clay to Scott, August 17, 1828, in 7:430-31. See also Clay to Whittlesey, Dec. 25, 1829, in 8:880.   14. In a recent House debate on proposals to modify the tariff, Polk had moved to allow a drawback of 4½ cents per square yard on foreign cotton bagging exported either in the original packages, or around the cotton bale, to any foreign country. He had argued that the five cent tax on foreign cotton bagging provided for in the Tariff of 1828 had been designed to benefit Kentucky hemp and bagging producers but it had not done so. Washington *Daily National Intelligencer*, March 16, 1830.   15. See 8:178.   16. See 8:132, 204-5, 214.   17. See 8:169.

UNKNOWN DOCUMENT

Probably Washington,
between May 15-27, 1830[1]

We regard it as a great misfortune that Kentucky should, at this interesting period, be represented in the Senate of the U. States by two gentlemen[2] decidedly opposed to those important measures of National policy, so essential to her prosperity as well as that of the Union at large, and at the same time in favor of those monstrous and violent doctrines of South Carolina,[3] which would be alarming but for the impotence which threatens by civil war and an appeal to arms to support them. Upon no National questions have the feelings and opinions of the people of this State ever been more frequently or more explicitly expressed than upon those which relate to Internal Improvements and the Tariff. More feelings and opinions have been avowed again and again in popular meetings, at celebrations of the anniversary of our independence and on other festive occasions, and by the collected wisdom of the State, in the General Assembly. At its very last Session it adopted a report and resolutions, characterized by uncommon ability, instructing our Senators and requesting our representatives, to support both of those systems. Yet our Senators are known to entertain sentiments in direct opposition to both, and one of them (Mr. Bibb) has recently given a practical exhibition of his opinions by voting against an appropriation of $150.000 for the Maysville and Lexington road[4] the first and only appropriation of the money of the U. States ever made to improve any road within the limits of Kentucky. Mr. Clay is known to have this measure long since in view. For that, amongst other reasons, he constantly supported the Cumberland road to Wheeling, afterwards urged and carried an appropriation to conduct it from the point opposite to Wheeling to Zanesville, and contemplated subsequently to propose the extension of that National road from the Muskingum or Scioto through Kentucky, Tennessee and Alabama to the gulph of Mexico. The road from Maysville to Lexington is but a section of this great National scheme. And the appropriation at this day demonstrates the wisdom of the doctrines for which that Citizen always contended, and the forecast which he manifested in laying National plans in other States which ultimately if not immediately would reach his own. By this course he secured the co-operation of the members from the States N.W. of the Ohio, every one of whom voted for the late appropriation, and of the friends of the system generally. The Argus lately reproached Mr. Clay with having done nothing for Kentucky on the subject of Internal Improvements, and boasted that the first appropriation directly beneficial to her proceeded from Genl [Andrew] Jackson's administration.[5] The reproach was unjust, as the boast was unfounded and ill timed. It was the principles so successfully established by Mr. Clay's exertions that carried the appropriation. It was his foresight, an[d] pushing forward the Cumberland road to Zanesville, that tended to secure it. And the ayes and noes in both houses will shew whether we are indebted to Mr. Clay's friends or Genl. Jackson's for the passage of the bill.

How Mr. Bibb will answer to his constituents for his recent flagrant abandonment of their interests, we know not. He has not only voted against the Maysville road, but it appears by the [Washington *Daily National*] Intell[*igence*]r. that on the 19th. Ulto. he was one of the 14 Senators (all but himself and Col. [Thomas Hart] Benton from the South and South Western States) who voted against the bill to enforce the Laws against smuggling to the prejudice of the revenue and of our manufactures.[6] He thus stands completely identified with the Southern policy, and opposed to that of his own State. He is understood to have pledged himself, when elected to the Senate, to sustain both the Tariff and Internal Improvements. He was bound to have resigned his seat or to have conformed his votes to the known wishes of his constituents, and to have redeemed the pledge solemnly given to the General Assembly of K[entucky].

But the course of his colleague (Mr. Rowan) appears to us equally exceptionable. He is know to have repeatedly declared that he believes that power exercised by the Genl. Governmt. over Internal Improvements to be unconstitutional. Sometimes he is absent when those questions arise in the Senate; and sometimes he votes for them. He voted for appropriations to complete the Canal at the falls, in which he is personally and largely interested; and he voted for the Maysville road. But if he believes the Genl. Govt. has no power over the subject, how can he consistently with his oath to support the Constitution of the U.S. vote for *any* appropriation? It may be said that his votes are in obedience to instructions. But no one has ever contended that a member can be rightfully instructed to violate the Constitution of the U.S. acco[r]ding to his convictions & to its meaning. In such cases he ought to resign, or in extraordi[nary] instances to comply with the obligations of his oath, and throw himself upon his Constituents. Mr. Rowan is equally known to be opposed to the Tariff. Whether he believes that to be also unconstitutional or not we have not understood. We observe that when the bill to enforce the Tariff was read a third time he was out of his seat and did not vote upon it.

But the most objectionable course of Mr. Rowan is that of his having recently adopted the nullifying doctrines of South Carolina. According to him any one of the 24 States can nullify, repeal and render void, within the limits of such State, an act of the Congress of the U.S.! A part, and a small part, agreeably to the new fangled doctrines of this Kentucky Senator is not merely equal but parmount to the whole! He would thus hitch Kentucky to the car of mad South Carolina, and drive her on into rebellion and disunion. His speech is before the public,[7] widely diffused by himself and his friends, to promote his re-election to the Senate. We invite the sober and thinking part of the State, to read that speech, if they can command the patience to trade through its metaphysical abhorations, and say if they can approve its principles, or retain any confidence in a public man who avows such principles. This is the same Speech which has been lately so much lauded by the K[entucky]. Argus.

AD, written in third person. DLC. 1. Possibly written for a newspaper; however, no publication of this document has been found. Dated by editors on the basis of internal evidence. 2. George M. Bibb and John Rowan. 3. See 8:598. 4. See 8:205, 214. 5. See Frankfort *Argus of Western America*, May 12, 1830. 6. The bill "For the more effectual collection of the impost duties," which included a provision against smuggling, passed the House on May 13, 1830, and the Senate on May 20. The president approved the act on May 28, 1830. U.S. H. of Reps., *Journal*, 21 Cong., 1 Sess., 216, 645, 685; U.S. Sen., *Journal*, 21 Cong., 1 Sess., 343. 7. For Rowan's speech, see *Register of Debates*, 21 Cong., 1 Sess., 128-45.

To JONATHAN THOMPSON[1]   Harrodsburg, Ky., July 25, 1831

A short retreat to this watering place affords me an opportunity to acknowledge the receipt of your favor of the 7h. inst.[2] As you anticipated, I have been well advised of the movements of our friends in N. York.[3] They have been, from your great meeting in Decr. to the late convention at Albany well timed and judicious.[4] From all that I learn your greatest difficulty in N. York is that of effecting a co-operation between the N[ational]. Republicans and the Anti Masons. That, if it can be accomplished at all, will, I think, be best secured by the resolution you have formed of hoisting your banner, and inviting the Antis' as well as all other friends of their Country to rally under it. Their course has been to *force* you to join them. Yours' it appears to me should be to persuade them to unite with you. By abstaining from bringing forward your own Candidates, and supporting those of the Antis', you deceived them and the public generally, as to their real numbers. If a separation, at the next fall elections, should take place between them and you, the legitimate strength of both parties will be developed; and by the next fall twelvemonth, the necessity of union being felt, concert and co-operation may follow.[5]

Upon the principles professed by Antimasons, we can see an adequate motive for their endeavoring to possess themselves of the power of a State Government. But what motive can they have at aiming at the acquisition of that of the Federal government? What part of its Constitution delegates any authority to promote the views either of Masons or Anti Masons?

Our elections will be decided next week. The friends of our cause are fully sensible of their importance, and are making corresponding exertions. Prodigious efforts are making on the other side, seconded by a vast expenditure of money, and other profligate means. Nevertheless we shall more than ever be mortified and disappointed if we do not get a large majority of the Legislature and of the members of Congress.[6]

Should you have occasion, as you intimate, to correspond with gentlemen in this State, in reference to any subject, you may address, with perfect confidence, Francis Johnson at Louisville, Jacob Swigert[7] at Frankfort or Richard H. Chinn,[8] or Thomas Smith at Lexington.

ALS. KyLoF.   1. For Thompson, see 4:548.   2. Not found.   3. See, for example, 8:306-7, 310-11.   4. See 8:307, 310-11, 371-72.   5. See 8:204-5, 381-82, 492-93.   6. See 8:332.   7. For Swigert, see 4:399.   8. For Chinn, see 1:707.

Speech at Hagerstown, Md., *ca.* late November, 1831. Thanks them for their expressions of esteem, noting that he met many of them nearly twenty-five years ago when he was on his way to Washington for a similar purpose to that which now takes him there. Asserts that "I go to the Senate with no anticipation of personal satisfaction, nor with any expectation of my being able to render any signal public service." Promises to "faithfully adhere to the Constitution, to the Union, and to those great principles of public liberty and public policy by which I have ever been guided." Copy. Printed in Washington *Daily National Intelligencer,* December 13, 1831.

Note to Speech of January 25, 1832. Controversy had arisen over a statement made in the speech criticizing Gen. Samuel Smith for introducing a bill in 1826 which provided terms for the U.S. to comply with the British act of July, 1825, regarding trade with British colonies. Smith had refuted Clay's statements in a speech in the Senate.

Now, Clay picks up the argument. States that in the speech of Gen. Samuel Smith, published in the Washington *Daily National Intelligencer* on February 7, 1832, "He [Smith] says he asked me [in 1825-26] whether the terms proposed by the British act of Parliament of July, 1825, were satisfactory; and that I said I 'considered they were all we could ask.'" Avers that Smith's memory is inaccurate, "and that I never did say to him that the terms proposed by the act were all we could ask." Asserts that he could not have made the remark, because the terms of the act required that "to entitle Powers not colonial (and of course the United States) to its privileges, those Powers are required to place the commerce and navigation of Great Britain (European as well as colonial) upon the footing of the most favored nation. . . . The vessels of Great Britain, therefore, would have been at liberty to import into the United States, on an equal footing with our own, the productions of *any* part of the globe, without a corresponding privilege on the part of our vessels, in the ports of Great Britain." Calls on Smith to publish the note "which he says he received [from me] accompanying the draft of the bill introduced by him." Copy. Printed in Washington *Daily National Intelligencer*, February 9 and again on February 14, 1832. For Clay's speech of January 25, 1832, see 8:450.

On February 12, 1832, Samuel Smith addressed a note to the *Intelligencer* asking them to publish a statement in which he refutes the note attached to Clay's speech and states that his personal papers are in Baltimore, and he cannot determine whether or not he has preserved Clay's note of 1826. Therefore, Smith calls on the testimony of Churchill C. Cambreleng to prove his point. In a letter to Smith, dated February 11, 1832, Cambreleng asserts that he had understood Clay to say in 1826 that the United States should adopt some reciprocal measure toward Britain. He further notes that Smith later showed him a note from Clay, "stating, according to my recollection, that when he had conferred with me he had expressed an opinion in favor of legislation—that upon reflection he thought it would be best to secure this trade by negotiation—but . . . if Congress should legislate, the government ought to acquiesce." Adds that he never heard "any objection made to the terms of the act of Parliament." Washington *Daily National Intelligencer*, February 14, 1832. For Clay's letter to Smith of January 31, 1826, see 5:75-76. For Cambreleng, see 3:335. For the British act of July, 1825, see 4:180, 941-42.

In an undated letter to Joseph Gales, Jr., and William W. Seaton, editors of the *Intelligencer*, Clay replies "That the point in issue, between Gen. Smith and me is, whether I told him that the terms contained in the British act of Parliament, of July, 1825, were considered by me to be 'all we could ask.' He alleges that I so informed him; I deny it, and have said and repeat, that I could not have so informed him." Avers that Cambreleng's letter does not touch on the point at issue. In fact, it "evinces more that ever the expediency of the exhibition of my letter to Gen. Smith," because Cambreleng asserts "that I had expressed, in that letter, a *preference for negotiation*." Adds that "I hope the great distance from this City to Baltimore, and the want of communication between the two places will be overcome, and that the letter will be procured and published."

Concludes: "The attempt now to prove that the ill judged and ineffectual movement of Gen. Smith, in the session of 1825-26, to provide for the Colonial Intercourse, by legislation, was, at the instance of, or sanctioned by the Department of State, surely needs no refutation. For six years past, the charge has been made and reiterated in a thousand forms, (and by no one more frequently than by Gen. Smith himself) against the late Administration, that it sought to accomplish by negotiation what ought to have been attained by legislation." Copy. Printed in Washington *Daily National Intelligencer*, February 15, 1832.

To John Marshall, Washington, February 9, 1832. Clay and Philemon Thomas, chairmen of the joint committee of the Senate and House, which has been given the responsibility to make arrangements for the celebration of George Washington's birthday, write asking him to give the oration. Copy. Printed in Washington *Daily National Intelligencer*, February 14, 1832.

Marshall replies on February 10, stating that the press of official duties and his physical condition make it impossible to accept. Notes the "My voice has become so weak as to be almost inaudible even in a room not unusually large."

Avers that nothing would have given him more pleasure than to honor "the memory of the Father of his Country." Copy. *Ibid.* For Thomas, see 8:183.

From HENRY BALDWIN[1]

Washington, *ca.* February or March, 1832[2]

I have this moment come from Bamford's [*sic,* George Bomford's] through the rain. The first thing I read was a paper containing your remarks on [Albert] Gallatin's pamphlet.[3] It is, in the language of Scripture, health to my soul, and marrow to my bones. It is, as we say in Pennsylvania of apple-toddy—meat, drink, washing, and lodging. Here is a token from one who always respected you as his old speaker, and schoolmaster in politics, elections, and candidates—*non obstanti*—and who in times of the highest excitement, never said of you as a statesman, a harsher thing than is in the pamphlet he put into your hands.

(Any thing connected with the pending election, to the contrary notwithstanding, which has nothing to do with personal accounts of H.B. and H.C.)

Here is a drop of the honest stuff—genuine Pennsylvania, the true extract, the essence of the American system, the produce of the same soil which gave us birth, and whence we derive our bread. It will suit an American palate, and raise no conscientious, constitutional scruples in an American stomach. Take a drop of it to my health in memory of Auld Lang Syne.

This Florida case is a tough one.[4] I shall have three or four evenings of leisure. When you, [William] Creighton, [Joseph] Vance, and [Thomas] Ewing[5] are disposed to bury old grudges, let me know it. Mrs. Bamford[6] has a small moiety of the self same, and you will all be as welcome as the flowers of May.

This is for your eye and those named, but for no others.

Copy. Printed in Colton, *Clay Correspondence,* 4:445.   1. For Baldwin, see 1:181 and *DAB.*   2. Colton dates this letter "_____ 1840"; however, editors have determined from its content that it was written soon after Clay's speech of Feb. 2, 3, 6, 1832 [8:455-56] in defense of the American system.   3. Gallatin's pamphlet, *Memorial of the Committee Appointed by the Free Trade Convention* (Philadelphia, 1831), an outgrowth of the 1831 free trade convention, argued for a 25% ad valorem tax on imports. Clay sharply attacked this position in his speech on Feb. 2. *Register of Debates,* 22 Cong., 1 Sess., 257-96; *Sen. Docs.,* 21 Cong., 1 Sess., no. 135, p. 32; Chien Tseng Mai, *The Fiscal Policies of Albert Gallatin* (New York, 1930), 34.   4. In the *United States* v. *Arredondo et al.,* the Supreme Court ruled that the grant of land in Florida from Spain to Don Fernando de la Maza Arredondo and son was valid under the U.S. treaty with Spain of 1819. 31 Peters, 691-759.   5. For Ewing, see 8:286 and *DAB;* for Vance, 3:259 and *BDAC.*   6. Probably Mrs. George Bomford. See his entry in *CAB.*

From George D. Prentice, Louisville, March 14, 1832. On behalf of a number of Clay's friends, asks that he use his influence, "if consistent with your many engagements, toward procuring satisfaction for the French Spoliation claims, which originated prior to the 30th of September, 1800." Adds that "I have never heard you speak on the subject of those claims, but am told, that you consider them just." Notes that some "of the claimants, with whom I am acquainted, are persons of great moral worth, and some of them, owing, perhaps, to the tardiness of the Government in rendering them justice, are in indigent circumstances."

Mentions that "We have not yet received your great speech [8:455-56], but, if Report has done it no more than justice, I would a thousand times rather be the author of it than President of the United States." ALS. PSC.

For Prentice, see 8:332-33. For the French spoliation claims, see France: U.S. relations with, in index in 8:919-20.

To WILLIAM L. STONE[1]   Washington, March 19, 1832

I have received your two favors of the 15h.[2] & 16h.[3] instant. With respect to the article in Mr. [Benjamin Franklin] Hallet's paper, I do not think that it is of a nature which requires any direct or *authorized* notice from me.[4] Possessing as he does a denial of my having ever written the paragraphs which he imputes to me, his article is undoubtedly wicked and malignant. But what does he expect? Merely that the paragraph stands *before the world uncontradicted by me.* Now this is true—I have never made any public contradiction of the paragraph, because I have not felt myself bound to notice every anonymous or irresponsible calumny. If I were now to do it, or to authorize it, where would it stop? Would he not be justified in putting afterwards any interrogatory he pleases to me in respect to Masonry? Or to make any assertion, and then if I did not contradict it, to assume its truth?

Besides, I think if you will look deliberately at the paragraph, erroneously imputed to me, you will see there is not much in it. It asserts 1st. that I knew from *my own* experience that Masonry had done more good than harm & 2dly. that it was susceptible of doing more good than harm, and must continue to do so. Now the paragraph does not make me speak of any Masonry but that of which I had experience. It does not make me speak of it, as it existed in N. York. And it is only by comparing & confounding the Kentucky Masonry, of which I had knowledge, with the N. York Masonry, of which I had no experience, that conclusions of an injurious character can be drawn. Mr Hallet wishes to draw me into the papers on the subject of Masonry, and I think I ought to keep out of them. Suppose I was to authorize a contradiction of the paragraph, would he not then demand of me whether I thought Masonry had done more *harm* than good? Would he not claim, indeed, that the contradiction itself implied the pernicious character of the institution? The consequences you can well imagine. We must never forget that there are two sides to that controversy, much incensed and embittered against each other, and that I have taken the ground that neither has any thing to do legitimately with national politics.

If you take any notice of the article, it should be to say that the paragraph had been repeatedly denied in the public prints; and to ask when & to whom was the letter written? And if Mr. Hallet himself does not know that there is no such genuine letter in existence?

I thank you for the slip containing the article and letter of Dr [Henry] Perrine, respecting the Tropical plants.[5] It may be useful to make an experiment towards naturalizing them, but I am afraid we must import the Tropics with the plants to be sure of success.

I shall be glad to hear from you, when at Albany.

ALS. KyLoF.   1. For Stone (1792-1844)—a New York City journalist and historian—see *DAB.*   2. See 8:476.   3. Not found.   4. For Hallet, see *DAB;* for the article, see 8:476.   5. Perrine had proposed a plan in 1832 for establishing a tropical plant introduction station in southern Florida on land which he hoped would be granted him by Congress. See *DAB*.

To Thomas C. Hambly, York, Pa., April 10, 1832. State: "We can only say, that so far as we, or either of us, is concerned or has any knowledge, this *whole* statement, by *whomsoever* it may have been *published,* or *authorised,* is *false* and *calumnious,*—We *never* attended any such *caucus*—never *heard* of any such, and have not the slightest reason to believe that any thing of the kind ever took place." Copy, extract, signed also by Daniel Webster and Edward Everett. Printed in *Niles' Register* (April 28, 1832), 42:155. Written from Washington, D.C. Hambly has not been identified.

This letter was written in response to a charge allegedly first made by Congressman Adam King of York, Pa., that Clay, Webster, and Everett had held a caucus with Supreme Court justices John Marshall, Smith Thompson, and Joseph Story in which it was determined that the Cherokee case should be decided "solely upon political grounds." *Ibid.*

In a decision rendered on March 3, 1832, the Supreme Court had ruled in the case of *Worcester* v. *Georgia* that the statutes of Georgia were unconstitutional as applied to the Cherokee tribes. White, *The Marshall Court,* 730-40.

From Robert Baird *et al.,* Newark, N.J., *ca.* May 2, 1832. Report a series of resolutions adopted by a meeting of journeymen who work at William Rankin's Hat Manufactory in Newark. Note that "we as Journeymen Hatters view with deep Solicitude the present agitation of the Tariff question; one that directly involves our interest, Since a material diminution of duties on Foreign hats will tend to introduce a large supply of that article into market—thereby lessening the demand for American Manufacture, and consequently operating against our interests—" Resolve, therefore: (1) to oppose any reduction in the duty on hats; (2) that it is a false assertion "that Americans pay an enormous advance for Hats manufactured in this country in consequence of the Tariff . . . the fact being well established that Hats in Great Britain are sold at higher prices, than in our own country"; (3) that the custom in some cities of putting foreign stamps in American hats is a "forgery tending to raise the reputation of foreign work at the expence of our own"; (4) that American hats are better in "workmanship and appearance" than imported hats; (5) that the journeyman hatters thank the members of Congress "who have nobly supported the American protective System"; (6) that no one is due more of their gratitude than Henry Clay; (7) that a hat from them be presented to Clay; and (8) that Peter S. Duryea be requested to make the presentation to Clay of the hat and a copy of the resolutions. ADS. DLC-HC (DNA, M212, R6).

For Baird, see 5:806 and *DAB*. For Clay's reply to these resolutions, see 8:507.

To J. Vincent Browne, Boston, July 1, 1832. Has received Browne's letter of June 27 [not found], "respecting Cordage and Teas." Reports that the Senate Committee of Manufactures "is now acting on the Tariff and will report tomorrow." Adds that "we hope to remedy the evils suggested by you." ALS. AzTeS.

Browne was appointed Navy agent for the port of Boston on December 23, 1841, and confirmed on March 10, 1842. U.S. Sen., *Executive Journal,* 6:6, 37. He later served as appraiser in the custom house in San Francisco. *NUC,* 79:568. For the report on the tariff from the Committee of Manufactures, see *Sen. Reports,* 22 Cong., 1 Sess., no. 116, pp. 2-4.

Speech to the Association of Mechanics and Other Workingmen, Washington, July 4, 1832. Thanks them for the manifestation of their friendship, and asserts that "All essential branches of domestic industry should be protected, or none. . . . For if particular branches were singled out and protected to-day, whilst others were sacrificed, the immunity would be temporary, and in the end those branches themselves would experience the same fate of destruction." Adds: "Let us, then, never forget the maxim of our fathers who achieved the independence which we this day commemorate, that 'United, we stand—Divided we fall.'"

Believes a few weeks ago "that the whole system of Protective Policy was threatened with total subversion," but now feels that the bill passing through Congress will provide adequate protection for American industry. Also, "it will, in a true spirit of harmony and union, be accompanied with important concessions to that quarter of the Confederacy which thinks itself aggrieved."

Accepts their gift of a silver pitcher which he will preserve "as one of the most precious memorials I have ever received." Copy. Printed in Washington *Daily National Intelligencer,* July 10, 1832.

The pitcher was made by Charles Pryse of Washington, D.C., "one of the best artists in his line in the country." *Ibid.*

To JONATHAN THOMPSON   Washington, July 20, 1832

I have duly recd. your favor of the 14h.[1] and feel much indebted to you for the information it contains. I am perfectly persuaded of the inclination and intention of Mr. [William] Wirt which you ascribe to him. As to the particular moment of his retirement, that I presume is a matter which will be arranged between him and the Anti Masons. I think the time is near at hand, but perhaps not yet arrived, when that ought to be done.[2] There ought to be a full and free consultation between him and the Anti Masons on that subject, and I suppose it will take place. If it can be *safely* done as to N. York, at this time, the effect every where else would be good.

The prospects of success are extremely flattering. Indeed my belief is that [Andrew] Jackson will not get 100 Electoral votes.[3] In this estimate, I of course take from him N. York, which I am happy to hear from all quarters that he will lose.[4]

Matters are in great confusion in Pennsa. The elements are there and at work which must deprive him of the vote of that State, if, as we have reason to hope a principle of cohesion can be found.[5]

I shall leave here in a few days for Kentucky, proceeding slowly through Virginia, and stopping at the White Sulphur Springs. As I shall remain at them until the 20h. of Aug. I shall be glad to receive at that place a letter from you communicating the results of the Convention of the 25h. inst.[6] and any thing else interesting.

ALS. KyLoF.   1. Not found.   2. For Wirt's nomination for president by the Antimasonic party, see 8:365. For rumors of his withdrawal from the race, see, for example, 8:446, 448, 468, 497.   3. See 8:368.   4. *Ibid.*   5. *Ibid.*   6. No such letter has been found. For the New York State National Republican convention, held at Utica, see 8:504.

To JONATHAN THOMPSON   Lexington, August 27, 1832

Our Kentucky elections have terminated in the election of the [Andrew] Jackson candidate for Governor [John Breathitt] by a majority of

1260 votes, The N[ational]. Republican Candidate for Lieut. Governor [James T. Morehead] by a majority of 2500 votes, and in 50 out of the 100 members that compose our H. of Representatives, as well as in securing the Senate, where the majority was against us last year, a majority of 22 out of the 38 members composing that body.[1]

We have been so often mortified with the issue of elections in this State, that I do not know whether you will take any interest in the causes of our recent partial defeat. They were 1st the employment of extraordinary means by the Jackson party, within and without the state. On this point all their efforts were brought to bear; and every species of influence was exercised. The patronage and the means of that party were profusely used. 2dly an eruption of Tennessee voters who came to the polls in some of our border counties. Last year, official returns of all the voters, in all the countries, was made to form the periodical adjustment of the ratio of our representation. In some of those border counties, at the recent election, I understand that the *Jackson majorities,* exceeded the whole number of the voters according to those returns. But we should have been able to resist successfully the joint effect of both the above causes; if it had not been for a third, which operated most extensively. Our Candidate was a Presbyterian, and against that sect most deep rooted, and inveterate prejudices exist, the weight of which had not been sufficiently estimated when he was selected. Owing to this latter cause I believe we lost not less than probably three thousand votes.[2]

But it is less important to dwell on the past and [word illeg.] event of our Governor's election than to look forward and provide against future disaster. The spirit of our friends is unbroken, their zeal is increased in warmth, and they are full of confidence of success in November.[3] What is more encouraging, they are already engaged in the best plans to secure success. Far from being disheartened, their recent partial defeat, arouses them to exertion more vigorous than ever; and the exceptionable means employed by their opponents have fired their indignation. I think there is much reason to hope that the late event will lead to more certain success in November than if we had carried the election of the Governor by such a majority as the other side has obtained.

What is most absorbing of public attention at this time is the Bank Veto.[4] On that subject our opponents have been much more industrious in the circulation of documents, than the friends of the institution. The Presidents Message[5] and [Thomas Hart] Benton's rodomontade[6] have been scattered in countless thousands, and time enough to affect the election; whilst, on the other side, but little reached us before the election, except Mr. Clay's speech,[7] which had a limited circulation, as it arrived only at the moment of the election. A clear, intelligible, popular statement of the case, with a just account of the certain effects of the overthrow of the Bank is much needed.

I hope that our friends abroad will see in our election that the bad use of it has been neutralized by the good; and that they will derive from it fresh motives to spare no exertions to save the Country.

P.S. Your discretion will suggest you the inexpediency of the publication of this letter with my name; but you are at liberty to shew it to my friends.

LS, with postscript and numbers of votes for governor and lieutenant governor given in first paragraph in Clay's hand. KyLoF. Clay also sent Daniel Webster virtually the same letter but with a different postscript. See 8:565-66. 1. See 8:439. 2. See 8:566. 3. See 8:368. 4. See 8:434. 5. For the message, see *MPP*, 2:576-91. 6. See 8:553. 7. See 8:552-53.

From JAMES G. BIRNEY[1] Huntsville, Ala., August 28, 1832

The Board of Managers of the American Colonization Society have thought proper to offer me an Agency in the District composed of the States of Tennessee, Alabama, Louisiana & Mississippi, and the Territory of Arkansas. Altho', in doing so, I have to abandon entirely the profits of a lucrative professional business, yet, I have determined to accept it, believing this to be the way in which, under present circumstances, I can best serve my country and promote the great cause of humanity & religion.[2]

I look upon the Colonization scheme as the only one by which a large portion of our country can be saved from the ruin which the coloured population is inevitably preparing for it. All other plans of relief are, in my humble judgment, impracticable,—the progress and present state of the Colony of Liberia demonstrate that *this is feasible*. If the *South* can be persuaded to action upon this plan, before it be too late, something, I thin[k] may be done for the preservation of the *Union*. The danger in which its [in]tegrity now stands, I cannot doubt, has been produced almost entirely by the habits of *living* and *thinking* which this *population* engenders. In the comparative poverty of the native soil of S. Carolina—the continual decrease of her products, occasioned by the miserable system of husbandry always attendant upon Slavery—and the luxury and lordliness of her leading men, I am inclined to lay the *foundation* of discontent in that State. I am confirmed in this opinion from the fact—that in the states of Georgia, Alabama, Mississippi and Louisiana, where the soil is fresh & productive & the habits of the people, in general, more economical than they are in S. Carolina, the Tariff, as far as I observed, was never felt, and, therefore, never complained of, in its injurious oper[a]tion, until within a short time past, & since the latter state has contrived to make it a political or party question.[3] In the conduct of it, the Demagogues have had a decided advantage, for the ignorant and uninformed, as are the large mass of *our* population, are easily persuaded to jealousy, and to ascribe their unthriftiness, or their failure to make as much as a sanguine temperament anticipated, to any cause more willingly than to the *true* one.—Our country is in a critical condition—the most self-denying and disinterested efforts of patriotism, alone, can save her, if *any thing can*, from the madness of imbecility and ambition. The result of the late election in Ken[tuc]ky[4] has discouraged me more than any thing that has occurred since the elevation of Gen. [Andrew] Jackson to the Presidency. Not, that I believe the assistance of her vote [will be] lost in the

241

next Presidential election—[5] but, because it indicates, upon the part of the people, a readiness to follow, with a furious joy, a tyrant through the broken-down ramparts of the principles and constitution of this Republic. It is to do what little I can, in removing what I believe is at the very bottom of Southern discontent, that I have accepted this agency. For altho' the principles of the Am. Col. So. disclaim every thing like interference with private right, or with slaves, as [s]uch, yet, I cannot but hope, if the imposthume, which wastes and deforms our Country, be once fairly opened, the very *core* of it will be dissolved and finally discharged thro' this passage.

I propose to be in Jackson and New-Orleans d[ur]ing the [ap]-proaching sessions of the Legislatures of Missi[ssippi]. and Lou[isian]a. It will be my first object to conciliate these *bodies*, and prevail upon them, at least, to hear me on the *Col. Subject.* If a favorable impression can be made upon them, it will be a passport to every part of those States.—[words illeg.] then, sir, in aid of the cause in which you have manifested a zeal, which has in no small degree, contributed to kindle mine, ask of you letters of introduction to such members of the Legislatures of these two states, and to such other persons as will assist me in my [words illeg.] en[co]uraged to make this request—not only from your interest in the coloniz[ation] cause, but because your letters, so politely tendered to me on a former [occasion] secured me a reception in a land of strangers which no others did.[6]

I took the liberty, a short time since, of introducing to you, by letter, Mr. William Clarke,[7] a very sincere and undeviating friend of yours. If you will oblige me so far as to comply with the above request, the letters can be transmitted to me by him, should he call by the 15 September. Should he not call upon you before that time, it would oblige me, to have them transmitted by mail to this place. Any suggestion which your time and inclination would induce you to make in relation to my agency, will be [gla]dly received.

Present me very respectfully to Mrs. [Lucretia Hart] Clay—

ALS, manuscript marred. ICU. 1. For Birney, see 5:120 and *DAB*. 2. After accepting this post, Birney traveled throughout the South for some months, lecturing on behalf of the colonization movement. See *DAB*. 3. For South Carolina nullification, see, for example, 8:242-44, 269-70, 389, 473, 597-98, 603, 609, 615. 4. See 8:439. 5. See 8:368. 6. For example, Clay to Whom It May Concern, August 9, 1830, listed in the Calendar on 8:881. 7. Possibly William Clarke of Jessamine County. See 4:427-28.

To THOMAS H. BAIRD[1]   Lexington, September 8, 1832

I recd. your favor of the 23d. Ulto.[2] and hardly know what to say on the subject of it, and, but for my respect for you, I should say nothing. With respect to the few letters which I have written to friends in Pennsa. in regard to the existing Presidential contest, I believe every one of them contained the sentiment that it was not for me to interfere in it; & that if it were proper for me to offer any suggestions, our friends would be much more competent than I was to decide what was best to be done. This caution seemed to me more proper because I observed, with regret, that there was much difference of opinion even among our friends.

It has indeed appeared very clear to me that the next best thing to the vote of Pennsa. being given to our cause would be that it should not be conferred on Genl. [Andrew] Jackson.[3] But those, on the theatre of action, could best judge whether either of those objects were attainable, and of which there was the greatest probability.

Of the avowed principles of Govr. [George] Wolf[4] and his party, in respect to public affairs, I entertained the highest respect; but I have not been able to see how they can reconcile the support of those principles, independently and consistently, with the support of the General administration, directly and palpably at war with them. Nor have I been able to comprehend how, after in October, re-electing Govr. Wolf, under the Jackson flag, those who bring about that event can put aside that flag, and hoist another in November.

You state that you have understood that an arrangement has been made between the leading N[ational]. Republicans to the Eastward and the Anti Masons, by which the two parties are to unite in the election of [Joseph] Ritner[5] and the [William] Wirt ticket. If there be any such arrangement I have not been informed of it. On the contrary, I understood that the Central Comee. which lately met at Harrisburg deemed it most expedient not to recommend to the N. Rn. party to support either of the two Candidates for Pennsa. Govr. in particular; but to leave the individual members of that party at liberty to act on that subject as they thought proper; and that the Convention of which you are a member[6] was to be reassembled after the Governor's election in October to determine what, under all circumstances, was their best [manuscript torn; word illeg.] to be done. By this course I presumed they meant to disentangle the Presidt. from the Governor's Election, and to take a new survey of the whole ground.

I do not think that I have written to Mr. [Thomas] McGiffin[7] any letter for several months, although I must add that my confidence in him remains undiminished; and that I regret extremely that between yourself and him, two friends whom I have known so long and esteemed so highly, there should exist any alienation.

Of the general prospects of the P[residential]. contest I am happy to be authorized, from the information which reaches me, to assure you that they are highly encouraging. If Pennsa. should think proper either to support our cause, or to withhold her vote from Genl. Jackson, I should regard his defeat as *certain*. If her vote were ever given to Mr. Wirt, I believe your kind wishes in respect to the Presidential Election would be accomplished.[8]

I have to request that you will regard this letter confidential . . .

ALS. KyU. 1. For Baird, see 9:877. 2. Not found. 3. See 8:515. 4. For Wolf, see 8:78. For his defeat of Joseph Ritner in the 1832 Pennsylvania gubernatorial race, see 8:515. 5. For Ritner, see 8:78. 6. The standing committee of the Pennsylvania National Republican convention. See 8:514-15. 7. For McGiffin, see 4:382. 8. See 8:368, 515.

To SAMUEL B. BEACH[1]   Lexington, October 22, 1832
I duly received your favor of the 29th. Ulto.[2] and feel greatly obliged by the evidence which it affords of your continued allotment and

regard. You mention that you had not received answers to two previous letters. I have much indulgence to request at the hands of my correspondents, who are very numerous. Unless their letters seem absolutely to require answers, I am compelled sometimes to throw my self upon their kindness. I beg you to believe that my omission to answer your letter had not proceeded from any in difference to your esteem and friendship.

The prospect of the deliverance of our country from the abomination of a [Andrew] Jackson administration is now highly encouraging.[3] In this State I entertain no doubt of success. Our friends, well organized, are full of zeal animation and confidence. Your State, all unite in assuring me, is certainly against Jackson. Penna. has thrown off his yoke. Ohio I believe will go against him. These States with those which have never been questioned on the side of the National Republican Party would seem to justify the most sanguine anticipations.[4] A few weeks more will decide the fate of the Republic; and I sincerely hope that the decision may be gratifying to yourself and every other friend of his Country.

ALS. WRipC. Courtesy of Kimberly Shankman, Ripon College Library. 1. For Beach, see 6:7 and *DAB*. 2. Not found. 3. See 8:368. 4. For the states carried by each candidate, see *ibid.*

To SAMUEL L. SOUTHARD
Lexington, November 10, 1832

You will share with me in the pleasure I have experienced in the redemption of Kentucky.[1] Our cause has triumphed here, and triumphed nobly. Our majority cannot be less than from four to five thousand.

From Ohio and Penna. the accounts are gloomy. The result in Indiana is not certainly known but, as far as returns are recd. we hope and believe we have succeeded.[2]

ALS. Jervais Public Library, Rome, N.Y. 1. See 8:368. 2. For the states carried by each candidate, see *ibid.*

Speech to Manufacturers & Workingmen of Philadelphia, December, 1832. Notes that he is deeply touched by the importance they attach to his public services. States that "It was not himself alone, nor the district from which he came, neither the state in which he resided, that could be considered as *especially* interested in the American System, justly so called." Asserts that the American System is "the only system which can *secure the union.*" Adds, however, that should "the majority . . . reduce us to a system of *unfair foreign competition,* we must abide by that majority." Copy, excerpt. Printed in *Niles' Register* (December 29, 1832), 43:256.

Clay visited Philadelphia from December 13, 1832, to January 3, 1833, so this address was given sometime in the period from December 13 to December 29, when it was published. See 8:602, 613.

To [Manuscript torn] H. POWELL[1]
Lexington, *ca.* December 7, 1832[2]

I have perused your letter,[3] just receive[d; manuscript torn] feelings of gratification and melancholy—grate[ful; manuscript torn] thankfulness for the friendly sentiments towards [manuscript torn] you do me the honor to entertain—melanch[oly; manuscript torn] account of the too faithful picture which you [manuscript torn] of the sad condition of our Country. In all its [manuscript torn] I have never known any event which has filled me [manuscript torn] fearful apprehensions for the future. For if the [manuscript torn] which have been so successfully employed to [manuscript torn] the late election admit of no remedy (and I confess I know of no adequate Constitutional and peaceful remedy) what is to prevent their application again and again hereafter? But I will not dwell on this painful subject. Perhaps I ought not to touch it.

I hope an all wise Providence may disclose to us some means of deliverance. In the mean time, it will be the best rule for us all, in our respective spheres, public and private, to do our whole duty & confide [manuscript torn; test]ify to the great respect which I have ever [manuscript torn] name. I am acquainted with your brother,[4] [manuscript torn; shou]ld you ever come to Kentucky, it will [manuscript torn] great satisfaction to receive you here as [manuscript torn].

[P.S.; manuscript torn] me the favor to present [manuscript torn] to your neighbour S. Bailey Esqr[5] [manuscript torn] intentions in respec[t; manuscript torn] to me.

My lasting gratitude is due to the noble banner County of Virginia for the support which it gave me.

ALS, manuscript mutilated. CSmH. Letter marked "(Private)." 1. First name has been torn from the letter. Probably addressed to John Hare Powel, which Clay frequently spelled "Powell." For Powel, see 7:122 and *DAB*. 2. Date has been torn from letter except for "Ashland, 7h."; however, it was probably written on Dec. 7, 1832, following Andrew Jackson's defeat of Clay in the presidential election. 3. Not found. 4. Possibly Robert Hare, a noted chemist. See *DAB*. 5. Not identified.

Answer in the Case of Eliza Jane Weir, Washington, January 16, 1833. Asserts that the law of Kentucky, not the law of the U.S., governs whether or not Miss Weir, a minor and an American citizen now residing in Ireland, must appear in person to receive her share of the estate left by her uncle James Weir. Argues that the law of Kentucky does not require her presence. Rather, her rights can be asserted by her guardian during her minority and by herself through an agent once she attains full age.

Next, answers the question "whether a Guardian appointed by the Irish Court of Chancery to Miss Weir can by Letter of Attorney authorize an Agent in America to investigate" her claims, and what documents would such an agent need to have his authority recognized by the courts of Kentucky. States that a guardian appointed by the Court of Chancery in Ireland "may by Letter of Attorney Authorize an Agent in America to investigate Miss Weir's claims, receive what money or effects may be due to her" and to do all acts connected with her property that a guardian is allowed to do by the laws of Kentucky.

Admits that the "right of a guardian, the residence of whom and his ward, is in a foreign Country, to constitute an Agency to receive the effects and manage the estate of his ward in the State of Kentucky, is not expressly recognized by its Law; but I think results from their general principle." Suggests, however, that if the courts of Kentucky "should decide that the Irish Courts of Chancery cannot appoint a guardian to Miss Weir," then an alternative would be to appoint a guardian for her in Kentucky through the Fayette County Court. Suggests that should this course be followed, she should write to the Fayette County Court in Kentucky requesting by name a guardian to be appointed for her; also, her grandfather in Ireland [James Prenter] should, in a similar letter,

245

unite with her in this request, with both letters being duly notarized. Believes "the rights of Miss Weir are perfectly safe." Copy. KyU.

An attached document, to which the above is a response, is written in the same hand. It details the pedigree of the Weirs, indicating that William Weir, nephew of James Weir and father of Eliza Jane, married Eliza Prenter in Ireland and "shortly afterwards emigrated to America as a Presbyterian Clergyman." Eliza Jane was born "In or about 1820" in the United States and is thereby an American citizen. In 1822, William Weir died in the U.S., leaving Eliza Jane as his only child. Shortly thereafter, the widow, with her child, departed for Ireland; however, the widow died during the passage home, and Eliza Jane, on arriving in Ireland "was taken charge of by her natural Grandfather, Mr James Prenter who has ever since supported her in his own house and clothed and educated her." Her uncle, James Weir, a native of the county of Down, Ireland, died in Lexington, Ky., in February, 1832, "possessed as is believed of freehold & chattel property of very considerable value—intestate, unmarried, and without issue." His nephews, Henry and James Weir, had long resided with him, had become American citizens, and had obtained letters of administration for their uncle's estate. Henry Weir had traveled to Ireland, had called on James Prenter, and had informed him that it was "absolutely necessary" for Eliza Jane to appear in person to receive her share of the estate. Prenter was unwilling to part with his granddaughter and was afraid to trust her to the care of her uncle for the trip to the U.S. James Prenter then, having been informed that "a Guardian of the fortune of a Minor, duly appointed such by the court of chancery in Ireland, could authorise by Letter of Attorney an Agent in America" to act on behalf of Eliza Jane, petitioned the Lord Chancellor of Ireland "upon which the usual order was made refering it to one of the masters of the Court to approve of a proper person to be appointed such Guardian of the Minor." Before leaving Ireland, Henry Weir appeared before the master of the court and "opposed the appointment of a Guardian, alledging that it was necessary by the general law of the United States or by the Law of the state of Kentucky . . . that the minor should be exhibited in person . . . before her claim to any property would be recognized." Thus, the master of the court declined to appoint a guardian until this point of the law could be ascertained; therefore, "Counsel is requested to advise and say, if the Law of America or the Law of Kentucky, renders it imperative that the Minor Eliza Jane Weir . . . must be produced in person in the State of Kentucky to entitle here [sic, her] to receive and enjoy the share of the . . . Property of James Weir, deceased, to which she is entitled" and whether a guardian appointed by the Irish Court of Chancery to the Minor, can by Letter of attorney authorise an Agent in America to "do all acts connected with her property in America." Copy. Ibid.

On April 26, 1835, Clay wrote James Stewart [sic, Stuart] that at the "first term of the Court at which the subject of the Guardianship of Miss Weir could be moved since my return from Washington. . . . I obtained a rule against Mr. Love, the Guardian formerly appointed, to shew cause why his appointment should not be revoked, and a new appointment be made of me, according to the wishes of Miss Weir and Mr. Prenter." Reports that the case was continued until the June term, and the judge ordered Mr. Love to remit $500 to Ireland in the meantime for the support and education of Eliza Jane. Notes also that "The property assigned to Miss Weir in the division which has been made will yield an annual income of twelve to fifteen hundred dollars."

Asks Stuart to investigate charges that Prenter "is not a person of good character, that the Education of Miss Weir is neglected, that restraints are put upon her unnecessarily, so that no one can have access to her; or correspond with her, and that he is seeking to appropriate her property to his own

246

use."Although he supposes these reports "originated in jealousy and prejudice," he does not want "to be even an unconscious organ of prejudice to the interests of Miss Weir." ALS. *Ibid.* Love is possibly John Love. See 5:605.

Clay wrote James Prenter on July 9, 1835, reporting that at its June term, the court removed Mr. Love as Eliza Jane's guardian and appointed Clay in his place. Mentions that during the trial "a witness (a young Irishman) was introduced by Mr. Love who proved that you are a person of doubtful character . . . that you prevented her paternal relatives from seeing her. And . . . that her signature to the petition to have me appointed as her guardian was not written by her, but was affixed by you." Wants a response to these charges and hopes that Eliza Jane herself will answer the letter he encloses to her.

States that he has looked at the division made of James Weir's property when Eliza Jane had no one representing her interests. Thinks the division was unequal, since she received only 5 or 6 of the 60 slaves, and "Slaves are now worth nearly double what they were when the division was made; whilst real Estate (of which her portion chiefly consisted) has not advanced in the same proportion." Thus, he has filed an answer in the court of Chancery to obtain a new division.

Recommends that Eliza Jane come to America and attend a boarding school in Philadelphia. If she declines to come, asks "what sum will be annually necessary to her support and education in Ireland." Points out that under U.S. law, "no guardian has any power to sell her slaves or real Estate. He can only apply a reasonable proportion of the annual income to her maintenance and education." ALS. KyU.

On July 9, 1835, Clay wrote Eliza Jane informing her of his appointment as her guardian and suggesting "the propriety of your coming to America." Adds that "you might go to the best female academy in Philada. or elsewhere, and afterwards you could reside in some genteel family." Explains that her Weir uncles "are respectable men, but have strong prejudices against your Grandfather." ALS. *Ibid.*

Clay again wrote James Prenter on November 6, 1835, reporting that after being named Eliza Jane's guardian in the circuit court, he has also secured an appointment through the Fayette County Court and has given security in both instances. Yet, Mr. Love has "refused to surrender the papers &c. in his hands and I had to proceed against him for a contempt of Court, when he was compelled to give them up. He had hired to Mr. [James] Weir the slaves which were assigned to Miss Weir, on the division and rented to him one of the two houses allotted to her. Mr. J. Weir refuses to give me possession of this property, or to pay its hire." Adds that "I have taken legal measures to effect a new division," and "I have also instituted a suit against Mr. James Weir to have a settlement of his account of the administration of the Estate of his uncle, and to compel him to pay over the part to which Miss [Eliza] Jane is entitled."

Promises to send to Ireland $250 or $300 of the $345 he has so far received from her share of the property. Explains that "The Court expressed the opinion that more than $500 per annum ought not to be remitted for the support and education of Miss Weir," and "This sum must constitute a limit, which I must respect."

Concludes that "I appreciate and respect the feelings both of yourself and Miss Weir which oppose your separation, and her coming to America; but I still think it would be for her interest and advantage . . . to come here." ALS. *Ibid.*

Clay wrote Eliza Jane on April 29, 1839, reporting that by the division of her uncle's estate, "you get, in lieu of the House and lot formerly assigned to you by the first division, nine negro slaves (men and boys) and the hire of them from the date of the first division. These, with the five formerly allotted to you, make you the proprietor of fourteen slaves," the hire of which "amounts to upwards of $7500." Adds that "If I had authority to sell the slaves, which I cannot have during your minority, I would dispose of them, as they would now command about $10,000, a very high price, and as they are liable to casualties."

Notes that he has hired the slaves out for this year for $1,725 and rented the house and lot on Main Street in Lexington for $600 per annum. Will send "by the Mail that carries this letter $500 to be remitted to you; that being the sum to which the Court thought your annual expenses should be limited." ALS. *Ibid.*

On April 1, 1840, Clay again wrote Eliza Jane, reporting that he had remitted to her grandfather "the first number of a draft, the second of which I now send you . . . being the proceeds of $500." States that he has hired out her slaves again "on the same terms as I did last year, that is at an average hire of $125 cash." Adds that one of the slaves died last year. Inquires whether she plans to come to America, if she has any plans to marry, and when will she turn twenty-one, concluding: "As I am getting advanced in life I should be glad to terminate my guardianship, which I cannot do until you are married or obtain majority." ALS. *Ibid.*

Clay wrote Eliza Jane on June 22, 1840, introducing his friend Alexander Porter [5:93], who can "give you much information about the U. States, Kentucky and Lexington, which you might like to obtain." ALS. *Ibid.*

Clay wrote Eliza Jane on July 9, 1841, enclosing a bill for 100 pounds sterling. States that "I believe you are at full age in this month; and, if I am right in the supposition, I should be glad to hear from you in respect to your property in my hands, and your wishes in regard to it." Reports that in May "I settled my account, as your Guardian," with "a balance in my hands of about Eleven thousand dollars. . . . inclusive of your slaves and real Estate." Adds that "a large part of it is lent out at six per Cent. interest." ALS. *Ibid.*

On September 14, 1841, Clay wrote Eliza Jane that "If you do not choose to come to America, your presence is not indispensable." Advises selling her slaves at the end of the year, for which he will need her power of attorney. Promises to send 1,000 pounds sterling at the first of the year and more "if it should be returned to me"; otherwise, "the interest will be punctually paid and remitted." ALS. *Ibid.*

Clay wrote Eliza Jane on October 5, 1841, enclosing a copy of his account as her guardian. Notes that he has loaned out $5,000 at 6% interest, which will be paid in February, 1843, and "the residue . . . I can remit . . . early in the year 1842." However, he wants to hear her wishes, since "All your money could be loaned out if you desired it. . . . But, if you do not come to America, perhaps it had better be remitted to you."

Reports that the "suit which I brought against your uncle for the settlement of his administration of the Estate of James Weir deceased has not yet been finally decided. Your uncle claims for himself and his brother very high wages for transacting the business of their uncle James Weir. I do not think it just; but the Court has intimated an opinion in part in favor of it. You will recover something in any event in that suit." If she does not come to America, recommends selling the slaves but not the house and lot, because "at present . . . sales cannot be made of real Estate without some sacrifice." ALS. *Ibid.*

On January 11, 1842, Clay wrote Eliza Jane that he had delayed making a remittance because of the unfavorable rate of exchange. Sends a bill for 561:14:7 pounds sterling, for which "I had to pay 18 per Cent in Kentucky funds." Assures her that her property is safe, "notwithstanding the bad condition of the credit of some of our American States." Reports that since he did not receive her power of attorney, he has hired her slaves out for the present

248

year, at an average of $115 each, "with the exception of one, who proved himself a worthless fellow, ran away, and was lodged in Jail for two months. I have directed him to be sold." Because of the drop in prices, advises against the sale of the slaves for the present. ALS. *Ibid.*

On April 22, 1842, Clay wrote Eliza Jane, noting that "Exchange is much more favorable to you now than it was in the winter," and "I herewith transmit a bill" for 950:14:1 pounds sterling which he had procured at 6%. Hopes by the end of the year or early in the next "to collect and remit the residue of your funds in my hands." Mentions that "I am now on my return from Congress to my residence and when I get there I will write you again." ALS. *Ibid.*

On May 12, 1842, Clay wrote Eliza Jane, sending "the second of a set of Exchange, the first of which I transmitted about two weeks ago from Balto," 950:14:1 pounds sterling. Promises that "The residue of your money, I will remit early next year . . . as soon as I collect it." Adds that "Owing to the extreme severity of the times in the U. States, all descriptions of property, and the hire of Slaves, have very much fallen." Now advises, however, that the slaves be sold at the end of the year. ALS. *Ibid.*

For the Eliza Jane Weir case, see 8:718-20; 9:8-12, 400, 555-56, 790. For James Weir, see 1:189.

To FREDERICK RAPP[1]   Washington, January 27, 1833

I recd. your favor of the 21st inst.[2] The subjects of Endless Life to whom you refer are two persons residing in Mercer County (K) one by the name of Jones (the name of the other I do not recollect, and have not the petition by me) whom I personally know.[3] He was and I believe yet is a Shaking Quaker, and has such a mixture of sense and insanity as to make it difficult to decide what predominates.

The fate of Mr. [Gulian C.] Verplanks bill is doubtful.[4] But I greatly fear that the protective policy will be seriously impaired, if not entirely destroyed at this or the *next* Session.[5] It appears to be an object which the President [Andrew Jackson] has much at heart; and unfortunately the People appear disposed to support him in all his measures.

I have hopes that hostilities with So. Carolina will be avoided, although one cannot see distinctly how peace is to be preserved. She has put herself so clearly in the wrong that she must see the folly of provoking hostilities. I entertain no doubt that ample provisions of law will be made to maintain the authority of the Laws of the U.S. in South Carolina.[6]

Be pleased to communicate my best respects to your Father [George Rapp] and to your niece.

Copy. Printed in Karl J.R. Arndt (ed.), *Economy on the Ohio, 1826-1834* (Worcester, Mass., 1984), 844.   1. For Frederick Rapp, adopted son of George Rapp, see *ibid.*, and Karl J.R. Arndt, *George Rapp's Harmony Society, 1785-1847* (Rutherford, Pa., 1965).   2. Rapp had written Clay on Jan. 21, 1833, asking the names of the two persons "calling themselves 'Subjects of endless life' praying for a quantity of public Land etc.," for whom Clay had presented a petition in the Senate. Rapp asserts that this incident "would not have made so much Impression on me, had I not some reason to suppose that those Individuals, or two much like them reside in this county." Also notes that "Mr. Verplanks Bill to reduce the Duties on Imports has received the attention of Congress," and "I trust you will defend the great Interest of our Country, with the usual Zeal and perseverance heretofore peculiar to your principles and character." Concludes by asking "to hear your opinion on the subject of South Carolina, what course they will probably take etc." Copy. Printed in Arndt, *Economy on the Ohio,* 843-44.   3. Petitioners were Leonard Jones and Henry Banta. See 8:613.   4. For Verplank's bill, see 8:608.   5. For the Compromise Tariff of 1833, see 8:604, 619-22, 626-27.   6. For the Force bill, see 8:615.

To Citizens of Addison and Rutland counties in Vermont, January 31, 1833. States that "The support which I have hitherto given to the policy of protecting Domestic industry, has proceeded from a deep conviction of its propriety; and, considering the legislation of foreign powers, of its justice towards them. That conviction is unshaken." Adds, however, that continuation of the policy of protection depends, not on himself, but the people; if the people choose to allow freely into U.S. ports ships of powers that exclude American ships, they have the right to do so.

Also, thanks them for approving "my endeavors to make some permanent settlement of the public lands." Copy. Printed in Washington *Daily National Intelligencer,* February 23, 1834.

To JAMES TAYLOR Lexington, May 20, 1833

I have to thank you for your obliging letter of the 11h. inst.[1] Your detention at Washington must have become very disagreeable. I suppose that the destruction of the Office of the Treasury must have contributed to your delay.[2]

After having had a very dry spring, a rainy spell began about ten days ago and we have since been abundantly supplied with copious showers. The drought admitted of a great deal of farming labor, and before the end of April almost every body had completed their planting of Corn &c I do not think that there was any injury done by it. There is a great rage prevailing here for English Cattle. I sold a Calf which I had brought out from Philada. at 7 weeks old for $200. It is too violent to last.

I regret to hear of your son's misfortune.[3] The loss of children, under any circumstances, is a great affliction; but when occasioned by such means, as in his case, it is much more distressing.

Wishing you success in your business, health & prosperity[.]

ALS. OC1WHi   1. Not found.   2. The Treasury Office had been burned by "an incendiary." Green, *Washington Village and Capital,* 136.   3. Not found.

To BEAUFORT T. WATTS[1] Washington, May 25, 1833[2]

I recd. your favor of the 16h. inst. with the proceedings which it transmitted,[3] and I was glad to learn that you approved of the struggle which we are making here against the usurpations of the Executive. I am happy to assure you that we have reason to believe, from evidences which reach us from all quarters of the Union, that the present Admon will not retain much longer power to do mischief.

I regret the continuance of dissentions in So. Carolina.[4] I had hoped that they would have terminated with the Compromise of the Tariff.[5] My time has been so completely engrossed with Federal affairs that I have not looked into the question which separates the people of S. Carolina. Here we find its members in both houses, heartily cooperating in the endeavor to check the [a]larming progress of the Executive. Occasionally indeed they mix up some of their peculiar ideas about nullification; but as few agree with them, and as no present danger is apprehended from that heresy, any mischief which the expression of those ideas might do is overlooked on account of the greater good which those Gentlemen are now rendering.

When I can command the requisite leisure I will look into the cause of your present divisions, which I should rejoice to hear had been satisfactorily healed.

AL, manuscript torn. ScU. 1. For Watts, see 4:235. 2. Last numeral of date has been torn off; date supplied on the basis of internal evidence. See note 4, below. 3. Not found. 4. A bitter struggle raged in South Carolina between Unionists and Nullifiers for two years following passage of the Compromise Tariff of 1833. At issue was a test oath, demanded by Nullifiers and opposed by Unionists, requiring all state officials to pledge their primary allegiance to South Carolina. Eventually, a compromise was adopted with the declaration that "'the allegiance required by the oath . . . is the allegiance which every citizen owes to the State consistently with the Constitution of the United States.'" This allowed both sides to interpret the oath in a way consistent to their opposing views of the nature of the Union. John Barnwell, *Love of Order, South Carolina's First Secession Crisis* (Chapel Hill, 1982), 33; William W. Freehling, *Prelude to Civil War, The Nullification Controversy in South Carolina, 1816-1836* (New York, 1965), 263-70, 303-27. 5. See 8:604, 619-22, 626-27.

From John McKim *et al.*, Baltimore, October 8, 1833. Invite Clay to a public dinner in his honor "to be given at the City Hotel, on any day which may suit your convenience." State: "The sensitive and honorable delicacy by which your conduct has ever been distinguished, seems, while you were a candidate for the highest office of this country, to have denied to us the opportunity of illustrating to you the hospitality of Baltimore, and of affording the manifestation of that cordial respect and friendship, which are, at once, the fruit and the ornament of your conduct and fame." Copy. Printed in Colton, *Clay Correspondence*, 2:334. For McKim, see 1:640.

Clay's reply of October 9, 1833, declining the invitation, is summarized in 8:664. Printed also in Colton, *Clay Correspondence*, 2:334-35.

On October 11, 1833, Arnold Naudain *et al.* wrote Clay and invited him to visit Wilmington, Delaware, and to partake of a public dinner in his honor. Copy. Printed in Colton, *Clay Correspondence*, 2:335-36. Also printed in *Niles' Register* (November 9, 1833), 45:175. Clay replied on October 14, accepting their invitation to visit, but declining the offer of a public dinner. Copy. Printed in Colton, *Clay Correspondence*, 2:336. For Naudain, see 8:865-66.

On October 12, 1833, Clay wrote from Philadelphia to T. B. Wakeman *et al.* accepting their invitation to attend the exhibition of the American Institute in New York City. Copy. Printed in *Niles' Register* (October 19, 1833), 45:114.

On October 14, 1833, Mathew Carey *et al.* invited Clay to a public dinner in Philadelphia. Copy. Printed in Colton, *Clay Correspondence*, 2:337. Printed also in *Niles' Register* (October 19, 1833), 45:113. Clay replied the same day, declining the offer of a public dinner, and stating: "I regret that I have been able to do so little; but the time has arrived, which I long ago apprehended, when our greatest exertions are necessary to maintain the free institutions inherited from our ancestors. Yes, gentlemen, disguise is useless. THE TIME IS COME, when we must decide, whether the constitution, the laws, and the checks which they have respectively provided, shall prevail; or the will of ONE MAN shall have uncontrolled sway? In the settlement of that question, I SHALL BE FOUND WHERE I HAVE EVER BEEN." Copy. Printed in Colton, *Clay Correspondence*, 2:337-38. Also printed in *Niles' Register* (October 19, 1833), 45:113.

On October 16, 1833, Clay wrote to the New York and Boston Steamboat Company, which had offered to convey Clay and his party to Rhode Island. States he will avail himself of their offer and will take a passage for himself and his family "in the boat of Friday next, at the customary hour of her departure. I beg, however, that we may be considered as ordinary passengers, and that no exclusive arrangements may be made for us." Copy. Printed in Colton, *Clay*

Correspondence, 2:339-40. Also printed in *Niles' Register* (November 9, 1833), 45:176. Clay embarked on the steamer *President* for Boston on the 18th. Colton, *Clay Correspondence,* 2:340.

Clay wrote to David Graham *et al.* on October 17, 1833, on behalf of Mrs. Lucretia Hart Clay, whom they had invited to a ball in New York City. States that "If she had not ceased to participate in that description of entertainment, she would accept with pleasure, the offer of one from a source so highly respectable, and made with a motive so gratifying to her feelings. In declining it, she requests the young men, at whose instance it is tendered, to be assured, that she will long retain a grateful sense of friendly purpose." Copy. Printed in Colton, *Clay Correspondence,* 2:339. Also printed in *Niles' Register* (November 9, 1833), 45:175. For Graham, see 10:480-81.

Thomas H. Perkins *et al.* of Boston wrote Clay on October 18, 1833, inviting him to a public dinner at Faneuil Hall. Copy. Printed in Colton, *Clay Correspondence,* 2:342-43. Perkins has not been identified. Clay's reply, declining the invitation, is summarized in 8:665. Also printed in Colton, *Clay Correspondence,* 2:343-44. Nevertheless, Clay did visit Faneuil Hall and was called on to make some remarks. See Speech at Faneuil Hall, October 23, 1833.

O. Ellsworth Williams & Henry Barnard wrote Clay on October 21, 1833, inviting him to visit Hartford, Connecticut, especially the "American Asylum for the Deaf and Dumb." Copy. Printed in Washington *Daily National Intelligencer,* October 30, 1833. Clay answered the same day, declining, but expressing the hope that he could pass through Hartford. Copy. *Ibid.* For Henry Barnard, who later served as president of St. John's College, see *NCAB,* 1:505. Williams is not identified.

On October 25, 1833, Seth S. Lynde of Boston wrote Clay, offering "for the acceptance of Mrs. Clay, a straw bonnet—a specimen of an article manufactured in New England, in various styles, to a great extent." Reports that everything used in the bonnet is "truly American" and that it was made "at the establishment of Miss S. H. Bingham." Adds that he is "now putting in operation one hundred looms for the purpose of weaving straw, which will give employment to one hundred and fifty persons." Believes this gives evidence of "the success of those principles which you have advocated with so much zeal." Copy. Printed in Colton, *Clay Correspondence,* 2:348. Bingham is not identified. Lynde lived at 17 Cambridge, in Boston and his business was at Pemberton Hill, Tremont. Charles Stimpson, *Boston Directory* (Boston, 1833).

Clay replied to Lynde on October 28, 1833, offering thanks from himself and Mrs. Clay. States: "I am glad to hear of the success of this branch of manufactures. It proves that our women, no less than our men, are skilful in the application of their taste and ingenuity to any objects which engage their industry." Copy. Printed in Colton, *Clay Correspondence,* 2:348.

On October 28, 1833, Clay wrote to Ichabod Bartlett *et al.,* declining an invitation to visit Portsmouth, New Hampshire. Copy. Printed in Portsmouth (N.H.) *Journal of Literature and Politics,* November 2, 1833.

On November 16, 1833, Clay wrote Heman Allen *et al.,* declining an invitation to visit Burlington, Vermont. ALS. VtU.

Speech to Whig Young Men of Boston, October 21, 1833. Thanks them for their reception of him, stating that "his journey had no political bearing whatever, past, present, or to come,—that on his former visit to Boston, many years ago, he had experienced much hospitality, and that he could not but expect in visiting it again to meet with something of the same reception. But that he had hoped to pass along privately, and mingle in the society of Boston simply as a fellow citizen." Adds that "since I crossed the mountains, my liberty has been

252

taken away from me. I have been taken into custody, made captive of, but placed withal in such delightful bondage, that I could find no strength and no desire to break away from it." Says that on almost all great public questions he has acted in harmony with the views of the people of Boston. Copy, summary. Printed in Frankfort *Commonwealth,* November 5, 1833. Also printed in Washington *Daily National Intelligencer,* October 28, 1833, which gives the date of the speech as October 21.

Speech at Faneuil Hall, Boston, October 23, 1833. States that he had hoped on his journey "to pass on quietly, without attracting any notice on his own account, or coming into contact with large portions of his fellow-citizens," but nothing "could induce him to remain silent" after the "enthusiastic demonstrations, with which he had been received; and especially THIS DAY, in this venerable hall." Notes that among his earliest memories "were revolutionary events and incidents, of which this hall, this city, and this state, were the patriotic theatre." Expects that if "human liberty shall be ONCE MORE exposed to danger in this favored land . . . this hall will again resound with inspired eloquence, and that a spirit will here go forth to sustain its interests, and vindicate its rights." Copy. Printed in Colton, *Clay Correspondence,* 2:347. Dated from Boston *Evening Transcript,* October 23, 1833.

Speech at Bunker Hill, October 28, 1833. States: "I can not express to you the feelings of satisfaction with which I receive these assurances of your friendly feeling, on a spot so justly celebrated. I ascribe it to your partiality, rather than to any merit of my own, that you have been pleased to connect my name in so honorable an association, with the gallant and patriotic men, who, upon this distinguished spot, sealed their devotion to their country with their blood." Adds that if in his public service "I have in any degree cooperated in the great work which our fathers had at heart, as the final object of their toils," he will feel "more than compensated for the discouragements, which, according to the common estimate of things, have attended my public career." Copy. Printed in Colton, *Clay Correspondence,* 2:345.

Although Colton indicates Clay visited Bunker Hill on October 23, 1833, Clay stated in a letter to Edward Everett, dated October 23, 1833, that he would visit there on "Monday next," which was October 28. See 8:665 and Frankfort *Commonwealth,* November 12, 1833.

Speech at Danvers, Mass., October, 29, 1833. Expresses his pleasure at meeting the citizens of Danvers and at finding "that the measures I have advocated . . . meet the approbation of my friends at Danvers." Notes that "I long ago came to the conclusion, that a country possessed of all the means which this country possesses, was in duty bound to bring those means into action, and to unite in one common interest all the branches of useful industry of which it is capable." Believes "our prosperity as a nation" depends on this. Refers to the crisis during the last session of Congress: *"disunion* on the one hand—*destruction* on the other." Explains: "It then seemed to me, that, without abandoning any of those principles, for which I have always contended (for I have never changed in the least my opinion on this subject), a COMPROMISE was the only way in which these great principles could be secured." Is glad that "the bill of compromise [8:604, 619-22, 626-27], suggested upon the impulse of the moment, has met with such general approbation. I surely thought it, at the time, the only thing that could be done." Copy. Printed in Colton, *Clay Correspondence,* 2:349. Printed also in Washington *Daily National Intelligencer,* November 5, 1833.

Speech in Troy, N.Y., November 13, 1833. In reply to a group of young men, who had presented him with a rifle, states: "I reciprocate your kind wishes of a long life and a career of usefulness. But, my young friends, it is known to you all, that long life is not for the aged. In the course of human nature, we who are now upon the stage, must soon resign the bustle, the burden, and the cares of public toil—of upholding our republic, and of preserving our institutions and liberties. . . . Upon YOU, then, will rest all these responsibilities. Let me, therefore, exhort you—and through you, all with whom you stand connected, to prepare yourselves by your devotion to principles, and your attachment to virtue and religion—to GUARD THEM WELL—so that, when you, in your turn, cast off this 'mortal coil,' this priceless inheritance, our happy institutions, may still pass on to the next generation—and from generation to generation—pure and unimpaired." Copy, excerpt. Printed in Colton, *Clay Correspondence*, 2:352. Dating of this speech is based on the Washington *Daily National Intelligencer*, November 19, 1833, which states that Clay gave the speech on "Wednesday last," which was November 13.

Speech at Independence Hall, Philadelphia, November 26, 1833. Thanks them for the many expressions of kindness and respect which they have demonstrated during his visit. Adds that the reasons for his current trip were entirely private, and "I did not anticipate . . . the public character, which, involuntarily on my part, it has been made to assume." Asserts that in respect to the many public demonstrations made to him, "I have no other than an humble claim to them, founded upon ardent zeal, purity of purpose and long public service, in the support of our civil institutions, great principles and important measures of national policy." Regards these as "powerful and encouraging testimony to the goodness of the cause of liberty and Union and national prosperity, to which I have always faithfully devoted myself," and as "pledges of the firm and patriotic determination, among the People, to maintain that cause against all danger, and to transmit to posterity, as we received from our ancestors, our liberties and our inestimable institutions, unviolated, unabridged, and uncorrupted." Copy. Printed in Washington *Daily National Intelligencer*, November 29, 1833.

To John H. James, *ca.* January, 1834. States: "Our public affairs have arrived at a momentous crisis. . . . I shall continue to exert myself to preserve our institutions and our liberties. I have strong hopes, not unmixed with strong fears. As for myself, I mean to leave events to roll on as they may, remaining perfectly passive. If they should point the way to my retirement to Ashland, I shall be entirely content." Copy, extract. Printed in William & Orphia D. Smith, *A Buckeye Titan* (Cincinnati, 1953), 250.

From Campbell McIlwaine & Co., January 13, 1834. Complain of the "very great difficulty and trouble" in making the calculation of duties on imported cotton goods under the interpretation the Treasury Department has given to the Compromise Tariff of 1833 [8:604, 619-21, 626-27]. Fear that more mistakes will be made in the calculations, and more clerks will be needed in the custom house in order to prevent merchants from being inconvenienced by long delays in obtaining their goods. Suggest the passage of a law "excepting from the law now in operation, all Cotton Goods formerly paying duty on the minimum principle, and . . . let the 30 Cents Cottons be by degrees lessened a few cents, say 28.26 &c and the 35 Cents Cottons be lessened to 32.30 &c or any other deduction That may be agreed upon." Add that "we are inclined to think that you had been aware of the difficulties which we have pointed out you would have endeavoured to avoid them in framing the Bill." Note that "we are an old and long established House importing Goods from Europe and have no Interest in any manufacturing Establishment in this or any other Country." Copy. DLC-Papers of Alexander Brown & Son.

To HENRY A.S. DEARBORN[1]   Washington, February 1, 1834
Your favor of the 22d. Ulto. is recd.[2] You are right in your construction of the Compromise act[3] as to the Cotton duty.[4] But I incline to think we had better not at this Session disturb the last Treasury instruction. Such I find is the opinion of other friends.

We have some hopes that the party will give way in the House on the deposite question.[5] It is said that they cannot now command a majority of more than one. If public opinion continue to act in our favor we shall succeed.

ALS. KyU.   1. For Dearborn, see 4:670-71.   2. Not found.   3. See 8:604, 619-21, 626-27.   4. See 8:688-90.   5. See 8:583-84, 684-94, 710-12.

From "Senex," New England, March, 1834. Has read "with satisfaction" Clay's resolutions concerning appointments [8:703] but feels "they do not reach the main source of our political evils." Believes that source to be the offers of office and the establishment of partisan presses by those who are candidates for the presidency. Asserts that no law or constitutional amendment will "secure our country from the worst evils of corruption, without first introducing a provision that shall effectually prevent a candidate from influencing public opinion, and bribing the support of favorites."

Suggests that each state select one of its citizens to be a candidate for the presidency, and that the names of all those chosen be sent to the secretary of state under seal until election day. On that day the envelopes would be opened before the two houses of Congress by the Speaker of the House, who would put the name of every person nominated in a box which would be shaken. Then the Speaker, the president of the Senate, or some other designated person would draw out half the names, which would be discarded. The president would then be selected by the House from the remaining names before the congressman "are permitted to rise from their seats, a majority of the States making a choice." Thus, "no intrigue or personal influence can be exerted." Adds that "We may prate about the virtue of the People as long as we please, and about enlightening their minds by education and by the press, but" unless a method is developed to select a chief magistrate without corruption, no republic can endure. Copy. Printed in Washington *Daily National Intelligencer*, March 19, 1834.

To LEWIS WELD[1]   Washington, May 19, 1834
I find that I omitted to acknowledge, in proper time, your favor[2] by Mr Ellsworth,[3] and that of one of the Pupils of the American Asylum[4] presenting to me a box manufactured by them. And now the box, containing his letter is sent to Kentucky; which prevents my making suitable acknowledgments to him and his associates. I will thank you to accept an apology yourself, and to make one for me to my young friends, for this seeming neglect. Assure them that it has proceeded from no insensibility to the value of their token but entirely from my incessant labors

255

in the Senate, to promote their good, in common with the rest of our Countrymen. On my return to Ashland, I will answer[5] the letter which has gone there.

P.S. I send several Copies of two Speeches for yourself and such of the Pupils as you may think proper to give them to.[6]

ALS. American School for the Deaf, Hartford, Conn.   1. For Weld, at this time principal of the American Asylum for the Education and Instruction of the Deaf and Dumb, see 5:369.   2. Not found.   3. Probably Connecticut Congressman William W. Ellsworth. See *DAB*.   4. See 5:369.   5. Not found.   6. Not found.

To HENRY THOMPSON[1]   Washington, June 20, 1834

The bill to compensate for French Spoliations prior to 1800, you will have seen, has been postponed, for want of time.[2] I took the occasion of its postponement to express my conviction that there existed a well founded claim to some amount.[3] I fear the other bill alluded to by you will experience a similar fate, tho' it may possibly be passed.

The only Copy of the Blue Book which I possessed I gave away. I do not know one which can be procured. I observe an edition of the work is about to be published in Philada.

I hope the Asses will go off today or tomorrow.[4]

ALS. FU.   1. For Thompson, see 2:237.   2. See 8:448.   3. See 8:733.   4. See 8:729.

To John Harvie *et al.*, June 21, 1834.

Has received their letter of the 7th [not found] inviting him to attend a convention at Frankfort on July 4 to celebrate the recent triumph of supporters of civil liberty in Virginia [8:703] and New York [8:705] and "expressing a sanction of my conduct, in the present awful and alarming crisis in our public affairs." Would make any sacrifice to attend, except sacrificing public duty, and believes the ensuing week may be the most important of this session in the Senate. Thus, cannot accept the invitation.

Adds his opinion that "intelligence from all quarters" indicates that the people are shocked by the abuse of executive power and are "resolved to recall it to its duty, within the secure limits of the constitution and laws." Believes a great victory is at hand, but warns that "no error is greater or more fatal, in politics as well as in war, than that of despising or treating with contempt the power of the foe. Our present adversary possesses vast means; his forces, although scattered and dismayed, are yet numerous; and he will display a vigor proportionate to the desperation of his cause. We must expect and prepare for a terrible contest. Our vigilance should never sleep; our exertions never tire. . . . we should throw the undivided energy of our whole souls into the struggle. . . . Animated by such spirit, it is impossible that the people should not dissolve the dangerous union between the Purse and the Sword, and replace the government upon the sure pillars of the constitution." Expects Kentucky to discharge her duty in the coming elections [8:708]. Copy. Printed in Frankfort *Commonwealth*, July 15, 1834.

For Harvie, see 3:228.

To UNKNOWN RECIPIENT   Lexington, August 2, 1834

I thank you for the Address made by you at the Whig Festival on the 4th [word illeg.] a copy of which I recd. with your favor of the 22d of the same month.[1] I perused it with much pleasure, and found it distinguished by a bold and manly spirit and patriotic elegance. I fervently hope that the sentiments which it breathes may be shared by a sufficient portion of Pennsylvanians to array your important state against the present wicked and corrupt administration.[2] Louisiana,[3] we just hear, has opened the Campaign with vigor and gallantry. I trust that Kentucky[4] next week will be along side of her; but it is to the Fall elections we must look for a decisive blow.

I am greatly obliged by the kind interest which you take in the accident which recently befel me.[5] The injury which I received, although inconvenient, was slight, and is now healed.

Copy. Henry Clay Memorial Foundation, Lexington, Ky.   1. Not found.   2. See 8:726.   3. See 8:741.   4. See 8:708.   5. See 8:736.

To BENJAMIN WATKINS LEIGH   Lexington, September 2, 1834
Mr. M[ann]. Butler, who will present this letter, being engaged in writing the History of K[entucky]. and the Country N. West of the Ohio, is desirous of resorting to the archives of Virginia to aid him in his object.[1] I take pleasure in introducing him to you, & in recommending him to your friendly offices, as a gentleman of literary merit and high respectability.

ALS. ViRVal.   1. For Butler and his book, see 3:330.

To LEVI WOODBURY[1]   Lexington, September 2, 1834
I lose no time in acknowledging the honor of the receipt of your letter of the 25th Ulto.[2] communicating the sum to be allowed to the representative of James Morrison, according to the interpretation placed by you on the act of the last Session of Congress.[3] As I had been induced to place a construction on the act somewhat different from yours, I hope you will excuse the liberty I take of making a few suggestions for your consideration, especially as it is desirable to avoid any resort again to Congress for a fresh annunciation of its intention.

The act authorizes you to settle the claim against the U. States in favor of said representative for interest on a *liquidated* demand, on the principles of justice and equity. The liquidated demand referred to is the protested bill drawn on the Governor of Illinois,[4] of which the portion due to James Morrison was $4020:66. The mode of ascertaining what interest is due, upon principles of justice and equity, on that sum to Morrisons Exor, it appears to me, is to calculate interest upon that sum, from the 2d of June 1820 up to the time the payment was made under the act of 20th May 1830, and, adding the principal and interest togather, deduct the payment of $4020.66 from both, and then to calculate interest upon the balance up to the time of settlement under the late act, or up to its date. The rule of law and justice is to apply partial payments first to the extinction of the interest due at the time they are respectively made, and if there be a residue to apply it to the principal. If the interest due, at the time of a partial payment, exceed the amount of such payment, the excess is to be kept seperate from the principal, so as to avoid compound interest, and such excess is to be first extinguished by subsequent payments. This rule for calculating interest is

257

the prevailing lawful rule throughout Europe and America, as far as my information extends. On a discussion which arose on this subject in the Senate during the last Session, it was ascertained to be the legal rule established in all the States, as to which any information was obtained. I will add that if it be objected that it operates in favor of the Creditor to the disadvantage of the debtor, the Government is oftener a creditor than a debtor. But its operation is believed to be perfectly just. The objection to the mode which you have adopted is, that there is a period of near four years during which no interest is received upon a demand admitted to be liquidated.

I transmit herewith a sketch of the account[5] according to the mode in which it appears to me it ought to be stated and settled.

Your letter requires that I should pay the costs and charges of the pending suit. This I do not think is right. The Government pays costs in no case. Why should it exact them in any? but in this particular case the suit is depending on a plea of non est factum, which has been pled by the representative of Morrison. The U. States Atto. and the Solicitor of the Treasury will both inform you that that plea must prevail, and the U. States be turned out of court. Is it just then to require Morrisons Exor to pay the costs of a suit, in which, if it be prosecuted, he must certainly succeed? I do not ask the Govt. to pay my costs; and I think it but just that the suit should be dismissed neither party recovering costs of the other. Farther; what the Government shall eventually receive from me is so much absolutely saved. [Ashton] Garrett is insolvent, I am not liable as Exor of Morrison for the Debt; but it happens that a fund is in my hands, which I might have paid over to Garrett, out of which, by the arrangement contemplated with me, the Government will secure something. This is clear gain. Why should I then be subjected to the paym[en]t of any costs?

I hope on a review of the case I shall be fortunate enough to obtain your concurrence in the principles of adjustment now stated; and that the account may be closed accordingly. As soon as I hear from you to that effect, I will pay the bal. & obtain the receipts in duplicate as directed by you.

LS, with account in Clay's hand. DNA, RG56, Treasury Dept., Letters from Members of Congress, 1834-37, A–L.   1. For Woodbury, see 5:79 and *DAB*.   2. Woodbury writes on August 25, 1834, in conformity with the act of May 1, 1834, to provide for "'the relief of the legal Representatives of James Morrison, decd'.... I have decided that interest at the rate of six per centum, per annum be allowed from 2d of June 1820 ... to the 20th May 1830—on $4020 66/100 being the one third of said debt ... the said interest ... amounting to $2403.80." Continues: "By applying said interest therefore in part payment of the bonds of Ashton Garrett, late a Paymaster in the Army, ... in the penalty of $7000. to which bond the name of ... James Morrison has been affixed as one of the sureties." Adds that when Clay deposits in the bank to the credit of the Treasurer of the U.S. "such further sum as will satisfy the claims of the United States on said bond of Ashton Garrett, together with Cost and Charges the Solicitor of the Treasury will be instructed to dismiss the suit pending on the said Bond." Copy. DNA, RG56, Treasury Dept., Series E: Letters & Reports to Congress, vol. 8, pp. 170-71 (1833-36). See also Clay to Woodbury, Sept. 5 and Oct. 11, 1834.   3. For the May 1, 1834, act, see 6 *U.S. Stat.*, 560.   4. It is uncertain to which of the Illinois governors—Shadrack Bond (1818-22), Edward Coles (1822-26), Ninian Edwards (1826-30), John Reynolds (1830-34)—he refers.   5. The account, which accompanies the letter, shows "one third part of a protested bill drawn by the Government upon the State of Illinois.... $4020:66" and the same amount "By cash paid the 20h. May 1830." The amount of interest is left blank.

To LEVI WOODBURY   Lexington, September 5, 1834

Since I had the honor of addressing you a few days ago,[1] on the subject
of adjusting the case of James Morrisons representative, I have received from the Clerk of the Fed. Court the enclosed letter, from which
it appears that the suit of the U. States against Morrison's Exor as the
surety of [Ashton] Garrett is actually discontinued—probably because it
could not be maintained against the plea mentioned in my letter—and
that the costs on either side are a mere trifle. I presume they have
been paid. This will settle one of the points between us; and I cannot
but think that, as to the remaining one respecting interest, we ought
not to differ.

ALS. DNA, RG56, Treasury Dept. Letters from Members of Congress, 1834-37,
A–L.   1. Clay to Woodbury, Sept. 2, 1834.

To LEVI WOODBURY   Lexington, October 11, 1834

A short absence from the place of my residence has delayed my acknowledgment of the receipt of your letter of the 12h. Ulto.[1]

I am happy to perceive that I have the honor of coinciding so
nearly with you as to the principles which should regulate the allowance to be made to the legal representative of James Morrison, under
the act of Congress of the first of May last, that I have no difficulty in
acquiescing in your views. According to these I am to pay into the Treasury $4026:63 and to be allowed under the before mentioned act
$2973:37. These two sums together made $7000 the amount of the
penalty of the bond of Ashton Garrett late a Paymaster &c and for
which his sureties were liable.[2]

I have therefore in pursuance of the directions contained in your
letter of the 25h. August[3] last deposited with the Office of the B U S in
Lexington to the credit of the Treasurer of the U States the above sum
of $4026:63 for which I have taken a receipt in duplicate, one of which
I transmit enclosed and the other I forward by the present mail to the
3d. Auditor.

As I have been acting, in this business, in an official character, and
am bound periodically to settle my accounts before the proper tribunal,
I have to request of you the necessary voucher to enable me to effect
the proper settlement. I take the liberty of transmitting herein the
form of such a voucher as will satisfy the local tribunal, which, if you
approve of it, you will oblige me by executing and forwarding to me.

ALS. DNA, RG56, Treasury Dept. Letters from Members of Congress, 1834-37, A–L.
1. On Sept. 12, 1834, Woodbury writes that after examining Clay's letter of Sept. 2 [see
above], he thinks "there is some equity in the additional claim presented: and hence feel
inclined to regard the interest on that demand, from the 2d June 1820, to the 20th May,
1830, as constituting a balance on the last mentioned day & being so due, do regard
it as deserving interest from that time to the date of the Act of 1 May 1834." Thus, there
will be allowed under that act $2,973.37, which "Upon your depos[i]ting therefore in the"
bank "such an amount as will with the amount allowed as above stated, satisfy the claim
of the United States against the legal Representative of James Morrison decd. the 3d
Auditor . . . will be instructed to close the account of Paymaster Garrett's bond." This
letter appears in the Calendar in 8:890.   2. Clay to Woodbury, Sept. 2 and Sept. 5,
1834.   3. Clay to Woodbury, Sept. 2, 1834.

From James H. Causten, Washington, December 19, 1834. Suggests an amendment to a recent bill in the Senate regarding Revolutionary bounty land

warrants. Thinks the proposed amendment would have a "beneficial effect on many persons, whose claims to scrip are undisputed, and yet have to bear long and in some cases interminable delay only because of the negligence of unavoidable absence of other heirs." Submits "the proposition on its own merits & with entire confidence in its utility & safety."

The proposal reads: "That upon satisfactory evidence his [word illeg.] to the Com: of the Gen L[and] office, upon its presentation of any U S Mil[itary] Land Warrant by the heirs of deceased persons entitled to sc[r]ip, of the law to which the first section of this act shall apply, or to which any previous act shall apply, that some of the heirs so entitled are in parts unknown, or from any cause this authority cannot be had, that to receive such scrip he shall issue the proportion of scrip due to those heirs applying, and shall return the proportions due to those who shall not apply for the same." ALS. DLC-Causten/ Pickett Papers.

For Causten, see 4:287-88. The bill, which authorized the secretary of the treasury to issue scrip to officers, non-commissioned officers, and soldiers of the Revolutionary War, or their legal representatives, in satisfaction of warrants for military bounty lands, which had not been located on the lands of the U.S. reserved for that purpose, was read first on December 9, 1834, and referred to the Committee on Pubic Lands the following day. The bill did not pass. U.S. Sen., *Journal*, 23 Cong., 2 Sess., 32, 34.

To THOMAS HART CLAY   Lexington, April 23, [1835 or 1837][1]
I hardly know what to do about pressing my hemp. I went to see Warner's at Mr. [John W.] Hunts, and it was all out of order. I don't wish to go to the expence of purchasing one, without being sure that it will answer. Can you think of no other mode? In the mean time I hope you will not allow the hackled hemp [to] be injured.

I am now anxious to send off the bagging and all the Rope, including what you have lately made, as soon as possible. I have determined to send the greater part of it to Savannah.[2]

ALS. DLC-HC (DNA, M212, R6).   1. Although the year is not given, this letter was probably written in 1835 or 1837. The letter is addressed to Thomas at "Logan factory," and it is known he worked for Logan in 1836; however, Clay was in Washington during April, 1836, but at Ashland in April, 1835 and 1837.   2. In another undated letter addressed to Thomas at "Logan Factory," Clay writes: "I send Harvey to haul the Rails, and he takes a bedstead and some Chairs. Send him home as soon as he is done, as we are very busy." Sends Thomas a check for $20. ALS. *Ibid.* Harvey was a slave. See 10:107.

To George S. White, July 4, 1835. Has received "a copy of your prospectus for the publication of a memoir of the late Mr. Samuel Slater" and his "successful exertions to introduce the cotton manufacture in the United States." States that "I have now in my possession some cotton yarn spun by the first spindles which he put up." Adds that "Without being able to contribute to the accomplishment of your undertaking, I shall be glad to hear of its successful execution." Copy. Printed in *Niles' Register* (August 8, 1835), 48:396.

For White (1784-1850), a Presbyterian and later an Episcopal clergyman, see *NCAB*, 4:319. For Samuel Slater (1768-1835), founder of the American cotton industry, see *DAB*. White's book, *Memoir of Samuel Slater, the Father of American Manufactures*, was published in Philadelphia in 1836.

To James Taylor et al., Newport, Ky., September 4, 1835. Declines their invitation to a public dinner in his honor in Newport. Explains that before leaving home he had decided to confine his visit "to the sole object which brought me here, of visiting the exhibition . . . of products of agriculture and manufactures." Copy. Printed in Washington *Daily National Intelligencer*, September 22, 1835. Written from Cincinnati, where an agricultural fair was being held.

In their invitation, printed without a date, Taylor *et al.* urge Clay to accept their offer of a public dinner as testimony to his public service "especially within the few past years of executive misrule." Copy. *Ibid.*

To CHARLES F. MERCER[1] Lexington, October 19, 1835

I heard last evening that you were in Lexington and called this morning at Mr. Brenan's [*sic*, John Brennan][2] tavern to see you; but was informed that you were out, probably at Mr. Wickliffe's.[3] Raining as it was I would have gone there to see you, if I had been sure of finding you. This afternoon I have to attend the funeral of Mrs. [John W.] Hunt.[4]

Will you do me as the favor to dine with me tomorrow or wednesday at 2 OClock (as the day may best suit you?)

I should be mortified if you left Lexington without my having the pleasure of seeing you, and at Ashland.

Do me the favor to ask Mr. Wickliffe to accompany you to dinner.

ALS. KyHi. 1. For Mercer, see 2:420. 2. Brennan was proprietor of the Phoenix Hotel in Lexington. Julius P. B. MacCabe, *Directory of the City of Lexington. . . . 1838 & '39* (Lexington, 1838). 3. It is uncertain to which of the many Wickliffes this refers. 4. Catharine Hunt had died on Oct. 17, 1835, at age 57. Lexington *Observer & Kentucky Reporter*, Oct. 28, 1835.

To Committee for the Whig Celebration [Luke Tiernan *et al.*], Baltimore, November 4, 1835. Declines, with regret, their invitation [not found] to a Whig celebration in Maryland. Expresses the belief that Martin Van Buren's election to the presidency [8:785] "would be fatal to the purity and existence of our institutions." Offers "as a sentiment at your festival, *Union and concert*, and a sacrifice of all individual attachment, in support of a Presidential candidate opposed to the Baltimore nomination [8:796]." Copy. Printed in Washington *Daily National Intelligencer*, November 17, 1835; also in Frankfort *Commonwealth*, November 28, 1835.

To HENRY SHEPHERD[1] Washington, December 15, 1835

Your brother [Rezin D. Shepherd][2] will have informed you that we have made an arrangement about some of his Durham Cattle,[3] and that we purpose visiting you. I took the liberty to send to your care two Cows from New Jersey which I hope have safely arrived. I have also a Bull [Hector][4] from Col. Powell's [*sic*, John Hare Powel][5] stock now on his way from Philada. to your house, which I will thank you to receive.

We will leave Balto. Thursday morning the 24th inst (next week) in the cars for Harper's ferry, and, if we can, reach your house that night.

It is indispensable to have the Cattle shod if possible, especially the larger ones. I will thank you to engage some careful blacksmith to do it early next week, and I will pay him when I see you. If one cannot be got in the neighborhood, but can be procured elsewhere, I will thank you to send for him. I should be glad when they are shoeing the bulls if rings could be put in their noses.

I shall want some careful hand to accompany Hawkins as far as Wheeling with the Cattle. If the man (I believe [John] O'Hara is his name) who has charge of the Powell bull will engage to go on reasonable terms, I will be obliged to you to employ him for me. If he cannot be got, I wish you would get some other careful person.[6]

The Cattle etc. I hope will all be ready, shod etc. to start on their journey Xmas day or the next day.[7]

ALS. Courtesy of Prof. Wade Hall, Bellarmine College, Louisville, Ky.   1. For Henry Shepherd, see 9:174.   2. For Rezin D. Shepherd, see 8:804.   3. See 8:804-5.   4. For Hector, see 8:805.   5. For Powel, see 8:122.   6. Hawkins has not been identified. For O'Hara, see 8:670.   7. See also 8:806, 814, 827, 835-36.

Speech to American Colonization Society, Washington, December 15, 1835. States that he had "no intention of saying one word on the present occasion"; rather, "I came . . . merely to evince by my presence, and by presiding at your deliberations, that however others may flag and faulter in regard to your noble scheme, it has at least one faithful adherent, and one who was among the first who put in motion this grand project." Notes that the colonization society is "assailed on one side by those who represent it, as an ally of slavery, and on the other by men who accuse it, with equal vehemence, of being unfriendly to freedom." Asserts that "it is neither the one nor the other; and it is because it disclaims alike all interference with slave property, and all connexion with immediate emancipation, that it is the object of common attack from both parties."

Points out that colonization has liberated a large number of persons who would otherwise still be in bondage. Avers that abolition has not "lightened the chains of slavery," nor "smoothed the pillow of the slave," nor "addressed the humanity and the philosophy of his master. . . . But it has lighted the torch to inflame and to agitate the country." Adds that is has also resulted in more oppressive laws for regulating slaves. Yet, believes the intentions of most abolitionists are good, though they "are misguided" and "are deceived."

Refers to recent remarks of Gerrit Smith in relation to the right of free discussion. Argues that discussion is the first stage of the process for making a decision, while "deliberation [is] the intermediate stage, and decision the ultimate end." Argues, therefore, that "Abolitionists at the North must show that this discussion, . . . is in order to deliberation, which they may rightfully entertain, and to a decision which they have a right to make. If they have no right to deliberate, or no right to decide, they have no right to discussion. And that is their mistake. I admit that the right of free political discussion should know no restraint; it should be like the water or like the air, which coming to us from heaven, should know no human restraints; but it is free discussion in relation to *ourselves* and to *our own affairs.*" Contends that the "officious and improper interference with the concerns of others" will produce the "opposite effect from that at which it aims." Cites as an example that many who were formerly in favor of gradual emancipation "have been driven from their purpose."

Bears testimony to the good effects of the colonization society and says to "the young men who are to push forward this cause after I shall have left it . . . 'Go ahead.' Your object must succeed. It unites religion with patriotism, humanity with justice and safety." Copy. Printed in *African Repository and Colonial Journal* (January, 1836), 12:9-11.

For Gerrit Smith, see 9:298.

Report of Foreign Relations Committee, March 3, 1836. Clay reports for the committee on the May 30, 1834, nomination of Andrew Stevenson for the office of minister plenipotentiary and envoy extraordinary to Great Britain. States that on June 24, 1834, Stevenson's nomination was rejected by the Senate [8:631-32] and that the office has remained vacant since the rejection of Martin Van Buren on January 25, 1832 [8:344]. Asserts that there was "an indirect intervention, with Mr. Stevenson's knowledge and acquiescence, to prevail on the President [Andrew Jackson] not to make the appointment in the vacation of the Senate, in accommodation to the views of Mr. Stevenson and his friend Mr. [Thomas] Ritchie." Thus, although the secretary of state had first written to Stevenson concerning the appointment on March 15, 1833, the nomination was not presented to the Senate until May 30, 1834. In the meantime, Stevenson had been elected to Congress and then chosen as Speaker of the House. States that "That office, at all times one of great influence, possessed more than ordinary weight in the session of 1833-'4. The President . . . had directed the public deposites to be withdrawn from the Bank of the United States, and placed in the local banks. . . . It was at this extraordinary period that the Speaker of the House of Representatives, invested with the power of appointing and arranging the committees of the House, and wielding a great influence, secretly held a written official promise of the most important mission abroad, every body being ignorant of the fact except himself, the President, the Secretary of State, and a few confidential friends. It was under these circumstances that his nomination came up for consideration in the Senate." Notes that "It is a fundamental principle of free government that, in order to preserve the purity of their administration, each of the three departments into which . . . they are divided, should be kept independent of and without the influence of the others. But, if the head of one of these departments may, at a critical period, confidentially present, and for a long period of time hold up to the presiding officer of the popular branch of another, the powerful inducement of a splendid foreign mission, is there not immediate danger of undue subserviency?" Adds that the "Senate thought there was, and withheld its advice and consent to the nomination of Mr. Stevenson as minister to Great Britain. And now, after the lapse of near two years, with all the circumstances by which his original nomination was attended remaining in full force . . . the same individual is again nominated by the President for the same office. . . . Doubtless, no personal feelings or wishes to achieve a triumph over the Senate can have prompted the renewal of the nomination." Asserts, however, that "When the Senate has once decided upon a nomination, there ought to be an end of the matter." Adds that "Prior to the present administration, instances of renomination were rare, and are believed to have occurred only when some indication was given from the Senate of a desire that it should take place. It has of late become much more frequent. . . . if the practice of renomination is indulged, in process of time there will be danger of the existence or the imputation of corruption. The committee think that the practice ought to be resisted; that when the Senate has once rejected an individual nomination, the decision ought to be held as final and conclusive; and that it ought not to confirm the nomination of the same person when again made for the same office, without strong special cause." Thus, the committee recommends "That the Senate do not advise and consent to the appointment of Andrew Stevenson" as minister to Great Britain. U.S. Sen., *Journal*, 24 Cong., 1 Sess., 577-81.

Jackson's renomination of Stevenson was presented to the Senate on February 18, 1836, and it was referred to the Committee on Foreign Relations. The committee reported on March 3, and Clay moved that the nomination lie on the table. On March 16, the Senate took up the nomination and confirmed Stevenson by a vote of 26 to 19, Clay voting nay. U.S. Sen., *Executive Journal*, 4:509-10, 513-17, 523-24. For Stevenson, see 8:430.

To HENRY THOMPSON   Washington, March 10, 1836

I have your favor of the 8h.[1] I am greatly disappointed in the height of the Jack Ass Octavian (that is the name I gave him) and cannot imagine how the error in regard to it was committed.

I transmit you enclosed fifty dollars; and will thank you after paying out of that and the $30 the expences you will have incurred, to hand over the residue of both sums to Van Sant [*sic*, Richard W. Vansant][2] on his arrival, and tell him I wish him to proceed immediately to K[entucky]. with the Jack, and to write me from Uniontown and from Wheeling. Tell him to travel not more than 25 miles per day and to take the greatest pains to get the Jack out in good order. I write in haste[.]

ALS. Courtesy of William W. Layton, Millwood, Va.   1. See 8:830.   2. Vansant was a cattle drover. See 8:830, 836, 851.

To Henry Clay Walker, April 16, 1836. States that "Your father [William Walker] informs me that he has done me the honor to bestow my name upon you" and has "requested me to address a few lines to you." Hopes young Walker "may prove useful to your fellow men, a blessing to your parents and acceptable to God." Recommends "a constant and useful employment of your time, unweakening as hence to truth, strict fidelity to all your engagements, regular performance of your religious duties and avoiding all mean, low or vulgar speech." Copy. Printed in Kansas City *Kansan*, June 20, 1954.

William Walker, a full-blooded Wyandot, was appointed by the tribe in 1852 as the first territorial governor of Kansas. *Ibid.*

To RICHARD GRAHAM   Washington, June 16, 1836

I have this moment had the pleasure of seeing your son and receiving your letter by him.[1] He is very much like you and for *that* and other reasons I hope to see more of him. He gives me very gratifying accounts of James [Brown Clay].[2]

My land Speech[3] has not yet been published; and I do not know that I shall have time, nor when, to write it out. A favorable incidental vote has this moment taken place in the H. of R. but the fate of the bill there is uncertain.

The Senate has decided against the preemption laws;[4] and I think none will pass this Session. James must take his chance of purchasing the vacant land adjoining him, whenever it is sold.

Congress has fixed the 4h. of July for adjournment.

ALS. MoSHi.   1. Not found.   2. See 8:801.   3. See 8:812-13.   4. See 8:839.

To SETH C. HAWLEY[1]   Washington, June 22, 1836

I duly recd. your favor of the 8h. inst.[2] The memorial to which it refers came safely to hand; and, as I was detained from the Senate by the extreme indisposition of my youngest son [John Morrison Clay],[3] I confided it to the care of my Colleague Mr. [John J.] Crittenden, who presented it to the Senate[.] The Com[mitt]ee. of F[oreign]. Relations has since made a report, on the subject of the recognition of Texas,[4] which you will see in the public prints, and which I hope you will find satisfactory.

I have not the means of forming a correct judgment on the point of local politics which you state. There can be no doubt that the practice of granting acts of incorporation has been carried too far in some of the States; but the evil is more obvious than any remedy for the past.

Information from various quarters of the Union, I think, renders Mr. [Martin] V[an]. Buren's election very doubtful;[5] and he is evidently losing ground, and must continue to do so. The passage of the deposite bill,[6] now certain, has been effected in spite of the most strenuous opposition from the Adm[inistrati]on, and threatened the total dissolution of the party. I believe it cannot easily recover from the shock.

ALS. KyU.   1. Not identified.   2. Not found.   3. See 8:849-52, 866.   4. See 8:838-39, 855.   5. See 8:785.   6. See 8:813.

To Committee of Arrangements, Carthage, Ohio July 22, 1836. Declines with regret an invitation from the committee organizing a barbecue in honor of Bellamy Storer's work during the previous session of Congress. Adds, however: "I offer a sentiment which, if you please, may be proposed to the company: 'The distribution of the surplus revenue—the brightest ray of light during the seven years of political darkness.'" Copy. Printed in Washington *Daily National Intelligencer*, August 19, 1836.

For Storer, an Ohio congressman, see 10:429 and *BDAC*.

To DOLLEY P. MADISON   Lexington, August 18, 1836
If I am late, perhaps among the last, in tendering as I now do, my condolence on account of your late afflicting loss,[1] I beg you to be persuaded that you have not one friend who more truly laments the event or more sincerely sympathises with you than I do. And yet why should we be grieved? Mr. [James] Madison, after passing a well-spent life of virtue of philosophy and of eminent utility; after having rendered more important services to his Country than any other man, [George] Washington only excepted, has sunk down into the grave as tranquilly as he lived, at an unusually advanced age. His was not a case of death but of translation. We ought not to repine at the event but to be thankful that so good and so great a man was so long spared to us.

I took much pleasure in suggesting to Mr. [Benjamin Watkins] Leigh to move, as the Senator from your own State, the passage of the bill which extends the franking privilege to you.[2] And I am sure that he did not feel less in contributing to have that merited compliment paid to you.

I infer, from the general knowledge which I possessed of Mr. Madison's condition, and from what I have learnt of the dispositions of his last will, through the news papers, that he has left you the means of comfort and abundance. I sincerely wish that you may long live to enjoy them. In this and all other friendly sentiments, and assurances Mrs. [Lucretia Hart] Clay unites cordially with [me].[3]

AL, signature removed. NN.   1. James Madison had died on June 28, 1836. See 8:859.   2. See 8:859.   3. For Mrs. Madison's reply, see 8:868-70, and for Clay's response, see 8:870-71.

Speech to Kentucky Colonization Society, Lexington, August 26, 1836. Asserts that the amalgamation of the two races in the United States is "a thing impossible." Traces the early history of the society, the origin of the concept of colonization, and the planting of the society's first colony in Africa. This last demonstrates the "practicability of the object" of the organization. The success of the society "is the work of an overruling Providence," even though it was "surrounded by difficulties at its outset, and it has at all times encountered opposition and misrepresentation." Continues: "Recently, a new school has sprung up; one which maintains that slavery is a blessing; that it is an indispensable element for the preservation of our own freedom! Of this school . . . I AM NOT ONE. . . . *I consider slavery as a curse*—a curse to the master; a wrong, a grievous wrong to the slave. In the abstract, it is ALL wrong; and no possible contingency can make it right." Only a "stern political necessity . . . can excuse or justify it; a necessity arising from the fact that to give freedom to our slaves that they might remain with us, *would be doing them an injury, rather than a benefit*—would render their condition worse than it is at present." As to whether "slavery was condemned by religion," he would not say. But refers to those "advocates of immediate, unconditional, indiscriminate emancipation, without regard to consequences" as a "fanatical class." Prefers "old fashioned gradual emancipationists" like Benjamin Franklin and Richard Rush. Reminds his audience of his own efforts in Kentucky in 1798-1799 to insert a provision for gradual emancipation into the state constitution [1:5-7, 12-14]. Denies that there is any connection whatever "between the Colonization and Abolition Societies." Admits having had some correspondence with a leading New York abolitionist [Lewis Tappan. See 8:768, 773-74, 793], but only to "convince him of his error." Admits that Tappan's charge that colonization is a "design of *slaveholders*" is "in part true" since "one advantage of the scheme was its tendency, by the removal of a class, in *theory* freemen, but in *fact* NOT free, to contribute to preserve quiet and subordination among slaves. The removal of the free blacks would, while it conferred a vast good on them, render the slave more docile, manageable, and useful." Suggests, analogously, that the interference of New York abolitionists in slavery in Kentucky would be similar to "the organization of societies in Kentucky to regulate the tolls on the New York and Ohio canals." Believes that the transport of free blacks to Africa will induce "among her people our religion." Asserts his own belief in and love of the superior "religion of Christ." Calls attention to the problem of disposing of the nation's surplus revenue and asks: "can it be doubted that the means of this are sufficient to transport not only the free, but the slaves, should the States consent to their removal? True, this Society has nothing to do with slaves. Yet, some, it is true, have been manumitted, and with the consent of their owners, sent to Liberia." Thinks that the present Distribution Act of June 23, 1836 [8:813], will bring to Kentucky alone from $1,000,000 to $2,500,000, or money enough to afford "Colonization, Education and Internal Improvements"; and that future federal "Land Bills and Distribution Bills" will produce additional large sums for Kentucky to apply to these projects. Trusts "Colonization would come in for its due share—as our State was among the first to express favorable opinions of this cause." Will not urge "at present a large appropriation, but one which would be considered liberal." Notes that this must be "left to the judgment of the Legislature." Copy. Printed in Lexington *Intelligencer*, September 2, 1836 "by the aid of the brief notes taken by us at the time"; reprinted in Washington *Daily National Intelligencer*, September 10, 1836, and in *The African Repository and Colonial Journal* (October, 1836), 12:297-301.

From Peter Dudley, Frankfort, Ky., December 28, 1836. Announces to Clay and John J. Crittenden that the Kentucky legislature has passed resolutions "to procure, if practicable, the passage of a law allowing compensation to the Vol-

266

unteer Mounted Gunmen of this State, who were organized for the service of the United States, in its military operations on our South-western frontier, and disbanded by order of the President before the day of rendezvous." Argues that it is only "just and reasonable" that these men be compensated for their actual expenses in outfitting themselves for the service, especially since "the order of the President directing the troops to be disbanded, gave assurance that they should be paid as soon as Congress would make an appropriation, if at that time there was no funds in the Treasury applicable to that purpose." Encloses copies of the muster rolls of each company, and suggests that indemnities be made according to rank. Copy. Printed in Frankfort *Commonwealth*, February 8, 1837. Dudley was adjutant general of Kentucky. For Dudley, see 1:843-44.

Gen. Edmund P. Gaines, who commanded U.S. troops in the Southwest with orders to prevent the conflict between Texas and Mexico from spilling over into the United States, had called upon the governors of several states (including Kentucky) to raise volunteers. In an executive order of August 7, 1836, Jackson had countermanded the requisition on the grounds that it violated U.S. neutrality, but he expressed the opinion that Congress should compensate those who had been called out for the losses they had incurred. See George L. Rives, *The United States and Mexico 1821-1848*, 2 vols. (New York, 1913), 1:372-80; *MPP*, 3:234-36.

The resolutions on this matter had passed the Kentucky house on December 9, 1836, and the senate the following day. The governor approved them on December 16, 1836, and Congressman James Harlan presented the petition to Congress on January 3, 1837. Ky. Sen., *Journal* . . . 1836-37, pp. 34, 41, 116; U.S. H. of Reps., *Journal*, 24 Cong., 1 Sess., 159-60. For Harlan, see 5:295 and *BDAC*.

To CORNELIUS VAN HORN[E][1]   Washington, January 30, 1837

I recd. this moment your letter of the 16h. instant,[2] and hasten to say that no bill has passed the H[ouse]. of R[epresentatives]. at the present Session for the relief of the early Adventurers in the West, as you had been lead to believe. A bill to that effect passed at the last Session the House, but did not receive the concurrence of the Senate. And I doubt now whether the subject will be acted on in either House.

ALS. PMCHi.   1. Cornelius Van Horne—farmer, lawyer, and miller—was the father of railroad executive William Cornelius Van Horne. See the son's entry in *DAB*. 2. Not found.

To BENJAMIN WATKINS LEIGH   Washington, February 4, 1837

I am curious to know what the General Assembly of Va. has done with you. If they have hung you, I wish you would direct your Executors to inform me when the ceremony was performed and how you bore it.[1] You will have seen that we are all expunged here.[2] How happy you are to be absent from a place where ignorance and folly, corruption and ruffians have undisputed sway! As for me, do you think that my Legislature had any right to tye me for six years to such a mass of putrefaction—to *such* a body as the Senate will be with *such* a head as it is likely to have for the next six years?[3]

But, to be more serious, the state of affairs here is bad enough, God knows. We have been now a week on a Land bill,[4] with the imposing title of restricting Sales to actual settlers &c &c. And every wild scheme of graduation, preemption, floats, cultivation &c. has been proposed, and some of them adopted. Instead of the Senators from Va. that State which made to the Genl Government one of the most magnificent Grants that ever was made, opposing with resolute firmness the waste of the Public Domain, Mr. [William C.] Rives[5] is lending himself to these nefarious projects. He appears to be resolved that his competitor Col. [Thomas Hart] Benton shall not get ahead of him, in appeals for the support of the new States.

The fate of the bill is uncertain, and seems to vary every day, and at different parts of almost every day. But it is here perfectly manifest that the Public Lands are to be the fund of influence and corruption upon which the new Administration and those who look to the succession intend to trade. So perfectly persuaded of this are some of the Opposition that they are almost willing to cede the lands at once to the new States, within which they are situated; believing that the political advantages from such a cession will be greater than any pecuniary benefit which will accrue to the Country by retaining *the* Public lands, as things are likely to be managed now. I cannot yet consent to such a desparate remedy.

How changed is the Senate, even in one short year! I am truly sad when I reflect on our losses in that brief period, and look upon those who supply their places.

Our hopes, if that word be not too strong to express the present state of our feelings, are now turned upon the H. of R.[6] There, if any where, must commence that reform, without which we shall be hurled, with accelerated rapidity, into utter ruin. All that I can say is God save the Commonwealth; for I am sure the Devil has now got hold of it. Whether his Infernal Majesty can be driven off or not, and whatever may happen, I pray you to be assured of the sincere regard and attachment of . . .

ALS. ViRVal.   1. While serving as a U.S. senator from Virginia, Leigh had vigorously supported the censure of President Jackson for the removal of government deposits from the Bank of the United States. When the general assembly in 1836 instructed the Virginia senators to vote for the resolution to expunge Jackson's censure, Leigh refused either to resign or to vote for the expunging resolution. He did, however, resign for personal reasons on July 4, 1836, and the general assembly subsequently passed resolutions of censure against him. See *DAB* and 8:820.   2. See 8:735; 9:12-14.   3. William R. King was president pro tempore of the Senate.   4. See 8:873; 9:6-7   5. For Rives, see 5:128-29 and *DAB*.   6. See 8:709.

To JAMES KENT[1]   Washington, February 22, 1837

I hasten to acknowledge, with cordial thanks and inexpressible satisfaction, the receipt of your obliging letter of the 20th. inst.[2] The opinions I have advanced, and the views which I have presented, in the Speech to which you have alluded,[3] could have received no approbation from any person *living* that would have given me more confidence in their truth and justness. Ah! how would I rejoice if the genuine patriotism, which prompts you to render this highly valued testimony, were more generally shared by my Countrymen. Ever hoping, never despairing, I yet trust that the days of delusion are numbered, and that we may *both* live, once more, to witness the Government of our beloved Country confided to the care of wise heads and honest hearts. Whatever may be our doom, I pray you to be assured of my high esteem, my affectionate attachment & my great admiration.

ALS. NNC.   1. For Kent, see 3:473 and *DAB*.   2. On Feb. 20, 1837, Kent had written Clay saying: "I cannot refrain from declaring my admiration of the Speech delivered by you in the Senate in January last [9:12-14] on the expunging resolution [8:735], & which is published at large in the [Washington *Daily*] National Intelligence[r] of the 16h. Inst." Adds that "My Sympathies, & Judgment, & confidence, & Patriotism, & Grief, & Indignation are with you on every point. . . . You have vindicated the resolution of 1834 with irresistable force, & damned the other to everlasting fame. If you, & such men as you, who are stemming despotism & servile meanness in the Senatorial Hall, have no other recompense, It may possibly give you some Consolation to be assured, that you are receiving the silent admiration & Gratitude of thousands." ALS. DLC-HC (DNA, M212, R5). Printed in Colton, *Clay Correspondence*, 4:411.   3. See 9:12-14.

From Charles M. Thruston *et al.*, Louisville, May 24, 1837. Explain that the citizens of Louisville are planning a public barbecue for Daniel Webster on May 30 and invite Clay to attend. Note that they see Clay "as the unrivalled advocate not only of" the country's "own great interests, but of the cause of human liberty throughout the world." Add that "Your prophetic voice has been often heard, but the people would not be warned; as a faithful sentinel, you pointed to the coming storm, and foretold its ravages. It has come, and desolation marks its track." Copy. Printed in Louisville *Daily Journal*, June 2, 1837. For Thruston, see 3:4.

To UNKNOWN RECIPIENT[1]   Washington, December 25, 1837

I duly received your favor of the 18th inst.,[2] and although pressed for time, by far the most valuable thing in my estimate, I cannot deny myself the pleasure of acknowledging its receipt, and of saying that I feel gratified with retaining a friendly place in your recollection.

We have passed through many political trials, during the last ten years. I thank God to be allowed to believe that they are drawing to a close. Light is bursting upon us from all quarters! and that from your state is the most cheering. New England, the home of the Pilgrims, the land of Revolutionary patriots, is becoming itself again.[3]

We must not allow ourselves to be distracted or to be defeated by Presidential Candidates. Our country first; our Country always. Every thing should be subordinate to its character, its institutions, and its glory. The spoilers have yet three years possession. Let us drive them out, and then the house can be put in order. But they can only be expelled by union, concert and perseverance.

I know not what our rulers will do—they will doubtless persist in their mad purposes of putting down the local institutions of our country putting down credit, putting down commerce, putting down industry. But the people will, I trust, put them down, and all their wicked schemes.

Copy. Printed in Cincinnati *Daily Gazette*, August 24, 1844.   1. The newspaper entry identifies the recipient only as "a gentleman of Portland." He is possibly J. Wingate, Jr. See 4:121-22.   2. Not found.   3. For recent elections in Connecticut, Rhode Island, and Massachusetts, see, respectively, 9:43, 59-60, 100.

To NAPOLEON B. MONTFORT[1]   Washington, February 13, 1838

I received your letter of the 9th instant,[2] with the constitution & by-laws of the Whig Association, in the 16th Ward of the City of New

York, which I have perused, with interest & attention. I thank the Association for the friendly consideration of me, which induced them to transmit these documents, & I sincerely hope that their anticipations of the regeneration of that ward may be realized.

The administration of the general government is completely organized, both for purposes of party & of government. If it at any time desire an expression of popular opinion to sustain its measures, there cannot be a doubt that suitable orders emanate from Washington to produce the desired expression. In order to effect[3] a change of Administration, & to transfer power from the hands of those who are abusing it, to the destruction of the best interests of the country, & to the danger of the public liberty, there must be counter organization—An organized party will almost always prevail against a party which acts without concert or co-operation. I am glad that the whigs of the 16th Ward have perceived & have acted upon this indisputable truth. And if throughout the city, and throughout the country, there should be similar associations, no doubt can exist of the ultimate triumph of the people. . . .

LS. KyLxT.   1. Montfort resided at "126 Water h. Ave. 4th C. Twenty ninth d." in 1837. Thomas Longworth, *Longworth's American Almanac: New-York Register, and City Directory* (New York, 1837).   2. The abbreviation "ult." has been crossed out by Clay and "instant" inserted. Letter not found.   3. The word "produce" has been crossed out and "effect" inserted.

From John Scott, Aberdeen, Scotland, February 20, 1838. Recalls having been introduced to Clay in the New York City Hall "a few years since." Launches into a long discussion of the continuing agitation in Great Britain over the slavery question, pointing out that the emancipation act of August 23, 1833, which abolished slavery in the British colonies [8:641] was but a "fond delusion" of the "*soi disant* philanthropists," and that "that condition of the negro in our West India islands is far worse than it was previously." Condemns the interference of British abolitionists, who pompously call themselves "*universal* emancipationists," in the slavery controversy in the United States, and regrets they have been joined and encouraged by American "immediate Abolitionists," such as Judge William Jay. Singles out George Thompson as "the great demagogue of our 'Emancipationists.'" Notes that Thompson appeals almost entirely to the "lower classes including a large proportion of females" who are "led on by excitement & influenced by the blind impulse of passion" rather than the "sober dictates of reason." Reports with regret that the once "flourishing Auxiliary" of the American Colonization Society in Aberdeen had been taken over by the emancipationists. Believes that the act of petitioning for the abolition of slavery, which, originates in the "northern United States" is a constitutional right "essential to the very existence of a free form of government"; but insists, nonetheless, that such petitions cannot be "regarded by the south in any other light than that of a premeditated insult." Assures Clay "that there exists not a nobler minded, more patriotic & truly generous race than the citizens of the *slaveholding* states," and expresses the conviction that the South would "forthwith & unanimously" abolish slavery "if it could be done without substituting in its place a greater evil." Condemns the radical abolitionists, British and American, at great length and for a variety of reasons. Mainly emphasizes the likelihood of social disintegration in the South that immediate abolition would bring. Asserts that only Clay has the "necessary qualifications" to "silence the common enemy." Particularly lauds his "intellectual capabilities," about "moral issu[es]."

Sees serious racial problems ahead in the British colonies as the result of the emancipation of the slaves there, since "No law human or *divine* will equalize them with the whites. The former cannot compel the lords of the soil to employ them rather than others nor force them to recognize them as their equal. And the divine law takes for granted the existence of different grades in society as a necessary part of civil & political economy." Believes that the danger of immediate abolitionism in the United States can be thwarted if "some one *state* say Maryland or Kentucky [would] set the example to the others" with a policy of gradual, compensated emancipation. "Angry debates & perilous collisions in Congress would thus be avoided." The main point is to shift the power and responsibility of emancipation from "individuals to a collective body. Whatever is done must be done *voluntarily.*" Adds: "I know the state of society in your southern & southwestern sections too well to suppose that any plan however rational judicious & advantageous for the extinction of slavery would not be opposed if introduced at first on too large a scale." Warns Clay that "The power to abolish slavery not residing in Congress only throws the greater individual responsibility on the states within which it exists. If it were once demonstrated that the feelings of the south with all their chivalry & generosity were converged to some specific point so as to evince their sincere desire to be rid of the evil on *fair* terms an appeal for assistance would be responded to from many a quarter. Slavery must terminate some time in America. It is an anomaly & should be extirpated. It was virtually doomed when so many noble signatures were put to the Declaration of Independence, that celebrated charter of the 'rights of man', & why should its reprieval be so long protracted." Argues that the beginning of action on emancipation would "throw the Abolitionists into the shade & neutralize their opposition . . . by thus presenting to their energies a safe channel & a legitimate object." Asserts in closing that the British need much more information of "this peculiar southern institution" to counteract the fact that "so much of our papers are occupied with the detestable nonsense & inflammatory trash of the Abolitionists." Lauds Clay for having adopted as his motto "in medio tutissimus," and assures him that "There the truth lies, & on this terra firma you will doubtless conquer. It is a difficult as well as a dangerous position to stand between two fires, but you remain as proof against the fiercest assaults & you have been accustomed to 'stand fire.'" ALS. DLC-HC (DNA, M212, R5). Endorsed by Clay on verso: "Aberdeen—Scotland—Abolition." Postmarked New York, June 25, 1838.

For John Scott (1798-1846), a surgeon in London, England, and George Thompson, a British abolitionist, see *DNB*. For William Jay, see 8:768 and *DAB*. For more on the emancipation of slaves in the British West Indies in 1833 and the apprenticeship system which followed, see Jack Gratus, *The Great White Lie; Slavery, Emancipation and Changing Radical Attitudes* (New York, 1973), 228-50; William A. Green, *British Slave Emancipation, the Sugar Colonies and the Great Experiment 1830-1865* (Oxford, 1976), 129-61; William L. Mathieson, *British Slavery and Its Abolition 1823-1838* (New York, 1926), 243-304.

To ISAAC BELL[1]   Washington, June 2, 1838

I received your friendly letter of the 30th ult.,[2] & it afforded me great satisfaction to find that I still enjoyed your confidence & esteem. Although I have felt it my duty to abstain from all interference in the designation of a candidate for the Presidency, I can but feel highly gratified with the demonstrations of public attachment towards me, which have from time to time been made, & with none more than that at the recent meeting in New York, at which you assisted.[3]

It is, indeed, my dear Sir, wonderful that the public affairs of a great people should have been so wretchedly administered as ours have been, & it is also very wonderful & at the same time, creditable to the people of this country, that they have borne themselves with so much patience. At last, however, light has broken in upon us, & I cordially congratulate you on the occasion.

LS. KyLoF.   1. For Bell, see 4:819-20.   2. Not found.   3. See 9:189-90.

To S. Lisle Smith, June 22, 1838. Thanks him for the friendly motives evident in his letter to Clay of June 4 [not found]. States: "There was no full report made of what I said during the progress of the Pre-emption Bill [9:114, 133-38] through the Senate and none which was corrected by me. The [Washington] Globe habitually misrepresents me, and I am compelled to believe sometimes from design—I *never used* THE WORDS 'They are a graceless set of robbers—land pirates, poor miserable preemptioners.' The language I used was substantially the same as that employed by Mr. [Martin] Van Buren in his message at the opening of the session [9:136]." Asserts that "I certainly made strenuous opposition to the passage of the Preemption Bill; I did it on principle, and from a serious sense of duty. I thought, and still think, that the Public Lands, which are the common property of all the people of the United States, ought not to be liable to be *trespassed upon* and seized and appropriated by any person who chooses to enter upon them, not only without the authority of law, but against its positive commands. The experience of the Government had satisfied me that a system of Preemptions, especially in connection with that of floats, *was perverted to the worst purposes of fraud, perjury and speculation.*" Adds that despite his aversion to the principle of preemption, "I should have cheerfully acquiesced in the late Preemption bill . . . *if its friends would have consented* to insert a clause terminating for ever that mode of disposing of the Public Lands; but that they refused to do."

Directs that this letter is "not for publication." Predicts that "I have outlived other calumnies, and, by the blessing of God, shall survive this and all others." Copy. Printed in New-York *Daily Tribune,* September 12, 1844. Smith has not been identified.

To JONATHAN THOMPSON   Lexington, November 19, 1838
I have very great pleasure in acknowledging the receipt of your friendly letter of the 8h. inst.[1] addressed to me at Louisville and which I have just got here. The intelligence, which it communicates, and which has been confirmed through a variety of other friendly channels, as to the issue of the Election in N. York,[2] has filled me with inexpressible joy. The Republic is herself again; and we may proudly look forward to the fulfillment of her high destiny. I think that other people now will find the necessity of repairing their fences, as well as you and I, and I trust that they will 'ere long be sent home on that errand, which is much too good to expect of *them.*

The Whigs have now, with the blessing of God, the fate of the Country in their hands; and if they do not foolishly exhaust their power, in idle divisions among themselves, about this or that individual, they may bear it through gloriously. N. York, to which we all look with high satisfaction, should take the lead, which she so well deserves to take, and decide the future. Moderation, Conciliation and decision, but above all firmness and *decision* should be our course. May it be guided by wisdom and lead to victory!

ALS. KyLoF.   1. Not found.   2. See 9:151, 216-17.

To W. L. SLONE[1]   Washington, January 11, 1839

I recd. your two favors,[2] in regard to the wish of Mr. [Lewis P.] Clover to obtain my portrait for the purpose of having it engraved.[3] The artists (I am sure without their fault) have so often failed in producing a correct likeness of me, and I have so frequently sat to them that I have become almost as tired of the experiment as I am of some other *experiments* in our Country. But I cannot decline acceding to the request of Mr. C. especially as, in making the picture, he is good enough to offer to consult my convenience as to the time and place of my sitting. If the artist therefore will call on me, I will endeavor to arrange with him the meetings between us in a manner mutually satisfactory.[4]

ALS. KyLoF.   1. Not identified.   2. Not found.   3. For Clover (1819-96)—painter, engraver, and later an Episcopal clergyman—see George C. Groce & David H. Wallace, *The New-York Historical Society's Dictionary of Artists in America 1564-1860* (New Haven, 1957), 132. No portrait or engraving of Clay by Clover has been found.   4. Clay wrote Lewis P. Clover on June 1, 1839, stating that he had received Clover's letter [not found] "requesting my opinion of the portrait taken of me by Mr. [George] Linen last winter." Thinks "it was uncommonly good; and several of my friends . . . pronounced it the most accurate of any of me which they had seen." Adds that Linen "was more fortunate, in catching a good expression, than most Artists who had preceded him." ALS. KyLoF. For Linen, see 9:371.

To HORACE GREELEY[1]   Washington, February 11, 1839

I concur in thinking that the proposed pamphlet[2] on the public lands will be attended with excellent effect; but I regret that I cannot supply the documents you request. I have been so often written to for copies that my store is completely exhausted. I can point out however where you can obtain them.

    1st. My report in 1832[3]
    2. My Speech——[4]
    3. Jacksons Veto message returning the Land bill 1833[5]
    4. My report upon it.[6]
All these you can find in Niles's Register.

    My Speeches at this and several preceding Sessions have not been reported, with the exception of one at the last Session on the graduation bill,[7] which I think your pamphlet ought to include.

    My impression is very strong that the pamphlet will do much good.

ALS. ViU.   1. For Greeley, see 9:371, 890, and *DAB*.   2. Pamphlet not found.   3. See 8:494.   4. See 8:539-41.   5. See 8:610.   6. See 8:671.   7. See 9:170-71.

To A. A. HUNTINGTON[1]   Lexington, March 14, 1839

During the late Session of Congress, I omitted to acknowledge the receipt of your favor,[2] in consequence of the pressure of my necessary duties and engagements. I now take pleasure, in compliance with your request, in transmitting my Autograph. I also send you a Copy of a Speech which I addressed to the Senate, from a perusal of which you will perceive the sentiments I entertain on the subject of Slavery and

Abolition.[3] I dare not hope that these sentiments will be concurred in unanimously by my fellow Citizens; but they are conscientious convictions of my deliberate judgment.

ALS. CtHi.   1. Not identified.   2. Not found.   3. See 9:278-83.

To MARY S. BAYARD[1]   Lexington, May 3, 1839

I was this moment greatly shocked by reading in the [Washington *Daily*] Nat[*ional*] Intell[*igence*]r. an account of the sudden death of our estimable friend Dr. [Aaron] Tucker, on his way to Frederick.[2] Is it true? I should address myself directly to Mrs Tucker, instead of you, and convey to her the sincere condolence of a warm friend both of her and her late husband, if I knew where to send my letter. In this ignorance, I pray you to be the organ and interpreter of my feelings, and to say to her how deeply I deplore her bereavement, and how truly I sympathize with her. The event must have been inconceivably shocking to her. In the Cars of the Rail Road! Then so sudden. On their way, I presume, to visit Mrs. [Gideon] Lee;[3] and full of agreeable anticipations of a pleasant sojourn at Needwood. Uh! how treacherous and uncertain is this existence of ours! You know how often and how late I have had occasion to feel the force of this melancholy truth; for you have favored me with your friendly sympathy.

I reached home exactly one week after I parted from Mr. [Richard Henry] Bayard[4] and you at the Relay House; and here I have been quietly ever since. I find the occupations which Ashland affords are much more agreeable than those of the Senate Chamber, although not always free from hazard; for four days ago I received a very severe kick from a horse that has lamed me a little, without fracturing either flesh or bone. It was within an inch of my knee bone which would have been broken into fragments if it had been struck, so violent was it.[5]

I hope this letter will find Mr. Bayard and your dear children all in good health. Do me the favor to remember me to him & to them in the kindest manner.

AL. DeHi.   1. For Mary Bayard, see 9:311.   2. For Tucker and his death, see 9:311.   3. See Gideon Lee article in *NCAB*, 5:423.   4. For Bayard, see 9:311 and *DAB*.   5. This is the injury referred to in 9:311.

To BENJAMIN WATKINS LEIGH   Lexington, June 12, 1839

Concurring accounts which have reached me assure me of the entire re-establishment of your health. No friend that you have rejoices more cordially and sincerely than I do on the occasion; and I trust that you will long live to enjoy that first of blessings.

We have been much alarmed about the issue of your recent Elections.[1] Late intelligence has however dissipated our fears, and satisfied us that, if your triumph has not been equal to all our hopes, you have sustained no defeat. That it might have been more decisive, if there could have been, every where in Virginia, a more perfect cooperation between the Whigs and Conservatives,[2] is now clear, although it may not be so clear how that co-operation was to be effected.

Judging from what I have heard of in other States and witnessed in my own, I should say that it is essential to future success in Virginia that the Opposition should be completely organized. That was the condition of the other party, at the late election, and I have no doubt that they profited by it. Our friends were enabled to animadvert successfully on some of the elements which composed their Convention;[3] and certainly it was shockingly indecent and unbecoming in Judges &c to take part in its proceedings; but, after making every abatement for this reprehensible structure of it, I have no doubt that they derived material advantage from it. It may be assumed, I think, as a truth, both in war and politics, that, when contending forces are nearly balanced, that which, being disciplined, acts in concert, the other not being organized, will prevail in the struggle.

If these views are correct, should you not forthwith proceed to organize the whole State and every County and City? Can you succeed without Conventions, Committees of Correspondence, Vigilance &c? I am aware that to some extent this has been done; but is the organization perfect? I have heard of no general Convention of the Whigs, no Convention of the old men and of the young men. These Conventions collect information, create acquaintance, produce excitement and beget zeal. They affect also the pride and vanity of men. To be a member of one of these bodies is a distinction, of which, perhaps unfortunately for poor human nature, too many of us are disposed to be flattered with. But, dismissing all exceptionable feelings, I think there is no doubt that there is a real utility in these agencies. They enable a party to disseminate genuine information and to ascertain its actual strength.

We have a great struggle before us, involving, perhaps, the fate of our institutions. Most certainly, if we are beaten in it, I shall despair of any salutary change, during my life. We never expect again to have such great advantages in the contest. It is our duty then to employ all honorable means to insure success. And I cannot but think that, if that which I have taken the liberty to suggest, is used, the exertions of the Whigs of Virginia will be crowned with victory.

We are getting along pretty well in this State, a little embarrassed by the question of the So. Carolina Bank;[4] but I believe that we shall return to Congress the same number of Whigs that we did to the last, *possibly* with one exception. From Tennessee we have the most gratifying intelligence.[5] I hear but little from Ohio[6] or Indiana.[7]

There is now a fair prospect of the next H[ouse]. of R[epresentatives]. opening with a majority against the Administration of thirty. Against that single fact, provided the advantage be properly improved, it cannot stand. But we should make, if we can, assurance doubly sure; and hence it is incumbent upon us, I think, to omit no arrangement nor the performance of any duty which may contribute to the salvation of the Country. . . .

ALS. ViRVal. Letter marked "(Confidential)."   1. See 9:296.   2. For the "Conservatives," see 9:20.   3. See 9:302.   4. The charter of the Louisville, Cincinnati & Charleston Railroad [9:224-25] had been amended by the South Carolina legislature to give the railroad company banking privileges. The application to the Kentucky legislature in 1838 for the bank charter had failed by six votes and had failed again in Jan.,

1839. The issue remained devisive within the Whig party as the Democrats attempted to make the 1839 Kentucky elections turn on the question of "bank or no bank." Louisville *Daily Journal*, March 23, 28, and 29, 1839; Samuel M. Derrick, *Centennial History of South Carolina Railroad* (Columbia, S.C., 1930), 138-75. 5. See 9:316-17. 6. See 9:308. 7. *Ibid.*

To NATHANIEL BEVERLEY TUCKER

Lexington, October 10, 1839

Since my return home, I have received the letter which you addressed to me on the 10th ult.[1] Mr. [Henry A.] Wise[2] correctly reported to you the opinion I entertain on the several public matters mentioned in your letter: 1st, That I think the compromise of the tariff[3] ought to be maintained without violation. I have invariably defended it when assailed in the Senate, and declared my purpose to abide by it. When attacked, it has been by gentlemen from the North, professing to be friendly to Southern interests, or by Col. [Thomas Hart] Benton, or by gentlemen from the South. I have supposed the South much more interested than the North in keeping that controversy closed by the compromise. In the origin of the protective policy, it was never supposed by me or by others of its friends, as far as I know their views, that it was to be permanent. We intended it to be temporary, so as to enable the American manufacturers to get through their infancy, and to maintain something like an equal competition with foreign. If asked at that period whether we required a longer duration to the policy than the year 1843, when the compromise will take complete effect, I think no one would have demanded it; 2nd, I have repeatedly stated to the Senate, that considering what had been done by Congress for the States in the Distribution bill,[4] and what had been done by the States themselves in the prosecution of their own systems of internal improvements, I thought it inexpedient that Congress should continue to exercise that power by commencing any new work; and that all that I ever wished now to see done by Congress was to pass the bill to distribute the net proceeds of the public lands among all the States, leaving to their exclusive care the general subject of internal improvements; 3rd, I have said, again and again, and most sincerely hold, that the patronage of the general government, as exercised by the late and present administration, is fraught with imminent danger to the institutions and liberty of the country. I believe that, unless its exercise be restricted and controlled in the hands of the executive, our system will rapidly degenerate into an elective monarchy, or rather, what is a great deal worse, that the incumbent monarch will be able, by means of it, and by other corrupt influences, to designate his successor.[5] I wish that we may not have actually arrived at this point. I believe that the power of removal[6] is a subject of legitimate legislation; and that the concession of it to the president, by the Congress of 1789, was as unwarranted by the Constitution as it has proved, and is likely still more to be, pernicious in practice.

Copy, excerpt. Printed in Lyon Gardiner Tyler, *The Letters and Times of the Tylers*, 2 vols. (Richmond, Va., 1884), 1:601-2.   1. For Tucker, see 7:251 and *DAB*.   2. For Wise, see 9:20 and *BDAC*.   3. See 8:604, 619-21, 626-27.   4. See 9:167, 170-71, 251. 5. See 8:559-60, 703, 727.   6. See 8:703.

To WILLIAM TOMPKINS[1]　　　　Lexington, October 12, 1839

I duly received your favor of the 3d. inst.[2] I received a letter from Genl [William Henry] Harrison,[3] after my return home, in answer to the one which I had addressed to him,[4] on my passage through Ohio, to which you refer. It was written in the most friendly spirit, expressing his great satisfaction with mine, stating that he had never expected to be thrown into a competition with me, whose election he *had* desired, that he had never aspired to any thing higher than the second office, but that his *destiny* had cast him into his present position &c. I sent the letter to Mr [Benjamin Watkins] Leigh of Richmond, or I would transmit it to you for your perusal. He does not say, in terms, that he will abide by the nomination of the Convention, but that is clearly to be inferred from the tenor of the letter.

The results of the elections of this year are discouraging; and if they should continue throughout so, especially if that of N. York should be adverse,[5] it will be very questionable whether the nomination of the Whig Convention will be worth accepting by any one, to whom it may be offered.[6] These results shew that every where the Administration party has gained upon us. From them we may infer than some *general* cause has been in active operation. What is it? Have the people changed and become reconciled to the Sub treasury? I think not. What then is it? I confess to you, I fear, that besides the known contributions which have been levied upon the office holders, the Administration has put its hands, in its desperation, freely into the public treasury, and taken out hundreds of thousands of dollars to use in purposes of corruption. In every State, whilst the mass is pure and sound, there are corruptible voters enough, sufficient to turn the scale if all thrown into it. The Administration is in the market for them, without any competitor. And, if my fear be well founded, the calculation was that, if successful, they can conceal the peculation and fraud by complicating public accounts. It is remarkable that, whilst the Whig vote has every where been maintained or nearly so, all the increase is on the other side. Is this probable, upon any supposition of honesty and fairness? It is also remarkable that some states and districts which resisted and stood firmly up, during the admon of Genl [Andrew] Jackson seem to be giving way or tottering under that of his confessedly less popular successor. I am apprehensive that an observation, which I long ago made, is about to be realized, that was, that Jackson ruled by intimidation, and [Martin] V[an]. Buren would by corruption. I have no *sufficient* evidence of the truth of these apprehensions, although I have heard of some startling circumstances.

I have seen with great pleasure the proceedings of the Staunton Convention,[7] and I trust that they will tend to arouse the people of our native State to a due sense of the dangers which encompass them. The resolutions of Mr. Leigh,[8] describing the Mal-administration of the Government, are very ably drawn. They are clear, condensed and energetic. I hope they will be followed by a complete organization of every County in the State. If we succeed, we must reconcile all divisions, surrender minor to main points, take off our coats and roll up our sleeves to our shoulders, and resolve to conquer or to die. Our

277

misfortune is that we have weak stomachs; our opponents have the stomachs of Storks.

A fine spirit is prevailing in Tennessee, and they write me in great confidence that they will recover the lost ground. There, unquestionably, the most detestable frauds have been committed on the Elective franchise.[9] There was an irruption of voters, from Alabama. Nine men are stated to have voted eighty one times! If it be criminal to violate an existing law how much more severe ought to be the punishment for corrupting the very sources of legislation!

ALS. ViU. Letter marked "(Confidential)." 1. For Tompkins, a Louisville teacher and librarian, see Johnston, *Memorial History of Louisville*, 1:69, 173. 2. Not found. 3. See 9:342-43. 4. Not found. 5. See 9:174. 6. See 9:92, 117, 362-65. 7. See 9:258. 8. See 9:351. 9. See 9:317.

To BENJAMIN WATKINS LEIGH   Lexington, November 17, 1839

I recd. your favor[1] returning the letters of Genl. [William Henry] Harrison[2] which it had not been my intention to trouble you with doing. I have heard nothing since their date from him; but I should suppose that subsequent political events had inspired him and his friends, as they ought to inspire all of us, with a spirit of moderation & resignation.

The state of our information here is such as to cast a little brighter prospect on public affairs than that which they wore some weeks ago. We suppose, from the tenor of it, that we have gained the State,[3] by a small majority, altho' we have lost the City,[4] of N. York; and that the Whigs may have triumphed in Michigan.[5] From Mississippi[6] we have as yet nothing, and nothing good do I anticipate from it, altho' I shall be glad if it come.

I shall leave home on thursday next for Washn. City, where I hope to arrive on the saturday preceding the commencement of the Session. I should be pleased to intercept & meet you there on your way to Harrisburg. I have much to say to you. In the mean time, I transmit under another cover, a document or two which may deserve your perusal. That from N. York shows the predominance and activity of the spirit of intrigue.[7] An anonymous printed circular, from an assumed *friend of mine,* to influence the Whigs of N. York *against* me![8] As if any single individual, much less an anonymous one, could know more and decide wiser, than the Convention, bringing together the information which prevails in all the localities of the whole Union![9]

I was highly gratified with the proceedings of the Staunton Convention.[10] The composition of the resolutions was happy;[11] presenting, in a short compass, but in a vigorous and comprehensive form, the numerous misdeeds of the Administration. They constitute an admirable text, on which the press and the politician may dwell with profit and advantage.

I think we can yet beat these Goths & Spoilers, if we will pull off our Coats, roll up our sleeves, and go to work like men, resolved to conquer or to die. Any why should we not do this? Every thing is at stake which should animate patriotism and banish despair. But I forbear. I hope to see you at Washn. . . .

ALS. ViRVal.   1. Not found.   2. See 9:342-43.   3. See 9:174.   4. See 9:301.
5. On Nov. 4, 1839, Whig William Woodbridge had defeated Democrat E. Farnsworth for
the Michigan governorship by a vote of 18,195 to 17,037. *BDGUS*, 2:742. Also, the Michigan legislature in 1839 chose Whig Augustus S. Porter for the U.S. Senate. *Guide to U.S.
Elections*, 467.   6. See 9:299.   7. See 9:288.   8. Not found.   9. See 9:92, 117,
362-65.   10. See 9:258.   11. See 9:351; Clay to Tompkins, Oct. 12, 1838.

To PIERRE VAN CORTLANDT, JR.[1]

Lexington,
November 25, 1839

I recd. your favor of the 11th. inst.[2] and most cordially reciprocate the
congratulations which it contains on the recent glorious issue of the N.
York election.[3] It has filled me with astonishment and inexpressible
pleasure. Your State has now established her right to be considered the
Empire State by a much nobler title than any which mere courtesy or
custom could confer—by shewing that she deserves it.

May the great event lead to the revival of National prosperity and
lend to the perpetuity of free institutions.

Copy. Printed in Jacob Judd (ed.), *The Van Cortlandt Family Papers*, 4 vols. (Tarrytown,
N.Y., 1981), 4:292.   1. For Van Cortlandt (1762-1848), see *ibid.*, 3:xxxv-xlix and
BDAC.   2. Not found.   3. See 9:151, 256.

To JOHN STRODE BARBOUR[1]

Washington,
December 14, 1839

I am sorry to learn from your favor just received that you are still confined to your chamber.

The nomination at Harrisburg[2] appears to have produced elsewhere the same surprise that it ex[ci]ted[3] with you. It has however been
made by the representative body to which the subject was confided.
And no alternative remains to me but to acquiesce in it. This I do, and
I shall give it my support in good faith and with honor. What will be
the issue of the contest I cannot tell, but, be that what it may, the path
of my duty cannot be changed. The indications of acquiescence and
approval, among the Whigs, so far have been general and apparently
cordial.

I think it probable that the House will appoint a Speaker today.[4]

Copy. Courtesy of Mary Lightfoot Dunford, Wake, Va.   1. Addressed to Barbour at
"Catalpa," near Culpeper Court House, Va. It is possible, though not probable, that
this letter was addressed to John Strode Barbour, Jr., then age 18. For the J.S. Bar-
bours, father and son, see *BDAC*.   2. See 9:92, 117.   3. Word may read "created."
4. Robert M.T. Hunter (Va.) was elected Speaker on Dec. 16, 1839. *BDAC*.

To Henry S. Randall, New York, *ca.* 1840s. Reports that "I was induced to
discontinue breeding the Herefords in consequence of an apprehension that I
should breed in-and-in too far, which in some instances I found to be the case.
I could not obtain, conveniently, crosses from other females of the same race."

Writes again on a later occasion that "My opinion is that the Herefords
make better work cattle, are hardier, and will, upon being fattened, take themselves to market better than their rivals. They are also fair milkers. On the
other hand, the Durhams, I think, have the advantage of earlier maturity, in
beauty and in the quantity of milk which they will yield. They will also attain
great size and weight. . . . If one has rich, long and luxuriant grass, affording a
good bite, and has not too far to drive to market, he had better breed the

Durhams, otherwise the Herefords." Copy, extracts from two undated letters. Printed in Alvin H. Sanders, *The History of the Herefords* (Chicago, 1914), 266. Randall was a leading agricultural writer. *Ibid.*

Statement of Assets, *ca.* 1840s. Listed are: Ashland, consisting of 515 acres at $80 per acre, $41,200; 46 slaves, estimated at $250 each, $11,500; stock of all kinds, $5,000; furniture, plate, wines, $7,500; house and lot in Lexington, $10,000; Mansfield, 120 acres at $50, $6,000; Combs lot 38 acres at $60, $2,280; 1,500 acres of land in Illinois, $12,000; 680 acres between the Mississippi and Missouri rivers, $6,800; cash funds at New Orleans, $9,000; 400 acres in Ohio, $2,000; good debts due me, $2,000; state bonds $1,200 at 7.5, $800; Frankfort Bridge stock ($4,500), Maysville Road stock ($1,800), Lexington & Richmond Road ($1,000), and Winchester & Danville ($400), all estimated at $2,000 total; Northern Bank stock ($600) at $450; unimproved lot near Col. William Brands, $600; one-third of 2,000 acres of land including mills near Frankfort held with Thomas Smith, $1,500; cash in bank, $1,400; interest in the old Medical Hall, _____ ; two bonds in James Erwin's hand, exclusive of interest due thereon, $4,000 and $1,000. Total $127,030. AD. DLC-HC (DNA, M212, R6).

Document is undated but must have been written after the purchase of the Frankfort Bridge stock in November, 1840. See 9:451.

From Albert T. Burnley, Louisville, January 25, 1840. With hesitation, suggests "a few things which my observation in Europe, induced me to believe ought to influence the action of our National Legislature." Notes that the states "of this Union" have an aggregate debt in Europe of over $150 million and that "the credit of these securities is now depreciated to a point which is ruinous to the purchases, while it is injurious to the character, and mortifying to the feelings of every American." Since this "discredit of American Securities" defeated "the immediate object of my mission to Europe," considers the possible "*causes* of that discredit." Asserts that it is not because of a general scarcity of money, because England and Holland, with much greater debts than the U.S. can borrow money at lower interest. Believes this results from the fact that England and Holland never borrow money without providing "a specific, adequate, & certain fund out of which to pay the Interest promptly, & generally, to redeem gradually the principal," while states in the U.S. have borrowed "without ever Seeming to think of how principal & Interest were to be paid." Moreover, much which the states have borrowed has been "invested in unprofitable and injudicious works—And the only Security for a prompt payment of principal and Interest, was to be looked for from the firmness of our State Legislatures in taxing the people directly & heavily—This was not thought very good Security, & these stocks fell in value."

Recommends as the only means for restoring credit, that the states tax their citizens "heavily at once, for a Sufficient Sum . . . to pay promptly the accruing Interest, & gradually to discharge the principal." Adds, however, that "From what I have seen of State Legislatures, *I do not believe they will be found to have the courage to do it.*" Thus, "I know no other but for the *Genl. Government to assume all the state Debts,*" though "I am aware that there are *many* objections to that course." Further, believes "This measure might also . . . be made instrumental in establishing the *principles* of your Land Bill [8:539-41, 609-10] . . . and unless the public Lands are pledged for some special purpose very Soon, I think all the indications are, that it will be squandered away to aid in making some man President." Also, suggests an amendment to the U.S. Constitution preventing states from borrowing in the future.

Reports that the letters Clay provided him before his trip to Europe "were of much service to me" and "enabled me to procure for Texas a fair hearing." Reports that "We procured an advance of $400.000 for Texas before leaving the United States [9:227]." ALS. DLC-John J. Crittenden Papers. For Burnley, see 9:226-27.

To BENJAMIN WATKINS LEIGH
Washington,
February 17, 1840

I have received your favor of yesterday.[1] It was my most anxious wish, if I went to Richmond, to be allowed to go there quietly, without any parade on my account. Why will you not allow me to do so? I have no doubt of the kindness towards me which prompts a desire for public manifestations; but *you*, I think, ought to conceive that state of *my* feelings which impels me to prefer the avoidance of all ostentatious display.

Mr. [James] Lyons[2] wrote me something about a Public dinner, and the wish, which prevailed, to put it off from this to the next week. If I were to be prevented by a public dinner, I was for the longest day, and wrote him that I *submittted* to any postponement, prefering, as I will say to you, that it should be indefinite.

Before I heard from Mr. Lyons, I had thought of leaving Washn. for Richmond on thursday; but, now, I will not go until friday, altho' I don't like that hangman's day. I shall proceed in the Car directly to Richmond, without stopping in Hanover, which I purpose visiting during my sojourn in Virginia.[3]

ALS. ViRVal. Letter marked "(Private)." 1. Not Found. 2. Letter not found, but for Lyons, see 9:424-25. 3. See 9:386, 392.

To ALEXANDER HAMILTON, JR.[1]
Washington, June 30, 1840

I received your favor of yesterday,[2] and, contrary to Mrs. Hamilton's prediction, I have just attentively read the whole of it. It is all worthy of consideration, altho I differ with you in several particulars, which I have not time to discuss. In truth, my dear sir, the Presidential contest absorbs every thing else. If [William Henry] Harrison be elected, there will be some hopes, if [Martin] V[an]. Buren, none for the Country.[3]

I should be very glad to possess the whole of the volumes, containing the Biography and works of your father.[4] Whilst our Country remains, he will be remembered as among its most distinguished Statesmen. Of his ability and his patriotism none ought to doubt. He entertained some opinions which, if he had lived to this time, he would have modified or corrected; and those, who disagreed with him, on other points, have found that he was not as far from the mark as they were.

I would not trouble you to send me the work, as I shall probably be able to purchase it at the Bookstores of Lex[ingto]n near which I reside.

I pray you to communicate my warm regards to Mrs. H.

Copy. DSI. 1. For Hamilton, see 9:47. 2. Not found. 3. For the election, see 9:263. 4. *The Works of Alexander Hamilton . . .* , 3 vols. (New York, 1810).

Speech in Senate, January 6, 1841. Speaks to Sen. John J. Crittenden's January 5 amendment to the permanent preemption system bill [9:463-64] that would permit aliens who declare their intention to become naturalized citizens to enjoy the right of preemption provided in the proposed legislation. Criticizes the lack of a termination date in the substitute bill introduced by Sen. Samuel Prentiss (Vt.) which would otherwise raise the minimum age of preemptors to 21, exclude widows from such right, and require the potential preemptor actually to be resident on the land for four months preceding the final enactment of this legislation. Also attacks Sen. Silas Wright (N.Y.) for asserting yesterday, during his defense of the right of aliens to preempt public land, that each state has the power to prescribe suffrage qualifications for its own residents, even to the point, in Clay's words, that "it is competent to a state under the Constitution to admit an unnaturalized foreigner to vote in our elections." Flatly denies the existence of such state power. This power, Clay asserts, is held exclusively by the general government under the Constitution. Points out that [Martin] Van Buren had carried Illinois in the recent presidential election, thanks to the votes of "unnaturalized foreigners" there [9:444-45].

Remarks that he has not taken the floor to discuss the issue of voting by aliens, but to deal with "the fearful extension now proposed to be given to the pre emption system. We have now had a land system in operation for upwards of forty years. Is there any thing in the practical effect of this old and long tried system which should induce us to repudiate it for a new, untried, and wild experiment?" Refers to the success of the nation's public land policy these past 40 years in terms of encouraging population growth, and discusses the origin of the practice of preemption in Ohio, Louisiana, Illinois, and Indiana during the early years of the century. Discusses also the history of the Preemption Act of 1830 and the biennial renewals of it from 1832 to 1840 [9:133-35]. Explains that "The pre-emption laws, as altered in 1830 allowed a right of pre-emption to all settlers on the public lands from a specified day, who should assert their rights before the expiration of the law, the operation of which was limited to two years. This new principle continued to be periodically re-enacated till some seven or eight years ago." But since the renewal of the 1830 act in 1838, advocates of preemption, "not satisfied with pre-emption laws restricted in point of time, and limited as to the theatre on which they were to operate.... have suddenly become converts to log cabin doctrine, and, under a log cabin profession, they demand the passage of a new law, boundless in the space on which it is to operate, or restricted only by the limits of the public lands themselves, and illimitable as to time." This lack of space and time limitations can only benefit land speculators. Also, the legislation now proposed would place 120,000,000 acres of surveyed public land, no matter how long in the market, and in spite of a modest purchase price of $1.25 an acre, under the right of preemption. It is obvious that this involves "a complete change in our whole land system; a thorough, radical, entire change. It opens at once all the public lands, surveyed, and unsurveyed, to the operation of a pre-emption law." Calls attention to Van Buren's annual message to Congress in December, 1837, in which the president had praised "the old land system [9:136]," criticized trespassers and intruders upon the public land, and called for one final preemption law that would better handle the squatter problem. Believes, however, that Van Buren and Secretary of the Treasury Levi Woodbury have recently opened "their ears to the counsels of gentlemen who are strong advocates for pre-emption laws and for the practical appropriation of the public domain to the benefit of a few." Scoffs at the notion that the administration can increase total federal revenue from public land sales by reducing prices from $1.25 to 25 or 50 cents per acre. Charges also that the administration seeks to convert the existing cash system into a credit system, in that under the proposed law the preemptor will get a two year stay of payment, that is, "a credit of two years." Asks: "And who are they who propose this change? The very men who decry all credit, who clamor for hard money, who inveigh against banks, and denounce the credit system as the source of all our woes! and yet here, now, under the name of a pre-emption law, they propose to revive the whole credit system! Can it be doubted that such will be the result of the bill? Will any man, who can get his land on a credit of one or two years, buy it for cash?—especially when he can dispose of his cash at a rate of 18 per cent. interest, as prevails in Illinois and some other new States?" Denies the contention of the preemption advocates that the difference effected by this proposed preemption law in the level of receipts from the public land would be a reduction of only "some two or three cents per acre." Explains at length the peculiar bookkeeping that permits the treasury to arrive at this unrealistic figure.

Argues, in addition, that an outgoing administration should not attempt to push through such important legislation in its final few months, complaining that unlike the practice of constitutional governments in Europe, "here an Administration *may be dismissed and still remain four months in power.*" Remarks that after President John Quincy Adams was defeated in 1828, the Senate, controlled by the opposition, "refused to pass on important Executive nominations till after the 4th of March, and then several of them were withdrawn, and substitutes sent in by the new President. The Senate refused him the constitutional exercise of his official right from the time of his lost election till he went out of office." Hopes the Whigs will not now do this to Van Buren; but assures the Democrats that "General [William Henry] Harrison means to be the *President*" when he takes power on March 4 and that "no premature bill, no stretching out of the [patronage] policy of this into the next Administration" will deter him from deciding who will be appointed or reappointed and who discharged from public office. Thinks, also, that the preemption question should be postponed until after the 1840 census figures are available so that the population of the western states can be known and "we may judge whether any further stimulation is needed to quicken the rate" of increase of settlers to those states. Suggests also that the postponement of preemption would be wise because there may well be significant increases in the value of some public lands in the near future.

Criticizes the provisions in the proposed bill dealing with the administrative machinery for handling disputed land claims. Indeed, the bill provides that claims "shall be settled 'summarily' and definitely by the register and receiver of the land district in which the dispute arises, these officers to decide under instructions from the Commissioner of the General Land Office. So, the disputant is put under the register and receiver; the register and receiver are under the Commissioner; the Commissioner is under the Secretary of the Treasury, and the Secretary is under the President. Thus, you add immensely to the mass of Executive power, by drawing within its vortex all the disputed claims through all the land districts." Argues that putting such judicial power in the hands of registers and receivers is unconstitutional, and notes the obvious "temptation" thus placed before "public officers so situated."

Sen. Silas Wright, in response to Clay, argues again, and at some length, the case for the exercise of states' rights in the constitutional area of permitting resident aliens to vote in national elections. He also chides Clay for his reference to the treatment John Quincy Adams had received on patronage appointments from Democrats in the final four months of his administration. He points out that the situation then and now was quite different in that the Democrats had achieved majorities in both houses two years before the defeat of Adams, not during the same year of that defeat. Hence, they were merely beginning to implement policies long urged and anticipated by the people.

In response to this, Clay recalls that the Van Buren administration had pushed through its "Sub-Treasury scheme" in July, 1840 [9:75-80, 145-48,

378-82], a scheme that was "*their* measure, and not the measure of the people whom they represent." Asks Wright to bow now to the "Democracy of numbers" which he espouses and renounce his support of that legislation since it has been condemned by a majority of New York's 400,000 voters in the recent presidential election. Says that were he Senator Wright, "I will tell what I would do. So help me God, on my sacred honor, I would move to repeal the Sub-Treasury law. I would not say that I had changed my opinion—my pride of principle would prevent that—but, finding the measure not acceptable to my constituents, I would conform to their will."

Concludes with extensive remarks on the constitutionality of state laws which permit a resident alien to vote for national officers, noting that "this case of unnaturalized foreigners is an exception to the otherwise universal exercise of the State sovereignty." Also warns Wright that he is foolish to believe that preemption is so popular that if this bill passes it would be very difficult to repeal. "Why, sir, I should think that after setting land traps for the people for these twelve years past and all in vain, the Senator and his party would not be so very sanguine in their expectations of the success of a new one. You have had all these traps for the popular favor for a period now of twelve years, and what have you got by them? About as much as you are, likely to get hereafter: you have got four out of nine land States! The more traps you set, the fewer States you will catch. . . . HONESTY is the best POLICY." *Cong. Globe,* 26 Cong., 2 Sess., Appendix, 28-30, 32. This speech was introduced in the *Globe* with the caveat: "Mr. CLAY of Kentucky now rose and addressed the Senate nearly as follows." *Ibid.,* 28. This speech was inadvertently omitted from volume 9, where cross-references to it appear.

For Samuel Prentiss and Silas Wright, see *BDAC.* For further action on this legislation, see 9:464.

From William Hickey, Office of Secretary of the Senate, March 29, 1841. Sends, with apologies for the delay due to the closing of the legislative session, extracts of speeches of Elias Kent Kane, John C. Calhoun, and Thomas Hart Benton on the bill in 1833 "appropriating the proceeds of the public lands for a limited time [8:494, 539-41, 610, 671]" and "extracts and references shewing the sentiments of General [Andrew] Jackson, while President, respecting the tariff." Hopes that "no inconvenience has resulted to The Hon. Mr. Clay and that no other retribution may be awarded than a frequent repetition of such calls, which are appreciated as conferring honor and which it is hoped can be more promptly responded to hereafter." ALS. CLU.

For Hickey, see 10:803; for Kane, see 4:198 and *BDAC.*

To BENJAMIN WATKINS LEIGH
Wheeling, Va. (W. Va.),
March 29, 1841

Your familiarity with the Laws and decisions of the Courts of Virginia prompts me to trouble you with an enquiry, which I shall be greatly obliged if you will transmit me an answer to, directed to Lexington.[1]

By the Law of K[entucky]., as copied from that of Virginia, an interested party is allowed by bill in Ch[ancer]y. to contest the validity of a Will, which had been previously proved & admitted to record. The Statute directs the issue to be tried, that is whether the writing be the last will and testament of the testator or not. Now I understand that, according to the invariable practice of your Courts, no issue is permitted to be made up & submitted to the Jury, but that specific issue, which is prescribed by the statute. What I wish to be informed of is, the particular adjudged and reported case or cases by which that practice was settled and established. Will you do me the favor to inform me? Our Courts have recently fallen into the practice of permitting a special plea by which, instead of the issue of the Statute, another and a different issue is made up, which has a material bearing upon some of the rights of the litigants. My wish is to correct this practice by an appeal to the parent source of authority.

The papers having recently announced truly my illness at Balto.[2] and as the topic of my letter is *last wills* &c, to guard against erroneous inferences, I have the pleasure to inform you that I am quite well again.

ALS. ViRVal.   1. No answer has been found.   2. See 9:518.

To JAMES GORDON BENNETT[1]   Washington, June 7, 1841

I received your letter[2] upon the subject of the admission of stenographers in the Senate, and objecting to the restriction by which those only are admitted who report for some papers published within the District of Columbia.

Upon enquiry, I was informed that the restriction was introduced in consequence of the limited accommodations afforded by the Chamber of the Senate.

I should be glad that the reporters of your paper or that of any other could be admitted; provided always that whoever is received, in good faith, performs the duty of a stenographer.

I will see if your reporter cannot, by some modification of the rule, be admitted, as it would give me pleasure to be instrumental in rendering that accommodation to you.

Copy. Printed in Isaac C. Pray, *Memoirs of James Gordon Bennett and His Times* (New York, 1855), 290-91.   1. For Bennett, see 9:343 and *DAB*.   2. See 9:538.

To LESLIE COMBS[1]   Washington, December 29, 1841

I received your favor of the 19h. inst.[2] and sincerely sympathise with you on the fate of your Son.[3] If any interposition can be made in his behalf by our Governmt. it can only be upon the ground that he went neither as a combatant nor trader but as an American Citizen for the benefit of his health. Proof to that effect being placed in the hands of the Secy of State [Daniel Webster] will form a basis for an instruction to our Minister at Mexico [Powhatan Ellis].[4]

I am also extremely sorry for the unfavorable condition of your pecuniary affairs. I feared this result for some time past; but hoped that you might escape it. I hardly know what to advise you. My own affairs, in consequence of the pressure of the times, & the fall in the value of all property give me uneasiness. My confidence is unshaken that you will not allow Mr [Daniel] Vertner[5] and myself to suffer as your endorsers.

As to any official appointment, far from being able to serve you, any recommendation from me would probably prejudice rather than benefit you with Mr. [John] Tyler. How do you stand with [Henry A.] Wise? He has, I think, more ability to serve you, in that quarter, if he would exert than any body else. I doubt whether Genl. [Winfield] Scott could serve you. I do not visit Tyler.

The Currency plan meets with but little support from either party.[6] In its present form it cannot possibly pass; nor I think in any form that I can conceive of.

ALS. KyLoF.   1. For Combs, see 1:396.   2. Not found.   3. For the capture of Americans in Mexico, see 9:717.   4. For Ellis, see 9:171, 717.   5. For Vertner, see 1:108.   6. See 9:623.

To MRS. STEPHENS[1]   Washington, March 28, 1842

When your note and book were left with me, I was confined by indisposition. Altho' I am not yet entirely recovered, I will not longer delay a compliance with your friendly request. I have no notes of the passage in my Speech delivered on wednesday last in the Senate,[2] which you wish to preserve, nor have I yet received those of the Stenographer; but my recollection of it is, I think, sufficiently accurate to enable me to record it here substantially. Contrasting the power of the British Empire and that of the United States I said:

"Mr. President, our's is a glorious Country; and vast as is the power and extent of the British Empire, will not suffer by a comparison with it. The British Empire is spread over the four quarters of the globe, separated by boundless oceans, detached and dispersed, in broken fragments, insular and continental, inhabited by different and discordant races of men, speaking various and unknown tongues, obeying an infinite diversity of laws, originating in every stage of human society, from the highest state of refined civilization to the lowest depths of ignorance and barbarism, and worshiping both the Christian and Heathen Gods. Whenever the charm of her Naval power, the cement of these heterogeneous and incongruous elements, is broken, the future greatness and glory of old England will vanish forever.

Our young and immense Confederacy, washed by the Pacific and Atlantic Oceans, by the Gulph of Mexico, and the great Northern Lakes, exhibits one compact, consolidated, continuous, unbroken Territory, abounding in the most valuable productions of Asia, of Africa, of Europe, and of America, inhabited by one race of men—the descendants of the most renowned and glorious of all the races of the Family of Mankind—duplicating their numbers in terms of 25 years, speaking the same common language, living under one Constitution, and similar laws, enjoying the inestimable blessing of Civil Liberty, and freely worshiping at the pure Altar of the only true God.

How ought our hearts to overflow with dutiful thankfulness and gratitude to that God for his gracious bounty to us! And what an awful responsibility do we lie under to HIM, to mankind, to posterity and to our own consciences for a faithful administration of the great and sacred trust which he has confided to our hands.

I only regret that the passage is not more worthy of your acceptance.

ALS. MBU.   1. Not identified.   2. See 9:682-87.

286

To _____ HOPKINS[1]   Washington, April 15, 1842

I have received your friendly letter,[2] informing me of your having given my name to your infant son, born on the 4th instant. I thank you for the honor thus done me, and for the sentiments of respect and esteem, which prompted it.

Deeply regretting the present extreme embarrassments of the country, I saw no prospect of my being able to accomplish any good proportionate to the sacrifices I was making by my rerunning [*sic*, remaining] in the public counseling [*sic*, counsels], and therefore thought that, after my long service, I might retire.[3]

Be pleased to present my acknowledgements to Mrs. Hopkins for her concurrence or acquiescence in confering my name on her infant; and for that, for her, and for yourself, accept the best wishes. . . .

Copy, typed. Henry Clay Memorial Foundation, Lexington, Ky.   1. Possibly Arthur F. Hopkins, an admirer of Clay. See *DAB*.   2. Not found.   3. See 9:691-96.

To UNKNOWN RECIPIENT   Lexington, *ca.* June, 1842[1]

Many thanks for your acceptable salmon[?] I wish you were here to discuss it with me.

The Speech[2] is in the hands of the printer, with some improvement in parts of it, and some suppressions. The Editors cannot publish it till the last of next week. It will be time enough. Say to the Editors of the [Frankfort] Comm[onweal]th[3] that I thank them for their brilliant but flattering account of the Barbecue[.]

Thanks for the information from White.[4]

ALS. NcD.   1. Dated only "Ashland Saturday night"; however, editors have determined from internal information that it may have been written shortly after his Speech in Lexington on June 9, 1842.   2. Possibly that in 9:708-16.   3. Thomas Stevenson took over from Orlando Brown as editor of the *Commonwealth* in 1842. Willard Rouse Jillson, *The Newspapers and Periodicals of Frankfort, Kentucky 1795-1945* (Frankfort, 1945), 13-14. For Stevenson, see 9:836; for Brown, 5:976.   4. Possibly Speaker of the House John White. See 9:522.

To James T. Morehead, June 11, 1842. Sends bank note for Alexander Porter who wants to subscribe to the Washington *Independent*.

Reports that "They gave me a brilliant Barbecue [9:708-16]. There were, I think about 15.000 & some 3 or 4 hundred Carriages." ALS. KyLoF.

For Morehead, see 8:219, 439; 9:510 and *BDAC*. For Porter, see 5:93. For the Washington *Independent*, see 9:651-52.

To JOHN B. MORRIS[1]   Lexington, August 12, 1842

Your disappointment cannot possibly be as great as my mortification that the amount of the protested bills has not been before remitted to you. I had reason to believe, founded on his own letter, that Mr. [James] Erwin[2] would have been here two weeks ago. He annually passes the winter at N. Orleans, but has hitherto invariably come up to his summer residence, adjoining me, before the middle of July. What has detained him I am at a loss to conjecture, unless it be that he has passed up through Tennessee where three of this children are, and has been detained. I am perfectly confident that as soon as he arrives, and I look for him daily, the requisite remittance will be placed at my disposal.

This affair has given me great pain. I no more anticipated the protest of Mr. Woods[3] acceptance than I should have done that of John J. Astor. The bills were drawn upon funds of mine in his hands, and, as he assured me, on funds of his in Mr. Woods's. Not dreaming of a protest, I made no provision for such an event, limiting my arrangements to taking up my note in your hands.

I will write you again in a few days.

ALS. MoSW.   1. For Morris, see 3:898.   2. See 9:730.   3. Not identified.

From JOHN WHITE[1]   Washington, August 18, 1842

You will have seen before this reaches you—the veto of the *Great Tariff*[2]—I planned the movement for a *Select* Committee upon it to enable Mr [John Quincy] Adams to make out a formal *reply* & *report*[3]—There is still conflicting opinions with the Whig Party what ought to be done—My conviction, however, is that we shall adjourn without doing any thing or attempting any other measure—It is said the "Captain" [John Tyler] will call us together again *forthwith*. Be it so—Let him do it—I believe we will be able to pass him the very same Bill—and send it to him as the *ultimatum* of our action—we will make his *call* session end in about 48 hours—There will be some dissatisfaction with a few Northern members—at the decission, They are few—so upon the whole I believe we shall break with a good understanding.

ALS. DLC-John J. Crittenden Papers.   1. For White, Speaker of the House, see 9:522 and *BDAC*.   2. See 9:628.   3. See 9:755.

Speech in Frankfort, Ky., October 26, 1842. States that in the history of the U.S. government, 22 bills have received the executive's veto. Admits that George Washington's veto of an apportionment bill and James Madison's veto of a bill in relation to a religious corporation in the District of Columbia were correct, but denounces "every other instance of the application of the odious power." Asserts "that almost every evil suffered by the country, had its origin in the remorseless abuse of this power by various Presidents." Copy, summary. Printed in Louisville *Daily Journal,* November 5, 1842. Given at the Kentucky Whig convention.

To BENJAMIN WATKINS LEIGH   Lexington, April 6, 1843

There is such a tone of cheerfulness, pervading your letter,[1] indicative of good health and good spirits, that the perusal of it gave me great pleasure, independent of its otherwise interesting contents. Long may you continue to enjoy both!

I think your Convention[2] was right in acceding to the desire, manifested elsewhere, for a Nat. Convention.[3] Such a Convention, if not necessary to nominate any other Candidate than one for the V.P. was requisite for that, and for the adoption of measures of concert to secure the success of the Whig ticket. It may do good in Pennsa.[4] on which, if my information and observation do not deceive me, we have great reason to count. The objection to it is, the intermediate intrigues to which its call, at so distant a day, will give birth. You will hear of Judge [John] McLean, Genl. [Winfield] Scott &c &c[.][5]

But no state of division that is likely to be excited among us can equal the distraction which prevails, and I think is likely to increase, with our opponents. I wish Mr. [John C.] Calhoun had a little more of Mr. [Martin] V[an]. Buren's strength. I really think that the fairest contest would be between the Whig Candidate and Mr. Calhoun. That would present a plain and intelligible issue, the decision of which, one way or the other, might give lasting repose to the Nation. Mr. V. Buren's election would settle no controverted question.[6]

You ask me what personal offense I have given [Henry A.] Wise?[7] None none whatever. We never had any personal difference. If you read the correspondence which passed between us, in relation to the unfortunate affair of [Jonathan] Cilley,[8] you saw that I expressed in it my ignorance of the cause of the inimical relation, in which he had placed himself to me. I am yet ignorant of it. I can only conjecture it; and I suppose it to originate in his vanity, egotism & inordinate ambition of notoriety.

In the winter of 40-41 he began to display a spirit of discontent and disaffection. In a conversation with Mr. [John] Sergeant and him, at their lodgings, I think in Feby 1841, he exhibited very strongly those feelings. He was opposed to the Extra Session,[9] and opposed to every thing which the Whigs wished done at it. His subsequent conduct did not surprise me so much after that conversation; but I did not entirely despair that cool reflection might prompt him to take a patriotic course.

It has been supposed that his hatred of me is attributable to his disappointment in being elected Speaker, and to his belief that I prevented his Election.[10] I had no more to do with the election than you had. I never spoke to a member to vote for Mr. [John] White,[11] nor made any interest whatever for him.

In his recent address, he says that I *urged* him, more strongly than Mr. [John] Tyler ever did, to accept a foreign mission. I have not the most distant recollection of ever having even conversed with him about going abroad; certainly I never *urged* him to do so.[12]

I perceive that you entertain some hopes of our mother state.[13] It is more than I do; and yet I cannot help thinking, with you, that if the contagion of [John M.] Bott's[14] spirit and example could be caught in some dozen of places, that the old lady would recover the high ground on which she once stood.

What do you think of an old gentleman of 65, near 66, recommencing the practice of the law? Does he not merit some patronage? I hope you will shew towards him your accustomed kindness extended to cadets & young beginners.

I thought I might assist a son.[15] Then, being in the City, will save others the trouble of coming to Ashland, who have no other object than the idle curiosity of seeing me—I mean of course total strangers. I must add that good fees, if I should be so lucky as to pick up any, will not be wholly unacceptable.

My warm regards to all the Clay-men of your family, if you have not slandered them, will include Mrs. [Julia Wickham] Leigh, [and the] other ladies.

ALS. ViRVal.   1. Not found.   2. See 9:806.   3. See 9:754; 10:52.   4. See 9:752. 5. For Scott, see 1:990; 4:502; for McLean, see 3:103. For the possibility of their being candidates in 1844, see 9:721-22, 754, 821-22, 827-28, 830, 836, 854, 865.   6. See 9:681, 752, 854.   7. See 9:827.   8. See 9:153.   9. See 9:454, 514-16.   10. For the election of Speaker, see 9:522.   11. *Ibid.*   12. Wise's grandson alleged that "prior to the death of [William Henry] Harrison, Clay had urged Wise to accept any foreign appointment at the President's disposal." Barton H. Wise, *The Life of Henry A. Wise of Virginia, 1806-1876* (New York, 1899), 102. For Wise's rejection as minister to France and subsequent appointment to Brazil, see 9:804.   13. See 10:99.   14. For Botts, see 9:299 and *BDAC.*   15. James Brown Clay. See 9:812.

To Willis Green, May 4, [1843]. Recalls that when "We boarded together, and I had abundant opportunity to know your feelings and sentiment, in respect to" the Bankrupt law, "You were firmly, constantly, I thought almost obstinately, opposed to its passage, and in favor of its repeal. I believe you were accidentally absent on some of the decisive qu[es]tions, but I am sure it was without design." Adds that the considerations "which induced me to support the law were" the economic distresses of the time, the responsibility of the government, and "the Constitutional fact that the [Ge]neral Government could, and the States could not, pass a bankrupt law; and the duty, as I thought, of Congress exercising the power thus entrusted to it." Remembers also that "So far from my attempting to make you a convert to my opinion (it was never my habit to persuade my Colleagues to go along with me—I went on my own hook, without regard to the course of others) you attempted to make me a convert to yours; but we both retained our respective opinions." ALS, manuscript torn. KyLoF. Date torn off, but postmarked "May 4" and endorsed "1843" in a strange hand.

In an undated note, probably attached to the above, Clay states: "Confidential. I hope you will be the Candidate and be elected in your District. I would, with pleasure, do any thing I could with propriety to promote that object. I have spoken warmly of you today to Triplett & [Alfred] Allen from Owensborough [*sic*, Owensboro, Ky.]. Tell me how I can serve you." Adds that "You may use m[y] lett[er] enclosing this in any way you please . . . except that I do not wish it published. AL, initialed. *Ibid.*

For Willis Green, see 9:707. Clay and Green had boarded together in 1840-41. See 9:386. Green won the Whig nomination for Congress from the Litchfield district and subsequently the election. Frankfort *Commonwealth*, April 18, June 13, 1843; *BDAC.* For the Bankruptcy bill, its passage and repeal, see espec. 9:408-9, 418-20.

Alfred Allen of Daviess County (not to be confused with Alfred Allen of Breckinridge County) was a delegate to the Kentucky Whig State convention in 1843 and also a delegate to the 1844 Whig National convention at Baltimore. Frankfort *Commonwealth*, November 21, 1843.

Triplett is either George W. or his brother Philip, both of whom were active in Kentucky politics. George W. was defeated for the Kentucky house in 1843, while Philip, who had been elected to Congress in 1839, served as a presidential elector in 1844. *Ibid.*, August 15, November 21, 1843.

To John W. Dodge, July 10, 1843. Asserts that "your portrait of me, for accuracy of likeness and beauty of execution, is *unexcelled by any ever taken of me,* and is *greatly superior* to most of the previous ones." Copy. Printed in New-York *Daily Tribune*, February 23, 1844. For Dodge, see 9:880.

Speech in Defense of Cassius M. Clay, *ca.* September, 1843. Argues that C.M. Clay had acted in self defense in using his knife against Samuel M. Brown in an altercation on August 1, 1843. States: "You are bound, on your oaths, to say, was Clay acting in his constitutional and legal right? Was he aggressive, or resting peacably in the security of the laws which guard alike the safety of you, of me, and him? . . . Standing, as he did, without aiders or abettors, and without popular sympathy; with the fatal pistol of conspired murderers pointed at his heart, would you have had him meanly and cowardly fly? Or would you have him do just what he did do—there stand in defense, or there fall?" Adds: "*And, if he had not, he would not have been worthy of the name which he bears!*" Copy, excerpt printed in Roberta Baughman Carlee, *The Last Gladiator: Cassius M. Clay* (Berea, Ky., 1979), 38. The document is not dated, but the case was entered in the Fayette Circuit Court Order Book 29, p. 300, on September 30, 1843.

For C.M. Clay, see 9:887. For an eyewitness account of the fight, see David L. Smiley, *Lion of Whitehall* (Madison, Wis., 1962), 256.

To HENRY M. BRACKENRIDGE   Lexington, November 12, 1843

I received your favor,[1] and the sketch of your Speech[2] for which I thank you. I saw, with regret, the divisions between the Anti Masons and Whigs in your district, during the whole progress of the Canvass, and the result did not disappoint me. I hope that it may lead to harmony and a better state of feeling between those two parties.[3]

There is a great deal of what Govr. [Robert P.] Letcher calls "good reading" in your Speech, some sound views of policy, and much historical truth. On two points (the Compromise [Tariff of 1833][4] and the Bank)[5] I think your sentiments require some modification. The Compromise gave ample protection up to 1840. The biennial reductions were so small up to that period that they were not felt. It gave the Manufacturers *stability,* which is a great want. They flourished under it, during those seven years; and would never have flourished more, if it had not been for the disorders of the Currency and the disorders of the times, which were not produced by the Compromise. It was not the fault of the Compromise that, after 1840, the Compromise worked ill. That was the fault of the [Martin] V[an]. Buren Congress in failing to provide an adequate current revenue, and in failing to provide for the Tariff, as was expected and contemplated, when the Compromise was first introduced.[6]

As to a U.S. Bank, I think you concede too much in admitting that public opinion is against it. Such may be the fact in Pennsa; but not, I think, taking the Union in the aggregate. With a good Charter, the Stock could be now taken in sixty days. It was said to be an obsolete idea to [word illeg.] the [John] Tyler administration. I have been unable to conceive any safe mode of supplying a Nat. Currency of convertible paper but through a well restricted Nat. bank. Still I adhere to what I formerly said that no such institution should be established until called for by public opinion.

I reciprocate all your friendly wishes, and remain ever Truly Your friend . . .

ALS. KyLoF. Addressed to Brackenridge in Tarentum[?], near Pittsburgh, Pa. 1. Not found. 2. See 10:71. 3. A rivalry in the struggle for patronage continued in Pennsylvania between the old National Republicans and the Anti-Masons. Led by Thaddeus Stevens, the latter made a last ditch effort in 1843-44 on behalf of Winfield Scott for the Whig nomination in 1844. William P. Vaughn, *The Antimasonic Party in the United States 1826-1843* (Lexington, Ky., 1983), 112. 4. See 8:604, 619-21, 626-27. 5. See espec. 9:528-29, 565-66, 587-94. 6. See espec. 9:628, 646-47, 719-20.

To Enoch C. Wines, Princeton, N.J., November 27, 1843. Bears testimony to the quality of Wines's boarding school, noting that "one of my sons and two of my grandsons [Martin Duralde III and Henry Clay Duralde] were under your care," and "my son John [Morrison Clay] thinks that he derived more benefit under your auspices than he ever obtained from all the other schools which he ever attended." Extends "my cordial wishes for your success." Copy. Printed in Washington *Daily National Intelligencer,* September 20, 1844.

For Wines, see 8:742-43 and *NCAB,* 1:180; for Henry Clay Duralde, see 4:16. See also 8:847-48.

To Walnut Ward Clay Club of Philadelphia, December 8, 1843. Thanks them for their expression of friendly sentiments [not found] and apologizes for his tardiness in replying. Notes that "The time is rapidly approaching when I may have to announce a definite determination, whether I shall give my consent or not, to the use of my name as a candidate for the high office which the Walnut Ward club does me the honor to desire I should fill." Finds it "highly gratifying to witness the almost daily evidences of the concentration and consolidation of public opinion, on those great measures of Whig policy, to the establishment of which I have uniformly contributed my humble exertions." Asserts "that from my first entry into public life to the present moment, I do not recollect that I have ever differed with Pennsylvania on any great measure or principle of National policy, in peace or war," but adds that "I have had the misfortune to differ from her in respect to the election of distinguished men to high office . . . and out of that difference I have been exposed within the borders of Pennsylvania and elsewhere, to much bitterness, misrepresentation, and misconception. I regretted it, but was constrained to endure it, trusting to time, the great purifier and corrector of error, to supply that remedy which I was unable to prescribe." Has, nevertheless, always supported "those measures of public policy, in which she [Pennsylvania] felt so deep an interest. . . . because it was my honest conviction, that those measures would greatly tend to promote both her prosperity and that of the whole Union." Copy. Printed in Louisville *Daily Journal,* January 6, 1844.

To NATIONAL CLAY CLUB OF LYNCHBURG, VA.   Late 1843

If I could have had that satisfaction, it would have given me great delight to commune with my fellow citizens of Lynchburg, and the surrounding country, on the past, the present, and the future condition of our country[.] If in the disappointment of our hopes, growing out of the memorable struggle of 1840,[1] and the events which ensued,[2] we have much to deplore, I am sure that you will agree with me that our country has a just right to all our exertions to place her government once more on the lofty and patriotic position which it formerly properly occupied. You have, gentlemen, correctly enumerated the principles and the measures of the Whig party, in my humble opinion, by which that event may be brought about; and I tender you cordial congratulations of the bright and cheering prospects of its accomplishment which beam all around us. . . .

Copy. Printed in Philadelphia *United State Gazette,* Jan. 5, 1844.   1. See 9:263.   2. For Clay's ensuing struggles with the Tyler administration, see Tyler, John, in index in 9:963.

To ALFRED VAIL[1]   Lexington, September 10, 1844

Absence from home, and the pressure of a most burdensome correspondence, have delayed my acknowledgment of the receipt of your favor of the 15th ultimo.[2] I should be most happy to be able to give you a satisfactory response to your enquiries respecting the electro magnetic telegraph; but I fear I can say nothing that will be of the least benefit to you. Assuming the success of your experiment, it is quite manifest that it is destined to exert great influence in the business and affairs of society[.][3] In the hands of private individuals, they will be able to monopolize intelligence and to perform the greatest operations in commerce and other departments of business. I think such an engine ought to be exclusively under the control of government; but that object cannot be accomplished without an appropriation by Congress to purchase the right of the inventors. With respect to the practicability of procuring such an appropriation, from a Body governed by such various views, both of constitutional power and expediency, you are quite as competent to judge as I am. As the session of that body is now nigh at hand, I submit to you whether it would not be advisable to offer your right to it before you dispose of it to a private company or to individuals. If I understand the progress of your experiment, it has been attended with further and satisfactory demonstrations since the adjournment of Congress.

LS. DSI.   1. For Vail (1807-1859)—a telegraph pioneer and associate of Samuel F.B. Morse—see *DAB*.   2. Not found.   3. In March, 1843, Congress had appropriated money for an experimental telegraph line between Washington and Baltimore, and the first message was sent on it on May 24, 1844. Vail, however, never benefited financially from the invention. *DAB*.

To OLÉ BULL[1]   Lexington, *ca*. 1845[2]

I am truly sorry that my bad cold, which the change of weather and the prospect of rain induce me to apprehend I might increase by going out at night, deprives me of an opportunity of witnessing your performance from which I anticipated so much pleasure to-night. All the other members of my family, who are not indisposed, have gone to enjoy that satisfaction.

I made an unsuccessful effort to see you to-day, but left no card. I hope to pay my respects to-morrow, if you do not leave the city before the afternoon.[3]

Copy. Printed in Sara C. Bull, *Olé Bull, A Memoir* (Boston, 1822), 213-14.   1. For Bull, a violinist, see *NCAB*, 4:234.   2. Although this letter is undated and Sara Bull places it in 1852, it must have been written during Bull's 1845 tour of the U.S. since Clay was not in Lexington during 1852.   3. Sara Bull records: "Ole Bull the next morning went to Mr. Clay's house, taking with him his violin. He went into the room adjoining the one in which Mr. Clay was seated, and played in a low tone the great statesman's favorite melody, 'The Last Rose of Summer.'"

Speech to Citizens of Pittsburgh and Allegheny, Pa., *ca*. March 20-24, 1848.

Thanks the citizens of the two cities for their welcome to him as "a private Citizen." Adds that "Nor did I until recently anticipate that my brief stopping in these Cities, on my return home, was to be signalized by any such warm and enthusiastic demonstrations. I have come here on no political errand, for no public purpose, with no prepared Speech, nor any arranged phrases." Notes that "Alas! how many of my estimable friends, whose generous hospitality I enjoyed when I was in the habit many years ago of embarking at this port on my return home from Congress, are now no more! And how greatly changed is the mode of transportation since that period! Then, I have often purchased one of those Arks or Kentucky flat boats, as they were called, divided it & fitted it up into separate apartments of Stable, Kitchen & Parlour, and in that way floated my family and myself down the current of this beautiful River." Judges "from the countless multitude which rended the Air with shouts & cheers on my arrival, and from the portion of the City which I have seen," that the "predictions I made a long time ago . . . as to the growth & future greatness of this City have been accomplished." Recalls that his whole public life has been devoted to "the Peace and honor and the advancement of the prosperity of the Country, the developement of our vast resources . . . the facilities of commercial and social intercourse, the improvement of our Rivers and Harbors, and the Establishment of Home manufacturers." Concludes that "in my retirement at Ashland," he will cherish the "enthusiastic demonstrations of this memorable day." AD. KyU. Document is undated, but it seems most likely Clay made this speech on his trip through Pittsburgh in 1848. See 10:404, 419-20.

From DAVID LEE CHILD[1]   Northampton, Mass., July 26, 1848

This is the evening of the day on which we have held a convention for the 6th Con[gressional]. Dis[trict]. of Massachusetts in pursuance of the movement in this and other states for restricting slavery in our country to the territory, which it occupies.[2] As I sat in my cottage smoking my pipe and musing upon the varied events of the past, and deliberating upon the dangers and duties of the present, I was suddenly inspired with the resolution to address my thoughts, just as they bubbled up, to you, who was a prominent figure in my contemplations.

We were disastrously defeated in 1844, partly I think by fraud and still more by our own misconduct.[3] Had the Whig party held an unambiguous language on the subject of annexation, and Mr Clay abided *strictly* by his admirable and statesmanlike letter written on the eve of his nomination,[4] he would now have been President of the United States, and we should have been saved from the unconstitutional, profligate and disgraceful policy, which his trivial and tortuous competitor [James K. Polk] has pursued with a success, which has probably astonished none more than himself. We should have had the best President that has administered the government since the great [George] Washington, one whom we could with pride and gratitude, have named, as the Romans did their Cicero, "father second [?] founder of the Republic[.]" But is it even now too late? Might not these attributes be won by more signal benefits and won with more brilliancy after the crimes and harms, we have seen, than before? There is now a wide, deep and *pure* popular movement, such an one as I had never seen and scarcely hoped to see, one from which the elements of office seeking, selfishness and faction are thoroughly eliminated. It is to save the poor and oppressed of our country and kind from ages of unutterable woe, and our own posterity from the evils (to be infinitely aggravated in their case) which have disturbed and afflicted us. Man cannot realize the highest heroism of which his nature is capable, nor develope his noblest energies, when he works merely for himself. To be sublime he must go out of himself. Our country and the world are now in that plastic state, which capacitates them to receive readily the deepest and most permanent impression. Societies and governments, for good or evil, are to be moulded. What a privilege then to live now, if it be only for a few years or months! And especially for those whose well earned influence and fame are wide as the world, and whose arm reaches to its uttermost parts! And how heavy is their responsibility. The character of our country might have been a bright and shining light—a Pharos [?] to the tempest-tossed nations; instead of which it is a jack o' lantern flickering over a mingled and festering mass of low ambition, greed, cor[r]uption and oppression. The opinion is daily gaining ground that our government, as now & of late administered, is the most corrupt in the world. It is set in opposition to the government of God; vice is rewarded and virtue punished or neglected; the Heaven-ordained decay of a vicious institution and the natural decline of the unjust power, unhappily conceded to it, are repaired, and are to be repaired for an indefinite period, by usurpations at home and conquests abroad. We have entered upon a career of fraud, aggression carnage and robbery for the extension of slavery & the aggrandizement of the Slave Power. And while all other civilized nations, monarchical, democratic & even despotic are knocking off with a generous and venerable emulation the chains of servitude, this "virtuous" "this [word illeg.]" this "pattern republic," are to be the great countervailing power! Am I mistaken in thinking that Henry Clay would gladly contribute to prevent this mournful result, and to arrest the fatal tendencies of the time? A genuine and mighty spirit of regeneration is awakened and at work in the land, but it wants tongue and hand for adequate expression and effective action. Where can it find these better than in Henry Clay, if the angels still hover over him? If haply Heaven should inspire him with *thought* and *purpose* fitting the demands of the hour, then it *is* "the Hour" and he is "the Man." If he be, (as who can doubt?) opposed to the unprincipled and ruinous career that is begun,—the bloody, beastly vulgar career of *military* tyrants and corruptionists, (soon reduced to most abject slaves) who have overturned other republics, then he will not, he cannot be indifferent to the alarming state of things, nor unobservant of the signs of the times. If he is opposed to the further extension and to the artificial prolongation of the great evil, which has been the chief, almost sole, cause of our destractions and degeneracy, and thinks proper to imitate and to *better* a great but too tardy example of the venerated Father of our Country—his age, his reputation, his magnanimity, his unrivalled eloquence and statesmanship would relieve the *united party* from all embarrassment about persons and merit the godlike purpose which has called it into being our progress with such a head would be *immediately* irresistable. His hand would collect the electricity flashing round the whole horizon, and gathering it [in?] one good bolt of concentrated thunder, hurl it among the ungodly now at Washington. What has *he*, what has our country gained by his past temporizing? Nothing! On the contrary, lost everything most valuable, peace honor, kindly affection, almost, conscience. We "have treasured up wrath against the day of wrath." It is time for a higher, a more *comprehensive,* a heroic policy.

Jam nouus Rerum nascitur Ordo. His motives might be maligned for a moment, but would that be either a new or important thing?

May not I, humble as I am, a lover of my country and *all* my kind, exhort and entreat Henry Clay to arise and gird himself for action suited to the epoch, to his capacity and position? Let him signify to some of those attached & faithful of whom no man living has more, that he has unalterably determined that so much of the day as remains, shall be consecrated to the cause of Liberty & Humanity, the cause rightly understood of "our [country] our *whole* country." Then shall he go down in the west with an expanding effulgence, and "His bones When he has run his course & sleeps in blessings, Shall have a tomb of orphans' tears wept on 'em."

I was about to say much of the Philadelphia Convention & the Con-[gressional] Cabal[5] of which I suppose it [word illeg.] been the tool, of the intrigue, treachery, and *dissembling* which directed and marked its proceedings and their results, for these came in for a large share of my meditations; but I willingly throw a veil over this as the sons of Noah "took a garment and going back wards covered their father's shame."

I do trust in God that you will make somebody, whom I may meet at Buffalo,[6] the depository of a wise & righteous determination on this momentous matter.

Copy. MB. Courtesy of Prof. Carolyn Karcher, Temple University.   1. For Child, see 8:179, 899.   2. Child signed this letter as a "Del[egate] of the 6th Con[gressional]. Dis-[trict]. Mass[achusetts] to the Buffalo Convention." For the various conventions leading to the formation of the Free Soil party at Buffalo, see 10:416.   3. See 10:74-75, 152-53, 169-70.   4. See 10:40-46.   5. See 10:291, 406, 445, 474-76.   6. See 10:416.

To FREEMAN HUNT[1]   Lexington, July 20, 1849

I wish to express to you the gratification I derived, on receiving the July number of the Merchants' Magazine and Commercial Review, from viewing your portrait in the beginning, and from reading your address to your friends at the end of it. When we feel under obligations to those who have contributed to our information and amusement, we are naturally desirous to possess all the knowledge of them, of their appearance, of the features of their countenance, and of the character and habits of their mind, which we can acquire. You have placed your numerous readers, (at least you have me, if I may not speak for them,) under those obligations; and the number of your valuable work now before me, in some degree satisfies the desire to which I have alluded.

I have become quite familiar with the Magazine and Review; and have no hesitation in expressing my humble opinion that it is emi-nently entitled to the public regard and support. It collects and ar-ranges, in good order, a large amount of valuable statistical, and other information, highly useful, not only to the merchant, but to the states-man, to the cultivator of the earth, to the manufacturer, to the mariner, in short, to all classes of the business and reading community.

Entertaining this opinion, I am glad that it has been, and hope that it may long continue to be, liberally patronized.

Copy. Printed in *The Merchant's Magazine and Commercial Review* (July-Dec. 1849), 21:369.   1. For Hunt and his magazine, see 10:497.

To MARY S. BAYARD   *ca.* Spring, 1850[1]

I am very anxious my dear friend, to learn whether you have heard any thing further from poor Charles [Bayard].[2] Do inform me if you have, or whenever you may.

I cannot but hope and think that nothing, so serious as your affectionate regard and tenderness for him prompted you to apprehend, has happened. The fall of the Stone can only have stunned & bruised him, for the moment. But deeply sympathizing in your distress, I shall feel greatly relieved whenever you receive good tidings of these[.] I trust you will inform me without delay.

If the incident had been much more tragical than I am fully persuaded it is, I was struck with some lines which accidentally caught my eye, and which in that mournful contingency would be applicable to the event. I do not often quote poetry, but here they are:

"Should they who are dearest, the child
    of thy heart,
The friend of thy bosom, in sorrow depart;
"*Look aloft*," from the darkness and dust
    of the tomb,
To that soil where affection is ever in bloom."

I pray you to present my warm regards to Mr. [Richard Henry] Bayard & all your family.

ALS. DeHi.   1. Letter contains no date; however, date supplied on basis of internal information.   2. Mrs. Bayard's son Charles had been struck by stones when Mt. Vesuvius erupted while he was visiting it. His arm had to be amputated, and he later died as a result. Delaware *Gazette*, March 29 and April 30, 1850.

To GEORGE H. DERBY & CO.   Washington, May 24, 1850
& DAVID B. COOKE & CO.[1]

I recd. your letter expressing a wish that I would communicate my opinion of the Lives of Madison and Monroe, which you have recently published.[2] They are worthy of high consideration, as fair delineations of their respective characters, and of their distinguished and patriotic services. Such a work may be read with profit & advantage by all who take a lively interest in the eminent men of our Country.

Copy. Printed in Epes Sargent, edited and completed at Clay's death by Horace Greeley, *The Life and Public Services of Henry Clay* (Auburn, N.Y., 1852), flyleaf.   1. Not identified.   2. John Quincy Adams, *Lives of Madison and Monroe, Fourth and Fifth Presidents of the United States* (Buffalo and Boston, 1850).

Statement on Sectional Controversy, *ca.* December, 1850 to March, 1851. Members of the 31st Congress, "believing that a renewal of sectional controversy upon the subject of slavery would be both dangerous to the Union, and destructive of its objects, and seeing no mode by which such controversy can be avoided, except by a strict adherence to *The Settlement* thereof effected by the compromise acts passed at the last Session of Congress, *Do Hereby Declare* their intention to maintain the said settlement inviolate, and to resist all attempts to repeal or alter the acts aforesaid, unless by the general consent of the friends of the measures, and to remedy such evils (if any) as time and experience may develope: And for the purpose of making this resolution effective they *farther declare* that they will not support for the office of President or of Vice

President, or of Senator or of Representative in Congress, or as member of a State legislature, any man, of whatever party, who is not known to be opposed to the disturbance of *The Settlement* aforesaid, and to the renewal, in any form, of agitation upon the subject of Slavery." D, signed by Clay and thirteen other members of the 31st Congress. DLC-Thomas Ritchie Papers. For the Compromise of 1850, see 10:998-1000.

From JOEL T. HART[1]   Florence, Italy, May 10, 1852

Col. Grigsby,[2] whose acquaintance I have had the pleasure of making in Florence, will do me the favour of conveying to you a live-oak stick, which I cut from the tomb of Cicero.—the stone head I had broke from a footworn pebble, being part of the door-sill of the house in which Columbus is said to have been born: the medallions cut upon it, are by Saulini of Rome,[3] a pupil of Thorwalsden [*sic*, Bertel Thorwaldsen];[4] from the famous head of Cicero in the royal gallery at Florence, and my head of yourself.

I hope you will accept this little token as significant of what I can but illy express in words,—with my earnest desire for your health and happiness.

Col. Grigsby will inform you what I have been about &c.

Knowing, as I do, the value of your time, it is too much for me to expect from you even a line, yet how acceptable it would be coming from you.

Mrs. [Lucretia Hart] Clay will please accept with yourself and family, my warmest regards. . . .

ALS. KyLoF.   1. For Hart, see 10:242.   2. Not identified.   3. Not identified. 4. For Danish sculptor Thorwaldsen, see *Encyclopedia Britannica*, 11th edition.

CALENDAR OF UNPUBLISHED LETTERS
AND OTHER DOCUMENTS

Letters deemed to have slight historical importance to an understanding of Henry Clay and his career are listed below. Copies of them are on file in the Special Collections Department, Margaret I. King Library, University of Kentucky, Lexington, and may be consulted by interested persons. The locus of the original manuscript of each letter has been included below, as has an indication of the general subject matter of each. Subject classification code numbers have been employed as follows:

1 Requests for general assistance and government assistance, information, documents, reports, correspondence, books and other printed materials.

2 Transmission of routine information and documents, including that between the Executive and Legislative branches.

3 Applications, recommendations, appointments, and resignations pertaining to government employment and political office.

4 Correspondence and transmission of information relating to the claims of private citizens against the U.S. and foreign governments:
   a. United States
   b. Great Britain
   c. France
   d. Spain
   e. Holland
   f. Other European nations
   g. Latin American nations.

5 Correspondence and transmission of information relating to land grants, pensions, and related legal actions.

6 Routine correspondence relating to:
   a. Forwarding of mail
   b. Interviews and audiences
   c. Introductions & character references
   d. Invitations, acceptances, regrets, condolences
   e. Appreciation, gratitude, social pleasantries
   f. Subject matter not clear
   g. Applications, recommendations pertaining to private employment
   h. Autograph requests.

7 Routine legal correspondence and documents relating to:
a. Clay's law practice as counsel or executor
b. Cases in which Clay was plaintiff, defendant, witness, or deponent
c. James Morrison Estate management
d. Eliza Jane Weir guardianship
e. James and/or Ann Hart Brown Estate management.

8 Routine correspondence and documents (including deeds, agreements, leases) relating to Clay's land purchases and sales, livestock transactions and breeding, and investments.

9 Routine bills, receipts, checks, bank drafts, promissory notes, loans, payments, rents, mortgages, tax documents.

10 Correspondence relating to routine political and professional services rendered constituents, colleagues, friends, and other politicians.

11 Remarks in Senate:
a. Procedural matters
b. Petitions, resolutions, memorials
c. Asides, clarifications, brief answers
d. Routine business with Executive department
e. Printing of documents
f. Salaries, appropriations, etc. relating to government employees and expenditures [*Congressional Globe* is abbreviated *CG*].

12 Miscellaneous.

UNDATED DOCUMENTS

Account, DLC-TJC, 9
Account, KyLxT, 9
To John Q. Adams, MHi, 6d
To John Q. Adams, MHi, 6d
With Thomas Arnold, DLC-TJC, 7a
BUS v. *White*, ViHi, 7a
To BUS, NN, 9
To BUS, DLC-TJC, 9
To Nicholas Biddle, DLC, 6a
From William Bradley, DLC-HC, 9
Burton v. *Gilmore*, KyLoF, 7a
To John C. Calhoun, DNA, 3
From William B. Calwell, DLC-TJC, 9
To Mrs. Conrey, ICHi, 6d
From Mr. Drake, DLC-TJC, 9
From General Court in Chancery, KyLoF, 7a
To Benjamin Gratz, PHi, 6d
To Ralph Randolph Gurley, DLC, 1
From Thomas P. Hart, DLC-TJC, 9
From John Hockaday, KyLxT, 10
From Josiah Stoddard Johnston, InU, 9
To Robert P. Letcher, OCHP, 6d
To General Lyman, MH, 6d

From Mr. Maccoun, DLC-TJC, 9
MEMO re: estate of George Nicholas, KyLxT, 7a
From Charles Morehead *et al.*, DNA, 6c
To Miss Payne, J. Winston Coleman, Jr., Collection, Lexington, Ky. 6h
To Dr. Peter, NcD, 6d
To Thomas H. Pindell, IHi, 6d
Poem in Clay's hand, KyU, 12
To James Rees, NUtC, 1
To Samuel Southard, NjP, 6d
To Samuel Southard, NjP, 6d
Toasts, DLC-HC, 12
To Unknown Recipient, MiU, 6d
To Unknown Recipient, NN, 12
To Unknown Recipient, DLC, 6d
To Myndert Van Schaick, Burton Milward, Lexington, Ky., 6d
To Mr. Washington, MH, 6d
From H.T. Weightman, DLC-TJC, 12
To Robert Wickliffe, DLC-TJC, 7b

UNDATED DOCUMENTS WITH APPROXIMATE DATES SUPPLIED BY EDITORS

1800-1810   To Fayette County District Court, KyLoF, 7c
January 1804   To Lewis Sanders, KyLoF, 12
1805   To Fayette County Circuit Court, KyLoF, 12
1806-10   *Innis* v. *Wilkinson*, KyLoF, 7a
Feb. 1814   To Mary Cutts, MH, 6d
1817-24   From John Gaillard, MH, 1
1820s   To Norborne B. Beall, KyLoF, 6d
1820-early 1830s   To General Robert Taylor, ViU, 6c
1823-24   To Richard Hawes, Albert Hawes, Park Hills, Ky., 6d, 7c
1825   To James Monroe, DNA, 3
June 1828   Furniture Inventory, DLC-HC, 12
1825-29   To Francis Brooke, DLC-TJC, 6b, 6d
1827-28   Document, DLC-TJC, 7c
June 30-31, 1829   From S.S. Nicholas, DLC, 7a
1830s   To Bank of Ky.-Lex. branch, DLC-TJC, 9
1830s   From Josiah Downing, DLC-TJC, 9
1830s   From William Martin, DLC-TJC, 9
1830-32   To Jesse Burton Harrison, DLC, 6d
May 1831   To Richard Hawes, Albert Hawes, Park Hills, Ky., 7c
1833   To BUS, DLC-TJC, 9
1833-35   To William C. Johnson, ViU, 12
1834-35   To Willie P. Mangum, Shanks, *Willie P. Mangum Papers*, 5:448, 12
1835-40   Memo, DLC-TJC, 12
1837-51   Bill of Sale/Pedigree, Josephine Simpson Collection, Lexington, Ky., 8
1838 or 1842   To John P. Kennedy, MdBP, 6d
August 21, 1839   To Samuel Southard, NjP, 6d
1840s   To Mary S. Bayard, DeHi, 6a
1840s   To Octavia Walton LeVert, NBuHi, 6d
1849   To Lord Ashburton, ScU, 6c
1849-51   To Thomas Corwin, DLC, 3
1850   Brief in Ray Case, ViU, 7a
Nov. 1850-March 1851   To Unknown Recipient, DNA, 3

1793
January 9   To Thomas Tinsley, KyLxT, 12

1799
nd   *Robert* v. *Weible*, Henry Clay Memorial Foundation, Lexington, Ky., 7a
January 30   *Evans* v. *McKinney*, CHT, 9

July 21   From Peyton Short, DLC, 7a
July 22   From Peyton Short, DLC, 7a
September 6   From Peyton Short, DLC, 7a
September 21   From Peyton Short, DLC, 7a
October 2   *Hughes & Elliott v. Satterwhite*, KyLoF, 7a

1800
July 29   To Robert Craddock, KyBgW, 7a

1801
nd   *Barker v. Cleveland*, TNJ, 7a
February   From John Postlethwait, *Day Book of Phoenix Hotel*, 9
ca. March 10   To Clark County Chancery Court, Dr. George F. Doyle, Louisville,
      Ky., 7a

1802
September 18   Agreement with James Morrison and John Bradford, KyU, 9

1803
February 10   From William Taylor, KyU, 7a

1805
January 14   Bond for John Bradford, KyHi, 12
May 2   From Nathaniel Hart, Dr. Thomas D. Clark Collection, Lexington, Ky., 7a, 9

1806
March 31   To John Wigglesworth, KyLxT, 9
ca. June 5   From Cuthbert Banks, KyU, 9
June 16   To Elijah Craig, Fayette Circuit Court File No. 206, 7a
June 27   To Andrew English, DLC-TJC, 8

1808
November 2   To Isaac Shelby, KyU, 7a
December 15   To Thomas Jefferson, DNA, 3
December 21   To William Lewis, PWbH, 9
December 27   To Lewis Sanders, KyLoF, 12

1810
March 21   To James Madison, DNA, 3
August 31   To Unknown Recipient, KyLoF, 6c
September 28   To Robert Wickliffe, KyU, 9
November 12   Agreement, Fayette Circuit Court, File 259, 9
November 28   To John Hart, MHi, 6c

1811
March 3   To Robert Smith, DNA, 3
June   *Gilmore's Exors. v. Nicholas's Exors.*, 7th Circuit Court, Ky. District, 7a
August 10   From John Hoomes, DLC-TJC, 9
October 8   To Unknown Recipient, CtY, 12
October 11   To Ky. Insurance, Mary Clay Kenner Collection, Rogersville, Tenn., 9
December 10   To William Lewis, PWbH, 8

1812
January 1   From Return Jonathan Meigs, OHi, 2
February 15   To John Read, KyLoF, 7a
February 22   To Joshua Barney, PHi, 9
May 5   To Richard Rush, DNA, 1
May 7   From Robert Brent, DNA, 1
June 10   From William Simmons, DNA, 4a
August 6   To Unknown Recipient, CtHi, 3

September 26   From Peter Hagner, DNA, 3
November 16   To Paul Hamilton, CtHi, 3

1813
February 17   From Thomas Turner, DNA, 9
May 4   To Gustavus & Colhoun *et al.*, KyU, 9
July 31   Resolution, JSC, 1

1814
January   From Unknown Correspondent, NHi, 3
January 6   To William Simmons, DNA, 1, 2
January 8   From William Simmons, DNA, 1, 5
January 14   From George M. Bibb, KyLoF, 9
January 29   With Parroh & Co., KyU, 9
June 30   To Reuben G. Beasley, RPB, 2
July 1   To Reuben G. Beasley, RPB, 1
August 19   To William Jones, CtHi, 3
September 12   *Clay* v. *Cowan*, Fayette Circuit Court, File 309, 9
September 24   To British Ministers, RPB, 2
November 11   Certificate of Membership in the Societe Des Beaux Arts De Grand,
   InU, 12
November 17   To British Ministers, RPB, 1, 2
December 11   To British Ministers, RPB, 1, 2

1815
January 22   To William Crowninshield, NcU, 6c
June 13   *Castleman* v. *Clay et al.*, Fayette County Circuit Court, Box 823, 7b
June 24   To Henry Jackson, KyLoF, 6c
September 26   To BUS, KyU, 9

1816
February 5   From Robert Brent, DNA, 10
March 9   To Robert Brent, NhD, 1
March 12   From Robert Brent, DNA, 2
August 2   To William Jones, William & Tracye Emslie, Albuquerque, N.M., 6c
December 4   From Robert Brent, DNA, 2
December 7   To Robert Brent, DNA, 5
December 12   From Robert Brent, DNA, 2, 9
December 13   To Robert Brent, NhHi, 6c
December 24   From Charles Cassedy, DNA, 2

1817
January 4   To BUS, Mary Clay Kenner Collection, Rogersville, Tenn., 9
January 9   To George Graham, DNA, 5
February 3   To Unknown Recipient, CtY, 6c
February 6   To N.F. Jr. [?], DNA, 5
February 7   From Robert Brent, DNA, 9
February 8   From Robert Brent, DNA, 2, 5
February 17   To John C. Calhoun, DNA, 3
March 3   From Robert Brent, DNA, 9
March 3   From James Monroe, DNA, 1
May 10   From Robert Brent, DNA, 5
June 17   To Judge Miller, ViHi, 8
ca. July 5   Mr. Aldridge, Lexington *Kentucky Gazette*, July 5, 1817, 6e
July 10   To Samuel Harvey, KyU, 7a
July 23   Account, WvU, 9
August 2   Advertisement, DLC, 8
ca. Fall   For John Hart, DLC-TJC, 9
November 18   To George Graham, DNA, 6c
December 17   Bill, DNA, 1, 2

December 29   To John C. Calhoun, DNA, 3
January 16   From Daniel D. Tompkins, MH, 6c
January 22   To James Biddle, Biddle Family Papers, Andalusia, Pa., 6d
January 30   Signature Certification, *House Reports*, 15 Cong., 1 Sess., no. 111, p. 42, 2

1818
April 27   To Leslie Combs, KyU, 1
April 29   To Unknown Recipient, Frankfort (Ky.) *Argus*, Nov. 9, 1831, 6c
May 20   From James Tallmadge, CtY, 6c
June 8   From David Daggett, CtY, 6c
July 23   To Daniel Brent, DNA, 2
October 3   *Ellis Heirs v. Gaurney Heirs*, ViU, 7b
October 9   Power of Attorney, KEU, 8
ca. December 7   Bill, DLC-TJC, 1, 2
December 26   From Robert Brent, DNA, 2

1819
January 6   To John Q. Adams, DNA, 1
January 6   From Robert Brent, DNA, 5
February 2   From Robert Brent, DNA, 5
March 11   From Robert Brent, DNA, 5
October 11   *Clay v. Philips*, Fayette Circuit Court, File No. 456, 7a
October 18   To George Gibson, KyU, 6g
October 29   To Unknown Recipient, NhHi, 6c

1820
January 14   To Peter Hagner, KyU, 1
January 18   To John C. Calhoun, DNA, 6c
January 20   To John C. Calhoun, DNA, 1
January 22   To Benjamin Warfield, KyU, 6c
March 14   To Horace Holley, KyLxT, 6c
April 4   From Edward Dowse, MHi, 6d
April 12   *Clay v. Richardson*, Marshall, *Decisions of the Court of Appeals of Kentucky . . .* ,
    199-200, 7a
July 31   From William R. Thompson, DNA, 12
August 10   To John C. Calhoun, DNA, 6c
August 22   To John C. Calhoun, DNA, 6c

1821
February 13   To John C. Calhoun, DNA, 6c
March 6   From John Q. Adams, The Adams Family Papers, MR146, 6d
June 29   From Thomas Hempstead, CtY, 1, 6c
August 28   To Thomas Dougherty, NjMoHP, 9
October 8   To Maj. William S. Dallas, KyU, 9
November 30   To Unknown Recipient, NHi, 6c
December 20   To Julien Poydras, NjMoHP, 6c

1822
February 26   Proceeding of Meeting on Death of Justice Pinkney, *Niles' Register* (March
    2, 1822), 22:15-16, 12
September 8   To John Q. Adams, CLU, 2
October 28   To Unknown Recipient, DNA, 6c

1823
January 18   From Charles West, KyU, 9
February 21   To James Monroe, DNA, 3
March 1   To Jonathan Russell, KyU, 6a
April 5   To Samuel Southard, NjP, 6c
June 26   Account with Bruce & Gratz, KyLxT, 7c
October 29   To John C. Calhoun, DNA, 6c

November 8   Property deed to heirs of James Morrison, Fayette County Court, Deed Book 10, pp. 148-60, 176-78, 7c
November 8   To Hetty M. Hawes, Clark County, Deed Book 20, pp. 22-25, 7c
November 28   From Willis A. Lee, DNA, 6c
December 3   From H. Marshall, DNA, 6c
December 16   To John C. Calhoun, DNA, 6c
December 22   From John Marshall, *Hamers . . . Autograph Collection . . . June 12, 1990*, 1, 2

1824
February 17   To John C. Calhoun, DNA, 3, 6c
March 9   From Daniel W. Coxe, PHi, 1, 2
March 17   To Francis P. Blair, NjMoHP, 6c
March 22   To John White, MdHi, 1
March 24   To George Bomford, DNA, 1
April 17   To Tench Coxe, PHi, 7a
May 18   To John C. Calhoun, DNA, 6c
May 21   From James Smith, Jr., PHi, 7a
August 12   To George W. Jones, OCHP, 7a
December 22   To John C. Calhoun, DNA, 6c
December 23   To John C. Calhoun, DNA, 6c
December 30   From Nicholas G. Ridgely, KyU, 7a
nd   Order of the Board of the Trustees concerning the Morrison legacy, KyLxT, 7c
nd   *Wickliffe* v. *Clay*, DLC-TJC, 7c

1825
nd   *Gilmore* v. *Nicholas's Heirs*, KyLxT, 7b
nd   From William Wirt, ViU, 2
February 2   To James Monroe, DNA, 3
ca. February 17   To James Monroe, DNA, 3
February 22   To Nicholas Biddle, PHi, 6c
April 17   From William A. Camron, DNA, 6c
April 19   From Benjamin Reeder, DNA, 3
May 29   From James Brown, DNA, 2
June 13   From Abraham Gibson, DNA, 3
ca. July 1   Resolution of Board of Trustees of Transylvania, KyLxT, 7c
July 15   From Felix Cicognani, DNA, 2
August 10   From Isaac Shelby, *The Collector*, No. 918 (1987), 19-20, 3
August 25   To C.D.E. Bangeman Huygens, CSmH, 2
September 8   To Horace Holley, ICN, 6c
October 19   From Abraham Gibson, DNA, 12
October 30   From Roman Estko, DNA, 2
November 16   To Samuel B. Barrell, MHi, 6e
December 15   To Charles Miner, PWbH, 6d

1826
January 3   To J.W. Patterson, DNA, 3
January 7   From John McKee, DNA, 3
January 30   To U.S. House of Representatives, CtY, 1
January 31   To Richard C. Anderson, Jr., NhD, 6c
early Feb.   From Daniel Webster, DNA, 1, 2
February 1   To Mr. Bartley, MHi, 6d
February 14   From George Hay, ViW, 3
February 24   To Rufus King, Ford, *The 1826 Journal of John James Audubon*, pp. 277-78, 6c
March 10   From Charles Miner, PWbH, 6c
April 5   From Ellen Lucas, DNA, 1
April 14   From Mary F. Ward, DNA, 1
May 26   From George Sullivan, DNA, 1
June 8   To Joaquim Barrozo Pereira, CSmH, 6d
July 8   From Felix Cicognani, DNA, 1

August 29   From Felix Cicognani, DNA, 3
August 31   From Abraham P. Gibson, DNA, 2
October 5   From Abraham P. Gibson, DNA, 2
October 27   From Joseph R. Evans *et al.*, DNA, 3
December 19   From Unknown Correspondent, NNC, 12

1827
nd   With Jacoby, Price &c., DLC-TJC, 7a
January 8   To Victor Dupont, DeGe, 3
February 27   To James Brown, L-M, 6c
February 27   To Nathaniel Rochester, NRU, 5
February 27   To Nathaniel Silsbee, Paul C. Richards, *Autographs Catalogue 235*,
    1988, 6c
April 26   From Abraham P. Gibson, DNA, 2
May 11   To Thomas I. Wharton, Robert F. Batchelder *Autographs . . . Catalogue 69*, 12
May 18   From N.G.C. Slaughter, DNA, 6c
July 7   From Calvin J. Keith, DNA, 2
July 9   To A. Kelly, OClWHi, 6d
July 14   To James McBride *et al.*, OCHP, 6d
July 14   To James McBride *et al.*, OCHP, 6d
July 16   From Thomas Reynolds, DNA, 3
August 14   From J. Webb & Co., DNA, 1
August 21   To Jonathan Thompson, DNA, 12
August 29   From Thomas Reynolds, DNA, 6c
October 1   With Robert Scott, KyLxT, 9
October 1   With Robert Scott, KyLxT, 9
November 5   To Vincent Rumpff, CSmH, 12
ca. December 29   Memo, DLC-TJC, 12

1828
January 4   To E.I. Dupont, DeGE, 2
January 8   From Robert Monroe Harrison, DNA, 2
January 8   From James Maury, DNA, 2
January 9   From William Woodbridge, DNA, 3
March 14   From Charles A. Wickliffe, DNA, 2
March 15   From Jose S. Rebello, DNA, 12
March 28   To Ludwig Niederstetter, DNA, 3
ca. March 29   From John McLean, DNA, 3
ca. May   To John Q. Adams, MHi, 6d
June 14   To William Prentiss, DNA, 2
June 14   To Benjamin O. Tyler, DNA, 2
August 6   From Thomas Metcalfe, DNA, 3
August 6   With Robert Scott, KyLxT, 9
October 3   From Isaac Bell, DNA, 12
October 18   From Jonathan Dorr, DNA, 4g
October 22   From Stephen Pleasonton, DNA, 2
October 25   From Henry Eckford, DNA, 4g
November 1   From George Bibb, KyLxT, 7a
November 5   From John H. Lawrence, DNA, 4g
ca. November 26   From James Peabody *et al.*, DNA, 3
December 4   From Thomas Pearce, DNA, 4a
December 12   To Bushrod Washington, ViMtvL, 6c
December 23   From Ebenezer Huntington, DNA, 3

1829
January 9   To Nathaniel H. Whitaker, DLC, 12
February 2   To Mr. Stansbury, DLC, 1
February 20   To Lewis M.S. Holleville, Carter, *Territorial Papers*, 20:851, 5
April 11   To the Clerk of the Supreme Court of the United States, DNA, 1
May 27   From Thomas S. Page, KyLxT, 7c
October 9   To William B. Lawrence, *Magazine of American History*, 12:448, 6e

1830
April 1   To BUS, Sheilagh Hammond, Lexington, Ky., 9
April 13   To W.C. Pelham, *Catherine Barnes Catalogue 2*, p. 4, 6c

1831
March 7   To Baron de Neuville, KyLoF, 6c
June 11   To Richard Smith, ViU, 9
June 15   To John Woods, Joseph M. Maddalena, *Profiles in History*, p. 12, 12
August 11   To Mr. Baldwin *et al.*, West Virginia Department of Culture and
    History, 6d

1832
March 12   From James Brown, CSmH, 6c
August 11   From Unknown Correspondent, Colton, *The Life and Times of Henry Clay*,
    1:58, 6c
November 21   To BUS, Henry Clay Memorial Foundation, Lexington, Ky., 9

1833
April 7   To BUS, Henry Clay Memorial Foundation, Lexington, Ky., 9
May 4   Contract with Trustees of Transylvania University, *Record Book Transylvania Uni-
    versity June 9, 1827 to March 14, 1839*, pp. 238-85, 7c
December 26   To George Watterson, Washington *Daily National Intelligencer*, Jan. 13,
    1834, 6d

1834
February 24   To A. Harrison, Jr., KyMurT, 6e
May 2   To George Watterson, ViU, 6e

1835
January 9   To Mr. Batchilder, CLU, 6h
March 6   To Henry Barnard, CtHi, 6c

1836
May 14   To H.I. Brown *et al.*, PLF, 6d
November 11   To A.W. Stone, Kent M. Brown, Lexington, Ky., 6a

1837
December 11   To W. Jones, KyU, 12

1838
May   To Unknown Recipient, Raleigh *Register and North Carolina Gazette*, June 11,
    1838, 12
November 19   To Bank of Ky.-Lex. Branch, Henry Clay Memorial Foundation, Lexing-
    ton, Ky., 9

1839
January 21   To Nicholas Biddle, MnU, 6c
May 21   To Bank of Ky.-Lex. Branch, Henry Clay Memorial Foundation, Lexington,
    Ky., 9
June 5   To Bank of Ky.-Lex. Branch, Henry Clay Memorial Foundation, Lexington,
    Ky., 9
July 23   To Mrs. Gideon Lee, InU, 6d

1840
February 10   To L.P. W. Balch, DNA, 3

1842
January 5   From Alexander Brown, DLC, 9
February 1   From Alexander Brown, DLC, 9
April 4   To Miss Eliza R. Triplett, *History of Daviess County*, p. 219, 6h

July 4   From January & Son, R.M. Smythe & Co., Inc., p. 5, 9
December 6   To Joseph Combs, OYMHi, 6e

1843
May 28   To Bernard Myers, *House Ex. Doc.* 177, 28 Cong., 1 Sess., pp. 144-45, 1
June 18   To Joseph Vance, IGK, 12
December 9   To Thomas W. Newton, Cincinnati *Gazette*, Jan. 22, 1844, 6d

1847
July 12   To Lewis Sanders, KyLoF, 6c

1848
May 23   Statement re: James Morrison Estate, Mr. & Mrs. Sam Downing, Lexington, Ky., 7c

1849
May 10   To Thomas Ewing, AzTeS, 6c

1850
September 7   To Angeline A. Redmon, North Shore Manuscript Co., Inc., Catalog #1, 6h

1851
March 29   To Dr. Ninian Pinkney, DLC, 2

1852
February 2   To Seth Salisbury, Scott Smith, Bethlehem, Pa., 6e
March 15   From James Shields *et al.*, Bull, *Olé Bull, A Memoir*, pp. 214-15, 6d

THE PORTRAITS OF HENRY CLAY:
A BRIEF HISTORY AND A CALENDAR

CLIFFORD AMYX

Professor of Art Emeritus,
University of Kentucky

Henry Clay's political life covers almost exactly the first half of the nineteenth century. As a subject for artists, he was painted by itinerant or "saddle bag" artists on the early Western frontier, by the relatively untaught or "native genius" painters such as Chester Harding and George Caleb Bingham, and then by a host of accomplished and noted portrait painters of his time. An equal number of minor painters and sculptors sought him out, usually for their own aggrandizement. Finally, Clay "faced the light" of the cruel and searching cameras as the subject of daguerreotypes in the last decade of his life. Clay was hardly a discerning patron of the arts and only an indifferent member of certain cultural associations, but he tolerated and even enjoyed the company of artists, though he tired in the last years of his life of the tedium of sitting for painters and sculptors.

Clay may have been the most frequently depicted man of his time; competitors for this honor would have been John Quincy Adams and Daniel Webster. But Clay was a difficult subject for artists, especially painters. He was ever mobile, with a fleeting countenance. Webster's rock-hard presence always impressed the artists; Clay constantly seemed on the point of escaping them. Yet Clay's renown was such that images were necessary to him as well as to the artists. The host of engravings, lithographs, and cartoons in which he figured constituted his more public image.

Clay was relatively tall and thin, with a certain shambling gait. According to some of his contemporaries, he was ugly. He said himself that his mouth was so wide that he never learned to spit properly. His nose was slightly *retroussé* at the tip, which some painters acknowledge. They had trouble at times setting his ears to his head. His complexion was flush, his hair once very light. Most of these things the artists sought to modify, suppress, or omit as their abilities permitted. The sculptors did well by the structure of his face; the painters could hide a long neck in a very high stock, which was in any case fashionable for Clay the dandy.

In his old age Clay was much photographed. He and Daniel Webster were the subjects of the most reproduced portraits of Americans in the recent survey of historic American portrait daguerreotypes at the National Portrait Gallery in Washington. By the decade of the daguerreotype, Clay had been seared and worn by his last campaign and by his disappointment at not gaining the presidency. The daguerreotype turned everything black and white. Clay sat immobile for the necessary exposures. Thus he lost his mobility and the "color," for which he was famed.

When Clay was admitted to the practice of law in Kentucky he made his mark at the bench, in the debating societies, and in support of those institutions that were to make Lexington "The Athens of the West." Yet there was no established portrait painter in Lexington until Matthew Jouett returned from study in Boston in 1818. George Beck, primarily a landscapist, had advertised as a portrait painter, but there is little record of his work in Lexington.

The first portrait of Clay still preserved was long attributed to various unlikely hands. Jouett and William West, two candidates, were still too young to
be competent painters at the time. This earliest portrait is now attributed to
Benjamin Trott, a "saddle bag" artist who painted at least three miniatures in
Lexington in 1805.[1] The painting is now in the hands of a member of the Clay
family, and tradition has it that it was a present from Clay to his bride Lucretia
Hart at the time of their wedding. The date 1805 obviates that claim. Trott's
likeness shows Clay at the age of twenty-eight, with very blond hair, "frizzy" in
the Republican manner. His face is pleasant and smiling, with a certain plump-
ness that he was to lose by the time of Jouett's portrait in 1818. Mrs. Clay confirmed the whiteness of his hair: "He had, as a young man, the whitest head of
hair I ever saw."[2] The French manner of dress was fashionable in Lexington for
a time, but there is no full-length portrait of Clay to confirm at that early date
the figure of a "dandy."

In spite of Clay's appointment to the Senate when he was still under the
required age of thirty, and his election to the House in 1811, where he was
immediately chosen Speaker, there is no further portrait of Clay until he departed in 1814 to serve as a peace commissioner at Ghent, ending the War of
1812. Before he left for Europe he was painted by the mercurial John Wesley
Jarvis, possibly at the instigation of Mrs. Clay. She regarded the portrait as a
failure and gave it to her niece. It is a bland image, and the likeness is not
assured.

Very soon after Clay's return from Europe, the publisher of the Philadelphia
Port Folio, John Hall, wished to print an engraving of Clay by Thomas Gimbrede. It was so dubious a portrait that he sent it to Clay for his approval. Clay
inquired among his friends and replied that the print "resembles any other
person quite as well as the original."[3] The proof print was never published and
has remained in the Library of Congress unnoticed until recently. Whether
Gimbrede was the artist of the original portrait has not been determined; neither Clay nor the publisher mentioned an artist.

It was Matthew Harris Jouett of Lexington who was to paint the best-known
early portrait of Clay. Jouett had studied with the aged Gilbert Stuart in Boston and returned to settle in Lexington with a good practice as a portrait
painter. The portrait of Clay at age forty shows him mature and lanky rather
than plump, with his thinning hair brushed forward. The long neck is concealed by a high stock, and the shoulders fall away precipitously. The wide
mouth and thin lips are not denied. The portrait has become the canonical
early image of Clay. A copy made by Jouett for Joseph Delaplaine's Panzo-
graphia, a publishing venture, was never published, though it is probably the
original of the anonymous engraving made for the Analectic Magazine in 1820.[4]

Delaplaine may have "stung" certain congressmen with the proposal to have
their portraits painted for a national gallery, but there were to be other portraits for such a gallery, extending to 1826. The Philadelphia artist Charles Wilson Peale was in Washington in 1818 "capturing" notables for his gallery in
Philadelphia and trying to persuade them to have portraits in bronze made
from his drawings and paintings. Peale, father of a brood of artists almost all of
whom he named for famous members of the profession, proved to be an inept
salesman. His likeness of Clay, almost unnoticed among his works, is bland,
somewhat like Jarvis's portrait of 1814, and barely an advance on the earlier
work.[5]

In later years, when William Dunlap—artist, impresario, and the first historian of American artists—wrote to Clay asking for information about artists in
the West, Clay mentioned Jouett, of Lexington, and William Edward West,
then in Italy or England, where he painted Lord Byron and other famous persons. Clay also mentioned Chester Harding, but added that he did not believe

310

Harding was a Kentuckian.[6] Harding was self-taught and had a gift for "a truthful likeness." He painted portraits in Paris, Kentucky, at "$25. a head," which his father in the East regarded as a disgraceful way to make a living. Harding did not paint Clay until both were in Washington in 1822, after the artist had been in Missouri to paint the only authentic portrait of the aged Daniel Boone. The portrait of Clay is a sound confirmation of Jouett's likeness, though it shows Clay less "elevated" in the picture space.

By the early 1820s Clay had spent so much time in public service that he was forced to resign from Congress and return to Lexington to practice law and recoup his finances. Just before leaving Washington, in 1821, he was painted by Charles Bird King. Clay is shown seated with a copy of his resolution favoring independence for the colonies in Latin America.[7] He appears younger than his actual age, so much so that one popular history reproduced this painting as a portrait of the "war hawk" Clay. There is a certain dark intensity that is not characteristic of Clay portraits, especially in the large eyes. The content of the painting, however, was such that it was engraved by Peter Maverick with inscriptions in both Spanish and English especially for distribution in South America. As one of the "champions of freedom" for South America, Clay was served well by the engraving.

Clay returned to the House as Speaker in 1823. In 1825 he was made secretary of state in the John Quincy Adams administration, a chore he did not relish; he would rather have been in the Congress. The portraits near the time of his appointment as secretary of state are singular. A life mask made by the sculptor John H.I. Browere was completed as a bust. Browere intended to complete a series of notable Americans, especially the Founding Fathers still living in the mid-1820s. These likenesses based on life masks he called *facsimiles*, but they were despised by the academic sculptors. John Adams, Thomas Jefferson, and others were shown old and toothless, almost painfully aged and ugly. A rumor was spread that Browere had smothered the aged Jefferson, which Jefferson was courteous enough to deny, while admitting privately that the process was very painful. Clay, however, was still relatively young, perhaps the youngest of all of Browere's "gallery," and this bust was known and praised. When Clay was banqueted in Virginia, a toast mentioning Browere took the form of a verse.

> "Let Browere, the Artist, his genius display,
> In moulding from plaster the busts of our Sages:
> Dame Kentucky has made, from Virginia Clay,
> A statesman whose fame shall outlive future ages."[8]

As an "absolute" likeness, Browere's bust serves excellently to determine the authenticity of likenesses as Clay approached the age of fifty.

A striking portrait perhaps close to the time of Browere's bust has not been dated or firmly attributed to an artist. It was long attributed to Jouett, but one version of the portrait now at the Chicago Historical Society, said to be a gift from Clay himself to a family in Mississippi, is no longer believed to be by Jouett. It is a very fashionable portrait, Clay at his most jaunty, with a lace ruff at the stock, and is a sound if somewhat dramatized likeness. It is wholly unlike a Jouett portrait.[9]

A miniature of Clay by an unknown artist, engraved by James B. Longacre, pleased Clay so much that he asked to have it made into a locket, but the miniature and its artist have not been identified.[10] Longacre's engraving (1827) was to appear as the frontispiece to Clay's speeches printed by James Maxwell that year, and was to be reengraved later. It also appeared in *The Casket* in 1828. It was the standard public image of Clay until Longacre's engraving after William J. Hubard became popular, as one of the engravings in *The National Portrait Gallery* (1836).

Clay was nominated by the National Republicans in 1832 but was beaten soundly by Andrew Jackson. Most of the portraits made close to this time were of no special character. When Harriet Martineau visited "Ashland" in 1835 she claimed to have seen thirty portraits of Clay, none satisfactory.[11] It is doubtful she had seen that painted by James Reid Lambdin in 1831. Lambdin, from Pittsburgh, was painting along the Mississippi when he encountered Clay at Natchez. The young artist was carrying a letter of recommendation addressed to Clay from Judge Henry Baldwin.[12] A sitting was arranged for Lexington, and the resulting portrait shows a very jaunty Clay, alert, smiling, with slightly graying hair brushed back. There is a sense of vitality through the whole picture, and it is a sound likeness.

Clay enjoyed Lambdin's company. At a dinner at Ashland a certain Mr. Gray of Boston remarked to Clay, "'It is much to be regretted Mr. Clay that you never visited Boston, to sit for your portrait to the great artist Mr. [Gilbert] Stuart.' To which Clay replied in his blandest manner, 'I trust, Sir, that my young friend at my right will make it evident that there is no good ground for your regret.'" "The prettiest compliment I ever received," wrote Lambdin.[13] The "original" of Lambdin's three portraits of Clay at the time was sent to Philadelphia by wagon, only to be lost. The portrait now in Lexington, Kentucky, may be very close to that "original," while the version in Pittsburgh, at the Carnegie Institute Museum, adds a scroll in Clay's hand. This is a more statesmanlike painting which may have had more forthright implications for the campaign of 1832.

Clay's prospects for the presidency seemed bright in 1840, and his renown was such that he was asked to sit for a host of indifferent artists in the later 1830s, as well as for the Cincinnati school of young sculptors, then for the heroic paintings as he moved toward the campaign of 1844.

Among the young sculptors who learned the rudiments of their craft in Cincinnati were four notable artists—Hiram Powers, Shobal Vail Clevenger, Joel T. Hart, and Henry Kirke Brown. All four went on to Italy to work in pure white marble. Powers was the only one of the four to gain international fame, and this was for his ideal sculpture, especially the famous *Greek Slave*, rather than for his portraits. Powers was balked in his efforts to model Henry Clay in Washington in 1837. Clay had been disappointed recently in the work of the "artistes," especially Horatio Greenough, whose bust he considered a failure, and he found it inconvenient to sit for Powers. Powers felt that he had been snubbed by Clay, and the snub was to rankle him for at least two decades, though he admitted that Clay had been of great service to his country.[14] The bust of Clay attributed to Powers at the Old Capitol Museum in Frankfort, Kentucky, may not be the work of Powers. It seems more likely to be a shop production in Florence, possibly by some of Powers's assistants working from a model by Hart, or possibly from Hart's studio.

Shobal Vail Clevenger was younger than Powers, but he was possibly the most gifted of all the Cincinnati sculptors; he was in any case the only Ohioan. He made a journey to Lexington to model Clay and then went on to Washington. His completed bust (1838) was exhibited there to very great praise. Wayne Craven regards this bust as one of the triumphs of Neo-Classic portrait sculpture, possibly the best.[15] Clay is slightly idealized. His thin lips are not emphasized but they are not denied, nor is his mouth overly wide. The likeness is excellent, giving Clay a firm and solid presence.

Joel Tanner Hart was to carve busts of Henry Clay through much of his life. He and Mahlon Pruden of Lexington were said at one time to have "littered" the country with busts of Clay. But Hart's other contributions to the history of Clay are posthumous; he did not complete his first statue of Clay until seven years after Clay's death. These statues are considered below. The other Cincinnati sculptor, Henry Kirke Brown, returned from Florence close to the time of Clay's death and completed a small memorial bronze bust of him.

Of the painters from the years 1838 to 1844, most were indifferent, but a remarkable bust portrait by Edward Dalton Marchant painted the same year as Clevenger's completed marble confirms the marble bust as an excellent, if idealized, likeness. Marchant was working in Cincinnati when he came to Lexington to paint Clay in 1838. When Mrs. Clay saw the completed head she is said to have wept for joy. Some years later the portrait was purchased by the State Department to represent Clay as secretary of state, though it was painted nearly a full decade after Clay had left that office.[16]

In the interval between 1840 and 1844, while Clay waited out the presidencies of William Henry Harrison and John Tyler, there are engravings that make Clay's image more public. An engraving by Ian Forrest after Washington Blanchard's miniature shows Clay's hair well below his ears. The original miniature now in the Corcoran Gallery was called "theatrical" by Charles Henry Hart in 1897, but there are others that show Clay much as Blanchard portrayed him.[17] An engraving by John F.E. Prudhomme after a portrait by George Linen was published as the frontispiece to the *Life and Speeches of Henry Clay* (New York, 1843), a bland and perhaps indifferent portrait of Clay, directed toward the campaign in 1844. By the time of the campaign, lithographs, especially Currier and Ives prints and those of E.B. & E.C. Kellogg of Hartford, were becoming a very standard part of campaigning, and even profitable to the lithographic firms. Also, the daguerreotype was just becoming known, and many artists were challenged by these new images. Some were very good painters and should have done better by Clay. Henry Inman was a brilliant painter at times, but a portrait of Clay by him, obviously indebted to the daguerreotype, is a poorly made likeness, unworthy of his signature (1840). Charles Loring Elliot may have thought of making a portrait of Clay but settled for painting directly over Alexander H. Ritchie's engraving, which was indebted in turn to Marcus A. Root's daguerreotype.

A very startling and bright portrait of Clay in these years was made by the Portugese émigré Manuel Joachim De Franca. The portrait, now at Clay's home, was owned by the McCormick family in Chicago and came to "Ashland" with the tradition that it was painted in Europe and brought home by Clay himself. But a letter of 1842 by Clay commending De Franca has been discovered, and the letter has made the proper dating and attribution of the portrait possible. "Mr. Franconia [sic] . . . has made a good portrait of me, which, as far as I am able to judge, is a good likeness. He has succeeded in some features, in respect to which most artists have failed."[18] What these features were we shall not know from Clay himself, but the letter is an excellent representation of Clay's ability to praise artists, sometimes with the reservations inherent in "some features" or in "some respects." The proper attribution and dating of the painting were important enough to cause the editors of the first volume of *The Papers of Henry Clay* to reproduce the portrait and use the letter as a frontispiece.

Until 1837 there was no heroic portrait of Henry Clay. In that year he was painted by the Maryland artist George Cooke in a legislative setting, in the act of speaking to an occasion, with the usual columns and drapes and with a view of the United States Capitol in the distance. Clay stands by a table with relevant papers, and his right arm designates these papers as it crosses his body. Clay's "shanks" are somewhat thin, perhaps with a view to the portrait's being shown higher than the spectator, in an optical accommodation to the viewer. Cooke was then painting other noted Americans, including George Washington, John C. Calhoun, and Daniel Webster, primarily for exhibition or sale in the South. Of the three versions of Cooke's portraits of Clay, two are now in the South, and one at Chicago was destroyed by fire in 1954.[19]

Between 1840 and 1844 the Whigs of Philadelphia commissioned John Neagle to journey to "Ashland" to paint a heroic portrait for the Union League Club in Philadelphia. Clay was very greatly pleased with this portrait as well as with the bust portrait Neagle painted initially.

In the full-length portrait Neagle shows Clay in the act of speaking, gesturing downward toward a flag that discloses a globe turned so as to reveal South America, thus indicating Clay's long-time promotion of independence for the colonies in Latin America. To Clay's left are the elements of the "American System," a shuttle, a plow, an anvil, some cattle, and in the distance a ship at sea. Neagle surely discussed these elements with Clay if he did not already understand them. When Calvin Colton later wrote to Clay asking for symbols that might be appropriate for Clay's coat of arms, Clay declined the suggestion of a coat of arms but replied that consideration should be given to "interests I have sought to promote in the National Councils. A loom, a shuttle, anvil, plow, or other articles connected with manufactures, agriculture, commerce."[20]

Neagle's heroic portrait is almost surely the most complex of the state portraits in America. Yet it was popular and popularly understood. It was engraved immediately by John Sartain, who regarded it as equal to Neagle's portrait of Pat Lyon, perhaps the artist's most important contribution to the history of art in America.[21] Sartain also engraved a full-length portrait of Clay after a painting by a nearly unknown James Wise, and produced another variant that he claimed was made from his own drawings, published in Louisville. Thus Neagle's portrait was spread about as a document of the campaign of 1844 and remains one of the best-known portraits. A full-sized replica by Ambrose Andrews is at "Ashland," and Neagle himself painted a replica for the United States Capitol. Smaller replicas of varying merit and size and by other artists are known.

Also looking to the campaign of 1844, George Caleb Bingham painted campaign banners for the Whig convention at Boonville, Missouri. Bingham is best known today as one of the major early genre painters, especially of life on the Missouri River, but he was a fervent Whig and was himself elected to the Missouri legislature somewhat later. He intended the banners for the Boonville convention to be substantial oil paintings on good linen, but only the one of Clay as the "Mill Boy" remains. The banners representing Clay as the "Plain Farmer" and as the exponent of the American System were lost by fire. Still later Bingham painted Clay in heroic posture for the state capitol of Missouri, but this painting was also lost by fire in 1911.[22]

The state portrait began to lose character near the time of the Civil War, and the painters who show Clay later than 1844 were often content to pose him in a legislative setting, or merely at a table with papers suggesting such a setting. Chester Harding, who had painted a good likeness of Clay in 1822, was in Washington at the time of the campaign of 1844 and had a tentative commission to paint Clay full-length, for which subscriptions were being sought among Clay's friends and partisans. Having no real interest in the commission, Harding much preferred Webster. He wrote, "I suppose I am to paint Mr. Clay."[23] After Clay's defeat there was some difficulty in obtaining subscriptions, but the portrait was finally completed in 1848. It shows Clay full-length, not in heroic posture or with symbolic elements but merely standing beside a table and chair in front of legislative columns. Clay appears merely to pose rather than to be actively speaking. The portrait is now in the National Portrait Gallery, Washington.

Toward the end of Clay's life, certain painters were commissioned for heroic portraits. Charles Wesley Jarvis, the son of the mercurial John Wesley, painted for the Union League Club of New York (1851) a relatively bland but accurate portrait of the aged Clay standing at a table. After Clay's death, however, Jarvis was commissioned for a full-length portrait for the Aldermen's Chambers, City Hall, New York. Jarvis's likenesses may have been dependent on daguerreotypes rather than actual sittings, but they are accurate. He shows Clay somewhat hunched and without his former vitality. The gesture he makes in the posthumous portrait can be taken for a farewell at a portico as easily as for a more positive address.

Clay took no pleasure in the implications of a "hard cider" and "log cabin" campaign such as Harrison's in 1840. An image of Clay at home had therefore to be of a different order. His almost patrician feelings would not allow him to be less than the dandy, and the painters who chose to show him as "The Sage of Ashland" were more appropriate to the campaign of 1844. Clay appears in their portraits with his top hat, a long coat, and a walking stick, usually in the vicinity of a large tree, presumably an ash. Theodore Sidney Moïse painted Clay in three-quarter-length view in New Orleans with a lake in the distance. The painting, now at the Metropolitan Museum, New York, was long attributed, through a misreading of the signature, to Samuel F.B. Morse, a painter and later inventor of the telegraph.

John Wood Dodge made three small paintings of Clay on his estate at "Ashland" seated on a hillock with his dog at his feet but dressed as a gentleman. One of the three replicas of this painting was engraved by H.S. Sadd as a direct contribution to the campaign of 1844.[24] A cabinet size painting by the Philadelphia lithographic artist Alfred Hoffy, showing Clay standing, may have been intended for a lithograph, but no such print is known. None of these paintings of Clay on his estate is by a major painter, and though the intention of at least two of them was directed toward Clay's last bid for the presidency, there is no evidence that they served him as well as did Neagle's heroic portrait and the engravings and replicas made from it.

After his defeat in 1844 Clay retired to "Ashland" to turn farmer again. He was embittered for a while, but when Philip Hone visited him in 1847 he was again able to "talk like a book." The Irish-American painter G.P.A. Healy came to "Ashland" in 1845 to paint Clay on a commission from Louis Philippe, king of France. Healy had hurried to the Hermitage to paint Andrew Jackson, then near death. When he came to paint Clay he was given a room with good light, and Clay began to enjoy his company, especially his gossip of the European courts. His sittings were long, and the Lexington artist Oliver Frazer, who had known Healy in France, was able to sketch Clay once more while Healy was painting. Clay believed Healy could do justice to his mouth, and Healy in turn reported that Clay's mouth was a peculiar one—thin lipped and extending almost from ear to ear—and that Clay had tremendous individuality. Healy showed the portrait to James Frothingham, who remarked that Clay was "a fox, but a genial fox."[25]

Healy's bust is one of the major portraits of Clay. It has a certain "shimmer" rather than incisive lines. There are a number of replicas, at least four by Healy himself. One replica went to France, where Louis Philippe had already lost his throne, and another was copied by a Major Clark, of whose replicas there is at least one in Lexington. Oliver Frazer's drawing, possibly made while Clay was posing for Healy, reflects this same "shimmer," which is present also in Frazer's late paintings of Clay, sometimes attributed to Frazer's failing eyesight. While Frazer was working on a replica of his painting of Clay, one member of the Clay family removed the painting from his easel, saying that the portrait was precisely like Clay.[26]

315

At the time of Clay's death the Kentucky sculptor Joel Tanner Hart was in Florence with a commission to complete a full-length statue of Clay for the Ladies' Clay Association of Richmond, Virginia. Clay admired Hart, who had made busts of him and of Cassius M. Clay; it was on the basis of these busts that Hart was commissioned for the full-length life-size statue. Clay's opinion was that Hart had the greatest versatility of talents of any man he had known. It was this very versatility that delayed Hart's completing the commissioned Clay statues and monuments. After early delays caused by the loss of one of the models and by Hart's illness in Florence, he began intensive work on his pointing machine.[27] It was only in 1859 that the Clay statue for Richmond was completed. Meanwhile, Hart had accepted a commission for a monumental bronze for the city of New Orleans,[28] and both statues were in place by 1860. Hart heard "imputations of laziness" from Richmond and did not go there for the dedication of the statue of Clay when he returned briefly to America in 1860. Instead, he was in New Orleans for the dedication of that monument. He sought the commission for the Clay Monument in the Lexington Cemetery, but the initial figure of Clay was completed by G. Rossi and A. Bullett. (It has been struck by lightning at least twice and was reconstructed by Charles Mulligan at the turn of this century.) Hart accepted instead a commission for a statue for Louisville and returned to Florence, where he completed the work by 1867.

A small bronze bust of Clay was made by Henry Kirke Brown close to the time of Clay's death in June 1852. Brown had returned to America after having known Clevenger, Powers, and Hart in Cincinnati and then again in Florence. He made first a marble bust, engraved by William H. Dougal in profile as a frontispiece to the *Obituary Addresses in Congress . . . Hon. Henry Clay* (Washington, 1852); then he cast small memorial busts dated July 1852 with a patent assigned to G. Nichols. Such an assignment surely implies wide distribution of casts, but thus far only two have appeared in public collections. The likeness shows a much younger Clay, and though both Brown and Clay were in New York in the early 1850s, no record of a sitting by Clay is known.

A bronze statuette of Clay was made by the sculptor Thomas Ball in 1858 as a companion to his *Webster*. Ball was certain of his ability to do justice to Webster, less sure of his *Clay*. He was assured by Edward Everett, however, that the statue was effective, as animated as Clay could be, and liked by everyone who had seen it. Wayne Craven has suggested that this statuette, only thirty-one inches high, is better than Hart's life-size monumental figures.[29] A larger plaster version of the statue is in a collection at Yale.

Modern bronzes of Clay include a work of Charles H. Niehaus in Statuary Hall, Washington, and a lesser known work by Edmond Quinn, which represents the "Young Cockerel of Kentucky" with a scroll in hand striding into the oratorical fray. This statue was given to the nation of Venezuela in return for a statue of Simon Bolivar sent to the United States.

The last decade of Clay's life corresponds almost exactly to the introduction and wide use of the daguerreotype process in America. When Samuel F.B. Morse brought back the process from Paris, he envisioned a partnership with Louis J.M. Daguerre. But it was not to be, and soon there were daguerreotypists in the larger cities here. In the survey of Historic American Portrait Daguerreotypes at the National Portrait Gallery, Webster and Clay vie for the position of the most frequently photographed American statesmen.[30]

The principal photographs of Clay were made by the studios of Edward Anthony, Mathew Brady, and Marcus A. Root. Many have been lost. Anthony's portrait of Henry and Lucretia Hart Clay is known in originals and in copies. The couple is old, of course, and Clay has long "scraggly" hair, while Lucretia wears a bonnet. Brady's photographs are the best known and have survived in various forms, one a *carte de visite* from long after Clay's death, a memorial card. Brady's original portraits were known also through an edition of lithographs by D'Avignon in partnership with Brady, and through a painting by Henry F. Darby, made perhaps at the time of Clay's sitting for Brady. Root's image had a very long life, since it seems to have been the principal one for memorial engravings and then survived as bank note and even postage stamp engravings. Clay always wears a heavy coat in Root's photographs.

Clay belongs to that last half century when the painters and sculptors were the primary image makers for statesmen. He was ordinarily kind to the artists, who were necessary to his public career. He rarely found an artist wholly lacking in merit, and he was amenable to writing letters on their behalf. Sometimes these letters were adroit in avoiding the failures and in finding things to praise. This is true especially in the case of De Franca's portrait at "Ashland," which had such a curious history. Clay's letter on behalf of the elder Jarvis, whom John J. Audubon regarded as "cracked," and whom Clay recommended more as an interesting man than as a painter, is another such ambivalent statement. It was only Greenough whom Clay called a failure, though not in a letter intended to be made public.

When Harriet Martineau said that she had seen no worthwhile portrait of Clay, perhaps thirty attempts already existed. The list grew much longer as Clay became still more a public figure through his campaigns and his struggles in the Senate for compromise on the slavery question. Martineau said that Clay tempered his remarks too greatly to the wishes of his hearers. The painters were often puzzled by him, but there are now enough works by the artists to give Clay "the face that he ought to have." He was by no means elusive to all of them.

Clay's state portraits, that is, his full-length portraits in the act of speaking, have more scope than those of Webster and far more than those of John C. Calhoun, who was painted less frequently. The praise awarded Neagle's portrait was very great. Reporters in the western papers who found it filled with a symbolism appropriate for Clay's American System and the nation were too expansive, but they sensed the remarkable scope of such a painting.

Clay belonged to an age of courtesy and even courtliness. By the time of his death, heroic painting had begun a steady decline. He grew tired of the long sittings for artists. Edward D. Marchant and James R. Lambdin had painted him in the 1830s, and they did so again in the late 1840s. They saw him in the later years still active, alert, and, in Lambdin's case, even jaunty and forthright; Marchant shows him considerably aged but still somewhat idealized. The daguerreotype finally aged him more than the painters were willing to allow. They robbed him of his full presence, his mobility, his color, and his size.

Clay was actually a statesman of another age, an age in which artists still had the power to be primary image makers. That age ended finally in the great war that Clay never lived to see.

1. Theodore Bolton & Ruel P. Tolman, "Benjamin Trott," *Art Quarterly* (1944), 7:257-90. The catalogue of Trott's works is by Tolman.

2. James O. Harrison, "Henry Clay. Reminiscences by His Executor," *Century Magazine* (Dec. 1886), 33:179.

3. The original miniature has not been located. *The Papers of Henry Clay* (Lexington, 1956), 2:163-64, 166-67. Hereafter cited as *Papers*.

4. Clay paid Jouett $100 for the replica of his portrait sent to Delaplaine. See *Papers*, 2:245. But a reproduction of this portrait was not published by Delaplaine. It may have been the source of the engraving published in 1820 by the *Analectic Magazine*.

5. Charles Coleman Sellers, *Charles Willson Peale* (Philadelphia, 1947), 2:321, fig. 36.

6. Henry Clay to William Dunlap, Washington, December 14, 1833. *Papers*, 8:676. In his autobiographical notes, *My Egotistigraphy* (Boston, 1866), Harding makes no mention of his early portrait of Clay. However, the later full-length portrait in Washington, 1844-48, is discussed at some length.

7. Charles B. King was noted as a painter of Indian chiefs visiting Washington, and also an early allegorist of the poverty of the artist in America. He annoyed William Dunlap by showing too much interest in theory and social issues. The engraving by Maverick was advertised for sale in the New York *Daily Advertiser* and then in the Lexington *Kentucky Reporter*, June 3, 1822.

8. *Papers*, 5:661. The toast was offered at a dinner in Clay's honor at Lewisburg, Virginia, August 20, 1826.

9. The attribution of the so-called Jouett at Chicago has been rejected by the Society. Efforts to connect it with Healy failed, and a suggestion that it might be by Bass Otis has not been confirmed.

10. *Papers*, 6:432-33, 524. Correspondence with Thomas I. Wharton.

11. "It is only after much intercourse that Mr. Clay's personal appearance can be discovered to do him any justice at all. All attempts to take his likeness have been in vain, though upward of thirty portraits of him, by different artists, were in existence when I was in America." Harriet Martineau, *A Retrospect of Western Travel* (London and New York, 1838), 1:173.

12. The letter from Judge Baldwin to Clay. *Papers*, 8:280.

13. Lambdin's autobiographical notes, unpublished, are in the Archives of American Art, Washington. A typescript made some time ago, unpaged, is at the University of Kentucky Art Museum, Lexington.

14. Clay wrote to Charles Edward Lester that failures by artists made him reluctant to sit for Powers. Yet he admitted that his failure to do so was a mistake. In this letter he calls Greenough's bust a failure, one of the rare times when he found nothing appropriate in a work by an artist. (Letter of September 26, Massachusetts Historical Society, Boston). Mr. Richard P. Wunder, who catalogued all of Powers's works for the National Museum of American Art, doubts that Powers made a bust of Clay. Letter to the author, 1986.

15. Wayne Craven, *Sculpture in America* (New York, 1984), 182.

16. The Department of State acquired Marchant's portrait along with his portrait of John Quincy Adams after the painter's death. The story that Mrs. Clay wept for joy on seeing Clay's portrait was told by Marchant's daughter. *The Secretaries of State* (Washington, Nov., 1978), 21 (Department of State Publication 8921).

17. Charles Henry Hart published the first overview of Clay portraits, "Life Portraits of Henry Clay," *McClure's Magazine* (Sept., 1897), 9:941-48. He may not have known other portraits of Clay, equally "theatrical," at the time of Blanchard's miniature.

18. *Papers*, 1:frontispiece. The editors of the *Papers* at that time were James F. Hopkins and Mary W.M. Hargreaves.

19. The primary reference for Cooke is Mary Lou Alston Rudulph, "George Cooke and His Paintings," *Georgia Historical Quarterly* (June 1960), 44:117-53. See also my "Henry Clay and the State Portrait," *Kentucky Review*, Fall, 1990.

20. Calvin Colton, *The Private Correspondence of Henry Clay* (Cincinnati, 1856), 532.

21. Sartain's remarks on Neagle's portrait are in his *Reminiscences of a Very Old Man* (New York, 1899), 192.

22. E. Maurice Bloch, *George Caleb Bingham* (Berkeley and Los Angeles, 1967), 1:211.

23. Chester Harding, *A Sketch of the Artist* (1927), 186.

24. Clifford Amyx, "The Painters of Henry Clay as 'The Sage of Ashland,' " *Kentucky Review* (Spring, 1988), 8:69-80. There is a copy of the painting by Moïse at the Margaret I. King Library, University of Kentucky. There are three versions, very similar, of the painting of Clay by Dodge.

25. G.P.A. Healy, *Reminiscences of a Portrait Painter* (Chicago, 1894; reprint ed., 1978), 147-48.

26. William Barrow Floyd, *Jouett, Bush, Frazer* (Lexington, 1868). Mr. Floyd's work is the only substantial account of Frazer.

27. Letters by Frederick Gale and Thomas Buchanan Read, written surely at Hart's request, are in the Addison G. Foster Collection, Margaret I. King Library, University of Kentucky.

28. Hart was in competition for the monumental bronze at New Orleans with the sculptor Thomas L. Crawford. Crawford offered to cast and place the statue for $16,000; Hart offered to do so for $10,000 but was required to furnish bond, no doubt because the "imputations of laziness" had reached New Orleans. Crawford may have made a

model of a statue for Clay partisans in New York, especially Philip Hone; the statue was not completed.

29. Wayne Craven, *Sculpture in America* (1984), 202.

30. Harold F. Pfister, *Facing the Light: Historic American Portrait Daguerreotypes* (Washington, 1978), 203-6, 305-8.

CALENDER OF ART WORK
FEATURING HENRY CLAY

ARTIST	GENRE	DATE	PRESENT LOCATION
Allen, William	Marble bust	1844	Location unknown
Andrews, Ambrose	Oil/canvas	*ca.*1856	"Ashland," Lexington, Ky.
Anelli, Francesco	Miniature	*ca.*1840	MHi
Anthony, Edward	Daguerreo-type	1844	"Ashland," Lexington, Ky.
Baker, S.F.	Engraving	1847	Location unknown
Ball, Thomas	Bronze	1858	NeRMA
	Replicas		NjR; Newark Museum, N.J.; "Ashland," Lexington, Ky.
Bartlett, Jason R.	Oil/canvas	1831	Privately owned
Beard, James H.	Oil/panel	?	National Museum of the D.A.R.,Washington, D.C.
	Oil	1850	NHi
	Oil/canvas	?	MoSHi
Berger, Charles F.	Oil/canvas	?	PPAFA
	Oil/canvas	?	Hegley Museum, Wilmington, De.
Bingham, George C.	Oil/canvas	1841	Location unknown
	Oil/canvas	1844	Privately owned
Birch, William R.	Miniature	?	Location unknown
Blanchard, Washington	Minia./ivory	1842	DCA
Brady, Mathew B.	Daguerreo-type	*ca.*1850	NHi
	Daguerreo-type	*ca.*1851	DLC
	Daguerreo-type	*ca.*1851	NNMoMA
Briscoe, A.H.	Medallion	*ca.*1859	Location unknown
Browere, John H.I.	Plaster bust	1825	NHi
Brown, Henry K.	Marble bust	1852	Newark Museum, N.J.
	Marble bust	?	DSI-NPG
	Bronze bust	1852	KyU
	Bronze bust	1852	Newark Museum, N.J.
Brown, William H.	Silhouette	1844	Location unknown
Brumidi, Constantine	Monochrome	?	U.S. Capitol
Burt, Charles K.	Engraving	?	Location unknown
Bush, Joseph H.	Oil/canvas	1848	Privately owned
Buttre, John C.	Engraving	1856	Frontispiece in E. Sargent, *Life of Henry Clay*
Cafferty, James H.	Oil/canvas	1847	NjHi
Cannon, Hugh	Marble bust	1841	PPAFA
Carter, Dennis	Oil/canvas	?	Location unknown
Chappel, Alonzo	Engraving	1861	Location unknown
	Engraving	1873	KyU
Crehen, Charles G.	Print	1850	DSI-NPG
Clevenger, Shobal V.	Marble bust	1838	NNMM
	Plaster busts	*ca.*1840	NHi, MdHi, MBAt

319

ARTIST	GENRE	DATE	PRESENT LOCATION
Cohill, Charles	Oil/canvas	1837	Location unknown
Cole, Joseph G.	Pencil draw- ing	?	MBMu
Colton & Barnes	Engraving	?	Frontispiece in vol. 5 of Colton, *Clay Correspondence*
Cooke, George	Oil/canvas	1837	Hanover County Court House, Ashland, Va.
	Oil/canvas	ca.1837	Destroyed, 1954
	Replicas	?	AU, DLC
Cox, Allyn	Oil	1950	U.S. Capitol
Currier & Ives	Lithographs	?	See Gale Research Co. Cata- logue, *Currier and Ives* (2 vols.), Detroit, 1984
Danforth, Wright & Co.	Engraving	?	PPAFA
Darby, Henry F.	Oil/canvas	1850	U.S. Capitol
D'Avignon, Francis	Litho./stone	1844	Location unknown
	Lithograph	1850	KyU
	Lithograph	ca.1850	KyU
	Engraving	?	*Harper's Magazine*, 68:945
DeFranca, Manuel J.	Oil/canvas	1842	"Ashland," Lexington, Ky.
Dick, Archibald L.	Engraving	?	Location unknown
Dodge, John W.	Oil/canvas	1843	PPAFA
	Oil/canvas	ca.1843	Privately owned
	Miniature	ca.1843	Location unknown
	Miniature	ca.1847	MdBWA
Doney, Thomas	Engraving	1845	*American Review*, vol. 1, 1845
	Engraving	1845	DSI-NPG
	Engraving	1848	Location unknown
Doolittle & Munson	Engraving	1842	Frontispiece in R. Chambers, *Speeches of Henry Clay....*
Dougal, William H.	Engraving	1852	Frontispiece in *Obituary Ad- dresses ... Hon. Henry Clay....* Washington, 1852
Dubourjal, Savinien E.	Miniature	?	NNMM
Earl, Ralph E.	Oil/canvas	?	DSI
Eckstein, Fredrick	Bust/life mask	ca.1825	Location unknown
Edauort, Auguste	Silhouette	1841	Location unknown
Edwards, W.J.	Engraving	?	KyU
Elliott, Charles L.	Oil/paper	?	KyLoU
Fagnani, Giuseppe	Oil/canvas	1852	U.S. Capitol
	Pastel/paper	1850	NHi
Fenderich, Charles	Lithograph	1844	KyU
	Lithograph	?	DSI-NPG
Forrest, Ian B.	Engraving	ca.1846	Frontispiece in vol. 1 of Colton, *Life of Henry Clay*
Fowler, Trevor T.	Oil/canvas	1840	Location unknown
Frazer, Oliver	Oil/canvas	?	KyHi
	Oil	?	Privately owned
	Oil	?	"The Brook," New York, N.Y.
	Oil/canvas	?	PEL
	Pencil draw- ing	?	Privately owned
	Miniature	1850	Privately owned
Frye, William	Oil/canvas	1865	KyHi
"G.M."	Engraving	?	KyU
Garlick, Theodatus	Medallion	?	Location unknown
Gibert, Antoine P.	Oil/canvas	1845	NNNGB
	Drawing	?	Location unknown

ARTIST	GENRE	DATE	PRESENT LOCATION
	Lithograph	?	In Harold F. Pfister, *Facing the Light . . .*, p. 307
Gimbrede, Thomas	Engraving	1816	DLC
Gould, Walter	Oil/canvas	?	Privately owned
Greenough, Horatio	Marble bust	*ca.*1836	Location unknown
Greiner, Christopher	Enamel	*ca.*1844	Location unknown
Grimes, John	Oil/canvas	?	Location unknown
Gross, Jacob D.	Engraving	?	Location unknown
Haas, Philip	Lithograph	?	Pfister, *Facing the Light*, no. 746
Haines, Frederick W.	Engraving	1844	KyU
Harding, Chester	Oil/canvas	1821-22	MA
	Oil/canvas	1848	DSI-NPG
	Oil/canvas	?	DS
Hart, Joel T.	Plaster bust	1842	KyHi
	Marble bust	1847	"Ashland," Lexington, Ky.
	Marble bust	1873	KyHi
	Plaster bust	?	KyU
	Marble bust	?	NNMM
	Plaster bust	?	NHi
	Marble bust	1844	DCA
	Marble bust	?	KyLx
	Plaster bust	1847	MdHi
	Mar. statuette	?	Privately owned
	Mar./life size	1847-59	Capitol, Richmond, Va.
	Bronze	1847-59	Lafayette Square, New Orleans
	Stone monument	*ca.*1861	Lexington (Ky.) Cemetery
	Bronze bust	?	"Ashland," Lexington, Ky.
Haynes, C. Younglove	Plaster relief	1850	ViHi
	Replica	?	PPL
Healy, George P.A.	Oil/canvas	1845	DSI-NPG
	Oil/canvas	?	"Ashland," Lexington, Ky.
	Oil/canvas	?	Musee Nationale, Versailles, France
Henry, Albert P.	Marble bust	?	U.S. Capitol
Hoffy, Alfred G.	Oil/canvas	1844	KyU
Hubard, William J.	Oil/canvas	1831-32	ViU
	Minia./copper	*ca.*1832	NHi
Inman, Henry	Oil/canvas	1840	Berkshire Museum, Pittsfield, Mass.
Jackson, W.J.	Engraving	?	KyU
Jarvis, Charles W.	Oil/canvas	1851	NNUnionL
	Oil/canvas	1854	City Hall, New York, N.Y.
Jarvis, John W.	Oil/panel	1814	Percy Rockefeller Estate, New York, N.Y.
Johnson, T.	Engraving	?	*Century Magazine*, 30:480
Jones, Thomas D.	Marble bust	1844	Tenn. State Museum, Nashville
	Plaster relief	*ca.* 1853	MdHi
	Replica	?	MdHi
Jouett, Mathew H.	Oil/canvas	1818	"Ashland," Lexington, Ky.
	Oil/canvas	1822	KyLxT
	Oil/canvas	?	Privately owned
	Replica	1818	Location unknown

321

ARTIST	GENRE	DATE	PRESENT LOCATION
	Oil/canvas	1822	On loan to Westmoreland Co. Museum, Greenburg, Pa.
	Engraving	1820	*The Analect Magazine*, vol. 1, no. 3, March, 1820
Kellogg, E.B. & E.C.	Lithograph	1840	CtHi
	Lithograph	?	CtHi
	Lithograph	?	D.W. Kellogg & Co., Hartford, Conn.
	Lithograph	1844	D.W. Kellogg & Co., Hartford, Conn.
Kellogg, Jarvis G.	Engraving	1832	DSI-NPG
King, Charles B.	Oil/canvas	1821	DCA
Lambdin, James R.	Oil/canvas	1831	KyU
	Oil/canvas	1832	PPiC
	Oil/canvas	?	Ehrich Galleries, New York, N.Y.
	Oil/canvas	*ca*.1831	NBLiHi
	Oil/canvas	1846	DS
Linen, George	Oil/canvas	1838	Privately owned
Longacre, James B.	Engraving	1836	In Rice & Hart, *National Portrait Gallery*, 1:18
	Engraving	1827	Frontispiece in J. Maxwell, *Speeches of Henry Clay*. . . .
Macdougall, John A.	Miniature	1844	NNMM
McPherson, John	Print	?	DSI-NPG
Marchant, Edward D.	Oil/canvas	1838	DS
	Replica	?	DSI-NPG
	Oil/canvas	1850	KyLoU
Martin, John B.	Oil/canvas	?	NcU
Maverick, Peter	Engraving	1822	*Papers of Henry Clay*, 4:497 (copy)
Mayer & Co.	Engraving	1856	Frontispiece in Colton, *Last Seven Years*. . . .
Middleton, Wallace	Engraving	1858	Frontispiece in William Clarke, *Monument to the Memory of Henry Clay*
Mills, Clark	Life mask	*ca*.1843	NjP
Moïse, Theodore S.	Oil/canvas	1843	NNMM
	Replica	1931	KyU
	Oil/canvas	?	Tenn. State Museum, Nashville
Muckelbauer, J.A.	Oil/canvas	?	Location unknown (photocopy in KyLoF)
Muller, Carl	Metal bust	1856	NHi
Neagle, John	Oil/canvas	1843	Union League Club, Philadelphia
	Oil/canvas	1843	U.S. Capitol
	Oil/canvas	?	American Scenic and Historic Preservation Society, New York
	Oil/canvas	?	The Burlingham Sale
	Oil/canvas	?	Privately owned
	Engraving	?	KyU
	Engraving	?	Frontispiece in vol. 1 of Colton, *Life & Speeches*. . . .
	Engraving	?	KyU
Newsam, Albert	Lithograph	*ca*.1829	DSI-NPG
	Lithograph	1831	DSI-NPG
	Lithograph	1844	DSI-NPG
Niehaus, Charles H.	Bronze	1928	U.S. Capitol
Osgood, Samuel S.	Oil/canvas	1839	NHi

ARTIST	GENRE	DATE	PRESENT LOCATION
Otis, Bass	Oil/canvas	?	Privately owned
Packard, Rawson	Engraving	1851	*The American (Whig) Review*, 13:383
Packer, Francis	Plaster/ bronzed	1933	DSI
Pate, William	Oil/canvas	?	CtY
Peale, Charles W.	Oil/canvas	1818	PHi
Peale, Rembrandt	Oil/canvas	?	PPAFA
	Oil/canvas	?	DSI-NPG
Pettrich, Ferdinand	Plaster/ bronzed	1842	DSI
Plumbe, John	Daguerreo- type	1846	Location unknown (copy in Pfister, *Facing the Light*, p. 74)
Powers, Hiram	Marble bust	?	KyHi
Pruden, Mahlon J.	Plaster	?	KyLx
Prudhomme, John F.E.	Engraving	*ca.*1843	Frontispiece in J. Swain, *The Life and Speeches of Henry Clay*
Quinn, Edmond T.	Bronze	1925	Caracas, Venezuela
Reich, Jacques	Drawing	?	DSI-NPG
Ritchie, Alexander	Engraving	1852	KyU
	Engraving	?	"Ashland," Lexington, Ky.
	Engraving	?	KyU
Robinson, Henry R.	Lithograph	1848	KyU
Rocia	Marble bust	?	Location unknown
Root (Marcus A.) Studio	Daguerreo- type	1848	Privately owned
	Daguerro- type	?	PHi
	Daguerro- type	1851	Location unknown
Rothermel, Peter F.	Oil/canvas	?	Location unknown
Sadd, Henry S.	Engraving	1839	KyU
	Engraving	1843	KyU
Sartain, John	Engraving	?	KyU
	Engraving	1844	PPAFA
	Engraving	*ca.*1848	Location unknown
	Engraving	1852	KyU
Sartain, Samuel	Mezzotint	1865	DSI-NPG
Saunders, Henry	Marble bust	*ca.*1853	Location unknown
Sealey, Alfred	Engraving	1859	DSI-NPG
Shackelford, William S.	Bust	?	Location unknown
Shumway, Henry C.	Miniature	*ca.*1841	Location unknown
Simons, Montgomery P.	Daguerreo- type	1848	DSI
Sims	Sculpture/ wood	1825	Destroyed
Southworth & Hawes	Daguerreo- type	?	NNMM
Stanton, Phineas, Jr.	Oil/canvas	1847	City Hall, New York, N.Y.
	Oil/canvas	1865	Location unknown
Stout, Thomas	Medallion	1839	Location unknown
Trott, Benjamin	Minia./ivory	1805	Privately owned
Vannerson, Julian	Daguerreo- type	?	DSI-MHT
Volk, Leonard W.	Marble bust	1851	KyHi
Walcutt, William	Oil/canvas	?	KyHi
Warner, William	Oil/canvas	*ca.*1844	Location unknown
Whitechurch, Robert	Engraving	1850	Presented to U.S. Senate
Wier, Robert	Watercolor	1852	Location unknown

ARTIST	GENRE	DATE	PRESENT LOCATION
Willard, Asaph	Engraving	1831	Frontispiece in G. Prentice, *Biography of Henry Clay*
Wise, James	Oil/canvas	*ca.*1845	Location unknown
Wood, Joseph	Painting	1825	Location unknown
Woodcock & Harvey	Engraving	1839	KyU
Woodward, David A.	Oil/canvas	1850	Location unknown
Wright, Charles C.	Bronze medal	1850	DSI-NPG
Unattributed	Oil/canvas	?	Privately owned
	Bronze	?	Slater Memorial Museum, Norwich, Conn.
	Oil/canvas	*ca.*1849	DCA
	Oil/canvas	?	DCos
	Oil/panel	1826	ICHi
	Oil/canvas	?	The Masonic Club, Lexington, Ky.
	Oil/canvas	?	Old South Association, Boston, Ky.
	Bronze	?	"Ashland," Lexington, Ky.
	Life Mask	?	NjP
	Miniature	?	NHi
	Sculpture	?	PPL
	Oil/canvas	?	ViAsR
	Daguerreo-type	?	DSI-NPG
	Daguerreo-type	1847	Location unknown
	Daguerreo-type	?	Privately owned
	Talbottype	1850	ViU
	Daguerreo-type	?	KyLoU
	Daguerreo-type	1849	CtY
	Daguerreo-type	?	NRGE
	Daguerreo-type	*ca.*1848	"Ashland," Lexington, Ky.

324

COMPREHENSIVE BIBLIOGRAPHY
OF WORKS CITED

Abernethy, Thomas P. *The Burr Conspiracy*. New York, 1954.
——— . *The Formative Period in Alabama, 1815-1828*. Montgomery, Ala., 1922.
——— . *From Frontier to Plantation in Tennessee*. Chapel Hill, N.C., 1932; reprint ed., 1967.
An Act to Incorporate The New England Society of Louisiana. Approved, March 26, 1842. . . . New Orleans, 1842.
The Acts of the Apostles of the Sea, An Eighty Years Record of the Works of the American Seamen's Friend Society. New York, 1909.
Adams, Ephraim D. *British Interests and Activities in Texas, 1838-1846*. Baltimore, 1910.
Adams, Henry. *History of the United States of America*. 9 vols. New York, 1889-91.
——— . *The Life of Albert Gallatin*. Reprint ed. New York, 1943.
——— , ed. *The Writings of Albert Gallatin*. 3 vols. Philadelphia, 1879.
Adams, Herbert B. *The Life and Writings of Jared Sparks*. Cambridge, Mass., 1893.
——— . *Thomas Jefferson and the University of Virginia*. Washington, 1888.
Adams, John Quincy. *The Duplicate Letters and the Fisheries and the Mississippi. . . .* Washington, 1822.
——— . *Lives of Madison and Monroe, Fourth and Fifth Presidents of the United States*. Boston, 1850.
——— . *Memoirs of John Quincy Adams*. Edited by Charles F. Adams. 12 vols. Philadelphia, 1876.
——— . *Writings of John Quincy Adams*. Edited by Worthington C. Ford. 7 vols. New York, 1913-17.
Adams, Oscar F. *A Dictionary of American Authors*. Boston, 1904.
Adams, Randolph G. *The Case of the Columbus Letter. . . .* New York, 1939.
Adams, William Harrison. "The Louisiana Whig Party." Ph.D. dissertation, Louisiana State University, 1960.
——— . *The Whig Party of Louisiana*. Lafayette, La., 1973.
Address to the People of the United States in Relation to the People and Government of Rhode Island. Providence, 1844.
Albert, George D., ed. *History of the County of Westmoreland, Pennsylvania. . . .* Philadelphia, 1882.
Albion, Robert G. *The Rise of New York Port, 1815-1860*. Hamden, Conn., 1961.
——— . *Square-Riggers on Schedule, The New York Sailing Packets to England, France, and the Cotton Ports*. Princeton, N.J., 1938.
Aler, F. Vernon. *Aler's History of Martinsburg and Berkeley County, West Virginia*. Hagerstown, Md., 1888.
Alexander, DeAlva S. *A Political History of the State of New York*. 3 vols. New York, 1906.
Alexander, Holmes. *The American Talleyrand, the Career and Contemporaries of Martin Van Buren, Eighth President*. New York, 1935.
Alexander, Thomas B. *Sectional Stress and Party Strength*. Nashville, 1967.
Alison, Archibald. *The Principles of Population and Their Connection with Human Happiness*. 2 vols. London, 1840.
Allen, Jane M. *Henry Watkins of Henrico County. . . .* Baltimore, 1985.
Allen, Jeffrey B. "The Debate Over Slavery and Race in Ante-Bellum Kentucky, 1792-1850." Ph.D. dissertation, Northwestern University, 1973.
Allen, Lewis F. *History of the Short-Horn Cattle*. Buffalo, 1872.
Allen, Paul. *History of the Expedition Under the Command of Captains Lewis and Clark. . . .* 2 vols. Philadelphia, 1814.
Allen, William B. *A History of Kentucky. . . .* Louisville, 1872.
Alvord, Clarence W. *The Centennial History of Illinois*. 5 vols. Springfield, Ill., 1919.

Ambler, Charles H. *The Life and Diary of John Floyd*. Richmond, Va., 1918.
———. *Sectionalism in Virginia From 1776 to 1861*. New York, 1964.
———. *Thomas Ritchie, A Study in Virginia Politics*. Richmond, Va., 1913.
———. "Virginia and the Presidential Succession, 1840-1844." In *Essays in American History Dedicated to Frederick Jackson Turner*. New York, 1910.
Ambrose, Stephen E. *Duty, Honor, Country: A History of West Point*. Baltimore, 1966.
The American Almanac and Repository of Useful Knowledge. . . . Boston, yearly editions.
American Colonization Society, A View of Exertions Lately Made for the Purpose of Colonizing the Free People of Colour in the United States, in Africa, or Elsewhere. Washington, 1817.
The American Military Pocket Atlas. London, 1776.
Ames, William E. *A History of the National Intelligencer*. Chapel Hill, N.C., 1972.
Ammon, Harry. *James Monroe, The Quest for National Identity*. New York, 1971.
Amyx, Clifford. "The Portraits of Henry Clay." 2 vols. Typescript. Special Collections, University of Kentucky, 1980.
Anales de la Sociedad de Geografia e Historia de Guatemala. Vol. 27. Marzo, 1953.
Ancestry and Descendants of Sir Richard Saltonstall. New York, 1897.
Anderson, James D. *Making the American Thoroughbred Especially in Tennessee, 1800-1845. . . .* Norwood, Mass., 1916.
Andrews, Henry P. *The Descendants of John Porter of Windsor, Connecticut. . . .* Saratoga Springs, N.Y., 1882.
Annuaire de la Noblesse et des Familles Patriciennes des Pays-Bas . . . le Annee, 1871. Rotterdam, 1871.
Annual Announcement of Transylvania University for 1843-44. Lexington, 1844.
The Annual Register, or a View of the History, Politics and Literature for the year. . . . London, 1825.
Anthony, Irvin. *Decatur*. New York, 1931.
Anthony, Katharine S. *Dolley Madison, Her Life and Times*. Garden City, N.Y., 1949.
Archer, William. *Play-Making; a Manual of Craftsmanship*. Boston, 1913.
Ardery, Julia S. *The Duncans of Bourbon County. . . .* Lexington, Ky., 1943.
Armstrong, J.M., pub. *Biographical Encyclopedia of Kentucky*. Cincinnati, 1878.
Arndt, Karl J.R., ed. *Economy on the Ohio, 1826-1834*. Worcester, Mass., 1984.
———. *George Rapp's Harmony Society, 1785-1847*. Rutherford, Pa., 1965.
The Ashland Text Book, Being a Compendium of Mr. Clay's Speeches, on Various Public Measures, Etc. Etc. Philadelphia, 1844.
Atkins, Dudley, ed. *Reports of Hospital Physicians, and Other Documents in Relation to the Epidemic Cholera of 1832*. New York, 1832.
Atwater, Edward E. *History of the City of New Haven*. New York, 1887.
Audubon, John James. *Ornithological Biography, or An Account of the Habits of the Birds of the United States of America*. Edinburgh, 1831-49.
Bacon, David F. *Wanderings on the Seas and Shores of Africa*. New York, 1843.
Bailey, Frank. *British Policy and the Turkish Reform Movement*. Cambridge, Mass., 1942.
Bailey, Kenneth P. *The Ohio Company Papers, 1753-1817*. Arcata, Calif., 1947.
Bailey, Thomas A. *A Diplomatic History of the American People*. 10th ed. Englewood Cliffs, N.J., 1980.
Baines, Edward. *History of the Cotton Manufacture in Great Britain. . . .* 2nd ed. London, 1966.
Baker, Elizabeth F. *Henry Wheaton, 1785-1848*. 1st ed., 1937; reprint ed., New York, 1971.
Baker, Gary E. "The Flint Glass Industry in Wheeling, West Virginia: 1829-1865." Master's thesis, University of Delaware, 1986.
Baker, William M. *Life & Labours of the Rev. Daniel Baker, D.D.* Philadelphia, 1858.
Balch, Galusha B. *Genealogy of the Balch Family in America*. Salem, Mass., 1897.
Ballentine's Law Dictionary. 3rd ed. Rochester, New York, 1969.
Bancroft, Hubert H. *History of the North Mexican States and Texas*. 2 vols. San Francisco, 1889.
———. *The Works of Hubert Howe Bancroft*. 39 vols. San Francisco, 1882-90.
Banks, Henry. *The Vindication of John Banks of Virginia. . . .* Frankfort, Ky., 1826.
Banks, Ronald F. *Maine Becomes a State: The Movement to Separate Maine from Massachusetts, 1785-1820*. Middletown, Conn., 1970.
Barbe-Marbois, Francois. *Histoire de la Louisiane et de la cession de cette colonie par la France aux Etats-Unis de l'Amerique Septentrionale. . . .* Paris, 1829. English translation by William B. Lawrence. Philadelphia, 1830.

Barber, Noel. *The Sultans*. New York, 1973.

Barker, Eugene, ed. *The Austin Papers*. Austin, Tx., 1926.

Barker, Jacob. *Incidents in the Life of Jacob Barker.* . . . Washington, 1855.

Barker, Nancy N. *The French Experience in Mexico, 1821-1861.* . . . Chapel Hill, N.C., 1979.

Barlen, M.E. *The Foundations of Modern Europe*. London, 1968.

Barnard, Harry. *Rutherford B. Hayes and His America*. New York, 1954.

Barnes, Harry Elmer. *The Evolution of Penology in Pennsylvania*. Indianapolis, *ca.* 1927.

Barnes, James J. *Authors, Publishers and Politicians, The Quest for an Anglo-American Copyright Agreement 1815-1854*. Columbus, Ohio, 1974.

Barnes, Thurlow W., ed. *The Life of Thurlow Weed Including His Autobiography and a Memoir*. 2 vols. Boston, 1884.

Barnwell, John. *Love of Order, South Carolina's First Secession Crisis*. Chapel Hill, N.C., 1982.

Bartlett, Irving H. *Daniel Webster*. New York, 1978.

Bartlett, John. *Familiar Quotations.* . . . 13th ed. Boston, 1955.

Bascom, Henry B. *Methodism and Slavery: With Other Matters in the Controversy Between the North and the South.* . . . Frankfort, Ky., 1845.

Baskin, O.L. *History of Logan County and Ohio.* . . . Chicago, 1880.

Bassett, John S. *The Life of Andrew Jackson*. 2 vols. Garden City, N.Y., 1911.

Bastiel, Paul. *Les Institutions Politiques de la Monarchie Parlemintaire Francoise*. Paris, 1954.

Bateman, Newton & Paul Selby, eds. *Historical Encyclopedia of Illinois*. Chicago, 1899.

Bateman, Newton, ed. *Historical Encyclopedia of Illinois and History of Sagamon County*. 2 vols. Chicago, 1912.

Bauer, K. Jack. *The Mexican War, 1846-1848*. New York, 1974.

———. *Ships of the Navy, 1775-1969*. Troy, N.Y., 1969.

———. *Zachary Taylor: Soldier, Planter, Statesman of the Old Southwest*. Baton Rouge, 1985.

Baxter, Maurice G. *One and Inseparable, Daniel Webster and the Union*. Cambridge, Mass., 1984.

Bayley, Rafael. *The National Loans of the United States from July 4, 1776 to June 30, 1880*. Washington, 1881.

Bayliss, M.F. *The Matriarchy of the American Turf 1875-1930*. N.p., 1931.

Baylor, Orval W. *John Pope, Kentuckian*. Cynthiana, Ky., 1943.

Beach, Moses Y., ed. *The Wealth and Biography of the Wealthy Citizens of the City of New York*. New York, 1846.

Beach, Vincint W. *Charles X of France*. Boulder, Colo., 1971.

Beasley, Paul. "Isaac Shelby." Master's thesis, University of Kentucky, 1968.

Beatty, Adam. *Southern Agriculture, Being Essays on the Cultivation of Corn, Hemp, Tobacco, Wheat, Etc. and the Best Method of Renovating the Soil*. New York, *ca.* 1843.

Beers, W.H., pub. *The History of Brown County, Ohio.* . . . Chicago, 1883.

Beik, Paul H. *Louis Philippe and the July Monarchy*. Princeton, N.J., 1965.

Bell, Landon C. *The Old Free State*. 2 vols. Richmond, Va., 1927.

Bemis, Samuel F., ed. *The American Secretaries of State and Their Diplomacy*. 10 vols. New York, 1927-29.

———. *A Diplomatic History of the United States*. New York, 1936.

———. *John Quincy Adams and the Foundations of American Foreign Policy*. New York, 1949.

———. *John Quincy Adams and the Union*. New York, 1956.

Bender, Thomas. *Towards An Urban Vision*. Lexington, Ky., 1975.

Bennet, James A. *The American System of Practical Book-Keeping, Adapted to the Commerce of the United States, in its Domestic and Foreign Relations; Comprehending all the Modern Improvements in the Practice of the Art.* . . . New York, 1820.

Bennett, David H. *The Party of Fear from Nativist Movements to the New Right in American History*. Chapel Hill, N.C., 1988.

Benns, F. Lee. *The American Struggle for the British West India Carring Trade, 1815-1830*. Reprint ed. Clifton, N.J., 1972.

Benson, Lee. *The Concept of Jacksonian Democracy: New York as a Test Case*. New York, 1965.

Benton, Thomas Hart. *Thirty Years' View; or, A History of the Working of the American Government for Thirty Years, From 1820 to 1850*. 2 vols. New York, 1858.

Bergeron, Paul. *The Presidency of James K. Polk*. Lawrence, Kan., 1987.

Berkeley, Edmund & Dorothy. *John Beckley.* . . . Philadelphia, 1973.

Bevan, Wilson L., ed. *History of Delaware Past and Present*. New York, 1929.

Beveridge, Albert. *The Life of John Marshall*. 4 vols. New York, 1919.

Biggs, Nina M. & Mabel L. MacKoy. *History of Greenup County, Kentucky.* Louisville, 1951.
Billington, Ray Allen. *The Origins of Nativism in the United States, 1800-1844.* Reprint ed. New York, 1974.
———. *The Protestant Crusade, 1800-1860.* New York, 1938.
Binkley, William C. *The Texas Revolution.* Baton Rouge, 1952.
Biographical Annals of Franklin County, Pennsylvania. . . . Chicago, 1905.
Biographical and Historical Memoirs of Mississippi. . . . 2 vols. Chicago, 1891.
Biographical Directory of the American Congress. Washington, 1928.
Birkner, Michael. "Politics, Law, and Enterprise in Jacksonian America: The Career of Samuel L. Southard, 1787-1842." Ph.D. dissertation, Princeton University, 1981.
———. *Samuel L. Southard; Jeffersonian Whig.* Rutherford, N.J., 1984.
Bishop, Robert H. *An Outline of the History of the Church in the State of Kentucky, during a Period of Forty Years. . . .* Lexington, Ky., 1824.
Blackburn, Joyce. *George Wythe of Williamsburg.* New York, 1975.
Blackstone, William. *Commentaries on the Laws of England. . . .* 18th London ed. New York, 1832.
Bland, Richard A. "Politics, Propaganda, and the Public Printing: The Administration Organs, 1829-1849." Ph.D. dissertation, University of Kentucky, 1975.
Bobbé, Dorothie. *DeWitt Clinton.* New York, 1933.
Bode, Carl. *The American Lyceum, Town Meeting of the Mind.* New York, 1956.
Bodley, Temple. *George Rogers Clark, His Life and Public Services.* Boston, 1926.
———. "Introduction." In *Reprints of Littell's Political Transactions.* Filson Club Publications. No. 31. Louisville, 1926.
Bohner, Charles H. *John Pendleton Kennedy, Gentleman from Baltimore.* Baltimore, 1961.
Bolivar, Simon. *Selected Writings of Bolivar.* Edited by Harold A. Bierck, Jr. 2 vols. New York, 1951.
Bolles, Albert S. *The Financial History of the United States.* 3rd ed. New York, 1891.
Bonner, James C. *A History of Georgia Agriculture 1732-1860.* Athens, Ga., 1964.
Bonner, William T. *New York, The World's Metropolis 1623-4—1923-4. . . .* New York, 1924.
Bonney, Catharina Van Rensselaer, comp. *A Legacy of Historical Gleanings.* 2 vols. Albany, N.Y., 1875.
Booth, William A. *The Writings of William A. Booth, M.D. During the Controversy Upon Slavery Which Ended in the Division of the Methodist Episcopal Church.* Sommerville, Tenn., 1845.
Boreman, Robert. *The Triumph of Faith Over Death.* London, 1654.
Boston City Directory. Boston, 1837.
Botta, Carlo. *History of War of Independence of the United States of America.* Translated by George A. Otis. 3 vols. Philadelphia, 1820-21.
Bouchette, Joseph. *A Topographical Description of the Province of Lower Canada with Remarks upon Upper Canada, and on the Relative Connexion of both Provinces with the United States of America.* London, 1815.
Bourne, Edward G. *The History of the Surplus Revenue of 1837.* New York, 1885; reprint ed., 1968.
Bowers, Claude. *The Party Battles of the Jackson Period.* New York, 1922.
Bowie, Effie G. *Across the Years in Prince Georges; a Genealogical and Biographical History of Some Prince Georges County, Maryland and Allied Families.* Richmond, Va., 1947; reprint ed., Baltimore, 1975.
Bowker, Richard R. *Copyright, Its History and Its Law.* New York, 1912.
Boxer, C.R. *The Portuguese Seaborne Empire, 1415-1825.* New York, 1969.
Boyd, Julian P. *The Murder of George Wythe, Two Essays.* Williamsburg, Va., 1955.
Boyd, William H. *Auburn Directory, 1859-60.* New York, 1860.
Brack, Gene M. *Mexico Views Manifest Destiny, 1821-1846: An Essay on the Origins of the Mexican War.* Albuquerque, 1975.
Brackenridge, Henry M. *Speech Delivered in Broadhurst's Grove on the Evening of the 6th October, 1843.* Pittsburgh, 1843.
———. *Voyage to South America. . . .* 2 vols. Baltimore, 1819.
Bradley, Harold W. *The American Frontier in Hawaii; the Pioneers, 1789-1843. . . .* Palo Alto, Calif., 1942.
Brady, W. Strader, ed. *Rhode Island Manual.* N.p., n.d.
Brandon, Edgar E. *Lafayette: Guest of the Nation.* 3 vols. Oxford, Ohio, 1950-57.
Brant, Irving. *The Fourth President, A Life of James Madison.* Indianapolis, 1970.

————. *James Madison.* 6 vols. Indianapolis, 1940-61.

Brauer, Kinley J. *Cotton versus Conscience.* Lexington, 1967.

Brawley, James S. *The Rowan Story 1753-1953, A Narrative History of Rowan County, N.C.* Salisbury, N.C., 1953.

Brebner, John B. *North Atlantic Triangle, The Interplay of Canada, the United States and Great Britain.* New Haven, Conn., 1945.

Breckinridge, Sophonisba P. *Legal Tender: A Study in English and American Monetary History.* Chicago, 1903.

Brenaman, Jacob N. *A History of Virginia Conventions. . . .* Richmond, Va., 1902.

Brescia, Anthony M. *The Letters and Papers of Richard Rush.* Microfilm edition.

Brigham, Clarence S. *History and Bibliography of American Newspapers, 1690-1820.* 2 vols. Worcester, Mass., 1947.

Brinton, Crane *et al. A History of Civilization.* 2 vols. Englewood Cliffs, N.J., 1967.

British And Foreign State Papers, 1824-1825. London, 1826.

Brockett, Linus P. *The Silk Industry in America, a History. . . .* New York, 1876.

Brodie, Fawn M. *No Man Knows My History, The Life of Joseph Smith.* New York, 1971.

Bromwell, William J. *History of Immigration to the United States. . . .* New York, 1855; reprint ed., New York, 1969.

Brooke, Francis T. *A Family Narrative of a Revolutionary Officer.* Richmond, Va., 1849.

Bronson, Walter C. *The History of Brown University, 1764-1914.* Providence, R.I., 1914.

Brower, D.H.B. *Danville, Montour County, Pennsylvania.* Harrisburg, Pa., 1881.

Brown, Alexander. *The Cabells and their Kin.* Boston, 1895.

Brown, Everette S. *The Constitutional History of the Louisiana Purchase, 1803-1812.* Berkeley, Calif., 1920.

Brown, Lucy M. *The Board of Trade and the Free Trade Movement 1830-1842.* Oxford, England, 1958.

Brown, Norman D. *Daniel Webster And The Politics of Availability.* Athens, Ga., 1969.

Brown, Orlando. *Memoranda of the Preston Family.* Frankfort, Ky., 1842.

Brown, Thomas N. *Irish-American Nationalism.* New York, 1966.

————. *Politics and Statesmanship: Essays on the American Whig Party.* New York, 1985.

Browne, Jefferson B. *Key West, The Old and the New.* Gainesville, Fla., 1973.

Brownlow, William. *A Political Register . . . With the Life and Public Services of Henry Clay.* Jonesborough, Tenn., 1844.

Bruce, Philip A. *History of the University of Virginia, 1819-1919.* 5 vols. New York, 1920-22.

Bruce, S.D. *The Thoroughbred Horse.* New York, 1892.

Bruce, William C. *John Randolph of Roanoke.* 2 vols. New York, 1922.

Brugger, Robert J. *Beverley Tucker: Heart Over Head in the Old South.* Baltimore, 1978.

Brunhouse, Robert L. *The Counter-Revolution in Pennsylvania 1776-1790.* Harrisburg, Pa., 1942.

Brush, Edward H. *Rufus King and His Times.* New York, 1926.

Bryan, Alfred C. "History of State Banking in Maryland." In *Johns Hopkins University Studies.* Vol. 17. Baltimore, 1899.

Bryan, Michael. *Bryan's Dictionary of Painters and Engravers.* Revised by George C. Williamson. 5 vols. New York, 1903-5.

Bryan, William. *A History of the Pioneer Families of Missouri.* St. Louis, Mo., 1876.

Buck, Solon. *Illinois in 1818.* 2nd rev. ed. Chicago, 1918.

Bucke, Emory S., ed. *The History of American Methodism.* 3 vols. New York, 1964.

Buley, R. Carlyle. *The Old Northwest Pioneer Period, 1815-1840.* 2 vols. Bloomington, Ind., 1950.

Bull, Sara C. *Olé Bull, A Memoir.* Boston, 1882.

Bulloch, Joseph G.B. *A History and Genealogy of the Families of Bayard. . . .* Washington, 1919.

Burdette, Franklin L. *Filibustering in the Senate.* Princeton, N.J., 1940.

Burger, William J.B. *Historical Americana . . . Catalogue.* N.p., 1985.

Burgess, John W. *The Middle Period, 1817-1858.* New York, 1910.

Burgner, Goldene F. *Greene County, Tennessee Wills, 1783-1890.* Easley, S.C., 1981.

Burke, Edmund, comp. *List of Patents for Inventions and Designs, Issued by the United States from 1790 to 1847.* Washington, 1847.

Burleigh, Joseph B., ed. *The Legislative Guide.* 4th ed. Philadelphia, 1853.

Burnham, George P. *The History of the Hen Fever.* Boston, 1855.

Burnham, W. Dean. *Presidential Ballots 1836-1892.* Baltimore, 1955.

Burns, Annie W., comp. "Revolutionary War Pensions of Soldiers who Settled in Fayette County, Kentucky." Mimeograph. Washington, 1936.

Burr, Samuel J. *The Life and Times of William Henry Harrison.* New York, 1840.

Burrage, Henry S. *Maine in the Northeastern Boundary Controversy.* Portland, Me., 1919.

Burt, Jesse C. *Nashville, Its Life and Times.* Nashville, Tenn., 1959.

Bushnell, David. *The Santander Regime in Gran Colombia.* Newark, Dela., 1954.

Bushong, Millard K. *Historic Jefferson County.* Boyce, Va., 1972.

———. *A History of Jefferson County West Virginia.* Charles Town, W.Va., 1941.

Butel-Dumont, George Marie. *Memoires historiques sur la Louisiane, Contenant ce qui y est arrive de plus memorable depuis l'annee 1687. jusqu'a present.* . . . 2 vols. Paris, 1753.

Butler, Mann. *A History of the Commonwealth of Kentucky.* Louisville, Ky., 1834.

Butler, Pierce. *The Unhurried Years.* . . . New Orleans, 1948.

Byars, William V. *B. and M. Gratz, Merchants in Philadelphia, 1754-1798.* Jefferson City, Mo., 1916.

Byington, Ezra H. *Rev. John Wheeler, D.D. 1798-1862.* Cambridge, Mass., 1894.

Cabell, Joseph C. *Speech on the Anti-Tariff Resolutions passed at the Session of the Legislature of Virginia 1828-9.* Richmond, Va., 1831.

Cabell, Margaret C. *Sketches and Recollections of Lynchburg.* Richmond, Va., 1858.

Caffrey, Kate. *The Twilight's Last Gleaming, Britain vs. America 1812-1815.* New York, 1977.

Caldwell, Joshua W. *Sketches of the Bench and Bar of Tennessee.* Knoxville, Tenn., 1898.

Calendar of Virginia State Papers and Other Manuscripts . . . Preserved in the Capital, at Richmond. 11 vols. Richmond, Va., 1875-93.

Calhoun, John C. *The Papers of John C. Calhoun.* Edited by Robert L. Meriwether *et al.* 15 vols. to date. Columbia, S.C., 1959-.

Callahan, Edward W., ed. *List of Officers of the Navy of the United States and of the Marines Corps From 1775 to 1900.* Reprint ed. New York, 1969.

Callahan, James M. *American Foreign Policy in Mexican Relations.* New York, 1932.

———. *Semi-Centennial History of West Virginia.* . . . Charleston, W.Va., 1913.

Calogeras, Joao Pendia. *A History of Brazil.* Translated and edited by Percy A. Martin. Chapel Hill, N.C., 1939.

Campbell, James V. *Outlines of the Political History of Michigan.* Detroit, 1876.

Canning, George. *The Speeches of George Canning with a Memoir of His Life.* Edited by Roger Therry. 6 vols. London, 1828.

Cappon, Lester J. *Virginia Newspapers 1821-1935.* New York, 1936.

Carey, Charles H. *A General History of Oregon Prior to 1861.* 2 vols. Portland, 1936.

Carey, Mathew. *Mathew Carey Autobiography.* In Research Classics, no. 1. Brooklyn, N.Y., 1942.

———. *Miscellaneous Essays.* . . . Philadelphia, 1830.

Carlee, Roberta B. *The Last Gladiator: Cassius M. Clay.* Berea, Ky., 1979.

Carrier, A.H. *Monument to the Memory of Henry Clay.* . . . Cincinnati, 1857.

Carroll, Grady L.E., Sr. *They Lived in Raleigh.* Raleigh, N.C., 1977.

Carson, James P. *Life, Letters and Speeches of James Louis Petigru.* . . . Washington, 1920.

Carter, Clarence E., ed. *The Territorial Papers of the United States.* 26 vols. Washington, 1934-.

Casseday, Ben. *The History of Louisville From Its Earliest Settlement till the Year 1852.* Louisville, 1852.

Cassell, C. Abayomi. *Liberia: History of the First African Republic.* New York, 1970.

Cassell, Frank A. *Merchant Congressman in the Young Republic, Samuel Smith of Maryland, 1752-1839.* Madison, Wisc., 1971.

Catalog of Joseph Rubinfine. Pleasantville, N.J., 1981.

Catalog of the Medical Department of Transylvania University for the Session 1845-46. Lexington, 1846.

Catalogue and Circular of the State & National Law School, at Ballston Spa, N.Y. Troy, N.Y., 1850.

Catalogue de la biblioteque de Son Exc. M. le Comte D. Boutourlin. Florence, Italy, 1831.

Catterall, Helen T., ed. *Judicial Cases Concerning American Slavery and the Negro.* Vol. 3. *Cases from the Courts of Georgia, Florida, Alabama, Mississippi, and Louisiana.* Washington, 1932.

Catterall, Ralph C.H. *The Second Bank of the United States.* Chicago, 1903.

Catterill, Robert S. *The Southern Indians.* Norman, Okla., 1954.

Caughey, John W. *Rushing For Gold.* Berkeley, Calif., 1949.

330

Caulkins, Frances M. *History of Norwich Connecticut.* . . . Chester, Conn., 1976.

The Celebration of the Centenary of the Supreme Court of Louisiana. New Orleans, 1913.

Chadbourne, Ava H. *Maine Place Names and The Peopling of Its Towns.* Portland, Me., 1955.

Chaddock, Robert E. *The Safety-Fund Banking System in New York, 1829-1866.* Washington, 1910.

Chamberlain, William H. *History of Yuba County, California.* Oakland, Calif., 1879.

Chambers, William N. *Old Bullion Benton, Senator from the New West.* Boston, 1956.

Channing, William E. *Slavery.* Boston, 1835.

———. *The Works of William E. Channing.* 2 vols. in one. Reprint ed. New York, 1970.

Chapman, Charles E. *A History of the Cuban Republic.* New York, 1927.

Charlton, Thomas U.P. *Report of Cases Argued and Determined in the Superior Courts of the Eastern District of the State of Georgia.* N.p., 1824.

Chase, Harold *et al.*, eds., *Biographical Dictionary of the Federal Judiciary.* Detroit, 1976.

Chase, James S. *Emergence of the Presidential Nominating Convention, 1789-1832.* Chicago, 1973.

Chase, Philander. *The Reminiscences of Bishop Chase, (Now Bishop of Illinois).* 2 vols. New York, 1844.

Cherrington, Ernest H. *The Evolution of Prohibition in the United States of America.* Westerville, Ohio, 1920.

Chesney, Alan M. *The Johns Hopkins Hospital and the Johns Hopkins University School of Medicine.* 3 vols. Baltimore, 1943-63.

Childs, William T. *John McDonogh, His Life and Work.* Baltimore, 1939.

Chinard, Gilbert. *The Letters of Lafayette and Jefferson.* . . . In *The Johns Hopkins Studies in International Thought.* Baltimore, 1929.

Chitwood, Oliver P. *John Tyler, Champion of the Old South.* New York, 1939.

Cist, Lewis J. *Trifles in Verse.* Cincinnati, 1845.

Claiborne, John F.H. *Mississippi, as a Province, Territory and State.* . . . Jackson, Miss., 1880.

Clarendon, Earl of (Edward Hyde). *The History of the Rebellion and Civil Wars in England Begun in the Year 1641.* Oxford, Eng., 1826.

Clark, Allen C. *Greenleaf and Law in the Federal City.* Washington, 1901.

Clark, Aubert J. *The Movement for International Copyright in Nineteenth Century America.* Washington, 1960.

Clark, Joshua V.H. *Onondaga Reminiscences of Earlier and Later Times.* . . . 2 vols. Syracuse, N.Y., 1849.

Clark, Thomas D. *A History of Kentucky.* Lexington, 1954.

Clark, Victor S. *History of Manufactures in the United States.* . . . 3 vols. Rev. ed. New York, 1929.

Clarke, Matthew. *Laws of the United States . . . and Other Documents Respecting the Public Lands.* Washington, 1828.

Clay, Cassius M. *The Life of Cassius Marcellus Clay. Memoirs, Writings, and Speeches.* . . . Cincinnati, 1886.

Clay, Clement C. *A Digest of the Laws of the State of Alabama.* Tuscaloosa, Ala., 1843.

Clay, Thomas H. & Ellis P. Oberholtzer. *Henry Clay.* Philadelphia, 1910.

Clayton, W.W. *History of Davidson County, Tennessee.* Philadelphia, 1880.

Cleaves, Freeman. *Old Tippecanoe: William Henry Harrison and His Time.* New York, 1939.

Cleveland, Len G. "George W. Crawford of Georgia, 1798-1872." Ph.D. dissertation, University of Georgia, 1974.

Cleven, N. Andrew. *The Political Organization of Bolivia.* Washington, 1940.

Clift, G. Glenn. *History of Maysville and Mason Co.* Lexington, Ky., 1936.

———. *Kentucky Marriages, 1797-1865.* Baltimore, 1966.

———. *Kentucky Obituaries, 1787-1854.* Baltimore, 1977.

———. *Kentucky Soldiers of the War of 1812.* Baltimore, 1969.

———. *Remember The Raisin!* Frankfort, Ky., 1961.

———. *"Second Census" of Kentucky, 1800.* . . . Frankfort, Ky., 1954.

Clingman, Thomas. *Selections from the Speeches and Writings of Hon. Thomas L. Clingman of North Carolina.* Raleigh, N.C., 1878.

Cocke, Leonie D. & Virginia W. *Cockes and Cousins.* Ann Arbor, Mich., 1967.

Codificación Nacional de Todas las Leyes de Colombia desde el Ano de 1821, Hecha Conforme a la Ley 13 de 1912, por la Sala de Negocios Generales del Consejo de Estado. Bogota, Colombia, 1924.

Coffin, Tristram P. *Uncertain Glory: Folklore and the American Revolution.* Detroit, 1971.

Coffman, Edward. *The Story of Logan County.* Nashville, Tenn., 1962.
———. *The Story of Russellville.* . . . Russellville, Ky., 1931.
Cole, Arthur C. *The Whig Party in the South.* Washington, 1913.
Cole, Cyrenus. *A History of the People of Iowa.* Cedar Rapids, Iowa, 1921.
Cole, Donald B. *Jacksonian Democracy in New Hampshire, 1800-1851.* Cambridge, Mass., 1970.
———. *Martin Van Buren and the American Political System.* Princeton, N.J., 1984.
Coleman, Mrs. Chapman. *The Life of John J. Crittenden, With Selections from His Correspondence and Speeches.* 2 vols. Philadelphia, 1871.
Coleman, J. Winston, Jr. *The Beauchamp-Sharp Tragedy.* . . . Frankfort, Ky., 1950.
———. *Famous Kentucky Duels.* . . . Frankfort, Ky., 1953.
———. *Henry Clay's Last Criminal Case.* Lexington, Ky., 1950.
———. *Lexington's First City Directory: Published by Joseph Charles for the year 1806.* Lexington, Ky., 1953.
———, ed. *Lexington's Second City Directory, Published by William Worsley and Thomas Smith for the year 1818.* Lexington, Ky., 1953.
———. *Masonry in the Bluegrass . . . 1788-1933.* Lexington, Ky., 1933.
———. *The Springs of Kentucky.* Lexington, Ky., 1955.
———. *The Squires Sketches of Lexington.* Lexington, Ky., 1972.
Coleman, Peter J. *The Transformation of Rhode Island, 1790-1860.* Providence, R.I., 1963.
Coles, Harry L., Jr. "A History of the Administration of Federal Land Policies and Land Tenure in Louisiana, 1803-1860." Ph.D. dissertation, Vanderbilt University, 1949.
———. *The War of 1812.* Chicago, 1965.
Collier's Encyclopedia. New York, 1985.
Collins, George C. *Fifty Reasons Why the Honorable Henry Clay Should Be Elected President of the United States, by an Adopted Citizen.* Baltimore, 1844.
Collins, Lewis & Richard H. *History of Kentucky.* 2 vols. Cynthiana, Ky., 1874; reprint ed., 1966.
Colton, Calvin. *The Life, Correspondence, and Speeches of Henry Clay.* 6 vols. New York, 1864.
———. *The Life and Times of Henry Clay.* 2 vols. New York, 1846.
———. *The Private Correspondence of Henry Clay.* New York, 1856.
———. *The Works of Henry Clay.* New York, 1855.
Colvin, John B., comp. *Laws of United States, Mar. 4, 1789-Mar. 4, 1815, Including Constitution of United States, Old Act of Confederation, Treaties, and Many Other Valuable Ordinances and Documents.* . . . 5 vols. Philadelphia, 1815.
Commemorative Biographical Record of Wayne County, Ohio. Chicago, 1889.
Congressional Quarterly's Guide to U.S. Elections. Washington, 1975.
Congressional Quarterly's Guide to U.S. Supreme Court. Washington, 1979.
Congressional Quarterly, Inc. *Presidential Elections Since 1789.* Washington, 1975.
Connable, Alfred & Silberfarb. *Tigers of Tammany, Nine Men Who Ran New York.* New York, 1967.
Connelley, William E. & E.M. Coulter. *History of Kentucky.* Edited by Charles Kerr. 5 vols. Chicago, 1922.
Conover, George S., ed. *History of Ontario County.* Syracuse, N.Y., 1893.
Conrad, Howard L. *Encyclopedia of the History of Missouri.* 6 vols. New York, 1901.
Cook, Anna M.G. *History of Baldwin County, Georgia.* Anderson, S.C., 1925.
Cooper, James F., ed. *Correspondence of James Fenimore-Cooper.* 2 vols. New Haven, 1922.
———. *The Letters and Journals of James Fenimore Cooper.* Edited by James F. Beard. 4 vols. Cambridge, Mass., 1960.
———. *Notions of the Americans: Picked up by a Travelling Bachelor.* London, 1828.
Cooper, William J., Jr. *The South and the Politics of Slavery, 1828-1856.* Baton Rouge, La., 1978.
Corey, Albert B. *The Crisis of 1830-1842 in Canadian-American Relations.* New Haven, Conn., 1941.
Corlett, Earl. *The Iron Ship.* New York, 1975.
Corning, Howard, ed. *Journal of John James Audubon Made during His Trip to New Orleans in 1820-21.* . . . Boston, 1929.
Coues, Elliott, ed. *The Journal of Jacob Fowler.* 2nd ed. Lincoln, Neb., 1970.
Coulter, E. Merton. *College Life in the Old South.* Athens, Ga., 1928.
———. *A Short History of Georgia.* Chapel Hill, N.C., 1933.

Cox, Isaac J. *The West Florida Controversy, 1798-1813, A Study in American Diplomacy.* Baltimore, 1918.
Cox, Norman W. *Encyclopedia of Southern Baptists.* 2 vols. Nashville, Tenn., 1958.
Coyle, William. *Ohio Authors and their Books . . . 1796-1950.* Cleveland, 1962.
Cralle, Richard K., ed. *The Works of John C. Calhoun. . . .* 6 vols. New York, 1853-55.
Cramer, Clarence H. *Case Western Reserve: A History of the University 1826-1976.* Boston, 1976.
Creasy, Edward S. *History of the Ottoman Turks. . . .* London, 1878; reprint ed., Beirut, 1961.
Cresson, William P. *James Monroe.* Chapel Hill, N.C., 1946.
Crittenden, H.H., comp. *The Crittenden Memoirs.* New York, 1936.
Cross, Whitney R. *The Burned-Over District: The Social and Intellectual History of Enthusiastic Religion in Western New York, 1800-1850.* Ithaca, 1950.
Crouthamel, James L. *James Watson Webb, A Biography.* Middletown, Conn., 1969.
Crum, Mabel T. "The History of the Lexington Theatre from the Beginning to 1860." 2 vols. Ph.D. dissertation, University of Kentucky, 1956.
Crumrine, Boyd. *The Courts of Justice, Bench and Bar of Washington County, Pennsylvania.* Washington, Pa., 1902.
———, ed. *History of Washington County, Pennsylvania. . . .* Philadelphia, 1882.
Cullinan, Gerald. *The Post Office Department.* New York, 1968.
Cumberlege, Geoffrey, ed. *The Oxford Dictionary of Quotations.* 2nd ed. London, 1953.
Cuming, Fortescue. *Sketches of a Tour to the Western Country. . . .* Pittsburgh, 1810.
Cunningham, Auburn S. *Everything You Want to Know About the Presidents.* Chicago, 1931.
Curran, Thomas J. *Xenophobia and Immigration 1820-1930.* Boston, 1975.
Current, Richard N. *Daniel Webster and the Rise of National Conservatism.* Edited by Oscar Handlin. Boston, ca. 1955.
Curtis, George T. *Life of Daniel Webster.* 2 vols. New York, 1870.
———. *Life of James Buchanan.* 2 vols. New York, 1883.
Curtis, James C. *The Fox at Bay, Martin Van Buren and the Presidency, 1837-1841.* Lexington, Ky., 1970.
Curtiss, George B. *The Industrial Development of Nations. . . .* 3 vols. Binghamton, N.Y., 1912.
Cushing, Caleb. *Brief Sketch of the Life . . . of William Henry Harrison of Ohio.* Augusta, Me., 1840.
Cutler, Wayne, ed. *Correspondence of James K. Polk.* Vol. 5. Nashville, Tenn., 1979.
Cutter, William R. *New England Families Genealogical and Memorial.* 4 vols. New York, 1914.
Dahl, Robert A. *Who Governs? Democracy and Power in an American City.* New Haven, Conn., 1961.
Dakin, Douglas. *British and American Philhellenes During the War of Greek Independence, 1821-1833.* Thessaloniki, Greece, 1955.
———. *The Greek Struggle for Independence, 1821-1833.* Berkeley, Calif., 1973.
Daley, John M. *Georgetown University: Origin and Early Years.* Washington, 1957.
Dana, James G. *Reports of Select Cases Decided in the Court of Appeals of Kentucky, During the Year 1835.* Cincinnati, 1835.
Dangerfield, George. *The Awakening of American Nationalism 1815-1828.* New York, 1965.
Darling, Arthur B. *Political Changes in Massachusetts 1824-1848.* New Haven, Conn., 1925.
Daughters of the American Revolution Lineage Book. Vol. 108. Washington, 1914.
Daveiss, Joseph H. *The Sketch of a Bill for an Uniform Militia of the United States. . . .* Frankfort, Ky., 1810.
Davidson, Robert. *History of the Presbyterian Church in the State of Kentucky. . . .* New York, 1847.
Davis, David B. *The Slave Power Conspiracy and the Paranoid Style.* Baton Rouge, La., 1969.
Davis, Dorothy. *John George Jackson.* Parsons, W.Va., 1976.
Davis, Harold A. *An International Community on the St. Croix.* Orono, Me., 1950.
Davis, James P. *History of Memphis.* Memphis, Tenn., 1873.
Davis, Jefferson. *The Papers of Jefferson Davis.* Edited by Haskell M. Monroe *et al.* 6 vols. to date. Baton Rouge, La., 1971-.
Davis, Varina A. *An Irish Knight of the 19th Century; Sketch of the Life of Robert Emmet. . . .* New York, ca. 1888.

Dawson, Moses. *A Historical Narrative of the Civil and Military Services of Major General William Henry Harrison. . . .* Cincinnati, 1824.

Dawson, Sarah M. *A Confederate Girl's Diary.* Edited by James I. Robertson, Jr. Bloomington, Ind., 1960.

Debates and Other Proceedings of the Convention of Virginia . . . for the purpose of deliberating on the . . . Federal Constitution. 2nd ed. Richmond, Va., 1805.

Debo, Angie. *The Rise and Fall of the Choctaw Republic.* Norman, Okla., 1934.

DeGregorio, William A. *The Complete Book of U.S. Presidents.* New York, 1984.

DeKnight, William F. *History of the Currency of the Country and the Loans of the United States from the Earliest Period to June 30, 1896.* Washington, 1897.

Delafield, Joseph. *The Unfortified Boundary. . . .* Edited by Robert McElroy & Thomas Riggs. New York, 1943.

DeLeon, Thomas C. *Belles Beaux and Brains of the 60's.* New York, 1907.

Demaree, Albert L. *The American Agricultural Press, 1819-1860.* New York, 1941.

Demarest, William H.S. *A History of Rutgers College, 1766-1924.* New Brunswick, N.J., 1924.

Dennison, George M. *The Dorr War: Republicanism on Trial, 1831-1861.* Lexington, Ky., 1976.

Derrick, Samuel M. *Centennial History of South Carolina Railroad.* Columbia, S.C., 1930.

DesCognats, Anna. *William Russell and His Descendants.* Lexington, Ky., 1884.

Desilver's Philadelphia Directory and Stranger's Guide, for 1828. Philadelphia, 1828.

Desilver's Philadelphia, Pa. Directory, 1833. Philadelphia, 1833.

Desmond, Alice C. *Bewitching Betsy Bonaparte. . . .* New York, 1960.

Dewey, Davis R. *Financial History of the United States.* New York, 1903.

Dexter, Franklin B. *Sketch of the History of Yale University.* New York, 1887.

Dickey, Dallas C. *Seargent S. Prentiss; Whig Orator of the Old South.* Baton Rouge, La., 1945.

Dickson, Harold E. *American Painter, 1780-1840, with a Checklist of His Works.* New York, 1949.

Diccionario de Historia de Espana desde sus Origenes hasta el Fin del Reinado de Alfonso XIII. 2 vols. Madrid, Spain, 1952.

Diccionario Enciclopedica Del Peru. 3 vols. N.p., 1966-67.

Dictionnaire de Biographie Francaise. Paris, France, 1969.

Didier, Eugene L. *The Life and Letters of Madame Bonaparte. . . .* New York, 1879.

Digested Summary and Alphabetical List of Private Claims Which Have Been Presented to the House of Representatives from the First to the Thirty-first Congresses. . . . 3 vols. Washington, 1853.

Document Transcriptions of the War of 1812 in the Northwest, Letters to the Secretary of War. . . . Columbus, Ohio, 1961.

Dodd, Dorothy. *Florida Becomes A State.* Tallahassee, Fla., 1945.

Dodwell, Henry H. *The Founder of Modern Egypt: A Study of Muhammad Ali.* London, 1931; reprint ed., 1967.

Doggett, John, Jr. *The New-York City Directory. . . .* New York, 1843, 1844, 1848.

Donald, Aida & David, eds. *Diary of Charles Francis Adams.* Cambridge, Mass., 1964.

Donaldson, Thomas. *The Public Domain, With Statistics. . . .* Washington, 1884.

Donnan, Elizabeth, ed. *The Papers of James A. Bayard.* In *Annual Report of the American Historical Association for the Year 1913.* 2 vols. Washington, 1915.

Donovan, Herbert D.A. *The Barnburners, A Study of the Internal Movements in the Political History of New York State and of the Resulting Changes in Political Affiliation 1830-1852.* Philadelphia, 1974.

Dorman, John F. *The Prestons of Smithfield and Greenfield in Virginia; Descendants of John and Elizabeth (Patton) Preston Through Five Generations.* Louisville, 1982.

Dorr, Harold M., ed. *The Michigan Constitutional Convention of 1835-36.* Ann Arbor, Mich., 1940.

Dougall, Richardson & Mary P. Chapman. *United States Chiefs of Missions, 1778-1973.* Washington, 1973.

Douglass, Ben. *History of Wayne County Ohio.* Indianapolis, 1878.

Drake, Thomas E. *Quakers and Slavery in America.* New Haven, Conn., 1950.

Drane, Maude J. *History of Henry County Kentucky.* N.p., 1948.

Draper, Lyman C. *King's Mountain and Its Heroes.* New York, 1881; reprint ed., 1971.

Drews, Toby. *Genealogies of Virginia Families From The Virginia Magazine of History and Biography.* Baltimore, 1981.

Drury, A.W. *History of the City of Dayton and Montgomery County, Ohio.* 2 vols. Chicago, 1909.

Duberman, Martin B. *Charles Francis Adams*. Cambridge, Mass., 1961.
DuBois, W.E.B. *The Suppression of the African Slave-Trade to the United States of America, 1638-1870*. New York, 1896.
Duckett, Alvin L. *John Forsyth, Political Tactician*. Athens, Ga., 1962.
Duffy, John, ed. *The Rudolph Matas History of Medicine in Louisiana*. Baton Rouge, La., 1958.
Duke, Basil W. *History of The Bank of Kentucky 1792-1895*. Louisville, Ky., 1895.
Dunbar, Willis. *Michigan Through the Centuries*. 4 vols. New York, 1955.
Dunham, Chester G. "The Diplomatic Career of Christopher Hughes." Ph.D. dissertation. Ohio State University, 1968.
Dunlap, William. *Diary of William Dunlap*. . . . New York, 1930.
Dunn, Jacob P. *History of Indianapolis*. 2 vols. Chicago, 1910.
———. *Indiana and Indianans, A History of Aboriginal and Territorial Indiana and the Century of Statehood*. 4 vols. Chicago, 1919.
Dunncomb, Samuel W. *Bankruptcy, A Study in Comparative Legislation*. New York, 1893.
Dunne, Gerald T. *Justice Joseph Story and the Rise of the Supreme Court*. New York, 1970.
DuPratz, M. LePage. *Histoire de la Louisiane*. . . . 3 vols. Paris, France, 1758.
DuVal, Miles P., Jr. *Cadiz to Cathay, The Story of the Long Diplomatic Struggle for the Panama Canal*. 2nd ed. Palo Alto, Calif., 1947.
Duvergier, Jean Baptiste, ed. *Collection Complete des Lois*. . . . Vol. 26. Paris, France, 1829.
Eaton, Clement. *Henry Clay and the Art of American Politics*. Boston, 1957.
———. *The Mind of the Old South*. Baton Rouge, La., 1964.
Edsall, Lillie T. *Chiles Tavern in Fayette County, Kentucky*. Lexington, Ky., 1944.
Edwards, Ninian. *The Edwards Papers*. . . . Edited by E.B. Washborne. Chicago, 1884.
———. *History of Illinois from 1778 to 1833*. Springfield, Ill., 1870.
———. *Life and Times of Ninian Edwards*. Springfield, Ill., 1870.
Eiselen, Malcolm Rogers. *The Rise of Pennsylvania Protectionism*. Philadelphia, 1932.
Eldredge, Zoeth S., ed. *History of California*. 5 vols. New York, 1914.
Elliot, Jonathan. *The American Diplomatic Code*. . . . *1778 to 1834*. . . . 2 vols. Reprint ed. New York, 1970.
Elliott, Charles W. *Winfield Scott, The Soldier and the Man*. New York, 1937.
Elliott, Robert N. *The Raleigh Register, 1799-1863*. Chapel Hill, N.C., 1955.
Elliott, Samuel. *A Humble Tribute to My Country*. . . . Boston, 1842.
Ellis, Franklin. *History of Monmouth County, New Jersey*. Philadelphia, 1885.
Ellis, Joseph & Robert Moore. *School for Soldiers: West Point and the Profession of Arms*. New York, 1974.
Ellis, William E. *et al. Madison County: 200 Years in Retrospect*. Madison County, Ky., 1985.
Elzas, Barnett A. *The Jews of South Carolina*. . . . Philadelphia, 1905; reprint ed., Spartanburg, S.C., 1972.
———. *The Old Jewish Cemeteries at Charleston, S.C.* Charleston, S.C., 1903.
Emery, William M. *The Salters of Portsmouth, New Hampshire*. New Bedford, Mass., 1936.
Emmanuel, Conte de Las Cases. *Memorial de Sainte Helene. Journal of the Private Life and Conversations of the Emperor Napoleon at Saint Helena*. . . . 6 vols. Philadelphia, 1823.
Enciclopedia Universal Ilustrada. 70 vols. Barcelona, Spain, 1907-30.
The Encyclopedia Americana, International Edition. 30 vols. Danbury, Conn., 1986.
The Encyclopedia Britannica. 11th ed. Cambridge, England, 1911.
Ershkowitz, Herbert. *The Origin of the Whig and Democratic Parties: New Jersey Politics 1820-1837*. Washington, 1982.
Esarey, Logan, ed. *Governors Messages and Letters. Messages and Letters of William Henry Harrison*. Vols. 7 & 9. Indianapolis, 1922.
———. *History of Indiana*. Dayton, Ohio, 1922.
———. *A History of Indiana from Its Exploration to 1850*. Indianapolis, 1915.
Espil, Felipe A., ed. *Once Anos en Buenos Aires, 1820-1831; las cronicas diplomaticas de John Murray Forbes*. Buenos Aires, Argentina, 1956.
Eubank, Sallie C. "The Iron Industry in Kentucky." Master's thesis, University of Kentucky, 1927.
Evans, Charles *et al. American Bibliography*. . . . 14 vols. Chicago & Worcester, Mass., 1903-59.
Evans, Henry R. *Old Georgetown on the Potomac*. Washington, 1933.
Evans, Melvin. "A Study in the State Government of Louisiana." In *Louisiana State University Studies*. No. 4. Baton Rouge, La., 1931.

Evans, Oliver. *The Young Mill-Wright and Miller's Guide*. 9th ed. Philadelphia, 1836.

Everett, Dick. "The Adventist Crisis, 1831-1844." Ph.D. dissertation, University of Wisconsin, 1930.

Everson, Zola G. *George Henry Calvert, American Literary Pioneer. . . .* New York, 1944.

Ezell, John S. *Fortune's Merry Wheel, The Lottery in America*. Cambridge, Mass., 1960.

Fairburn, William A. *Merchant Sail*. 6 vols. Center Lovell, Me., 1945-55.

Fallenbach, Joseph & Jessamine. *American State Governors 1776-1976*. 2 vols. Dobbs Ferry, N.Y., 1977.

Fasel, George. *Europe in Upheaval: The Revolutions of 1848*. Chicago, 1970.

Faux, W. *Memorable Days in America. . . .* London, 1823.

Federal Writers' Project. *Military History of Kentucky*. Frankfort, Ky., 1939.

Federal Writers' Project. *Washington City and Capital*. Washington, 1937.

Fehlandt, August F. *A Century of Drink Reform in the United States*. Cincinnati, 1904.

Feldberg, Michael. *The Philadelphia Riots of 1844*. Westport, Conn., 1975.

Ferguson, Russell J. *Early Western Pennsylvania Politics*. Pittsburgh, 1938.

Fielding, Mantle. *Dictionary of American Painters, Sculptors and Engravers*. Philadelphia, 1926.

Fields, Carl J. "Making Kentucky's Third Constitution 1830-50." Ph.D. dissertation, University of Kentucky, 1951.

Filler, Louis. *The Crusade Against Slavery, 1830-1860*. New York, 1960.

Finlay, George. *A History of Greece from Its Conquest by the Romans to the Present Time B.C. 146 to A.D. 1864*. Edited by H. F. Tozer. 7 vols. Revised ed. Oxford, England, 1877.

Finley, Alex C. *The History of Russellville and Logan County, Ky. . . .* 3 vols. Russellville, Ky., 1878-90.

First Anniversary Meeting of the Baltimore Sabbath Association Held on the 13th January, 1845. Baltimore, 1845.

Firth, C.H. *Oliver Cromwell and the Rule of the Puritans in England*. London, 1901.

Fischer, Jacques. *Sculpture in Miniature*. Louisville, Ky., 1969.

Fish, Carl R. *Civil Service and the Patronage*. Cambridge, Mass., 1920.

Fitzpatrick, John C., ed. *The Autobiography of Martin Van Buren*. New York, 1969.

———. *The Writings of George Washington from the Original Manuscript Sources. . . .* 39 vols. Washington, 1931-44.

Fladeland, Betty. *James Gillespie Birney: Slaveholder to Abolitionist*. Ithaca, N.Y., 1955.

———. *Men and Brothers, Anglo-American Antislavery Cooperation*. Chicago, 1972.

Fleming, Thomas J. *West Point: The Men and Times of the United States Military Academy*. New York, 1969.

Flint, David. *William Lyon MacKenzie, Rebel Against Authority*. Toronto, Canada, 1971.

Folkman, David I., Jr. *The Nicaraguan Route*. Salt Lake City, 1972.

Foner, Philip S. *Business and Slavery, The New York Merchants and the Irrepressible Conflict*. Chapel Hill, N.C., 1941.

Foote, Henry S. *Casket of Reminiscences*. 1874; reprint ed., New York, 1968.

Ford, Alice. ed. *The 1826 Journal of John James Audubon*. Norman, Okla., 1967.

———, *John James Audubon*. Norman, Okla., 1964.

Ford, Henry A. *History of Cincinnati, Ohio*. Cleveland, 1881.

Ford, Paul L., ed. *The Works of Thomas Jefferson. . . .* 12 vols. New York, 1904-5.

Forrester, Frank. *The Horse of America*. 2 vols. New York, 1857.

Fortier, Alcee. *A History of Louisiana*. 4 vols. New York, 1904.

Fortune, Alonzo W. *The Disciples in Kentucky. . . .* Lexington, Ky., *ca.* 1932.

Fowler, Ila Earle. *Captain John Fowler of Virginia and Kentucky. . . .* Cynthiana, Ky., 1942.

Fox, Dixon R. *The Decline of Aristocracy in the Politics of New York*. New York, 1919.

Fox, Early L. *The American Colonization Society, 1817-1840*. Baltimore, 1919.

Franklin, Benjamin. *The Works of Benjamin Franklin*. Edited by John Bigelow. Federal edition. 12 vols. New York, 1904.

Franklin, Walter S., comp. *Resolutions, Laws, and Ordinances Relating to the Pay, Half Pay, Commutation of Half Pay, Bounty Lands, and Other Promises Made by Congress to the Officers and Soldiers of the Revolution. . . .* Washington, 1838.

Freehling, William W., ed. *The Nullification Era, A Documentary Record*. New York, 1967.

———. *Prelude to Civil War, The Nullification Controversy in South Carolina 1816-1836*. New York, 1965.

Freeman, Douglas S. *R.E. Lee, A Biography*. 4 vols. New York, 1944.

336

Freeman, Frederick. *A Plea for Africa, Being Familiar Conversations on the Subject of Slavery and Colonization.* . . . 2nd ed. Philadelphia, 1837.

Freidel, Frank B. *Francis Lieber, Nineteenth-Century Liberal.* Baton Rouge, La., 1947.

Friis, Herman R., ed. *The Pacific Basin: A History of Its Geographical Exploration.* New York, 1967.

Fuess, Claude M. *Daniel Webster.* 2 vols. Boston, 1930.

————. *The Life of Caleb Cushing.* Reprint ed. Hamden, Conn., 1965.

Furness, Horace H., ed. *A New Variorum Edition of Shakespeare.* 27 vols. Philadelphia, 1871-1956.

Gagliardini, Elise C.B. *From My Journal Random Thoughts.* New York, 1958.

Gainer, William H., Jr. *Thomas Mann Randolph, Jefferson's Son-in-Law.* Baton Rouge, La., 1966.

Galdames, Luis. *A History of Chile.* Edited and trans. by Isaac J. Cox. Chapel Hill, N.C., 1941.

Gallatin, Albert. *Memorial of the Committee Appointed by the Free Trade Convention.* Philadelphia, 1831.

————. *Peace With Mexico.* New York, 1847.

Gallatin, Count, ed. *The Diary of James Gallatin.* . . . New York, 1926.

Galloway, Howard S. *The Shelby Family Ancestry and Descendants.* . . . Mobile, Ala., 1964.

Galpin, W. Freeman. *Pioneering for Peace: A Study of American Peace Efforts to 1846.* New York, 1933.

Gammon, Samuel R., Jr. *The Presidential Campaign of 1832.* Baltimore, 1922.

Gardiner, C. Harvey, ed. *Mexico, 1825-1828, The Journal and Correspondence of Edward Thornton Tayloe.* Chapel Hill, N.C., *ca.* 1959.

Garland, Hugh A. *The Life of John Randolph of Roanoke.* 2 vols. New York, 1859; reprint ed., 1969.

Garnett, James M. *Biographical Sketches of Hon. Charles Fenton Mercer 1778-1858.* . . . Richmond, Va., 1911.

Garraty, John A. *Silas Wright.* New York, 1949.

Garrett, William. *Reminiscences of Public Men in Alabama.* Atlanta, Ga., 1872.

Gates, Paul W. *History of Public Land Law Development.* . . . Washington, 1968.

Gayarre, Charles. *History of Louisiana.* 4 vols. New York, 1854.

Geddes, George, comp. *Report on the Agriculture and Industry of the County of Onondaga State of New York.* Albany, N.Y., 1860.

The General Stud Book, Containing Pedigrees of English Race Horses. . . . 3 vols. Baltimore, 1834.

Genêt, Edmund C. *Address on the Several Subjects of Science, Useful Knowledge, Public Improvements.* . . . *Delivered on the Fifth of February, 1824, in the Assembly Room of the Capitol.* Albany, N.Y., 1825.

Georgia Official and Statistical Register 1977-1978. Atlanta, 1978.

Gettleman, Marvin E. *The Dorr Rebellion: A Study in American Radicalism, 1833-1849.* New York, 1973.

Gibbon, Edward. *The History of the Decline and Fall of the Roman Empire.* 6 vols. 5th American ed. New York, 1836.

Gibson, John. *Gibson's Guide and Directory of the State of Louisiana and the Cities of New Orleans and LaFayette.* . . . New Orleans, 1838.

Gibson, John & Albert A. Fossier. *New Orleans, the Glamour Period, 1800-1840.* New Orleans, 1957.

Gieysztor, Alexander *et al. History of Poland.* Trans. by Krystyna Cekalska *et al.* Warsaw, Poland, 1968.

Giles, William B. *Mr. Clay's Speech Upon the Tariff.* . . . Richmond, Va., 1827.

————, comp. *Political Miscellanies.* Richmond, Va., 1829.

Gillies, John. *The History of Ancient Greece.* . . . 4 vols. New York, 1814.

Gilpin, Alec R. *The Territory of Michigan 1805-1837.* East Lansing, Mich., 1970.

Glenn, Thomas A., ed. *Some Colonial Mansions and Those Who Lived in Them.* . . . 2 vols. Philadelphia, 1897.

Goebel, Dorothy B. *William Henry Harrison, A Political Biography.* Indianapolis, 1926.

Going, Charles B. *David Wilmot, Free Soiler.* . . . New York, 1924.

Goldman, Perry M. & James S. Young. *The United States Congressional Directories 1789-1840.* New York, 1973.

Gollancz, Israel, ed. *The Works of Shakespeare*. . . . 12 vols. London, 1899-1900.
Goode, George B. *The Fisheries and Fishery Industries of the United States*. . . . 7 vols. Washington, 1884-87.
Goodrich, Carter, ed. *Canals and American Economic Development*. New York, 1961.
Goodspeed, Weston A. *History of Lincoln County, Missouri*. . . . Chicago, 1888.
———. *History of Southeast Missouri*. . . . Reprint ed. Cape Girardeau, Mo., 1955.
———. *History of Tennessee*. . . . Nashville, Tenn., 1886.
Goodykootz, Colin B. *Home Missions on the American Frontier*. Caldwell, Idaho, 1939.
Gorin, Franklin. *The Times of Long Ago*. Louisville, Ky., 1929.
Gouge, William M. *An Inquiry into the Expediency of Dispensing with Bank Agency and Bank Paper in Fiscal Concerns of the United States*. Philadelphia, 1837.
———. *A Short History of Paper Money and Banking in the United States*. . . . Philadelphia, 1833.
Govan, Thomas P. *Nicholas Biddle, Nationalist and Public Banker 1786-1844*. Chicago, 1959.
Graebner, Norman A. *Empire on the Pacific*. New York, 1955.
Graham, A.A. *History of Fairfield and Perry Counties*. . . . Chicago, 1883.
Graham, William B. "Railroads in Kentucky Before 1850." Master's thesis, University of Kentucky, 1931.
Grande Enciclopedia Portuguesa e Brasiliera. Lisbon, Portugal, 1940.
Grant, Ulysses S. *Personal Memoirs*. . . . 2 vols. New York, 1885-86.
Grattan, Peachy R. *Reports of Cases Decided in the Supreme Court of Appeals of Virginia*. . . . 3rd ed. Richmond, Va., 1897.
Gratus, Jack. *The Great White Lie; Slavery, Emancipation and Changing Radical Attitudes*. New York, 1973.
Gray, Lewis C. *History of Agriculture in the Southern United States to 1860*. 2 vols. Washington, 1933.
Graydon, Alexander. *Memoirs of a Life*. . . . Harrisburg, Pa., 1811.
Greeley, Horace, ed. *The Life and Public Services of Henry Clay, Down to 1848*. New York, 1860.
———. *Recollections of a Busy Life*. . . . New York, 1868.
Green, Constance. *Washington Village and Capital, 1800-1878*. Princeton, N.J., 1962.
Green, Edwin L. *George McDuffie*. Columbia, S.C., 1936.
Green, Raleigh. *Genealogical and Historical Notes on Culpeper County, Virginia*. Culpeper, Va., 1900.
Green, William A. *British Slave Emancipation, the Sugar Colonies and the Great Experiment 1830-1865*. Oxford, England, 1976.
Green, William M. *Memoir of Rt. Rev. James Hervey Otey*. . . . New York, 1885.
Greene, Boutell E. & Clarence Alvord, eds. *The Governors' Letter-Books, 1818-1834*. Vol. 4. Springfield, Ill., 1909.
Greene, Welcome A. *The Providence Plantations*. Providence, R.I., 1886.
Greenbie, Sydney & Marjorie B. *Gold of Ophir: The China Trade in the Making of America*. Rev. ed. New York, 1937.
Gregory, Martin T. "A History of the Kentucky State Treasury From 1792 to 1860." Master's thesis, University of Kentucky, 1928.
Gregory, Winifred, ed. *American Newspapers, 1821-1836*. . . . New York, 1937.
Gresham, John M., comp. *Biographical Cyclopedia of the Commonwealth of Kentucky*. Chicago, 1896.
Greve, Charles T. *Centennial History of Cincinnati and Representative Citizens*. 2 vols. Chicago, 1904.
Grey, Anchitell, comp. *Debates of the House of Commons from 1667 to 1694*. 10 vols. London, 1769.
Griffin, Charles C. *The United States and the Disruption of the Spanish Empire, 1810-1822*. . . . New York, 1937.
Grigsby, Hugh B. *Discourse on the Life and Character of the Hon. Littleton Waller Tazewell*. . . . Norfolk, Va., 1860.
Groce, George C. & David H. Wallace. *The New-York Historical Society's Dictionary of Artists in America 1564-1860*. New Haven, Conn., 1957.
Guedalla, Philip. *Wellington*. American ed. New York, 1931.
Gunderson, Robert G. *The Log-Cabin Campaign*. Lexington, Ky., 1957.
Gurney, Joseph J. *A Winter in the West Indies Described in Familiar Letters to Henry Clay, of Kentucky*. London, 1841.

338

Gusfield, Joseph R. *Symbolic Crusade: Status Politics and the American Temperance Movement.* Urbana, Ill., 1963.

Gwathmey, Edward M. *John Pendleton Kennedy.* New York, 1931.

Gwathmey, John H. *Historical Register of Virginians in the Revolution; Soldiers, Sailors, Marines, 1775-1783. . . .* Richmond, Va., 1938.

——— . *Twelve Virginia Counties: Where the Migration Began.* Richmond, Va., 1937.

Haddock, John A. *The Growth of a Century: As Illustrated in the History of Jefferson County, New York, from 1793 to 1894. . . .* Albany, N.Y., 1895.

Haight, Frank A. *A History of French Commercial Policies.* New York, 1941.

Hale, Will T. *A History of Tennessee and Tennesseans.* 7 vols. New York, 1913.

Hall, Claude. *Abel Parker Upshur.* Madison, Wis., 1963.

Hall, G.K. & Co. *The Mariners Museum, Newport News, Virginia, Catalog of Marine Prints and Paintings.* 3 vols. Boston, 1964.

Hall, James. *A Memoir of the Public Services of William Henry Harrison of Ohio.* Philadelphia, 1836.

——— . *Statistics of the West, at the Close of the Year 1836.* Cincinnati, 1836.

Hallam, Henry. *The Constitutional History of England, From the Accession of Henry VII to the Death of George II.* 2 vols. London, 1827.

——— . *History of Europe During the Middle Ages.* 3 vols. Paris, France, 1820-21.

——— . *View of the State of Europe During the Middle Ages. . . .* 4 vols. Philadelphia, 1821.

Hamersly, Thomas. *Complete Regular Army Register.* Washington, 1880.

Hamilton, Alexander. *The Papers of Alexander Hamilton.* Edited by Harold C. Syrett. 26 vols. New York, 1961-79.

Hamilton, Holman. *Prologue to Conflict, The Crisis and Compromise of 1850.* Lexington, Ky., 1964.

——— . *Zachary Taylor, Soldier of the Republic.* Indianapolis, 1941.

——— . *Zachary Taylor, Soldier in the White House.* New York, 1951.

Hamilton, Joseph. *Party Politics in North Carolina 1835-1860.* In *The James Sprunt Historical Publications.* Vol. 15. Chapel Hill, N.C., 1916.

Hamilton, Milton W. *The Country Printer, New York State, 1785-1830.* 2nd ed. Port Washington, N.Y., *ca.* 1964.

Hamilton, Robert S. *Discourse on the Scheme of African Colonization, Delivered Before the Colonization Society of Greene County, Ohio, at Zenia, July 4, 1849.* Cincinnati, 1849.

Hamlin, Talbot. *Benjamin Henry Latrobe.* New York, 1955.

Hammond, Bray. *Banks and Politics in America.* Princeton, N.J., 1957.

Hammond, Jabez D. *The History of Political Parties in the State of New York. . . .* 3 vols. Syracuse, N.Y., 1842-52.

Hammond, Mrs. L.M. *History of Madison County, State of New York.* Syracuse, N.Y., 1872.

Hampel, Robert L. *Temperance and Prohibition in Massachusetts 1813-1852.* Ann Arbor, Mich., 1982.

Hanover County Historical Society. *Old Homes of Hanover County Virginia.* Hanover, Va., 1983.

Hansard, T.C., comp. *The Parliamentary Debates. . . .* London, 1803-.

Hargraves, Mary W.M. *The Presidency of John Quincy Adams.* Lawrence, Kan., 1985.

Harman, John N. *Annals of Tazewell County, Virginia, from 1800 to 1922. . . .* 2 vols. Richmond, Va., 1922-25.

Harmon, George D. *Sixty Years of Indian Affairs, Political, Economic, and Diplomatic, 1789-1850.* Chapel Hill, N.C., 1941; reprint ed., 1969.

Harmon, Robert. "Government and Politics in New Jersey: An Information Source Survey." In *Public Administration Series: A Bibliography.* No. 197. Monticello, Ill., 1979.

Harper, J. Henry. *The House of Harper, A Century of Publishing in Franklin Square.* New York, 1912.

Harris, Alexander. *A Biographical History of Lancaster County.* Lancaster, Pa., 1872.

Harris, Malcolm H. *A History of Louisa County.* Richmond, Va., 1936.

Harrison, Fairfax. *The Roanoke Stud, 1795-1833.* Richmond, Va., 1930.

Harrison, Gabriel. *John Howard Payne, Dramatist, Poet, Actor. . . .* Philadelphia, 1885.

Harrison, John H. *Settlers by the Long Grey Trail.* Dayton, Va., 1935.

Harrison, Lowell. *John Breckinridge, Jeffersonian Republican.* Louisville, Ky., 1969.

——— , ed. *Kentucky's Governors 1792-1985.* Lexington, Ky., 1985.

Hartley, William & Ellen. *Osceola: The Unconquered Indian.* New York, 1973.

Hasse, Adelaide. *Index to United States Documents Relating to Foreign Affairs, 1828-1861*. 3 parts. Washington, 1914-21.

Haswell, John H., ed. *Treaties and Conventions Concluded Between The United States of America and Other Powers Since July 4, 1776*. Washington, 1889.

Hatcher, William B. *Edward Livingston, Jeffersonian Republican and Jacksonian Democrat*. Baton Rouge, La., 1940.

Hatsell, John. *Precedents of Proceedings in the House of Commons . . . with Observations*. 4 vols. London, 1781.

Hawgood, John A., ed. *First and Last Consul, Thomas Oliver Larkin and the Americanization of California*. 2nd ed. Palo Alto, Calif., 1970.

Hay, George. *A Treatise on Expatriation*. Washington, 1814.

Hay, Melba P. "Madeline McDowell Breckinridge: Kentucky Suffragist and Progressive Reformer." Ph.D. dissertation, University of Kentucky, 1980.

Hayden, Horace E. *Virginia Genealogies*. Reprint ed. Washington, 1931.

Haynes, George H. *The Senate of the United States; Its History and Practice*. Cambridge, Mass., 1938.

Hazard, Samuel, ed. *The Register of Pennsylvania Devoted to the Preservation of Facts and Documents. . . .* Philadelphia, 1830.

Heath, James E. *Edge-Hill, or The Family of the Fitzroyals*. N.p., 1828.

Hecht, Marie B. *John Quincy Adams*. New York, 1972.

Heitman, Francis B. *Historical Register and Dictionary of the United States Army. . . .* Washington, 1903; reprint ed., 1965.

Henao, Jesus Maria & Gerardo Arrubla. *History of Colombia*. Edited and trans. by J. Fred Rippy. Chapel Hill, N.C., 1938.

Henderson, Daniel. *The Hidden Coasts: A Biography of Admiral Charles Wilkes*. New York, 1953; reprint ed., Westport, Conn., 1971.

Hendricks, John R. "The Liberty Party in New York State." Ph.D. dissertation, Fordham University, 1959.

Hening, William W. *The Statutes at Large; Being a Collection of All the Laws of Virginia, from the First Session of the Legislature, in the year 1819*. 13 vols. New York, 1809-1823.

Henkle, M.M. *The Life of Henry Bidleman Bascom, D.D., LL.D.* Nashville, Tenn., 1891.

Henry, H.M. *The Police Control of the Slave in South Carolina*. Reprint ed. New York, 1968.

Herbert, Henry W. *Frank Forester's Horse and Horsemanship of the United States and British Provinces of North America. . . .* 2 vols. New York, 1857.

Herman, Arthur. *Metternich*. New York, 1932.

Hervey, John. *Racing in America*. New York, 1944.

Hewitt, W.T. *Landmarks of Tompkins County New York*. Edited by John H. Selkrey. Syracuse, N.Y., 1894.

Hibbard, Benjamin H. *A History of the Public Land Policies*. New York, 1939.

Hickey, William. *The Constitution of the United States of America. . . .* 4th ed. Philadelphia, 1851.

Hildreth, Richard. *The Contrast: or William Henry Harrison Versus Martin Van Buren*. Boston, 1840.

Hildt, John C. "Early Diplomatic Negotiations of the United States with Russia." In *Johns Hopkins Studies in Historical and Political Science*. Series 24, nos. 5-6. Baltimore, 1906.

Hill, Sam E. *Report of the Adjutant General of the State of Kentucky. Soldiers of the War of 1812*. Frankfort, Ky., 1891.

Hinds, Asher C. *Hinds' Precedents of the House of Representatives. . . .* Washington, 1907.

Hirst, Margaret E. *Life of Friedrich List and Selections From His Writings*. New York, 1909.

The Historical Annals of Cornelius Tacitus. Philadelphia, 1829.

Historical and Biographical Memoirs of Mississippi. . . . 2 vols. Chicago, 1891.

Historical Catalogue of Brown University, 1764-1914. Providence, R.I., 1905.

Historical Collection of the Mahoning Valley. . . . Youngstown, Ohio, 1876.

History of Logan County and Ohio. Chicago, 1880.

The History of Montgomery County, Ohio. . . . Chicago, 1882.

History of the Ohio Falls Cities and Their Counties. . . . 2 vols. Cleveland, Ohio, 1882.

History and Record of the Proceedings of the People of Lexington . . . in the Suppression of the "TRUE AMERICAN". . . . N.p., n.d.

Hitsman, J. Mackay. *Safeguarding Canada 1763-1871*. Toronto, 1968.

Hochschild, Harold K. *Township 34: A History with Digression of an Adriandad Township in Hamilton County in the State of New York*. New York, 1952.

Hockett, Homer C. *The Constitutional History of the United States, 1776-1866.* New York, 1939.

Hodges, Todd, & Pruett, pub. *The Campaign of 1844.* Frankfort, Ky., 1844.

Hoefer, Jean C.F. *Nouvelle Biographie Generale depuis les Temps les Plus Recules jusqu'a Nos Jours. . . .* 46 vols. Paris, France, 1952-66.

Hoffman, L.G. *Albany Directory and City Register, 1846-7.* Albany, N.Y., 1846.

Hoffman, William. "Andrew Jackson and North Carolina Politics." In *The James Sprunt Studies in History and Political Science.* Vol. 40. Chapel Hill, N.C., 1958.

Hofstadter, Richard & Michael Wallace. *American Violence.* New York, 1970.

Hogan, William R. & Edwin A. Davis, eds. *William Johnson's Natchez. . . .* Baton Rouge, La., 1951.

Holley, Horace. *Discourse Occasioned by the Death of Col. James Morrison, Delivered in the Episcopal Church, May 19, 1823.* Lexington, Ky., 1823.

Holli, Melvin G. & Peter Jones, eds. *Biographical Dictionary of American Mayors 1820-1980.* Westport, Conn., 1981.

Holmes, John. *The Statesman, or Principles of Legislation and Law.* Augusta, Me., 1840.

Holt, Edgar Allen. *Party Politics in Ohio, 1840-1850.* Columbus, Ohio, 1931.

Hooper, George. *Wellington.* London, 1908.

Hopkins, James F. *A History of the Hemp Industry in Kentucky.* Lexington, Ky., 1951.

Horine, Emmet F. *Daniel Drake, 1785-1852, Pioneer Physician of the Midwest.* Philadelphia, 1961.

Horn, D.B. & Mary Ransome. *English Historical Documents 1714-1783.* London, 1957.

Horseman, Reginald. *The War of 1812.* New York, 1969.

Houck, Louis. *A History of Missouri.* 3 vols. Chicago, 1908.

Hough, Franklin B. *A History of Jefferson County in the State of New York, from the Earliest Period to the Present Time.* Albany, N.Y., 1854.

Houston, David. *A Critical Study of Nullification in South Carolina.* Cambridge, Mass., 1896.

Howard, Benjamin C. *Reports of Cases Argued and Adjudged in the Supreme Court of the United States, January Term, 1848.* Boston, 1854.

Howard, George W. *The Monumental City, its Past History and Present Resources.* Baltimore, 1873.

Howard, Perry H. *Political Tendencies in Louisiana.* Baton Rouge, La., 1957.

Howarth, Thomas E.B. *Citizen-King, The Life of Louis-Philippe King of the French.* London, 1961.

Howe, Henry. *Historical Collections of Ohio in Two Volumes.* Cincinnati, 1907.

Hoxie, Leslie R. *The Hoxie Family, Three Centuries in America.* Ukiah, Ore., 1950.

Hoyt, W.H. *The Mecklenburg Declaration of Independence.* New York, 1907.

Hubbell, Walter. *History of the Hubbell Family.* New York, 1881.

Hudson, Frederick. *Journalism in the United States, 1690-1872.* New York, 1873; reprint ed., Ann Arbor, Mich., 1964.

Hughes, Philip. *The Catholic Question 1688-1829.* London, 1929.

Humboldt, Alexander de. *Political Essay on the Kingdom of New Spain. . . .* Trans. by John Black. 2 vols. New York, 1811.

Hume, David. *The History of England . . . Designed As a Continuation of Mr. Hume's History.* London, 1785.

Humphreys, James. *Observations on the Actual State of the English Laws of Real Property; with Outlines for a Systematic Reform.* 2nd ed. London, 1827.

Hungerford, Edward. *The Story of the Baltimore & Ohio Railroad 1827-1927.* New York, 1928.

Hunt, Gaillard, ed. *The First Forty Years of Washington Society.* New York, 1906.

———. *The History of the Seal of the United States.* Washington, 1909.

———, ed. *The Writings of James Madison.* 9 vols. New York, 1900-1910.

Hunt, Rockwell D., ed. *California and Californians.* 5 vols. New York, 1926.

Hunter, Louis C. *Steamboats on the Western Rivers.* Cambridge, Mass., 1949.

Hurd, D. Hamilton. *History of Fairfield County, Connecticut. . . .* Philadelphia, 1881.

Huston, Charles. *An Essay on the History and Nature of Original Titles to Land in the Province and State of Pennsylvania.* Philadelphia, 1849.

Hyde, William & Howard L. Conrad, eds. *Encyclopedia of the the History of St. Louis. . . .* 2 vols. St. Louis, 1899.

Hynds, Ernest C. *Antebellum Athens and Clark County, Georgia.* Athens, Ga., 1974.

Incidents in the Life of Jacob Barker, of New Orleans. . . . Washington, 1855.

Ingersoll, Charles J. *Historical Sketch of the Second War Between the United States of America, and Great Britain, Declared By Act of Congress, the 18th of June 1812, and Concluded By Peace, the 15th of February, 1815*. 2 vols. Philadelphia, 1845-49.

Innis, Harold A. *The Cod Fisheries, the History of an International Economy*. Revised ed. Toronto, Canada, 1954.

Ireland, Tom. *Ireland Past and Present*. New York, 1942.

Irvine, Baptis. *On the Commerce of South America, A Canal at the Darien*. Philadelphia, 1822.

Irwin, Ray W. *Daniel D. Tompkins: Governor of New York and Vice President of the United States*. New York, 1968.

Jackson, Andrew. *Correspondence of Andrew Jackson*. Edited by John S. Bassett. 7 vols. Washington, 1926-35.

Jackson, Ronald V. *et al.*, eds. *Kentucky 1830 Census Index*. Bountiful, Utah, 1976.

——, eds. *Kentucky 1840 Census Index*. Bountiful, Utah, 1978.

Jacobus, Donald L., ed. *Families of Ancient New Haven*. Baltimore, 1974.

Jacoby, John W. *History of Marion County, Ohio, and Representative Citizens*. Chicago, 1907.

James, D. Clayton. *Antebellum Natchez*. Baton Rouge, La., 1968.

James, Edward T. *et al.*, eds. *Notable American Women, 1607-1950, A Biographical Dictionary*. 4 vols. Cambridge, Mass., 1971-80.

James, Marquis. *Andrew Jackson: Portrait of a President*. Indianapolis, 1937.

——. *The Life of Andrew Jackson*. New York, 1938.

——. *The Raven; A Biography of Sam Houston*. Indianapolis, *ca.* 1929.

Jameson, J. Franklin, ed. *Correspondence of John C. Calhoun*. In American Historical Association *Annual Report, 1899*. Vol. 2. Washington, 1900.

Jarvis, Russell. *To the Public, Statement of Russell Jarvis Regarding the Difficulties Between Himself and Duff Green Arising Out of the Dissolution of Their Partnership in the United States Telegraph*. Washington, 1829.

Jay, William. *Letter of the Honorable William Jay, to Hon. Theo. Frelinghuysen*. New York, 1844.

Jefferson, Thomas. *A Manual of Parliamentary Practice.* . . . Washington, 1801.

——. *The Writings of Thomas Jefferson*. 20 vols. Monticello ed. Washington, 1904-5.

Jeffrey, Thomas E. *State Parties and National Politics: North Carolina, 1815-1861*. Athens, Ga., 1989.

Jegli, John B. *Louisville, New-Albany, Jeffersonville, Shippingport and Portland Directory, For 1845-1846.* . . . Louisville, Ky., 1845.

Jenkins, John H., comp. *The Papers of the Texas Revolution, 1835-36*. Austin, Tx., 1973.

Jenkins, William S. *Pro-Slavery Thought in the Old South*. Chapel Hill, N.C., 1935.

Jennings, Kathleen. *Louisville's First Families, A Series of Genealogical Sketches*. Louisville, Ky., 1920.

Jennings, Thelma. *The Nashville Convention, Southern Movement for Unity, 1848-1851*. Memphis, Tenn., 1980.

Jennings, Walter W. *Transylvania, Pioneer University of the West*. New York, 1955.

Jervey, Theodore D. *Robert Y. Hayne and His Times*. New York, 1909.

Jillson, Willard R. *Early Frankfort and Franklin County, Kentucky*. Louisville, Ky., 1936.

——, comp. *The Kentucky Land Grants: A Systematic Index to all of the Land Grants Recorded in the State Land Office at Frankfort, Kentucky, 1782-1924*. Louisville, Ky., 1925.

——. *The Newspapers and Periodicals of Frankfort, Kentucky 1795-1945*. Frankfort, Ky., 1945.

——. *Old Kentucky Entries and Deeds: A Complete Index to All of the Earliest Land Entries, Military Warrants, Deeds and Wills of the Commonwealth of Kentucky*. Louisville, Ky., 1926.

——. *A Sketch and Bibliography of the Kentucky Historical Society 1836-1943*. Frankfort, Ky., 1943.

——. *Some Kentucky Obliquities in Retrospect: Meade, Rafinesque, Wilkinson*. Frankfort, Ky., 1952.

Joblin, M. & Co. *Cincinnati Past and Present*. Cincinnati, 1872.

——. *Louisville Past and Present*. Louisville, Ky., 1875.

Johannsen, Albert. *The House of Beadle & Adams and its Dime and Nickel Novels: The Story of a Vanished Literature*. Norman, Okla., 1950.

Johnson, E. Polk. *A History of Kentucky and Kentuckians*. 3 vols. Chicago, 1912.

Johnson, L.F. *The History of Franklin County, Kentucky*. Frankfort, Ky., 1912.

Johnson, Rossiter, ed. *The Twentieth Century Biographical Dictionary of Notable Americans.* . . . Boston, 1904.

342

Johnston, J. Stoddard, ed. *Memorial History of Louisville From its First Settlement to the Year 1896*. 2 vols. New York, 1896.

Johnston, William P., comp. *The Johnstons of Salisbury, With a Brief Supplement Concerning the Hancock, Strother and Preston Families*. New Orleans, 1897.

Jones, Elias. *History of Dorchester County Maryland*. Baltimore, 1902.

Jones, Oakah L., Jr. *Santa Anna*. New York, 1968.

Jones, Rufus M. *The Later Periods of Quakerism*. 2 vols. London, 1921.

Jones, Wilber D. *Lord Aberdeen and the Americas*. Athens, Ga., 1958.

Jones, Wilber D. & Arvel B. Erickson. *The Peelites, 1846-1857*. Columbus, Ohio, 1972.

Journal of the Common Council of the City of Philadelphia . . . October 15, 1847. . . . Philadelphia, 1848.

Journal of the House of Representatives of the State of Ohio. 43 Gen. Assembly, 1 Sess. Columbus, Ohio, 1844.

Joutel, Henri. *Journal Historique du Dernier Voyage que feu M. de LaSale fit dans le golfe de Mexique, pour trouver l'embouchure, & le cours de la riviere de Missicipi. . . .* Paris, France, 1713.

Judd, Jacob, ed. *The Van Cortlandt Family Papers*. 4 vols. Tarrytown, N.Y., 1981.

Juettner, Otto. *Daniel Drake and his Followers; Historical and Biographical Sketches*. Cincinnati, 1909.

Julian, George W. *The Life of Joshua R. Giddings*. Chicago, 1892.

Kallenbach, Joseph E. & Jessamine S. *American State Governors, 1776-1976*. Dobbs Ferry, N.Y., 1981.

Kane, Harnett C. *Gentlemen, Swords and Pistols*. New York, 1951.

———. *Natchez on the Mississippi*. New York, 1947.

Kane, Joseph. *Facts About the Presidents*. New York, 1974.

Kappler, Charles J., comp. & ed. *Indian Affairs: Laws and Treaties*. 2 vols. Washington, 1903.

Kaser, David. *A Directory of the Book and Printing Industries in Ante-Bellum Nashville*. New York, 1966.

Kass, Alvin. *Politics in New York State, 1800-1830*. Syracuse, N.Y., 1965.

Keeper, Horace A. *Early Iron Industries of Dauphin County*. Harrisburg, Pa., 1927.

Kellar, Herbert A., ed. *Solon Robinson, Pioneer and Agriculturist*. 2 vols. Chicago, 1936.

Keller, William F. *The Nation's Advocate: Henry Marie Brackenridge and Young America*. Pittsburgh, *ca.* 1956.

Kendall, Amos. *Autobiography. . . .* Edited by William Stickney. New York, 1949.

Kennedy, John Pendleton. *Defence of the Whigs, By A Member of the Twenty-Seventh Congress*. New York, 1844.

———. *Memoirs of the Life of William Wirt, Attorney General of the United States*. Philadelphia, 1849.

Kennedy, Mary C. "Silas Wright And New York Politics, 1795-1847." Ph.D. dissertation, University of Chicago, 1950.

Kennedy, Robert P. *The Historical Review of Logan County, Ohio*. Chicago, 1903.

Kenngott, George F. *The Record of a City, A Social Survey of Lowell, Massachusetts*. New York, 1912.

Kent, Frank R. *The Story of Alexander Brown & Sons. . . .* Baltimore, 1925.

Kent, James, ed. *The Charter of the City of New York. . . .* New York, 1836.

Kent, Sherman. *The Election of 1827 in France*. Cambridge, Mass., 1975.

Kentucky Writer's Project. *A Centennial History of the University of Louisville*. Louisville, 1939.

Kerr, Charles, ed. *History of Kentucky*. 5 vols. Chicago, 1922.

Kilbourn, John, comp. *Public Documents Concerning the Ohio Canals. . . .* Columbus, Ohio, 1828.

Kimball & James. *Business Directory for the Mississippi Valley: 1844, Including . . . Cincinnati*. Cincinnati, 1844.

King, Charles R., ed. *The Life and Correspondence of Rufus King Comprising His Letters, Private and Official, His Public Documents and His Speeches*. 6 vols. New York, 1894-1900.

King, Duane, ed. *The Cherokee Indian Nation*. Knoxville, Tenn., 1979.

King, Grace. *Creole Families of New Orleans*. New York, 1921.

Kingford, William. *History of Canada*. 10 vols. Toronto, 1898.

Kinglake, Alexander W. *Eothen, or Traces of Travel Brought Home from the East*. N.p., 1844.

Kingsbury, Henry D. *Illustrated History of Kennebec County Maine 1625-1892*. New York, 1892.

Kinley, David. *The Independent Treasury of the United States and Its Relations to the Banks of the Country*. Washington, 1910.

Kinne, Asa. *Kinne's Quarterly Law Compendium for 1845; or Digest of Cases Reported in the United States and Great Britain in 1843, 1844, & 1845*. New York, 1845.

Kirker, James. *Adventures to China; Americans in the Southern Oceans, 1792-1812*. New York, 1970.

Kirkland, Thomas J. & Robert M. Kennedy. *Historic Camden*. 2 vols. Columbia, S.C., 1905-26.

Kirwan, Albert D. *John J. Crittenden: The Struggle for the Union*. Lexington, Ky., 1962.

Kittler, Glenn D. *Hail to the Chief; The Inauguration Days of Our Presidents*. Philadelphia, 1965.

Kittrell, James B., Jr. *Thumbnail Sketches of Old Lexington (Ky.) Today*. Lexington, Ky., 1959.

Klein, Maury. *History of the Louisville & Nashville Railroad*. New York, 1972.

Klein, Philip S. *Pennsylvania Politics 1817-1832, A Game Without Rules*. Philadelphia, 1940.

————. *President James Buchanan: A Biography*. University Park, Pa., 1962.

Klotter, James C. "The Breckinridges of Kentucky, Two Centuries of Leadership." Ph.D. dissertation, University of Kentucky, 1975.

Knox, John J. *A History of Banking in the United States*. Reprint ed. New York, 1969.

Kraft, Myrtice C. *Campbell County Kentucky Marriages, 1795-1840*. N.p., 1961.

Krueger, David. "Party Development in Indiana 1800-1832." Ph.D. dissertation, University of Kentucky, 1974.

Kruman, Marc W. *Parties and Politics in North Carolina 1836-1865*. Baton Rouge, La., 1983.

Kunitz, Stanley J. & Howard Haycraft, eds. *American Authors, 1600-1900.* . . . New York, 1938.

Kuroda, Tadahisa. "The County Court System of Virginia From The Revolution to the Civil War." Ph.D. dissertation, Columbia University, 1970.

Kuykendall, Ralph S. *The Hawaiian Kingdom 1778-1854*. Honolulu, 1947.

Lafayette, Marquis de. *Mémoires, Correspondence et Manuscrits Du General Lafayette*. Paris, France, 1836.

Lamb, Martha J. *History of the City of New York*. 2 vols. New York, 1877.

Lambert, Oscar D. *Presidential Politics in the United States, 1841-1844*. Durham, N.C., 1936.

Langer, William L., ed. *An Encyclopedia of World History*. 4th ed. Boston, 1968.

Langhorne, John & William. *Plutarch's Lives, Translated From the Original Greek.* . . . 6 vols. 3rd ed. Philadelphia, 1822.

Langley, Howard D. *Social Reform in the United States Navy, 1798-1862*. Urbana, Ill., 1967.

Lanman, Charles. *Haphazard Personalities; Chiefly of Noted Americans*. Boston, 1886.

————. *Letters From the Alleghany Mountains*. New York, 1849.

————. *A Summer in the Wilderness; Embracing a Canoe Voyage Up the Mississippi and around Lake Superior*. New York, 1847.

Latimer, Elizabeth. *Russia and Turkey in the Nineteenth Century*. Chicago, 1894.

Laurie, Robert & James Whittle. *The United States of America . . . According to the Preliminary Articles of Peace*. Map. London, 1794.

Laws of the State of Mississippi, Passed . . . in January, February And March, A.D. 1846. Jackson, Miss., 1846.

Learned, Henry B. *The President's Cabinet; Studies in the Origin, Formation and Structure of an American Institution*. New Haven, Conn., 1912.

Leavy, William A. *A Memoir of Lexington And Its Vicinity*. Written in 1875. Lexington, Ky., 1944.

Lee, Edmund J. *Lee of Virginia 1642-1892, Biographical and Genealogical Sketches of the Descendants of Colonel Richard Lee*. Philadelphia, 1894; reprint ed., Baltimore, 1974.

Lee, Francis B. *New Jersey As a Colony and As a State*. Vol. 3. New York, 1902.

Lee, Rebecca S. *Mary Austin Holley: A Biography*. Austin, Tx., 1962.

Lee, Thomas. *Cases Argued and Adjudged in the Court of King's Bench, at Westminister in . . . the Reign of his Late Majesty, King George the Second*. London, 1825.

————. *A Dictionary of the Practice in Civil Actions, in the Courts of King's Bench and Common Pleas*. London, 1825.

Lefler, Hugh T. *North Carolina History Told By Contemporaries*. Chapel Hill, N.C., 1948.

Leggett, Conaway & Co. *The History of Marion County, Ohio.* . . . Chicago, 1883.

Leger, William. "The Public Life of John Adair." Ph.D. dissertation, University of Kentucky, 1953.

Leighton, Robert. *The Whole Works of Robert Leighton . . . To Which is Prefixed, A Life of the Author. . . .* Philadelphia, 1848.

Leonard, Ira M. "New York City Politics, 1841-1844: Nativism and Reform." Ph.D. dissertation, New York University, 1965.

——— & Robert D. Parmet. *American Nativism, 1830-1860.* New York, 1971.

Leonard, Lewis A., ed. *Greater Cincinnati and Its People, A History.* 4 vols. New York, 1927.

Lester, Charles E. *The Artist, the Merchant, and the Statesman, of the Age of the Medici and of Our Own Times.* New York, 1845.

Lester, William S. *The Transylvania Colony.* Spencer, Ind., 1935.

Letters of Gen. Adair & Gen. Jackson, relative to the Charge of Cowardice, Made by the Latter against the Kentucky troops at New Orleans. Lexington, Ky., ca. 1824.

Levene, Ricardo. *A History of Argentina.* Edited and trans. by William S. Robertson. Chapel Hill, N.C., 1937.

Levin, H., ed. *The Lawyers and Lawmakers of Kentucky.* Chicago, 1897.

Lewis, David W. *Transactions of the Southern Central Agricultural Society from its Organization in 1846 to 1851.* Macon, Ga., 1852.

Lewis, Enoch. *The Arithmetical Expositer. . . .* Philadelphia, 1824.

Lewis, Oscar. *Sea Routes to the Gold Fields. . . .* New York, 1949.

Lewis, Virgil A. *How West Virginia Was Made. . . .* Charleston, W.Va., 1909.

Lexington, Kentucky, Trustees Record Book, 1781-1811. 2 vols. N.p., n.d.

Lieber, Francis. *Legal and Political Hermeneutics; or, Principles of Interpretation and Construction in Law and Politics. . . .* Boston, 1839.

———. *Manual of Political Ethics. . . .* 2 vols. Boston, 1838-39.

Lieven, Daria K.B. *The Private Letters of Princess Lieven to Prince Metternich, 1820-1826.* New York, ca. 1938.

Lignades, Amestasios D. *The First Loan of Independence.* Athens, Ga., 1970.

Lincoln, Abraham. *Complete Works of Abraham Lincoln. . . .* Edited by John Nicolay and John Hay. 12 vols. New York, 1905.

Lincoln, Anna T. *Wilmington, Delaware: Three Centuries Under Four Flags, 1609-1937.* Rutland, Vt., 1937.

Linn, E.A. & Nathan Sargent. *The Life and Public Services of Dr. Lewis F. Linn.* New York, 1857.

Lippincott's Gazetteer of the World. Philadelphia, 1922.

Liston, Ann E. "W.C. Rives: Diplomat and Politician, 1829-53." Ph.D. dissertation, Ohio State University, 1972.

Littell, William, comp. *Cases Selected from the Decisions of the Court of Appeals of Kentucky. . . .* Louisville, Ky., 1899.

——— & Jacob Swigert. *Digest of the Statute Law of Kentucky.* Frankfort, Ky., 1822.

———. *Littell's Political Transactions In and Concerning Kentucky. . . .* Louisville, Ky., 1926.

———. *The Statute Law of Kentucky. . . .* 5 vols. Frankfort, Ky., 1809-19.

Little, Lucius P. *Ben Hardin: His Times and Contemporaries, with Selections from His Speeches.* Louisville, Ky., 1887.

Livermore, H.V. *A History of Portugal.* Cambridge, England, 1947.

Livermore, Shaw, Jr. *The Twilight of Federalism, the Disintegration of the Federalist Party, 1815-1830.* Princeton, N.J., 1962.

Lobanov-Rostovsky, Andrei. *Russia and Europe, 1789-1825.* Durham, N.C., 1947.

Lockey, Joseph B. *Pan-Americanism: Its Beginnings.* New York, 1920.

Logan, Rayford W. *The Diplomatic Relations of the United States With Haiti 1776-1891.* Chapel Hill, N.C., 1941.

Long, David L. *Nothing Too Daring: A Biography of Commodore David Porter.* Annapolis, Md., 1970.

Longworth, Thomas. *Longworth's American Almanac: New-York Register, and City Directory.* New York, 1835, 1836, 1837, 1840.

Low, J. Herbert. *English History. . . .* Chicago, 1928.

Lowrie, Walter, ed. *American State Papers, Documents . . . in Relation to Public Land.* Washington, n.d.

Lowry, Robert & William H. McCardle. *A History of Mississippi. . . .* Jackson, Miss., 1891.

Lucas-Dubreton, Jean. *Le Comte d'Artois, Charles X, Le Prince, L'Emigre, Le Roi.* Paris, France, ca. 1962.

345

———. *The Restoration and the July Monarchy*. Trans. by E.F. Buckley. New York, 1929.

Luckhurst, Kenneth W. *The Story of Exhibitions*. London, 1951.

Ludewig, Hermann E. *Literature of American Local History*. New York, 1946.

Lumpkin, Wilson. *The Removal of the Cherokee Indians from Georgia, 1827-1841*. New York, 1907.

Lynch, Denis T. *An Epoch and a Man: Martin Van Buren and His Times*. New York, 1929.

Lyons, Joseph A., comp. *Silver Jubilee of the University of Notre Dame, June 23rd, 1869*. 2nd ed. Chicago, 1869.

Mabee, Carleton. *The American Leonardo, A Life of Samuel F.B. Morse*. New York, 1944.

McAfee, Robert. *History of the Late War in the Western Country . . . From the Commencement of Hostilities at Tippecanoe. . . .* Lexington, Ky., 1816.

MacCabe, Julius P.B. *Directory of the City of Lexington . . . 1838 & '39*. Lexington, Ky., 1838.

McCain, William D. *The Story of Jackson, A History of the Capital of Mississippi*. 2 vols. Jackson, Miss., 1953.

McCaleb, Walter F. *The Aaron Burr Conspiracy*. New York, 1936.

McCarthy, Charles. *The Antimasonic Party: A Study of Political Anti-Masonry in the United States, 1827-1840*. Washington, 1903.

McCormac, Eugene I. *James K. Polk, A Political Biography*. Berkeley, Calif., 1922.

McCormick, Richard P. *The Second American Party System*. Chapel Hill, N.C., 1966.

MacCracken, Henry N. *Blithe Dutchess, The Flowering of An American County From 1812*. New York, 1958.

McCrary, Royce C., Jr. "John MacPherson Berrien of Georgia (1781-1856): A Political Biography." Ph.D. dissertation, University of Georgia, 1971.

M'Elroy's Philadelphia Directory. . . . Philadelphia, 1839, 1842, 1844, 1845.

McGrane, Reginald C., ed. *The Correspondence of Nicholas Biddle dealing with National Affairs, 1807-1844*. Boston, 1919.

———. *Foreign Bondholders and American State Debts*. New York, 1935.

———. *The Panic of 1837, Some Financial Problems of the Jacksonian Era*. Chicago, 1924.

McIlhany, Hugh M., Jr. *Being the Genealogies of the Kinney . . . and Other Families of Virginia*. Staunton, Va., 1903.

McKay, Richard C. *South Street: A Maritime History of New York*. New York, ca. 1934.

McKee, Thomas H. *The National Conventions and Platforms of All Political Parties, 1789 to 1905; Convention, Popular and Electoral Vote*. New York, 1906; reprint ed., 1971.

McKelvey, Blake. *Rochester, The Water-Power City 1812-1854*. Cambridge, Mass., 1945.

MacKenzie, William L. *The Life and Times of Martin Van Buren. . . .* Boston, 1846.

Mackoy, Mabel L. *History of Greenup County, Ky.* Louisville, Ky., 1951.

McLaren, Moray. *Sir Walter Scott*. London, 1970.

McLaughlin, Andrew C. *Lewis Cass*. Boston, 1891.

MacLean, John P. *Shakers of Ohio. . . .* Columbus, Ohio, 1907.

McLean, Malcolm D. *Papers Concerning Robertson's Colony in Texas*. 3 vols. Fort Worth, Tx., 1974.

McLemore, Richard A. *Franco-American Relations, 1816-1836*. Baton Rouge, La., 1941.

———. *A History of Mississippi*. 2 vols. Hattiesburg, Miss., 1972.

Macloy, Edgar S. *A History of American Privateers. . . .* 1899; reprint ed., 1924.

MacMaster, John B. *A History of the People of the United States, From the Revolution to the Civil War*. 8 vols. New York, 1897-1914.

———. *The Life and Times of Stephen Girard, Mariner and Merchant*. 2 vols. Philadelphia, 1918.

McMeekin, Isabel M. *Louisville, The Gateway City*. New York, 1946.

The Macmillan Dictionary of Canadian Biography. 3rd ed. New York, 1963.

McMurtrie, Henrico. *Sketches of Louisville And its Environs*. Louisville, Ky., 1819.

McNall, Neil A. *An Agricultural History of the Genesee Valley, 1790-1860*. Philadelphia, 1952.

McPherson, Elizabeth G. "The History of Reporting the Debates and Proceedings of Congress." Ph.D. dissertation, University of North Carolina, 1940.

McRaven, Henry. *Nashville, "Athens of the South"*. Chapel Hill, N.C., 1949.

McRaven, William. *Life and Times of Edward Swanson*. Nashville, Tenn., 1837.

McReynolds, Edwin C. *The Seminoles*. Norman, Okla., 1957.

Madariaga, Salvador de. *Bolivar*. New York, 1952.

Madsen, A.W. *The State as Manufacturer and Trader . . .* London, 1916.

Madison, James. *Exposition of the Federal Constitution Contained in the Report of the Virginia House of Delegates . . . in answer to the resolutions of the General Assembly . . . commonly called Madison's report. . . .* Richmond, Va., 1819.

———. *Letters And Other Writings of James Madison.* 4 vols. Philadelphia, 1865.

———. *The Papers of James Madison.* Edited by William T. Hutchinson *et al.* 16 vols. to date. Chicago & Charlottesville, 1962-.

Mahon, John K. *History of the Second Seminole War, 1835-1842.* Gainesville, Fla., 1967.

Mahony, Cornelius R. *Everyman His Own Landlord. . . .* Dublin, Ireland, n.d.

Mai, Chien Tseng. *The Fiscal Policies of Albert Gallatin.* New York, 1930.

Maitland, James. *An Inquiry into the Nature and Origin of Public Wealth, and into the Means and Causes of its Increase.* London, 1804.

Maizlish, Stephen E. *The Triumph of Sectionalism: The Transformation of Ohio Politics, 1844-1856.* Kent, Ohio, 1983.

Mallory, Daniel. *The Life and Speeches of the Hon. Henry Clay.* 2 vols. New York, 1843.

Manning, William R., ed. *Diplomatic Correspondence of the United States, Canadian Relations, 1784-1860.* 4 vols. Washington, 1940-45.

———, ed. *Diplomatic Correspondence of the United States Concerning the Independence of the Latin-American Nations. . . .* 3 vols. New York, 1925.

———. *Diplomatic Correspondence of the United States, Inter-American Affairs 1831-1860.* 12 vols. Washington, 1932-39.

Marcandier. *An Abstract of the Most Useful Parts of a Late Treatise on Hemp. . . .* Boston, 1766.

Marshall, Humphrey. *The History of Kentucky. . . .* 2 vols. 2nd ed. Frankfort, Ky., 1824.

Marshall, James W. *The Presbyterian Church in Alabama.* Montgomery, Ala., 1977.

Marshall, John. *The Life of George Washington.* 5 vols. Philadelphia, 1804-7.

Martens, George de. *Nouveau Recueil De Traites De L'Europe.* Gottingen, Germany, 1829.

Martin, Christopher. *The Amistad Affair.* New York, 1970.

Martin, William E. *Internal Improvements in Alabama.* In *Johns Hopkins University Studies in Historical and Political Science.* Vol. 20, no. 4. Baltimore, 1902.

Martin, William T. *History of Franklin County. . . .* Columbus, Ohio, 1858.

Martineau, Harriet. *Society in America.* 2 vols. New York, 1837.

Mason, Richard. *The Gentleman's New Pocket Farrier. . . .* Philadelphia, 1853.

Massie, David M. *Nathaniel Massie, a Pioneer of Ohio. . . .* Cincinnati, 1896.

Masur, Gerhard. *Simon Bolivar.* Albuquerque, N.M., 1948.

Mathew Carey Autobiography. Research Classics, no. 1. Brooklyn, N.Y., 1942.

Mathews, John J. *The Osages, Children of the Middle Waters.* Norman, Okla., *ca.* 1961.

Mathieson, William L. *British Slavery and Its Abolition 1823-1838.* New York, 1926.

Mattes, Merrill J. *Indians, Infants and Infantry, Andrew and Elizabeth Burt on the Frontier.* Denver, Colo., 1960.

Maxwell, William, ed. *Virginia Historical Register and Literary Advertiser.* 6 vols. Richmond, Va., 1848.

Mayer, Brantz. *Mexico As It Was and As It Is.* New York, 1844.

———. *Mexico; Aztec, Spanish and Republican: A Historical, Geographical, Political, Statistical and Social Account of Country. . . .* 2 vols. Hartford, Conn., 1851.

Mayfield, John. *Rehearsal for Republicanism: Free Soil and the Politics of Antislavery.* Port Washington, N.Y., 1980.

Mayhew, Henry. *The Mormons: Or Latter-Day Saints. . . .* 3rd ed. London, 1852.

Mayo, Bernard. *Henry Clay, Spokesman of the New West.* Boston, 1937.

———, ed. *Jefferson Himself, The Personal Narrative of a Many-sided American.* Boston, 1942.

Mayo, Lawrence S. *The Winthrop Family in America.* Boston, 1948.

Meigs, William M. *The Life of Thomas Hart Benton.* Philadelphia, 1904.

Melcher, Marguerite F. *The Shaker Adventure.* Reprint ed. Cleveland, 1960.

Mellor, George R. *British Imperial Trusteeships.* London, n.d.

Mering, John V. *The Whig Party in Missouri.* Columbia, Mo., 1967.

Merk, Frederick. *Albert Gallatin and the Oregon Problem.* Cambridge, Mass., 1950.

———, ed. *Fur Trade and Empire, Simpson's Journal. . . .* Revised ed. Cambridge, Mass., 1968.

———. *The Oregon Question, Essays in Anglo-American Diplomacy and Politics.* Cambridge, Mass., 1967.

———& Lois Merk. *Fruits of Propaganda in the Tyler Administration.* Cambridge, Mass., 1971.

Metternich, Richard, ed. *Memoirs of Prince Metternich.* 5 vols. New York, 1880-82.

347

Meyer, Leland W. *Georgetown College, Its Background and a Chapter in Its Early History*. Louisville, Ky., 1929.
———. *The Life and Times of Colonel Richard M. Johnson of Kentucky*. New York, 1932.
Michel & Company's New Orleans Annual and Commercial Register for 1846. New Orleans, 1846.
Mikkelson, Dwight L. "*Kentucky Gazette*, 1787-1848: 'The Herald of a Noisy World.' " Ph.D. dissertation, University of Kentucky, 1963.
Miles, Edwin A. *Jacksonian Democracy in Mississippi*. Chapel Hill, N.C., 1960.
Miller, Charles G. *Donn Piatt: His Work and His Ways*. Cincinnati, 1893.
Miller, David H., ed. *Treaties and Other International Acts of the United States of America*. 8 vols. Washington, 1931.
Miller, Robert D.L. *Past and Present of Menard County, Illinois*. Chicago, 1905.
Miller, Stephen F. *The Bench and Bar of Georgia.* . . . 2 vols. Philadelphia, 1858.
Miller, William. *The Ottoman Empire and Its Successors, 1801-1927.* . . . Revised ed. London, 1966.
Mills, J. Thornton, III. *Politics and Power in a Slave Society, Alabama, 1800-1860*. Baton Rouge, La., 1978.
Minor, Benjamin B. "Memoir of the Author." In George Wythe, *Decisions of Cases in Virginia, by the High Court of Chancery.* . . . Richmond, Va., 1852.
Minutes of the General Assembly of the Presbyterian Church . . . 1839. Philadelphia, 1839.
Mitchell, Brian R., ed. *Abstract of British Historical Statistics*. Cambridge, England, 1962.
Michie, Thomas J., ed. *Virginia Reports . . .* Charlottesville, Va., 1903.
Molhuysen, Philip *et al.*, eds. *Nieuw Nederlandsch Biografisch Woordenboekonder.* . . . 10 vols. The Netherlands, 1911-37.
Monceau, Henri du. *A Practical Treatise of Husbandry.* . . . London, 1759.
Monroe, James. *The Writings of James Monroe*. Edited by Stanislaus M. Hamilton. 7 vols. New York, 1898-1903.
Montague, George W. *History and Genealogy of Peter Montague . . . And His Descendants, 1621-1894*. Amherst, Mass., 1894.
Moon, Anna M. *Sketches of the Shelby, McDowell, Deaderick, Anderson Families*. Chattanooga, Tenn., 1933.
Mooney, Chase C. *William H. Crawford, 1772-1834*. Lexington, Ky., 1974.
Moore, Albert B. *History of Alabama*. Tuscaloosa, Ala., *ca.* 1934.
Moore, D. Lynn. "Benjamin Orr Peers and the Beginnings of the Public School Movement in Kentucky, 1826 to 1842." Ed.D. dissertation, University of Kentucky, 1981.
Moore, Glover. *The Missouri Controversy 1819-1821*. Lexington, Ky., 1953.
Moore, John B. *A Digest of International Law*. Washington, 1906.
———. *History and Digest of the International Arbitrations to Which the United States Has Been a Party.* . . . 6 vols. Washington, 1898.
———. *The Works of James Buchanan*. 12 vols. Reprint ed. New York, 1960.
Moore, J.H. *Defense of the Mecklenburg Declaration of Independence*. Raleigh, N.C., 1908.
Moore, Thomas R. "The Virginia Supreme Court, An Institutional and Political Analysis." Ph.D. dissertation, University of Virginia, 1975.
Moore, Virginia. *The Madisons, A Biography*. New York, 1979.
Morais, Henry S. *The Jews of Philadelphia*. Philadelphia, 1894.
Morgan, Robert J. *A Whig Embattled, The Presidency of John Tyler*. Reprint ed. Hamden, Conn., 1974.
Morison, Samuel E. *Harrison Gray Otis 1765-1848, The Urbane Federalist*. Boston, 1969.
———. *The Life and Letters of Harrison Gray Otis*. 2 vols. Boston, 1913.
Morris, John D. "The New York Whigs, 1834-1842: A Study of Political Organization." Ph.D. dissertation, University of Rochester, 1970.
Morris, Richard, ed. *Encyclopedia of American History*. New York, 1953.
Morrison, A.J., ed. *College of Hampden-Sydney Dictionary of Biography, 1776-1825*. Hampden-Sydney, Va., 1921.
Morrison, Chaplain W. *Democratic Politics and Sectionalism:The Wilmot Proviso Controversy*. Chapel Hill, N.C., 1967.
Morse, Edward L. *Samuel F.B. Morse, His Letters and Journals*. 2 vols. Boston, 1914.
Morton, Oren F. *A History of Rockbridge County Virginia*. Staunton, Va., 1920.
Moser, Harold D. "Subtreasury Politics and the Virginia Conservative Democrats, 1835-1844." Ph.D. dissertation, University of Wisconsin-Madison, 1977.

Mott, Frank L. *A History of American Magazines 1741-1850.* New York, 1930.

Moulton, Gary E. *John Ross.* Athens, Ga., 1978.

Mowry, Arthur M. *The Dorr War or the Constitutional Struggle in Rhode Island.* Providence, R.I., 1901.

Mudd, Richard D. *The Mudd Family of the United States.* 2 vols. N.p., 1951.

Mueller, Henry R. *The Whig Party in Pennsylvania.* New York, 1922.

Mulkearn, Lois & Edwin V. Pugh. *A Traveler's Guide to Historic Western Pennsylvania.* Pittsburgh, 1954.

Mullett, Charles F. *The British Empire.* New York, 1938.

Munford, Beverley B. *Virginia's Attitude Toward Slavery and Secession.* New York, 1909.

Munn, Glenn G. *Encyclopedia of Banking and Finance.* 5th ed. Cambridge, Mass., 1949.

Munroe, Ira T. *History of the Town of Livermore....* Lewiston, Me., 1928.

Munroe, John. *Louis McLane: Federalist and Jacksonian.* New Brunswick, N.J., 1973.

Murphy, John, pub. *The Baltimore Directory for 1845.* Baltimore, 1845.

Murray, Paul. *The Whig Party in Georgia, 1825-1853.* In *James Sprunt Studies in History and Political Science.* Vol. 29. Chapel Hill, N.C., 1948.

Mushkat, Jerome. *Tammany, The Evolution of a Political Machine 1789-1865.* Syracuse, N.Y., 1971.

Musser, Clifford S. *Two Hundred Years' History of Shepherdstown.* Shepherdstown, W.Va., 1931.

Myers, Gustavus. *The History of Tammany Hall.* New York, 1917.

Nagel, Paul C. *The Adams Women, Abigail and Louisa Adams, Their Sisters and Daughters.* New York, 1987.

Nance, Joseph M., ed. *Mier Expedition Diary, A Texan Prisoner's Account.* Austin, Tx., 1978.

Nathans, Sydney. *Daniel Webster And Jacksonian Democracy.* Baltimore, 1973.

The National Union Catalog Pre-1956 Imprints. Chicago, 1979.

Neal, Julia. *By Their Fruits; The Story of Shakerism in South Union, Kentucky.* Chapel Hill, N.C., 1947.

Nederland's Adelsboek 1923. The Hague, 1906.

Nesbit, Robert C. *Wisconsin, A History.* Madison, Wis., 1973.

Nevins, Allan & Milton H. Thomas, eds. *The Diary of George Templeton Strong, Young Man in New York, 1835-1849.* New York, 1952.

Nevins, Allan, ed. *The Diary of John Quincy Adams.* New York, 1928.

——— , ed. *The Diary of Philip Hone 1828-1851.* Reprint ed. New York, 1970.

——— . *Fremont, Pathmaker of the West.* New York, 1939.

——— . *Hamilton Fish: The Inner History of the Grant Administration.* 2 vols. New York, 1957.

——— . *Ordeal of the Union.* 8 vols. New York, 1947-71.

New Catholic Encyclopedia. Washington, 1967.

Newman, Harry W. *The Maryland Semmes and Kindred Families.* Baltimore, 1956.

New-York City Directory For 1844 and 1845. New York, 1845.

Nicholas, Samuel S. *Letters on the Presidency, by a Kentucky Democrat....* Louisville, Ky., 1840.

Nicholson, Irene. *The Liberators: A Study of Independence Movements in Spanish America.* New York, 1969.

Nicholson, Margaret. *A Dictionary of American-English Usage.* New York, 1957.

Niles, William O. *The Tippecanoe Textbook, Compiled From Niles' Register....* Baltimore, 1840.

Niven, John. *Martin Van Buren: The Romantic Age of American Politics.* New York, 1983.

Northern, William. *Men of Mark in Georgia.* 4 vols. Atlanta, Ga., 1910.

Notable Names in American History. Clifton, N.J., 1973.

Nott, Charles & Samuel H. Huntington, eds. *Cases Decided in the Court of Claims of the United States at the Dec. Term for 1866.* Washington, 1868.

Nottingham, Stratton. *Revolutionary Soldiers and Sailors from Accomack County, Virginia.* Onancock, Va., 1927.

Nowell, Charles E. *A History of Portugal.* New York, 1952.

Oates, Stephen B. *The Fires of Jubilee: Nat Turner's Fierce Rebellion.* New York, 1974.

Oberholtzer, Ellis P. *Robert Morris: Patriot and Financier.* New York, 1903.

O'Brien, John G. *Philadelphia Wholesale Business Directory and United States, South America and West Indian Circular for the Year 1845.* Philadelphia, 1845.

O'Byrne, William R. *A Naval Biographical Dictionary....* London, 1849.

Oehser, Paul H. *Sons of Science, The Story of the Smithsonian....* New York, 1949.

Officers and Graduates of Columbia University, General Catalogue 1754-1900. New York, 1900.
Ohio General Assembly. *Acts Passed at the First Session of the Nineteenth General Assembly*. . . . Columbus, Ohio, 1821.
Osae, T.A. *A Short History of West Africa*. New York, 1968.
Padover, Saul K. *Jefferson*. New York, *ca.* 1942.
Page, Richard C.M. *Genealogy of the Page Family in Virginia, Also a Condensed Account of the Nelson, Walker, Pendleton and Randolph Families.* . . . 2nd ed. New York, 1893.
Paine, Ralph. *Joshua Barney: A Forgotten Hero of Blue Water*. New York, *ca.* 1924.
Pakalin, Mehmet Z. *Dictionary of Ottoman Historical Expressions and Terms*. 3 vols. 2nd ed. Istanbul, Turkey, 1971.
Palacio, Fajardo. *Outline of the Revolution in Spanish America.* . . . New York, 1817.
Palgrave, Robert H., ed. *Dictionary of Political Economy*. 3 vols. London, 1925.
Park, Hugh. *Reminiscences of the Indians by Cephas Washburn*. Van Buren, Ark., 1955.
Parker, Donald D., ed. *The Recollections of Philander Prescott, Frontiersman of the Old Northwest, 1819-1862*. Lincoln, Neb., 1966.
Parker, Margaret T. *Lowell, a Study of Industrial Development*. New York, 1940.
Parker, Richard G. & J. Madison Watson. *The National Fifth Reader.* . . . New York, 1863.
Parks, Joseph H. *Felix Grundy, Champion of Democracy*. Baton Rouge, La., 1940.
——— . *John Bell of Tennessee*. Baton Rouge, 1950.
Parrish, Gladys V. "The History of Female Education in Lexington and Fayette County." Master's thesis, University of Kentucky, 1932.
Parrish, William E., ed. *History of Missouri*. Vol. 2. Columbia, Mo., 1972.
Parry, Clive, ed. *The Consolidated Treaty Series*. 231 vols. Dobbs Ferry, N.Y., 1969.
Parsons, Stanley B. *et al. United States Congressional Districts, 1788-1841*. Westport, Conn., 1978.
Parton, James. *Life of Andrew Jackson*. 3 vols. New York, 1860.
——— . *The Presidency of Andrew Jackson*. Edited by Robert V. Remini. New York, 1967.
Pattee, Fred L., ed. *The Poems of Philip Freneau, Poet of the American Revolution*. 2 vols. Princeton, N.J., 1903.
Patten, James M., ed. *Patten's New Haven Directory for the Year 1840*. New Haven, Conn., 1840.
Paullin, Charles O. *American Voyages to the Orient, 1690-1865.* . . . Annapolis, Md., 1971.
——— . *Commodore John Rodgers: Captain, Commodore, and Senior Officer of the American Navy, 1773-1838*. Cleveland, 1910.
——— . *Diplomatic Negotiations of American Naval Officers*. Baltimore, 1912.
Paxton, W.M. *The Marshall Family*. Baltimore, 1970.
Pease, Theodore C. *The Centennial History of Illinois* . . . Springfield, Ill., 1918.
——— . *Illinois Election Returns 1818-1848*. Springfield, Ill., 1923.
Pease, W.H. & J.H. *The Anti-Slavery Argument*. New York, 1965.
Pennypacker, Samuel W. *The Autobiography of a Pennsylvanian*. Philadelphia, 1918.
Percival, W.P. *The Lure of Quebec*. Toronto, Canada, 1941.
Perkins, Dexter. *The Monroe Doctrine, 1823-1826*. Cambridge, Mass., 1932.
Perkins, George. "The Ohio Canal: An Account of its Completion to Chillicothe." In *Ohio Archaelogical and Historical Publications*. Vol. 34. Columbus, Ohio, 1926.
Perrin, William H. *History of Bourbon, Scott, Harrison and Nicholas Counties*. Chicago, 1882.
——— , ed. *History of Fayette County, Kentucky*. Chicago, 1882.
——— . *History of Scott County*. Georgetown, Ky., 1964.
——— *et al. Kentucky, A History of the State.* . . . 8 vols. 1887; reprint. ed., Louisville, 1979.
——— . *The Pioneer Press of Kentucky.* . . . Filson Club Publications. No. 3. Louisville, 1888.
Peter, Robert. *The History of the Medical Department of Transylvania University*. Louisville, 1905.
——— . *Transylvania University: Its Origin, Rise, Decline, and Fall*. Filson Club Publications. No. 11. Louisville, 1896.
Peters, Richard. *The Public Statutes at Large of the United States of America*. Boston, 1846.
——— . *Reports of Cases Argued and Adjudged in the Supreme Court of the United States. January Term, 1833*. Philadelphia, 1851.
Peters, Virginia B. *The Florida Wars*. Hamden, Conn., 1979.
Petersen, Svend. *A Statistical History of the American Presidential Elections*. New York, 1968.

350

Peterson, Harold F. *Argentina and the United States, 1810-1960.* New York, 1964.
Peterson, Merrill D. *Democracy, Liberty and Property, The State Constitutional Conventions of the 1820's.* New York, 1966.
——— . *The Great Triumvirate: Webster, Clay, and Calhoun.* New York, 1987.
——— , ed. *James Madison.* New York, 1974.
——— . *The Jeffersonian Image in the American Mind.* New York, 1960.
——— . *Olive Branch and Sword—The Compromise of 1833.* Baton Rouge, La., 1982.
Peterson, William J. *The Story of Iowa.* 4 vols. New York, 1952.
Peyton, J. Lewis. *History of Augusta County, Virginia.* Staunton, Va., 1882.
Pickard, John B., ed. *The Letters of John Greenleaf Whittier.* 3 vols. Cambridge, Mass., 1975.
Philip, Cynthia O. *Robert Fulton, A Biography.* New York, 1985.
Phillips, Charles. *Recollections of Curran. . . .* New York, 1818.
Phillips, Mount Vernon. "History of the Independent Toll Bridge in Kentucky 1792-1850." M.A. thesis, University of Kentucky, 1930.
Phillips, Ulrich B. *Georgia and State Rights. . . .* In American Historical Association, *Annual Report . . . for 1901.* Vol. 2. Washington, 1902.
Pidgeon, Norman L. *The Commonwealth of Massachusetts Manual for the General Court.* Boston, 1971.
Pierce, Arthur D. *Family Empire in Jersey Iron.* New Brunswick, N.J., 1964.
Pierce, Bessie Louise. *A History of Chicago.* 3 vols. New York, 1937.
Pitkin, Timothy. *A Political and Civil History of the United States. . . .* 2 vols. New Haven, 1828.
——— . *A Statistical View of the Commerce of the United States. . . .* Hartford, Conn., 1816.
Pletcher, David M. *The Diplomacy of Annexation: Texas, Oregon, and the Mexican War.* Columbia, Mo., 1973.
Plutarch. *The Lives of the Noble Grecians and Romans.* Trans. by John Dryden and rev. by Arthur H. Clough. New York, 1932.
Poage, George R. *Henry Clay and the Whig Party.* 1936; reprint ed., Gloucester, Mass., 1965.
Poems by the Late Henry John Sharpe, Esq. London, 1859.
Polk, James K. *Correspondence of James K. Polk.* Edited by Herbert Weaver *et al.* 6 vols. to date. Nashville, Tenn. 1969-.
Pollard, James E. *The Presidents and The Press.* New York, 1973.
Poore, Ben. Perley, comp. *A Descriptive Catalogue of the Government Publications of the United States. . . .* Washington, 1885.
——— . *Perley's Reminiscences of Sixty Years in the National Metropolis. . . .* 2 vols. Philadelphia, *ca.* 1886.
Pope, William F. *Early Days in Arkansas.* Little Rock, 1895.
Porter, Kenneth W. *John Jacob Astor, Business Man.* 2 vols. Cambridge, Mass., 1931.
Porter, Sir Robert K. *Travelling Sketches in Russia and Sweden During the Years 1805-1808.* Philadelphia, 1809.
Pothier, Robert J. *A Treatise On the Law of Obligations, or Contracts.* 2nd American ed. Philadelphia, 1839.
Potter, E.B. & J.R. Fredland, eds. *The United States and World Sea Power.* Englewood Cliffs, N.J., 1955.
Potter, George. *To the Golden Door, The Story of the Irish in Ireland and America.* Boston, 1960.
Potter, John. *The Antiquities of Greece or Archaeologia Graeca.* 2 vols. Oxford, England, 1697-98.
Powell, John H. *Richard Rush: Republican Diplomat.* Philadelphia, 1842.
Powell, Mary H. *The History of Old Alexandria, Virginia From July 13, 1749 to May 24, 1861.* Richmond, Va., 1928.
Power, John C. *History of the Early Settlers of Sangamon County, Illinois.* Springfield, Ill., 1876.
Pray, Isaac C. *Memoirs of James Gordon Bennett and His Times.* New York, 1855.
Prentice, George D. *Biography of Henry Clay.* New York, 1831.
Prentiss, George L., ed. *A Memoir of S.S. Prentiss.* 2 vols. New York, 1858.
Presidential Elections Since 1789. Washington, 1975.
Prevost, M., ed. *Dictionnaire de Brographie Francaise.* Paris, 1956.
Price, Benjamin L. *John Price, the Emigrant Jamestown Colony 1620. . . .* Alexandria, La., 1910.

351

Prince, Benjamin F. *A Standard History of Springfield and Clark County, Ohio.* 2 vols. Chicago, 1922.

Pritchett, John P. *The Red River Valley, 1811-1849, A Regional Study.* New Haven, Conn., 1942.

Proceedings and Debates of the Virginia State Convention of 1829-30. Richmond, Va., 1830.

Prokhorov, A.M., ed. *Great Soviet Encyclopedia.* New York, *ca.* 1973.

Prucha, Francis P. *American Indian Policy in the Formative Years.* Cambridge, Mass., 1962.

——— . *The Sword of the Republic: The United States Army on the Frontier, 1783-1846.* New York, 1969.

Puryear, Vernon J. *France and the Levant from the Bourbon Restoration to the Peace of Kutiah.* Berkeley, Calif., 1941.

Quaife, Milo M., ed. *The Diary of James K. Polk.* 4 vols. Chicago, 1910.

Quenzel, Carrol H. *Samuel Snowden, a Founding Father of Printing in Alexandria.* Charlottesville, Va., 1952.

Quisenberry, A.C. *The Life and Times of Hon. Humphrey Marshall. . . .* Winchester, Ky., 1892.

Racing Calendar . . . in Great Britain and Ireland. . . . London, 1773.

Railey, William E. *History of Woodford County.* Versailles, Ky., 1968.

Ranck, George W. *History of Lexington Kentucky.* Cincinnati, 1872.

Ranck, James B. *Albert Gallatin Brown, Radical Southern Nationalist.* New York, 1937.

Rand McNally's *1982 Commercial Atlas and Marketing Guide.* New York, 1982.

Randall, Emilius O. *History of Ohio, The Rise and Progress of an American State.* 5 vols. New York, 1912.

Randall, Henry S. *The Life of Thomas Jefferson.* 3 vols. New York, 1858.

Raney, William F. *Wisconsin, A Story of Progress.* New York, 1940.

Ratchford, Benjamin U. *American State Debts.* Durham, N.C., 1941.

Ratner, Lorman. *Antimasonry: The Crusade and the Party.* Englewood Cliffs, N.J., 1969.

Rauch, Basil. *American Interest in Cuba: 1848-1855.* New York, 1948.

Rayback, Robert J. *Millard Fillmore, Biography of A President.* Buffalo, N.Y., 1959.

Raynal, Guillaume-Thomas. *Histoire Philosophique et Politique des etablissemens et du commerce des Europeens dans les deux Indes.* Amsterdam, 1770.

Reader, Francis S. *History of the Newspapers of Beaver County, Pennsylvania.* New Brighton, Pa., 1905.

Reed, George I., ed. *Bench and Bar of Ohio. . . .* 2 vols. Chicago, 1897.

Reeves, J.S. *American Diplomacy Under Tyler and Polk.* Baltimore, 1907.

Register of Graduates and Former Cadets of the United States Military Academy. West Point, N.Y., 1960.

A Register of Officers and Agents, Civil, Military, in the Service of the United States. . . . Washington, 1825.

Reid, Richard. *Historical Sketches of Montgomery County.* Lexington, Ky., 1926.

Reid, Samuel C., Jr., ed. *The Case of the Private Armed Brig of War Gen. Armstrong. . . .* New York, 1857.

Remini, Robert V. *Andrew Jackson and the Course of American Empire, 1767-1821.* New York, 1977.

——— . *Andrew Jackson and the Course of American Freedom.* New York, 1981.

——— . *The Election of Andrew Jackson.* Philadelphia, 1963.

——— . *Martin Van Buren and the Making of the Democratic Party.* New York, 1959.

The Rendells, Inc. *The American Frontier . . . Exploration and Settlement to the Mississippi River.* Vol. 1. Newton, Mass., 1982.

Reniers, Perceval. *The Springs of Virginia.* Chapel Hill, N.C., 1941.

Rennick, Robert M. *Kentucky Place Names.* Lexington, Ky., 1984.

The Report of the Select Committee . . . Charging Benjamin Sebastian . . . with Having Received a Pension from the Spanish Government. Frankfort, Ky., 1806.

Resolutions and Addresses of the Convention . . . of New York . . . 1828, Nominating John Quincy Adams . . . for President. . . . Albany, N.Y., 1828.

Return. Members of Parliament. 2 vols. London, 1878.

Rhodes, Irwin S. *The Papers of John Marshall: A Descriptive Calendar.* 2 vols. Norman, Okla., 1969.

Rice, Madeleine H. *Federal Street Pastor, The Life of William Ellery Channing.* New York, 1961.

Richards, John A. *A History of Bath County.* Yuma, Az., 1961.

Richards, Paul C. *Autographs, Catalogue 235*. Templeton, Mass., 1988.

Richardson, James D., comp. *A Compilation of the Messages and Papers of the Presidents 1789-1902*. 10 vols. plus supplements. Washington, 1904.

Richardson, Robert, ed. *Memoirs of Alexander Campbell*. 2 vols. Cincinnati, 1872.

Richardson, Rupert *et al. Texas, the Lone Star State*. 3rd ed. Englewood Cliffs, N.J., 1970.

Ridley, Jasper. *Lord Palmerston*. London, 1970.

Riker, Dorothy, ed. *Executive Proceedings of the State of Indiana, 1816-1836*. Indianapolis, 1947.

———— & Gayle Thornbrough. *Indiana Election Returns, 1816-1851*. Indianapolis, 1960.

Rippy, J. Fred, ed. *History of Colombia*. Chapel Hill, N.C., 1938.

————. *Joel R. Poinsett, Versatile American*. Durham, N.C., 1935.

Rives, George L. *The United States and Mexico 1821-1848*. 2 vols. New York, 1913.

Robbins, Roy M. *Our Landed Heritage, The Public Domain, 1776-1936*. Lincoln, Neb., 1962.

Robert, Joseph C. *The Road from Monticello: A Study of the Virginia Slavery Debate of 1832*. Durham, N.C., 1941.

Robertson, George. *An Outline of the Life of George Robertson, Written by Himself*. . . . Lexington, Ky., 1876.

Robertson, William. *The History of the Reign of Charles the Fifth, Emperor of Germany*. 3 vols. Philadelphia, 1770.

Robertson, William S. *France and Latin-American Independence*. . . . Baltimore, 1939.

————. *The Life of Miranda*. 2 vols. Chapel Hill, N.C., 1929.

Robinson, Merritt M. *Reports of Cases Argued and Determined in the Supreme Court of Louisiana*. New Orleans, 1845.

Rockey, J.L. & R.J. Bancroft. *History of Clermont County, Ohio*. Philadelphia, 1880.

Rodgers, Andrew D., III. "Lucas Sullivant and the Founding of Columbus." In *Ohio Archaeological and Historical Society Publications*. Vol. 37. Columbus, Ohio, 1928.

Rogers, Amelia C. "Ashland, Home of Henry Clay." Master's thesis, University of Kentucky, 1934.

Rogers, Joseph M. *Thomas H. Benton*. Philadelphia, 1905.

————. *The True Henry Clay*. Philadelphia, 1905.

Rogers, Sophie S. *et al. Selden Ancestry, A Family History*. Oil City, Pa., n.d.

Rogin, Michael P. *Fathers and Children: Andrew Jackson and the Subjugation of the American Indian*. New York, 1975.

Roseboom, Eugene H. & Francis P. Weisenburger. *A History of Ohio*. . . . New York, 1934.

Rosenberg, Charles. *The Cholera Years*. Chicago, 1962.

Rosenbloom, Joseph R. *A Biographical Dictionary of Early American Jews, Colonial Times through 1800*. Lexington, Ky., *ca.* 1960.

Rothbard, Murray N. *The Panic of 1819; Reactions and Policies*. New York, 1962.

Rothert, Otto A. *A History of Muhlenberg County*. Louisville, Ky., 1913.

Rowe, Kenneth W. *Mathew Carey: A Study in American Economic Development*. Baltimore, 1933.

Rowland, Dunbar. *History of Mississippi the Heart of the South*. 2 vols. Chicago, 1925.

————, ed. *Official Letter Books of W.C.C. Claiborne 1801-1816*. 6 vols. Jackson, Miss., 1917.

Rowland, Kate M. *The Life of Charles Carroll of Carrollton, 1737-1832*. . . . 2 vols. New York, 1898.

Royce, Charles. *The Cherokee Nation of Indians*. Chicago, 1975.

————. *Indian Land Cessions in the U.S.* Washington, 1900.

Ruchames, Louis. *The Abolitionists, A Collection of Their Writings*. New York, 1964.

Rudd, Murpha T. *1850 Census Tennessee*. Evanston, Ill., 1975.

Rush, Richard. *Memoranda of a Residence at the Court of London*. 2 vols. Philadelphia, 1833-45.

Russell, William. *The History of Modern Europe . . . to . . . 1763*. 6 vols. Philadelphia, 1800-11.

Sabin, Joseph. *Bibliotheca Americana, A Dictionary of Books Relating to America, from Its Discovery to the Present Time*. 29 vols. New York, 1868-1936.

Saffell, W.T.R. *Records of the Revolutionary War: Containing the Military and Financial Correspondence of Distinguished Officers, Names of the Officers*. . . . New York, 1858.

Safford, William H. *The Blennerhassett Papers*. . . . Cincinnati, 1864.

————. *The Life of Harman Blennerhassett*. . . . Chillicothe, Ohio, 1850.

Sainty, J.C., comp. *Office-Holders in Modern Britain, III, Officials of the Board of Trade, 1660-1870*. London, 1974.

Salem (Mass.) Directory. Salem, Mass., 1837.

Salisbury, Edward. *Family-Histories and Genealogies*. 3 vols. N.p., 1892.

Sanderlin, Walter S. *The Great National Project, A History of the Chesapeake and Ohio Canal*. In *Johns Hopkins University Studies in Historical and Political Science*. Vol. 64. Baltimore, 1946.

Sanders, Alvin H. *The History of the Herefords*. Chicago, 1914.

Sant'Angelo, Orazio de Attellis. *The Texas Question Reviewed by an Adopted Citizen*. . . . New York, 1844.

Sargent, Emma W. & Charles Sprague Sargent, eds. *Epes Sargent of Gloucester and His Descendants*. Boston, 1923.

Sargent, Epes. *The Life and Public Services of Henry Clay*. . . . New York, 1842; revised editions, 1844, 1848, 1852, 1855.

Sargent, Nathan. *Brief Outline of the Life of Henry Clay*. Washington, 1844.

————. *Public Men and Events*. 2 vols. Philadelphia, 1875.

Satz, Ronald N. *American Indian Policy in the Jacksonian Era*. Lincoln, Neb., 1974.

Schachner, Nathan. *Aaron Burr, A Biography*. New York, 1937.

————. *Thomas Jefferson, A Biography*. 2 vols. New York, 1951.

Scharf, J. Thomas. *The Chronicles of Baltimore*. . . . Baltimore, 1874.

————. *History of Maryland*. . . . 3 vols. Baltimore, 1879.

————. *History of Philadelphia, 1609-1884*. 3 vols. Philadelphia, 1884.

————. *History of Saint Louis City and County*. . . . 2 vols. Philadelphia, 1883.

————. *History of Western Maryland*. . . . 2 vols. Philadelphia, 1882.

Schauinger, J. Herman. *Cathedrals in the Wilderness*. Milwaukee, Wis., 1952.

Schlesinger, Arthur M., Jr. *The Age of Jackson*. Boston, 1953.

————. et al. *History of American Presidential Elections 1789-1968*. 4 vols. New York, 1971.

————. *History of U.S. Political Parties*. 4 vols. New York, 1973.

Schmeckebier, Lawrence. *Government Publications and Their Use*. 2nd ed. Washington, 1969.

Schmitz, Joseph W. *Texan State Craft 1836-1845*. San Antonio, Tx., 1941.

Schuckers, J.W. *The Life and Public Services of Salmon Portland Chase*. . . . New York, 1874.

Schurz, Carl. *Life of Henry Clay*. 2 vols. Boston, 1887.

Scobey, F.E. & E.W. Doty. *The Biographical Annals of Ohio*. 3 vols. Springfield, Ohio, 1902.

———— & B.L. McElroy. *Historical Collections of Ohio*. . . . 2 vols. Cincinnati, 1907.

Scott, Franklin W. *Newspapers and Periodicals of Illinois, 1814-1879*. Revised ed. Springfield, Ill., 1910.

Scott, James G. & Edward A. Wyatt. *Petersburg's Story: A History*. Petersburg, Va., 1960.

Scott, Mary W. & Louise F. Catterall. *Virginia's Capitol Square, Its Buildings & Its Monuments*. Richmond, Va., 1957.

Scott, Nancy N., ed. *A Memoir of Hugh Lawson White . . . with Selections from His Speeches and Correspondence*. Philadelphia, 1856.

Scott, Sir Walter. *St. Ronan's Well*. Edinburgh, Scotland, 1823.

Scott, Winfield. *Memoirs of Lieut.-General Scott, LL.D*. 2 vols. New York, 1864.

Seager, Robert, II. *And Tyler Too: A Biography of John and Julia Gardiner Tyler*. New York, 1963.

Sears, Alfred B. *Thomas Worthington, Father of Ohio Statehood*. Columbus, Ohio, 1958.

Seaton, Oren A. *The Seaton Family with Genealogy and Biographies*. Topeka, Kansas, 1906.

Secomb, Daniel F. *History of the Town of Amherst . . . New Hampshire*. . . . Concord, 1883.

Seitz, Don C. *Famous American Duels*. . . . New York, 1929.

————. *The James Gordon Bennetts*. . . . Indianapolis, 1928.

Sellers, Charles Coleman. *Dickinson College, A History*. Middletown, Conn., 1973.

Sellers, Charles G. *James K. Polk, Continentalist, 1843-1846*. Princeton, N.J., 1966.

————. *James K. Polk, Jacksonian, 1795-1843*. Princeton, N.J., 1957.

Seltzer, Leon E., ed. *The Columbia Lippincott Gazetteer of the World*. New York, 1952.

Semmes, Samuel M. *Extracts from a Pamphlet Entitled: "Religious Liberty in Danger"; A Vindication of the Whig party from the Charge of Hostility to Catholics and Foreigners, By a Catholic Layman*. N.p., 1844.

Seton-Watson, Robert William. *Britain in Europe, 1789-1914*. New York, 1938.

Seward, Frederick W. *Autobiography of William H. Seward From 1801 to 1834 with a Memoir of His Life*. . . . New York, 1877.

Sewell, Richard H. *Ballots for Freedom: Antislavery Politics in the United States, 1837-1860*. New York, 1976.

Shaffer, James F. et al. *Piatt's Landing Eastbend*. Cincinnati, 1978.

354

Shanks, Henry T., ed. *The Papers of Willie Person Mangum*. 5 vols. Raleigh, N.C., 1953.
Shannon, J.B. *Presidential Politics in Kentucky, 1824-1948: A Compilation of Election Statistics and an Analysis of Political Behavior*. Lexington, Ky., 1950.
Sharp, James R. *The Jacksonians Versus the Banks: Politics in the States After the Panic of 1837*. New York, 1970.
Shaw, William H. *History of Essex and Hudson Counties, New Jersey*. 2 vols. Philadelphia, 1884.
Shelby, Lucy G. *Grassland Days and Grassland Ways*. Lexington, Ky., 1957.
Shenton, James P. *Robert John Walker: A Politician from Jackson to Lincoln*. New York, 1961.
Shepard, Edward M. *Martin Van Buren*. Boston, 1890.
Sherman, Neil W. *Taliaferro-Toliver Family Records*. Peoria, Ill., 1960.
Shipman, Paul R. *A Handful of Bitter Herbs. . . .* Lexington, 1953.
Shipp, John E.D. *Giant Days or the Life and Times of William H. Crawford*. Americus, Ga., 1909.
Shoemaker, Floyd C. *Missouri & Missourians*. 5 vols. Chicago, 1943.
Shoemaker, Richard H. *A Checklist of American Imprints for 1828*. Metuchen, N.J., 1971.
Shultz, Gladys. *Jenny Lind: The Swedish Nightingale*. Philadelphia, 1962.
Shultz, William J. & M.R. Caine. *Financial Development of the United States*. New York, 1937.
Siegel, Stanley. *A Political History of the Texas Republic, 1836-1845*. Austin, Tx., 1956.
Silber, Kate. *Pestalozzi: the Man and His Work*. New York, 1973.
Simms, Henry H. *The Rise of the Whigs in Virginia 1824-1840*. Richmond, Va., 1929.
Simpson, Craig M. *A Good Southerner, The Life of Henry A. Wise of Virginia*. Chapel Hill, N.C., 1985.
Simpson, Elizabeth M. *Bluegrass Houses and Their Traditions*. Lexington, Ky., 1932.
Simpson, Henry. *The Lives of Eminent Philadelphians*. Philadelphia, 1859.
Simpson, Louisiana W. *The Colonel's Lady*. Lexington, Ky., 1981.
Sinclair, Bruce. *Philadelphia's Philosopher Mechanics. . . .* Baltimore, 1974.
Singletary, Otis A. *The Mexican War*. Chicago, 1960.
Sistler, Byron & Barbara, transcribers. *1850 Census Tennessee*. Evanston, Ill., 1976.
Skeel, Emily E.F. "Not Quite Spurlos Versunkt." *Bookmen's Holiday*. New York, 1943.
Skinner, J.B. *The Gentleman's New Pocket Farrier. . . . and Stud Book*. Philadelphia, 1853.
Slaughter, Philip. *Genealogical and Historical Notes on Culpeper County, Virginia*. Culpeper, Va., 1900.
Smiley, David L. *Lion of Whitehall*. Madison, Wis., 1962.
Smith, Allen W., ed. *Beginnings at "the Point": A Documentary History of Northern Kentucky and Environs, the Town of Covington in Particular, 1751-1834*. Park Hills, Ky., 1977.
Smith, Benjamin E. & William D. Whitney, eds. *Century Dictionary and Cyclopedia*. 12 vols. New York, 1911.
Smith, Clifford L. *History of Troup County*. Atlanta, Ga., 1933.
Smith, Elbert B. *Francis Preston Blair*. New York, 1980.
——— . *Magnificent Missourian*. New York, 1958.
——— . *The Presidencies of Zachary Taylor & Millard Fillmore*. Lawrence, Kan., 1988.
Smith, George G. *The Story of Georgia and the Georgia People*. Macon, Ga., 1900.
Smith, George W. & Charles Judah, eds. *Chronicles of the Gringos, The U.S. Army in the Mexican War, 1846-1848*. Albuquerque, N.M., 1968.
Smith, H. Perry. *History of the City of Buffalo and Erie County*. 2 vols. Syracuse, N.Y., 1884.
Smith, James W. *Sojourners in Search of Freedom, The Settlement of Liberia by Black Americans*. Lanham, Md., 1987.
Smith, John E. *Our Country and Its People: A Descriptive and Biographical Record of Madison County, New York*. Boston, 1899.
Smith, Joseph. *History of the Church of Jesus Christ of Latter Day Saints*. 6 vols. 2nd. rev. ed. Salt Lake City, Utah, 1948-51.
Smith, Junius. *Essays on the Cultivation of the Tea Plant*. New York, 1948.
Smith, Justin H. *The Annexation of Texas*. Corrected ed. New York, 1941.
——— . *The War with Mexico*. 2 vols. New York, 1919.
Smith, Mark A. *The Tariff on Wool*. New York, 1926.
Smith, Oliver H. *Early Indiana Trials: and Sketches, Reminiscences*. Cincinnati, 1858.
Smith, Sarah B. *Historic Nelson County*. Louisville, Ky., 1971.
Smith, Solomon F. *Theatrical Management in the West and South for Thirty Years. . . .* New York, 1868.

Smith, Walter Buckingham. *Economic Aspects of the Second Bank of the United States.* Cambridge, Mass., 1953.

Smith, Wilbur W. "The Whig Party in Maryland, 1826-1856." Ph.D. dissertation, University of Maryland, 1967.

Smith, William E. *The Francis Preston Blair Family in Politics.* New York, 1933.

———— & Orphia D. Smith. *A Buckeye Titan.* Cincinnati, 1953.

Smith, William Henry. *Charles Hammond and His Relations to Henry Clay and John Quincy Adams.* . . . Chicago, 1885.

————. *A Political History of Slavery.* Reprint ed. New York, 1966.

Smith, Zachary F. & Mary Rogers Clay. *The Clay Family.* Filson Club Publications. No. 14. Louisville, Ky., 1899.

Smith & DeLand, pub. *Northern Alabama Historical and Biographical.* Birmingham, 1888.

Smylie, James. *Brief History of the Trial of the Rev. William A. Scott.* . . . New York, 1847.

Smyth, Samuel G. *A Genealogy of the Duke-Shepherd-VanMetre Family.* Lancaster, Pa., 1909.

Snyder, Charles M. *The Jacksonian Heritage, Pennsylvania Politics 1833-1848.* Harrisburg, Pa., 1958.

————. *Oswego From Buckskin to Bustles.* Port Washington, N.Y., 1968.

Sobel, Robert & John Raimo, eds. *The Biographical Directory of the Governors of the United States, 1789-1978.* 4 vols. Westport, Conn., 1978.

Sonne, Niels H. *Liberal Kentucky, 1780-1828.* New York, 1939.

Sorin, Gerald. *Abolitionism, A New Perspective.* New York, 1972.

Sowers, Don C. *The Financial History of New York State from 1789 to 1912.* In *Columbia University Studies in History, Economics, and Public Law.* Vol. 57, no.2. New York, 1914.

Spalding, Martin J. *Sketches of the Life, Times, and Character of the Rt. Rev. Benedict Joseph Flaget, First Bishop of Louisville.* Louisville, Ky., 1852.

Spalding, Mattingly. *Bardstown: Town of Tradition.* . . . Baltimore, 1947.

Sparks, Jared. *A Historical Outline of the American Colonization Society.* . . . Boston, 1824.

Spaulding, E. Wilder. *His Excellency George Clinton, Critic of the Constitution.* New York, 1938.

Special Staff of Writers. *History of North Carolina.* 6 vols. Chicago, 1919.

The Speeches, Addresses and Messages of the Several Presidents of the United States at the Openings of Congress. . . . Philadelphia, 1825.

Speed, Thomas. *Records and Memorials of the Speed Family.* Louisville, Ky., 1892.

Spelman, Georgia P. "The Whig Rhetoric of John Pendleton Kennedy, Spokesman for Industry." Ph.D. dissertation, Indiana University, 1974.

Spencer, Ivor D. *The Victor and the Spoils; a Life of William L. Marcy.* Providence, R.I., 1959.

Spencer, John Henderson. *A History of Kentucky Baptists from 1769 to 1885, Including More than 800 Biographical Sketches.* 2 vols. Cincinnati, 1885.

Spiller, Robert E. *Fenimore Cooper, Critic of His Times.* New York, 1931.

Spraker, Hazel A., comp. *The Boone Family.* . . . Rutland, Vt., 1922.

Stanwood, Edward. *A History of the Presidency.* New York, 1898.

Staples, Charles R. *The History of Pioneer Lexington, 1779-1806.* Lexington, Ky., 1939.

Starbuck, Alexander. *The History of Nantucket.* Rutland, Vt., 1969.

Starkweather, Carlton L. *A Brief Genealogical History of Robert Starkweather of Roxbury & Ipswich, Mass.* Auburn, N.Y., 1904.

Starling, Edmund L. *History of Henderson County, Kentucky.* . . . Henderson, Ky., 1887.

State Papers and Publick Documents of the United States. . . . 10 vols. Boston, 1817.

The Statistical History of the United States from Colonial Times to the Present. Stamford, Conn., 1965.

Staudenraus, P.J. *The African Colonization Movement, 1816-1865.* New York, 1961.

Stearns, Peter N. *1848: The Revolutionary Tide in Europe.* New York, 1974.

Steele, Robert. *Early Dayton.* Dayton, Ohio, 1896.

Steffen, Truman G., ed. *Byron's Don Juan.* 4 vols. Austin, Tx., 1957.

Stephenson, George M. *The Political History of the Public Lands From 1840 to 1862.* Boston, 1917.

Stephenson, Wendell Holmes. *Alexander Porter, Whig Planter of Old Louisiana.* Baton Rouge, La., 1934.

Stevens, Harry R. *The Early Jackson Party in Ohio.* Durham, N.C., 1957.

Stevens, Kenneth R. "The *Caroline* Affair: Anglo-American Relations and Domestic Politics, 1837-1842." Ph.D. dissertation, Indiana University, 1982.

356

Stevens, Lewis Townsend. *The History of Cape May County, New Jersey.* . . . Cape May, N.J., 1897.

Stevens, Sylvester K. *American Expansion in Hawaii 1842-1898.* Harrisburg, Pa., 1945.

Stevens, William O. *Pistols at Ten Paces.* . . . Boston, 1940.

————. *The Shenandoah and its Byways.* New York, 1941.

Stevenson, Burton, arr. *The Home Book of Proverbs, Maxims and Familiar Phrases.* . . . New York, 1948.

Stewart, James B. *Joshua R. Giddings and the Tactics of Radical Politics.* Cleveland, 1970.

Stickney, William, ed. *Autobiography of Amos Kendall.* New York, 1949.

Stimpson, Charles. *Boston Directory for 1847/48.* Boston, 1848.

Stokes, Anson P. *Church and State in the United States.* 3 vols. New York, 1950.

Stone, John S. *A Memoir of the Life of James Milnor, D.D., Late Rector of St. George's Church, New York.* New York, 1849.

Stone, Richard G. *H. Niles as an Economist.* In *The Johns Hopkins University Studies in Historical and Political Science.* Vol. 51, no. 5. Baltimore, 1933.

Stone, William L. *History of New York City from the Discovery to the Present Day.* New York, 1872.

Stoner, Robert. *A Seed-Bed of the Republic, Early Botetourt.* Radford, Va., 1962.

Story, Joseph. *Commentaries on the Constitution of the United States.* . . . 2 vols. 4th ed. Boston, 1873.

————. *The Public and General Statutes Passed by the Congress from 1789 to 1836.* . . . 4 vols. Boston, 1827-37.

Story, William W. *Life and Letters of Joseph Story.* . . . 2 vols. Boston, 1851.

Strange, Sir John. *Reports of Adjudged Cases in the Courts of Chancery, King's Bench . . . in the Second Year of King George I to . . . Twenty-first Year of King George II.* 2 vols. London, 1855.

Stratton, Margaret B. *Place-Names of Logan County and Oft-Told Tales.* Russellville, Ky., *ca.* 1950.

Strauss, W. Patrick. *Americans in Polynesia, 1783-1842.* East Lansing, Mich., 1963.

Stuart, Graham H. *The Governmental System of Pennsylvania.* Washington, 1940.

Stuart, Robert, pseud. *A Descriptive History of the Steam Engine Illustrated.* 3rd ed. London, 1825.

Stuart-Wortley, Lady Emmaline. *Travels in the United States, etc. During 1849 and 1850.* London, 1851.

Studer, Jacob H. *Columbus, Ohio: Its History, Resources, and Progress.* Washington, 1873.

Styran, Arthur. *The Last of the Cocked Hats, James Monroe & the Virginia Dynasty.* Oklahoma City, Okla., 1945.

Subject Matter Index of Patents for Inventions Issued by the U.S. Patent Office, 1789-1873 inclusive. Washington, 1874.

Summers, Thomas J. *History of Marietta.* Marietta, Ohio, 1903.

Sumner, W. G. *et al. A History of Banking in all the Leading Nations.* 4 vols. New York, 1896.

Swain, James B., ed. *The Life and Speeches of Henry Clay.* 2 vols. in 1. New York, 1843.

Swann Gallerier Catalogue. *Autographs and a Private Collection of Printed & Manuscript Americana.* New York, 1986.

Swearinger, Mack Buckley. "The Early Life of George Poindexter, a Story of the First Southwest." Ph.D. dissertation, University of Chicago, 1934.

Swinford, Frances K. & Rebecca S. Lee. *The Great Elm Tree, Heritage of the Episcopal Diocese of Lexington.* Lexington, Ky., 1969.

Swisher, Carl B. *Roger B. Taney.* New York, 1935.

————. *The Taney Period, 1836-64.* Vol. 5. In *History of the Supreme Court of the United States.* Edited by Paul A. Freund. New York, 1974.

Sydnor, Charles S. *Development of Southern Sectionalism, 1819-1848.* Baton Rouge, La., 1964.

Tanner, Earl C. *Rhode Island, A Brief History.* Providence, R.I., 1954.

Taussig, Frank W. *The Tariff History of the U.S.* New York, 1888.

Taylor, George R. *The Transportation Revolution, 1815-1860.* New York, 1964.

Taylor, John. *Construction Construed and Constitutions Vindicated.* Richmond, Va., 1820.

Taylor, Orville W. *Negro Slavery in Arkansas.* Durham, N.C., 1958.

Teague, William. "An Appeal to Reason: Daniel Webster, Henry Clay, and Whig Presidential Politics, 1836-1848." Ph.D. dissertation, North Texas State University, 1977.

Teeter, Negley K. & John D. Shearer. *The Prison at Philadelphia: Cherry Hill*. New York, 1957.

Tefft, B.F., ed. *Speeches of Daniel Webster*. New York, n.d.

Temin, Peter. *The Jacksonian Economy*. New York, 1969.

Temperley, Harold. *The Foreign Policy of Canning, 1822-1827....* London, 1925.

Tercentenary Handlist of English and Welsh Newspapers, Magazines and Reviews. London, 1966.

Terrell, John U. *Furs by Astor*. New York, 1963.

Thacher, John B. *Christopher Columbus: His Life, His Work, His Remains....* 3 vols. New York, 1903-4.

Thacker, Joseph A., Jr. "The Kentucky Militia from 1792 to 1812." Master's thesis, University of Kentucky, 1954.

Thane, Elswyth. *Mount Vernon is Ours, The Story of Its Preservation*. New York, 1966.

Theirs, Adolphe. *Histoire de la Revolution Francaise*. 10 vols. Paris, n.d.

Thomas, Clayton L., ed. *Taber's Cyclopedic Medical Dictionary*. Philadelphia, 1979.

Thomas, James W. & T.J.C. Williams. *History of Allegany County, Maryland*. 2 vols. N.p., 1923.

Thompson, Benjamin F. *History of Long Island*. 2 vols. New York, 1839-43.

Thompson, Charles M. *The Illinois Whigs Before 1846*. Urbana, 1915.

Thomson, Peter G. *A Bibliography of the State of Ohio*. Cincinnati, 1880.

Thornton, J. Mills, III. *Politics and Power in a Slave Society, Alabama, 1800-1860*. Baton Rouge, La., 1978.

Thornton, William. *Outlines of a Constitution for a United North & South Colombia....* Washington, 1815.

Thorp, Willard L. *Business Annals....* New York, 1926.

Thurston, David. *A Brief History of Winthrop....* Portland, Me., 1855.

Thwaites, Reuben G. *Early Western Travels, 1748-1846....* Cleveland, Ohio, 1905.

Tischendorf, Alfred & E. Taylor Parks, eds. *The Diary and Journal of Richard Clough Anderson, Jr., 1814-1826*. Durham, N.C., 1964.

Tombstone Inscriptions and Burial Lots Compiled by Bee Line Chapter, National Society Daughters of the American Revolution. Marceline, Mo., n.d.

Tooker, Elva. *Nathan Trotter, Philadelphia Merchant 1787-1853*. Cambridge, Mass., 1955.

Toullier, Charles B.M. *Le Droit Civil Francais, Suivant l'order du Code....* Paris, various editions.

A Treatise of the Diseases of the Chest. Philadelphia, 1823.

Tregle, Joseph G. "Louisiana In The Age of Jackson: A Study In Ego-Politics." Ph.D. dissertation, University of Pennsylvania, 1954.

Trend, J.B. *Bolivar and the Independence of Spanish America*. Clinton, Mass., 1951.

Trevelyan, George M. *British History in the Nineteenth Century (1782-1901)*. New York, 1923.

The Tribune Almanac for the Years 1836 to 1868.... 2 vols. New York, 1868.

Trimble, David. *Address of David Trimble, to the Public, containing proof that he did not make statements attributed to him, in relation to charges against the President of the United States, and Mr. Clay*. Frankfort, Ky., 1828.

Triplett, Robert. *Roland Trevor: Or, the Pilot of Human Life*. Philadelphia, 1853.

Troutman, Richard L. "Plantation Life in the Ante-Bellum Bluegrass Region of Kentucky." Master's thesis, University of Kentucky, 1955.

True, Webster P. *The First Hundred Years of the Smithsonian Institution 1846-1946*. Washington, 1946.

Truett, Randle B. *Trade and Travel around the Southern Appalachians before 1830*. Chapel Hill, N.C., 1935.

Trumbull, J. Hammond, ed. *The Memorial History of Hartford County, Connecticut, 1633-1884*. 2 vols. Boston, 1886.

Tucker, Ebenezer. *History of Randolph County, Indiana, with Illustrations and Biographical Sketches....* Chicago, 1882.

Tuppen, John N. *Studies in Industrial Geography: France*. Kent, England, 1980.

Turner, Frederick J. *The United States 1830-1850*. New York, 1935.

Tuttle, Mary & Henry B. Thompson. *Autobiography and Correspondence of Allen Trimble Governor of Ohio*. Reprint ed. Columbus, Ohio, 1909.

The Twentieth Century Bench and Bar of Pennsylvania. Vol. 2. Chicago, 1903.

Twitchell, Ralph E. *The Leading Facts of New Mexican History*. Albuquerque, N.M., 1963.

358

Tyler, David B. *Steam Conquers the Atlantic*. New York, 1939.
Tyler, Lyon G. *The Letters and Times of the Tylers*. 2 vols. Richmond, Va., 1884.
———. *Parties and Patronage in the United States*. New York, 1891.
The Universal Jewish Encyclopedia. New York, 1943.
University of Kentucky Library Associates. *Cholera in Lexington*. Lexington, Ky., 1963.
United States Beet Sugar Association. *The Beet Sugar Story*. Washington, 1959.
U.S. Bureau of Census. *The Statistical History of the United States from Colonial Times to the Present*. Stamford, Conn., 1965.
U.S. Continental Congress. *Secret Journals of the Acts and Proceedings of Congress. . . .* 4 vols. Boston, 1820-21.
U.S. Department of Agriculture, Bureau of Statistics. *Cotton Crop of the United States 1790-1911*. Washington, 1912.
U.S. Military Academy. *Register of Graduates and Former Cadets of the United States Military Academy*. West Point, N.Y., 1960.
·U.S. Senate. *Journal of the Executive Proceedings of the Senate of the United States of America*. 3 vols. Washington, 1828.
U.S. Superintendent of Documents, comp. *Checklist of United States Public Documents, 1789-1909. . . .* 3rd ed. Washington, n.d.
Utter, William T. *The Frontier State, 1803-1825*. Columbus, Ohio, 1942.
Valentine, Alan. *Lord Stirling*. New York, 1969.
Van Deusen, Glyndon G. *Horace Greeley, Nineteenth Century Crusader*. New York, 1953.
———. *The Jacksonian Era, 1828-1848*. New York, 1959.
———. *The Life of Henry Clay*. Boston, 1937.
———. *The Rise And Decline of Jacksonian Democracy*. New York, 1970.
———. *Thurlow Weed: Wizard of the Lobby*. Boston, 1947.
———. *William Henry Seward*. New York, 1967.
Van Wyck, Frederick. *Recollections of an Old New Yorker. . . .* New York, ca. 1932.
Varg, Paul A. *United States Foreign Relations, 1829-1860*. East Lansing, Mich., 1979.
Vaughn, William P. *The Antimasonic Party in the United States 1826-1843*. Lexington, Ky., 1983.
Vedder, O.F. *History of the City of Memphis and Shelby County, Tennessee. . . .* 2 vols. Syracuse, N.Y., 1888.
Viola, Herman J. *Thomas L. McKenney: Architect of America's Early Indian Policy, 1816-1830*. Chicago, 1974.
Vital Records of Norwich 1659-1848. Part II. Hartford, Conn., 1913.
Voltz, Harry A., III. "Party, State, and Nation: Kentucky and the Coming of the Civil War." Ph.D. dissertation, University of Virginia, 1982.
Von Holst, Harold. *The Constitutional and Political History of the United States*. 8 vols. Chicago, 1881-92.
Wager, David E., ed. *Our County and its People, A Descriptive Work on Oneida County, New York*. Boston, 1896.
Walker, Thomas L., comp. *History of the Lexington Post Office From 1794 to 1901*. Lexington, Ky., 1901.
Wallace, George S. *Cabell County Annals and Families*. Richmond, Va., 1935.
Wallace, William S. *A Dictionary of North American Authors Deceased Before 1850*. Toronto, Canada, 1951.
Walsh, James J. *History of Medicine in New York*. 5 vols. New York, 1919.
Walters, Raymond, Jr. *Albert Gallatin, Jeffersonian Financier and Diplomat*. New York, 1957.
Walton, Joseph S. *Conrad Weiser and the Indian Policy of Colonial Pennsylvania*. Philadelphia, 1900.
Ward, Henry G. *Mexico in 1827*. 2 vols. London, 1828.
Ward, John W. *Andrew Jackson—Symbol for an Age*. London, 1953; reprint ed., 1968.
Ware, Caroline. *The Early New England Cotton Manufactures*. Boston, 1931.
Warfield, Joshua D. *The Founders of Anne Arundel and Howard Counties, Maryland, a Genealogical and Biographical Review. . . .* Baltimore, 1905.
Warner, Ezra J. *Generals in Blue*. Baton Rouge, La., 1964.
Warner, Oliver. *Captain Marryat, a Rediscovery*. London, 1953.
Warren, Charles. *The Supreme Court in United States History*. 2 vols. Boston, 1937.
Warren, Harris G. *The Sword Was Their Passport, a History of American Filibustering in the Mexican Revolution*. Baton Rouge, La., 1943.
Washburne, Elihu B., ed. *The Edwards Papers . . . .* Chicago, 1884.

———. *Sketch of Edward Coles*. Chicago, 1882.

The Washington Directory. . . . Washington, 1827.

Washington, George. *Official Letters to the Honourable American Congress, Written during the War between the United Colonies and Great Britain. . . .* 2 vols. Boston, 1795.

Wayland, Francis F. *Andrew Stevenson, Democrat and Diplomat 1785-1857*. Philadelphia, 1949.

Webb, Lester A. *Captain Alden Partridge and the United States Military Academy 1806-1833*. Northport, Ala., 1965.

Webb, R.K. *Harriet Martineau, A Radical Victorian*. London, 1960.

Webb, Walter P. *The Handbook of Texas*. Austin, Tx., 1922.

Weber, Ralph E. *Diplomatic Codes and Ciphers 1775-1938*. Chicago, 1979.

Webster, Charles K. *Britain and the Independence of Latin America 1812-1830*. New York, 1970.

———. *The Congress of Vienna 1814-1815*. New York, 1963.

Webster, Daniel. *The Papers of Daniel Webster: Correspondence*. Edited by Charles M. Wiltse *et al.* 7 vols. Hanover, N.H., 1974-86.

———. *Works. . . .* 6 vols. 5th ed. Boston, 1853.

———. *The Writings and Speeches of Daniel Webster. . . .* Edited by James W. McIntyre. 18 vols. National Edition. Boston, 1903.

Wedgwood, William B. *Civil Service Reform*. Portland, Me., 1883.

Weed, Harriet A., ed. *Autobiography of Thurlow Weed*. 2 vols. Boston, 1883.

Weigley, Russell F. *History of the United States Army*. New York, 1967.

Weise, Arthur J. *Troy's One Hundred Years*. Troy, N.Y., 1891.

Weisenburger, Francis P. *The Life of John McLean, A Politician on the United States Supreme Court*. Columbus, Ohio, 1937.

Weiss, Harry B. *Rafinesque's Kentucky Friends*. Highland Park, N.J., 1936.

Welsh, Samuel. *Home History, Recollections of Buffalo*. Buffalo, N.Y., 1891.

Weld, Ralph F. *Brooklyn Village, 1816-1834*. New York, 1938.

Wellington, Raymond G. *The Political and Sectional Influence of the Public Lands, 1828-1842*. New York, 1914; reprint ed., 1970.

Werner, M.R. *Tammany Hall*. New York, 1928.

West, Elizabeth H., comp. *Calendar of the Papers of Martin Van Buren. . . .* Washington, 1910.

West, Richard S., Jr. *Gideon Welles, Lincoln's Navy Department*. Indianapolis, *ca.* 1943.

West, Sue C. *The Maury Family Tree. . . .* Birmingham, Ala., n.d.

Weston, Florence. *The Presidential Election of 1828*. Philadelphia, 1974.

Wheaton, Henry. *A Digest of the Law of Maritime Captures and Prizes*. New York, 1815.

The Whig Almanac 1845. New York, 1845.

Whipple, Charles. *Relation of the American Board of Commissioners for Foreign Missions to Slavery*. 1861; reprint ed., New York, 1969.

Whitaker, A.P. *The United States and the Independence of Latin America, 1800-1830*. Baltimore, 1941.

White, G. Edward. *The Marshall Court and Cultural Change, 1815-35*. New York, 1988.

White, George. *Historical Collections of Georgia*. New York, 1855.

White, George F. *A Century of Spain and Portugal, 1788-1898*. London, 1909.

White, George S. *Memoir of Samuel Slater, Father of American Manufactures*. Philadelphia, 1836.

White, James T. & Co., pub. *National Cyclopedia of American Biography*. New York, 1898-.

White, Laura A. *Robert Barnwell Rhett: Father of Secession*. New York, 1931.

White, Leonard D. *The Jacksonians, A Study in Administrative History 1829-1861*. New York, 1954.

White, Ronald F. "A Dialogue on Madness: Eastern State Lunatic Asylum and Mental Health Policy in Kentucky, 1824-1883." Ph.D. dissertation, University of Kentucky, 1984.

Whitlock, Brand. *LaFayette*. New York, 1929.

Whitley, Edna T. *Kentucky Antebellum Portraiture*. Paris, Ky., 1956.

Whitney, Ellen M., ed. *The Black Hawk War of 1831-1832*. 2 vols. Springfield, Ill., 1970.

Whittaker, Genevieve S. *Some Notes on the Shelton Family of England and America*. St. Louis, 1927.

Who Was Who in America, Historical Volume 1607-1896. Chicago, 1963.

Wiecek, William M. *The Sources of Antislavery Constitutionalism in America, 1760-1848*. Ithaca, N.Y., 1977.

Wikander, Lawrence E. *et al.*, eds. *The Northampton Book . . . A New England Town 1654-1954*. Northampton, 1954.

Wilburn, Jean A. *Biddle's Bank: The Crucial Years*. New York, 1967.

Wilcox, Cadmus. *History of the Mexican War*. Edited by Mary R. Wilcox. Washington, 1892.

Wiley, Bell I. *Slaves No More, Letters from Liberia 1833-1869*. Lexington, Ky., 1980.

Wilkins, Thurman. *Cherokee Tragedy: The Story of the Ridge Family and the Decimation of a People*. New York, 1970.

Williams, C.S. *Lexington Directory, City Guide, and Business Mirror*. Lexington, Ky., 1859.

Williams, David H., ed. *The American Almanac and Repository of Useful Knowledge for the Year 1841*. Boston, 1841.

Williams, Harold A. *History of the Hibernian Society of Baltimore 1803-1957*. Baltimore, 1957.

Williams, Samuel C. *Beginnings of West Tennessee . . . 1541-1841*. Johnson City, Tenn., 1930.

Williams, Stephen K., ed. *Cases Argued and Decided in the Supreme Court of the United States 1850-1851. . . .* Rochester, New York, 1901.

Williams, Thomas J.C. *History of Allegany County, Maryland*. 2 vols. N.p., 1923.

———. *A History of Washington County Maryland. . . .* Baltimore, 1968.

Williams, William W. *History of Ashtabula County, Ohio. . . .* Philadelphia, 1878.

———. *History of the Fire Lands, Comprising Huron and Erie Counties, Ohio*. Cleveland, Ohio, 1879.

Willis, Jean L. *Historical Dictionary of Uruguay*. Metuchen, N.J., 1974.

Williston, Ebenezer B. *Eloquence of the United States*. Middletown, Conn., 1827.

Willson, Beckles. *America's Ambassadors to England (1785-1929)*. New York, 1929.

Wilmerding, Lucius, Jr. *James Monroe: Public Claimant*. Trenton, N.J., *ca.* 1960.

Wilson, Charles M. *Liberia, Black Africa in Microcosm*. New York, 1971.

Wilson, Joseph M. *Presbyterian Historical Almanac and Annual Remembrance of the Church*. N.p., 1860.

Wilson, Major L. *The Presidency of Martin Van Buren*. Lawrence, Kan., 1984.

Wilson, S. *1844 Albany City Guide*. Albany, N.Y., 1844.

Wilson, Samuel M. *History of Kentucky*. 2 vols. Louisville, Ky., 1928.

Wilson, Samuel R. *History of the United States Court for the Eastern District of Kentucky*. Lexington, Ky., 1935.

Wilson's Business Directory for New York City. New York, 1848.

Wiltse, Charles M. *John C. Calhoun: Nationalist, 1782-1828*. Indianapolis, 1944.

———. *John C. Calhoun: Nullifier, 1829-1839*. Indianapolis, 1949.

———. *John C. Calhoun: Sectionalist, 1840-1850*. New York, 1951.

Wingerter, Charles A. *History of Greater Wheeling and Vicinity*. 2 vols. Chicago, 1912.

Wingfield, Marshall. *A History of Caroline County, Virginia, 1827-1924*. Richmond, Va., 1924.

Wire, Richard A. "John M. Clayton and the Search for Order: A Study in Whig Politics and Diplomacy." Ph.D. dissertation, University of Maryland, 1971.

Wise, Barton H. *The Life of Henry A. Wise of Virginia, 1806-1876*. New York, 1899.

Wise, Henry A. *Seven Decades of the Union . . . Illustrated by A Memoir of John Tyler*. Philadelphia, 1872.

Wissett, Robert. *On Cultivation and Preparation of Hemp*. London, 1804.

Witherspoon, E.D. *Directory of the Presbyterian Church, U.S., 1861-1967*. Doraville, Ga., 1967.

Wittke, Carl, ed. *The History of the State of Ohio*. 6 vols. Columbus, Ohio, 1941-44.

———. *We Who Built America, The Saga of the Immigrant*. Rev. ed. Cleveland, Ohio, 1964.

Wood, Edwin T. *Wood's Mobile Directory for 1844*. Mobile, Ala., 1844.

Woodberry, George E. *The Life of Edgar Allan Poe, Personal and Literary*. 2 vols. New York, 1909.

Woodford, Frank B. *Lewis Cass: The Last Jeffersonian*. New Brunswick, N.J., 1950.

Woodhouse, C.M. *The Greek War of Independence*. London, 1952.

Woods, Alva. *Literary and Theological Addresses*. Providence, R.I., 1868.

Woods, Edgar. *History of Albermarle County in Virginia*. Charlottesville, Va., 1901.

Wooldridge, J., ed. *History of Nashville, Tenn*. Nashville, 1890.

The Works of Alexander Hamilton. . . . 3 vols. New York, 1810.

World Book Encyclopedia. Chicago, 1984.

Wright, Buster W., comp. *Abstracts of Marriages Reported in the Columbus (Georgia) Enquirer 1832-1852*. Columbus, Ga., 1980.

Wright, John D., Jr. *Transylvania: Tutor to the West*. Lexington, Ky., 1975.

Wyatt-Brown, Bertram. *Lewis Tappan and the Evangelical War Against Slavery*. New York, 1971.

Yerby, William E.W. *History of Greensboro, Alabama*. Northport, Ala., 1963.

Young, John P., ed. *Standard History of Memphis, Tennessee*. Knoxville, Tenn., 1912.

Young, Sarah S. *Genealogical Narrative of the Hart Family*. Memphis, Tenn., 1882.

Zetlin, Mikhail. *The Decembrists*. New York, 1958.

Ziegler, Philip. *King William IV*. London, 1971.

Zinny, Antonio. *Historia de los Gobernadores de las Provincias Argentinas*. . . . 4 vols. Revised ed. Buenos Aires, 1920.

ERRATA

Since the publication of Volume 7, the editors have made a systematic attempt to compile a list of all errors found in that and subsequent volumes. These include misspelled names, errors in transcription, dates, or other basic information, clarifications, and significant additional information uncovered too late for inclusion in the proper place. This list does not include simple typographical errors except those concerning proper names or dates. Although no such list is available for Volumes 1-6, those errors found through everyday usage or marked by previous editors in office copies are given.

Volume One

Page

16   **Property Deed,** May 15, 1799. Note 1. Date of Dr. Richard Pindell's death should be 1833, not 1813.

33   **Receipt from Edmund Thomas,** June 26, 1800. Second paragraph of notes. Name should be Wade Mosby, not Moseby.

72   **To Francis T. Brooke,** Dec. 30, 1801. Note 4. Should indicate that Anderson was the principal surveyor of bounty lands in Ohio as well as Kentucky.

146   **From Montgomery Bell,** August 25, 1804. Note 1, line 4. Should read "the Virginia and Kentucky Resolutions of 1798 and 1799."

410   **Bond to John Winn,** May 8, 1809. Line 2 of notes. Editors have determined that John Winn was a resident of Fayette County, Ky., not Fleming County.

430   **Promissory Note from Prettyman Merry,** Dec. 15, 1809. Note 1. The case was against Norborne B. Beall in U.S. Circuit Court, 7th Circuit, District of Kentucky, G, 427ff.

432   **Credentials as United States Senator,** Jan. 6, 1810. Line 3. Date should read Nov. 19, 1806, not Dec. 29, 1806.

559   **To _____ ,** June 10, 1811. Note 1. Edward Church was not appointed U.S. consul at L'Orient, France, until 1817.

561   **From Alexander Stephens,** June 14, 1811. Note 2. "Brenham &c." was probably the Frankfort, Ky., firm of Brenham & Marshall (Robert Brenham & John J. Marshall).

575   **To Caesar A. Rodney,** August 17, 1811. Note 4. The name of the new Supreme Court Justice was Gabriel Duvall, not Duval. Note 7. Martin Duralde, Jr., had been appointed marshal of Orleans Territory but had declined due to ill health. See *Letter Books of W.C.C. Claiborne,* 5:143, 183-84.

585   **Deed of Trust From Samuel Hopkins,** Oct. 1, 1811. Note 1. Robert Crockett was also the son of Joseph Crockett.

630   **To James Morrison,** Feb. 6, 1812. Last line of letter. A superscript note reference number 7 should appear after "Worseley."

645-48   **Newspaper Editorial,** April 14, 1812. The editorial was written by James Monroe, not Henry Clay. (A correction was printed and attached to this page.)

705   **From William Coleman to Clay and Robert Wickliffe,** *ca.* August 7, 1812. Note 3. Possibly Ward & Johnson (Robert J. Ward & James Johnson).

805   **Property Deed, Clay and Others to John L. May and Polly Epes,** June 18, 1813. Note 5. Jephthah Dudley was the nephew of William Dudley, not his brother.

832   **Receipt from Grinstead and Davis,** Oct. 11, 1813. Source note. The court file number is 412, not 442.

Volume Two

Hart constituted the "&c." Case began in 1808 and was settled in 1821. See Federal Circuit Court, Complete Record Book Q, 1-10 and Complete Record Book P, 335-37. The earlier case mentioned was *Beall's Exors* v. *Nicholas's Exors*. Note 5. Date of American Commissioners to Monroe is July 3, 1815.

Volume Three

319	**From Langdon Cheves,** Nov. 9, 1833. Note 12. The last name should be spelled "Whittelsey."
333	**From John Breathitt,** Dec. 8, 1822. Line 2 of letter. A superscript reference number "1" should appear after the name Wm. Y.C. Ewing. Note 1. W.Y.C. Ewing was the son of Urban Ewing.
525	**Statement of Account with Bank of Kentucky,** Nov. 20, 1823. Line 4 of document. The name should be John Tilford.
596	**From Baptis Irvine,** Jan. 18, 1824. Note 6. This missing name is possibly Sistare.
786	**Mortgage Deed from John Tilford,** June 25, 1824. Source note. This mortgage is also recorded in Fayette County Deed Book Y, p. 53.
880	**Agreement with George J. Brown and Others,** Nov. 6, 1824. Heading. Brown's middle initial was "I.," not "J."
925	**Index.** Listing for Northeast Boundary Commission should be Northern Boundary Commission.

Volume Four

62	**From Nicholas Biddle,** Feb. 9, 1825. Note 1. The name should be Abram Claypool, not Abraham.
112	**From Josephus B. Stuart,** March 15, 1825. Note 1. Noah's former publication was being managed by Thomas Snowden and edited by James Gordon Bennett.
141	**To the Baron de Tuyll [Van Serookskerken],** March 25, 1825. Name should be Van Serooskerken.
291	**From Langdon Cheves,** April 26, 1825. Line 6, paragraph 3. The enclosed documents have not been found and are not in DNA, RG76, Indemnity for Slaves.
564	**From William Lytle,** August 3, 1825. Line 1 of letter. The superscript reference number "1" should go after the date "28th."
571	**From Susan Clay Duralde,** August 8, 1825. Note 7. The name should be John Morrison Clay.
586	**To John J. Crittenden,** August 22, 1825. Note 3. The date of Bodley to Clay was August 23, 1825.
599	**From David B. Macomb,** August 29, 1825. Lines 6-7. D.B. Macomb was a cousin and brother-in-law of Gen. Alexander Macomb, not a brother. *Florida Historical Quarterly*, 32:189-201.
919	**From Bartlett Yancy and Hutchins G. Burton,** Dec. 15, 1825. The name should be "Yancey," not Yancy.
926	**From Charles Yancy,** Dec. 19, 1825. Name should be "Yancey."
949	**From John J. Crittenden,** Dec. 26, 1825. Note 5. The date of the annual message was Dec. 6, 1825.
967	**Index.** Listing for John Minor Clay. The entry should be John Morrison Clay.
987	**Index.** Listing for Samuel Swartwout. Numbers should include page 46.
991	**Index.** Listings for Bartlett Yancy, Charles Yancy, and Joel Yancy should all be spelled "Yancey."

Volume Five

31	**From James Brown Clay,** Jan. 13, 1826. Note 11. For the actions of the Adams administration on these claims, see 6:143.
61	**From Samuel L. Southard,** Jan. 25, 1826. Line 8. The name of the frigate should be *Macedonian*.
90	**From Archibald Gracie,** Feb. 7, 1826. Line 4. The ship and cargo had been seized in 1824, not 1821.
136	**From Philip Robinson,** Feb. 27, 1826. Lines 4-5. Robinson received the appointment in March, 1827, and resigned later the same year.
258	**From Frederick Smith,** April 19, 1826. Last line. Philip S. Markley received the appointment as naval officer under the Adams administration in 1826. See 5:821.

266   **From Thomas R. Mercein,** April 21, 1826. Line 1. The memorial given as "not found" is that of Mary Ward to Clay of April 14, 1826, prepared by her lawyer Mercein. It is listed in the calendar items, this volume.

349   **From William B. Rochester,** May 9, 1826. Note 5, last line. The cross-reference should be to Rochester to Clay, Nov. 18, 1826.

359   **From Aaron Vail,** May 10, 1826. Identification of Vail should include that he received the position of clerk in the State Department on March 3, 1827.

439   **To Thompson, McCulloch, & Pryor,** June 17, 1826. Last line. Pryor held the job of Norfolk customs collector until he died in April, 1827.

618   **Account with Thomas Smith,** *ca.* August 12, 1826. Note 3, last line. The Rental Agreement of August 8, 1826, appears above, not below.

690   **From John Rainals,** Sept. 15, 1826. Line 2. The town's name is Kronstadt, not Cronstadt.

739   **From Claiborne Watkins,** Sept. 30, 1826. Note 3. Randolph was defeated by John Tyler, not Philip P. Barbour. See 5:1030-31.

826   **To C.D.E.J. Bangeman Huygens,** Oct. 25, 1826. Source note. A draft, dated Oct. 18, 1826, is in CSmH.

952   **From John J. Crittenden,** Nov. 25, 1826. Note 7. Information from the Allen book is incorrect. Buckner was not reelected until 1827.

964   **From James Brown,** Nov. 29, 1826. Note 6, line 7. The citation in parenthesis should be "3:155n."

975   **From John M. Forbes,** Dec. 4, 1826. Line 4. The signature was by J. Dn. Mendenhall.

981   **From Gulian C. Verplanck,** Dec. 7, 1826. Line 3 from bottom. The instructions given as "not found" are on 5:267n.

986   **From Jacob Harvey,** Dec. 9, 1826. Line 1. Should read "encloses a recommendation for Reuben Harvey."

1031   **From John H. Pleasants,** Dec. 24, 1826. Note 7, last line. The *Princeton* was a steam frigate, not a battleship.

1092   **Index.** Listings for James Tallmadge and James Tallmadge, Jr., should all be under the latter name.

Volume Six

378   **From James Tallmadge,** March 30, 1827. Line 1. Reference number "1" should appear after "22th. [*sic*]."

406   **To Pablo Obregon,** April 6, 1827. Line 10. The draft in CSmH is dated April 2, 1827.

727   **From James Brown,** June 28, 1827. Note 2. This and numerous other citations of Clay to Taylor, April 4, 1827, in reference to the 1827 Kentucky elections should also include Clay to Adams, August 19, 1827.

877   **From Charles Hammond,** August 10, 1827. Note 2. Cross-reference should be to Clay to Crittenden, Feb. 14, 1828, not Feb. 16.

1420   **Index.** Listing for Phillip R. Fendall should be Philip.

Volume Seven

22   **From Peter B. Porter,** Jan. 8, 1828. Line 1. The cross-reference to "6:194-6" should be to 6:1394-96.

30   **From Robert Scott,** Jan. 11, 1828. Line 3. The amount advanced by Scott and Clay was $6,000, not $600. For a summary of their agreement of April 25, 1828, see above, this volume.

77   **To William B. Lawrence,** Feb. 4, 1828. Date of letter should be Feb. 21, 1828.

170   **To Charles A. Wickliffe,** March 17, 1828. Note 1. Wickliffe to Clay, March 14, 1828, was not included in Volume 7. It appears in the calendar of this volume.

247   **From James Brown,** April 28, 1828. Line 16 from bottom. The word "scarcely" should read "securely."

299   **From Sidney Breese,** May 25, 1828. Line 3, paragraph 2. The word "positions" should read "partisans."

337-38 **To Washington Daily National Intelligencer,** *ca.* June 9, 1828. Date of letter was Nov. 15, 1822. It is published under correct date in 3:322-23.

402 **From William Plumer,** July 26, 1828. Line 2 of letter. The word "duply" should read "deeply."

433 **From William Tudor,** August 20, 1828. Line 8, second full paragraph. The words "any impression" should read "my impression."

490 **To James Brown,** Oct. 11, 1828. Note 1. The date should be August 10, 1827, not 1828.

591 **From James Erwin,** Jan. 6, 1829. Note 2. Anne Erwin's daughter was named Lucretia Clay Erwin, not Lucretia Hart Erwin.

604 **From Richard Henry Lee,** Jan. 23, 1829. Note 1. The history Lee intended to write was probably one about the Adams administration, which he never did, rather than the one about Arthur Lee. See 8:34.

624 **To John Quincy Adams,** Feb. 20, 1829. Note 2, last line. The citation "R9" should read "R19."

664 **Index.** Listing for Lucretia Hart Erwin should be Lucretia Clay Erwin.

688 **Index.** Listing for Robert Walsh. Page number after "work in JQA campaign (1828) should be 481, not 482.

708 **Index.** Listing for "Columbia" should be "Colombia."

——— **From Henry Shaw,** Nov. 24, 1828, accidentally omitted from Volume 7, is published above, this volume. Cross-references to it may appear in Volume 7.

——— **From William W. Worsley,** March 30, 1828, accidentally omitted from Volume 7, is printed above, this volume. Cross-references to it may appear in Volume 7.

Volume Eight

85 **From John G. Simpson,** August 10, 1829. Line 14, paragraph 3. The words "public goods" should read "public gaols."

96 **From S. Newton Dexter,** Sept. 9, 1829. Date. ALS version, which is found in NIC, is dated Sept. 10, 1829.

106 **From William L. Brent,** Oct. 2, 1829. Line 4 from bottom. "Opponents" should read "appointments."

107 **From Peter B. Porter,** Oct. 2, 1829. Line 4, paragraph 3. Word "representatives" should read "representations."

108 **From Peter B. Porter,** Oct. 2, 1829. Line 3, paragraph 2. Probably should read "[from] persons," not "how persons." Manuscript is torn at this point.

121 **From George Smith Houston,** Oct. 31, 1829. Lines 4, 7. Name should be Elijah Hayward, not Haywood.

130 **To Nicholas Biddle,** Nov. 28, 1829. Line 3. Word "entrance" should be "enhance."

199 **To Josiah S. Johnston,** April 30, 1830. Note 4. Citation of Clay to Brooke, April 24, 1830, was taken from Colton, *Clay Correspondence*, 4:262-63, where the date appears as 1830. Actually, the letter was written in 1831, rendering it incorrect as a cross-reference in this instance. See 8:337-39.

253 **From William Greene,** August 19, 1830. Line 3. The word "[re]vision" should read "view."

267 **From Hezekiah Niles,** Sept. 17, 1830. Line 6. The word "cast" should read "east."

319 **From James Brown Clay,** Jan. 11, 1831. Date should be "1831 [*sic*, 1832]."

321 **From John Morrison Clay,** Jan. 14, 1831. Date should be "1831 [*sic*, 1832]."

328 **From John L. Lawrence,** March 29, 1831. Line 2 from bottom. Date in Webster to Clay, March 4, 1831, should be April 4, 1831.

343 **To Francis T. Brooke,** May 1, 1831. Line 3. The name should read "Judge [William] Smith."

349 **To Peter B. Porter,** May 14, 1831. Note 1. Date of Porter to Clay, Feb. 10, 1830, should be Dec. 10, 1830. Note 4. Reference should be to Letcher to Clay, Dec. 21, 1829.

365 **From Josiah Randall,** June 24, 1831. Line 4. Cross-reference should be to Letcher to Clay, Dec. 21, 1829.

383   **From Josiah S. Johnston,** August 2, 1831. Note 1. Reference of Lawrence to Clay, Dec. 21, 1829, should be Letcher to Clay, Dec. 21, 1829.

405   **To Edgar Snowden,** Sept. 25, 1831. Line 1, paragraph 3. The word "extension" should read "extinction."

415   **To John Sloane,** Oct. 4, 1831. Note 4. Reference is to the bonus paid by the Bank of the U.S. for its charter, not the treasury surplus.

429   **From Anne Brown Clay Erwin,** Dec. 8, 1831. Line 3, third full paragraph. Name Lucretia Hart Erwin should be Lucretia Clay Erwin.

432   **To Samuel L. Southard,** Dec. 12, 1831. Note 3. Quotation attributed to Jackson's Third Annual Message is from his Fourth Annual Message on Dec. 4, 1832. *MPP*, 2:597.

434   **From Henry Clay, Jr.,** Dec. 16, 1831. Note 1. Name Lucretia Hart Erwin should be Lucretia Clay Erwin.

434   **To James Brown,** Dec. 18, 1831. Line 3, paragraph 2. Should be Philip P. Barbour, not James.

438   **To William Greene,** Dec. 26, 1831. Note 2. Reference of Webster to Clay, Jan. 1, 1832, should read "Jan. 8, 1832."

451   **From Henry Clay, Jr.,** Jan. 27, 1832. Line 3, paragraph 8. Name Lucretia Hart Erwin should be Lucretia Clay Erwin.

456   **From Hezekiah Niles,** Feb. 3, 1832. Line 5. The "*great rejected*" refers to Martin Van Buren, not Jackson.

461   **From Hiram Ketchum,** Feb. 12, 1832. Line 2, first full paragraph. The word "around" should read "aroused."

464   **From Thomas Metcalfe,** Feb. 14, 1832. Note 4. Reference should be to Van Buren's reputed drafting of Jackson's Maysville Road veto.

469   **From Hexekiah Niles,** Feb. 28, 1832. Name should read "Hezekiah."

474   **To Peter B. Porter,** March 10, 1832. Note 2. The name James Barbour should be Philip P. Barbour.

486   **To Francis T. Brooke,** April 1, 1832. Note 2. The name James Barbour should be Philip P. Barbour.

529   **From Francis T. Brooke,** June 7, 1832. Line 2, paragraph 2. Cross-reference should be Webster to Clay, Jan. 8, 1832.

531   **From Fortunatus Sydnor,** June 9, 1832. Line 4, paragraph 2. The name James Barbour should be Philip P. Barbour.

543   **To Charles Hammond,** June 22, 1832. Note 10. The name James Barbour should be Philip P. Barbour.

558   **To Phillip R. Fendall,** August 4, 1832. Heading. "Phillip" should read "Philip." Note 1. Reference should be Webster to Clay, Jan. 8, 1832.

573   **From William B. Rochester,** Sept. 8, 1832. Line 6. The name "Jesse Buell" should read "Jesse Buel."

574   **To Charles H. List,** Sept. 10, 1832. Line 6. Cross-reference should be Smith to Clay, Dec. 27, 1831.

575   **To Samuel L. Southard,** Sept. 11, 1832. Note 1. Cross-reference should be Smith to Clay, Dec. 27, 1831.

586   **To Samuel P. Lyman,** Oct. 22, 1832. Note 5. Vote totals for Clay and Jackson are reversed.

613   **Comment in Senate,** Jan. 14, 1833. Cross-references to the issue of French spoliations inadvertently mixes the claims for spoliations committed before and after 1800.

635   **From James Madison,** April 2, 1833. Line 16. "Embris" should read "Embrio."

649   **From Robert P. Letcher,** June 8, 1833. Line 7. Cross-reference for James Harlan should read "[5:295]."

657   **To Henry Clay, Jr.,** July 7, 1832. Heading. Date should be 1833, not 1832.

659   **To Edward Everett,** July 23, 1833. Date. Colton, *Clay Correspondence*, 4:425-26 misdates this as July 22.

667   **To Phillip R. Fendall,** Nov. 24, 1833. Name should be "Philip."

684   **Speech in Senate,** Dec. 26, 1833. Line 4. Should say William J. Duane refused to remove the deposits.

687   **From Peter B. Porter,** Jan. 5, 1834. Last paragraph of letter and note 9. "The Spy" probably refers to Matthew L. Davis, who wrote a newspaper column called "The Spy in Washington," rather than to Alexis de Sarcy.

690   **To John Pendleton Kennedy,** Jan. 15, 1834. Line 1, paragraph 2. Instead of "[John] McLean's," this should read "McLean's [*sic*, Louis McLane]."

741   **To Bellamy Storer,** August 8, 1834. Line 5, paragraph 4. The word "secretary" should read "scrutiny." Storer is identified in 10:429.

782   **To John M. Bailhache,** July 14, 1835. Lines 15-16, paragraph 2. Word "forcing" should read "fearing."

757   **To Francis T. Brooke,** Jan. 16, 1835. Note 5. Should mention the indefinite postponement in March, 1835, of Taney's nomination as associate justice of the Supreme Court.

795   **From James Barbour,** August 2, 1835. Lines 3, 9. The word "Inglers" should read "Juglers"; the word "pigling" should read "Jugling."

796   **Ibid.** Lines 3-4, 11, 16. Phrase "or that heard" should read "on that head"; "Families" should read "Fanatics"; "three" should read "their."

809   **To Lucretia Hart Clay,** Dec. 9, 1835. Note 4. Name Lucretia Hart Erwin should be Lucretia Clay Erwin.

822   **To John Forsyth,** Jan. 27, 1836. Note 2. Should read "The following day, Jan. 28."

825   **Draft of Undelivered Senate Speech,** *ca*. Late Jan., 1836. Line 3, second full paragraph. Barton was U.S. chargé d'affaires, not U.S. minister.

860   **Speech at the Woodford Festival,** July 26, 1836. Line 2. Word "house" should read "hours."

902   **Index.** Listing for "Jesse Buell" should be "Jesse Buel."

918   **Index.** Listing for Lucretia Hart Erwin should be Lucretia Clay Erwin.

922   **Index.** Listing for Elijah Haywood should be Elijah Hayward.

931   **Index.** Listing for Charlotte Mentelle should be "(Mrs. Augustus Waldemarde)" and listing for Walderman Mentelle should be Augustus Waldermarde Mentelle.

941   **Index.** Omitted is "Stevens, John A.: from, 816-17; to, 817."

942   **Index.** Listing for Bellamy Storer should include "to, 741." Listing for William L. Stone should include page 476.

Volume Nine

153   **To Thomas Speed,** March 2, 1838. Note 3, fifth line from bottom. Cross-reference should be Clay to Wise, Feb. 28, 1842.

421   **To Stephen [*sic*, Steven] Whitney,** June 8, 1840. Heading. The spelling "Stephen" is correct.

498   **To Peter B. Porter,** Feb. 7, 1841. Note 3. Date for suspension of specie payment by Trotter's bank should be Feb. 5, not Feb. 4.

688   **To Lucretia Hart Clay,** March 27, 1842. Note 3. R. W. Thompson was Richard W. Thompson, secretary of the navy from 1877-81. See *DAB*.

731   **To Oliver H. Smith,** July 10, 1842. Note 3. Should read "did not provide for home valuation."

796   **To Lucretia Hart Clay,** Jan. 3, 1843. Line 1, fifth full paragraph. Name should be William N. Mercer.

801   **To Lucretia Hart Clay,** Feb. 10, 1843. Line 8. Name should be William N. Mercer.

841   **To Robert Garrett & Sons,** July 31, 1843. Garrett is identified in 10:56.

870   **From Peter B. Porter,** Oct. 11, 1843. Third full paragraph. The Maryland congressional elections were postponed from the fall of 1843 to the spring of 1844. See 10:15 for correction.

894   **To John Pendleton Kennedy,** Dec. 3, 1843. Note 1. Clay was president of the American Colonization Society until his death in 1852.

921   **Index.** Listing for Carter Beverley should include the following numbers under the subentry for "Corrupt Bargain" issue: 648-49, 659, 696-97, 709-10.

951   **Index.** Listing for Michigan should give subentry for 1837 instead of 1839 state and U.S. House elections in, and the page number should be 148, not 147.

959   **Index.** Listing for William H. Seward should read: "from, 335," not 334.

———   **To James Kent,** Feb. 22, 1837, accidentally omitted from Volume 9, is printed above, this volume. Cross-references to it may appear in Volume 9.

— **To Napoleon B. Montfort,** Feb. 13, 1838, accidentally omitted from Volume 9, is printed above, this volume. Cross-references to it may appear in Volume 9.

— **From John Scott,** Feb. 20, 1838, accidentally omitted from Volume 9, is printed above, this volume. Cross-references to it may appear in Volume 9.

— **Speech in Senate,** Jan. 6, 1841, accidentally omitted from Volume 9, is printed above, this volume. Cross-references to it may appear in Volume 9.

NAME & SUBJECT INDEX: SUPPLEMENT

Botts, John M., 289-90
Bouligny, Dominique, 180, 182
Bourbon County, Ky., 158
Bowling Green, Ky., 142
Boyd, George: to, 71; mentioned, 65
Brackenridge, Henry M.: to, 291; mentioned, 70
Bradford, Fielding, Jr., 51, 179
Bradford, John: from, 56-57; mentioned, 51, 53
Brady, Mathew, 316-17, 319
Branch, John, 208
Brand, William, 280
Brazil: relations of with Portugal, 44-46; *Spark* incident, 204; mentioned, 290
Breathitt, John, 239
Breck, Samuel, 127
Breckinridge, Mr., 119
Breckinridge, J. Cabell, 125
Breckinridge, John, 148
Breckinridge County, Ky., 290
Brennan, John, 261
Brent, Mr., 162
Brent, Robert: from, 29, 53-54, 60-61, 65; to, 54
Brest, France, 41, 46-48
Briscoe, A. H., 319
Brodhead, Lucas: to, 82-83; mentioned, 134
Brooke, Francis T., 186, 226
Brooke, John, 226
Browere, John H. I., 311, 319
Brown, Ann Hart "Nancy" (Mrs. James), 63, 178-79
Brown, Henry Kirke, 312-13, 316, 319
Brown, Jacob J., 42
Brown, James: to, 33; travels in Europe, 63; alleged debt of, 119; mentioned, 7-8, 148-49, 187
Brown, John, 119-20
Brown, Orlando, 287
Brown, Samuel M., 290
Brown, William H., 319
Brown and Bell, 119
Browne, Thomas C., 117, 128
Browne, J. Vincent: to, 238
Brown's Hotel (Washington), 103
Brown University, 179
Brumidi, Constantine, 319
Brush, Henry, 149
Brussels, Belgium, 41
Bryan, Daniel, 24
Buchanan, James, 206-7
Buckner, Richard A., 203
Buenos Aires, Argentina, 70

Buffalo, N.Y., 191, 211, 296
Bulama (now Bolama) Island, 73-74
Bull, John, 56, 211-12
Bull, Olé: to, 293
Bullett, A., 316
Bunker Hill, Mass.: C. speech at, 253
Bunker Hill Association, 186
Burlington, Vt., 252
Burnet, Jacob, 124-25, 139, 155
Burnley, Albert T.: from, 280-81
Burr, Aaron: alleged conspiracy of, 9-10; mentioned, 17
Burt, Charles K., 319
Bush, Joseph H., 319
Bushnell, Mr., 20
Butler, Anthony, 67
Butler, Mann, 257
Buttre, John C., 319
Byrd, Charles W., 89
Bywaters, Robert, 70

Cadore, Duc de, 14-15
Cafferty, James H., 319
Cahaba River, 72
Caldwell, Phillips, 7-8
Calhoun, John C.: from, 184; to, 63-66, 71, 90-91, 102; appointed secretary of war, 60; as 1824 presidential candidate, 100-101, 104-6, 109-10, 129, 144-45, 163, 173, 181-82; influences Monroe's appointments, 144; mentioned, 92, 122, 125, 165, 201, 229, 284, 289, 314, 317
Cambreleng, Churchill C., 235
Cambridge, Mass., 69, 71
Campbell, Duncan G., 184
Campbell, George Washington, 65, 116
Campbell, John, 70
Campbell, William, 136
Campbell County, Ky., 96-97, 153
Campbell's Well, Ky., 55
Cana, Frederick, 44, 47-48
Canby, Israel T., 138, 140, 152, 160-61
Cannon, Hugh, 319
Cannon, Newton, 116-18, 121
Canrzlaar, _____ , 168
Canton, Mass., 171
Cape Girardeau, Mo., 180
Caraman, Count de (Georges-Joseph-Victor de Riquet), 34-35

Cardell, William S.: from, 84-85; to, 86
Carey, Mathew: from, 251; to, 166, 171, 251; retirement of, 171; support of for protective tariff, 171; mentioned, 225
Carlisle, John W., 75-76
Carneal, Thomas D., 98, 111-13, 123, 126-27, 138, 140-41, 143, 147, 152, 154, 159-60
Carneal, Thomas D. (Sr.), 98
Carnegie Institute Museum, 312
Caroline (slave), 196
Carr, Charles, 54
Carr, Francis, 144
Carr, William, 56
Carroll, Henry, 34-35, 65
Carroll, William, 115-16, 121
Carter, Dennis, 319
Castlereagh, Lord (Robert Stewart), 24, 37-38, 40, 49
"Catalpa," 279
Causten, James H.: from, 259-60
Chambers, James: from, 101
Chappel, Alonzo, 319
Chase, Philander, 196
Chase, Samuel, 10
Chauncey, Isaac, 34-36
Cheltenham Springs, England, 191-92
Chelt River, 192
Cherokee Indians, 68-69, 238
Chesapeake (ship), 18
Cheves, Langdon: from, 110-11; to, 83-84, 104; mentioned, 19, 81, 86, 91, 105, 111, 125, 127
Chicago Historical Society, 311
Child, David Lee: from, 294-96
Chile, 199
Chiles, Richard, 229, 231
Chiles Tavern, 231
Chillicothe, Ohio, 56, 94, 96, 101, 149-50
Chilton, Thomas: leaves Jackson party, 230-31
Chinn, Richard H., 234
Church, Thomas, 74-75
Cicero, 298
Cilley, Jonathan, 289
Cincinnati, Ohio, 1, 83-84, 94, 96-98, 110-15, 125, 127, 137, 139, 143-44, 147-49, 152, 155-56, 158, 161, 165, 182, 188-90, 208-9, 261, 312-13, 316
Claiborne, William C. C., Jr., 211

feelings of on election of Jackson, 214; contemplates returning to U.S. House, 106, 109; attitude of toward Jackson and Van Buren administrations, 223-27, 229-30, 244, 250, 256-57, 263, 269-70, 276-77, 283; love of Union, 228, 261; on admitting newspaper stenographers into the Senate, 285; opposes nullification doctrine, 231-33; on Masons v. Antimasons, 237, 243; C. denies trying to influence Supreme Court on *Worcester v. Georgia*, 238; attitude of toward compromise, 253; resolutions of concerning appointments, 255; attitude of toward public lands issue, 272-73, 276, 281-84; on president's power of removal, 276; retires from Senate, 287; on use of presidential veto, 288
—religion & religious issues: supports religious toleration, 170; attitude of toward Shakers, 228-29
—slaves & slavery: buys, sells, hires out slaves, 26, 196; escape of slave George, 56-57; opposes slave trade, 73; supports gradual emancipation in 1799 Kentucky constitution, 148-49, 266; believes slavery is a state issue, 149; seeks to find and free slave belonging to N. G. Hart, 178-79; assists Abduhl Rahahman, 213; speech of to American Colonization Society, 262; speech of to Kentucky Colonization Society, 265-66; attitude of toward slavery, 266, 273-74; C. urged to rise up and oppose, 294-96
—war, peace, & foreign policy views: on war with Britain, 18-20, 23-24, 59, 226-27; serves as peace negotiator, 30-33, 35; discusses peace negotiations, 35-37, 41-42, 44, 216-21; goes to England to negotiate treaty of commerce, 48-50; support of for independence of Spanish America, 64-65, 67, 73,

76-77, 90, 135, 194-95, 226-27; compares U.S. and Britain, 286
Clay, James Brown (son): visits Philander Chase, 196; mentioned, 264, 290
Clay, John (brother): financial problems of, 16-17; mentioned, 1
Clay, John Morrison (son): illness of, 264; educated at E. C. Wines's school, 292; mentioned, 196, 226
Clay, Lucretia Hart (wife): suffers ill health, 196; mentioned, 16, 23, 30, 32, 55, 63, 66, 69, 117, 178, 198, 211, 225, 242, 252, 265, 298, 310, 313, 316, 318
Clay, Lucretia Hart (daughter), 30, 143
Clay, Porter (brother): to, 54-55
Clay, Sidney P.: to, 74
Clay, Susan Hart (daughter): *See* Duralde, Susan Hart Clay
Clay, Theodore Wythe (son): attends Bancel's Academy, 53; goes to Harvard, 69; mentioned, 26, 30, 56, 58, 71, 200
Clay, Thomas Hart (son): to, 260; attends Bancel's Academy, 53; goes to Harvard, 69; goes to U.S. Military Academy, 85-86, 90-91, 99-100; C. problems with, 100, 102-3, 221-22; works at Logan Factory, 260; mentioned, 26, 30, 56, 58
Claypool, Abram G., 89
Cleveland, Ohio, 208
Clevenger, Shobal V., 312, 316, 319
Clinton, DeWitt: as possible 1828 presidential candidate, 191; death of, 191, 209-10; mentioned, 76, 129, 161, 164-65, 168-69, 184, 186. *See also* Election of 1824
Clinton, George, 193
Clover, Lewis P.: to, 273
Coburn, John: to, 72-73; mentioned, 10
Cocke, John, 17, 117-18, 121, 165
Cocke, William, 8
Coghill, Sir John, 51-52
Coghlan, John, 25
Cohill, Charles, 320

Cole, Joseph G., 320
Coleman, William, 38
Coles, Edward: to, 128; mentioned, 117, 258
Collins, Mr., 212
Collins, Joel, 142
Colombia, 104, 135, 197
Colton, Calvin, 314
Colton & Barnes, 320
Columbus, Christopher, 298
Columbus, Ohio, 83, 89, 97-98, 106, 112, 118-20, 123-24, 127, 129, 132-33, 140-41, 147-48, 150-52, 155-56, 161-62, 165, 168-69, 194
Combs, Leslie: to, 285-86; capture of son of in Mexico, 285-86; financial condition of, 285-86
Compromise of 1850, 297-98
Compromise Tariff of 1833. *See* Tariff of 1833
Concord, Mass., 209
Congress of the United States: act authorizing detachment from militia, 13; discussion of proposed Ohio Canal, 13; 1810 adjournment of, 14; opposition in (1810) to military preparedness, 14-15; bills in for raising additional troops, 18-20; bill authorizing loan, 20-21; declaration of war against Britain, 19-20, 22-23; Boston merchants petition to withdraw property from Britain, 21; bills and resolutions in for relief of individuals, 22-23, 75, 186-87; House resolution concerning Berlin and Milan decrees, 25; act for support of military, 25-26; tax act, 29; act providing pension to widows and orphans of slain militiamen, 29, 60-61; appropriation of to build steam battery, 31-32; treaty-making power of, 52; act for improving public square, 57-58; House resolutions concerning sales of public lands in Alabama, 71-72; bill to prohibit exportation of produce to British possessions in North America, 76; act empowering federal marshals to hire a jail when necessary, 93-94; P. P. Barbour elected Speaker, 99; C. contem-

376

378

Washington, Pa., 168
Washington *Daily National Intelligencer*, 194-95, 200, 206, 232, 234-35, 269, 274
Washington *Daily National Journal*, 200, 206, 223
Washington *Globe*, 272
Washington *Independent*, 287
Washington *National Intelligencer*, 69-70
Washington *United States Telegraph*, 200
Washington (Ky.) *Mirror*, 51
Wasp (ship), 36
Watauga, 68
Waters, Richard L., 91, 93
Watkins, Henry, 20
Watkins, John, 20, 53
Watkins, Tobias, 205, 222-23
Watts, Beaufort T.: to, 250-51
Webster, Daniel: to, 191-92, 213-14; and Tariff of 1824, 174-75; elected to U.S. Senate, 204-5; barbecue for in Louisville, 269; mentioned, 85, 231, 238, 241, 285, 309, 314, 316-17
Webster, Dudley, 27-28
Weible, Daniel, 7
Weir, Eliza Jane: to, 247-49; mentioned, 245-49
Weir, Henry, 246
Weir, James, 245-49
Weir, James (nephew of James), 246
Weir, William, 246
Weld, Lewis: to, 255-56
Wellesley, Richard Colley, 14-15
Wellington, Lord, 41
West, William, 310
West Indies, 50, 270-71
West Middleton, Pa., 20
West Point. *See* United States Military Academy
Western Quarterly Reporter of Medical, Surgical, and Natural Science, 103
Wharton, Arabella Griffith, 199
Wharton, Thomas I.: to, 193, 199-203, 222, 225; serves on Pennsylvania commission to revise penal codes, 202-3; mentioned, 318

Wheaton, Henry: appointed chargé to Denmark, 201; mentioned, 90
Wheaton, Joseph, 75
Wheeling, Va. (W. Va.), 72, 107, 141, 150, 206, 222, 232, 261, 264
Whig party: C. urges organization of in Virginia, 275; 1838 victory of in New York State, 272-73; 1839 national convention of, 279; C. urges national convention for 1844 presidential election, 288-89; mentioned, 256, 261, 269-70, 274, 276-78, 283, 290-92, 294, 314
Whitaker, William W., 67
White, George S.: to, 260
White, Hugh L., 124
White, John: from, 288; mentioned, 287, 289
White, Lee, 207
Whitechurch, Robert, 323
White Sulpher Springs, Va. (W.Va.), 211, 239
Whom It May Concern: to, 11-12, 78-79, 134, 213
Wickliffe, _____ , 261
Wickliffe, Charles, 224
Wickliffe, Charles A.: reelected to U.S. House, 207; claims C. tried to get him to vote for Adams in 1825, 207
Wickliffe, Robert: to, 67; mentioned, 18, 25, 159, 190
Widgery, William: to, 28-29
Wier, Robert, 323
Wilkins, Charles, 11
Wilkins, John, Jr., 11
Wilkins, William: to, 19-20
Wilkinson, James: investigation and trial of, 15; financial problems of, 15-16; mentioned, 17
Willard, Asaph, 324
Williams, John, 116-18, 121, 198
Williams, Jonathan, 22
Williams, O. Ellsworth: from, 252
Williamsburg, Va., 226
Williston, Ebenezer B.: to, 194-95
Wilmington, Del., 47, 251
Wilson, Alexander, 78-79

Wilson, S.: to, 85-86
Wilson, Samuel, 85
Wilson, Thomas, 82-83, 123, 126, 152, 154, 156
Winchester, James, 29
Winchester & Danville Road, 280
Winer, Benjamin: to, 208-9
Wines, Enoch C.: to, 292
Wirt, William: from, 75; on role of attorney general, 75; nominated for president by Antimasonic party, 239; mentioned, 60, 243
Wise, Barton H., 290
Wise, Henry A.: enmity with C., 289; on Graves-Cilley duel, 289; diplomatic appointments of, 290; mentioned, 276, 286
Wise, James, 314, 324
Wolf, George, 243
Wood, Joseph, 324
Woodbridge, William, 279
Woodbury, Levi: from, 258-59; to, 257-59; mentioned, 204, 282
Woodcock & Harvey, 324
Woods, Mr., 288
Woodward, David A., 324
Woolley, Abram R., 63
Worcester v. *Georgia*, 238
Worsley, William W.: from, 51, 211-12; mentioned, 222
Worth, Gorham A.: from, 81-82; to, 81-82, 89-91, 93-97
Worthington, Dr., 15-16
Worthington, Thomas: presidential or vice presidential aspirations of, 141-42; mentioned, 121
Worthington, William M., 82, 89, 95, 115
Wright, Charles C., 324
Wright, John C., 79
Wright, Silas, 282-84
Wyandot Indians, 264

Yale University, 316
Yancey, Joel, 203
Yeatman, Griffen, 127, 152, 154, 159
York, Pa., 238
Young, John D., 26
Yverdon, Switzerland, 40

Zanesville, Ohio, 63, 150, 232

engravings, and daguerreotypes that featured Clay as the subject. Appended to the essay is a calendar listing each major work, the artist, date of completion, and present location.

A comprehensive bibliography of works cited in the entire series of *The Papers of Henry Clay* will benefit researchers seeking information in addition to that provided in the annotations. This supplement is an essential addition to the earlier volumes in the series.

Melba Porter Hay was associate editor of volumes 8 and 9 and editor of volume 10 of *The Papers of Henry Clay*.